Philosophy
Themes and Thinkers
JW Phelan

CAMBRIDGE
UNIVERSITY PRESS

To my parents

CAMBRIDGE UNIVERSITY PRESS
Cambridge, New York, Melbourne, Madrid, Cape Town, Singapore, São Paulo

Cambridge University Press
The Edinburgh Building, Cambridge CB2 2RU, UK

www.cambridge.org
Information on this title: www.cambridge.org/9780521537421

First published 2005

Printed in the United Kingdom at the University Press, Cambridge

A catalogue record for this publication is available from the British Library

ISBN-13   978-0-521-53742-1 paperback
ISBN-10   0-521-53742-8 paperback

ACKNOWLEDGEMENTS

Bridgeman Art Library/Getty Images, p. 329*t*; Bridgeman Art Library © Munch Museum/Munch-
Ellingsen Group, BONO, Oslo, DACS, London 2005, p. 318; Fotomas Index UK, pp. 5, 19, 24, 29, 56,
64, 78, 109, 117, 150, 168, 201, 212, 252, 265; Hulton Archive/Getty Images, pp. 68, 93, 129, 224, 294,
317; Time & Life Pictures/Getty Images, pp. 48, 108, 133, 287; Tracey Emin © Tracey Emin, courtesy
Jay Jopling/White Cube (London), photo Stephen White, p. 329*b*

Cover design by Tim Elcock, cover image *The Philosopher's Trouble* by Giorgio de Chirico
© Alinari Archives/ CORBIS

Illustrations on pages 8, 84, 105 and 126 by Gerry Ball

Contents

Part 2 Thinkers

Author's acknowledgements

Many thanks to all those who have assisted in the preparation of this textbook, especially to my head of department Peter Holmes for encouraging me in this task and for reading the chapters on the philosophy of mind and the theory of knowledge. Thanks also to the following stalwarts for their individual contributions: Louise Aspinwall for her comments on the philosophy of science, Mark Hogarth for his comments on dualism and induction, Anthony Finnerty and Kerri Fox for their careful readings of the chapter on the philosophy of religion, James Hunter for his suggestions on Aristotle and Ann O'Quigley for her patient editing.

I continued to teach philosophy while writing this textbook and would like to thank the current and former students of Hills Road Sixth Form College, Cambridge, for their immediate and constructive feedback. I also owe a debt of gratitude to David Jacques, Mark Hogarth and Darryl Hinchliffe for supplying much-needed social vitamins, and to Catherine and Laurence Dixon for providing inspiration and solace in equal measures at the Champion of the Thames. The final and most important tribute must go to my parents, to whom this book is dedicated, and who courageously supported me throughout this project. I only regret that my father did not live to see its completion … i bParthas na nGrást go rabhaimíd.

Introduction

A philosopher is a blind man in a dark cellar at midnight, looking for a black cat that isn't there. (Anon)

Philosophy is at one and the same time a fascinating and frustrating subject. It deals with the big questions in life and can leave one equally inspired or bewildered. In essence, philosophy seeks to do two things:

- Separate good arguments from bad arguments.
- Give useful advice on how to live our lives.

These tasks are in no way mutually exclusive. Plato, the founding father of philosophy, criticised his adversaries the Sophists for using bad arguments when selling their advice to the citizens of Athens.

Many students approach philosophy with the desire to learn an ancient wisdom from aged professors who stroke their grey beards contemplatively. They may be surprised to learn that such beards have long since been shaved and that many philosophers today are more interested in science, psychology or logic than in asking whether our souls survive beyond the grave.

Two distinct styles of philosophy prevail, and they are often referred to as the analytic and continental schools. Analytic philosophy became popular in the English-speaking world, and as a result is often referred to as the Anglo-Saxon tradition. This tradition emphasises logic, linguistic analysis and the classification of formal types of argument, casting philosophy as a branch of science. Chapter 15 of this book examines the writing and inheritance of A. J. Ayer, a philosopher in the analytic tradition, who sought to separate philosophical questions into two piles, the meaningful and the meaningless, and to set fire to the latter. For Ayer, questions such as 'How does one live a good life?' do not have a definitive answer and philosophers are wasting their time in trying to find one. Much of Ayer's work seems dated, but the school of thought to which he belonged, known as logical positivism, still exerts an important influence in philosophy and is far from passé.

The continental school embraces various attempts to answer the question 'What is the meaning of life?' and is often explored through literature. Continental philosophy seeks to incorporate the grey area of emotions into its analysis of the human condition. In addition, continental philosophy attaches greater importance to the historical context of a thinker's work. This textbook examines both schools of thought, focusing on continental thinkers such as Nietzsche, Heidegger and Sartre as well as analytic philosophers such as Hume, Russell and Ayer. But one must bear in mind that philosophy is a value-laden operation!

There is, nevertheless, solace to be found in contemplating life's imponderables. The activity raises one above the banal world of everyday existence. It encourages one to formulate opinions, carefully articulate them and creatively defend them against attack. It is hoped, therefore, that whatever you conceive philosophy to be and whatever your interests – whether religious, political or scientific – you will find something of use in this book. I have endeavoured to include as many relevant points as time and space permit, but the resultant work aims to be comprehensive rather than definitive. It provides a useful guide that will hopefully inspire you to find out more about the subject yourself. I wish you the best of luck.

Preliminary reading

- Baggini, J. (2002) *Philosophy Key Texts*, Basingstoke, Macmillan Palgrave
  Baggini's work provides a clear introduction to select philosophical themes and authors

- Baldwin, T. (2001) *Contemporary Philosophy*, Oxford, OUP

  An accessible introduction to philosophy in English since 1945

- Blackburn, S. (1999) *Think*, Oxford, OUP

  A rich introduction that tracks the course of prominent arguments

- Craig, E. (2002) *Philosophy: A Very Short Introduction*, Oxford, OUP

  A useful survey of various thinkers in their historical context

- De Botton, A. (2000) *The Consolations of Philosophy*, London, Pantheon

  A readable introduction to the advice philosophers have given on how to live

- Horner, C. and Westacott, E. (2000) *Thinking through Philosophy*, Cambridge, CUP

  A fluent introduction to philosophical themes

- Morton, A. (1999) *Philosophy in Practice*, Oxford, Blackwell
  An interactive textbook covering the theory of knowledge, moral philosophy and the philosophy of mind

- Nagel, T. (1987) *What Does It All Mean?*, Oxford, OUP

  A collection of short essays on the main philosophical puzzles

- Warburton, N. (1999) *Philosophy: The Basics*, London, Routledge
  This provides clear outlines of many of the central arguments and is useful for preliminary reading

PART 1 Themes

1 Theory of knowledge

Only a shallow man doesn't judge by appearances. (Oscar Wilde)

Aims

On completion of this chapter you should be able to:

- evaluate rationalism
- evaluate empiricism
- distinguish between *a priori* and *a posteriori* knowledge and account for the tensions between these categories
- evaluate the foundationalist, coherentist and reliabilist theories of justification
- outline and evaluate the tripartite definition of knowledge
- explain the difference between ordinary and philosophical doubt
- evaluate traditional and modern sceptical arguments
- evaluate the naive realist theory of perception
- evaluate the representative realist theory of perception
- evaluate the idealist theory of perception
- evaluate the phenomenalist theory of perception.

It is characteristic of philosophy to step back from familiar facts and figures and to talk in more general terms. Plato (c. 427–347 BC), one of the first philosophers, describes this approach in *The Republic* as 'the study of essential natures'.[1] The theory of **knowledge** lies at the very heart of the philosophical enterprise, which is in essence a quest for meaning. The essential questions surrounding knowledge concern its nature and whether we can categorise different types of knowledge, as well as the possibility of there being limits to what we can know. **Epistemology**, as the study of knowledge is called, inevitably connects with the philosophies of mind, science and language. Let us begin by examining the notion of knowledge itself.

Knowledge

The history of western epistemology (a word that derives from the Greek word *episteme*, which means 'knowledge') is the history of two schools of thought that seek to define knowledge in different ways. **Rationalism** sees knowledge as the product of reasoned reflection capable of operating independently of experience. **Empiricism**, on the other hand, views knowledge as the product of sensory experience. Rationalists believe that we arrive at knowledge by thinking about relations between concepts. We know, for example, that there are 60 seconds in a minute by learning the meanings of the terms 'second' and 'minute'. In the same way, we know that there are 60 minutes in an hour, from which we can deduce that there are 3,600 seconds in an hour. This type of knowledge is called *a priori* knowledge. One does not even have to leave the comfort of one's armchair to discover it, as the operation involves thought alone. In contrast, we acquire empirical or *a posteriori* knowledge from examination and observation. Thus we know from sensory experience that barium burns with an apple-green flame: all we need to do is perform the experiment and note the results.

The phrase *a priori* derives from the Latin meaning 'from what comes before' and the phrase *a posteriori* means 'from what comes after'.

Rationalists, like Plato, believe that human beings are born with a body of knowledge already stored in the mind that enables us to recognise truths when we unearth them. Plato tells the story of Meno's slave to illustrate the point that each of us has an innate capacity to reason.[2] The narrator, Socrates, draws a number of geometric figures in the sand in front of Meno's slave who, when asked a series of questions, recognises the right answers despite never having done any mathematics before. Empiricists, on the other hand, believe that all knowledge needs to be learnt and that there is no such thing as innate knowledge. The most famous empiricist, John Locke, described the human mind as a *tabula rasa*, a blank slate upon which facts acquired through experience are written.

Attempts have been made to bring together rationalism and empiricism. The most famous was made by the German philosopher Immanuel Kant (1724–1804), who saw the role of reason as one of organising phenomenal experience – that is, experience gained from the senses. The post-Kantian rationalist tradition has refined its standpoint from the days of Plato. It accepts that we acquire genuine knowledge from experience, but holds that we are born with the innate capacity to reason, which means that we know what to do with the information received from experience. A rationalist would agree with an empiricist that we cannot know that there are 3,600 seconds in an hour without having been told that that there are 60 seconds in a minute and 60 minutes in an hour. But a rationalist would argue that in order to have reached the correct conclusion we require certain innate cerebral capacities such as an understanding of language and an ability to work out the relationship between the concepts that we acquire.

A priori knowledge is that body of information we know to be true from thinking about the concepts involved: from a logical examination we can conclude that there is something permanent, universal and necessary about this knowledge. Contrariwise, *a posteriori* knowledge is that body

John Locke
(1632–1704)

Born in the Somerset village of Wrington in the summer of 1632, John Locke became one of the most prominent English empiricists of his age, as well as writing influential pieces on political philosophy. Locke's contribution to empiricism consists in his idea that all our knowledge is accrued through the senses from birth. He explains sensory perception in terms of 'primary and secondary qualities' of objects. Primary qualities include size, shape and movement, and belong to objects irrespective of whether or not they are being perceived, while secondary qualities are imposed on objects by the observer and include colour, smell and taste.

Locke's father wanted his son to study for the religious ministry, but the gaunt, scholarly student pursued various courses in medicine and philosophy in his intermittent time at Oxford, which lasted some thirty years. Locke was interested in politics, and during the English civil war supported the parliamentary party, who sought to reduce the power of the monarch and make him rule with parliament. Locke, as a supporter of the parliamentarians, fled to Holland but returned to England after William and Mary were brought to the throne during the Glorious Revolution. Locke's famous political work, the *Two Treatises of Civil Government* (1690), was published after this turbulent time, although recent scholarship suggests an earlier authorship. Having returned to England, Locke suffered bad health and died in 1704.

Significant works
Essay Concerning Human Understanding (1690)
Two Treatises of Civil Government (1690)

of information acquired through sensory experience: from observation we can accurately report something about the world we live in. At the heart of the rationalist–empiricist debate is the question of whether knowledge is innate or gained from experience. But why do we need to decide between these two categories? Many philosophers of knowledge reject such a stark choice.

Hume's fork

The Scottish philosopher David Hume (1711–1776) was the first thinker to propose an exhaustive account of knowledge that embraced both the *a priori* and *a posteriori* categories. He outlined his thoughts in his *Enquiry Concerning Human Understanding* (Section IV, Part 1) and his model is often referred to as Hume's fork. This has two prongs that are designed to spear either one of two types of **truth** claim – termed 'relations of ideas' (*a priori*) and 'matters of fact' (*a posteriori*). Hume's outline of knowledge consists in a clear-cut division between the self-evidently true (tautological) and the empirically verifiable (proved through experiment). Hume's analysis may be represented as a diagram. Hume is a committed empiricist, yet admits to a category of knowledge gained from reason alone. This fact helps us to refine our definitions of rationalism and empiricism. A rationalist is any philosopher who believes that knowledge gained through reason is more immune from sceptical attack and therefore more fully 'knowledge', whereas an empiricist is any philosopher who argues that knowledge gained through the senses is informative and therefore more worthy of the title 'knowledge' than that gained from reason alone.

Humes' fork divides the categories of statements with its two prongs, so that any statement must fall into all three categories on the same side: it must be either *a priori*, analytic and necessary, or it must be *a posteriori*, synthetic and contingent. The semantic categories 'analytic' and 'synthetic' refer to the kinds of statement. Hume holds that claims to knowledge are either true by definition (analytic) or can be tested by an experiment (synthetic). An example of an analytic statement is 'All bachelors are unmarried' whereas an example of a synthetic statement is 'Potassium burns with a lilac flame'.

The category 'modal' describes logical possibilities and is described in terms of possible worlds. A possible world is the same kind of thing as the world we are experiencing at the moment but with room for conjecture and imaginary differences. I might imagine a possible world, for instance, in which I am made of

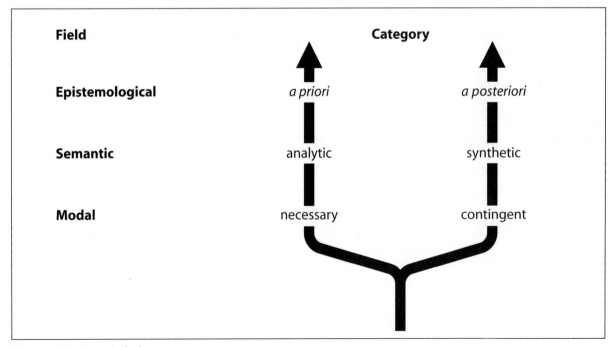

Figure 1.1 *Hume's fork*

potassium and burn with a lilac flame! Possible worlds entertain the most weird and wonderful options. Consider the possible world of cartoons where it may be possible for a character's head to expand and reduce in a second or for someone to run as fast as a speeding train. Yet even in this most creative of fantasy worlds, the laws of logic can never be compromised. Even the most inventive animator cannot draw a square circle or represent a married bachelor. Anything that is the case in this world but doesn't have to be true in all worlds is called 'contingent' whereas anything that has to be the case in all possible worlds is termed 'necessary'.

Such a statement as 'All sisters are female' is necessary, analytic and *a priori*. Indeed Hume assumes that all necessary, analytic truths are *a priori*. Similarly a statement such as 'Sodium burns with a yellow flame' is contingent, synthetic and *a posteriori* as we have gained this knowledge through observation and can entertain the idea of sodium burning with a different coloured flame. Other thinkers, however, have attempted to criticise this categorisation as being overly simplistic. Let us examine two such cases.

Bending Hume's fork

The most famous attempt to bend Hume's fork is to be found in Kant's *Critique of Pure Reason* (first edition, 1781). Kant draws a similar distinction between analytic and synthetic judgements to Hume's. He draws our attention to the fact that basic sentences are made up of subjects (what the statement is about) and predicates (words used to describe the subject). Thus the sentence 'Some roses are red' features 'Some roses' as its subject and 'are red' as its predicate. Kant held that analytic statements are those in which the subject contains the predicate and which do not supply any additional information; an example would be the sentence 'Red roses are red'. Synthetic statements do not have predicates which are contained in the subject and as a consequence give us new information; an example would be 'This rose is red' (it would still be a rose if it were another colour).

Kant, however, suggested that there are certain sentences that can be established as true by the operation of thought alone (*a priori*) and in which the predicate is not contained in the subject (synthetic). He gives the following examples:

$7 + 5 = 12$

Every event has a cause.

There is nothing inherently present in the concept of '7' that makes it evident that when it is added to '5' the result will be '12'. Likewise, there is nothing present in the concept of 'an event' that makes us immediately aware that it has been caused. Kant called such sentences synthetic, *a priori* statements, and this categorisation set the tone for a ferocious subsequent debate. Much of the argument centres on the clarity of the distinctions drawn and the issue of whether the above categories of *a priori* and *a posteriori* are mutually exclusive. Kant's notion of the synthetic *a priori* is significant as it challenges the **belief** that there are two mutually exclusive accounts of knowledge termed 'rationalist' and 'empiricist' that can never be reconciled. Kant argues that **sense-data** are important building blocks of knowledge but points out that reason has an equally important role in organising this data. A similar position was developed by W. V. O. Quine, who is discussed later in the chapter.

A more recent protagonist who has stepped into the ring to challenge Hume's fork is the American philosopher Saul Kripke (born 1940). He tries to prove the existence of a necessary, *a posteriori* category. Many of Kripke's examples focus on the nature of proper names. Kripke holds that names behave in a very different way to straightforward descriptions such as 'red' or 'female'.

- Proper names do not appear in dictionaries.
- Proper names possess only one bearer (signified by the intention of the speaker).
- Proper names are 'rigid designators' as distinct from general descriptions.
- Proper names once learnt have a necessary, *a priori* standing as one knows what is referred to without investigation.

Despite it only being a contingent fact that my parents baptised me by a certain name (they might have chosen another one), I can nevertheless travel through any number of possible worlds and know that the inhabitants of each possible world are referring to me when they address me by means of my name. My proper name is a rigid designator and when used in context can only point to me. My proper name provides an example of a necessary, *a posteriori* truth. It is necessary because I retain my identity in all possible worlds, but it is *a posteriori* because you have to meet me first in order to find out who I am. Kripke supplies some scientific examples to act as exceptions to Hume's fork. His favourites include:

Water is H_2O.

Gold has atomic number 79.

Kripke argues that we need to perform an experiment in order to discover such information (so the truth is *a posteriori*), but water is the name of the substance H_2O, and so the truth that water is H_2O is necessary; similarly gold is the name of the substance with the atomic number 79. Like Kant's argument, Kripke attempts to show that Hume's position is not watertight.

Review questions

1 Briefly explain the difference between the rationalist and empiricist accounts of knowledge.

2 Briefly explain the difference between *a priori* and *a posteriori* knowledge.

The twentieth-century logician and philosopher Willard Van Orman Quine was one thinker who questioned the profitability of a war between rationalism and empiricism. Indeed, the philosopher's lexicon offers the verb 'to quine' as a denial of any absolute distinction. Quine sought a coherent philosophy of knowledge that incorporated logical truths and scientific discoveries. He attacked the false dichotomy between the analytic and the synthetic on the

W. V. O. Quine (1908–2000)

Quine has emerged as one of the most significant intellects of the later twentieth century. He was born in Akron, Ohio, and majored in mathematics in Harvard where he gained a Ph.D. in only two years. Renowned as a logician and mathematical philosopher, he developed more original ideas in the years after his influential paper 'Two Dogmas of Empiricism' (1951) in which he challenged the synthetic–analytic distinction. Quine held that to suppose there is a boundary to be drawn between the synthetic and analytic is to adopt an unwarranted 'article of faith'. His philosophy, which is firmly rooted in the Anglo-Saxon analytic school, was greatly influenced by Bertrand Russell. He sought to unify the scientific and philosophical enterprises, and believed that epistemology, rather than being some elevated discipline, was firmly rooted in mathematics and science. Quine served as a code-breaker for the navy in the Second World War before returning to a fellowship at Harvard. He wrote in a crisp, elegant style and lectured in a fast, machine-gun-like monotone. He enjoyed Dixieland jazz and travelling; indeed his interest in the latter is well attested in his autobiography *The Time of My Life* with details of routes and timetables. Quine's other hobbies were stamp-collecting, map-reading and tracing the origins of words (especially words beginning with Q).

Significant works
From a Logical Point of View (1953)
Word and Object (1960)
Web of Beliefs (1978)
Quiddities (1987)

grounds that there is no such thing as pure *a priori* knowledge, and believed that everything is capable of being revised in the light of experience. Quine held that if one squeezes an analytic statement such as 'All bachelors are unmarried' hard enough then it turns into a set of synthetic propositions: that some men are not married, and that these men are collectively given the English name 'bachelor'. At some moment in time someone had to point out an unmarried man and tell us that the English word 'bachelor' is used as a rigid, synthetic description. As he declares in 'Two Dogmas of Empiricism', 'the lexicographer is an empirical scientist'. Synthetic descriptions remain open to revision at some time in the future: another term might be used or a new discovery made. Like Kant, Quine finds a role for reason in organising sensory perceptions into what he terms 'a web of beliefs'. Each belief gains its meaning from the other beliefs to which it stands in relation and each individual thinker spins and repairs their own web of beliefs in order to catch the truth. Quine's most famous attack on the analytic–synthetic distinction appears in 'Two Dogmas of Empiricism'. The two unfounded beliefs or dogmas are: an unwavering conviction in the existence of pure, analytic truths and the belief that all meaningful statements can be reduced to verifiable sense-data. Both dogmas are mistaken in assuming that one can easily separate language and experience.

Justification

Knowledge has traditionally been defined as 'justified true belief'. This idea is called the tripartite definition of knowledge (see pp. 13–14) and finds its origins in Plato's *Theaetetus*. Plato argues that knowledge cannot just consist in true belief alone and a further ingredient is required, namely **justification**. He gives the example of a jury who have a hunch that the accused is guilty and are in fact correct in this assumption but states that we would not be right in condemning the accused without some form of evidence.[3] Plato declares that the jury's true belief does not count as knowledge without proof, warrant or justification. It is this notion, that of justification,

that concerns us in this section.

Knowledge is not based on guesswork or chance, but on having a good reason for holding a belief. Thus guessing a stranger's name correctly would not count as knowledge. This is what is meant when we say that a belief is 'justified'. There are three principal explanations as to what constitutes a good reason for holding a belief: foundationalism, coherentism and reliabilism. Let us examine each in turn.

Foundationalism

Foundationalists divide all beliefs into two main groups:

- basic beliefs – i.e. beliefs that support themselves and are, therefore, not inferred from other beliefs (non-inferential);
- non-basic beliefs – i.e. beliefs that need to be supported by other beliefs, which are inferred from other beliefs (inferential).

Foundationalism is often seen as a superstructure of non-basic beliefs that are built on a firm foundation of basic beliefs; such an image has led philosophers to call this theory of justification 'the pyramid model'. Foundationalism is favoured by empiricists, who are intent on building a structure of scientific knowledge. An empiricist model that uses scientific facts verified by sense-data as the candidate for basic beliefs

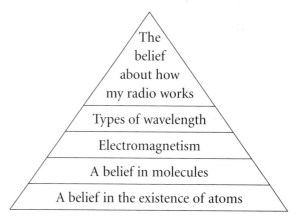

may run as follows:
Each level of beliefs builds on the previous stratum; one might say that each belief is inferred from what has already been established. In this example, the pinnacle belief acts as a test of the basic beliefs. Thus, if one is engaged in the

activity of manufacturing some device, the main endorsement for the validity of your beliefs is if the end product works.

Foundationalism is not an exclusively empiricist model. Descartes (1596–1650) is one rationalist who constructs a pyramid from what

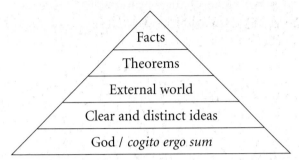

he holds to be *a priori* beliefs:

Descartes uses as his foundations the premises 'God exists' and 'I think therefore I am' (*cogito ergo sum*). He holds that such clear and distinct ideas are self-evidently true and from this firm basis we can demonstrate the existence of an external world of objects and even go as far as to

Task

Invent your own pyramid of basic and non-basic beliefs to illustrate the foundationalist theory of justification. Draw on any subject area, e.g. economics, history or the sciences, and set it out as above.

discover laws governing how they work.

For non-basic beliefs to be justified they need to rest on basic beliefs. In many cases, these basic beliefs appeal to present sensory experiences. For instance, an empiricist might use as a basic belief an observation such as litmus paper changing colour or the atomic structure of a substance as seen through a microscope. Underlying this view is the conviction that sense-data are reliable, to the point of being privileged as basic beliefs. In turn, non-basic beliefs are justified on a scale of probability in relation to the concrete, infallible foundations of empirical data. For this reason, foundationalism has been termed an error-avoidance theory: foundationalists seek to avoid false beliefs and may make use of **scepticism** (see pp. 14–17) to rid the superstructure of any dubious beliefs that may lead to its collapse. Every level of the pyramid needs to be secured

before it is built on. One might argue, however, that no basic belief is truly simple. So, for example, something as seemingly fundamental as a white sense-datum nevertheless implies a spectrum, an object to hold the property of whiteness or an area in which to be white. Basic beliefs are subject to two problems: either the basic belief is so basic that nothing of interest can be inferred from it or it yields too many possible but indeterminate beliefs.

Criticisms of foundationalism

There are two further strands of criticism of the foundationalist theory. The first we shall call the regress argument and it may be summarised as follows:

1 In the foundationalist model, each belief relies on another belief for its justification.
2 Basic beliefs cannot be treated as an exception and must in turn rely on a further set of beliefs for their justification.
3 There is no end to this process of justification, which must continue *ad infinitum*.

Philosophers term such a never-ending sequence an 'infinite regress', and consider it to be extremely problematic in any explanation.

The two pyramid models cited above create infinite regresses: the Cartesian model begs warrant for a belief in God; the empiricist model assumes a correspondence between sense-data and reality. Foundationalists respond either by accepting that a regress occurs *ad infinitum* in any case of justification or by denying this fact. The second line of defence (denying infinite regress) sees hard-line foundationalists arguing that basic beliefs, by definition, do not need any further justification. Soft foundationalists view basic beliefs as lying beyond *reasonable* doubt and argue that accurate observation is the best we can hope for as the foundation to our knowledge.

The second major criticism of foundationalism rests on the fallibility of the sense-data (i.e. the possibility that sense-data are wrong). The English philosopher Bertrand Russell (1872–1970) argues in the following example that a more sophisticated way of determining truth and falsity is needed as opposed to an uncritical reliance on sense-data:

Domestic animals expect food when they see the person who usually feeds them. We know that all these rather crude expectations of uniformity are liable to be misleading. The man who has fed the chicken every day throughout its life at last wrings its neck instead, showing that more refined views as to the uniformity of nature would have been useful to the chicken.[4]

Russell's sentiment, inherited from Humean scepticism, is that one cannot rely on any necessary connection between sense-data. This is a particular problem for empiricism. Underlying Russell's concerns is the fact that just because something happens in a certain way does not mean that it always will (see section on the problem of induction, pp. 123–24). No belief can realistically be termed 'infallible', and as a consequence one cannot use basic beliefs as an indubitable foundation as even they might turn out to be unjustified. In response to this, some foundationalists argue more humbly that basic beliefs can at least provide us with a useful working model.

Coherentism

The coherentist theory of justification stresses the consistency, connectedness and cohesion of justified beliefs and is sometimes referred to as holism for this reason. A belief coheres with a general pattern of beliefs if:

- it is based on adequate evidence;
- it is not disproved by one's current pattern of beliefs.

Thus I believe that an acid turns litmus paper red as I have observed the reaction take place and it fits in with my other convictions about chemistry. Coherentism may be compared to a raft on which each proposition is a length of driftwood bound together in order to float on a sea of uncertainty. Foundationalists, in contrast, set out to construct an oil-refinery-like superstructure. The coherentist aim is to sail on a self-contained body of knowledge in which:

- each proposition is to be judged on its own merits;
- each proposition is connected to at least one other proposition;

- no proposition can stand separately from the rest.

Beliefs in a foundationalist model have an asymmetrical structure, i.e. belief A is justified because it is based on basic belief B. Coherentism, contrariwise, operates a symmetrical relation between beliefs, i.e. belief A justifies belief B as much as belief B justifies belief A. For example, Eddington used planetary motion to prove Einstein's predictions, yet Einsteinian physics can equally be employed to explain the position of Uranus. The two beliefs are mutually explanatory. Coherentists are reluctant to change the mutually reliant structure, as its main aim is to stay afloat. For this reason, the model has been called an ignorance-avoidance theory. It seeks to offer an explanation, accepting the likelihood of some falsehoods in order to obtain beliefs about the world around us and avoid drowning. As the set of justified beliefs expands, each belief in turn is better explained by the additions. An expansion of the set of justified beliefs must result in an improved, more comprehensive explanation than was previously offered. Cosmology is one example, where in ancient times poetic creation stories were told in order to fill an unsettling void. In due course, a more refined 'big bang theory' has replaced mythology as it dovetails with other scientific theories. It, nevertheless, remains a conjecture.

Three strands of coherentism may be identified: positive, negative and mixed. Positive coherence involves beliefs being justified if there is evidence for their truth. This approach is favoured in hard sciences such as physics and chemistry. Negative coherence involves beliefs being accepted until one unearths evidence against them. One might think of an archaeologist devising a likely explanation for a given feature that may be revised in the face of contrary evidence that comes to light. In practice, most theories are mixed.

Criticisms of coherentism

Let us examine two criticisms of coherentism. The first argument runs as follows:

1 Coherentists seek to offer a complete and comprehensive explanation made up of justified beliefs.

2 There might be more than one complete and comprehensive explanation made up of these justified beliefs, given that each belief has an equal and opposite possible belief. (For example, for my belief that Nelson's Column is in London, there is an equal and opposite belief that Nelson's Column is not in London.)

3 Coherentism does not provide adequate criteria with which to judge rival explanations.

4 Therefore, coherentism is an inadequate theory of justification.

This accusation is a powerful one: if every belief has an equal and opposite belief floating on the sea of uncertainty, how does one choose between them? One would have to argue in defence that the truth is somehow unique and that a truthful answer is the only answer where each belief coheres properly.

The argument from plurality may be refined in a second criticism. According to coherentism, any system of beliefs works if, and only if, it coheres. However, the entire system could be wrong or misinterpreted. Surely the justification of a belief needs to be linked to the truth of that belief. Yet no criteria are supplied by coherentists that enable us to test for truth. How do we judge rival explanations for the origins of the universe if each appears to cohere with what we already know about physics?

Review questions

1 Identify and explain two differences between foundationalism and coherentism.

2 Briefly explain the view that knowledge is justified true belief.

Reliabilism

The third theory of justification examined in this chapter is termed reliabilism. This account holds that a belief is justified if and only if it is the product of a reliable method. Reliabilists are not as much concerned with the ins and outs of how a method comes to be reliable as with the realisation that it is. Consider the following examples of reliable methods:

- *Testimony:* historians are able to work with primary sources to generate valuable information (such as 'The battle of Hastings was fought in 1066'). They work with first-hand testimonies to elucidate facts and figures about past events.

- *Memory:* doctors use memory to remember the symptoms of various diseases in order to diagnose accurately.

- *Perception:* scientists use sensory perception in their day-to-day experiments. We learn that copper burns with a blue-green flame through observation.

- *Inference:* logicians use inference as a fail-safe method for deducing a valid conclusion. This may take the basic form, 'Either p or q: not p: therefore q' (see appendix 2 on critical thinking).

In practice, many reliable methods may be used together. Consider the example of a person who discovers a potentially valuable painting in her attic. She takes it along to an expert, who tells her that it is indeed a priceless work. On discovering another painting in this style she is even more delighted. This person relies on the art expert's testimony. He is able to remember details and recognise them in works of art. In turn, given that one work is valuable and a second bears sufficient resemblance to the first, one may infer that the second piece is also valuable. One might express the conviction that the second work of art is of value in terms of probability. Indeed reliabilism is linked to probability:

1 It is reasonable, all things considered, to believe p (where p is some proposition).

2 p makes q (another proposition) highly probable.

3 So, all things considered, it is reasonable to believe q.

Reliabilism differs from foundationalism and coherentism in that it is concerned with the processes involved in generating justification rather than the relationship between beliefs. For this reason, it is termed an externalist theory of justification. Reliability does not depend on human beings but on an external process that is noted by them. Foundationalism and coherentism are termed internalist theories of justification. To illustrate the difference, consider the scenario where an internalist and an externalist enjoy a day at the races. The internalist spends all day considering the form, the going, which trainers and jockeys are in luck, the age, weight and breeding of the runners. The externalist, however, spends an hour in the bar talking to his contacts, who he knows will give him a winner. The reliabilist or externalist does not understand how his contacts come up with so many successful tips at each meeting, but is eternally grateful that they do. Note that both punters might bring home equal winnings.

Criticisms of reliabilism

One frustration that is encountered in pursuing the reliabilist theory of justification is that no method of justification is infallible (i.e. reliable) in every instance. Your watch may have always provided reliable information about the time in the past but might stop tomorrow! In addition, one might imagine a historian being misled when looking at the Bayeux tapestry depiction of the battle of Hastings, thinking that Harold was shot in the eye with an arrow when, in fact, the character with an arrow in his eye might not have been Harold. Similarly, we might be forgetful or be impeded so we are unable to perceive accurately. Lastly, inference may supply a valid method, though not necessarily true conclusions. For example, one might argue flawlessly as follows without realising the ornithological error in the first sentence (not all swans are white!):

1 All swans are white.
2 Frank is a swan.
3 Therefore, Frank is white.

A second criticism of reliabilism stems from the circular nature of the reliabilist reasoning. The argument runs:

1 Reliable methods generate knowledge.
2 Knowledge is what is generated by reliable methods.

When laid out like this it becomes evident that the theory does not present clear criteria against which knowledge or reliability can be judged. Taken together these criticisms from error and circularity prove difficult for reliabilists to argue against. Yet, as we have seen, criticism can be waged against each of the three theories of justification: foundationalism, coherentism and reliabilism. Is it then ever possible to achieve certainty? One group of philosophers who believe that every form of justification and knowledge can be challenged are called 'sceptics'. We shall meet some of their arguments later in this chapter.

The tripartite definition of knowledge

So far we have surveyed theories of knowledge and justification. We shall now look at the relationship between these concepts and explain the tripartite definition of knowledge. The term 'tripartite' means divided into three parts and refers to the traditional conception of knowledge as justified true belief. The definition may be expressed more formally in the following way:

For person X to know that *p*:

1 *p* must be true.
2 Person X must believe that *p* is true.
3 Person X must have some reason for believing (evidence or assurance) that *p* is true.

I can be said to know that Mercury is the nearest planet to the Sun because it is, I accept that it is, and have assurance every time I scan the sky with my telescope.

The most famous objection to the tripartite definition of knowledge comes from E. L. Gettier's short paper 'Is Justified True Belief Knowledge?' (1963). Gettier (born 1927) maintains that in certain circumstances all three elements are present, yet the resulting intellectual state cannot be counted as a genuine instance of knowledge. Such scenarios have been called 'Gettier counter-examples'. Imagine yourself at a party; you gaze across the dance floor and notice that your friend Ben happens to be dancing. In fact, it is Ben's identical twin brother Bill, but coincidentally Ben is also dancing close by:

1 It is true that Ben is dancing.

2 You believe Ben is dancing.

3 You have a good reason to believe that Ben is dancing.

Yet the above instance, according to Gettier, does not warrant the description of knowledge.[5] Gettier's examples dwell on the fact that the justification does not relate to the truth of the situation. Is there a clause that we can insert to rescue the tripartite definition from the scrap-heap of invalid arguments? Perhaps one might try the following to counter the effect of coincidence:

> The justification for *p* must correspond to the truth of *p*.

Thus, one might add to the previous example that you are justified in believing that Ben is on the dance floor if, and only if, the person you have observed is indeed Ben. In practice, it will be extremely difficult to prove this link for every supposition one makes.

Task

Invent your own Gettier counter-example. Explain how each of the three elements of truth, belief and justification are present and why your belief cannot, according to Gettier, be classed as knowledge.

Other wounds have been inflicted on the tripartite definition of knowledge. As we have previously seen, there is little agreement as to what constitutes justification. The tripartite definition does not specify which account of justification (foundationalism, coherentism or reliabilism) is to be accepted, nor does it specify what counts as truth.

There are rival epistemological theories as to the definition of truth (e.g. coherence, correspondence, performance and pragmatism). The tripartite definition of truth makes no attempt to resolve this wrangling.

Finally, one may accuse exponents of the tripartite definition of knowledge of overcooking the definition. In many cases we take knowledge to be self-evident and do not need to carry out laborious examinations. Self-evident knowledge,

such as the mathematical truth $2 + 2 = 4$, appears to be beyond the need for justification.

Scepticism

Doubt

When we say a person is sceptical, we usually mean that that person is not easily convinced and doubts any claim that is not well founded. Scepticism is also the term used for a philosophical school of thought that has its origins in ancient Greece and which has had many famous advocates over the centuries. Sceptics believe that if they apply a systematic method of doubt to what is taken for granted some indisputable truths will be established. Philosophical doubt is used to discover the indubitable, i.e. that which cannot be doubted. Philosophical doubt differs from ordinary doubt in a number of ways:

- Philosophical doubt is concerned with the big questions in life.
- Philosophical doubt examines the justification of truths.
- Philosophical doubt does not need to have any practical benefits.
- Philosophical doubt challenges our idea of what counts as knowledge.

One of the earliest sceptics was the ancient Greek philosopher Pyrrho of Elis. He concluded that we could not know anything for certain and that this yielded a calm detachment from life known as *ataraxia*. Another ancient Greek philosopher, and follower of the Pyrrhonian school, was the stoic Agrippa. He challenged people, in what became known as 'Agrippa's trilemma', to find a claim to knowledge that did not involve dogmatism, regress or circularity:

- *Dogmatism* is the entrenched commitment to a belief even in the face of contrary evidence. For example, members of some ancient tribes retain their beliefs about the nature of the world even when faced with contrary evidence.
- *Regress* is an endless sequence of justification where successive beliefs justify the next *ad infinitum* (we have already encountered this problem when looking at foundationalism).

- *Circularity* occurs when a set of beliefs justify each other. One might imagine a religious person arguing that they believe in God because God's existence is documented in scripture, which should be believed because it is the word of God.

Agrippa reached the conclusion that we can never assert a genuine claim to knowledge. Many centuries later, however, the French philosopher René Descartes believed that, through using sceptical arguments as a tool, he could engineer a whole epistemic structure founded on **certainty**. Unlike the previous Pyrrhonian scepticism, which has as its end uncertainty, Cartesian scepticism aims for truths that cannot be doubted. Note, however, that both Pyrrho and Descartes are global (radical) sceptics in that they cast doubt over *all* claims to knowledge rather than over claims in a localised area, such as morality, religion or science.

Cartesian scepticism

Descartes used a system of methodological doubt for a positive end in order to establish what is indubitable and to extinguish any trace of uncertainty. His conclusions sound surprising to the modern ear, which is used to hearing words such as 'scientific' and 'empirical' as bywords for assurance and authoritativeness. Instead, Descartes held that we cannot be certain of scientific truths and can only be sure about the existence of God, the existence of our souls and self-evident truths such as those found in mathematics. He used three main sceptical arguments to reach this conclusion. These arguments can be phrased in the form of questions:

- How do we know that our senses are delivering reliable information to our brains about what reality is like? (the argument from illusion)
- How do we know that what we experience is not a dream? (the argument from dreaming)
- How do we know that all that we believe is not deliberately created in our minds by an evil deceiver? (the argument from deception)

Descartes concluded that even if we were being deceived we could still be sure of our own existence, as it is impossible for someone to be deceived and not exist. He went on from this basic conclusion to derive certainty about the existence of God and the truths of mathematics.

Modern 'brain in a vat' arguments are direct descendants of Cartesian doubt, and take the form of asking the disquieting question 'How do you know that you are not a brain in a vat having your experiences controlled by some super-psychologist?' Hilary Putnam (born 1926) describes the scene thus:

> The person's brain (your brain) has been removed from the body and placed in a vat of nutrients which keeps the brain alive. The nerve endings have been connected to a super-scientific computer which causes the person whose brain it is to have the illusion that everything is perfectly normal.[6]

Every brain wave that we experience, whether it is a memory, personal experience or feeling, is the result of controlled electronic impulses and it is possible that every human being is fed these impulses artificially, as in the film *The Matrix*. Putnam operates in the same way as Descartes in using scepticism for an anti-sceptical purpose. Like Descartes, Putnam hopes to establish a positive conclusion. His brain in a vat argument differs from the Cartesian account of an evil deceiver in some notable ways. Putnam dispenses with a malign genius whose intent is to feed false beliefs into people's brains. Instead Putnam talks about all sentient beings suffering from a collective hallucination that is controlled by a self-refuting system. That we are all brains in a vat of nutrients would be admittedly a strange quirk of nature, but not inconceivable. Having sketched out the scene, Putnam goes on to argue that the expression 'I am a brain in a vat' is in fact a self-refuting proposition – that is, one which if true proves to be false. Putnam belongs to the analytic school of philosophy that defines meaningful statements as those which are either obviously true or provable by experiment. For Putnam, the sentence 'I am a brain in a vat' is factually meaningless as it suggests something that goes beyond the evidence for or against. The idea of being a brain in a vat has no external reference point that we can investigate and as such goes beyond belief and disbelief. If we are to refer to some object or property in the physical world with any degree of meaning then we need to establish a causal link between our description and the thing itself. It is as if our description exists as a balloon that needs to be tied to physical evidence. Such a declaration as 'We exist as brains in a vat' is like an untied balloon or free-floating belief that exists beyond our reach and beyond the realm of reasonable doubt. Expressed more formally Putnam's anti-sceptical arguments runs:

1 I know that I am here talking to you.
2 Sitting here talking to you entails that you are not a brain in a vat.
3 Therefore, I know that you are not a brain in a vat.

Review question

Identify two ways in which a sceptic can doubt that what we see is what there is.

Humean scepticism

Descartes was one of several philosophers to successfully use sceptical methods to establish a certainty (that thinking entails existence). Scepticism has also been used in the empiricist tradition to clarify the nature of our knowledge. Two powerful arguments put forward by Hume illustrate the limits of the scientific enterprise. Hume states that just because we have observed the same effect follow an event on a myriad of previous occasions it does not mean that there is a necessary relationship between the cause and the effect. A sceptic is justified, therefore, in questioning such seemingly indubitable notions as that the sun will rise tomorrow by asserting that there is no logical justification for supposing that the sun will rise rather than that the darkness will remain.

The philosopher's second argument warns of the dangers of classifying general laws as indisputable, owing to the fact that we can never complete an infinite number of observations. We might embark on a number of experiments to test the hypothesis 'All frogs can swim'. Even if all the frogs in our experiment took to the water with consummate ease, it is still a leap of faith to move from the premise 'All observed frogs can

swim' to the conclusion 'All frogs can swim'. If we can theoretically conceive of an amphibian still wearing frog-sized armbands that hasn't learnt to swim yet, then we cannot say that we have discovered a certainty about all frogs.

Russellian scepticism

Bertrand Russell was another empiricist philosopher who added to the mêlée of sceptical challenges. He focused on the distinction between appearance and reality (see chapter 14) and his argument can be laid out as follows:

1 Appearances differ from reality.
2 We are only acquainted with the appearances of things.
3 Therefore, we can never pronounce with certainty on the reality of things.

Russell's argument is classed as sceptical as it sows the thought in our minds that reality might be different from the world as depicted by our sense-data. He concludes that we can only talk meaningfully about our sense-data and not about a separate reality, but he remains open to the possibility that there is such a separate reality.

In summation: the various strands of scepticism mentioned above all focus on the inadequacy of sense-data. Cartesian scepticism doubts that knowledge gained from sensory evidence could be as assured as knowledge gained from reason. Humean scepticism acknowledges information gained through the senses but doubts that this informs us of necessary truths. Russellian scepticism doubts that sense-data give us a true picture of what lies behind the world of everyday experience.

Solipsism

Descartes, Hume and Russell attempted to achieve a positive result from their sceptical challenges. For Descartes, it was the assurance of his own existence through the activity of thinking; for Hume, it was contingent truths gained from observation of the world around us; and for Russell, it was the fact that we can only meaningfully describe sense-data. The most extreme form of doubt is called **solipsism**, and yields a different conclusion. Solipsism is the view that you alone are the only object of real knowledge and source of existence – that is, other objects only exist when and because you perceive them. The term is coined from two Latin words: *solus* meaning 'alone' and *ipse* meaning 'self'.

The position divides reality into two conceptual frameworks or matrices. The first matrix consists in a familiarity with one's own thoughts, experiences and emotions. The second comprises everything else, including other minds, the external world, time and space. While we can have certain knowledge of the first matrix, references to the second cannot be held as claims to knowledge.

Solipsism is in turn subject to the following criticisms:

- Language is too complicated to be invented by any one person and similarly could not be authentically maintained by only one user.

- Solipsism seems to offer a poor account of our existence in that even if it were true it does not supply an account of where our thoughts, experiences and emotions come from.

- Solipsism poses the wrong sort of questions. While in the past philosophers investigated things like consciousness and existence, today such topics belong in the remit of scientific investigation.

No mainstream philosophical movement has ever adopted a seriously solipsistic standpoint, perhaps due to the perceived lack of an audience, but it is nevertheless an interesting notion to explore! Solipsism raises uncertainties about the true nature of our perceptions. How do we know that what we see is what there is? The last section of this chapter supplies an outline of the four main accounts of **perception**.

Perception

We gain knowledge of the external world from sensory data: touch, sight, smell, hearing and taste. For this reason philosophers are interested in the mechanisms of sensory perception and pose the question, 'What is going on when something is perceived?' Four possible accounts are explored below: naive realism, representative realism, **idealism** and **phenomenalism**.

Naive realism

Any theory of perception that is described as 'realist' holds that we perceive the world as it really is and that there is no difference between appearance and reality. Naive realists believe that we have direct access to a naked, unmediated and unadorned reality. It is the commonsensical view that what we see is what there is; thus, observing a bowl of ripening fruit involves nothing more than opening my eyes and seeing what is really there. In addition, the term 'naive' has a technical meaning in the philosophy of perception, namely that objects contain the same properties when they are not being perceived as when they are being perceived. So, for instance, if I were to leave the kitchen for a moment or two, the oranges in the fruit bowl would continue being orange and the bananas would still be banana-shaped. In summary, the two principles of naive realism are as follows:

- the principle of direct realism, i.e. the belief that the relevant physical object and your immediate perception of it are indistinguishable in every way;

- the principle of innate properties, i.e. the belief that properties intrinsically belong to objects and that objects hold their properties even when they are not being perceived – this is to deny any distinction between primary and secondary qualities raised by representative realists (see below).

Naive realism runs into problems as there is clearly a complex process involved in perception that consists in an image of an object being presented to the mind's eye. Science explains this in terms of light rays hitting the retina and producing brain waves. To argue that we have unmediated access to the external world is to ignore the role of the sense organs as instruments of perception. Secondly, naive realism seems to hold that whatever is immediately perceived must immediately exist. This is not true in cases of time lag, as when I see a star that ceased to exist years ago. Thirdly, arguments from illusion successfully counter the theory by showing how mistaken one can be when perceiving the world. The most effective arguments of this type involve cases of hallucination, where there is a radical discrepancy between our perceptions and relevant physical objects – there are no relevant physical objects present when a hallucination takes place.

Naive realism may be summarised in the following diagram:

Perceiver ⟶ World

Representative realism

Representative or indirect realism seeks to incorporate the scientific analysis of perception by talking about two worlds: the world around us and the world of images or representations that are presented to me. To use the example of sight: light reflects from objects in the external world (perhaps a bunch of grapes from our earlier example), my eyes are stimulated and a brain wave is produced. As a result I enjoy a visual experience of the grapes draped over the fruit bowl. Representative realists talk in terms of the actual grapes as they exist in the real world and the visual experience, representation or perception I have of the fruit.

The English empiricist John Locke advances a further notion concerning how we perceive the features of objects in the real world. Locke argues that some features (termed primary qualities) belong to the objects themselves and include shape, size and movement while other features (termed secondary qualities) are added by our sensory systems and include colour, texture and sound. Returning to our fruit example, a pear possesses the primary quality of being pear-shaped while also possessing the power to induce the secondary quality of a sweet taste as experienced by the perceiver. This secondary quality of sweetness is perceived by the person who eats the fruit but it is not said to belong to the pear itself.

Representative realists are left with an important question as to how the mental image corresponds to what exists in the real world. Some philosophers, called idealists, have even doubted that the real world exists, arguing that all that exists are our minds and their perceptions. For the moment let us summarise representative realism in the following diagram:

Perceiver ⟶ World I ⟶ World II
(in our mind)　(in reality)

Idealism

Idealism (and phenomenalism) may be described as anti-realist theories of perception in that they hold that there is no independent reality 'out there'. The most prominent idealist was the Anglo-Irish bishop George Berkeley (1685–1753), who posed the question 'How do we know that a material world exists?' Berkeley's conclusion was that there was no good reason for believing in the existence of material objects and that the notion of matter as an independently existing substance was groundless and unintelligible. For Berkeley, we can only be sure of three things: the existence of our own mind, the existence of ideas and the existence of God. It is God who keeps ideas in existence when they are not entertained in our minds. The idealist philosophy of existence and perception consists entirely of non-physical entities. Thus you may believe that the book you are currently reading exists in solid material form, but it is in fact a series of mental images perceived by your mind's eye and stored in the library of God's imagination when not 'in use', i.e. being perceived. Berkeley summed up this notion in his famous epigram *esse est percipi* – to be is to be perceived.

The idealist theory of perception has made many enemies down the years since its first formulation, but one must admire Berkeley's originality. He is not questioning the existence of matter in order to be irritating but raises the question, 'What good reason do we have for believing in a material realm?' One of Berkeley's contemporaries Samuel Johnson famously kicked a stone outside Berkeley's church and declared, 'I refute it thus'. His point was that it is obvious that the material world exists, yet his refutation is no refutation at all, as the stone, the act of kicking and Johnson's exclamation would, according to idealism, all belong to the immaterial world of ideas. A more successful criticism may be made through countering Berkeley's question 'How do we know that matter exists?' with a further question, 'Is there a good reason for supposing that matter does not exist?' This return fire suggests that idealism itself lacks justification and is, as a consequence, unlikely.

George Berkeley (1685–1753)

George Berkeley was born near Thomastown, County Kilkenny, in Ireland. The previous generation of his family had moved to Ireland from England, and Berkeley was to work in Ireland intermittently for the rest of his life. He attended school in Kilkenny before moving to Dublin where he studied and taught theology at Trinity College. Berkeley took holy orders in the Protestant clergy in 1713 and left Dublin for London that same year. He returned to Ireland, but later he embarked on a project to build a college for Christian education hundreds of miles away in Bermuda. Many of his friends agreed to assist him financially, but when he eventually travelled to America in 1728 much of this money fell through and he settled on a farmstead on Rhode Island. By this time Berkeley was married and spent some pleasant years writing, teaching and founding a philosophy society in this rural outpost. Life in the new world was not to last, however, and the clergyman travelled back to London in 1732 before being made Bishop of Cloyne in Cork in 1734. He spent many years there before retiring to Oxford to be with his son.

Significant works
Theory of Vision (1709)
The Principles of Human Knowledge (1710)
Three Dialogues between Hylas and Philonous (1713)

Idealism took a different form in the eighteenth century with the theory of perception advanced by Immanuel Kant, which became known as 'transcendent idealism'. Whereas Berkeley believed that no material objects existed and that the 'physical things' that appear to us are ideas and nothing more, Kant held that these appearances have material counterparts but that they are permanently hidden from view. Kant argued that this real or 'noumenal' world of things-in-themselves was permanently off limits and that our minds could only conceive the phenomenal realm or 'how things seem'. The phenomenal world is organised into sensations or concepts and put into a context of space and time by the human mind.

The next period of perceptual philosophy was the nineteenth- and twentieth-century versions of phenomenalism. Some phenomenalists agreed with Berkeley that there was no material reality beyond the phenomena we perceive. Other phenomenalists agreed with Kant that there is another realm beyond the phenomena we experience. All phenomenalists hold, however, that whether there is a reality beyond phenomena or not we can only talk meaningfully about the sense-data we experience. The next section explores phenomenalism in more detail.

A summary of subjective idealism (Berkeley)

perceiver → phenomena (termed 'ideas')   no material reality beyond

A summary of transcendent idealism (Kant)

             senses
perceiver → concepts → phenomena ← noumena
             space/time

Phenomenalism

Elements of phenomenalism are found in the works of Berkeley, but are more fully developed in the writings of the British philosophers J. S. Mill (1808–1873), Bertrand Russell (1872–1970) and A. J. Ayer (1910–1989). Phenomenalists do not agree with the realist claim that there is no difference between appearance and reality, and question the representative realist claim that sense-data match reality. Some phenomenalists deny an independent reality altogether, while some believe that the noumenal world exists as an inaccessible mystery. As a straightforward sense-datum theory, which asserts that we can only be aware of sensory information, it seems relatively uncontroversial. A more controversial version, however, attempts to bridge the gap between the appearance of things and real things by asserting that the essence of objects consists in the sensations we perceive and nothing more.

Remember when we looked at how representative realists talked about the image presented to us being different from the object itself. Phenomenalists agree that we can only talk intelligibly about the representations or phenomena that are presented to us. Some phenomenalists argue that there is no reality behind the sense-data that we experience when we see an object.

Phenomenalists refer to the realm of phenomena as the 'veil of perception'. This phrase sounds like an oxymoron (an apparent contradiction in terms), as the purpose of a veil is to impede perception, not enhance it. Phenomenalists humbly admit that we can only talk meaningfully about sense-data.

The phenomenalist theories of Russell and Ayer may be classified as linguistic theories in the style of emotivism and behaviourism (see pp. 43–44 and 83–86), as they assert that all statements about perception can be translated into statements about phenomena or sensations. Just as emotivists assert that statements such as 'Murder is wrong' can be translated into statements about feelings, e.g. 'I find the idea of murder repulsive', so phenomenalists believe that statements about perception, such as 'I see a custard pie', can be translated into statements to do with sense-data, e.g. 'I am having a yellow, pie-shaped, custardy sensory experience and will call this experience a custard pie'.

Phenomenalism is, however, subject to the following philosophical 'razors'. Firstly, as a compromise between realism and idealism, it can be attacked from both sides of the fence, so phenomenalists who presume that an external world exists cannot prove that our sense-data are not illusory. Alternatively, phenomenalists who deny the existence of an external world are led to the solipsistic conclusion that other people are only ideas in our mind, which seems counter-intuitive. Secondly, as a philosophical theory it is a poor explanation: it does not tell us where sense-data come from, how sense-data are related or even what kind of thing sense-data are. Thirdly, phenomenalism does not tell us why we

---

Task

The hallmark of a good theory of perception is how successful it is in repelling sceptical attack. In the following table the columns are headed by four theories of perception and the rows by three sceptical arguments. Complete the table, placing a cross if the theory of perception succumbs to the sceptical argument and a tick if it resists it. Judging by your results, which account of perception is the most successful?

	Naive realism	Representative realism	Berkeleyan idealism	Phenomenalism
Argument from illusion				
Argument from dreaming				
Argument from deception				

should expect the same kind of sense-data every time. For example, it is natural but not necessary to expect a lemon to instil sour sense-data rather than sweet because every lemon in the past has tasted bitter.

In summation, philosophy has challenged the notion that we can perceive the world around us directly. Representative realists argue that our senses project an exact copy of the real world in a way that enables us to know what is going on. Idealists and phenomenalists argue that we only have access to these projections and entertain the idea that there might not even be anything other than sensory experience.

Review questions

1 Identify two differences between naive and representative realism.
2 Identify two differences between idealism and phenomenalism.

Revision questions

1 Evaluate one account of knowledge.
2 Assess the claim that coherentism provides a better account of justification than foundationalism.
3 Briefly explain what is meant by philosophical doubt.
4 Assess sceptical arguments concerning our knowledge of the external world.
5 Assess the merits and demerits of the common-sense view that the world is just as it appears to be.

Discussion questions

- Briefly explain the differences between 'I feel certain', 'I am certain' and 'It is certain'.
- Outline and illustrate one difference between knowledge and belief.
- Outline and illustrate two differences between representative realism and phenomenalism.
- Explain and illustrate the contention that all our perceptions necessarily involve interpretation.
- Does idealism offer a convincing account of what we know and how we know it?

Glossary of key terms

Belief: a unit of thought that is subject to proof but which contains some degree of conviction on the part of the thinker.

Certainty: the absence of doubt as to whether something is true. Certainty differs from knowledge, as one can be certain of something that isn't true.

Empiricism: empiricists believe that we gain knowledge through observation and experience.

Epistemology: the philosophical study of the nature and limitation of human knowledge.

Idealism: the theory of perception that holds that only our minds and their ideas exist.

Justification: a good reason for holding a belief. There are different theories of justification.

Knowledge: the traditional account of knowledge defines it as justified true belief.

Perception: the process of gaining information about the world or oneself via the senses of touch, taste, sight, smell and hearing.

Phenomenalism: the theory of perception that states that we only have access to our own sense experiences, which are called 'phenomena'. This sense-data theory differs from idealism as it holds that possible perceptions exist as a potential experience even when not being perceived.

Rationalism: rationalists emphasise the role of reason in establishing knowledge. Many believe that we are born with this preformed capacity.

Scepticism: philosophical doubt that challenges our claim to knowledge.

Sense-data: information conveyed by the senses in a perceptual experience, for example the taste, sight and smell of an orange.

Solipsism: the belief that only you exist and everything else, including other people, is an illusion.

Truth: there are several theories of truth. One theory holds that the truth is that which is the case: statement p is true if and only if p.

Suggested reading

- Audi, R. (1998) *Epistemology: A Contemporary Introduction to the Theory of Knowledge*, London, Routledge
  Complete coverage of the course in bite-sized pieces
- Dancy, J. (1996) *Introduction to Contemporary Epistemology*, Oxford, Blackwell
  A detailed and scholarly guide to the theory of knowledge that would suit an advanced reader
- Morton, A. (2001) *A Guide through the Theory of Knowledge*, Oxford, Blackwell
  A textbook that explores many issues in epistemology in an entertaining way
- Trusted, J. (1997) *An Introduction to the Philosophy of Knowledge*, Basingstoke, Macmillan
  A clear and comprehensive coverage of all the main epistemological arguments
- Williams, M. (2001) *Problems of Knowledge*, Oxford, OUP
  A modern introduction to epistemology that includes background for students to explore

Notes

1 Plato (1987) *The Republic*, trans. Desmond Lee, London, Penguin, 476.

2 Plato (1956) *Protagoras and Meno*, trans. W. K. C. Guthrie, London, Penguin.

3 Plato (1987) *Theaetetus*, trans. Robin Waterfield, London, Penguin, 200d.

4 Russell, B. (1912, 1988) *The Problems of Philosophy*, Oxford, OUP, p. 35.

5 For other Gettier counter-examples, see J. Dancy (1996) *Introduction to Contemporary Epistemology*, Oxford, Blackwell, pp. 25, 27 and 38.

6 Putnam, H. (1999) 'Brains in a Vat', in K. DeRose and T. Warfield, *Skepticism*, Oxford, OUP.

2 Moral philosophy

There is nothing either good or bad, but thinking makes it so.
(William Shakespeare)

Aims

On completion of this chapter you should be able to:

- distinguish between normative and meta-ethical theories
- understand and evaluate the different versions of utilitarianism
- understand and evaluate Kant's deontological moral philosophy
- understand and evaluate Aristotelian and other forms of virtue theory
- understand and criticise the various arguments for and against abortion
- understand and criticise the various arguments for and against euthanasia
- understand and criticise the various arguments for and against the contention that non-human animals deserve rights
- comprehend and assess the main cognitive meta-ethical theories, i.e. moral realism and intuitionism
- give a critical account of the is–ought gap and attempts to bridge it
- comprehend and assess the main non-cognitive meta-ethical theories, namely emotivism, prescriptivism, relativism and nihilism.

From ancient times to the present day, philosophers have sought to give guidance on how we should behave and have theorised about what constitutes a good life. Socrates famously declared that the unexamined life is not worth living. The same sentiment lies behind the various moral philosophies outlined in this chapter, which examine who we are, how we should act and the nature of right and wrong. Many of the themes raised in the following pages are explored in more detail in the later chapters on Plato, Aristotle, Nietzsche, Ayer and Sartre. Let us begin by exploring the principal normative ethical theories.

Normative ethics

A **normative ethical** theory is any theory that helps us find our way through life's moral maze. It should help us to see more clearly what makes a problem difficult and how we might find a solution. Meta-ethics, by contrast, is the study of ethical concepts (such as goodness) and does not aim to give moral advice. Moral questions arise in many varied fields: for example, personal

relationships, economic life, health care and environmental concerns. There follows a brief examination of how three philosophical theories seek to give helpful advice as to how moral problems can be solved through applying a simple principle. Firstly, utilitarianism emphasises the importance of maximising happiness. Secondly, Kant's rule-based (deontological) ethic, known as the 'categorical imperative', stresses the roles of duty and reason. The third theory, virtue theory, states that we should concentrate on cultivating a virtuous character, from which right actions will follow.

Utilitarianism

To use as a starting point the fact that human beings seek out pleasure may seem like stating the obvious. Yet philosophical enquiries into the nature of happiness are fraught with difficulties. This poses a perennial problem for utilitarians, who view the worth of an act in relation to how much happiness it produces and how much unhappiness it prevents. As the first advocate of utilitarianism, Jeremy Bentham, declared, 'nature has put mankind under two sovereign masters: pain and pleasure'. Bentham believed that there was an implicit principle in all ethical judgements. This became known as the principle of utility:

> What is good is what leads to the greatest happiness of the greatest number.

Bentham first encountered this formula in an economics textbook, and became convinced that happiness was a measurable quantity. He devised a method of calculation that any individual might use in order to work out whether the action produced a sufficient amount of pleasure. This hedonic (*hedone* is the Greek for 'pleasure') calculus proceeds in seven steps and is summarised below in the form of a series of questions:

1 How intense is the pleasure?
2 What is the duration of the pleasure?
3 How certain are you that pleasure will be generated?
4 Is the pleasure immediate or in the future?
5 Will the pleasure be followed by pleasures of a similar kind?
6 Will the pleasure be followed by pain?
7 How many will be affected by the pleasure?

For example, on wondering whether to return a mislaid wallet you would consider the intensity of that warm glow of satisfaction gained from returning a lost item. You would weigh this against the weeks of good fortune you might enjoy spending the contents. You might wonder whether the wallet's owner could easily be found and weigh this against the immediate pleasure of buying things you would enjoy with this new-found wealth. You might also reflect on whether buying luxuries would in fact make you happy. And you might also consider the possibility of being caught using somebody else's money and, if so, whether this might upset your friends and family. These would be some of the considerations in the utilitarian calculation.

Jeremy Bentham (1748–1832)

Jeremy Bentham was born in London into a family of wealthy lawyers. He displayed a precocious intellect from an early age and started to learn Latin at three. His family sent him to study at Queen's College, Oxford, when he was twelve and he trained as a lawyer. Bentham did not write a great deal but involved himself in social projects to enhance the lives of his fellow Londoners. One such project was the designing of a new kind of prison called the Panopticon, a plan that in the end did not reach fruition. Bentham was one of the inspirations behind the founding of University College London, though he was too old to take an active part himself. His preserved skeleton, resplendent in a full set of his own clothes, may be found at the end of South Cloisters to this day, though Bentham's head is secured elsewhere. There are many stories told about this so-called auto-icon. It allegedly attended a meeting of the UCL Council in 1996 to mark the 150th anniversary of the university's founding, the minutes recording that 'Bentham was present but not voting'. Bentham's head was once stolen and deposited in a left luggage locker in Aberdeen railway station, and has variously been used in football practice and attended dinners, once falling into a bowl of soup. Bentham's first time away from UCL was in 1992 when he accompanied a group of students to a philosophy conference in Germany, after which it was rumoured that he attended a nearby beer festival. The reason behind the philosopher's strange desire to be preserved is not clear.

Significant works
An Introduction to the Principles of Morals and Legislation (1789)
The Theory of Legislation (1802)

Strengths of ultilitarianism

- Utilitarianism has a certain intuitive appeal. Most people say that they want to be happy and want other people to be happy.
- The theory provides a useful procedure for weighing the benefits and concerns of any course of action.
- Utilitarianism is a secular ethic that requires minimum commitment but is accessible, egalitarian and consistent.
- Utilitarianism incorporates subjectivity in acknowledging individual likes and dislikes.

Criticisms of utilitarianism

Bentham's hedonistic utilitarianism runs headlong into some preliminary difficulties:

- There is disagreement between individuals as to what counts as a pleasurable experience, and individuals may even change their minds. If pleasure is a matter of personal preference, then the theory does not supply proper criteria by which we can judge between pleasures and, in so doing, decide how to act.
- Bentham's hedonic calculus could be used to justify the oppression of any minority by any majority. This seems to conflict with other principles such as justice and liberty.
- While some aspects of pleasure, such as duration, can be measured, how can we measure the intensity of pleasure? It is telling that the philosopher found his formula in an economics textbook and he seems to conceive of pleasure in quantitative terms.
- It is not clear whose happiness is relevant and whether we extend the calculation to all sentient creatures, even the lowliest worm.
- One might wonder when the calculation of future pleasure would stop; it could continue *ad infinitum*.

The theory appears to reduce the **moral agent** to the status of an ethical barometer registering the fluctuations between pleasure and pain.

Mill's utilitarianism

The nineteenth-century philosopher John Stuart Mill advanced a more sophisticated version of utilitarianism that meets some of the criticisms above.

Mill suggests that when we attribute moral praise or blame we are really talking about the happiness-generating capacity of acts. He did not want to deny, however, that some people have plainly wrong views on what is good.

Mill defines happiness as 'pleasure and the absence of pain'. However, he distinguishes between higher and lower pleasures. Mill argues that one pleasure is superior to another pleasure if those acquainted with both 'decidedly prefer' one to the other. When there is disagreement on the superiority of a particular pleasure, then it is the view of the majority acquainted with it that must prevail. In Mill's writing, higher pleasures tend to be of the mind, such as poetry, whereas lower pleasures are more sensory and superficial, such as sports and games.

There is a difficulty in the theory if people choose lesser pleasures at the expense of higher ones. Mill replies by asserting that these are not majority preferences and are often the choices of individuals with blunted sensibilities. It is also possible for people to choose lower pleasures while still acknowledging the more valuable character of some neglected higher pleasure. This last point is problematic, as the criterion of a higher pleasure seems no longer to be the empirical fact that it is preferred but the fact that it is recognised as preferable. We will now consider some more general objections to utilitarianism, and see how Mill responded to these criticisms:

- Utilitarianism is misguided as it encourages the pursuit of an unattainable or at any rate unsustainable goal, which is happiness. Mill replies that by happiness is meant not a state of ecstatic pleasure but an active life with the predominance of pleasure over pain and where expectations do not exceed life's capacity to deliver.
- Utilitarianism destroys the connection between good actions and good people. One might picture a cruel, despotic ruler revitalising culture, education and economic prosperity in a state and being judged by utilitarians as good. Mill disagrees and defends his position by asserting that the best proof of character is good actions.

- Some acts are just wrong whether they produce happiness or not: utilitarianism as a theory cannot defend the absolute rightness or wrongness of certain acts. Mill asserts that there are no actions that are right or wrong in themselves.

- The principle of utility conflicts with justice. The theory would encourage us to lie to someone whose partner we know is having an affair, but we may inform them of this fact out of a sense of fair play despite knowing the unhappiness it will bring. Mill argues that it is impossible to give an account of justice without falling back on the principle of utility.

- Lastly, one might assert that the future cannot accurately be predicted and so we can never be sure of the consequences of our actions. Mill replies that, on the contrary, we generally know enough about the likely consequences of a particular act.

To summarise: we have so far examined the hedonistic utilitarianism of Bentham and cited some obvious problems. Mill's version of utilitarianism was then examined as a refinement of Bentham's theory. To check whether you have understood utilitarianism consider the examples in the task below.

Task

Read the following scenarios and discuss whether these examples pose a problem for utilitarians:

- Suppose that there is one cream bun on a plate. I love cream buns but I offer it to you. You enjoy it, but not much. Have I done the right thing?
- In humiliating Bob, the class as a whole has a good laugh. Not to remark on his appearance leaves them in the doldrums. Ought we to humiliate him, therefore, as a matter of moral obligation?
- I have promised to pay back the five pounds you lent me. However, I hear of the unhappiness of a beggar and decide that he will be made happier if I donate the fiver to him. What should I do?
- If I must maximise happiness, is it not my duty to have as many children as possible so long as they all can achieve a measure of happiness (i.e. a balance of pleasure over pain) in their lives?

Other forms of utilitarianism

Utilitarianism is an easy theory to grasp and still easier to criticise. It nevertheless carries a lasting appeal perhaps because of its capacity to evolve in various forms in order to combat counter-arguments.

Act utilitarianism and rule utilitarianism

Act utilitarianism judges every act on its own merits and deems it necessary to calculate the resultant pleasure and pain in every instance. 'Rules of thumb' may be used on occasion to speed up the calculations but are only generalisations that should not be accepted as always being true. The act utilitarian is always prepared to break rules such as 'promises should be kept' if he or she considers that in a particular case a balance of pleasure over pain is produced by so doing.

Rule utilitarianism respects those rules established in society to maximise happiness. Strong rule utilitarianism adheres to such rules irrespective of individual circumstances on the grounds that such consistency has a more satisfactory outcome in overcoming potentially misguided personal judgements. Weak rule utilitarianism argues that such rules should in certain circumstances be overridden by personal judgements so more pleasure can be generated.

Positive and negative utilitarianism

Positive utilitarianism is concerned with the maximisation of pleasure, and has been criticised by some philosophers as an overly idealistic aim. The alternative is negative utilitarianism, which is concerned with the minimisation of pain and is seen by many to be more pragmatic, as one's goal is to eradicate identifiable hardships rather than to identify what leads to happiness.

Ideal utilitarianism

The term 'ideal utilitarianism' has been applied to aspects of the moral philosophies of Mill and the Cambridge philosopher G. E. Moore (1873–1958). The theory holds that happiness is not the only thing that is independently good; other ideals are suggested, such as beauty, truth, education, freedom and virtue. In this way, ideal utilitarianism meets the criticism that utilitarianism conflicts with other principles or ideals by embracing these ideals in a bear hug. In so doing it seems close to virtue theory (discussed later in this chapter).

Preference utilitarianism

Preference utilitarianism attempts to counter problems inherent in any crude form of hedonism by taking into account our plans in life or sets of desires and interests (our 'preferences'). An act is therefore deemed good if it leads to these preferences being satisfied, and bad if our preferences are frustrated. For preference utilitarians like Peter Singer (born 1946), there is an intrinsic worth in preference satisfaction. Singer also argues that we should take into account other species when doing our calculations.

To make the differences between these versions of utilitarianism clear let us examine how each might respond to a specific ethical issue, namely euthanasia. An act utilitarian would proceed with a calculation of an individual's suffering weighed against his or her quality of life. In contrast, rule utilitarianism may decide that in so far as the ethical imperative 'You should not kill' contributes to the greatest happiness of the greatest number, euthanasia as an instance of killing would be unjustifiable. Positive utilitarians might reflect on the residual quality of life a terminally ill patient has, while a negative utilitarian would seek to minimise the suffering endured. For preference utilitarians the issue of whether the patient's preferences could still be met decides the course of action, while ideal utilitarians might point to additional considerations with regard to happiness such as freedom of choice or personal dignity.

Conclusion

The feature that is most striking about the principle of utility is its generality, which renders it user-friendly but also imprecise. It is difficult to identify a situation where we would evaluate an act as right and where we would clearly not be falling back upon the principle of utility; it is equally difficult to point to an instance where we are quite genuinely seeking to promote the greatest happiness of the greatest number. As a practical method of weighing up the benefits and concerns of a difficult situation, utilitarianism has many merits but it doesn't provide an analysis of right and wrong that can be deemed definitive. Opposing theories such as Kant's deontology promise to do exactly that.

Deontology

A deontological ethical theory is one which denies that an action is right or wrong because of its consequences, and as such is the opposite of **consequentialist** theories such as utilitarianism. The term **deontology** literally means 'a duty-based morality'. There are many strands of deontology, ranging from religious ethics to the moral philosophy of Immanuel Kant; we shall examine the latter in this section. According to Kant, the outcome of an act is irrelevant to its moral standing. Instead, acts are considered moral or immoral according to whether they are right or wrong 'in themselves'. A problem is immediately created in that, if I am told that certain rules have moral worth independently of the consequences, then how do I know that the moral rule I ought to obey is authoritative? What is needed is some sort of test to enable us to decide what laws ought to be obeyed. Kant's method of determining right and wrong is known as the categorical imperative.

The categorical imperative

The word 'categorical' means unqualified, absolute or without exception, while the noun 'imperative' means a command or order; in the context of Kant's philosophy it means a moral injunction telling someone what they ought to do. In his philosophical works, Kant distinguished between a categorical imperative and a hypothetical imperative. A hypothetical imperative tells us what actions would be good as a means to an end, e.g. if you eat less and exercise then you will lose weight. Eating less is not good in itself but only as a means to an end. The categorical imperative, however, informs us as to what an end is in itself. Kant gives three versions of the categorical imperative:

1 Act only on that maxim whereby you can, at the same time, will that it should become a universal law.

Universalisability is the most important feature of the categorical imperative. What Kant meant was that we will know where our duty lies if we ask ourselves the fundamental question: 'Would I wish everyone to behave as I am now proposing to do in these circumstances?' If the answer is 'no', then the moral agent is treating himself or herself as an exception, and this is logically flawed. If the answer is 'yes', then one has discovered a rule that does not lead to contradiction and can be elevated to the status of a universal law, such as 'Thou shalt not lie' or 'Thou shalt not steal'.

> 2 Act in such a way that you always treat humanity, whether in your own person or in the person of any other, never simply as a means but always as an end.

At the heart of this version of the categorical imperative stands the belief that rational beings should always treat other rational beings equally and in the same way that they would wish to be treated; this is often referred to as 'the golden rule'. The value of human beings does not consist in how they can be used, but is intrinsically part of each of us. For example, Kant condemns suicide as wrong because it involves treating oneself as a means to an end, that end being escape from an intolerable situation.

> 3 Act as if you were, through your maxims, a law-making member of a kingdom of ends.

The third formulation of the categorical imperative combines the first and second principles in asserting that it should be universal that everyone treats each other as ends rather than as means. We are invited to imagine a utopia in which everyone acts in this way. The implication of this theory of ethics is that people should do what is morally right because it is morally right and not because they have been instructed to act in a certain way.

Kant, as a typical Enlightenment thinker, placed great importance on an individual's ability to reason, i.e. to be able to think objectively. He believed that this capacity to think rationally distinguishes human beings from all other creatures. Reason binds humans together in so far as it enables individuals to resolve problems in a way more or less acceptable to everyone.

According to Kant, if one person reasons logically then they will arrive at the same conclusion as another person who reasons logically.

Task

What judgement would the categorical imperative make on the following statements?
- 'Lying is always wrong.'
- 'Never kill another human being.'
- 'Always be kind to other people.'

Is the theory useful in deciding what action to take?

Kant's moral theory

Kant believed that the only good is the 'good will' – that is, our unconditional motives when we decide to behave in a particular way in our dealings with other people. Being a good person means having a good will, and not seeking any selfish reward when we help someone. Good will is not concerned with the results of an action, as consequentialists declare, but with a pure intention. Kant illustrates his idea of good will by describing a grocer who fixes his prices, not in order to attract more customers or undercut his competitors but because it is right in itself to ask a fair price. But how can I be sure that I am acting with the right intentions? Kant's answer to this difficult question was simple and direct. The person of good will acts solely in accordance with duty and for the sake of duty; their only motive for doing what is right is their awareness that it is the right thing to do. The individual does what is right because it is right, and for no other reason. The secret in understanding Kant's theory is to understand the interplay of the following concepts:

- A *good act* is one which is committed through good will
- *Good will* fulfils our duty
- *Duty* satisfies absolute moral rules
- *Rules* are worked out through reason
- *Reason* establishes right and wrong through asking two questions:
  1 Can the action be universalised?
  2 Am I treating another person as an object (wrong) or as a subject (right)?

Immanuel Kant (1724–1804)

Although as a philosopher Kant soberly advocated moral imperatives, in his private life he was known as a socialite, bon viveur and engaging conversationalist at his frequent dinner parties. The nineteenth-century utilitarian John Stuart Mill, on the other hand, philosophically praised happiness but seemed to live a particularly restrictive and puritanical life. Immanuel Kant was the son of a saddler, and never ventured beyond the environs of his home town of Königsberg (now Kaliningrad) in East Prussia. He was a university lecturer and, while being well versed in many subjects from geography to mathematics, believed that philosophy was the crowning glory of the human intellect, as in philosophy human beings are able to reflect on the nature of knowledge itself. Kant's writings extended to moral philosophy, aesthetics, epistemology and metaphysics. As an Enlightenment thinker, he was keen to emphasise humanity's coming of age and ability to find solutions to life's problems through the exercise of reason. Kant enjoyed a regular walk, and would be accompanied by his servant Old Lampe, holding an umbrella if it was raining. Indeed, it was said that the housewives of Königsberg would set their clocks when he passed due to the precise timing of these outings.

Significant works
Critique of Pure Reason (1781, 1787)
Critique of Practical Reason (1788)
Critique of Judgement (1790)

Let us survey the strengths of this theory:

- Many people have found the idea of universalisability a useful rule of thumb when facing a moral dilemma. The categorical imperative makes decision-making clear-cut, as there is a specified rule to follow.

- Unlike utilitarianism, it takes account of justice, correcting the presumption that the innocent can be punished as long as the majority benefit.

- Kant elevates human beings to the high point of creation as rational creatures. Humans are given dignity and the chance of not being exploited by others.

- The fact that each individual is their own moral authority awards an important degree of autonomy and responsibility to humans, and lifts the moral decision-making process above that of personal gratification or the pursuit of pleasure.

- The theory distinguishes between duty and inclination. It prevents individuals assuming

that what brings them pleasure or benefit is morally good, i.e. good for everyone.

Kant's theory also has its weaknesses:

- It does not explain how we are to reconcile a clash of duties: to one's family, one's employer, one's country, even to God. One might, for example, imagine a religious person experiencing some moral scruples about going to war to defend their loved ones.

- Kantian deontology seems to undervalue the role of emotions in moral decision-making. Surely a sense of satisfaction is relevant in moral decision-making?

- The concept of duty tends to lead to an unquestioning acceptance of authority. Consider the excuses put forward by Nazi functionaries that they were only obeying orders.

- The ability of a rule to be universalised does not of itself guarantee that the rule will be morally good or even moral at all. I can imagine such a rule as 'Take what you want' being universalised and, although the society would be degenerate, my condemnation would have to appeal to something outside the categorical imperative.

- Kant appears to overlook the fact that, while all people may be rational, we do not all have the same temperaments or desires and, consequently, we do not all find the same situations tolerable or intolerable.

- Any absolutist philosophy that uses the terms 'always' or 'never' seems bound to run into exceptions.

- In addition, many high-sounding laws, such as 'Always act in the best interests of another person', leave the field open for a wide-ranging variety of actions, and in practice become vacuous.

- Kant's theory tells us what we should *not* do rather than what we ought to do. As the virtue theorist Alasdair MacIntyre (born 1929) writes: 'Morality [as presented by the categorical imperative] sets limits to the ways in which and the means by which we conduct our lives: it does not give them direction'.[1]

Despite its widespread influence and growing resurgence, it seems that the categorical imperative, which may well have looked straightforward enough at first glance, is somewhat difficult to apply in practice. Let us see whether MacIntyre's own theory of virtue ethics can fare any better.

Virtue theory

An alternative moral philosophy is virtue theory. Initial formulations are to be found in the writings of Plato and Aristotle, whose ethical theories have more in keeping with the literal meaning of the Greek word *ethos*, meaning 'character'. A virtue theorist is more concerned with what constitutes a noble character than in the specifics of a particular action. This assumes that once a virtuous disposition is achieved one will know what to do for the best. Any exploration of virtue theory has to start with Aristotle (see chapter 8).

Aristotle and the importance of being mean

In his masterly manual of virtue theory, *Nicomachean Ethics*, Aristotle describes the ultimate virtue and how to achieve it through the doctrine of the mean. The author suggests that, on asking members of the public what they most desire, one receives a variety of answers such as love, pleasure, money and fame. Aristotle maintains that these are only secondary goals to the ultimate goal of happiness or *eudaimonia*, which is often translated as 'flourishing' or 'personal fulfilment'. *Eudaimonia* is concocted from a variety of ingredients, among them good health, friends, long life, a reasonable amount of money and sufficiently good looks. *Eudaimonia* requires two further virtues for its consummation. One needs to be able to calculate how one should act in a given situation (intellectual virtue) and act in the right manner (moral virtue). The former is achieved through applying the doctrine of the mean, the latter through a process of conditioning where one is trained to act in the right manner.

Aristotle defines virtue as that which 'hits the mean point between two vices, one of excess and the other of deficiency'.[2] The text of *Nicomachean Ethics* consists of the author's lecture notes, and it is thought that at this stage of his delivery Aristotle would produce a chart of three columns – the excessive, the virtuous and the deficient – to illustrate his point. This annotation is reconstructed in Book II of the Penguin edition and provides us with clear examples of what the ethicist means when he exhorts us to choose the midpoint. In the case of fear and confidence, for instance, the excess may be termed rashness, the deficiency would be cowardice, and, through contrasting these two extremes, we are able to establish the desirable mean of courage or bravery.

Virtue theory received a new lease of life in the twentieth century, mainly through the writings of Elizabeth Anscombe and Alasdair MacIntyre, who sought to bring Aristotle's position back to popularity.

Alasdair MacIntyre

The main thesis in MacIntyre's work *After Virtue* is that there is a central problem affecting all contemporary ethical debate: what we have in the way of moral language is left over from a way of thinking long since abandoned; what we say is no longer understood by us and cannot adequately explain what we believe. One might liken this to a modern-day Christian who, despite having a religious faith, finds the language used in church, which talks of sin and grace, difficult to understand. MacIntyre gives two parallel examples in the text to illustrate this predicament:

- the situation found in eighteenth-century Polynesia, where the vocabulary of taboo had no rational explanation either for anthropologists or for the native language users;
- the imaginary situation where an attempt has been made to systematically eliminate science, leaving odd reports, stories of experiments, bits of theories in place without there being any real internal coherence.

MacIntyre tries to provide a historical explanation of how this situation has come to pass and how we are left with our current state of radical confusion. Some critics have found that his reliance on pseudo-historical defences fails to provide a reason as to why virtue theory is a more tenable position than its alternatives. To inform us that we are at a crossroads does not make it clear as to which road to take. For MacIntyre, virtue theory should be revived as a solution to society's moral malaise. He argues that most of our moral debates are potentially indeterminable and indecisive. We have discussions on such subjects as war, abortion and equal opportunities with a semblance of rationality and an appeal to impersonal standards that might settle the issue one way or another. However, such standards are illusory, since the participants in the debates begin with different premises, which they consider fundamental.

One theory that offers an explanation of the paradoxical character of rational debate is emotivism, i.e. the belief that moral judgements are ultimately nothing but expressions of preference, attitude or feeling, and are consequently neither true nor false (see section on emotivism, pp. 43–44). According to MacIntyre, we live in an emotivist culture. Virtue theory is viewed as an alternative meta-ethical

theory, but more importantly one which at the same time has a normative aspect that instructs us on how to live. In an emotivist culture there is no final difference between aesthetic and ethical goals, as all are dependent on how one feels. There is no hierarchy of ends, since ends and goals have value through being preferred or chosen. The result of this is that there is no rational basis for elevating one goal above another.

The degeneracy of our society is epitomised for MacIntyre by the proliferation of certain types of individual who contrast with the virtuous type:

- those who tend to manipulate means to further given ends, who work efficiently but view their work as existing outside the moral realm (bureaucratic managers);
- those who discriminate effectively between given means for purely subjective reasons (aesthetes);
- those who use expertise to achieve certain ends irrespective of whether or not these ends ought to exist, who oil the wheels of a corrupt system with sound-bites and sycophantic superficiality (therapists).

All three stock characters of our civilisation reveal its character, its abandonment of rational debate and its preoccupation with satisfying our emotions. The virtue theory of MacIntyre is a community-based ethic, in marked contrast to the individualism that surrounds us. We are, according to MacIntyre, living amidst the ruins of the Enlightenment project that attempted and failed to find a rational basis for morality. The historic period spanning the seventeenth and eighteenth centuries was known as the Enlightenment as it felt as if humanity had come of age and had gained knowledge of important truths. For MacIntyre the Enlightenment began with a systematic debunking of Aristotelian philosophy, especially the notion that everything worked towards some purpose or end. The Aristotelian account, however, offers humanity a rational goal and a framework within which certain moral statements such as 'arrogance is good' are plainly wrong as they conflict with the facts. If one discovers that arrogance hinders the development of humankind, then one can conclude that arrogance is wrong. This cuts across a basic distinction, dear to subsequent generations influenced by the Enlightenment, that there is an unbridgeable logical chasm between matters of fact and matters of value. Conventional wisdom states that these are entirely different enterprises, yet this was not the case in Aristotle's theory. A person's actions would be more or less related to the achievement of his or her goal, and thus from a factual description of this one may infer whether acts are good or bad in the same way as one might infer from a list of details about the functioning of a device as to whether it is good or bad. We are therefore faced with a choice: either to adopt an Aristotelian outlook or to sign up to the emotivist conclusion, argued so eloquently by the German philosopher Friedrich Nietzsche (1844–1900), which views moral debate as nothing more than the clamour of the discrepant preferences of arbitrary wills.

The value of virtue

Modern virtue theorists draw our attention to the many merits of the theory:

- Virtue theory focuses on the individual moral agent and not on the moral nature of specific acts.
- Virtue theory takes an integrated and holistic approach to ethics and includes the emotional and social side of human nature.
- Virtue theory is compatible with justice and reason.
- Virtue theory is easily taught through example.
- Virtue theory takes into consideration the context of each situation.

Like daily vitamins, virtues abound in various forms. One problem with such a plurality of values is that they tend to embrace less desirable traits that are nonetheless advantageous, such as cunning or greed. To this accusation, virtue theorists reply that such beneficial vices are false friends and 'inevitably carry an undesirable cost' to the moral agent, unlike virtues.

More successful criticisms of virtue theory include:

- The idea of *eudaimonia* is overly abstract (cannot be calculated) and idealistic (cannot be achieved).

- The doctrine of the mean does not take into consideration such virtues as accuracy, happiness, sincerity and reliability, which have one opposite not two. Thus someone is either accurate, happy, sincere, reliable or not.
- Virtue theory does not supply clear moral advice. Proponents might argue that this fact makes virtue theory flexible, but one expects a normative ethical theory to yield a conclusion.
- Virtue theory does not supply us with a clear way of deciding between preferences if faced with a choice between two potentially virtuous alternatives. Should I donate money to a local homeless charity or aid famine relief overseas?
- Virtues appear to be relative to one's community or culture. One culture might promote courage while another might promote compassion.

Review questions

1 Briefly distinguish between a consequentialist and deontological ethical theory.
2 Choose three virtues and explain why they are classed as such.

Task

Is the distinction between vice and virtue as clear-cut as virtue theorists maintain?

Imagine that you are travelling in a balloon in the hope of founding a new state in some remote part of the world. Your travelling companions are Reason, Humour, Lust, Kindness and Anger, but it becomes necessary for one to bail out. Appoint speakers to argue the case for each of the named characteristics and decide which has to go overboard. Which other traits might have been useful passengers in the balloon? What are the implications for virtue theory of any difficulties experienced in this discussion?

Practical ethics

If we have established useful action-guiding principles on a normative level, then practical moral issues ought to be easy to solve. They aren't. Practical ethics covers moral dilemmas faced in the fields of medicine, sexuality and politics. Three such issues – abortion, euthanasia and animal rights – are examined below.

Abortion

Medical ethics developed beyond all recognition in the last decade of the twentieth century and now constitutes a highly specialised study that includes in its remit the ethics of human cloning, genetic engineering, resource allocation and trans-species organ transplant, to name but a few. The question as to whether abortion is morally justifiable, however, has been with us for a lot longer. Irish monks in the Middle Ages gave a fourteen years' penance of bread and water for aborting a foetus after conception. The anti-abortion campaign still has a strong voice but, whereas no one can be said to be actively in favour of abortion, the pro-choice lobby also employ powerful philosophical arguments to aid their cause. The philosopher's role in this debate is to draw helpful distinctions and to separate the wheat of solid argumentation from the chaff of propaganda. Yet philosophers must not lose sight of the fact that this topic, like many others in practical ethics, is about real people facing heart-wrenching decisions.

Pro-choice arguments

Pro-choice arguments concern a woman's right to choose whether to let the pregnancy run to term or not. This can be a lonely decision, as depicted by Jean-Paul Sartre (1905–1980) in *The Age of Reason*, when the pregnant heroine is awaiting her lover Mathieu, suffering from morning sickness and considering having a termination. Such a stark existentialist choice may be eased, however, if we view the foetus not as a person but as a mere collection of cells. A discrete collection of cells, so the argument would run, cannot be placed in the moral realm, and we are justified in dealing with it as we would other cellular growths such as a tumour. Owing to the medical advances in stem cell research, both a foetus and a tumour have the potential to grow into fully-fledged human beings, but does this grant them the same rights?

Peter Singer is one ethicist who rejects the argument from potentiality (that we should award potential human beings the same rights as actual human beings) on the grounds that this does not apply in other cases. Prince Charles, for instance, is not granted the privileges of a monarch when he is still heir apparent. Similarly,

we do not have the same qualms about crushing an acorn as we would about chopping down a mature oak. A potential human being is not the same as an actual human being.

The pro-choice position so far stated may be summarised as follows:

1 Only a moral agent can have their rights violated.
2 A foetus is not a moral agent.
3 Therefore, a foetus cannot have its rights violated and abortion is acceptable.

The arguments for or against abortion vary according to whether the pregnancy is unwanted or whether the life of the foetus or the expectant mother is at risk. The most extreme case of an unwanted pregnancy would be if the mother had been raped. Judith Jarvis Thomson argues that, even under more mundane circumstances, if the pregnancy was not desired then the prospective mother is justified in terminating it. In her essay 'In Defence of Abortion' Thomson[3] gives the example of a woman who wakes up in hospital back-to-back with a famous violinist plugged into some of her vital organs and who is told that she will have to remain in such a state for nine months in order that he might live. Although it was not her fault that a group of fanatical violin-lovers tracked her down as a perfect match for the violinist's organs and plugged her in while she was asleep, the fact remains that if she unplugs him he will die. Thomson argues in this analogy that no one has the right to ask her to remain plugged in and she has no duty to the violinist, as she did not give her permission for him to be attached. An unwanted pregnancy engenders the same moral response: there is the opportunity to do something noble in letting the pregnancy run to term, but there is no moral requirement.

People who are pro-choice often invoke the principle of double effect as philosophical warrant for terminating the life of a foetus. The principle holds that for any action there may be certain secondary, oblique effects produced, which are not desired by the moral agent. It is naive to suppose that a nurse administering a large dose of morphine in the case of euthanasia, or a doctor who uses his instruments to fatal effect in the case of abortion, is not aware that such an action will result in death. The point is that the secondary or double effect is known about, and yet the action is still deemed the right thing to do in light of this knowledge. There are no surprises or accidents involved. Such an action is the result of the moral agent becoming aware that the desired result is necessarily connected to a tragic one. The ideal in any pregnancy is a healthy mother and child, but in circumstances where we can only be guaranteed either a healthy mother or a healthy baby, we feel it incumbent to pursue one end and sacrifice the other. The principle of double effect can only work in a scenario where one is forced to choose between two evils. In a situation where both mother and baby will die if the baby is not aborted, then the lesser of two evils is abortion. Abortion, in this case, is the secondary or double effect of the primary goal, which is to save the mother's life.

Anti-abortionist arguments

Many people oppose abortion on religious grounds and, whereas this is convincing to those with religious faith, to philosophers it is question-begging and therefore inconclusive. While not signing up to the doctrine that human life is sacred, many medical ethicists nevertheless believe that the conviction that 'all human life is important' is a useful rule of thumb in decision-making. In extreme cases such as anencephelia, a medical condition for which the longest recorded life span is a couple of weeks and death usually occurs in a matter of days, few exponents of the sanctity of life or its secular equivalent would justify allocating resources to keep the **moral patient** alive.

While Kantian deontology and virtue theory are normative standpoints that tend to be anti-abortionist, they are not necessarily so. Utilitarians support abortion if the happiness of the mother and wider family (whose socio-economic conditions might be worsened) are affected. Likewise, on a societal level, utilitarians have argued that abortion helps population control, lessens the market for back-street abortions and can produce cells that are used in the therapeutic treatment of diseases such as Parkinson's and Alzheimer's. These are all sound

utilitarian justifications for allowing an abortion to proceed. For Kantian deontologists, contrariwise, the right to kill an innocent human being could never be universalised as one could never will such an unjust and unstable society. The corollary of this runs:

1 It is always wrong to kill an innocent human being.
2 An unborn child is an innocent human being.
3 Therefore, it is wrong to kill an unborn child.

We have seen earlier that it is not uncontentious to describe the foetus as a human being. It may be more accurate to describe the unborn as a potential human being. Aristotelian virtue theory and Roman Catholic ethical teaching, which is influenced by Aristotle, argue that it is the denial of the opportunity to achieve *eudaimonia* (see p. 30) that makes abortion reprehensible. A further Catholic argument against abortion is based on the notion of time as a continuous process of becoming. From the fusion of the sperm and ovum, the human develops, and any time between conception and death that we mark as a watershed when we are justified in terminating life is arbitrary and unwarranted. Pre-natal abortion has as much justification as post-natal infanticide, according to proponents of this position.

Another school of thought that has advanced anti-abortion arguments is feminism. Many feminists of course champion the woman's right to choose, but others have stressed that the movement embraces the rights of all human beings, and this includes the right of the unborn to be born. Feminism rejects the use of force to dominate and control, and sees a logical contradiction in arguing for equality and non-violence and at the same time adopting a pro-abortion stance. Feminist anti-abortionists argue that it is as wrong for women to treat foetuses as their property as it is for men to treat women as their chattels. Our attention is drawn to the fact that in many cases abortion is chosen because of a lack of resources and emotional support for women. The choice, therefore, should not be limited to abortion or hardship, but should involve increased support for struggling families.

Euthanasia

The word 'euthanasia' is derived from two Greek words meaning 'well' and 'death' (*thanatos*). The crucial criterion in defining euthanasia is that the moral patient must be suffering from a terminal illness (such as cancer); this distinguishes euthanasia from cases of assisted suicide. Death is viewed as a release from incurable and unbearable suffering. Patients may leave express wishes, possibly in the form of a living will, to have their lives terminated in the event of their contracting a terminal illness. This is known as 'voluntary euthanasia'. If the patient's wishes are not known, then members of the family may be consulted; this is termed 'non-voluntary euthanasia'. If the patient has expressly stated that they do not want euthanasia and it is administered anyway, then this is classified as 'involuntary euthanasia'. One might imagine a scenario where a permanently comatose patient is costing valuable medical resources that could be better used elsewhere.

Pro-euthanasia arguments

Pro-euthanasia arguments aim to eliminate as much pain as possible and are broadly versions of negative utilitarianism. Pro-euthanasiasts might also embrace Freud's notion that, just as each human being possesses a *libido* or life instinct, so we also possess a *thanatos* or death instinct, and it is only natural for us to desire release from this mortal coil at the end of life. Many pro-euthanasia arguments emphasise the patient's autonomy as the only person who can make a decision on their future in keeping with modern guidelines in medical ethics, known as the four principles approach.

The four principles of medical ethics

1 *Autonomy:* patients have the right to make an informed choice as to their treatment when faced with the options. It is a legitimate exercise of this choice to refuse any treatment at all.
2 *Beneficence:* in keeping with the Hippocratic tradition (from Hippocrates, a doctor in ancient Greece, who said that the role of doctors is to help cure disease and save lives), medical professionals should aim to do the kindest thing.
3 *No harm:* phrased in more negative terms than the second principle, this reminds health professionals that no treatment should cause the patient harm. It is not easy to square this with euthanasia without recourse to the principle of double effect.
4 *Justice:* one ought always to pursue what is considered the fairest line in allocating resources and deciding on who should be treated first.

In light of the grim reality of interminable suffering, the contemporary American ethicist James Rachels (1941–2003) has argued that it is more praiseworthy to administer a lethal injection (active euthanasia) than to let the patient die (passive euthanasia), perhaps by denying them nutrition, water or life support. Rachels makes the point that the justification and outcome of both active and passive euthanasia are the same, and it is only the fact that passive euthanasia prolongs the patient's suffering that separates the two and makes the latter a more cruel alternative. He believes that, for the purposes of moral assessment, inaction such as the withdrawal of treatment counts as a type of action, albeit a peculiar one, 'just as one may insult someone by way of not shaking hands'.[4]

There are, in addition, utilitarian arguments in favour of euthanasia, such as the pragmatic point that if a patient is terminally ill and requiring extraordinary medical means to keep them alive, then euthanasia would enable such resources to be allocated to better effect. Another utilitarian defence of euthanasia takes the line, based on Mill's writings, that freedom of choice entails a greater chance of happiness, and that arguments against euthanasia seem to exercise a well-meaning but tyrannical paternalism.

Anti-euthanasia arguments

Kantian deontology is often cited as the opposite view to utilitarianism, and in keeping with Kant's arguments against suicide we might infer that he would also have been against euthanasia. It is not clear, however, why a Kantian philosopher could not justify euthanasia as universalisable in the case of excruciating, debilitating diseases such as ovarian cancer.

In practice many virtue theorists are against euthanasia providing that there is a residue of quality of life for the terminally ill patient. This is not a blanket view, however, and some virtue theorists would argue that a good death (*euthanasia*) given unbearable suffering is a necessary condition in a good life (*eudaimonia*).

The increased interest in living wills has tried to sidestep the anti-euthanasiast allegation that no one who is crazed with pain can be *compos mentis* enough to make a rational choice. Many believe that such living wills, in which the author's preferences are spelt out should such tragic circumstances arise, commit the individual to too restrictive a course of action. There may always be a glimmer of hope that a cure will be found for the disease. In addition, lawyers might feel that their professionalism is compromised in arbitrating over life and death in the midst of complex family tensions. Similarly, some doctors believe that euthanasia is contrary to the Hippocratic tradition and, in the event of euthanasia being legalised, they would want it to be administered by a distinct body of 'euthanisers'. A utilitarian argument against euthanasia invites us to consider whether or not society at large will experience a sense of anxiety, especially among the marginalised and vulnerable. Any climate of mistrust in health care and legal matters must be damaging.

Arguments against euthanasia include: it devalues life, creates too many problems in legislation and is readily open to abuse. In addition, there seems to be a problem in drawing a clear separation between meaningful and merely biological life. Despite suffering, those in the last throes of life often experience significant moments with their loved ones that would not have occurred had euthanasia taken place.

The most powerful argument against voluntary euthanasia is the argument from palliative care, which states that there is a third alternative in addition to terminal suffering or death, and that is the alleviation of suffering as carried out by the many medical workers and volunteers in hospices. Palliative care retrieves a degree of quality of life for those who are terminally ill, and counters the devaluing of life that is set in motion by pro-euthanasia arguments.

Briefly explain one deontological argument against either abortion or euthanasia.

Animal rights

The assumption behind the debate is that human beings have rights and that humans have duties towards other humans. The crucial question is how far the differences that exist between humans and animals properly justify the different moral attitudes that we have towards them. It is argued that there are few absolute differences between us and animals, and those differences that undoubtedly exist are differences of degree and not of kind. After all, we are members of the animal kingdom.

No-rights theories
No rights because of no consciousness

Descartes argued that animals were organic automata (machines) and, though they had passions, they lacked consciousness. One could thus endanger their bodily structure and terminate their action, but one could neither hurt them nor give them pleasure. Thus, in at least one sense, they could not be harmed and we are free to treat them as we wish. Animals may writhe (show pain behaviour) and evade torment, but they cannot consciously suffer. The belief that animals are conscious Descartes described as a 'prejudice', totally lacking in evidential support. This view, however, seems debatable since, as the French materialist La Mettrie (1709–1751) pointed out after Descartes, the same approach could be adopted towards fellow human beings. Can we be sure they are conscious? Descartes' view is inconsistent with how we talk and feel about animals and with common sense; this is not a conclusive argument, but it does throw the burden of proof back on the Cartesian standpoint. Such a view has not been found helpful in describing and explaining the way in which animals behave. Zoologists find it useful to ascribe to some animals intentions, foresight, beliefs and concept formation. The programme Descartes urged of a purely mechanistic explanation of animal behaviour avoiding the postulate of animal consciousness has not in its entirety been a successful one.

No rights because of no language

Some argue that animals cannot have consciousness because they do not have language. This is a dubious line of reasoning, since it is clear that some higher primates can be trained in some kind of language mastery and that babies, who presumably have rights, can be totally deficient in language while being conscious enough to learn it. There seems no clear connection between the absence of language and the absence of consciousness.

No rights because of no moral sense

Kant assumes, like Aristotle, that animals are not rational, and claims further that animals are not moral agents. For Kant, morality is very much to do with rationality, and moral decisions are decisions of reason. However, we can readily accept that animals do not have a moral nature even if we doubt that they lack rationality and even if we doubt that morality is based on reason. Kant moves from the true proposition that animals are amoral to the conclusion that we can owe them no duties. Kant believed that animals are not moral agents, and duties are only owed to moral agents by other moral agents. You could adopt a similar view if you saw morality as having its foundation in contract, that contract being between moral agents and no one else. This would not be a Kantian view of morality but it would arrive at the same conclusion: that animals have no rights and we owe them no duties. Kant views animals as simply means to whom we owe no direct duties, but we may owe them indirect duties, in so far as they are owned by other people. We are then obliged to look after others' property.

Kant also agreed that treating animals badly encourages us to develop a cruel disposition and, since we owe it to our neighbour as a direct duty not to develop such a disposition, we have an indirect duty not to maltreat animals. Animals represent an arena for moral practice where the right virtues can be inculcated and applied properly on a subsequent occasion. Looking after animals makes for a better human nature, which we then exercise in the human world. Animals are thus, even when treated decently, no more than means, and not genuine moral concerns. The problem with Kant's view is that it rests on the contentious premise that we have obligations only to moral agents. Clearly, babies and the severely mentally handicapped are not moral agents and, in the case of the latter, unlikely to become moral agents. It would be a brave philosopher who could argue that we do not have direct responsibilities to people in these categories.

Rights theories

Utilitarians have a fine track record in the encouragement of animal welfare. Bentham's famous remark was: 'The question is not, "Can they reason?" nor, "Can they talk?" but, "Can they suffer?" '

Many of his disciples worked actively for animal welfare and argued that when one was considering 'the greatest happiness of the greatest number' one must include all sentient beings. However, utilitarianism can be used to justify conventional uses animals are put to, which animal rights theorists deplore. If I gas a baby seal humanely, it feels practically no pain; however, the purchaser of the coat made from seal skin may derive intense pleasure, and so may many future owners of this highly durable product. In this case, the greater happiness consideration seems to justify seal slaughter, especially if the subsequent owners and people in general have no inkling of the origin of the fur. As a result of unfortunate outcomes like this, Peter Singer has devised a new theory called preference utilitarianism. Here, a different form of calculation is called for. Instead of weighing the minimal unhappiness of an anaesthetised animal's death against the obvious enjoyment of people using the resultant products, we should weigh the pleasures that would follow if the creature were allowed to continue to exercise preferences over an assumed normal lifetime. Only when we compare the satisfaction of one set of preferences over another can we decide on the morally correct course of action. However, Singer's version of utilitarianism would justify me in killing a creature and so diminishing its opportunities for happiness if in so doing I could thereby create new life. I could thus justify the use of monkey glands to make women fertile. It is not obvious that Singer's preference utilitarianism avoids the difficulties of ordinary utilitarianism in justifying the unjust.

Thomas Regan (born 1938) puts forward a theory of animal rights on intuitionist grounds, arguing that there is a difference between gut reactions (pre-reflective intuitions) and genuine intuitions (reflective). Our moral code should be based on the latter, i.e. the basic beliefs we are driven to that underpin real moral thinking. One of these is the conviction that all sentient creatures who have desires, beliefs and preferences are of equal, inherent value. He believes some animals have this value irrespective of their utility. We should respect any creature who has such a value and show this respect by an unwillingness to harm such creatures. Regan thinks that what he calls the 'rights view' obliges us to be active vegetarians opposed to a whole range of animal uses, so long as the animals concerned are sophisticated enough, i.e. have sufficient intellectual capacity.

Task

Complete the following table by placing a tick if you think that the normative ethical theory would be in favour of abortion, euthanasia and animal rights in most circumstances or placing a cross if you think that it would be against. Compare your answers. Do you agree?

	Abortion	Euthanasia	Animal rights
Utilitarianism			
Deontology			
Virtue theory			

Cognitive meta-ethics

The above normative ethical theories (utilitarianism, deontology and virtue theory), despite offering different guides to action, have one thing in common: they presuppose that there is such a thing as moral advice to give. According to these moral philosophies, we are able to work out what our behaviour should be through reason or cognition. Hence we can apply the principle of utility, the categorical imperative or the doctrine of the mean to a given situation. Philosophers who believe that such moral truths can be discovered are called **cognitivists**, and the branch of philosophy that studies ethical theories is referred to as **meta-ethics**. The prefix 'meta' means to rise 'above' or go 'beyond' the subject area; in this case one rises above the moral theory in order to devise a theory about the theory. Those individuals who study meta-ethics are especially interested in the type of language used in moral discussions. It is as if they put each kind of sentence under a microscope to examine what kind of thing it is. Cognitivists classify moral language as expressing an important type of fact, just as scientific truths are important types of fact. Non-cognitivists, on the other hand, believe that moral language expresses an opinion and cannot be awarded the same objective status as scientific facts or logical certainties. So the statement 'Torture is wrong' may be equivalent in status to 'I like the taste of citrus' but not equivalent in status to 'Water boils at 100 °C'.

Cognitive meta-ethics embraces two main strands worthy of investigation: moral realism and intuitionism.

Moral realism

Moral realists point to the fact that most people hold that it is morally compelling to, for example, help those less fortunate than themselves, keep promises and act responsibly. They infer from these injunctions that there are such things as moral truths. Moral truths exist as independent categories of right and wrong, the 'moral reality'. Moral realist theories seek to explain the nature of goodness itself and, despite offering different accounts as to what this nature is, agree that there is a definitive answer to the question, 'Are there moral truths?' Moral realism is a cognitive theory, as it holds that ethical principles have an objective foundation and that we can acquire knowledge of these principles. Moral realists employ a selection of arguments to defend their position; we shall consider two of the most prominent, starting with the argument from self-appraisal:

1 If there were no objective moral truths, then human beings would not experience remorse, regret, guilt or moral pride.

2 Self-appraisal as outlined in premise 1 does occur.

3 Therefore, there must be objective moral truths.

Non-cognitivists complain that such an argument is founded on dubious premises, and that features such as remorse, regret, guilt or pride are nothing more than emotions personal to the individual experiencing them. What is one man's regret is another man's triumph.

A second defence of moral realism is known as the argument from moral convergence:

1 On the surface there seems to be a great diversity of moral opinion in this world.

2 If one looks more carefully, these divergent moral systems converge towards a set of shared values.

3 These shared values constitute objective moral truth.

This strand of moral realism has a more empirical flavour, and argues that if we ignore the superficial differences between various cultures' ethical codes, which are as irrelevant as differences in diet or dress, then we are left with a set of core values that transcend the diversity and may include such truths as 'Murder is wrong' or 'Helping someone less fortunate than yourself is good'.

Moral realists believe that there is no difference in epistemic status between facts and values. They argue that the above assertions are to be granted the same truth-value as scientific facts such as 'Lithium burns with a bright red flame'. For moral realists, ethical principles exist independently of people's personal beliefs about what is right or wrong, and hence are not based on social convention but are universally discoverable by anyone seeking the truth.

One of the first moral realists was Plato, who describes the philosopher's search for the truth about right and wrong in his famous dialogue *The Republic* (see pp. 156–160). Platonic epistemology distinguishes between an ephemeral, everyday world of decision-making and an unchanging, eternal world of moral truth in which reside the essences of holiness, justice, prudence and equality, amongst other forms. For Plato, moral principles are as certain and accessible as mathematical proofs and constitute a moral reality. Just as we are able to find the right answer in mathematics, so there is a moral answer to be found. And, just as we are liable to make mistakes in any field before we become proficient, so in the moral sphere immoral actions are a necessary evil along the path to becoming a good person.

A criticism of moral realism

One sceptical attack emphasises the fact that we lack knowledge and justification in moral decision-making:

1 If there were moral truths then there would be no disagreement or contention.

2 The field of morality abounds with disagreement and contention.

3 Therefore, there are no moral truths.

If moral realism were true, then one would have expected some obvious candidates for moral reality to emerge during human history, and it is at least uncertain as to whether they have emerged. Many people, however, believe that when faced with the alternative to moral realism, i.e. a valueless world, then it is necessary to award fact status to moral judgements to avoid a descent into nihilism.

Task

Make a list of what might count as a moral truth. Include both positive and negative imperatives: for example, it is right to help the aged; it is wrong to steal other people's property. Does every society hold these values as important?

Intuitionism

Intuitionists walk a tightrope between moral realism and non-cognitive meta-ethical theories. Like moral realists, intuitionists hold that there are such things as moral facts, which can be known. But unlike moral realists, intuitionists believe that we discover these moral facts not through reason but through a sixth sense called 'moral intuition'. The word 'intuition' is derived from the Latin *intueri* meaning 'to look into'. Just as the immediate perception of material objects by our senses is called by some philosophers sensuous or empirical intuition, the immediate apprehension by the intellect of how we ought to behave is called intellectual intuition or moral sense. The theory has its origins amongst British philosophers who were writing in the period between the First and Second World Wars. They heard about the inevitable wartime atrocities and felt that they had good grounds for condemning such actions, but they were unable as philosophers to give a logical explanation for their moral sentiments. As a result, they advanced an argument known as intuitionism or moral sense theory, which holds that if we are of sufficient maturity then we just know whether something is right or wrong. It is as clear-cut as visual or auditory perception.

For exponents of moral sense theory, goodness is both self-evident and indefinable. One may compare the intuitions of moral sense theory to the work of a water diviner who can accurately calculate the whereabouts and even the pumping capacity of a water source with the use of hazel rods but is unable to provide an account of why this method works. Intuitionists believe that people's moral sense yields a correct result that can be termed a moral fact, for example that murder is wrong. If someone believes that murder is right, then there is something wrong with his or her moral sense, just as one's eyesight can be defective. However, unlike the physical senses, for which one can supply a scientific explanation, intuitionists do not believe an account can be given of how the moral sense works. It is a bone of contention as to whether an explanation can ever be given or whether we just cannot explain moral sense at this moment in time.

Intuitionists hold that moral sense only works if the moral agent is of a mature mind and has allotted sufficient time for reflection. Such a moral sense needs regular exercise to develop, like muscle tone. Certain moral properties exist in a given situation and present themselves to the moral faculty, making the right course of action clear. Consider one's sense of injustice, for instance, at hearing of a multi-million-pound conglomerate steam-rolling someone's vegetable patch as a joke, or one's immediate connection,

on an intuitive level, with an anonymous victim of crime in a news report. Despite features of goodness being instantly recognisable, for G. E. Moore, the most famous intuitionist, goodness remains in a realm beyond definition. He likens goodness to yellowness in so far as we can point to things that are yellow but not explain the colour itself.

Certain strands of intuitionism, such as the version outlined by W. D. Ross in the 1930s, have been described as deontological, i.e. rules-based. Ross identifies the following duties that do not require proof but can be seen as the right thing to do when faced with an ethical dilemma. Ross holds that they are not absolute rules but rules of thumb that may change according to the particular circumstances:

- fidelity, refraining from telling lies;
- keeping our promises;
- reparation, making amends for having done wrong;
- gratitude, acknowledging kindness shown to us;
- justice, to ensuring a fair distribution of benefits;
- beneficence, seeking to make life better for other people;
- self-improvement, maintaining and improving one's own virtues, promoting one's own happiness;
- non-maleficence, not injuring others.

Not all intuitionists agree on every one of these principles. There is disagreement, for instance, as to whether the promotion of personal happiness should be listed as a duty.

Criticisms of intuitionism

The main criticism alleged against intuitionism is lack of clarity. It does not seem to explain how moral knowledge is possible, despite its conviction that there are such things as moral facts. In addition, it does not even explain why it is important to make the right moral decisions. Philosophers sometimes refer to this lack of explanation as 'explanatory poverty'. A theory may be judged weak if it raises more questions than it answers. This is certainly the case with intuitionism, and we are left with many unanswered questions: How do we tell what is right or wrong? What does it mean to be described as having a mature mind? What is this mysterious faculty known as intuition? Isn't moral sense just a matter of social conditioning? Why is there such a divergence of moral beliefs in society if right and wrong are discoverable truths?

The is–ought controversy

One problem that is often associated with cognitive theories like moral realism and intuitionism is called the **is–ought controversy** or the problem of moral compulsion. The problem of moral compulsion poses the question, 'Why *should* I behave in a certain way if I do not want to?' Many philosophers believe that facts and values are fundamentally different and that one cannot logically derive a compelling 'You *ought* to do X' from 'The fact *is* that X'. Thus we cannot say that euthanasia ought to be practised just because it is a fact that it alleviates suffering. Those thinkers who believe in a fact–value distinction assert that facts are objective in that they can, in principle, be discovered to be true or false. Facts relate to the world and are something we can be said to have knowledge of. Values, contrariwise, cannot be known to be true or false, as they relate to what we personally find important and describe how the world ought to be. Attempts to bridge the gap between fact and value are discussed below.

The Platonic attempt

In Book VII of *The Republic*, Plato describes the epistemological enterprise in terms of a journey from the observation of dimly lit objects to the contemplation of abstract principles that will always exist in an immutable realm of knowledge called the world of forms. He believes that the same journey can be made in the moral sphere, as when an ethical agent, contemplating a selection of good acts, discovers what goodness is in essence. For this ancient Greek philosopher, the good and what we ought to do are synonymous, and once the seeker of daylight has become enlightened and learnt what goodness is, then they will know automatically what they ought to do. The is–ought gap is thus bridged in Plato's world of forms as what we ought to do is

what the inhabitants of this ideal world would be doing anyway. Platonists do not think that the fact–value distinction holds, as the same method of attaining truths applies in both the case of fact-finding and that of discovering what should be valued. If it did not, then we are misguidedly using words such as 'good', 'beautiful' and 'just', as we cannot explain what these words mean.

The Aristotelian attempt

Aristotelians hold that the is–ought gap can be bridged for two reasons:

- Facts are not only about the way things are but also about the way things function.
- Logic is distinct from reason.

Let us start with the first point. Consider the example of a malfunctioning lawnmower which, instead of cutting the grass, miraculously encourages it to grow. The fact that it is performing this strange operation (as a 'lawngrower') shows us the discrepancy between the true function of the machine and how it is actually functioning. For thinkers who follow the Aristotelian tradition, anything that doesn't fulfil its function has somehow gone wrong as, by definition, it ought to be fulfilling its function. It it legitimate to say that lawnmowers ought to cut grass.

Secondly, Aristotelian philosophers accept that there is a distinction between fact and value; they acknowledge that there is a gap between 'is' and 'ought'. They even admit that non-cognitivists are right to claim that you cannot logically derive an 'ought' conclusion from an 'is' premise in an argument. However, they reject the view that the lack of a strict logical connection between fact and value means that we cannot discover moral truths that help us live our lives. Aristotelian philosophers maintain that we can argue from facts to values in a reasonable and persuasive manner. Thus one can reach a reasonable ethical conclusion but one that does not rely on formal logic.

The formal attempt

A formal attempt to bridge the is–ought gap relies on adding a further premise. Strict logical proof forces you to accept the conclusion of an argument, i.e. the argument moves in such a way that having accepted the premises you would contradict yourself in denying the conclusion (you simply have to accept it logically). For example:

- Premise 1: All men are mortal.
- Premise 2: Socrates is a man.
- Conclusion: Therefore, Socrates is mortal.

It is logically impossible to accept the premises of this argument and deny the conclusion. Why is this? Because the conclusion is already 'in' the premises – it simply states what is already implied (speaking technically, one might say that the conclusion is entailed by the premises). The conclusion tells us nothing new given that we already know the truth of the premises.

Now the claim 'no ought from is' is correct if made on the basis of strict logical proof, since no set of 'is' premises (facts) can entail an 'ought' conclusion (value judgement). For such an argument to work another premise containing an 'ought' needs to be added. An example may help:

- Premise 1 (fact): People desire happiness.
- Conclusion (value): Therefore, we ought to promote happiness.

The factual premise, while true, does not entail the conclusion. In other words, I can accept the premise, yet deny the conclusion without falling into logical contradiction (I might argue that, while it is true that people desire happiness, moral obligation may lie somewhere else, such as doing one's duty). In order to convert the argument into a strict logical proof, another premise needs to be added:

- Premise 1 (fact): People desire happiness.
- Premise 2 (value): We ought to satisfy our desires.
- Conclusion (value): Therefore, we ought to promote happiness.

The premises now entail (logically force you to accept) the conclusion. However, this has only been achieved by adding a new premise, and the new premise (2) is not a factual premise, but a statement of value. The gap has been moved rather than bridged.

Searle's promise

The American philosopher John Searle (born 1932) disagrees with the absolute distinction and unwavering separation of facts and values. He argues that there are certain kinds of facts which give us values, known as institutional facts. Institutional facts are those that occur in the context of an agreed set of rules and provide moral obligation. Consider the following example concerning promising. Do you think that it successfully moves from an 'is' to an 'ought' as Searle hopes it does?

1 Jones promises to pay £5.
2 Jones is heard to say, 'I promise to pay Smith £5'.
3 Jones puts himself under the obligation to pay £5.
4 Jones is under the obligation to pay £5.
5 Jones ought to pay £5.

Critics accuse Searle of distorting the meaning of 'fact' and draw attention to the hidden value in the above argument, namely that one ought to keep promises. According to Searle's critics, facts are not things that can be agreed upon but stand on their own epistemic merit. So-called 'institutional facts' are only of value if you support the institution, e.g. doctor–patient confidentiality.

A final attempt

The philosophical problem known as the is–ought gap is to an extent a misnomer, as there is no logical contradiction in moving from a premise containing 'is' to one containing 'ought' if contained within the moral sphere. Consider:

1 Abortion is wrong.
2 Therefore, I ought not to abort my foetus.

The fallacy is supposed to occur when I try and move from a non-moral premise to a moral conclusion:

1 My foetus is 14 days old.
2 Therefore, I ought not to abort my foetus.

However, it is a mistake to suppose that there is a generic fault in moving from non-moral premises to a moral conclusion. Consider the following two examples in which the argument legitimately moves from a non-moral premise containing 'is' to a moral conclusion containing 'ought':

1 What God says is true.
2 God says that one should not abort a foetus.
3 Therefore, I ought not to abort my foetus.

Or:

1 Either 'the sun is shining' or 'abortion is wrong'.
2 The sun is not shining.
3 Therefore, abortion is wrong.

Both of the above arguments are formally valid, while at the same time they move from non-moral premises to a moral conclusion. As a consequence, it is not clear as to the logical error being made when one asserts that one ought to do something.

For many philosophers, none of the above attempts is sufficient to bridge the is–ought gap, as the fact–value distinction is an absolute one. This band of thinkers is examined in the next section on non-cognitive meta-ethics.

Review questions

1 Identify one similarity and one difference between moral realism and intuitionism.

2 Briefly explain what is meant by the is–ought gap.

Non-cognitive meta-ethics

Emotivism

Emotivism is by far the most prominent school of **non-cognitivism**. The theory has its origins in the writings of Hume, though it would be imprecise to call Hume an emotivist. We learnt in chapter 1 that Hume drew a clear distinction between self-evident truths and matters of fact. These two categories were believed to be an exhaustive account of knowledge, and anything that fell beyond their bounds was categorised as belief or opinion. Emotivists such as the English philosopher A. J. Ayer (1910–1989) applied Hume's fork to ethics and concluded that, because moral statements were not claims to knowledge, they were not fit for philosophical study and should be consigned to a separate class

of statements, which he termed 'factually nonsensical' (see chapter 15).

Ayer's theory of language

For Ayer, a fact has to be either one of two things:

- a tautology, i.e. a statement which is true by definition, such as 'All sisters are female';
- empirically verifiable, i.e. provable by experiment, such as 'Elephants are grey'.

Where do moral statements fit in? Let us consider the simple ethical statement, 'Pulling the cat's tail is wrong'. This statement is not true by definition, and the only empirical observation we can make is that someone is pulling the cat's tail. One can see immediately, therefore, that this sentence is not a candidate for being awarded fact status. It is a factually meaningless value judgement. But that is not to say that emotivists are advocating cruelty to animals; they are meta-ethical philosophers who seek to inform us as to the nature of morality and the classification of moral language.

The Boo/Hooray theory

Ayer believed that morality was motivated by desire not reason, and that ethics had more in common with aesthetics than science in so far as what counts as 'good' boils down to personal taste. Emotivists argue that morality is an expression of one's emotions and nothing more. One is reminded of Lady Cheveley's words in Oscar Wilde's play *An Ideal Husband*: 'Morality is simply the attitude we adopt towards people whom we personally dislike.' In other words, if we condemn someone or something as immoral then we mean that we do not like it, and if we praise something for being moral then we are declaring our admiration. For emotivists, there are no independent criteria of moral rectitude against which ethical actions can be judged. Emotivists believe that moral judgements have no literal meaning at all and are only expressions of emotion, like grunts, sighs or laughter. So when someone says 'Torture is wrong' or 'You ought to tell the truth', they are doing little more than showing how they feel about torture or truth-telling. What they say is neither true nor false: it is more or less the same as shouting 'Boo!' at the mention of torture or 'Hooray!' at the mention of truth-telling. Indeed, emotivism is sometimes referred to as the Boo/Hooray theory.

The American linguistic philosopher C. L. Stevenson (1908–1979) added another dimension to the emotivist analysis of language by arguing that when someone issues a moral statement they are not just expressing their emotions but are engaged in an act of persuading other people to share their feelings on a given issue. Just as when someone shouts 'Boo!' or 'Hooray!' they are not simply showing how they feel but are usually trying to encourage other people to join them on their side of the debate. For emotivists, ethical discussions are nothing but propaganda and persuasion.

> **Task**
>
> Write a short dialogue between two people who disagree on abortion, euthanasia or animal rights. Start your dialogue halfway through so that the argument is in full swing. When you have finished go over the conversation carefully, marking (with two different-coloured pens) what may be classed as 'factual utterance' and what may be classed as 'value judgement'. Is there as clear a distinction as emotivists would have us believe?

A criticism of emotivism

Many statements are judged factually nonsensical when in fact they seem very significant. Take, for example, the following categories:

- scientific theories, e.g. the space–time continuum or quarks;
- talk about past or future events, e.g. 'There will be a nuclear holocaust in the future';
- counterfactual statements, e.g. 'What would have happened if the Nazis had won the Second World War?';
- statements about other people's experiences, e.g. 'Mary is in a good mood today';
- statements of general laws, e.g. 'Metals will always expand when heated'.

Emotivists believe that all genuinely factual statements could in principle be verified by reducing or analysing them into basic sentences

that could then be checked directly against the reports of our senses. They were, however, unable to agree amongst themselves on what such a sentence would look like or how the mechanics of checking would work. In addition, the statement 'Emotivism is true' would have to be judged factually meaningless by its own standards. In a lecture delivered to mark the fiftieth anniversary of the publication of Ayer's *Language, Truth and Logic*, the author tried to defend the theory as a tautology to escape this last embarrassing point. He argued that morality is concerned with emotions by definition.

Prescriptivism

Prescriptivism is a non-cognitive, linguistic theory like emotivism, but prescriptivists such as R. M. Hare (1919–2002) believe that their analysis offers a more complete picture of morality. Hare argues that morality is an expression of human emotion and as such cannot be granted fact status, but he also believes that emotivists fail to acknowledge the following features of ethical discourse:

1 Morals are prescriptive.
2 Morals are expressed through reasoned arguments.
3 Morals act as action-guiding principles.
4 Morals are used consistently.

Let us examine each of these points in turn in order to understand the prescriptivist argument.

Descriptive and prescriptive

Prescriptivism is a meta-ethical argument, and Hare does not seek to tell us what we should or shouldn't be doing. Normatively, Hare was a utilitarian and incidentally a survivor of a Japanese prisoner-of-war camp. Hare concluded, on analysing moral statements, that they were in essence prescriptive. Prescriptivists are not prescribing any particular actions, but are arguing that moral language is prescriptive. Just as when a doctor writes a prescription he or she is informing you of what you should do in order to get better, so those who declare something right or wrong are issuing prescriptive advice: either to follow a course of action (commendatory) or to avoid it (discommendatory). Emotivists believe that moral discourse arouses feelings and is used by those intent on persuasion. Prescriptivists harden this outlook, arguing that moral agents are not only desirous of persuading individuals of a specific course of action but are explicitly advising and prescribing.

Hare explains the difference between 'descriptive' and 'prescriptive' in his work *The Language of Morals* (1952) by citing the example of a strawberry. I might describe a strawberry as being large, red and juicy but if I evaluate a strawberry as 'good' then I am prescribing a course of action – you should eat it! All moral language according to Hare is prescriptive and as such:

- is either commendatory or discommendatory;
- is action-guiding;
- takes the form of imperatives (commands);
- carries universal application.

The role of reason

Prescriptivists see the emotivist view of moral language as fruitful yet incomplete. One bone of contention is the role that reason plays in ethical discussion. Prescriptivists are keen to point out that people use basic forms of inference when making ethical judgements (perhaps there is an example of this in the dialogue you wrote for the last task). For thinkers like Hare, moral discourse can only exist if those involved are able to understand certain logical root words such as 'all' in the case of:

1 All instances of X are wrong.
2 Y is an instance of X.
3 Therefore, Y is wrong.

We can see how this works by looking at an example involving a teacher, Mr Osbourne, and a student, Wally:

1 It is always wrong for a teacher to hit his students.
2 Mr Osbourne hit Wally.
3 Therefore, it was wrong for Mr Osbourne to hit Wally.

Hare believed that many moral judgements exhibit rational justification and may be criticised on rational grounds. Admittedly, the above inference is based on the first premise, which is a value judgement, but this in no way detracts from it being a good inference.

The role of principles

Prescriptivists suggest that particular moral judgements are derived from more general principles. The judgement that it was morally unjustifiable for Mr Osbourne to hit Wally was derived from a more general principle, 'It is always wrong for a teacher to hit a child'. The author of *The Language of Morals* argues that if it were not the case that principles were involved in moral decision-making then no one would be able to decide what to do. He illustrates the importance of principles through the following thought experiment:

> Let us suppose that a man has a peculiar kind of clairvoyance such that he can know everything about the effects of all the alternative actions open to him. But let us suppose that he has so far formed for himself, or been taught, no principles of conduct. In deciding between alternative courses of action, such a man would know, fully and exactly, between what he was deciding. We have to ask to what extent, if any, such a man would be handicapped, in coming to a decision, by not having any formed principles.[5]

Hare concludes that such a power as seeing the future and being able to predict the consequences of actions would be useless without the direction supplied through the application of principles. From this thought experiment, Hare goes on to conclude:

1 Morality consists in something more than brute feelings.
2 This something more consists in using principles in making moral decisions.
3 Principles relate to the effects of an action.
4 Such principles are not necessarily permanent.
5 Principles of conduct are learnt.
6 Principles adapt and progress through a system of choice from rival principles, e.g. the new against the old.

The role of consistency

The fourth aspect of the prescriptivist analysis is that moral language is consistent. We usually expect moral agents to be consistent in the judgements they make, and we might consider it incoherent if we spotted someone campaigning for pacifism every Tuesday and war-mongering on Wednesdays. In addition, we expect certain types of judgement to have more weight than others. We would regard it as more justifiable to hit someone because they insulted your sister than because you disliked their tie. Prescriptivism seems successful in filling the gaps left by emotivism. One criticism is that moral commendation is not always prescriptive. We could admire a character from history such as St Francis of Assisi without recommending that we adopt his radical views on poverty.

Two associated problems

Both Ayer and Hare present versions of non-cognitivism that analyse moral statements and the nature of moral discourse. Hare's theory appears to sidestep many of the traps that emotivism falls into and as such seems to be the most rounded non-cognitive account. Indeed, critics might allege that it only informs us of what we know to be the case already. One is still left wondering, however, whether there is more to morality than our feelings. If we agree with non-cognitivists that there isn't, then we encounter two further problems, those presented by the theories of relativism and nihilism.

Relativism

To many thinkers, the fact that different cultures have different moral codes suggests that there is no universal truth in ethics. The relativist argument runs as follows:

1 Different cultures have different moral codes (e.g. female circumcision is the norm in some African countries but is considered unacceptable in Europe).
2 Therefore, there is no objective truth in morality, and right and wrong are only matters of opinion that vary from culture to culture.

This is not a formally valid argument, however, as the conclusion does not follow from the premise. Those who believe in an objective moral code may say that there is one moral code, which is right, and some cultures have got it wrong. According to the laws of logic both standpoints are equally consistent.

Cultural relativism is a popular argument today, and seems compatible with non-cognitive standpoints such as emotivism and prescriptivism. One can imagine someone believing that morality is an expression of emotion and that our feelings are influenced by our upbringing. For other philosophers, relativism presents a serious moral problem. Consider the consequences of accepting these moral relativist arguments:

- Are we prepared to accept a society that is violently racist? Cultural relativism would not allow us to say that such practices were wrong. We would not be able to say that from a meta-ethical perspective a society tolerant of Jews is better than an anti-Semitic society, only that it is different.

- The only way that we could decide whether an action is wrong or right would be to consult the standards of our own society. After all, if right and wrong are relative to culture, this must be true for our own culture, just as much as for others.

- If we accept the relativist argument, then the idea of moral progress is called into doubt. Consider the changes over the centuries in the status of women. The relativist can only say that there have been changes in the position of women in society but not that this is a good thing, as this would assume an objective standard by which a comparison could be made.

- The relativist cannot recommend tolerance as an objective value (i.e. everyone should, objectively, respect the different values of other cultures) because this contradicts their basic position. If all values are relative, then tolerance must be relative too!

We have already encountered the moral realist claim that it is inaccurate to overestimate the extent of cultural differences (called the argument from moral convergence). On the surface, practices may appear very different, whereas on closer inspection the underlying moral value might be the same. The Inuit put their ill, elderly relatives on the ice floe, whereas in Europe they may be housed in old people's homes or hospices. What differs here are the factual beliefs of different cultures about how the good for the infirm is to be achieved and is relative to the environment in which the moral community lives. There is a shared moral value, however, in not wanting unnecessary suffering for the aged. Consider other values that are universal and cross cultural boundaries: truth-telling, promise-keeping and the prohibition of murder. Imagine a society where these values were not well established (the stuff of nightmares and science-fiction films).

Relativism nevertheless warns us about the dangers of assuming that all preferences are based on some absolute standard. Many of our practices (but not all) are merely peculiar to our society, e.g. our attitude to the dead, nudity and sexuality. Consider the case of female circumcision in Somalia: western disapproval of the practice is based on the values of female autonomy, avoidance of unnecessarily inflicted pain and individualism, whereas Somalian society might place emphasis on the ritual passage to womanhood, the need for clearly defined roles and the security of group identity, even at the expense of individual satisfaction. How are we to respond in this situation? Should each culture understand each other's values and accept the differences, particularly if all those involved are 'happy'? (It is much more difficult to accept the situation in cases where there is unhappiness to do with a practice.) Or should we attempt to reform cultural practices that differ from our way of living?

Right and Wong
The ethical relativist David Wong believes that one could give an account of the variations in moral belief by suggesting that there are different ways of fulfilling underlying human needs. Wong's relativism identifies two approaches:

1 Western thought: based primarily on individual rights and happiness, where acting freely is seen as the major good.
2 Traditional cultures (Africa, Asia): where the group has greater moral significance.

Wong argues that a good and fulfilling life could be lived in either of these cultures, and claims that a good life can be had in a variety of ways, so that there is not one set of morally correct positions. A moral system is just in so far as it meets human needs. If these needs can be met in different ways, then there can be different moral systems and practices.

Nihilism
Many people look to moral philosophy for advice on how to live and an explanation as to why we exist. If we conclude that there is no such advice or explanation to give, then we might be left with a sense of confusion and uncertainty. The non-cognitive meta-ethical theory that states that morality is illusory and that there is no pre-ordained purpose in living is called nihilism. The word is derived from the Latin *nihil* meaning 'nothing'. Nihilists are agreed that there is no meaning to life, nor is there any category of objective moral truth. The two most prominent nihilists in the history of western philosophy were Arthur Schopenhauer (1788–1860) and Friedrich Nietzsche (1844–1900). Nihilism has its origins in Schopenhauer's *The Fourfold Root of Sufficient Reason* (1813), in which he argues that in order to call something true we must have a sufficient reason to believe it:

- One can gain a sufficient reason from a causal explanation, e.g. that a plant grows where a seed is sown.

- One can gain a sufficient reason from the concept of a thing, e.g. if an entity X fits the concept of a tree then we can be reassured that it is a tree.

- One can gain a sufficient reason by calculating an answer using geometry or arithmetic.

- One can gain a sufficient reason from our inner sense or will.

Schopenhauer believed that there was no sufficient reason to believe in moral truth. Our lot in life, according to Schopenhauer's pessimistic philosophy, is to turn away from the world. His philosophy is often referred to as 'weak nihilism'.

A fellow German who was influenced by Schopenhauer's work was Friedrich Nietzsche (see chapter 11), whose views became known as 'strong nihilism'. Nietzsche agreed with Schopenhauer's diagnosis that there is no ultimate goal, design, purpose or reason for living. He declared:

> One sees a sad, hard but determined gaze – an eye which looks out, as an isolated Arctic explorer looks out (perhaps in order not to look in? in order not to look back? ...). Here is snow, here life is silenced; the last crows whose cries can still be heard here call 'Why?', 'In vain!' 'Nothing!'[6]

Nietzsche uses some dramatic imagery in the above quotation to describe our existence in the harsh, barren Arctic wasteland of life where meaning and morality are illusory. In contrast to Schopenhauer, Nietzsche says that this conclusion provides the very reason for seizing life by the throat and demanding of it whatever you seek. Nietzsche's view of morality is essentially existentialist, in that he believed that we are free to create our own picture of the world and are free to make this portrait as beautiful and life-enhancing as we can. (See chapter 16 on Sartre for a discussion of existentialism.) The white expanse of snow that confronts our timid gaze is at the same time a blank canvas upon which we can inscribe something great and beautiful.

Review question

Briefly explain two reasons for believing that morality is a matter of opinion and nothing more.

Arthur Schopenhauer (1788–1860)

Arthur Schopenhauer was born in the Prussian city of Danzig, which is present-day Gdansk in Poland. He was the son of a wealthy businessman of Dutch extraction and inherited a great deal of money on his father's death, when the young philosopher was in his twenties. Indeed, this change in lifestyle allowed Schopenhauer to live a life of scholarly retirement. He was greatly influenced by the writings of his fellow German Immanuel Kant but, unlike Kant, who emphasised the importance of autonomy and the individual will, Schopenhauer concluded that every human being was in a relationship with one will that exists in the universe. He described this will as the will to life and construed it as an essentially deterministic desire to reproduce. Sadly, Schopenhauer did not have much success on this front, and this led to feelings of inadequacy, misplacement and eventually misanthropy. He developed a particular mistrust of women, whom he described as 'childish, frivolous and short-sighted'. Schopenhauer's depression worsened when he was involved in an argument with a seamstress who had been chatting loudly outside his room. The philosopher, who hated noise, ended up pushing the woman down the stairs and was forced by a Berlin court to pay her an allowance every month for the rest of her life. She lived for another twenty years. Schopenhauer found consolation in playing the flute before lunch and taking regular walks with his favourite poodle, Atma.

Significant works
The Fourfold Root of Sufficient Reason (1813)
The World as Will and Representation (1819, 1844)
The Two Fundamental Problems of Ethics (1841)

We have defined a normative ethical theory as one that gives advice and a meta-ethical theory as one that consists in an analysis of morality itself. You should at this stage be clear as to what each meta-ethical theory asserts. In order to test your understanding, write a sentence in each box below that describes how the meta-ethical theorist would interpret the normative theory. For example, an emotivist would point to utilitarianism and say: 'This theory is based on happiness and happiness is an emotion therefore this is further evidence that all morality is an expression of emotion.'

	Utilitarianism	Deontology	Virtue theory
Moral realism			
Emotivism			
Prescriptivism			

Revision questions

1 Explain and illustrate one argument that states values can be based on reason.

2 Assess whether it is useful to focus on virtue when deciding on how to act.

3 Outline and illustrate one strength and one weakness of the prescriptivist account of the nature of moral language.

4 Explain what is meant by the is–ought gap. Can it be bridged?

5 Outline and illustrate one argument that a utilitarian might use to oppose abortion.

Discussion questions

- Assess the merits and demerits of utilitarianism as a guide to moral conduct.
- Can ethical disagreements be resolved by an appeal to intuition?
- Briefly explain what a moral philosopher means when he calls morality a subjective matter.
- Describe two moral problems raised by voluntary euthanasia.
- If animals kill each other, why can't we kill them?

Glossary of key terms

Cognitivism: the belief that ethical statements can be understood as truths.

Consequentialism: the belief that the moral standing of an action depends on its outcome.

Deontology: the belief that there are moral rules that correspond to absolute categories of right and wrong.

Is–ought controversy (naturalistic fallacy): the accusation that an error in reasoning is made through moving from an analysis of facts about human nature to moral judgements.

Meta-ethics: the philosophical discipline, usually of a linguistic nature, that analyses ethical theories.

Moral agent: the person who engages in any moral or immoral activity.

Moral patient: the person who bears the outcome of any moral activity.

Non-cognitivism: the belief that statements to do with right and wrong are value judgements.

Normative ethics: any moral theory that equips the moral agent with a means of working out how to act in a given situation.

Suggested reading

- Glover, J. (1990) *Causing Death and Saving Lives*, London, Penguin
  A clearly written companion to practical ethics
- Norman, R. (1998) *The Moral Philosophers*, Oxford and New York, OUP
  A thinkers-based work on moral philosophy
- Rachels, J. (1975) *The Elements of Moral Philosophy*, London, McGraw Hill
  An impressive companion to ethics
- Raphael, D. D. (1994) *Moral Philosophy*, Oxford and New York, OUP
  A themes-based work on moral philosophy
- Singer, P., ed. (1993) *A Companion to Ethics*, Oxford, Blackwell
  A comprehensive volume and useful source book for meta-ethics

Notes

[1] MacIntyre, A. (1966) *A Short History of Ethics*, London, Macmillan, p. 197.

[2] Aristotle, *The Nicomachean Ethics*, Book IX, Chapter 2.

[3] Thomson, J. J. (1986) *Rights, Restitution and Risk*, Cambridge, CUP.

[4] Rachels, J. (1975) 'Active and Passive Euthanasia', *The New England Journal of Medicine*, vol. 292, pp. 78–80.

[5] Hare, R. M. (1970) *The Language of Morals*, Oxford, OUP, p. 58.

[6] Nietzsche, F. (1998) *On the Genealogy of Morals*, Oxford, OUP, Third Essay (III) Section 26, p. 131.

3 Philosophy of religion

I believe because it is absurd. (Tertullian)

Aims

On completion of this chapter you should be able to:

- evaluate the traditional divine attributes
- evaluate the problem of religious language
- give a critical account of the cosmological argument
- give a critical account of the teleological argument
- give a critical account of the ontological argument
- give a critical account of the argument from religious experience
- appreciate the intellectual tensions between faith and reason
- give a critical account of the pragmatic argument and Pascal's wager
- give a critical account of the argument from faith and the illative sense
- explain and evaluate the problem of evil and attempts at solving this problem
- give a critical account of the argument from miracles
- give a critical account of the moral argument.

The philosophy of religion, that branch of philosophy that deals with questions surrounding God's nature and existence, appears out of fashion in much mainstream philosophy at the moment. To an extent questions concerning the nature of human consciousness and the metaphysics of personal identity have stolen the thunder of theological philosophy. Yet the philosophy of religion has enjoyed the attention of great minds for centuries. For many thinkers, arguments for the existence of God have as credible a standing as any other branch of metaphysics. Whether you are religious or not the following sketches and summations will provide food for thought if not food for the soul.

The meaning and justification of religious concepts

Divine attributes

Philosophers have become well known for starting any enquiry with the question, 'What do

you mean by…?'; in the philosophy of religion the question is: 'What do we mean by God?' The concept of God advanced by most religious believers is of an **omnipotent** (all-powerful), **omniscient** (all-knowing) being who is morally perfect and the creative force behind the universe. According to different versions of **theism**, God may also be described as omnipresent (everywhere), eternal, perfectly free, worthy of devotion, the source of moral obligation, immutable (unchanging), necessarily existent and responsible for sustaining the universe. Indeed, it is this last characteristic that separates the theistic standpoint from the **deistic** one. The term 'deism' describes belief in a God who is not engaged in active service but who has wound up the world like a watch to let it keep time in accordance with itself.

The properties of God, known as 'divine attributes', as conceived by traditional theism raise some important questions in the philosophy of religion. One question that is raised is whether these divine properties can exist together (are compossible) or whether the likes of omniscience, presence in our universe and perfect freedom are incompatible. Other queries surround the intelligibility of terms such as 'omnipotent' and 'omniscient'. The word 'omnipotent' means having power to do whatever is not logically inconceivable. This belief has led to the formulation of paradoxes such as 'Can God create a stone too heavy for Him to lift?' or 'Can God create something that He cannot destroy?' Some religious believers maintain that God can transcend the logically impossible, whereas those who occupy a less hard-line standpoint assert that God is bound by the laws of logic like the rest of us. The second school argue that the terms 'omnipotent' and 'omniscient' mean that God possesses certain powers analogous to our own but to a considerably greater degree. The question of what sort of knowledge God possesses is equally intriguing. Does God know the same sort of things that we do? Does God acquire such knowledge by the same methods? Does God have foreknowledge, and can God ever be surprised? Such questions raise deeper concerns over the divine nature and raise the issue as to whether, in order to possess knowledge, God needs to be corporeal. As the psalmist in Hebrew scripture said, 'Is the creator of the eye unable to see?'

The problem of religious language

It is appreciated by both religious and non-religious writers that there are special difficulties in using language, primarily developed to describe everyday things, to express beliefs about an other-worldly being. Some theists have even gone so far as to allege that the only things that we can justifiably say about God must be expressed in negative statements and that nothing positive can be adequately defended. This tradition is known as apophatic theology. **Apophaticism** is typified by the anonymous, fourteenth-century spiritual classic *The Cloud of Unknowing*, which, as its name suggests, pictures God as a being that surpasses all understanding and can only be experienced through love and grace:

But now you will ask me, 'How am I to think of God himself, and what is he?' and I cannot answer you except to say 'I do not know!' For with this question you have brought me into the same darkness, the same cloud of unknowing where I want you to be! For though we through the grace of God can know fully about all other matters, and think about them – yes, even the very works of God himself – yet of God himself can no man think.[1]

According to the apophatic tradition (sometimes referred to in the literature as the *via negativa* or negative way), if we cannot think about God then we cannot speak about God either.

Other Christian thinkers, such as St Thomas Aquinas (1225–1274), have alleged that talk of God rarely amounts to direct description but is 'analogical', i.e. concerned with drawing comparisons and similarities between God and things within our experience. In the Bible, God is referred to as the rock of ages and the lion of Judah. We understand that such analogies are intended to evoke steadfastness and nobility rather than asserting anything literal about God being a geological formation or a big cat. The difficulties in talking about God have in recent times become the source of a negative critique of religion itself. The ball was set rolling by Hume, who suggested that we make a bonfire of all books that did not justify their claims by experimental or mathematical reasoning:

If we take in our hand any volume of divinity or school metaphysics, for instance let us ask, 'Does it contain any experimental reasoning concerning matter of fact and existence'. No. Commit it then to the flames for it can contain nothing but sophistry and illusion'.[2]

This attack on theological statements was revived in the twentieth century by a group of scientifically minded philosophers known as logical positivists. They declared there to be two sorts of statement: the meaningful and the meaningless. A meaningful statement had to be true by definition or provable through observation. This was called the 'verification principle' and it clearly left most religious statements, as well as a good deal of ordinary speech, in the meaningless category. The workings of the verification principle are well illustrated in a radio debate between the philosopher of religion F. C. Copleston (1907–1994) and the most famous advocate of logical positivism, A. J. Ayer. Ayer starts:

> Suppose I suggest 'There's a "Drogulus" over there,' and you say 'What?' and I say 'Drogulus,' and you say 'What's a Drogulus?' Well I say 'I can't describe what a Drogulus is, because it's not the sort of thing you can see or touch, it has no physical effects of any kind, but it's a disembodied being.' And you say 'Well how am I to tell if it's there or not?' and I say 'There's no way of telling. Everything's just the same if it's there or it's not there. But the fact is it's there. There's a Drogulus there standing behind you, spiritually behind you.' Does that make sense?[3]

Ayer believed that such assertions about a Drogulus did not make sense and that religious language is equally meaningless for the same reasons. Logical positivism is now a discredited philosophy, but it is important to realise that the trend it set in thinking is far from being obsolete. The verification principle eventually died the death of a thousand cuts, but from its grave there arose the principle of falsification. This stems from the work of the philosopher Karl Popper (1902–1994), an ardent critic of logical positivism since his early life in Austria when he was excluded from meetings of the Vienna Circle.

The principle of falsification is a method for distinguishing good science from bad science. Popper suggests that a scientific theory is worth persevering with if, and only if, one is able to say under what circumstances it could be falsified; that is to say, one ought to be able to think of a situation for which, if it occurred, the theory would be found wanting (falsified). According to Popper, good science ought to be falsifiable, though not of course false. The statement 'My brother is a man of distinction and over five foot tall' is quite acceptable because it is falsifiable; but it might be false. The point about good science is that we do know how to falsify it, and so we set about trying to do just that: we put it to the test, and if we fail, we hold the theory to be unrefuted and so as true as any theory can be. There are good reasons for believing that Popper has given us a good rule of thumb for eliminating bad theories in science, but one would hesitate to elevate the falsification

principle to the status of a logical principle. Many respectable theories in science are unfalsifiable, as even when they are put to the test our interpretation of the test results and our methodology in the test itself are conditioned by our acceptance of the theory. Our assurance that Newtonian mechanics, for example, is correct is founded on certain background assumptions concerning planetary motion. Religious believers, so the argument would run, have certain background assumptions as well. Secondly, there are some quite acceptable statements that are not in principle falsifiable, and yet it would not do to disallow them. Hick gives the example that there are three successive sevens in the decimal expansion of *pi*. This is only falsifiable if we had an infinite length of time to analyse the endless refinement of 3.142.

Flew's challenge

The erstwhile atheist Anthony Flew (born 1923) devised a 'challenge' that rests upon the principle of falsification. His challenge is fundamentally the assertion that religious statements are non-falsifiable, and so can be called 'meaningless' or 'factually meaningless'. Let us begin with a parable, recalled by Flew, about two explorers who find a clearing in the jungle that contains flowers and weeds. One alleges that a gardener tends this plot. The other contradicts him. They watch. No one comes. 'Perhaps,' says the believer, 'he is an invisible gardener.' They set traps, electrify fences, patrol with bloodhounds etc.; still nothing. The believer still persists in his faith in an invisible, intangible, soundless, scentless gardener. 'How, though,' says the unbelieving explorer 'does your gardener differ from no gardener at all?' This little parable, originally told by the Cambridge philosopher John Wisdom (1904–1993), is the basis of Flew's challenge. If the religious believer allows nothing to count against belief in God, can visualise no situation that would be incompatible with belief in God, can anticipate no situation in which belief in God would have to be given up, then isn't belief in God so much empty talk? If there is something that a belief asserts, urges Flew, then it must also deny or rule out something. What would have to occur or to have occurred to constitute a disproof of the divine attributes or the very existence of God?'

On the surface this challenge seems open, fair-minded and convincing. Flew asks for details of a situation in which belief in God would be untenable; the situation need not be real but simply hypothetical. Yet to specify to conceptual atheists the conditions under which religious belief may be falsifiable is no easy matter. We must dream up a situation to meet a very tough specification; the circumstances must be:

- unambiguous, i.e. interpretable in only one way;
- inter-subjective, i.e. identifiable by anyone;
- non-jargonistic, i.e. fully describable without the use of any religious or metaphysically loaded terminology.

Task

Draw up a list of examples of religious language. Choose quotations from each of the major world faiths: Hinduism, Buddhism, Sikhism, Judaism, Christianity and Islam.

Responses to Flew

Agnostics and atheists have been only too ready to agree that religious propositions are vacuous; yet some attempts to answer Flew's challenge have emerged.

The Roman Catholic linguistic philosopher R. M. Hare (1919–2002) replied with two parables, the first about a man with a pathological but irremovable conviction that all university dons are out to kill him, a belief unshaken by the apparent kindness most show towards him. The second story is about a man who is deeply suspicious about the strength of metal, to the extent that when he drives his car he drives with fear and trepidation lest the working parts of it suddenly become elastic. Both these people have what Hare somewhat inadequately calls 'a blik'. Bliks affect their behaviour and judgement of events occurring around them. A blik is a neologism coined by Hare that corresponds roughly to what we might term 'psychological conditioning'. Religious beliefs, Hare suggests, are a sort of blik, but are in no way inferior to non-religious bliks. Hare

alleges that we humans cannot do without some kind of blik and that no one, religious or irreligious, lives blikless. What Hare seems to be doing is echoing Wittgenstein's point that religious beliefs are used to evaluate reality, rather than something that one checks against reality.

Basil Mitchell (born 1917) provides another response that similarly begins with a parable, this time about a French resistance fighter (the religious believer) who meets a stranger who claims to be on the side of the resistance. The resistance fighter is deeply impressed by him. Subsequently, some actions of the stranger seem to benefit the resistance, but at other times seem to favour the Gestapo. It is not at all obvious whose side he is on. The resistance fighter nevertheless persists in his claim that the stranger is on his side. Mitchell points out that the believer allows much to count against his belief (suffering the betrayals of the stranger), but he does not allow anything to count finally and decisively against his faith. Mitchell concludes by arguing that the encounter of the believer with God, through religious experience, is of such a quality that it will not be abandoned in the face of contrary evidence; rather, such experience will be seen as a test of faith. In this he seems to have correctly isolated a feature of how religious people think and believe and of how religious beliefs are established. He has not, however, finished the job and provided a thorough account of faith. Is there anything about religious faith that makes it irrevocable once found, and if not, then how is religious faith tested?

The English philosopher John Hick (born 1922) responds to Flew's demands by arguing that if a belief can only be meaningful if it can be verified or falsified, then religious belief can certainly be verified, since much religious belief is committed to an after-life, and the existence of one would count in support of this belief. This notion is termed 'eschatological verification', a phrase derived from the theological term *eschaton*, which refers to any event associated with the end of the world: death, judgement, heaven or hell. Hick's notion of eschatological verification is, however, subject to attack. The Danish philosopher Kai Nielsen (born 1915) has argued that an after-life would not confirm religious belief, since it might just be a fact of nature that some people live on after death and this fact need not be interpreted in religious terms. One can easily imagine some experiences after death that decisively lend support to religious belief while conceding with Nielsen that not every post-mortem experience would do so. This last objection of Nielsen is in itself very revealing for it shows that what is required by Flew's challenge is not a state of affairs that could be seen as confirming or disconfirming religious belief, but a state of affairs which is objectively and unambiguously clear-cut in its interpretation.

Flew's challenge itself is proof that such a specification is not unintelligible. The challenge supposes that there exists a rationally convincing proof of either the falsity or the meaninglessness of religious beliefs that would create a situation in which one would have to give up religious belief. There is no difficulty in thinking of propositions that would be true if religious beliefs were false. For example, the belief that God exists and loves us would be falsified if it could be shown that the world works ultimately against our welfare. If that situation can be identified as existing, then it would be foolish to maintain beliefs in the existence and **omnibenevolence** of an omnipotent deity. One could not hold such beliefs if it were found to be the case that we are all totally at the mercy of a demonic power. In such circumstances belief in theism would be clearly falsified.

Review question
Briefly explain how religious language differs from the descriptions we give of everyday objects.

Arguments for the existence of God

St Augustine of Hippo (354–430) said that questions about God were the most important that any philosopher could consider. They still represent a series of questions that ought to be considered important in philosophy. This section begins by looking at the traditional attempts to prove God's existence, before focusing on a set of problems concerned with faith and the problem of evil. For many people today, belief in a supreme being is untenable because God's existence cannot be proved. Let us briefly examine the nature of proof.

Proof differs from justification in that it not only provides a good reason for believing something but a logically compelling argument that forces us to believe it. However, seriously sceptical arguments suggest that there is no absolute proof for anything at all. A number of arguments have been suggested by theistic philosophers for the existence of God and fall into two general categories: proofs from premises and proofs from religious experience. Some apologists have felt that the only way to fill the void of uncertainty and disbelief is by providing a neat deductive argument for the existence of God. We shall begin with a brief exposition of these proofs from premises before the notion of faith is explored.

The cosmological argument
It seems appropriate to start with the first cause argument. One of the deepest human intuitions, prevalent in most cultures, is the idea that the universe depends on something else for its existence. One Hindu creation myth describes how the world is set on the back of an elephant, which is balanced on the back of a turtle, which is itself part of an infinite line of turtles. Such an image is an example of what philosophers call an **infinite regress**, i.e. something that goes on for ever without an end. The infinite regress explanation for the origin of the universe still begs the question, 'Why is the universe existent?' Another suggestion is that of a prime mover or uncaused cause. Such a solution has been championed in the west by thinkers such as St Thomas Aquinas, and is termed the **cosmological** or first cause argument. Aquinas believes that the universe was caused by, and is dependent on, an intervening God.

Aquinas' proofs of the existence of God are framed in the Five Ways, though only the first three may be accurately termed cosmological:

Way 1 (causal argument)
1 The world is in motion due to change.
2 All changes in the world are due to some prior cause.

3 There must be a cause for this entire sequence of changes.

4 We call this cause 'God'.

Way 2 (causal argument)

1 The world consists of a sequence of events.

2 Every event in the world has a cause.

3 There must be a cause for the entire sequence of events.

4 We call this cause 'God'.

Aquinas' second way is a prime example of a causal argument for the existence of God. The second premise presumes that nothing can cause itself to come into existence but, rather, everything comes into existence as a consequence of something else. The argument denies the possibility of backwards or circular causation. The third premise is based on the medieval formula *ex nihilo nihil fit*, which translates as 'nothing comes from nothing' and is an intuitively attractive notion. Note also that big-bang cosmology does not imply that anything comes into existence without a cause.

Way 3 (contingency argument)

1 The world might not have been.

2 Everything that exists in the world depends on some other thing for its existence.

3 The world itself must depend upon some other thing for its existence.

4 We call that which sustains the world's existence 'God'.

'Contingency' is the word used by philosophers to describe anything that exists but might not have existed and is contrasted with 'necessity', which is the term used to describe anything that could not have failed to exist. The contingency argument as stated above holds that the universe

Thomas Aquinas
(1225–1274)

Thomas Aquinas was born into a noble family near the small town of Aquino, which lies between Naples and Rome. He became a Dominican friar in 1244 much to the consternation of his family, who hired a prostitute to tempt him away from the order, but he fled in horror. Aquinas was a heavyweight scholar in both senses of the word. Weighing in at around twenty stone, it is rumoured that this doctor of the church worked at a specially designed desk to fit around his corpulence. Despite a peripatetic life of preaching and teaching, Aquinas penned over two million words of in-depth theology, his best-known works being the *Summa Theologica* and the *Summa Contra Gentiles*. A *summa* (summary) was a comprehensive exposition of a theological or philosophical matter. There was little to distinguish between theology and philosophy until the Enlightenment; before this time philosophy was referred to as the handmaid of theology.

In Aquinas' writings, faith and reason are harmonised in a grand theologico-philosophical system that inspired the medieval philosophical tradition known as Thomism and which has been favoured by the Roman Catholic church ever since. There are many areas of interest to philosophers in the work of Aquinas, such as Aquinas' theory of knowledge, his analysis of causality, his writings on God (the Five Ways and the doctrine of analogy) together with his neo-Aristotelian **teleological** theory of ethics called 'Natural Law'. Like many people who have firmly held religious convictions, Aquinas wrestled with the tension between faith and reason. He is recorded as having described his work as 'so much straw' compared with the quality of religious experience. He is, nevertheless, an influential figure, and one saint who also had a Ph.D. He remains the patron saint of philosophers, students and scholars, and his feast day is 28 January.

Significant works
Summa Contra Gentiles (1259–1264)
Summa Theologica (1265–1274)

is contingent and that all contingent things can be explained with recourse to necessary things. This is achieved by the simple deduction that if other contingent things were used as an explanation then the question would remain as to their origins. So there must be a necessary being that figures in the explanation of contingent entities. The universe itself cannot enter the candidature of necessary beings, as it is made up of particles and planets that exist contingently. Theists term the necessary being 'God' and, while it is legitimate to point out that it takes a pretty large leap of the imagination to get from a philosophical first cause to the theistic concept of God as outlined above, it nevertheless remains that the cosmological argument seems plausible independent of traditional theism.

The fourth way is a version of the moral argument and the fifth way constitutes a teleological argument. Both are presented below for the sake of completeness:

Way 4

1 There are degrees of perfection in the world.
2 Things are more perfect the closer they approach the maximum.
3 There is a maximum perfection, which we call 'God'.

Way 5

1 Each body has a natural tendency towards its goal.
2 All order requires a designer.
3 End-directedness of all natural bodies must have a designing force.
4 There is such a designer, which we call 'God'.

Aquinas' arguments have been reformulated by neo-Thomists (the name given to contemporary adherents of Aquinas' philosophy) in an attempt to avoid the problem of infinite regress. Aquinas postulates God as the prime mover or uncaused cause of the universe but admits that there is a difficulty in excluding an endless regress of events requiring no first state. Thomist scholars interpret the endless series of events that Aquinas' argument seeks to exclude as an infinite and therefore eternally inconclusive regress of explanations. If fact A is made intelligible by its relationship to facts B, C, D, where each fact is

rendered intelligible by its relationship to others, then at the back of the complex there must be a reality that is self-explanatory and whose existence constitutes the ultimate explanation of the whole. If no such reality exists then the universe is merely an unintelligible, brute fact. This latter view was considered legitimate by philosophers such as Bertrand Russell, who declared, 'I should say that the universe is just there and that's all.' This is an unimaginative response that could be applied to any problem with the same sterile result. It is also a contravention of Leibniz's principle of sufficient reason, which states that for every state of affairs there must be a reason why it is not otherwise. To prosaically assert that something just is is not to explain why it is not otherwise.

Criticisms of the cosmological argument

- One might attack the need to have an explanation as to the origins of the universe by arguing that the universe does not need a causal explanation but just exists. This appears to be suggesting that every event does not need a cause.

- One might attack the notion of God as an uncaused cause as being absurd especially if the major premise in the cosmological argument is that every event has a cause.

- One might accuse proponents of the cosmological argument of not telling us anything about this cause, only that it exists. There is a significant leap of faith from accepting such a cause exists to accepting other tenets of theistic belief.

The teleological argument

The cosmological argument starts with a basic, coarse-grained fact concerning causality, whereas the teleological argument begins with a special fact: that intelligent design implies an intelligent designer. The teleological argument (*telos* is the Greek word for 'goal' or 'purpose') focuses on the existence of purpose or design in nature. Despite the teleological argument possessing an important *a posteriori* element through our observation of patterns and sequences in the world, the argument can nevertheless be stated in neat, deductive fashion:

1 There is evidence of order in the universe.

2 All order requires a designer.

3 The universe has a designer, whom we call 'God'.

One of the argument's chief exponents, William Paley (1743–1805), drew an analogy between the universe and a watch to help illustrate the argument. Paley invites us to imagine that, while out on a country ramble, we come across a watch and a stone lying on the ground. He says that we would be acting quite reasonably if we supposed that chance and natural forces had laid the stone in that particular spot, but we would not be justified in accounting for the presence of the watch in the same way, owing to it being a complex and deliberate arrangement of high-precision parts: the chains, springs, wheels, pointers and transparent cover. Paley argues that the conclusion that this object has been made is 'an inevitable inference'. Paley's intention is to draw a comparison between the watch and the world, suggesting that both are purposeful systems that function in an exact and accurate way, unlike the stone.

Task

Paley is careful to emphasise the self-contained, interconnected, precise and purposeful elements of the watch. What features of the natural world would he draw our attention to as evidence of design in the universe? Draw up a list and discuss whether such features might be explained in any other way.

To say that the universe is fine-tuned is an understatement, and one must bear in mind when reading Hume's criticisms of the argument from design in the next section that he was not aware of how intricate our universe is. The best candidate for design must be the existence of rational animals like human beings. This has led philosophers to refer to the special conditions required for life to develop as 'the anthropic principle' after the Greek *anthropos* meaning 'human being'. Advocates of the anthropic principle point to the fact that if these conditions were minutely different (e.g. if the atomic mass of oxygen had not remained constant) then life would not have been created. But are we not presuming that life in general and rational life in particular is a good thing? Perhaps we make this value judgement because we find our universe more interesting than a universe full of hydrogen, which would be a world of snowy randomness like a television screen that is stuck between channels.

Criticisms of the teleological argument

Authors such as the atheist scientist Richard Dawkins (born 1941) in his work *The Blind Watchmaker* have criticised the first premise that there is evidence of order in the universe. For Dawkins, any apparent order in the natural world is due to non-intelligent causes such as evolution, natural selection and environmental adaptation. A teleologist might reply, however, that evolution is a process that itself requires, and is proof of, a designer, whom we may call God.

In turn, the second premise may be rendered invalid if one could point to an instance where order did not require a designer. Biologists distinguish between designed and 'designoid' objects, citing in the former class any artefact that has been fashioned intelligently for a specific purpose and counting as 'designoid' anything that is made out of instinct. A wasp's nest, which appears complex and intricate enough to fulfil Paley's criteria, has been produced on evolutionary auto-pilot and cannot, therefore, count as evidence of intelligent design.

The third avenue of criticism is pursued by Hume in his *Dialogues Concerning Natural Religion* (1779). The text constitutes a sustained sceptical attack on the teleological argument. During the dialogue a character called Philo advances some powerful objections to the argument from design, though it is a source of scholarly disagreement as to whether in voicing such criticisms he is acting as the mouthpiece for Hume himself. Philo's refutation centres around three primary contentions:

- The argument from design offers more proof in favour of polytheism, belief in many gods, than monotheism, belief in one God.

- The argument from design offers more proof that the creator of the universe is dead rather than alive.
- The argument from design offers more proof that the universe has been created by a malevolent force rather than a benevolent one.

In Part V of the text, the author invites us to contemplate the construction of a ship, stating that, as such complexity is more likely to be the handiwork of many rather than one, so the universe is less likely to have been created by a single deity. Hume extends the analogy to make the point that such construction is achieved by imitation and not intelligence, and thus infers that the creation of the universe does not necessarily entail omniscience. In Part VI, Hume chooses Demea as the messenger who announces the weight of criticism against the argument from design:

> While we are uncertain, whether there is one deity or many; whether the deity or deities, to whom we owe our existence, be perfect or imperfect, subordinate or extreme, dead or alive; what trust or confidence can we repose in them? What devotion or worship address to them? What veneration or obedience pay them?[4]

The position is strengthened later in the text (Parts X and XI), where the reality of suffering is commented on and the tempered conclusion reached that, if God did create the universe, He has left it incomplete, 'so little finished in every part and so coarse are the strokes with which it is executed' (Part XI). This argument appears an inverse teleological argument, i.e. one that argues against the existence of God from facts about the universe. This is essentially the line taken by exponents of the problem of evil.

It is impossible to escape analogy in any analysis of the teleological argument, as the argument itself relies on the comparison between designed objects and the universe. Yet the parallel drawn above reaches the conclusion that the universe has come about and is maintained in existence out of necessity. This conclusion has been dismissed in an earlier discussion of the cosmological argument, but the concept of necessity requires further exploration. One

argument that holds that God's existence is necessary is the **ontological** argument.

The ontological argument

The German philosopher Arthur Schopenhauer (1788–1860) described the ontological argument as a charming joke, while the late Cardinal Basil Hume once described it as a good intuition. Both views are fairly damning for an argument that seeks to set out a deductive proof of the existence of God. The first version of the argument appears in the meditations of St Anselm of Canterbury (c. 1033–1109) in the third and fourth chapters of his *Proslogion*. Anselm quotes the beginning of Psalm 53: 'The impious fool says in his heart, "There is no God" '. From this verse Anselm argues that the fool must have a conception of what God is, in order to deny this belief. One's idea of God embodies certain features: that God is a rational, conscious person rather than an impersonal force; in addition, that God can do things that we cannot do, know things that we cannot know, is always good and is the creator of the universe. Implicit in this description of God, as sketched out in the opening section, is the belief that God exists. For the twelfth-century monk, to assert that God does not exist would be tantamount to asserting a straight logical contradiction. Let us express the Anselmian version of the ontological argument more formally:

1 We have an idea of God.
2 Our idea is of a being than which no greater can be thought.
3 Either this being exists only in our minds or it exists in reality as well.
4 If this being exists only in our minds, then it cannot be thought of as a being than which no greater can be thought. (We could think of a greater being, viz. one that exists in reality as well.)
5 Therefore, we are to think of God as existing in reality. Therefore, God exists.

The word 'ontological' stems from the Greek *ontos*, which means 'being' or 'existence'. As can be seen from the above argument, Anselm tries to prove God's existence from the idea of what sort of being God is. The third premise offers us a choice; the first alternative is then ruled out in the fourth premise, leaving us with the conclusion that if God is a supreme being, then He must exist, as otherwise He would lack a feature of supremacy or perfection. Needless to say, this deduction (formally termed a *reductio ad absurdum*) has left thinkers suspicious, as if some intellectual sleight of hand has been committed.

The first critic was Gaunilo, a French monk writing at the time of Anselm, whose essay 'On Behalf of the Fool' started a benign theological disagreement. Gaunilo objects to the ontological argument because the same reasoning could be applied to anything we consider ideal. He uses the example of a perfect island and substitutes it as follows:

1 We have an idea of a perfect island.
2 Either this perfect island exists in our imagination or else it exists in reality as well.
3 If this island only existed in our imagination then it would not be perfect.
4 This perfect island must exist in reality.

Gaunilo's argument helps to clarify Anselm's proof that God is a unique case of necessary existence. Anselm replies to Gaunilo's criticism by noting that the greatness, perfection or supremacy referred to is not spatial magnitude but 'greatness in goodness and value, like wisdom'. The Anselmian influence continued and one should more accurately refer to the ontological argument not as one argument but as a family of arguments that has had an eclectic mix of advocates.

Descartes (see chapter 9) reformulated the argument in such a way as to emphasise some aspects that lacked clarity in Anselm's version. He argued that:

1 Everyone, even atheists, can understand the idea of God as the most perfect being.
2 The most perfect must, by definition, possess all perfections.
3 To exist in reality is greater than to exist simply as an idea.

The Cartesian reformulation attracted new attention to the argument and raises the assumption that existence is a predicate, i.e. a property or characteristic of a thing; this idea was later challenged by Kant.

The German philosopher G. W. Leibniz (1646–1716) follows Descartes in advancing a version in his *Monadology* (1714):

> Thus God alone (or the Necessary Being) has the privilege that he must exist if he is possible. And as nothing can prevent the possibility of that which has no limits, no negation, and consequently no contradiction, this alone is sufficient for us to know the existence of God *a priori*. We have proved it also by the reality of eternal truths. And we have now just proved it *a posteriori* also, since there exist contingent beings, which can only have their ultimate or sufficient reason in the Necessary Being, who has the reason for his existence in himself.[5]

In the above version of the argument the existence of contingent beings is supplied as justification for the existence of a supreme, necessary being who keeps them alive.

The modal ontological argument

Alvin Plantinga (born 1932) was one of the first philosophers to argue that God as 'a being of maximal greatness' necessarily exists in all possible worlds. This version of the proof may be expressed formally as follows:

1 Any perfect being must possess all perfections.
2 Necessary existence is a perfection.
3 Any perfect being must necessarily exist.
4 It is possibly true that such a perfect being exists.
5 Therefore, it is necessarily true that such a perfect being exists.
6 Therefore, a perfect being exists whom we call God.

The argument moves from asserting that the existence of God is conceivable, i.e. there is nothing logically contradictory being advanced. To be possibly true means to be true in at least one possible world, but it is the nature of the beast in the case of theism that to be true at all is to be necessarily true. One cannot construe a state of affairs in which God exists in some worlds and not in others. So if theism is true in one world then it must be true in all worlds. One of those worlds is the actual world that we inhabit; therefore, theism must be true in this world. The argument holds, but would also hold if we were to argue the case for atheism, and there lies the catch. Consider the argument that atheism is possible. If it were possible in one world then it is necessarily true, because it is concerned with denying the existence of God and not a contingent human life. If atheism is necessarily true then theism is necessarily false. If both the above modal arguments are formally valid, it is hard to see how we could ever establish whether God exists at all.

Criticisms of the ontological argument

Three main strands of criticism have developed over the centuries:

- St Thomas Aquinas criticised Anselm's argument on the straightforward basis that the conclusion does not follow from the premises. It is simply not the case that we can assume God's existence in the real world, as opposed to the realm of understanding, merely from the fact that God is taken to mean a being than which no greater can be conceived. He goes on to add that atheists do not accept that there is anything in reality that fits Anselm's definition of God. Implicit in this Thomist criticism is an important logical point. We call any statement that asserts that something exists 'an existential proposition', and we term any statement whose negation is self-contradictory 'a logically necessary statement' or 'tautology'; tautologies are true by definition. Consider as an example the statement, 'Eggs are eggs'. To assert the opposite, 'Eggs are not eggs', does not make sense. Anselm puts the statement 'God exists' in the class of propositions called tautologies, yet the assertion 'God does not exist' seems to make sense. It appears that no existential proposition can be logically necessary.
- The second strand of criticism is linguistic in nature and originates from the writings of Immanuel Kant, the first person to coin the term 'ontological argument'. Kant believed that the word 'exists' does not behave in the same way as other predicates such as 'woolly', 'small' or 'turquoise'. Kant believed that existence was

not a predicate at all. The difference, he says, between a real and an imaginary sum of money is that one actually exists and the other exists only in the imagination. What would be at issue if you wanted someone to extend credit on the surety of a sum of money, perhaps one thousand pounds, would be proof that you were telling the truth about the state of your finances, and this would not be available from any analysis of the concept of 'one thousand pounds'. The logician Gottlob Frege (1848–1925) adds that the term 'exists' does not inform us about the nature of the entity referred to.

- The third criticism of the ontological argument focuses on Anselm's presumption that it is better to exist than not to exist. Why does he suppose this to be the case? It is a value judgement, and may be challenged by asserting either that both states are neutral descriptions or that not to exist is better. The onus is thrown back on Anselm, as God's existence remains subject to proof. Alternatively, one might assert that, by definition, ideals cannot exist, but occupy an imaginary realm similar to that of Plato's forms. I have an ideal meal in mind that any actual meal will somehow fall short of. Even unpleasant entities such as overdrafts can have an appropriately unpleasant yet perfect form; thus one cannot say whether it is better to exist or not to exist but only assert something exists as a matter of verifiable fact.

Review question

Briefly explain the meaning of two of the following terms: cosmological, teleological, ontological.

The argument from religious experience

When Mole and Rat, those well-known philosophers of religion, go in search of the lost otter in *The Wind in the Willows*, they enjoy a religious experience:

Then suddenly Mole felt a great Awe fall upon him, an awe that turned his muscles to water, bowed his head, and rooted his feet to the ground. It was no panic terror – indeed he felt wonderfully at peace and happy – but it was an awe that smote and held him and, without seeing, he knew it could only mean that some august Presence was very, very near. With difficulty he turned to look for his friend, and saw him at his side cowed, stricken, and trembling violently. And still there was utter silence in the populous bird-haunted branches around them; and still the light grew and grew.[6]

There are a number of important features in this narrative that correspond to the argument from religious experience: the author strives to express the characters' feelings in a way that exposes the inadequacy of language; the experiences themselves occur in the private rather than the public sphere; and one might question why these individuals and not others have been awarded the elite privilege of religious experience. Why were the weasels excluded from such mystical enchantment?

The argument itself might be expressed formally as follows:

1 I have an experience X.
2 Experience X is of such a quality that it can only be attributed to a divine source.
3 Therefore, the Divine exists.

One of the most detailed studies of religious experience was undertaken by William James (1842–1910) and published under the title *The Varieties of Religious Experience*. James came from a well-known Bostonian family and was the elder brother of the novelist Henry James. *The Varieties of Religious Experience* was originally delivered as a series of lectures at Edinburgh University and published as a complete volume in 1902. In this volume, James embarks upon the study of religion from a psychological perspective. Throughout the text, many specific cases and instances are cited in the hope that philosophy can extract general facts about religious experience upon which everybody can agree. Many accounts are recorded from people who have sensed the presence of something not directly perceived by their senses. These include among other things visualised hallucinations, mystical seizures (rapture, ecstasy), photisms (sensations of bright light) and a sense of the presence of God. Testimonies regarding religious experience come from people of different sexes and ages who believe that they have had intimate

contact and communion with the Divine and that this constitutes proof of His existence. James' survey, however, does not conclude that religious experience has a divine origin, and many rationalisations are examined. One such rationalisation is the thought that religious experience is a substitute for sexual expression or the product of an overactive adolescent mind. James discusses these arguments, and points out that it is not only the sexual life but the entire higher mental life that awakens during adolescence, and that adolescence can equally determine resolute atheism as well as religious zeal.

An interesting distinction is drawn in lectures 4 and 5 between the everyday, mundane, perfunctory aspects of life and the higher mental life. James infers that religious experience consists of moving from the shallow nature of humanity to the profound. One might view religious experience as the antidote to feelings of dissatisfaction and uneasiness felt by some people when reflecting on the human condition (described in religious terms as sinful). Is religious experience an escape route manufactured in the recesses of the subject's own mind or is it directed by God? Does religious experience need an external cause to generate an internal effect, or can it be self-generated? In the course of lectures 9 and 10, James points out that religious experience can be induced by post-hypnotic suggestion. However, he states that a purely psychological explanation for religious experience does not exclude the notion of the direct presence of the deity perhaps working through a natural process.

The remaining lectures comprise a description of holiness and an examination of its value. James concludes in *The Varieties of Religious Experience* that there is a body of experience 'something larger than ourselves' and that human beings can find solace in its contemplation.

Each world faith lays claim to some sort of religious experience, and philosophers of religion have wrestled with the problem of conflicting truth claims for some time. John Hick is one contemporary theologian who advocates a Copernican shift, which deposes God as the focal point of such experiences in favour of what he calls 'the Real', thus incorporating Buddhist and non-theistic Hindu traditions. His critics allege, however, that such a focus is so general as to be meaningless. Further arguments centre around a wholly physical explanation of the psychology of religious feeling. Consider the example of Pittinger's helmet, which when worn is a device capable of manufacturing religious experiences in some people.

> ## Task
>
> Type out the above proofs for the existence of God as they appear, in neat, deductive form. With a pair of scissors, cut each of the arguments into their constitutive sentences and place in an envelope. When you come to revise, open the envelope and reform the jumbled sentences into the original arguments.

Faith and reason

The pragmatic argument

The pragmatic argument, as developed by the Oxford philosopher Richard Swinburne (born 1934), states that the existence of God becomes incrementally more certain as we look at an increasingly wide range of evidence. Swinburne holds that any useful causal explanation shares certain features:

- It is not needlessly complex.
- It fits in with our background knowledge.
- If present then it seems to make the occurrence more probable.
- If absent then it seems to make the occurrence less probable.

Granted these criteria, Swinburne argues that God is the most likely explanation for the observed evidence of a universe governed by simple scientific laws, fine-tuned to produce conscious animals and humans, and various historical phenomena and the religious experience of humans. Alternative explanations such as the existence of multiple universes are less likely, and any argument from chance is no explanation at all. Swinburne argues from probability theory that it is only theism that takes sufficient account of man's moral and religious experience as well as giving all the material aspects of the universe their proper place.

This theory does not, however, help us to discover very much about the existence of God, because, as Hume points out, there is only one universe, and so we cannot make definitive judgements about it. If there were, say, ten universes and we knew for certain that half of them were God-produced, then we could infer that the probability of our own universe being also God-produced would be 1 in 2. To say that one statement is more reasonable than another is to say that when they are both considered against a common body of prior, evidence-stating propositions, it is more reasonable to believe one than the other. However, the fact that there are no propositions existing independently of the universe that provide evidence for God's existence is problematic. There is, as far as we know, only one universe, and it is capable of being interpreted both theistically and non-theistically.

Pascal's wager

What is interesting about the religious writings of Pascal is the manner in which they show the deep combination in his personality of both the scepticism of the scientist and the faith of the religious convert. Pascal is often compared with the Danish philosopher Søren Kierkegaard (1813–1855) in terms of his belief in the need for existential religious commitment rather than a faith based on reason alone. Kierkegaard wrote of the necessity for a 'leap of faith'. Pascal's famous 'wager' was formulated in his *Pensées* (1670), a classical text of devotional literature in which the author argues that we are incapable of finally knowing whether or not God exists. Nevertheless, even if metaphysical argument fails, we can still ask if it is better to believe in God than not to do so. This remains a legitimate question.

The argument runs as follows:

1 If God exists, then it is clearly sensible to worship him, since the prospect of eternal life in Heaven [for believers] is preferable to damnation in Hell [for non-believers].

2 If, on the other hand, God does not exist, then we have lost nothing by living a life based on our religious faith, and may even have gained in terms of the quality of our moral and spiritual self-development.

Blaise Pascal (1623–1662)

Blaise Pascal was a French physicist, philosopher and mathematical prodigy. By the age of sixteen he was publishing mathematical papers, and his friendship with Pierre Fermat laid the foundation of the modern theory of probability. Pascal's mother died when he was three years of age, and his father took on the responsibility of the education of young Blaise and his two sisters. They were taught at home, but Pascal was such a sickly child that he was often confined to his bedroom to recuperate. It was in these quiet moments that the philosopher developed a fascination with mathematics and in particular with geometry. He discovered many geometric truths without any teaching, which constitutes a good example of how *a priori* knowledge can be acquired. In 1654, Pascal, who came from a religious family (they followed the teachings of the Roman Catholic sect called Jansenism), underwent some kind of intense religious experience in which Christ appeared to him, the effects of which led him away from mathematics and science and towards philosophy and theology. This change was compounded by the effects of a serious accident that the philosopher only just survived, when a coach and horses ran away with him and he was narrowly saved by the tackle breaking before his carriage was about to run into a river. Pascal documented this incident on a tiny piece of parchment, which he kept about his person at all times, and he saw it as God's way of telling him that he should not marry but concentrate on academic and religious life.

Significant works
Provincial Letters (1656)
Pensées (1670)

---

3 Therefore, Pascal argues, belief should always be our dominant strategy since, while it can win, it can never lose.

In Pascal's own terms, the odds of the wager are *infini–rien*, infinity to nothing; we should, therefore, avoid scepticism and develop faith. On realising that it is impossible simply to choose to believe in God, Pascal argues that religious faith should be gradually developed in a person. He thought that belief was contagious and could be passed from person to person simply as a result of association and normal social intercourse. Through this social intercourse and the faithful carrying out of religious duties throughout life, a person would end up developing faith and achieving the most desirable and prudent state of being.

There are two standard criticisms of Pascal's argument. First, that if we really are ignorant about the existence of God, then we are also ignorant as to the kinds of reward and punishment that God might make use of. In addition, no punishment will be administered by a compassionate God who sympathises with our uncertainty. Secondly, the wager, unlike most arguments for belief, makes no reference to the likelihood of truth, but only probability concerning an individual's belief.

The argument from faith

We have examined the traditional proofs for the existence of God established through reason; let us proceed to arguments from faith and religious experience. The argument from faith is the furthest removed from the above deductions, and may be described as anti-rationalist in so far as it does not hold that God's existence can be proved through logical means but can only be discovered through a journey of faith. The most dramatic exponent of this view was Kierkegaard. This view is termed 'fideism', a word derived from the Latin *fides* meaning 'faith'.

Fideism

The debate about what constitutes religious faith has a great deal to do with the credibility that we award this notion. To have faith in something is to be sure about it, although not in any normal sense of assurance. Synonyms for 'faith', such as 'trust', 'confidence' and 'certitude', attest to this fact. Faith may strike you as being a difficult and paradoxical notion, and one that requires you to choose freely to give assent to 'truths' for which there is no empirically verifiable evidence. What you need to decide is whether or not you feel able to accept that, in the case of religious faith, you feel justified in setting aside all of the standards by which you usually assess the reliability of knowledge in favour of another, rather more mysterious, set of standards. This is, clearly, a very personal decision.

Kierkegaard argued that all truth is subjective and that each of us perceives the truths by which we live as true for us, regardless of what others may or may not believe. All our thinking about life is based upon our own individual existence and the needs which this generates in us, because we exist as concrete and autonomous individuals possessed of the ability to choose. From this, it followed for Kierkegaard that there can be no answer to the question 'Why do I exist?' except that we exist to make choices, each of which we make, in the last analysis, for reasons that may seem sufficient only to us. He defined this act of choice as 'a leap of faith' into the unknown and offers, in his work *Fear and Trembling*, the biblical example of Abraham and Isaac (Genesis 22), in which Abraham is prepared to sacrifice the life of his son in order to demonstrate his faith in God, while Isaac is willing to keep faith with his father's love for him. Clearly, this is not behaviour that most fathers and sons would find easy to subscribe to! Kierkegaard is trying to demonstrate that religious faith is the means by which human beings confront the deepest mysteries of our existence, which, he argues, have to do with such complex states of mind and emotions as despair and fear of death. When we make an act of religious faith, therefore, we are choosing the means by which we intend to resolve our questioning and concern about those issues in our lives that seem to us intractable and insoluble in any other terms.

The illative sense

The next account of faith to be examined is advanced by the Christian writer John Henry Newman (1801–1890) in his *Essay in Aid of a Grammar of Assent*. Newman's argument moves from a recognition of the intellectual arguments for the existence of God as outlined above to a celebration of religious experience in the form of devotional feelings and a moral conscience. The author terms his conviction that God exists 'certitude', and holds that it is the product of an individual's illative sense. This term is derived from the Latin *illatio* meaning 'to carry into' in the sense of being directed or guided. It consists in nothing more than linking together smaller features into a unified interpretation of the whole, just as on first meeting someone you form an opinion about them from more discrete aspects of their appearance. Newman uses the image of a rope made out of individually weaker threads that form a strong cable when bound together. In turn, one can climb this rope to reach a position of certainty that God exists. Indeed, it is necessary to make a concerted physical effort in order to reach this position of faith, just as it is useless to know in theory how to climb without ever having tried it. Newman's theory of assent emphasises the personal, experiential and intuitive aspects of religion, but is not a theory immune from criticism. One might accuse Newman of expounding a theory that is neither definable nor verifiable. In addition, one might question his method of asserting that the whole is greater than the sum of its parts.

Review questions

1 Briefly explain Pascal's wager.
2 Briefly explain the view that faith and proof are incompatible.

Implications of God's existence

The problem of evil

The problem of evil counts as a deductive argument against the existence of God, and may be formally expressed as follows:

1 We conceive of God as an omniscient, omnipotent and omnibenevolent being.
2 The existence of evil is incompatible with the existence of an omniscient, omnipotent and omnibenevolent God.
3 Evil occurs.
4 Therefore, there is no omniscient, omnipotent and omnibenevolent God.

The term 'evil' referred to in the third premise requires further classification. Certain rough-and-ready categories present themselves in the form of moral evil and physical suffering.

The extent of 'man's inhumanity to man' in cases such as rape, murder and genocide constitutes moral evil, whereas the experience of famine, flood and disease may be cited as instances of unmerited physical suffering. Both categories point to a marked incompatibility with an able and compassionate deity. Even proponents of the teleological argument are forced to admit that the design of the universe is flawed. General explanations that 'pain and accident and loss are inevitable aspects of an evolving organic world' point to the underlying question of why didn't God do better.[7] This sentiment led the comedian Woody Allen to say that the best thing that could be said about God is that he is an under-achiever. In medieval times, the problem of why the universe did not exhibit a perfect design was known as the problem of metaphysical evil.

Theistic replies to the problem of evil are called **theodicies**, and generally involve a reinterpretation of premises **1** and **2**, with only a minority of thinkers challenging the validity of the third premise in arguing that evil is illusory. Traditional theodicies defend God's part in allowing suffering, whereas post-Holocaust theodicies attempt to redefine the divine attributes as described in the first premise.

Traditional theodicies

The two most enduring theodicies belong to the Early Church fathers St Irenaeus (130–202) and St Augustine of Hippo (354–430). Both assert that evil is present in order for some greater good to occur that could not have been achieved in any other way.

The Irenaean theodicy

Both Irenaeus' and Augustine's arguments refer to the Old Testament Book of Genesis (Chapter 1, Verse 26), which states that God made human beings in His image and likeness. From this, Irenaeus argues that there are two distinct phases of evolution in the human race. The first sees us created as intelligent though imperfect creatures, possessed of enormous capacity for moral and spiritual development, even if it is over a huge span of time. We were immature, as if at the beginning of a vastly extended childhood, but promisingly full of potential for an unforeseeable future. During the second stage of our evolution, through which we are currently living, human beings are being transformed from what might be called 'human animals' into what Irenaeus calls 'children of God'. Importantly, Irenaeus argues that we have reached this evolutionary point not through coercion by God but as a result of our own freely chosen movement towards Him, our own free responses. For Irenaeus, God has always wanted and intended to create human beings in this way, so that they would grow towards Him naturally and freely as they learned the true nature of their moral and spiritual selves. The 'distance' that He has maintained from us has always been a strategy deliberately chosen as a means of encouraging human beings to seek out knowledge and understanding, to move forward in their journey towards God and so become more fully human.

According to Irenaeus, suffering exists as a necessary condition for the creation of humanity in the likeness of God. The Irenaean theodicy is an interesting argument and it raises some important questions:

1 Is the saint correct in asserting that all the richest human virtues would never have developed in a world devoid of risk, danger or difficulty?
2 Since it is clear that we are not morally perfect beings when we die, does the process of soul-making continue beyond the grave?
3 Does any ideal, spiritual state 'closer to God' justify the suffering of innocent people?

Dostoevsky posed the last question in his work *The Brothers Karamazov* when he declares:

> Tell me frankly, I appeal to you – answer me: imagine that it is you yourself who are erecting the edifice of human destiny with the aim of making men happy in the end, of giving them peace and contentment at last, but that to do that it is absolutely necessary, and indeed quite inevitable, to torture to death only one tiny creature, the little girl who beat her breast with her little fist, and to found the edifice on her unavenged tears – would you consent to be the architect on those conditions? Tell me and do not lie?[8]

The Augustinian theodicy

Augustine's defence consists of three strands of argument: malfunction, moral balance and appreciation. The first point asserts that creation is as God intended it to be and is inherently good, only becoming corrupt or 'evil' when part of it malfunctions. The example of a human eye used by Augustine echoes a previous theodicy suggested by St Basil the Great (c. 329–379), and holds that the human eye is good in itself until it ceases to function properly in the case of blindness, when evil is said to have occurred. Augustine faces the problem of applying this argument to the universe as a whole in order to solve the theological problem of the existence of evil. On the basis of this highly charged theological argument, Augustine felt able to state categorically that 'all evil is either sin or the punishment for sin'. The idea that Augustine is developing here has subsequently come to be referred to as the argument from moral balance:

sin is punished as justice dictates it should be. The institution of justice is a greater good than the suffering experienced, and a moral balance cannot be achieved in any other way. The third spin to this argument is that evil exists as a contrast to, and even a complement to, goodness. Augustine argues that pain is needed in order to appreciate pleasure in the same way that an artist uses a dash of black to make the colours in a painting stand out. The suffering we experience in this life, according to the saint, is for our own private good.

These three arguments yield three major criticisms that have evolved over the centuries:

- The first asserts that a universe created by a God who possesses absolute power cannot be conceived to be capable of going wrong, as the idea of a perfect creation that can malfunction is self-contradictory.

- Irenaeus and Augustine cannot build a philosophical defence on a religious document such as the Eden story. Despite it being a fantastically rich text, a philosophical proof is required.

- Finally, the responsibility for the presence of evil in the world must lie with God. This point, clearly formulated by the eighteenth-century German theologian Friedrich Schleiermacher (1768–1834), makes the important philosophical point that, since it would have been logically possible for God to have created beings incapable of sin, we must ask why He did not do so. Was it not possible for God to create each citizen of the universe as a determined robot who always chooses the most benign course of action? Why is free will so precious in the face of suffering?

Process theodicy

The major difference between this theodicy and the previous two is that process theodicy admits that God does not have limitless and absolute power to act but is part of a universe that is uncreated. Process theologians liken the uncreated world to an object that seems solid yet, when looked at with the aid of a sufficiently powerful microscope, is revealed to be not 'solid' at all, but made up of vast numbers of moving

Augustine of Hippo (354–430)

Augustine of Hippo was a North African saint of European extraction. He was born in present-day Algeria in 354 to a pagan father and Christian mother, who brought him up in the Christian faith. Augustine is held to be one of the most important theologians in the western tradition, and has made a unique contribution to the philosophy of religion. As a person he was self-important, scholarly and promiscuous; he famously declared, 'Lord, make me chaste but not today.' From his sexually charged teenage years, when he fathered a child at eighteen years of age, Augustine wrestled with the Christian ethic of self-denial and sexual responsibility. He left North Africa for Rome in his late twenties in order to pursue a career in academia and prospered in the intellectual climate that he found there. Augustine was next appointed to a professorship in the Italian city of Milan where he studied under the watchful eye of St Ambrose, who persuaded him that Christianity was a tenable position for a philosopher to hold. His new-found faith was consolidated by a religious experience in a Milan garden when he heard a child's voice whispering to him, 'Take up and read.' He opened a copy of the New Testament that had been lying nearby and read the powerful prose of the thirteenth chapter of Paul's letter to the Roman church, which ends 'make no provisions for the flesh, to gratify its desires'. Augustine had flirted with many heresies in his intellectual life but had settled on a fundamentally dualist view of life that consisted of a recognition of the dichotomies: mind and body, right and wrong, existence and non-existence. This famous thinker became bishop of Hippo in 395 and remains known as Augustine of Hippo to the present day to distinguish him from his English namesake, Augustine of Canterbury.

Significant works

Confessions (400)
On the Trinity (420)
The City of God (426)

particles, each of which seems to contain its own source of energy. The supply of this energy seems infinite, since the particles never stop or slow down but move apparently randomly, round and round. Their lives seem to be made up of vast numbers of momentary individual events during which they change direction, or collide, only to be cast on some journey, the purpose of which seems either inexplicably complex or simply non-existent. What is interesting about this array of particles is that there is within each of them individually and within all of them collectively a sense of creative power, the consequence of which is that the solid object that 'contains' them and is made up of them actually works: the bar stool supports your weight, and your pint doesn't cease to exist or disintegrate into a cloud of atomic particles before you drink it. Although God may be a part of this unending process, He is certainly not in control of it but is if anything controlled by it. Many people living in our Einsteinian and Darwinian age find this notion attractive.

Harmony and intensity of experience do not always make easy bedfellows, as to experience anything very intensely is to run the risk of losing the comfortable sense of harmony that is provided by the same experience at a lower level of intensity. The pleasurable sense of having eaten well may provide a sense of harmony, but keep on eating past this point and see what happens. The same is true of most intense human experiences: enough is as good as a feast. Failure to understand this may lead to endlessly repeated experiences, none of which live up to their imagined potential. For process theologians, evil may be defined as the failure of an occasion or a moment of experience to achieve 'the highest appropriate intensity'. The universe, it would seem, lives in a permanent state of tension between these two polarities of good and evil, and it is only under these conditions that God may function.

Criticisms of process theodicy
- The God of process theodicy is too far removed from the traditional concept of God to carry any ring of authenticity.
- Process theodicy seems to supply a poetic meta-narrative, i.e. a story about how the world works, but is it grounded in anything that we can prove?
- Process theodicy seems to attach warrantless value on to contemporary scientific ideas.

The argument from miracles

The term 'miracle' does not simply refer to 'something to be wondered at' as its Latin derivation, *miraculum*, suggests, but is used to describe any event that is attributed to direct, divine intervention: 'things which are done by divine agency beyond the order commonly observed in nature'.[9]

On the face of it, this appears to have the most potential of all the traditional arguments as, if divine intervention necessarily entails divine existence and God does indeed intervene in the world, then we can assert with impunity that God exists. The argument from miracles has nevertheless ignited a Catherine wheel of criticisms, not least of which is the assertion that if 'miracle' is defined as a breach of natural law then one can *a priori* declare that there are no miracles.

The most famous exposition of miracles occurs towards the end of Hume's *Enquiry Concerning Human Understanding*. The author is responding to a school of thought prevalent at the time, advocated by the so-called natural theologians, who sought to distinguish between bogus and *bona fide* religious authority by appealing to revelation through the miraculous. Hume advises caution in any treatment of miracles and issues the following maxim as a guideline: 'That no testimony is sufficient to establish a miracle, unless the testimony be of such a kind, that its falsehood would be more miraculous, than the fact, which it endeavours to establish'.[10]

According to this method, any miraculous accounts from whatever culture should be treated equally. Hume notes in passing that miracles appeal to the human passion for story-telling and are often more plentiful in remote, rural cultures. Does the above dictum leave any room for miracles occurring? He asserts that it has ruled out any occurrences to date, but is aware that this does not mean that there cannot be any in the future. In addition, to speak of miracles running against the law of nature implies that we understand all the principles upon which nature works and that such laws are regular and reliable. This is not the case, but it would be equally prejudicial to assert that the possibility of miracles can always be excluded. Many scientifically minded philosophers assert that the best we can do at the moment is to talk in terms of probabilities, and it is more helpful when trying to understand something to talk in terms of the frequency of occurrence of particular outcomes. Thus, the same event, described by the theist as 'a miracle', rationalised by the scientist as 'a probability of very low likelihood', may be reconciled by the philosopher as an impossible event that may have a divine cause if the divine exists. On the whole, Hume's scepticism is shown to be not so much destructive as pragmatic when applied to a real philosophical case study.

> **Task**
> Make your own philosophical case study of a miracle that has been documented in any major world faith. Describe the miracle first and how the religious community interprets it. Then assess whether any other explanations might be given.

The moral argument

The moral argument alleges that the existence of God can be proved from the existence of moral imperatives. The argument claims that ethical experience, and especially our sense of moral obligation, entails the existence of God as the sole source or basis of this obligation. The moral argument for God's existence has received less attention than the other 'traditional' proofs, but is advanced by Kant in his work *The Critique of Practical Reason* (1788).[11] Kant's formulation of the moral argument gives us a 'strong' version of the proof, which may be summarised in the following deduction:

1 Unless there is a God there cannot be objectively binding moral obligations.
2 There are objectively binding moral obligations.
3 Therefore, there is a God.

Other formulations of the moral argument exist. St Thomas Aquinas argues from the existence of degrees of value to the existence of absolute value, the source of which we call God. Implicit in the Thomist moral philosophy, called 'natural law,' is the conviction that law requires a lawgiver, whom we call God. It has been argued by thinkers such as Newman that it is impossible to feel any moral compulsion without a sense of someone who puts us under compulsion; that is to say, we cannot imagine a command without the existence of a commander. Critics of this argument point out that the origin of moral commands is cultural conditioning and not the divine will. This spurs the second, thinner strand of moral arguments, viz. the view that anyone seriously committed to respecting moral values as exercising a claim over his or her life must believe in the reality of a transhuman source or basis for these values, as otherwise these commands are devoid of significance or moral compulsion. In conclusion, rather than being a successful argument for the existence of God, the moral argument draws our attention to the ethical implications following from God's existence as laid out in such codes as the Ten Commandments. Any alternative source of moral guidance, such as pleasure-seeking, individualism or the cultivation of virtues (see chapter 2), are all rival explanations to the theistic account.

Review questions

1 Briefly explain one reason for God to allow evil to occur.
2 Briefly explain the view that morality only makes sense if God exists.

Task

Read the section in chapter 2 on non-cognitive meta-ethics and make notes on the possible criticisms that such thinkers would use against the moral argument.

Revision questions

1 Briefly explain Pascal's wager.
2 Assess the assertion that God's existence is necessarily true.
3 Outline and illustrate two criticisms of the argument from religious experience.
4 Assess the view that religious language is factually significant.
5 What philosophical problems arise in attempting to prove that a given event was miraculous?

Discussion questions

- If God's existence were proved, would faith be rendered meaningless?
- Does the existence of moral evil in the world mean that God does not exist?
- Does religious experience constitute adequate evidence for God's existence?
- What differences are there between scientific analogies and religious ones?
- Which, if any, is the most successful argument for the existence of God?

Glossary of key terms

Apophaticism: the view, popular in the fourteenth century, that the idea of God is beyond our understanding and that we can only describe the divine negatively as 'indescribable'.

Cosmological: refers to the cosmos or universe; the cosmological argument tries to infer the existence of God from the existence of the world and our presence in it.

Deism: the belief that a single deity exists but cannot intervene or is not interested in intervening in the course of history or in the laws of nature.

Infinite regress: refers to any sequence that is never-ending. Any philosophical theory that leads to an infinite regress of explanations/deductions is considered an inadequate explanation.

Omnibenevolence: the description of God as all-good or morally perfect.

Omnipotence: the description of God as all-powerful.

Omniscience: the description of God as all-knowing.

Ontological: refers to anything to do with being or what there is; the ontological argument holds that God necessarily exists.

Teleological: derived from the Greek word *telos*, meaning 'goal' or 'purpose'; the teleological argument attempts to infer the existence of God from the evidence of purpose or design in the universe.

Theism: belief in a God who actively intervenes in our world, as opposed to belief in a God who is a remote and unconcerned force.

Theodicy: a term coined by Leibniz (1646–1716), derived from two Greek words: *theo*, meaning 'God', and *dike*, meaning 'justice'. It is a technical term used in theology and philosophy to describe an argument that attempts to defend God's honour against the accusation that God has permitted the existence of evil in creation.

Suggested reading

- Davies, B. (1993) *An Introduction to the Philosophy of Religion*, Oxford, OUP
  This classic introduction to the philosophy of religion has been through many editions and is justifiably as popular today as when it first came out
- Peterson, M. *et al.* (1991) *Reason and Religious Belief*, Oxford, OUP
  A useful source with which to enter the faith versus reason debate

- Stephen Evans, C. (1982) *Philosophy of Religion*, Leicester, InterVarsity Press
  A textbook designed for the philosophy of religion component in religious studies courses
- Swinburne, R. (1996) *Is There a God?* Oxford, OUP
  This notable philosopher and theist seeks to defend his position in a short, readable work
- Vardy, P. (1995) *The Puzzle of God*, London, Fount
  A concise and readable introduction to the traditional proofs and divine attributes

Notes

[1] Walter, C., trans. (1978) *The Cloud of Unknowing and Other Works*, London, Penguin, p. 67.

[2] Davies, B. (1993) *An Introduction to the Philosophy of Religion*, Oxford, OUP, p. 2.

[3] Rogers, B. (2000) *A. J. Ayer: A Life*, London, Vintage, p. 225.

[4] Hume, D. (1993) *Dialogues Concerning Natural Religion*, Oxford, OUP, p. 72.

[5] Leibniz, G. W. (1988) *Philosophical Writings*, London, Dent, p. 186.

[6] Grahame, K. (1961) *The Wind in the Willows*, London, Methuen, p. 134.

[7] Hebblethwaite, B. (1979) *Evil, Suffering and Religion*, London, Sheldon Press, p. 77.

[8] Dostoevsky, F. (1967) *The Brothers Karamazov*, Harmondsworth, Penguin, p. 287.

[9] Aquinas, T. *Summa Contra Gentiles*, III.100.

[10] Hume, D. (1996) *Enquiries Concerning Human Understanding*, Oxford, Clarendon Press, pp. 115–116.

[11] Book II, Chapter 2, Sections 4 and 5.

4 Philosophy of mind

Dualism ... is usually adopted on the grounds that it must be true, and rejected on the grounds that it can't be true. (Thomas Nagel)

Aims

On completion of this chapter you should be able to:

- evaluate substance and property dualism
- evaluate the different versions of physicalism (identity theory, eliminative materialism and biological naturalism)
- explain and criticise philosophical behaviourism
- explain and criticise functionalism
- outline evidence in support of each of these theories of mind and understand the tensions between them
- outline the main arguments advanced in the artificial intelligence debate
- understand key notions in the philosophy of mind such as supervenience, qualia, consciousness, privileged access and intentionality
- appreciate the difficulties in explaining how the mind and the body interact
- appreciate the problem of establishing whether other individuals have minds
- appreciate the problem of self-ascription
- appreciate the problem of establishing criteria for continued personal identity through time.

Philosophy has been likened to a conversation spanning over two millennia. If this is so, then the philosophy of mind represents its latest pronouncement, as it combines twentieth-century scientific knowledge with a timeless fascination as to the nature of human thought. The present age sees philosophers in conference with neurobiologists and computer scientists in an attempt to offer an explanation for mental activity, or what is generally termed 'consciousness'. Three approaches are presented below. The first standpoint, known as dualism, holds that there are two separate and mutually exclusive kinds of thing: the physical and the mental. **Physicalism**, on the other hand, holds that consciousness is entirely explicable in terms of physical processes in the brain. The third category of theories, which includes behaviourism and functionalism, tries to sidestep the dualist/physicalist stalemate by arguing that we can only talk meaningfully about minds in terms of behaviour or causal roles. Let us examine the strengths and weaknesses of each position in turn.

Dualism

Dualism is the assumption that there are two worlds: the observable, physical world of brain states and the private, psychical world of mental states. These two realms interact with each other, so that we can talk about a mental event causing a physical one (for example, the desire for a cup of tea causes me to make one) or a physical event causing a mental one (for example, drinking a nice cup of tea causes the feeling of satisfaction). As the opening quotation to this chapter shows, dualism has a popular and intuitive appeal. To assert that we are conscious creatures with private, non-spatial, qualitative thoughts while being physically embodied seems self-evident. Indeed, for a long time the governance of mind over matter was accepted as true without dispute. A popular analogy for the relationship between mind and body was that of master and slave.[1] One of the earliest written accounts of dualism, recorded in a dialogue attributed to Plato, *Alcibiades I*, claimed that as the soul uses, rules and has authority over the body, any definition of humanity that involves awarding the body significance should be rejected.

Substance dualism

Substance dualism, which is also referred to as Cartesian or classical dualism, asserts that there are two kinds of things or 'substances' in the world. The term 'substance' refers to any entity that does not depend on anything else for its existence, in contrast to features or 'properties', which by definition belong to something else. Descartes is often referred to as the founding father of modern philosophy of mind, and was influenced by the dualism of Plato. Indeed, there are many passages in his *Meditations* (see chapter 9) that could have been penned by the ancient Greek.[2] It is in Descartes that substance dualism finds its most eloquent advocate. Throughout the *Meditations* Descartes reflects on his innermost thoughts in a method known as **introspection**. He retreats from everyday life to the seclusion of his study and then retreats from the surroundings of his study to the dark recesses of his thoughts. This inner world becomes a private laboratory in which he performs certain thought experiments, which confirm that the physical and mental are distinct yet interactive substances. Let us examine his main arguments in favour of dualism.

The argument from doubt

1 I can doubt that my body exists.
2 I cannot doubt that I exist.
3 Therefore, I must be distinct (a different substance) from my body.

There seems to be a property (let us call it indubitability) that I possess but that is not shared by any physical thing. This property assures me of my own existence, and is cited as proof that the mind and body are separate. Many have argued, however, that the above syllogism (logical deduction) does not stand up. Let us make the error conspicuous by forming a parallel argument that makes the same move but is obviously false. Imagine Elizabeth II declaring:

1 I can doubt that a queen of England exists.
2 I cannot doubt that I exist.
3 Therefore, I am not the queen of England.

But at the time of her declaration she is the queen of England! In asserting the above, she makes herself the victim of mistaken identity. Physicalists argue that the same case of mistaken identity surrounds the 'I' in the argument from doubt.

Many philosophers accuse Descartes of committing a fallacy in his use of introspection, as one cannot speak objectively about oneself, but only about things that are outside one's experience. If he is alleging that there is, within his constitution, a part of himself that is neutrally observing and another bit that is being impartially observed, then this seems an arbitrary distinction and one that leads to an infinite regress of observer and observed. One might allege that there is a further part observing the observer, and another observing this observer like a series of Russian dolls. Critics call this error in reasoning the 'homunculus fallacy' as it depicts lots of little observers in one's mind (*homunculus* is Latin and means 'little man').

The argument from indivisibility

Descartes' Sixth Meditation offers an argument in favour of dualism known as the argument from indivisibility, which has in turn led to a sister argument known as the argument from irreducibility. The argument from indivisibility is presented below:

1 The body is divisible into parts.
2 The mind is not divisible into parts.
3 Therefore, the mind must be of an entirely different nature from the body.

While it is not possible to cleave the mind in two with an axe (as the mind is non-spatial), one can perform such a gruesome deed to a brain; therefore, minds and brains must be different types of thing. Yet to assert that the mind cannot be 'divided' appears to fly in the face of the categories that we impose on thoughts, dividing them into perceptions, personality traits, emotions, memories etc. What dualists mean is that these things cannot be reduced to the physical. Yet isn't this a case of pantomime philosophy where one side asserts one thing, i.e. that mental states cannot be reduced, while the other side asserts the opposite, i.e. 'Oh yes they can'? We wait to see how this disagreement can be resolved.

The argument from irreducibility

1 Mental activities such as reason, intuition, language-use and subjective experience cannot be reduced to physical explanations.
2 Things either have a physical or a mental explanation.
3 There must be non-physical explanations for these activities.

Advocates of the above argument include John Foster[3] and Richard Swinburne,[4] who hold that no physicalist theory could offer an adequate account of the mental. Even if this is correct, the question of how a dualist theory could explain the mental remains and has not been sufficiently well answered.

In his meditations on dualism, Descartes invites us to picture imageless thoughts: our disembodied selves, God, and mathematical figures such as a chiliagon (a thousand-sided figure). Our capacity to conceive of such imageless thoughts gives Descartes sufficient grounds to conclude that our thoughts are not physical entities. This doctrine became known as rationalism. We are born with certain God-given intuitions that are incorruptible by space, time or matter. Dualism fits readily into a religious view of the world, and many theistic philosophers subscribe to dualism, as they cannot see how a physicalist account of human beings is compatible with the survival of the soul. Of course, one does not have to be a member of an institutionalised religion to have a sense of a mysterious, other-worldly realm beyond the material world. Strange occurrences such as telepathy (mind-reading), precognition (seeing the future), telekinesis (thought control of material objects), clairvoyance (knowledge of distant objects), and astral projection (mind leaving the body) have been documented, and so far appear to defy physicalist explanation. There seems to be more in this world than can ever be dreamt of by any physicalist philosophy.

Versions of dualism

Epiphenomenalism is a dualist theory of mind–body interaction that maintains that all mental events are causally dependent upon physical states (i.e. brain states). Mental activity is an epiphenomenon: something that is caused but itself causes nothing, like a cog in a machine that is turned, but which does not itself turn any other cogs. According to this theory, brain events cause mental events, but mental events, although existing in their own right, do not cause any events.

Interactionism, on the other hand, claims that there is a two-way causal connection between mind and body. This means that the body (specifically the brain) can cause mental events such as pain, and also that mental events such as the desire to avoid pain can have a causal influence on the body, as when a person moves her hand away from a fire.

Occasionalism holds that there is no causal interaction between minds and bodies. Instead, mental events are caused by God to occur in synchrony with physical events, so that mind and body only interact via God. This is a version of parallelism, which also maintains that mental and physical events run on a parallel course but do not causally interact with each other. A popular illustration of this theory depicts two watches keeping exactly the same time because they are in harmony and not because there is a causal connection between them.

Criticisms of dualism

Minds are not the genuine article

The term 'mind' occurs in our everyday conversations, but the fact that we talk about minds does not necessarily mean that minds exist.

An objection to dualism is to say that the mind is not a genuine entity, so that to talk about X's mind is comparable to talking about X's sake. When we say, 'Person Y did this for X's sake', the sake is not a genuine object in its own right. Dualists might claim, however, that a relationship exists between a person's brain and their mind analogous to that between an orchestra and its music. The instruments are the only way the music can be presented; music, however, can be considered a genuine entity.

Dualism is never a tenable position for Hume, as it wallows in the muddy waters of metaphysics. He seeks to replace traditional armchair questions such as 'What is the mind?' with questions that can be empirically investigated, such as 'What kind of things are my beliefs about?' and 'What are the sources of my beliefs?' Like Descartes, Hume tries to meditate on the nature of self, but unlike the Frenchman he concludes that there is no self independent of experiences to meditate on. Instead, the self is a bundle of different impressions (see chapter 10). A version of Hume's bundle theory is defended by the philosopher Derek Parfit (born 1942).

The argument from category error

The most famous criticisms of dualism appear in the first chapter of Gilbert Ryle's book *The Concept of Mind* (1949). Ryle (1900–1976) accuses substance dualists of making a category error, i.e. a mistake in classification. The argument from category error separates the meaningful from the meaningless in the style of logical positivism. Whereas for Ryle it makes perfect sense to say 'My football team won the game' or 'There are 15 individual members in the team', it does not make sense to assert 'The team exists in addition to its members'. It is this exact fault that Ryle accuses dualists of making. Thus one cannot say that the mind exists in addition to the mental activity and behaviour displayed. Note that this problem is shared by descriptions of the body, which raise similar metaphysical questions such as: What makes something my body? Am I and my body two things or one? Could two people share a single body?

Ryle seeks to reduce the concept of mind to such a degree as to render it redundant. He stresses the absurdity of what he pejoratively calls the 'ghost in the machine theory' by stating that it forces us to think of our lives as running two parallel courses, one mental and one physical, like two disparate autobiographies. In addition, he asserts that when one talks of minds and thoughts occurring 'inside', one is only talking metaphorically, and therefore the content is not an expression of literal truth. One further criticism focuses on causality and language, and runs as follows:

1 Any chain of cause and effect can always be traced back to a single physical cause.
2 A mental event can only cause another mental event if mediated through the physical.
3 It is not necessary to talk in terms of mental activity.
4 The concept of mind is a redundant one.

Scientific evidence

Another criticism of dualism may be taken from the many examples that seem to prove the dependency of the mental on the neurological. One such instance is the case of a nineteenth-century railway worker, Phineas P. Gage, whose story was reported in a publication of the Massachusetts Medical Society (1868), which described the normally placid and reliable man turning into an aggressive alcoholic after surviving an accident in which a steel rod pierced his lower jaw and stuck through his head. Dualists might respond by denying any necessary connection between brain damage and personality change, but case scenarios pointing to the opposite conclusion abound.

There are cases of people whose *corpus callosum*, the conduit of information unifying the left and right hemispheres of the brain, has been severed, resulting in the unusual effect that the two sides of the brain know different things. For instance, the right side of the brain will pick up information from the left visual field and the left side of the brain will pick up information from the right visual field.

This plethora of criticisms has led Daniel Dennett to describe dualism as 'not so much a philosophical position but more of a cliff over which you push your opponents'. **Property dualism** is one theory that attempts to retrieve the situation.

Property dualism

Can we dispense with the idea of a distinct, metaphysical substance called 'the mind' but retain the 'otherness' of thoughts? Property or attributive dualism attempts such a move. The American philosopher Thomas Nagel (born 1937), in his influential essay 'What Is It Like to Be a Bat?' (1974), seeks to reconcile the existence of subjective experience with the materialism of a scientific age. Nagel asserts that only the physical exists, but that brain waves curiously exhibit a second class of characteristics in addition to material properties, which we might call mental properties. He begins by stating that one cannot reduce consciousness and that consciousness entails subjective experience: 'the fact that an organism has conscious experience *at all* means, basically, that there is something it is like *to be* that organism. We call this the subjective character of experience'.[5] Focusing on the nature of subjective experience, he concludes that it is inexplicable in terms of its purpose, the content of thought or any causal relationship. And any physicalist analysis is at present inadequate in providing an explanation.

Moving on to the illustration promised in the essay's title, Nagel argues as follows:

1 Bats have experience, i.e. there is something like 'being a bat'.
2 Human beings are restricted to the resources of their own minds.
3 Therefore, human beings cannot feel what it is like to be a bat.

The above argument seeks to highlight the exclusivity of subjective experience. It concludes that consciousness exhibits both a private, subjective property and a public, objective property and that these are irreconcilably different. Yet property dualism still appears to skirt around the issue, as it fails to explain what such private, mental properties consist in and how they are related to physical, neuro-physiological activity. It is not clear what the assertion that 'mental properties are not physical properties' actually means other than to say that science in its present form is not advanced enough to understand mental states.

Supervenience

Crude substance dualism gives rise to other theories such as epiphenomenalism and property dualism. These theories attempt to assert in different ways that there exists first and foremost a physical system that gives rise to a mental experience. Respectively, these theories construe the mental as a causal relationship or a distinct set of attributes. Each theory believes that there is a necessary connection between the mental and the physical. This necessary connection is known as **supervenience**, a term that here means 'emergence from'. Supervenient features (the mental) arise out of a subvenient base (the physical). Supervenient features exist in their own right, although they change if the subvenient base changes. Consider the illustrations in figure 4.1; both are made up of different patterns of dots, but one is able to make

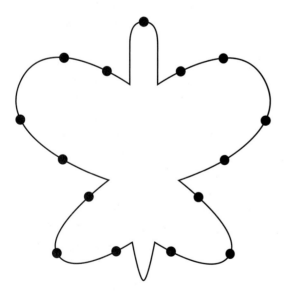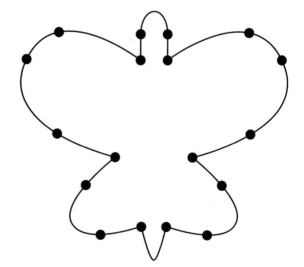

Figure 4.1 *Supervenience*

out the outline of a butterfly in each case. The two different patterns of dots are examples of subvenient bases, while the image of a butterfly may be said to supervene on these patterns. In a similar way, according to supervenience theorists, thoughts can be said to emerge from neural sequences in our brains. Let us move on to examine the physicalist theories of mind.

Review question

Describe and illustrate one argument in favour and one argument against substance dualism.

Physicalism

In contrast to dualism, theories that offer a purely physical explanation of consciousness are called physicalist or materialist theories. Physicalism is a form of **monism** – that is, the belief that the universe is made up of only one kind of substance, physical or mental, but not both. One advantage of monism is that there is no need to try to explain any mysterious interaction between such radically different things as minds and bodies. If you are a monist and an idealist, you think that the only things in existence are minds and their perceptions; if you are a monist and a physicalist, then you think that only material things exist and that philosophers of mind should only be interested in brains. Three versions of physicalism are examined below: identity theory (reductive materialism), eliminative materialism and biological naturalism.

Identity theory (reductive materialism)

Identity theory, or the Australian Heresy as it came to be known, was popular during the 1950s. It should not, however, be viewed as a mere historical stepping stone across the river of progress but a worthwhile spot to pause and fish for arguments. Identity theorists maintain that mental events are identical with events taking place in the brain. This is to say that the relationship between mind and brain, between thoughts and the firing of neurones, is the same as that between, for example, lightning and electrical discharge. This is not to say, however, that the firing of a neurone means the same thing as a thought. Similarly, 'lightning' has a different meaning from the term 'electrical discharge'. I do not look out of the window during a storm and say 'I've just had a certain sequence of neurological firings' but 'I have seen some lightning'. The point is that I can use two different terms, which carry with them different qualitative elements, while still referring to the same thing.

One of the most famous examples of this is the fact that the terms 'morning star' and 'evening star' both refer to the planet Venus, yet have different subjective meanings. The descriptions don't mean the same, or else the ancient Babylonians could have discovered their shared identity *a priori*, without any astronomical research. In the same way, talk about thoughts and the firings of neurones differ in meaning yet have the same reference. Identity theorists argue that mental states are identical to physical states of the brain. The mind is the brain. They believe that brain research will be able to show how consciousness is generated, and the term 'mind-brain' may be favoured in the future to explain this feature. Identity theorists point to the widespread and systematic correlations between mental states and brain states. Yet correlations are not explanations, and many philosophers remain unconvinced.

A problem for identity theory arises when one asserts that if two people are having the same thought about something then they are sharing the same brain state also. If you and I are both looking at a beautiful coastline and we express the thought of its beauty, then identity theory asserts that an identical process will be going on in each of our brains. The problem with this is that my thought about the picturesque coastline is wrapped up with my past experiences of coastlines and with what I consider beautiful in general. For your part, your thought about the coastline is inseparable from all your past experiences in a similar way. If this is true, then the sense in which we can both be said to be having the same thought is weakened, and the sense in which the whole of our mental life can be compared disappears. If we cannot say that two people are having the same thought, then the idea of identifying thoughts with brain processes becomes problematic, because it assumes that if you can identify the same brain process in one person as in another then you are entitled to hold the belief that they have the same thought.

Leibniz's law

Statements concerning identity have held a peculiar fascination for many philosophers. One was the German philosopher Gottfried Wilhelm Leibniz, who formulated a special law of identity used to test whether two or more seemingly different descriptions are about the same thing. The usual formulation of **Leibniz's law** runs as follows:

> If X = Y, then X has the property F if and only if Y has the property F.

This version presumes that we can first establish that X = Y, which seems to jump the gun. A more accurate phrasing of Leibniz's law may be presented as follows:

> All the properties of X and Y are identical if and only if X = Y, that is to say if X and Y are the same thing.

One can see that this works perfectly in the previous examples, where X might represent lightning and Y electrical discharge.

As it stands, Leibniz's law seems like a good principle of logic, if not a scintillatingly interesting one. However, there have been challenges to it, and the case of the two electrons is cited as a possible exception. One is invited to imagine that the universe consists of only two electrons. They share every property (mass, spin etc.) and, not surprisingly, they are the same distance from each other. Spatial position is irrelevant, as they are the only two things in the universe. According to Leibniz's law, they must be the same electron, but there are two!

If identity theorists are right and mental states are identical to physical states of the brain then, according to Leibniz's law, they must be identical in every way. Opponents of identity theory use Leibniz's law to assert that mental states are not numerically identical (one and the same thing) with brain states. Consider the following two examples.

Gottfried Leibniz (1646–1716)

Gottfried Wilhelm Leibniz was the son of a professor of moral philosophy from Leipzig, Germany. His father died when he was just six years old, and the young Gottfried made an effort to learn Latin and Greek from an early age in order to read his father's books. Leibniz was brought up in the German Lutheran tradition and became interested in theological questions. He published his work entitled *Theodicy* in 1710, which inspired Voltaire's satirical novel *Candide* in which Leibniz is caricatured as the indefatigable Dr Pangloss, who believed that everything was for the best in the best of all possible worlds, despite evidence to the contrary. During his lifetime, Leibniz was described as a stooped figure of medium height, broad-shouldered but bandy-legged, who was capable of sitting in the same chair and thinking for several days. This thinking paid off, and Leibniz became an immensely influential figure in mathematics and logic, developing the binary system of arithmetic as well as differential and integral calculus. Like many philosophers, he never married. He worked in Hanover from 1676 at a strange selection of jobs, from library work and teaching to designing a wind-driven pump to drain water from a nearby mine. Leibniz was also a prodigious letter writer and had over 600 scholarly correspondents across Europe. He died in 1716, plagued with gout but leaving the world of philosophy a richer place.

Significant works
New Essays on Human Understanding (c. 1705)
Theodicy (1710)
Monadology (1714)

Example 1: a Cartesian argument

1 All entities fall into two mutually exclusive categories: space-occupying entities and conscious, non-extended entities.

2 The spatial location of brain processes can be specified with a high degree of accuracy.

3 The spatial location of thoughts or emotions cannot be identified at all.

4 If the brain is spatial and the mind is non-spatial, then, according to Leibniz's law, the brain cannot be numerically the same as the mind.

Example 2: an argument from **intentionality**

1 Mental states are about states of affairs external to themselves, e.g. beliefs, desires, dreams, hopes, thoughts are about something apart from the thought itself.

2 For a thought to be about something means that it represents something.

3 No physical state can possess representational content.

4 Therefore, mental states cannot be, according to Leibniz's law, numerically identical with physical states.

The debate takes the following twists and turns. First, identity theorists inform us that the mind is the brain. This is a statement of identity, and as such should fit with Leibniz's law. Critics of identity theory assert that it doesn't, and cite examples such as spatial location and representational content as instances where minds and brains differ.

Task

Can our thoughts be reduced to brain waves?

Consider whether the following statements are successful in identifying a difference between mind and brain:

1 Brain waves occupy space; thoughts do not.

2 Thoughts are about something, whereas brain waves are not.

3 I can keep my thoughts private, but a neuroscientist can measure my brain activity in public.

4 I can attribute value to my thoughts (e.g. a naughty suggestion), but my brain activity exists in a realm of fact, not value.

---

5 Our thoughts have distinct felt qualities, e.g. pangs of jealousy, but our brain activities do not.

6 I can know what my thoughts are by virtue of the fact that I am me, but in order to understand my brain activity I need to study neuroscience.

The type–token distinction

Identity theorists have attempted to refine their theory using the type–token distinction.

The term 'type' is any kind of thing, which is shared by many particular entities. The term 'token' refers to a particular instance or exemplar of a type, which is located in some particular space or time. Consider the following sentence:

The bat sat on the mat.

There are six individual words in this sentence that we might call specific instances or tokens. When we look closer we see that there are two specific instances of the word 'the', so the word 'the' can be classed as a type. Type identity refers to the kind of thought we might be experiencing, whereas token identity describes specific thoughts. For example, type identity theorists argue that pain and the firing of C-fibres in my brain are identical. Both arms of the identity (pain and the firing of C-fibres) are construed as the same type of thing. This account runs into difficulties if it turns out that pain can be realised in another way, perhaps by the activity of B-fibres. In this case the claim that pain and the firing of C-fibres are identical is proved false. In order to maintain identity theory one needs to frame a version in terms of tokens. So, for instance, one would say that a particular token of pain is identical to C-fibres firing, while a different token is identical to B-fibres firing.

Kripke's criticism

A further criticism waged against identity theory issues from the American philosopher Saul Kripke, who argues that 'The mind is the brain', as a statement of identity, should be a necessary truth but isn't. This accusation is based on the fact that statements of identity are necessary truths and that if different names refer to the same thing (for example, the terms 'morning star' and 'evening star' both refer to the planet Venus), then this is a necessary truth in every possible world. The fact that one can conceive of a possible world in which the mind is not the brain means that identity theory does not advance anything that may be classed as a necessary truth. Let us phrase this objection formally:

1 Identity theorists assert that 'mental states are physical states' is a necessary truth about the world.

2 To be a necessary truth about the world, a statement needs to be true in this actual world and true in all possible worlds (e.g. water is H_2O).

3 We can, however, imagine a world where there is brain activity, e.g. C-fibres fire in the brain (physical state), but the individual, for whatever reason, does not feel pain.

4 Therefore, it is possible to conceive of a brain state occurring without the presence of a corresponding mental state. Therefore, mental states and physical states are not identical.

The fallacy of intentionality

Identity theorists attempt to dodge the above criticisms by catching their critics out on a technicality. They assert that all the examples cited in the task on page 79 commit the fallacy of intentionality. This occurs when an argument refers to the arguer's beliefs and not to the object of those beliefs. So, for instance, if I were to argue that my belief in God proves that God exists, this would commit the fallacy of intentionality, as my belief does not affect God's existence in any way but only tells you something about me. Identity theorists assert that one's belief in doubt, privacy, value-attribution, after-images, subjective experience and introspection go a long way in telling us about our own thoughts, but this does not prove identity theory wrong, as it does not conclusively show that these features belong to minds rather than brains. A more hardline theory that challenges the notion of mental states altogether is eliminative materialism.

Eliminative materialism

In order to understand **eliminative materialism**, one needs to establish exactly what is being eliminated. The theory is in the tradition of logical positivism, the twentieth-century movement of scientifically minded philosophers who sought to distinguish the factually meaningful from the factually meaningless according to whether the statement under analysis is true by definition or provable by experiment (these are meaningful statements; other types of statement are meaningless). Contemporary eliminativists, such as the Canadian philosophers Paul and Patricia Churchland (born in 1942 and 1943 respectively) and the American philosopher Daniel Dennett (born 1942), seek to perform the same linguistic operation on descriptions of mental states. Their conclusion is that any notions of free-floating thoughts or beliefs are factually nonsensical. They believe that such 'hornswoggle' or 'gobbledegook' is the product of an unscientific method, and should be heaped under the pejorative label of **folk psychology**. This phrase may conjure up images of bearded fiddle players discussing the works of Freud, but here it means any non-empirical theory that conjectures a non-physical realm of thought.

According to the Churchlands, it is the job of science to eliminate conceptual frameworks that misinterpret the phenomena. Historical examples abound, such as the concept of witches and demonic possession in the field of mental health or ancient alchemical arguments over how base metals are turned into gold. Such superstition has been dispelled by science as nonsensical and has now only minor historical significance. Eliminativists believe that the same fate awaits the concept of mind:

> Eliminative materialism is the thesis that our common-sense conception of psychological phenomena constitutes a radically false theory, a theory so fundamentally defective that both the principles and the ontology of that theory will eventually be displaced.[6]

The Churchlands' argument against what they call folk psychology proceeds along the following lines. First, they classify folk psychology as a scientific theory, as it uses rules and laws to make predictions. Then they point out that the theory fails in offering an explanation in a number of important cases, such as mental illness, the psychological function of sleep, and child development. Indeed folk psychology as a research project, which has its origins in ancient Greece, has been failing for over two thousand years. Further confirmation that folk psychology is redundant is found in the fact that it does not cohere with the current canon of scientific theories, including particle physics, atomic and molecular theory, organic chemistry, evolutionary biology, physiology and materialistic neuroscience. While eliminativists such as Dennett see some role for folk psychology's continuation in the future, the Churchlands believe that its obvious explanatory poverty should spell elimination. This presents a problem for them, as it is not clear how we could communicate without a hopelessly uneconomical and complicated reliance on neurological facts. We are not all neurologists.

At first glance it seems strange that a group of philosophers of mind should become famous for denying the existence of minds. What does this leave them with? The answer is philosophy, which they view as complementary to science, and they hold that it is only through neuroscience that philosophical problems concerning consciousness can be solved. Indeed, Patricia Churchland's *magnum opus* is entitled *Neurophilosophy* to emphasise the synthesis of philosophy and neuroscience. She identifies a further candidate for elimination in her article 'The Hornswoggle Problem' (1996). In this piece of work she berates the false distinction between the difficult, philosophical question concerning the nature of consciousness (termed the 'hard problem') and all other unsolved mysteries in neuroscience (termed 'easy problems'):

> Although consciousness is, certainly, a difficult problem, difficulty *per se* does not distinguish it from many other neuroscientific problems such as how the brains of homeotherms keep a constant internal temperature despite varying external conditions, or the brain basis for schizophrenia and autism, or why we dream and sleep.[7]

The author invites us to imagine a ledger of two columns entitled respectively 'hard problems' and 'easy problems'. To cite only one entry, i.e. the philosophical problem of consciousness, under the heading 'hard problems', while listing every other research project concerned with the human brain in the other column is, for the author, ungrounded and ill-informed. If one studies scientific progress, then it is reasonable to assume that thirty-first century neurobiology will have explained what consciousness is. Not to accept this position is to commit the informal fallacy *argumentum ad ignorantiam* (an argument based on ignorance) as one asserts:

1 Phenomenon P (in this case the mind) is not understood.
2 Therefore, we know that phenomenon P can never be understood.

This argument is fallacious because we cannot say that we know that we will never know at all.

Criticisms of eliminative materialism

Eliminativists seem to commit two informal fallacies themselves: firstly, in defending their standpoint with an argument from analogy, e.g. in comparing consciousness to witchcraft; and, secondly, in presuming that the answer to the problem of consciousness is a physical one. Like many physicalists who approach the problem of personal identity, an unfounded shift is made by moving from asserting (1) I am a physical thing to the conclusion (2) I am essentially a physical thing or I am only what I can be proved to be through science.

The argument from the conservation of energy

Eliminativists argue that if the physical domain is a closed causal network, then there is no place for non-physical entities such as the mind. In other words, there cannot be an interaction between mind and matter in terms of energy exchange, as dualists would have to assert. This is known as the argument from the conservation of energy and may be summarised as follows:

1 The total net energy of any closed system always remains the same (the law of conservation of energy).
2 The physical world is a closed system.
3 If the physical world interacted with something non-physical (e.g. a mind) then its total net energy would increase or decrease.

4 Therefore, the physical world cannot interact with anything non-physical.

This seems like a good argument, but it isn't. We do not know that the physical world is a closed system; science has not shown that every physical event must have a physical cause. The argument from the conservation of energy demonstrates the confidence that eliminativists have in science to provide a Theory of Everything (TOE). This is by no means a clear-cut assertion.

A further criticism, which is often dismissed by philosophers as *ad personam* (an argument based on personal interest), is that a theory such as eliminative materialism is counter-intuitive. Many feel that if they accept such a clinical diagnosis of the human condition then life would lose its value. How was it possible, they might argue, for Paul and Patricia Churchland to fall in love? Was their union sealed in a heady biochemical surge of testosterone, serotonin and nothing more? One physicalist theory that leaves the door ajar for qualitative experience is biological naturalism.

Task

Imagine a society where any references to minds or emotions have been eliminated and replaced with scientific jargon. Write a short dialogue between two lovers replacing any expressions of feeling with scientific language. Do we lose anything by changing register from the romantic to the biological? If so, then what is lost?

Biological naturalism

The description 'biological naturalism' refers to the fact that this school of thought holds that consciousness is completely explicable in terms of the physical sciences. Biological naturalists believe that the question 'What is the mind?' cannot be separated from the question 'What is human nature?' Their answer casts us in the role of 'human animals' who interact with our environment, reproduce, eat, sleep and perform other biological processes. For biological naturalists, our mental life is as natural a part of this material existence as respiration or defecation. Two arguments are employed by biological naturalists to defend this position.

The first is an argument from evolution that states that consciousness, like any other biological process, is the product of evolution, and that it is this fact that enables us to account for the complexity and sophistication of the human brain. Expressed formally it would run:

1 Every aspect of human beings (like other animals) has purely physical origins.
2 Consciousness is an aspect of human beings.
3 Consciousness has a purely physical origin.

Secondly, biological naturalists distinguish between human activity on a macro-level, such as social behaviour, and human activity on the ordinarily unobservable level of our micro-particles, which includes consciousness. They maintain that the workings of the mind can be explained most effectively on a cellular level and that we ought to resist the temptation to search out non-scientific explanations for macro-level activity. A comparison is drawn between hydrogen and oxygen combining on a molecular level to create the feeling of wetness on a macro-level. The same can be said of C-fibres firing on a micro-level to produce feelings of pain on a macro-level scale.

Biological naturalists such as John Searle (born 1932) attempt to provide a holistic account of human thought that is neither reductive nor eliminative, but includes the distinctive quality of experiences and acknowledges that perceptions have representational content. Consider what happens when someone looks at a bright light. The light entering the eye causes a reductive chemical reaction in the cells of the retina on which it falls; the chemical reaction causes an electrical current in the neighbouring nerve cells; this current stimulates more nerve cells in the brain and elsewhere in the nervous system; some of the nerve cells stimulated are connected to muscles, for instance in the iris, and the current in them causes these muscles to contract. A chain of cause and effect is generated, with each event being the cause of further events. The cells of the retina, nervous system, muscles and so forth are like components in a very complex machine that enables the human body to respond in a more or less sophisticated way to stimuli. In fact, machines can be built to mimic some features of the human body. Certain cameras, for instance, can automatically match the size of their aperture to the intensity of the surrounding light, just as the human eye does. But something else happens when a person looks at a bright light, provided that the person's sight is not impaired in any way. The person 'sees' the light. They have something we call a visual experience.

We know what such experiences are like because we are having them all the time. Biological naturalists assert that, whereas scientists such as anatomists, biochemists and neurologists can explain how we perceive things, there is in addition a value-added component, which we term 'consciousness'. This remains mysterious at present, but science will eventually be able to give an account of what it is. Biological naturalism is an attractive theory that maintains a degree of scientific credibility (although there is some disagreement as to what constitutes science) while admitting that there is a quality about experience that is part of the distinctly human aptitude to understand the representational content of thoughts. The term used by philosophers to describe the representational content of thought is 'intentionality', and Searle argues that this quality cannot be reduced to a physicalist, non-philosophical explanation and that thought-content implies qualitative experience.[8]

In some ways, John Searle is the natural successor to Descartes, in that both authors compare and contrast human intelligence to non-human intelligence. In the case of Searle it is **artificial intelligence** and in the case of Descartes it is animal intelligence. Indeed, it is this fact that leads us to the accusation that biological naturalism is really dualism in sheep's clothing. Biological naturalists want to remain scientifically credible while acknowledging subjective experience (or what philosophers term **qualia**) and intentionality. This standpoint does not escape the mind–body problem. Indeed, the similarity is clearly seen when one concedes that any coherent dualist philosophy of mind would never deny that consciousness is inextricably linked to physical brain activity. Descartes' view of science might have been the mechanistic,

clockwork conception promulgated in the seventeenth century but it was, nevertheless, an attempt to explore the relationship between thought and matter. In many of the most important respects biological naturalism is indistinguishable from property dualism, as advanced by Nagel, who ends his essay 'What Is It Like to Be a Bat?' on a note of scientific optimism while terming his position 'dualist'.

This highlights a depressing fact about the philosophy of mind. The fact is that thinkers are still searching in the dark for an elusive explanation, and have to date only offered an incomplete picture of how the brain works to which they attach (in the case of biological naturalism), superimpose (as in the case of supervenience theory) or dangle (in the case of Davidson's anomalous monism, which is discussed later in this chapter) subjective experience and the content of thoughts. It is hard not to read such attempts as nothing more than restatements of dualism.

Review question

Describe and illustrate one physicalist account of the mind.

Behaviourism and functionalism

Philosophical behaviourism

Philosophical behaviourism is from the same stable as logical positivism, and holds that we can only talk meaningfully about what can be verified. Behaviourists believe that due to the private nature of mental states philosophers of mind should concern themselves with behaviour. We can talk meaningfully about behaviour because it can be directly observed. In practice, what this means is that a word like 'pain' does not refer to some set of inner mental events but to a certain set of behaviour such as wincing, shrieking and hopping around. Psychological statements are verified by observing how people behave. It is important to note that philosophical behaviourists do not dismiss the idea of mental phenomena completely, and, while the theory is compatible with staunch physicalism, it does not entail it.

Knowing how and knowing that

Ryle sought to dismiss dualism, which he described in the first chapter of his classic study *The Concept of Mind*, as the dogma of the 'ghost in the machine'. Yet Ryle runs into a problem in reducing everything to acts and utterances, as to how we might distinguish between 'knowing how' and 'knowing that'. The category of 'knowing how' is not problematic as it is concerned with practical, behavioural skills, but 'knowing that' appears non-behavioural and suggests a mind that does the knowing. Ryle attempts to meet this criticism by explaining away intelligence as nothing above or beyond knowing what is required in a given situation. 'Knowing that' is the act of having practised certain strategies and, as a consequence, having met certain performative standards. He states the following examples:

> It was because Aristotle found himself and others reasoning now intelligently and now stupidly and it was because Izaak Walton found himself and others angling sometimes effectively and sometimes ineffectively that both were able to give their pupils the maxims and prescriptions of their arts.[9]

Conditional statements

Ryle and like-minded philosophers set out to develop a theory that would allow one to paraphrase any sentence about mental states in a way that completely captures the meaning of the original but that makes no use of mental language. The fact that such an operation is possible in theory, though not necessarily practicable, holds philosophical significance for behaviourists. It would enable human beings to completely eliminate mental language, and with it the pseudo-questions that arise from a mistaken understanding of the function of such terms. The best way of seeing how the paraphrasing of mind-talk into talk about behaviour works is to cite an example.

Behaviourists seek to offer definitions of mental activity using 'If … then' formulae. Consider the following sentence:

> If X were put in unsaturated water, then X would dissolve.

This is an operational definition of solubility, and similar operational definitions can be offered to explain behaviour:

Gilbert Ryle
(1900–1976)

The most famous philosophical behaviourist was the Oxford philosopher Gilbert Ryle, although Quine and Wittgenstein (later in his career) had behaviourist leanings. Ryle was the epitome of a pipe-smoking, tweed-clad Oxford professor. The son of an Anglican bishop, Ryle studied as an undergraduate at Christ Church, Oxford, and stayed on as tutor in philosophy. He greatly aided A. J. Ayer in his career by persuading him to visit Vienna on honeymoon and to find out what the Vienna Circle was doing. He also introduced Ayer to Wittgenstein when they visited Cambridge. On another occasion reported by Ayer, the two scholars were driving across France on their way to a European philosophy conference when the conversation quickly dried up. In an effort to start it again, Ayer asked the shy professor whether he was a virgin, to which he answered 'yes'. Ayer then asked Ryle whether he preferred boys or girls, to which he replied 'probably boys' and remained in stony silence for the rest of the journey. Like Ayer, Ryle was a staunch advocate of analytic philosophy, and believed that many philosophical dilemmas were caused by logical or grammatical mistakes. He edited the philosophy journal *Mind* for nearly twenty-five years before his retirement.

Significant works
The Concept of Mind (1949)
Dilemmas (1954)
Collected Papers (1971)

If X were asked, then X would give answer Y.

According to behaviourists, every mental ascription is equivalent to asserting an 'If ... then' statement. The assertion 'Person X is thirsty' is equivalent to asserting 'If there were water available, then Person X would drink some'.

'If' clauses are always about stimuli, whereas 'then' clauses are always about behaviour. The fact that both stimuli and behaviour are physical makes this linguistic operation compatible with physicalist theories of mind.

In summation, any description about my beliefs can be paraphrased in a statement about how I would behave in various circumstances. Thus we can use the idea of dispositions to give a better statement of the behaviourist position, which is that the real function of mental language is to provide an economical way of talking about the ways people behave if they are in a given situation. According to the behaviourist, any sentence in which a mental term occurs can be paraphrased in a way that makes no reference to the mental but that instead refers to behavioural tendencies.

Criticisms of behaviourism
Behaviourism is an inadequate linguistic theory
The best that behaviourists can offer is an open-ended set of hypotheticals: 'If X were asked, then X may give answer Y.' Behaviourists cannot assert, as they claim, 'If X were asked, then X will/must give answer Y'. One could imagine a state of affairs where someone might be contrary, weak-willed, careless or having a siesta, and would not act in the way predicted. Behaviourists can only offer a 'for the most part' prediction. Imagine if in the above example an ascetic deliberately sought to be thirsty. The list of conditionals needed before we can make any kind of accurate prediction seem problematically long, open-ended and apparently unpredictable in the face of choice.

Pretence
A further problem with behavourism is that people can pretend to be in pain as well as actually being in pain. I can wince, shriek, hop around and, if my behaviour is all there is, then you would have grounds for supposing that I am in pain despite the fact that I might be malingering. Actually, this is not such a problem for behaviourists, as they include in the term 'behaviour' all sorts of reactions that are non-voluntary. To be in pain means not just crying out or limping but also evincing a range of physiological characteristics such as uncontrollable sweating or a high temperature. If we include all the non-voluntary facets of behaviour in our definition of pain, then the behaviourist becomes less vulnerable to the charge of deception through pretence.

Paralysis
A criticism which is more difficult to meet concerns people who are paralysed. Such individuals may not be able to move in even the simplest of ways, and they may need ventilator machines to keep them alive. From the behaviourist point of view, there is nothing to suggest that such people have any inner mental life at all. Yet we know that such individuals do have a mental life. The French journalist Jean-Dominique Bauby, for instance, after suffering a massive heart attack and slipping into a coma, dictated his reflections by moving his left eyelid, signalling his choice of letter as the alphabet was read to him; the result was his book *The Diving Bell and the Butterfly*. If behaviour is the sum total of meaning and in these cases there is no behaviour, then no account can be given about these patients with regard to mind or meaning.

A criticism from introspection
An odd consequence of behaviourism is that it seems to imply that if I want to know about my own feelings or beliefs I should not do so by introspection but by observing my own behaviour. Behaviourism seems to deny the 'inner' aspects of mental states, for example that pain has an intrinsic, qualitative, introspective nature separate from pain behaviour. Behaviourist assertions about dispositions seem frustrating in ignoring such 'inner aspects'. A strictly behaviourist account seems to omit meaningful distinctions such as the difference between being thoughtful and being taciturn, as the resultant behaviour remains the same. Talk about dispositions can only be hypothetical,

when something positive, categorical and explanatory is needed. Would behaviourists have to check in a mirror to see whether they were in a good mood or not? And would a behaviourist lover ask, 'I know it was good for you but was it good for me?'

Philosophical behaviourism is nevertheless of historical significance in the philosophy of mind and has left as its legacy an important theory known as functionalism.

Functionalism

Functionalists are concerned with the causal role of mental states, expressed in terms of cause and effect. They want to know what sort of job the mind performs. Functionalism retains the main insight of behaviourism, in preserving the link between mental states and behaviour. Yet the functionalist avoids some of the principal pitfalls of behaviourism in maintaining that mental states have an inner component. Functionalists, such as Hilary Putnam (born 1926), accept that mental language is about what it appears to be about, i.e. mental states. Functionalism attempts to give a complete account of mental events through highlighting the causal relationship between input, what may be called 'inner workings' or psychological states, and output.

To make this clearer, let us consider how a function works.

Consider the workings of a security system. Having been burgled, you decide to install a security system, which involves lights on the outside of the house and sensors, which are activated by movement within a certain range. This system can be described in terms of its purpose or function as in figure 4.2.

Functionalists describe the workings of our brains in terms of a function. The experience of pain, for example, may be summarised as in figure 4.3.

Functionalists point to the fact that many things are functionally equivalent: one might, for instance, employ a watchful student armed with a hooter instead of installing a burglar alarm at great expense. In this case the student and the alarm are functionally equivalent. This presents a useful response on the part of functionalists to the problem of multiple realisability. They assert that it does not matter whether a creature's brain is made of something totally unlike our own; as long as it does the same job then it can be classed as a mind. Functionalism appears to have offered us a fairly holistic picture of mental properties despite its rather formulaic appearance.

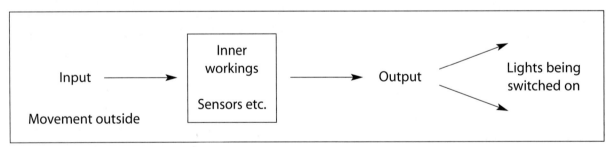

Figure 4.2 *Function of a security system*

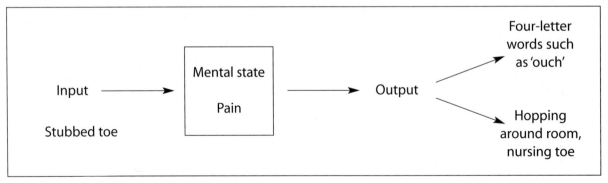

Figure 4.3 *The experience of pain*

Complete the table below with likely scenarios to show the relationships between input, mental states and output.

Input	Mental state	Output
Tissue damage	Pain	Groaning, wincing, nursing injury
	Perception	
	Anger	
	Dream	
	Hope	
	Jealousy	
	Love	

Functionalists also find it useful to talk in terms of belief and desire, which are termed 'propositional attitudes'. Beliefs and desires seem to be inferred from an analysis of stimuli and behaviour. So, for instance, if I observe you stubbing your toe and hopping around I can justifiably infer that you are experiencing pain and desire not to have such an unpleasant experience again.

Criticisms of functionalism

There are two main criticisms of the functionalist account. The first is that the theory fails to account for the subjective 'feel' of these mental states. Philosophers term this ineffable 'what-is-it-like-ness' of an experience a 'quale' (plural 'qualia'). Secondly, functionalism seems comfortable with the notion that humans are functionally equivalent to machines, a view not shared by many thinkers. Let us explore each of these areas in more detail, starting with qualia.

Qualia

Qualia are the various subjective qualities in our sensations that cannot be expressed in causal terms. I might have studied types of exotic fruit but until I sink my teeth into a juicy guava I cannot claim to have enjoyed the qualitative sensory experience of tasting one. Qualia are derived from the senses, but are part of the process of introspection. They vary between individuals despite stemming from the same stimulus; thus, having halved the guava, I might offer you some, which you duly savour but appear to relish less than I do. We are experiencing different qualia, although there is a necessary connection between the properties of the fruit and the mental properties of our thoughts.

Mental states in possession of qualia may be categorised under the following headings:

- perceptual experience, e.g. seeing red;
- bodily pain, e.g. the itchiness of an itch;
- felt reactions, e.g. the pangs of jealousy;
- felt moods, e.g. a roller-coaster weekend of elation and despair.

Since ancient times, human beings have been intrigued by the possibility of other beings imitating humans in such a way as to remain undetected. Thought experiments surrounding the notion of qualia have considered the case of zombies and mutants that display all the roles and reactions that we do without any of the 'felt quality'. Such meditations are intended to raise the question as to whether any significance needs to be attached to qualia at all. Some philosophers such as Daniel Dennett have argued that qualia are nothing more than a philosophical myth, and consequently do not present any real problems for functionalists. However, the Australian philosopher Frank Jackson tells the following story in order to prove that qualia do exist.

The two Marys

Jackson was not convinced by his fellow Australian physicalists (although he has subsequently succumbed to their arguments), due to the felt quality of experience appearing to be something more than the physical. He invites us to imagine that we live in an age where science has explained everything and in which there are no more mysteries. Imagine two scientists who are both called Mary, who have spent their lives in a strictly controlled room that displays only various shades of black, white and grey. The Marys are so pale themselves as to appear on this black and white spectrum and they dress in black and white clothes. Despite the absence of colour in their lives they have become world authorities on the physics of colour, and understand everything there is to know about wavelengths and the various chemical compounds needed to yield each subtle hue. Imagine what would happen if one of the Marys were suddenly released from her black and white chamber and shown a colourful object such as a vibrant red tomato! She would experience redness, rather than just know what the colour is in theory, and it is this personal experience, termed qualia, that presents functionalists with a problem. Let us call the cloistered Mary Mary 1 and the released Mary Mary 2. Mary 1 and Mary 2 are functionally equivalent as a computer and human brain might be, according to the functionalist account of things, yet their mental states are different. Mary 2 enjoys qualia, for example 'redness', yet for Mary 1 qualia are absent.

The possibility of inverted qualia is even more problematic for functionalists. This point has its origins in Wittgenstein's private language argument. Consider the possibility of two people's qualia being different.

Person	Quale observed	Quale termed
Bill	Red	Red
Ben	Green	Red

Both Bill and Ben are the same in terms of output in so far as they might exclaim 'I understand redness!' but they have different experiences. On the surface this argument seems straightforward, but the more you mull it over in your mind, the more you realise what difficulties it creates.

The Chinese room argument

In a similar vein, the American philosopher John Searle offers an argument from intentionality or 'aboutness' as a criticism of the functionalist view of intelligence. It is known as the Chinese room argument. Searle does not agree that humans and machines are functionally equivalent, due to the latter being incapable of feeling and understanding. The following thought experiment is intended to illustrate what is happening when a machine, e.g. a computer, is solving a problem. Imagine that it is someone's job to live in a room all by themselves and to reply to messages posted to them through a slot on one side of the room. The messages are written in Chinese characters and correspond to a set of replies, which are stored inside the room. The person who is replying, however, does not speak Chinese and only recognises which replies to post back by virtue of the same squiggles appearing on both message and reply. The worker can become really fast at posting the right answers to the questions that he is receiving but can never learn the meanings of those symbols.

The point of Searle's thought experiment is that the inmate is imitating what goes on in the central processing unit (CPU) of a computer, and this symbol manipulation cannot lead to any kind of understanding of the characters that are being manipulated. Searle draws a distinction between the 'syntactic' manipulation of symbols and the 'semantic' understanding of ideas. Searle's Chinese room argument rests on the inadequacy of the person in the room to assign meaning to the symbols. Critics have tried to rectify this by building a bigger and better computational model called a Chinese gym, which enables the inmate to consult with a speaker of both Chinese and English, and eventually familiarise himself with what is going on.

Artificial intelligence

A central feature of functionalism is that human intelligence is viewed as functionally equivalent to other types of intelligence. According to functionalists, to deny this is to be guilty of speciesism in the case of animal intelligence or bio-chauvinism in the case of artificial (silicon-based) intelligence. George Graham illustrates what functionalists would consider as unfounded prejudice in the following story:

Imagine that a creature from another planet lands in your backyard and tells you (in perfect English) that it is going to enroll for courses at Princeton University. Then the creature dresses up like a human (suppose that otherwise it looks most unhuman and that the creature is devoid of anything which we would classify as a brain) and enrolls at Princeton. Within three months it is awarded a Ph.D. in Comparative Literature! What should you say? Should you say that brains are essential for belief or that they are inessential?[10]

This story may seem outlandish to more down-to-earth readers, but it intends to make the philosophical point that it is conceivable for something to exist that does what we do but has a very different anatomy and psychology. Functionalists draw on arguments from technological development to conjecture that machines essentially behave like brains, and so have the potential to become conscious. If you think that conjecturing what computers will be like in the twenty-fifth century is mere science fiction, then more recent reports should be of interest. An article in the *New Scientist*[11] describes how artificial intelligence experts are aiming to produce self-managing, self-repairing computers by engineering the machines to mimic the biochemistry of genes and proteins. Such 'software enzymes' evolve in the same way as biological enzymes, suggesting a future possibility of computers that grow to be more intelligent than their designers. Indeed, the American artificial intelligence expert Marvin Minsky believes that computers will eventually dominate society and keep us on as their pets.

The Turing test
The myth of Pygmalion[12] describes a statue coming to life and winning the heart of the eponymous hero. Of course the statue wasn't truly human, but its successful deception raises important questions. If X looks like a human and is functionally equivalent in terms of roles and reactions, then how are we justified in not classifying X as one of us? The same dilemma is faced in differentiating between carbon-based human intelligence and silicon-based artificial intelligence. If computers can do everything that we do then why not include them in our community of intelligence?

Alan Turing proposed in the journal *Mind* (1950) that if a computer could communicate with a human being in such a way that the human being could not tell the difference between conversing with the computer and with another human being, then it would be arbitrary (mere bio-chauvinism) to deny that the computer can think simply because it is a computer. By following an algorithm (a series of simple, discrete steps), computers can perform many of the functions that humans perform. What then is the difference between brains and motherboards, the computational equivalent of brains? Turing suggested that a two-way input–output device be set up between a person and two rooms. There would be a human being in one of the rooms and a pre-programmed computer in the other. If the person outside the rooms who was communicating with the inhabitants of each could not decide which room contained the human and which the machine, then one is forced to admit that there is no functional difference between them, at least inside these narrowly defined parameters.

Task
Are there any absolute differences between minds and machines?

Alicebot was a winning attempt at satisfying the Turing test. Search for winners of the Loebner prize (this is awarded each year for the program which comes closest to passing the Turing test) on the Internet and converse with artificial intelligence. Record what differences you notice between talking to Alicebot and a human. Vague, irrelevant and incoherent responses do not count as differences! Draw up a list of general differences between minds and machines. For example, the philosopher Hubert Dreyfus has suggested that 'common sense' is an attribute of the minded but not of the mechanical.

Review questions

1 Outline and illustrate the view that talk about mental states is talk about actual or potential behaviour.

2 Outline and illustrate what is meant by the term 'multiple realisability'.

Problems in the philosophy of mind

Let us next examine the four main problems encountered by theories of mind: the mind–body problem, the problem of other minds, the problem of self-ascription and the problem of personal identity.

The mind–body problem

Questions concerning the relationship between the mind and body are controversial from the outset, as they assume the existence of minds. Hard-nosed physicalists and behaviourists with materialist leanings dispute the existence of minds, and as a consequence assert that there is no such problem. But for those thinkers who do posit a mind, two central questions are raised:

- What is the mind? This is the problem of classification.
- What is the mind's relationship with the body? This is the problem of interaction.

There are many more tributary questions feeding into these main headings. One might ask when classifying the mind: What is it made of? What size is it? Where is it located? Similarly, when exploring how the mind relates to the body one might ask: Does the mental depend upon the physical or vice versa? Where do thoughts come from? What gives thoughts their content? Any cursory look at the mind–body problem will yield the conclusion that there isn't just one problem but many. Looking at their resolution helps to clarify the philosophical views already discussed in this chapter. These views are represented in the following table.

Task

For each of the theories listed across the top of the table below, write a paragraph summary of its response to the mind–body problem. Which do you find the most convincing reply?

The mind–body problem has spawned other interesting responses, one of which is called anomalous monism and is an account of the mind–body interaction proposed by the American philosopher Donald Davidson (1917–2003). As its name suggests, the theory holds that there is only one existent substance; Davidson believes that this is physical. The description 'anomalous' derives from the Greek *anomie*, meaning 'lawlessness', and refers to Davidson's conviction that there are no law-like connections between thoughts and brain states. Davidson believes that given the uncertainties and plasticity surrounding consciousness we can only talk about accidents, coincidences and exceptions.

As a term, 'consciousness' is often used in the philosophy of mind; yet it requires further analysis. It may accurately be defined as an awareness of external phenomena, an access to memories and an ability to monitor one's feelings. In addition, theorists have drawn a distinction between intransitive and transitive accounts of consciousness. The former refers to the sense of being awake or aware of one's faculties, and may be termed 'self-consciousness'; whereas the latter may be characterised by statements that take the form, 'I am conscious that there is something there'. Two rival camps emerge in the debate as to how consciousness

	Cartesian dualism	Identity theory	Eliminative materialism	Behaviourism	Functionalism
Do thoughts exist?	Yes	Yes	Brainwaves exist	Most say no	Yes
How are thoughts caused?	No answer	Possibly physical	Brains	Caused physically	No answer
What does it mean to have a mind?	To possess a soul?	To possess brain states	Nothing	To behave	Input relates to output
Does the mental depend on the physical?	No	Yes	Only the physical exists	Yes	No answer
Do thoughts have both mental and physical properties?	No, only mental	Yes	No, only physical	Yes	No answer

may be explained. The first is the view that consciousness is a mysterious, non-physical substance along the lines of an aura or soul, which does not seem to fit into any of the physical stories we tell about what goes on in the body. This theory, sometimes called transcendentalism or mysterianism, holds that conscious experiences occur in the mind and, in some more extreme versions, suggest that God is responsible for the mind's interaction with the body. The best that can be said for this view is that it is an ignorance-avoidance theory that does not contain any logical contradictions. The contrary view is founded in physicalism and holds that consciousness is nothing more or less than brain waves. An example of this might be the token-identity theory (see p. 79).

The problem of other minds

We have direct experience of our own sensations, feelings and perceptions. If we consider the experiences of others, however, we do not have access to such directness. This gives rise to the problem of other minds, which constitutes a sceptical challenge that states that we can never know whether other human beings have minds or whether their inner mental life is the same as our own. We become aware of other people's feelings and thoughts through observing their behaviour; from this we infer whether they are in a good mood or not. Behaviourists boast that their theory renders the problem of other minds redundant, but, as we have seen, there are many other difficulties with behaviourism, such as pretence and deception. And any reference to predisposition is as hard to prove as the existence of other minds.

On the face of it, these ideas may seem eccentric, but to dismiss the problem of other minds on the grounds that it does not fit in with our common sense is not to give a reasoned refutation of it. The problem of other minds, as one philosopher[13] has pointed out, sheds uncertainty on whether we can establish the minded status of aliens, animals and automata as well as other human beings. Expressed more formally and with specific reference to other human beings, the contention runs:

1 I cannot know exactly what sorts of experience other people have but can only observe their behaviour.
2 There is no necessary connection between mental states and behaviour.
3 We cannot possess knowledge of another person's mental states.

This conclusion leaves the door open for some hard-line sceptics to advance an extreme position known as solipsism (see pp. 16–17). Certain solutions have been suggested; one of the most popular until recently was the argument from analogy.

The argument from analogy

Traditionally, philosophers have tried to meet this sort of sceptical position by arguing from analogy. Arguments from analogy rely on the comparison of similar things. If one thing is like another in some respects, then it is thought it will be like it in others. Since I am like other individuals in my appearance and behaviour, the argument from analogy suggests that it is reasonable to assume that other individuals have the same mental life as I do. So when they do something to themselves that would cause me pain, such as stubbing a toe, I believe that it is likely that they are in pain. One may back this assertion up with scientific evidence concerning their nervous systems. The argument from analogy may be summarised as follows:

1 I am familiar with my own mind and body.
2 I am familiar with other people's physical behaviour and aware that it resembles my own.
3 I can infer that other people's minds resemble my own.

Despite being a commonsensical argument, it runs into problems if one pushes the possibility that other people's minds don't resemble one's own mind. There are many possible entities that are minded but do not resemble the human mind, e.g. gods, floridly psychotic human beings, animals and aliens. Why do proponents of the argument from analogy such as Bertrand Russell presume that, just because people's behaviour resembles his, their minds also resemble his mind?

Wittgenstein and language use

Ludwig Wittgenstein (1889–1951) was one of the most subtle and engaging thinkers of the twentieth century, and frequently turned his attention to questions in the philosophy of mind. His rebuttal of the argument from analogy has been labelled 'the beetle in the box criticism', in reference to a famous passage occurring in *Philosophical Investigations*:

> Suppose everyone had a box with something in it: we call it a 'beetle'. No one can look into anyone else's box, and everyone says he knows what a beetle is only by looking at *his* beetle. – Here it would be quite possible for everyone to have something different in his box. One might even imagine such a thing constantly changing. – But suppose the word 'beetle' had a use in these people's language? – If so it would not be used as the name of a thing. The thing in the box has no place in the language-game at all; not even as a *something*: for the box might even be empty.[14]

Let us consider an analogy along similar lines. Imagine entering a warehouse that is full of crates. All the crates look similar to each other in that they are all the same size and weight and have the same labels. We are curious about the contents of the crates, so we decide to open one up to see what is inside. By analogy from the one instance we have knowledge of, we may expect all the other crates to have similar contents to the one we have opened. However, any such assumption would be philosophically unfounded. Just because we know the contents of one of the crates does not mean that we can infer the contents of the others. The one difference between the case of the crates and our attempt to claim knowledge of the existence of other minds is that, in the case of the crates, we at least have the possibility of opening up a few more to confirm our suspicions. In the end, we may even decide to open all the crates and make absolutely sure that the contents of the first, second or third are substantially similar to all the rest. In the case of minds, we are only able to open and directly look into the one 'crate' that is our own mind. As far as other people are concerned, we have to rely on the markings on the sides of the crates or, to put it another way, the behaviour of other people. Wittgenstein goes further in inviting us to imagine lots of people peering into the various crates and advancing descriptions about what they contain, but having no method of verifying whether they are talking about the same thing. Such descriptions do not abide by the rules of normal language, according to Wittgenstein, and it would be irresponsible to draw conclusions from it. The argument from analogy does not solve the problem of other minds.

This depressing thought is salvaged by Wittgenstein when he goes on to show that the existence of language implies the existence of other minds. According to Wittgenstein, words have meanings because of the rules that are associated with their use. The word 'chair' can be used correctly or incorrectly depending on whether we use it within the bounds of the rules for its application or not. If I assumed that I was the only being in the universe then it would be impossible for me ever to be certain that I was using the words of my language correctly. All that I would have to go on to tell me that I was applying a word today in the same way that I applied it yesterday would be my own memory. To use Wittgenstein's own example, I would be like a person who in seeking to confirm his opinion that a train arrives at a particular time could only do so by referring to his own memory rather than to a timetable that exists independently of that memory. The private language argument attempts to show that built into our language about our own consciousness is a set of assumptions about the existence of other minds, and that to raise sceptical doubts about the existence of such minds is therefore to undermine our ability to say anything not just about other people's experience but about our own.

Wittgenstein believes not only that any private language invented by oneself is impractical, but also that it is an impossibility. Why is private language impossible? First of all, we would not have the power of mind to create it on our own. More significantly, any language could not be verified or falsified if we were the sole language-user. He compares this state of affairs (*Philosophical Investigations* (265)) to someone buying several copies of the same newspaper to check the validity of stories they read in the first. Equally, there could be no sustained rules of the language game, and nothing would stop the solitary language-user changing the rules at will. But language does have rules, and the fact that we infer from such rules that other minds exist depends on the use of language and not its meaning. For Wittgenstein, meaning is use; thus to talk meaningfully about love stems from the fact that we have learnt how to use the language of love. We have been taught by other language-users the words for certain experiences and sensations. We have been able to compare these descriptions with the descriptions from people around us. We have been able to measure the intensity of these feelings, and have been corrected by others when we have made mistakes in describing our story. Such language use would be impossible without other minded individuals.[15]

The problem of self-ascription

Imagine that you are standing in front of a mirror, looking at your reflection. You might assert:

Ludwig Wittgenstein (1889–1951)

Wittgenstein has been hailed as the most important philosopher of the twentieth century and someone who breathed fresh ideas into the subject. He remained concerned with how language represents both ideas and the external world throughout his life, although he changed his approach after publishing the *Tractatus*, leading commentators to refer to early and later Wittgenstein. He is remembered for many things: as the heir to a multi-million-pound fortune inherited from his steel baron father; as someone who gave up his inheritance to ensure the security of his sisters from Nazi anti-semitism; as an ascetic who renounced attachment to material possessions and sought solitude variously in Ireland, Iceland and Norway; as a talented mathematician and logician; as an architect, inventor, choleric primary school teacher (the only work other than the *Tractatus* published in his lifetime was a children's dictionary); as a suicidal, tortured genius with ambiguous sexuality. One might say that he had it all. He is most famously associated with the Cambridge school of philosophy, and is considered as the immediate successor to Bertrand Russell. He found the atmosphere at Trinity College precious and restrictive, but inspired a band of acolytes who dressed as he did with open-necked shirts and adopted his militaristic, purposeful walk and mimicked his gestures, contorted grimaces, catchphrases and Austrian accent. It was at a famous meeting of the Moral Sciences Club at King's College in October 1946 that Wittgenstein was said to have threatened the visiting speaker, Karl Popper, with a poker. Reports differ as to the accuracy of this story, and it is noteworthy that this encounter took place in a dim, firelit room where most people were smoking. Hence it must have been hard to ascertain important details. If a reliable account is unobtainable, the story attests to the fiery, domineering egomania that made Wittgenstein such a charismatic and ebullient character. He sadly died of cancer in 1951. During his illness he would regularly take a walk, despite his growing frailty, to visit a tree which grew near Churchill College. He found comfort in hugging this tree, and when it was cut down to make room for a car park was heard to exclaim 'My tree, my life!' The famous philosopher died the day after. For many, Wittgenstein exhibited an other-worldly intelligence and mysticism; yet for many of his critics he was a confidence trickster who left philosophy no richer by his presence.

Significant works
Tractatus Logico-Philosophicus (1921)
The Blue and Brown Books (1958)
Philosophical Investigations (1953)

1 I have grey hair.

2 I am feeling contented.

Both statements may be described as 'self-ascriptions', but whereas the first statement is a bodily self-ascription the second statement is a mental self-ascription. Our concern in this section is with the latter.

Many philosophers believe that we can self-ascribe about perceptions, feelings, memories and the like through an inner sense. One is present to oneself as an object of introspective self-awareness. On the basis of this self-awareness any first-person statement such as 'I am feeling contented' is immune from error through misidentification. It is impossible to be wrong about your own mental state. This conviction is linked to three notable doctrines in the philosophy of mind: immediate, privileged and infallible accessibility. Let us define each in turn:

- *Immediate accessibility* is the first-hand, transparent quality of self-awareness. It would not make sense to assert, 'I don't know whether I am contented'.

- *Privileged accessibility* refers to the fact that I am in a uniquely authoritative position to comment on my own mental state. This is not enjoyed when commenting on other people's mental states (the problem of other minds).

- *Infallible accessibility* refers to the truth value of my mental self-ascriptions. By virtue of the fact that I am the subject of experience X, I know experience X is true.

How then is it possible to question self-ascriptions and why is it a problem? The problem lies in the fact that mental self-ascription carries with it the baggage of a dualist conception of the self. Hardline sceptics such as Lichtenberg (in his criticism of Descartes) and Hume (in his bundle theory) deny the existence of a self and as a consequence deny the validity of self-ascription. Thus the 'I' in the statement 'I am feeling contented' does not correspond to any independent reality but is just a feature of language. A weaker sceptical argument holds that a self exists but is caught in an introspective twilight and thus cannot pronounce on mental states. The fact that many mental states are

unconscious may be cited in support of this argument. The line being advanced here is that any view of introspection as a searchlight that illuminates our experiences with exact detail is plainly not true. Such an argument fans the flames of Colin McGinn's conviction that we cannot meaningfully advance theories about our own mind as we only have our mind as the medium of investigation.

Colin McGinn (born 1950) argues that human beings cannot understand how the mind works, as the only tools they have at their disposal are minds, and this creates a cognitive closure. We cannot understand how technicolour phenomenology arises out of soggy, grey matter, or as he puts it, 'how the water of the physical brain is turned into the wine of consciousness'[16] because we are like a five-year-old child trying to learn about the theory of relativity. We do not have access to any mind–brain link, as we cannot get out of our minds.

Task

Discuss possible answers to the following questions on self-ascription:

1 What would a behaviourist say about mental self-ascription?

2 Do animals self-ascribe?

3 At what stage do humans gain the power to self-ascribe?

Review questions

1 Outline and illustrate one response to the mind–body problem.

2 Outline and illustrate one response to the problem of other minds.

The problem of personal identity

In essence, philosophy is an exercise in self-reflection: How should I behave? What do I know and believe? And more fundamentally still, what is it to be human? Not surprisingly, physicalists respond to this last question in a physicalist vein and dualists in a dualist one. Respectively, one might call these physical and psychological accounts of personal identity. There is a third approach, most recently advocated in the philosophy of mind by Derek

Parfit, which is termed 'bundle theory'. The problem of personal identity comes to a head in examining philosophical difficulties in establishing our continued identity through time. Is there an enduring self? Scientists inform us that over a period of time all the molecules in our body change. Cells are replaced in the gut after two days, red blood cells after one hundred days and brain cells over a period of years. If Sleeping Beauty fell asleep for seven years then all of the cells in her body would have been replaced by the time she woke up. So would she remain the same person? Can philosophers suggest watertight criteria that prove she was the same person at time 1 (t_1), when she was put under the spell of the evil witch, as she was later at time 2 (t_2), when kissed by the handsome prince?

Physical continuity

Physicalists maintain that we recognise people as individual and distinct by physical criteria of identity, in other words that they are 'flesh and blood'. One might summarise the argument:

1 Personal identity consists in my being a flesh-and-blood body and being biologically alive.
2 There is continuity between my being alive at t_1 and t_2; therefore, I am the same person at t_1 and t_2.

One might even take one step further and cite DNA as the best criterion for physical continuity, with the unique hallmark of our existence contained in each of our cells. Yet our physicality can be manipulated, either in the realm of science, or at least through the philosopher's imagination in the realm of science fiction. One might conceive of someone who had their DNA removed from each cell, leaving the cell structure intact, before someone else's DNA was inserted. Would they remain the same person? This operation might seem highly improbable, but it illustrates the problem of advancing purely physical grounds for personal identity.

One refinement, advanced by Thomas Noonan, of the physical continuity theory admits that any person at t_1 and t_2 does not have to be materially identical, but suggests that all the matter constituting the person at t_2 needs to have resulted from that constituting the person at t_1 by a series of more or less gradual replacements. This still creates an identity crisis for recipients of organ donations, and raises the question of whether those people in the future who have received transplants from other species will be classed as only partly human.

Psychological continuity

Theories of psychological continuity inherit a long tradition in western philosophy, stretching back to Plato's *Phaedo* and including theistic notions of body and soul, with the latter possessing the ability to survive death. Later in the tradition, atheistic existentialists argue that if we are free to create ourselves as works of art then this unique blend of character traits and the ability to choose which course of action to take constitutes ourselves. Memory has been hugely important in all psychological accounts of personal identity and may be outlined as follows:

1 Personal identity consists in my remembering the events that have occurred throughout my life.
2 There is a continuity in my memory at t_1 and t_2; therefore, I must be the same person at t_1 and t_2.

Certain criticisms challenge this notion:

• Memory can be manipulated through hypnosis or suggestion. Conceive a Ministry of Truth, in the spirit of Orwell's *1984*, which manufactures a series of photographs with you airbrushed in, despite the fact that you weren't there. Through such devilry, the men from the Ministry set about conditioning you to believe that you were present. Memory can be artificially manufactured, and as a consequence seems a weak candidate for identity.

• Memory can also be lost, as in the case of amnesia or just general forgetfulness. Thomas Reid (1710–1796) offers the following story in disagreement with an argument from memory proposed by John Locke (1632–1704). There was a soldier who, when he was a boy, had stolen apples from an orchard and was flogged as a consequence. That same boy later became a brave ensign who won honours in battle. Afterwards, the ensign gained promotion and subsequently became a famous general. If memory is supposed to be necessary for personal identity, what happens if the brave ensign can remember stealing the apples as a boy and the general can remember winning honours in battle but not stealing apples? Are we to say that they are not the same person? Clearly, personal identity is an all-or-nothing thing, but are we really expected to remember every experience? One might counter Reid's argument by asserting that there is still a continuity of connectedness between boy, ensign and general; therefore, they are one and the same person. Noonan suggested physical continuity based on gradual replacement; one might make a similar move here and advance an argument from overlapping memories.

- One might argue that it is wrong to force an 'either/or' decision between physical and psychological approaches. Instead, one might champion the existence of an indivisible unity between mind and body that constitutes the whole. Such a unity exists even in the case of multiple personalities, which pose an exception to purely psychological accounts; any such unity is vehemently denied by bundle theorists.

Bundle theories

The contemporary bundle theorist Derek Parfit contrasts both physical and psychological accounts, which he collectively terms 'ego theories', with a standpoint called the bundle theory. The thoughts we experience are not connected through a separate 'ego' but exist in a haystack-like bundle and are loosely linked through their contiguity in space and time. Parfit argues against the notion of a unified, underlying person. He states that when we talk of personhood we usually mean a single entity but that such an account is unintelligible. Parfit cites two cases of bifurcation as evidence: one physical and one psychological. Firstly, we are to imagine a case of artificial replacement when parts of our body are replaced or swapped. Secondly, we are to imagine certain facts about our brain (content, psychological make-up) being scanned

and duplicated in an exact replica. In both cases, we do not remain a single, unified entity. Parfit argues that these cases prove problematic for ego theories, which posit an underlying self, but not for bundle theories, which define personhood in terms of a changing collection of thoughts, sensations and experiences.

In western philosophy, bundle theories are the natural heirs to Georg Lichtenberg (1742–1799) and Hume (1711–1776), but many counterparts exist in eastern philosophy, where the position is termed the doctrine of *anatman* (no self). The Buddha likens the mistaken belief in a self to someone who believes that a carriage exists in addition to its parts. Ryle would have said the person was making a category error.

As well as Buddhists, certain contemporary thinkers have denied that a self exists at all and have put forward the view that the idea is nothing more than the product of social convention. The psychologist Susan Blackmore (born 1951) has argued from a physicalist perspective that the notion of selfhood is a lie, an illusion or an evolutionary trick.[17] She argues that thoughts are generated physically, and that such beliefs as religion, science and the idea of personal identity have originated by accident but are so beneficial to the survival of the species that they are passed on like genes from person to person. These skills, habits and ideas that are imitated through the medium of language are termed 'memes', though it remains unclear why each person and their *a priori* receptiveness to memes cannot count as grounds for personal identity.

Revision questions

1 In what ways can the mental and the physical be distinguished?

2 Assess the strengths and weaknesses of eliminative materialism as a theory of mind.

3 Assess the problems involved in arguing from our own case to the existence of other minds.

4 Describe and illustrate three difficulties in establishing our continued identity through time.

5 Examine the difficulties that intentionality presents for theories of the relationship between mind and body.

- Describe and illustrate what is meant by qualia.
- Assess the arguments for and against the survival of disembodied consciousness.
- Behaviourism, in none of its versions, can account for the fact that an inner mental life exists with no behavioural manifestations. Discuss.
- Assess the implications of artificial intelligence for the view that the mind is the brain.
- Assess whether any form of dualism offers a plausible account of the nature of mind.

Glossary of key terms

Artificial intelligence: the study of silicon-based systems that display skills such as problem-solving.

Eliminative materialism: the view that one can eliminate the concept of the mental without loss of meaning.

Epiphenomenalism: the dualist doctrine that the physical can cause the mental but the mental cannot cause the physical, e.g. you feel hot because you are hot not because you are thinking about heat.

Folk psychology: a pejorative term coined by eliminativists to describe homespun psychological theories that have evolved to explain other people's behaviour.

Intentionality: the content of a thought. Mental expressions have to be about something, and what a specific thought or belief is about is termed its intentionality.

Introspection: the process whereby we gain information about ourselves by thinking about our own thoughts.

Leibniz's law: Leibniz asserted that for two things to be the same then they must be numerically identical. This may be expressed formally: If every property of X is also a property of Y then X = Y.

Monism: the view that there is only one substance of which the universe is made. This may be mental, as in the case of Berkeley's immaterialism, or physical, as in the case of modern materialist philosophies of mind.

Physicalism: the group of philosophical theories which hold that questions concerning consciousness and the mind can be resolved by physical explanations.

Property dualism: the view, advanced by thinkers such as Nagel, that asserts that the mental and the physical exhibit different attributes and should, therefore, be considered as distinct.

Qualia: the qualitative, subjective characteristics of experience – for example, how something tastes to a particular person.

Supervenience: this refers to the process whereby a further layer of meaning emanates from particular entities. For example, if one calls someone's face cute, one is describing cuteness supervening or emanating from the particular features of the individual's face.

Suggested reading

- Churchland, P. (1999) *Matter of Consciousness*, London and New York, MIT Press
  A short volume introducing the various schools of thought, including the Churchlands' own eliminativism

- Graham, G. (2000) *Philosophy of Mind: An Introduction*, Oxford, Blackwell
  The most accessible introduction to the subject with interesting links to other philosophical issues

- Lyons, W. ed. (1995) *Modern Philosophy of Mind*, London, Dent
  An anthology of essays and articles covering a wide spectrum of thought

- Maslin, K. T. (2001) *An Introduction to the Philosophy of Mind*, Oxford, Polity
  An in-depth survey of all the relevant arguments

- Smith, P. and Jones, O. R. (1986) *The Philosophy of Mind*, Cambridge, CUP
  An undergraduate text on the philosophy of mind that nevertheless includes some useful introductory material

Notes

1 Ryle. G. (1949) *The Concept of Mind*, Harmondsworth, Penguin, p. 25.

2 Descartes, R. (2000) *Meditations and Other Metaphysical Writings*, Harmondsworth, Penguin, pp. 20, 22, 33, 40, 52, 56 and 58.

3 Foster, J. (1991) *The Immaterial Self*, London, Routledge.

4 Swinburne, R. and Shoemaker, S. (1989) *Personal Identity*, Oxford, Blackwell.

5 Nagel, T. (1995) 'What Is It Like to Be a Bat?', in W. Lyons, *Modern Philosophy of Mind*, London, Dent, p. 160.

6 Churchland, P. (1999) 'Eliminative Materialism and the Propositional Attitudes', in W. G. Lycan (ed.), *Mind and Cognition*, Oxford, Blackwell, p. 206.

7 Churchland, P. (1996) 'The Hornswoggle Problem', Internet.

8 Searle, J. (1994) *The Rediscovery of Mind*, Massachusetts, MIT Press.

9 Ryle, G. (1949) *The Concept of Mind*, Harmondsworth, Penguin, p. 31.

10 Graham, G. (2000) *Philosophy of Mind: An Introduction*, Oxford, Blackwell, p. 88.

11 'Evolve or Die', *New Scientist*, 27 October 2001.

12 Ovid (1988) *Metamorphoses*, Harmondsworth, Penguin, Book X.

13 Churchland, P. (1984) *Matter and Consciousness*, London, MIT, p. 67.

14 Wittgenstein, L. (1958) *Philosophical Investigations*, Oxford, Blackwell, p. 100.

15 For a detailed analysis of Wittgenstein's private-language argument see A. Kenny (1973) *Wittgenstein*, London, Penguin, pp. 178–202.

16 McGinn, C. (1995) 'Can We Solve the Mind–Body Problem?', in W. Lyons, *Modern Philosophy of Mind*, London, Dent, p. 272.

17 Blackmore, S. (1999) 'Meme, Myself, I', *New Scientist*, 13 March, pp. 40–44.

5 Political philosophy

Never exceed your rights, and they will soon become unlimited.
(Rousseau)

Aims

On completion of this chapter you should be able to:

- outline and evaluate liberalism, conservatism, socialism and anarchism
- provide a critical account of positive and negative freedom
- outline and assess the different accounts of natural rights
- explain the basis for and status of the law and how it affects the freedom of the individual
- explain the nature and competing claims of freedom, justice and law
- explain and evaluate the various theories of punishment and their justification
- outline and assess the nature and forms of authority
- consider the definition and role of the state.

Political philosophy is, to an important extent, concerned with moral questions that arise from people living together in community. This study in applied ethics affects our lives both on a global and local level. Indeed, it is worth noting that the record of history is written in the blood and suffering of men and women who died or were killed because of the passion inspired in them, or their leaders, by political ideas. This chapter seeks to demonstrate the complexity of these ideas and offer some insights into the various philosophical contexts in which they appear. Our route through political philosophy takes the form of a series of questions: What set of beliefs should we live by? What restrictions should be imposed on our actions? What rights do we possess? How are restrictions to be formulated and implemented? What sanctions exist for those who ignore the laws of a state? From what authority are they passed down? And, finally, what do we mean by the term 'state'? These issues pose living questions and are not merely interesting areas of academic dispute; it is the job of a political philosopher to convince their audience of the accuracy of a particular understanding. Let us begin with a brief survey of political ideologies.

Political ideologies

A political **ideology** provides the theoretical basis for political beliefs. The earliest ideology is known as liberalism. It maintains that an individual's liberty should be cherished and cultivated by the **state**. It is in response to this belief that conservatism (**right-wing** ideology), socialism (**left-wing** ideology) and anarchism (anti-statism) have arisen.

Liberalism

The political ideology known as liberalism is characterised by the twin principles of individuality and freedom. The most famous defence of these values was undertaken by John Stuart Mill in his essay *On Liberty* (see chapter 13), but defences of liberalism have historically deeper roots in an Aristotelian argument known as the 'shoe-pinching argument'. It proceeds as follows:

1 Individuals have their own interests and preferences.
2 Each individual has the right to pursue these interests and preferences.
3 A society that encourages individuality and liberty provides the best setting where this legitimate right can be met.

4 An individual member of such a society knows when their interests and preferences are being violated.

The image of shoe-pinching refers to the conviction in **4** that it is the individual who knows best when their interests are being compromised, just as the shoe wearer knows exactly where the shoe pinches. The liberal argument admits not that all people's rights will be violated, just as not everyone has ill-fitting shoes, but that the needs of those whose rights are violated need to be addressed. Note that there is a moral 'ought' at the bedrock of liberalism, which is compatible with any normative ethical theory, as outlined in chapter 2. Note also that the liberal argument describes a type of ideal state and not a type of government, as the government cannot, by virtue of its role, determine where the shoe pinches. One might assert that a democracy is the type of government that best achieves maximum liberty, tolerance and individuality, but it does not necessarily entail these ideals. A benign dictatorship by a platonic elite may also nurture such values. To borrow an illustration from Plato's parable of the ship, the government is like a helm directing the society to an ideological destination but it is not instrumental in deciding what this goal should be.

Mill defends liberalism in his essay *On Liberty* on the grounds that through championing freedom, individuality and equality the greatest happiness of the greatest number will be achieved. This is a classic utilitarian defence, which is based on the **common good** of society. **Coercion** in the form of law or punishment is only to be exercised when the above values are being compromised. In this case, and in this case only, the state is justified in curtailing the freedom of the perpetrator. Even Mill, who is famous for supporting social freedom, allows coercion in this instance to limit the harm produced by those members of society with more dominant wills. Isaiah Berlin (1909–1997) quotes the adage 'freedom for the pike is death for the minnows' in his seminal essay 'Two Concepts of Liberty', but goes on to say that, although it is morally warranted for the freedom

of such domineering 'pikes' to be curtailed by law, a society is to be judged as successful if it possesses sufficient conscience not to need an overbearingly authoritarian state. Karl Popper (1902–1994) is another to take up this cudgel in *The Open Society and Its Enemies* by using the following epistemological defence of liberalism:

1 The ideal society is the most effective at problem-solving.

2 Problem-solving is dependent on the process of falsification.

3 The best society is one that has the freedom to challenge even the most basic beliefs and takes nothing for granted.

Popper believed that we obtain knowledge through a process of falsification (see p. 127) and condemned a society that did not allow such a falsification of erroneous beliefs to take place.

Criticisms of liberalism

Despite the above defences, liberalism has to face the following criticisms:

- The shoe-pinching argument is not justified in grounding rights in interests. In so doing a person's moral status is compromised by their desires or preferences. It might be in the interests of one state to take land from another, but this does not mean that this state possesses the right to engage in such an activity.

- Liberalism justifies **autonomy**, reason and choice on utilitarian grounds, and, as we have seen, utilitarianism has many flaws (see chapter 2).

- Liberty is an overly romantic notion. This criticism is sometimes called 'the myth of the free', as one might assert that our liberty is a fiction and that in reality our lives are totally determined by social and economic conditions.

Conservatism

While liberalism takes its name from the central notion of liberty, conservatism is so called due to the importance attached in this ideology to the conservation of traditional values and established customs. Conservatism recognises that we are determined by social and economic conditions, and holds that the most effective way to guard each individual's welfare is through the work of established institutions. The specialised functions of such institutions are:

- to ensure the practical efficiency of the system;
- to ensure an equilibrium;
- to protect against radical change;
- to protect valuable resources for future generations of citizens.

As a consequence, conservatives would condemn the label 'political ideology' as a straightforward contradiction, as anything political is necessarily practical. They would cite any form of radicalism (any set of beliefs that shakes the status quo) as dangerously unsettling. Conservatism advocates **justice**, self-reliance and prosperity as collective goals.

Conservatives admit that there will always be disadvantaged and marginalised members of society, but employ what has been known as the 'invisible hand argument'. This phrase comes from the writings of the Scottish economist Adam Smith (1723–1790), who defends the view that such an economic underclass fares better under a conservative government:

1 Social class is an inevitability, and there will always be a poorer underclass of people.
2 Conservatism encourages prosperity amongst the already prosperous.
3 Economic prosperity for those at the top will have an effect further down the economic scale.
4 Therefore, both poorer and richer classes benefit from a conservative approach to politics.

The invisible hand argument has its origins in the proto-industry of the eighteenth and nineteenth centuries. It holds that an increased prosperity for industry will help every member of the community as if an invisible hand were distributing benefits further afield. Each individual, while aspiring to maximise their own benefits, will in fact contribute to the common good. However, many disagree with Smith's evaluation. The most powerful arguments against conservative ideology spill from the pen of Karl Marx (see chapter 12), who accuses the fat cats of industry of dehumanising the work force. He argues that the productive forces unleashed under capitalism do indeed create unprecedented wealth, but the relations of production under capitalism will eventually act as fetters on the further development of these productive forces and, instead of any trickle-down effect of wealth, there will rather be a polarisation: great wealth for the few; grinding poverty for the multitude. For Marx, society should not have to rely on an invisible hand but on collective, rational human decision-making. Other problems arise for conservatives in the following forms.

Criticisms of conservatism

The following major criticisms are made of conservatism:

- No clear criteria can be supplied that inform us how to judge between what should and should not be conserved. Which values are to be conserved and which are to be forgotten? Should nation-states conserve institutions such as the monarchy?
- Change is inevitable, and the conservative ideology appears to deny this fact.
- Conservatism can harden to a *laissez faire* approach, where the government does not interfere with an individual's affairs. This fails to look after the marginalised and vulnerable of society.

Socialism

The socialist ideology sees society as the source of **power**, authority and justice. It stresses the importance of virtues such as equality, comradeship and fraternity over individualism and institutions. Socialists believe injustice in the form of class discrimination to be a force for evil that needs to be overcome. Many commentators have likened forms of the socialist movement to a religion. In the same way as a religion tells us where we have gone wrong, socialism diagnoses the ills of the human condition before offering a way of salvation. What cure does the left wing offer? A version of the socialist argument runs:

1 There is a marked inequality in the world community and, in particular, in sovereign states.

2 This is caused by the selfish and divisive notion of private ownership.

3 The distribution of resources should be re-allocated according to need rather than possession.

4 Only when a universal class is established with the shared values of the community prevailing over the individual can human beings live authentic lives.

Socialism is an ideology that is grounded in the empirical science of social observation. Indeed, Marx's co-author on many works, Friedrich Engels (1820–1895), wrote a detailed analysis of social history that recorded the atrocious conditions workers had to endure in the cotton mills of Lancashire in the 1840s. Socialism is the direct opposite of a conservative ideology that critics allege encourages greed, competition and exploitation.

Although the socialist ideology is essentially materialistic, maintaining that we are our physical existence and nothing more, it appeals to higher ideals such as fairness and a sense of the common good. Marx rejects the notion that socialism is ideological in the sense of being theoretical and idealistic, arguing instead that it is pragmatic and farsighted. Socialism advocates the values of productiveness and social unity just as, to borrow a popular political metaphor, all the bees in the hive work together for the good of their community.

Criticisms of socialism

The idyll of this socialist beehive has its critics:

• The great champion of socialism, Karl Marx, has been misinterpreted by cruel and despotic leaders such as Stalin, Mao and Kim Il Sung. This suggests that an ideology that places people on an even playing field encourages injustice and exploitation despite its opposite intention.

• The New Left movement, typified by the British prime minister Tony Blair's Third Way, seeks to combine profit with parity, thus reconciling what is thought to be the best of

liberalism and socialism while acknowledging the need for prosperity.

• Libertarians might criticise the socialist emphasis on freedom from injustice as leading to an unbalanced notion of liberty that ignores the positive freedom of self-expression and individuality.

Anarchism

Those disaffected with society often call themselves 'anarchists', but in a formal sense anarchism is the ideological standpoint that denies the need for any state at all. In practice, this may lead to minor insurrections such as the May Day riots that occurred in many European cities in 2000 or the forming of anti-state communes within a state. But what justification do anarchists provide for questioning the state orthodoxy set forward by liberalism, conservatism and, to a lesser degree, socialism?

Three main arguments are to be found. The first is a historical argument that draws our attention to the fact that, for over four-fifths of human existence, states did not exist and are hence surplus to requirements now. Anarchists trace the origins of any state to the first forms of specialisation; thus, before societies developed, every member of the community acted as carer, law enforcer and provider, and it is only when such functions are pursued exclusively that the state is born. Political philosophers refer to the time before societies and governments as 'a state of nature'. Anarchists believe that human beings are perfectly capable of thriving in a stateless condition without the trappings of statist orthodoxy.

A second anti-statist argument advanced by anarchists accuses states of putting the human species at greater risk. While the first anarchist contention holds the notion of 'state' to be a redundant one, the second argument holds the notion of statehood to be positively dangerous, as it causes wars, global pollution and regional conflict, which are all carried out 'for the good of the state'.

In the third argument against the state, anarchists point to the fact that statehood is constructed on top of the practical reality of life. One has only to look at the quasi-religious language of political philosophers in their descriptions of the state to understand the devotion it inspires. The English philosopher Thomas Hobbes (1588–1679), for instance, refers to the state as a 'mortal god' in *Leviathan*. This is evidence, so the anarchist argument would run, that the state is a top-down notion, i.e. one that is centred in theory rather than practice; and unless one adopts an alternative bottom-up approach then a solution to the problems of life cannot be found.

Before any critical questions are posed, one further argument needs to be mentioned that reflects the way anarchism as a political argument has straddled the left–right spectrum. While most anarchists make the journey from liberal individualism to socialism and then to a denial of the state apparatus as a useful functionary, an alternative path leads from ultra-conservatism to a position that can be termed anarcho-capitalism. The anarcho-capitalist point of view may be summarised as follows:

1 The purpose of a state is to protect the life, liberty and prosperity of individuals.
2 Each person should be able to retain what belongs to them.
3 A state which, in the name of equality, redistributes property and wealth is depriving the individual of the very protection which led to its formation.
4 Such protection is afforded by market forces and economics and any formal notion of the state is ineffective.

Robert Nozick (1938–2002) argues a similar position in *Anarchy, State and Utopia* (1974) and such a standpoint influenced the New Right

politics of Ronald Reagan and Margaret Thatcher in the 1980s, the latter famously declaring that 'there is no such thing as society'.

Criticisms of anarchism

Many thinkers disagree with the various shades of anarchism, putting forward the following arguments:

- Communities in the past were small, homogeneous and rural, and bear little resemblance to the densely populated, urban, ethnically heterogeneous and technologically advanced societies of the present. Whereas in the past order was maintained through ostracism, religious retribution, familial pressure and primitive bartering, it is necessary today to have a specialised police force to uphold the laws and protect each individual.
- The anarchist concept of a state of nature is insufficient and ignores the reality of the human situation.
- The emergence of super-states such as the European Union is evidence that humans need formal structure and cohesion.
- Free markets, as advocated by the New Right, have a divisive character when left to themselves.

Summary

The following table summarises the stance each political ideology takes on the central political issues of freedom, law, authority and the role of the state.

Review question

Describe and illustrate one argument in favour of the socialist ideology and one argument against.

	Liberalism	**Conservatism**	**Socialism**	**Anarchism**
Freedom	Negative freedom	Guarded by punishment	Positive freedom	Maximum freedom
Law	Guards rights	Administers justice	Ensures welfare	Autonomy
Authority	Consent	Obligation	Society	No specification of function
State	Weak paternalism	Coercion	Common good	Denial

Freedom

Anarchists advocate maximum freedom, whereas most other philosophical standpoints admit the need for some restrictions. But is it clear what the term 'freedom' means? 'Freedom' has a range of associations, not only in philosophy, but also in politics, literature, law and personal relationships. In daily usage, it would be next to impossible to pin down exactly the meaning intended each time the word is used. In each of the following sentences the word 'free' means something different:

- 'Are you free tonight?'
- 'Is this product free?'
- 'This is a free country.'

In the face of common sense, there seems little point in searching for a concept of freedom that is likely to be endlessly subject to an infinity of subtle changes. There are, however, a number of areas of human life in which the uses of the term 'freedom' are so important that it is necessary to struggle with confusions of meaning and attempt to resolve them, whatever the difficulties. This is referred to as the problem of freedom, and may be summarised as follows:

1 Every meaningful expression refers to a basic, discoverable reality.
2 The term 'freedom' is used and manipulated in a variety of contexts.
3 The basic, discoverable reality to which 'freedom' refers is concealed and obscured by the aforementioned contexts.

If a problem exists in defining freedom, then how do we know that we are free at all? Political philosophers have investigated the concept of freedom and draw a distinction between two senses: positive and negative freedom.

Positive and negative freedom

Freedom appears to be something that human beings feel naturally inclined to value. Such liberty takes two distinct forms, identified in Isaiah Berlin's famous essay 'Two Concepts of Freedom' (1958). Negative freedom, sometimes termed 'freedom from', is freedom from constraint, external barriers or interference in order to carry out a set of actions. Positive freedom, sometimes termed 'freedom to', is the freedom to take control of one's own life and experience some degree of self-fulfilment, self-governance and autonomy. Positive freedom requires:

- a minimum of negative freedom;
- rational intelligence to work out personal and collective goals, and how to overcome obstacles;
- a sense of self-realisation and self-direction.

I am free to develop if nothing prevents me. It appears, therefore, that negative freedom needs to exist as a condition of positive freedom; Berlin calls this 'minimum liberty'. Note that negative freedom involves freedom to do something as well as freedom not to do it, whereas positive freedom is an abstract ideal akin to 'personal fulfilment'. External obstacles to the desires of my will might take the form of physical obstacles, which I could move given sufficient power. The obstacle may consist in another person's contrary will, which I could circumvent given sufficient means. Once negative freedom is achieved, however, it has nothing to say about how a society should be governed, how a life should be lived or what the limits of state authority should be.

A helpful illustration of the difference between positive and negative freedom comes from the life of Berlin. As a political philosopher of Jewish origins he became interested in plans to found an independent state of Israel. Such a state granted the positive freedom for its inhabitants to attain self-mastery, independence and freedom to decide how they want to live. This positive freedom in turn entails the negative freedom to choose whether to live in accordance with a set of religious or cultural directives.

Positive freedom is necessarily bound by capacity: although no one will stop me trying to float to the moon, to assert that I am free to do so seems to miss the point that I lack the power. The fact that positive freedom has significance and is good for us has led some philosophers to assert that it should be made compulsory. Rousseau employs the following argument:

1 Human beings use reason.

2 The goals of rational beings must be harmonious and unified (as rational arguments are in mathematics and science).

3 Human beings are not necessarily aware of their status as rational beings.

4 Human beings do not necessarily distinguish effectively between free, rational desires and the passions that enslave us.

5 Thus it is legitimate to force human beings to do what those possessing authority on this know is in their interests.

This argument seems somewhat sinister, but raises the interesting question as to the relationship between freedom and authority. Should we, as Rousseau suggests, be forced to be free? A problem for positive freedom arises in the form of the often empty nature of the liberty awarded to the marginalised in society. Basic civil liberties may be important, but in the face of there being members of the community who are unable to acquire basic necessities, they appear as vacuous clichés. This difficulty has been ironically termed the 'freedom to starve'.

Rights

One of the great debates surrounding the issue of freedom and restriction has been concerned with the philosophical grounds for awarding human rights. Jeremy Bentham, in his *Fragment on Government* (1776), famously argued that talk of **natural rights** is 'nonsense on stilts'. Although it is not possible to go further into what Bentham was arguing here, his assertion does make clear the dilemma in hand: What is the origin and status of rights? 'Human rights' is a politically correct term for moral guidelines, and moral guidelines require philosophical justification. To state that rights rely on ethical imperatives begs

Isaiah Berlin
(1909–1997)

Isaiah Berlin was born in Latvia, where he grew up as a slightly smothered and hypochondriacal only child of a wealthy Jewish timber merchant. His family emigrated to London when he was twelve and his academic journey took him from St Pauls School to Oxford University, where he eventually became a fellow of the elite All Souls College and later in his life helped to found Wolfson College. When growing up, a blunt private tutor had once described Berlin as a superficial thinker and this accusation was to follow him throughout his academic career. Philosophically, he leant towards the sceptical position of logical positivism, which was prominent in 1930s Oxford courtesy of A. J. Ayer. Berlin's greatest contribution was his astute analysis of past political philosophers and his clarification of the concept of freedom. A gregarious, gifted linguist with an excellent memory, Berlin was very much aware that his talents lay in the more concrete disciplines of history and political analysis rather than philosophy; he saw himself as a historian of ideas. His philosophical insecurity can be traced back to a meeting of the Cambridge Moral Science Club in June 1940 when Wittgenstein destroyed his somewhat pedestrian paper on the problem of other minds. Berlin immersed himself in diplomatic duties during the later part of the Second World War and his first-hand experience of Stalinist Russia, McCarthyist America and the Zionist struggle to establish an independent state of Israel helped shape his characteristic political realism and liberal pluralism. His reports from various postings were of such clarity that Winston Churchill invited him to dinner when he heard that Berlin was in London. A confusion ensued and Downing Street ended up inviting the songwriter Irving Berlin. Churchill was bemused when his guest replied that he thought the greatest thing he had ever written was the song 'White Christmas'.

Significant works
Four Essays on Liberty (1969)

the question 'Whose ethical imperatives?' To assert that rights are the product of divine authorship begs the question 'How does one know that the divine exists?' Thus modern political philosophy occupies a position of uncertainty on this topic, on the one hand holding that rights are important but on the other finding it difficult to give a clear, unambiguous account of their justification.

As a single term, 'rights' can mean a lot of things. The government may claim the right to imprison a terrorist (power); a pacifist may claim the right not to fight (immunity); a farmer may exercise his right to hunt with hounds over his land (a liberty right); hunt saboteurs may exercise their right to protest (another liberty right) and say that animals have the right not to be hunted.

These differing rights give rise to a number of philosophical questions:

- Do we acquire rights by virtue of being members of a specific society?
- Are they given to us in return for our carrying out the duties and responsibilities of citizenship, so that we lose them if we breach the terms of the social contract within which we live?[1]
- Do we possess rights simply by virtue of being born?
- If so, on what authority, moral, religious or other, does this claim rest?
- Do other species apart from *homo sapiens* possess rights?

Political philosophers have attempted to answer these questions by looking at the problem of rights and trying to define the term more precisely.

Rights as renunciations

For the seventeenth-century political philosopher Thomas Hobbes, rights play an important part in explaining the origins of political society. Hobbes uses the term 'natural rights' to mean rights awarded to us because we share a human nature. Such natural rights are enjoyed in a state of nature, which was according to Hobbes a state of war and mutual threat. Everyone has a natural right to everything, even to kill one another. The advent of political society means that individuals wanting to participate in the state must renounce their natural rights and subject themselves to authority. For Hobbes, rights are acquired through subjection to 'Leviathan' (a special name he gives to any state with absolute authority).

Rights as moral entitlements

The conception of rights as advanced by John Locke is very different from the Hobbesian account. For Locke, natural rights bear divine authorship, and exist as ontologically independent entities that we may discover through reason. Such rights order our lives and enable us to live in harmony with one another. Locke's account of the origin of rights may be summarised as follows:

1 Natural rights exist.
2 At least one person must possess natural rights in a state of nature.
3 There are no grounds for denying anybody the same rights if at least one person possesses natural rights.
4 Therefore, everybody has the same entitlement to rights.

The main difference between the Hobbesian and Lockean accounts of rights is that, for Locke, people carry their natural rights of life, liberty and property forward into political society. As a consequence, each citizen of the state has a correlative duty not to harm the life, liberty and property of others.

Rights as trumps

Whereas in the past any theory of rights could be based on an unquestioning acceptance of God's existence, this luxury is not enjoyed by present-day theorists. One corollary of this is that the term 'natural rights' has been dropped in favour of 'human rights'. In *Taking Rights Seriously* (1978), the American philosopher Ronald Dworkin (born 1931) uses the phrase 'human rights' in a stronger sense than legal rights, which he views as particular instantiations. Dworkin characterises 'rights as trumps', drawing on an analogy from card playing. Just as a trump card beats cards of other suits, so rights trump other political considerations.

Rights as side constraints

Robert Nozick is a modern philosopher who writes on the morality of rights, viewing them as side constraints which provide the moral limits to any political argument. Nozick, writing in *Anarchy, State and Utopia* (1974), diverges from Dworkin's view in that he does not see the need for rights to be overriding all the time, but instead sees rights as providing a special reason for action.

Freedom and the law

So far we have celebrated the importance of freedom and human rights, but sometimes liberty needs to be curtailed. The warrant for such restriction is studied in the philosophy of law. Legal systems the world over are engaged, on a daily basis, in making decisions as to the justifiability and the legitimacy of human behaviour. On some occasions, however, appalling injustices are committed in the name of political advantage, as a result of which innocent men, women and children are imprisoned, brutalised, tortured, executed or simply left to serve out their time in gaol. Likewise, there are occasions on which guilty individuals are allowed to slip through the fingers of the law, escaping entirely the consequences of their conduct. At both extremes, such pronounced injustice is deeply troubling because it makes clear to each citizen that our belief in the ability of the state to protect our security is, depending upon our luck, more or less misplaced. The question then arises as to why we should fulfil our **obligations** to the state when it cannot or does not wish to do as much for us.

In his important book *The Concept of Law* (1961), H. L. A. Hart (1907–1992) argues that it is not possible to criticise a law effectively unless we know the moral basis upon which it rests and whether or not this moral basis is popularly acceptable. Hart makes a connection between law and morality, which for many philosophers is absolutely crucial. Only when we know this, he goes on, can we assess the extent to which a law is sensible, sound and consistent with the other legal principles to which it relates. Ronald Dworkin, in *Taking Rights Seriously*, makes essentially the same point when he asks whether or not judges follow rules that make a clear connection between legal issues and moral principles, the alternative being that they regard these issues merely as matters of legal fact and strategy. The willingness and ability of the law and its representatives to bring about just outcomes in the matters with which they deal is obviously a desirable end. Where this is not the case, there may well be a perception that the terms of the social contract are not being honoured and this, in turn, may lead to loss of trust in the institutions of government, a breakdown in social and political consensus and the kinds of conflict with which the media make us familiar. A social contract is an unwritten agreement between citizen and state founded on mutual responsibility. Thus when the contract is not honoured, as in the case of some criminal act, the citizen's right can be retracted by the state.

The issue that underlies all debate as to the justifiability of specific laws, the extent to which they promote justice and the welfare and happiness of those upon whom they are imposed, has to do with a single question: Which is more important, freedom or order? It is equally true, however, that too much or too little of either of these can be a very bad thing indeed and may serve to achieve the exact opposite of what was originally intended. What is needed is for the law to embody principles of liability which make clear that it always seeks to strike a balance between two conflicting but equally important goals: the protection of the freedom of the individual and the control or prevention of criminality and law-breaking in all their forms.

The ultimate justification of any legal system is that it promotes order by defining the limits of what is considered tolerable behaviour within a particular community or society, and so creates the stability and security necessary for the prosperity and happiness of the people. In addition to defining the rights and freedoms of individual citizens in this way, the law also makes clear the duties of the citizen, both to other citizens and to the state. In other words, we may individually need to restrain some of our wishes and inclinations in order to remain within the bounds of acceptable behaviour as defined by the law of our society, but, in return for this willingness to conform, certain liberties will be guaranteed to us by those in authority, which will enhance the quality of our lives and allow us the freedom and security to pursue our own goals. This is the foundation of social contract theory.

The problem inherent in this position has to do with authority and the extent to which each of us feels that we are governed in a manner and on the basis of values and attitudes to which we feel able to give our **consent**. We are, in agreeing to conform to the requirements of the law, being asked to give up our freedom of choice. This is a fundamental liberty without which the entire issue of the extent to which we may be held to be responsible for what we do becomes once again a matter of real importance. Fundamental questions as to the nature of the relationship between the individual and the state are being raised here. These questions have to do with the acceptable limits of the power wielded over us by the institution and its system of laws.

Review questions

1 Describe and illustrate one instance when social welfare might conflict with natural rights.

2 Describe and illustrate two differences between positive and negative liberty.

Law

The law and *Leviathan* (1651)

Leviathan is the greatest political text written in the English language, and was published two years after the execution of Charles I. Growing out of Hobbes' preoccupation with the events leading up to the first English Civil War (1642–1647) and the concern felt throughout society with such matters as the encroaching powers of the monarchy, individual rights, universal suffrage, the treatment of minorities and the ownership of property, the book caused shock waves even among Hobbes' friends and led to his becoming known as the 'Beast of Malmesbury'.

Hobbes saw humans as being motivated primarily by self-interest coupled with a desire for power and self-preservation. He believed that in a state of nature, where there is no single leader to prevent it, the consequences of uncontrolled human behaviour were bound to be terrible. Each person would seek to dominate and manipulate others, taking their goods and property. As a consequence of this anarchic and violent condition, life would be driven by fear and the insatiability of animal appetite.

The state of nature, then, is a state of conflict and war, in which each person has a natural right to get what he can and keep what he gets. This situation conflicts totally with the sense possessed by all rational human beings that the ideal state in which to live must be one of peace, harmony and security. Hobbes argues that individual human rights must be given up in favour of the acceptance of the authority of a

Figure 5.1 *The original (1651) title page of Thomas Hobbes'* Leviathan

leader elected by majority vote and given the sanctions necessary to hold civil society together, which his contract with the people will begin to make possible. What is important about the nature of this contract, which Hobbes so clearly favours, is that its arbitrators must be just.

> **Task**
>
> Look at Figure 5.1, taken from *Leviathan*, and explain in your own words how it reflects the political views of Thomas Hobbes on the nature of a state.

In *Leviathan*, Hobbes develops a set of rules, which he describes as 'natural laws'. He uses this term to indicate that they are the necessary preconditions for the existence of any kind of settled, secure community, out of which might develop a politically controlled society, rather than one at the mercy of random historical events. Natural laws, for Hobbes, are the conditions needing to prevail if life is to avoid anarchy. In Chapters 14 and 15 of *Leviathan*, he lists nineteen such rules, all of which he believes need to be met by any society wishing to escape the state of nature, in which, he argues, human life will be spent in a state of continual conflict that will make it 'solitary, poor, nasty, brutish and short'. He argues in addition that of the three traditional forms of government, monarchy, democracy and aristocracy, the most effective for the enforcement of law is monarchy because 'in Monarchy, the private interest is the same with the publique'. He goes on to add that citizens owe allegiance to their monarch only so long as the ruler continues to protect them successfully. The monarch does not, in other words, rule by divine right but by contract only. According to Hobbes, political institutions are intrinsically neither good nor evil, but simply more or less successful in fulfilling their function, which is to ensure security, avoid anarchy and sustain a status quo.

Hobbes defends what he describes as the contract between natural persons (individuals expressing their own views independently) and the rights of Leviathan by arguing that, in giving up the right to individual self-government and accepting the authority of the monarch or the state, the citizens achieve protection from each other under the law and from their external enemies also. Thus, within this commonwealth, they achieve security and can live and work happily and without anxiety. For Hobbes, it is clear that, whatever the tyrannies of the state, they are unlikely to be worse than the chaos

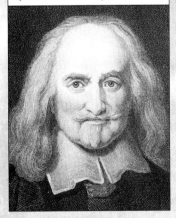

Thomas Hobbes
(1588–1679)

Thomas Hobbes was, in addition to being an eminent political philosopher, also a talented classicist, mathematician and logician. He was born in the Wiltshire town of Malmesbury, the son of a clergyman, though brought up by his uncle after his father was involved in a fight outside his church with another vicar. Young Hobbes was recognised as a clever child and sent to Magdalen College, Oxford, in 1603, where he excelled in logic and rejected the popular scholastic philosophy of his day. He pursued a career in teaching the aristocracy, and taught the future Charles II mathematics. Unlike John Locke, Hobbes supported the powers of the monarch during the English Civil War and defended the royal prerogative of Charles I. Indeed, he had to flee England for Paris in 1640 as he was a known Royalist, but soon returned and lived under protection. He died at the ripe old age of 91, his last scholarly project being translations of Homer's *Odyssey* and *Iliad* into English.

Significant works
The Elements of Law (1650)
Leviathan (1651)
Of Liberty and Necessity (1654)

and anarchy that prevail in a state of nature. The state has a duty to protect the people, and the people have a duty to the government on accepting Leviathan.

Natural rights have been given by the people to the monarch, who is the voice of Leviathan. But, because Hobbes sees Leviathan as what he refers to as an artificial person (as opposed to a real person), a commonwealth of citizens made up of all the individuals who have contracted to be governed in this way, then, he argues, the laws and rules that have to be enforced will, in practice, be enforced by the citizens upon themselves. It follows, therefore, that, however harsh the code of law of Leviathan may appear to be, the monarch can bring about no real injustice, since all of the powers and actions of the sovereign are, in fact, also those of the subjects themselves. One point stands out clearly from the complexities of Hobbes' arguments: that it is a great deal easier to attack individual instances of what we might regard as bad law than to oversee the creation of an integrated and comprehensive system of law.

The search for perfectly just law is not unlike a wild-goose chase. How is it possible to formulate a code to govern all the contingencies and individual variants likely to affect the lives of the many tens, hundreds and thousands of millions of people who, at any given time, are subject to the laws of the societies in which they live? In addition, how is it ever likely to be possible to achieve any kind of international agreement as to what constitutes just law between countries with widely differing attitudes to the rights of individuals, the nature of justice and the function of punishment?

Law, justice and morality

Laws are so formulated to protect society from unreasonable dangers, and to protect the rights of individuals in all of the many contexts of their lives. The argument may be phrased as follows:

1 Society consists of shared values.
2 Society also consists of physical structures.
3 Society can disintegrate morally as well as physically.
4 Society is entitled to protect itself from physical attack (as in the case of an invasion).

5 Therefore, society is entitled to protect itself from moral disintegration.
6 Society's power to protect itself from physical attack is limitless.
7 Therefore, society's power to protect itself from moral disintegration is also limitless.
8 Society is, therefore, entitled to make laws to protect its shared values.

The above argument is an argument from analogy, and it is not clear how one can detect moral disintegration. Some political philosophers assert that it may be measured according to whether inalienable rights, those rights that always stand, are being infringed. What rights an individual citizen has, however, may well be a subject of considerable disagreement within different societies, so that definitions of either natural or human rights may be less than easy to achieve. The same difficulty may arise in defining related terms such as 'duty', and in agreeing upon the nature and rationale of a just system of punishment.

One of the most famous expositions of justice occurs in Plato's *Republic*, where an answer is provided in the soul–state analogy (see chapter 7). Plato argues that justice in an individual involves the harmonious balance of reason over character and the emotions, and that a similar relationship should exist on a societal level. Alternative accounts of justice have nevertheless been provided, and the seminal work *A Theory of Justice* (1971) by the American philosopher John Rawls (1921–2002) provides good grazing for students seeking sustenance on this point. Let us examine the central tenets of Rawls' work:

1 *Retributive justice* – This is the idea of seeking to balance an injustice by rectifying the situation, or by regaining an equality that the injustice overturned. It is most simply summed up in the principle 'an eye for an eye, and a tooth for a tooth'. Rectification suggests taking from the offender and giving to the injured party, whereas retribution acknowledges that this is sometimes impossible (for example, if the victim is dead), but embodies the idea that an offence may 'cry out' for punishment, and

that the moral order is out of balance until this is administered.

2 *The veil of ignorance* – This is a metaphorical description of the barrier against using special concerns in order to assess principles of justice. Everyone is on an even playing field, and we are ignorant of whether that someone is a judge or a vagrant. It is as if all parties have to contract into basic social structures, defining the liberties that their society will allow and the economic structure it will recognise, but not knowing which role in the society they themselves will be allocated. Only if a social system can rationally be chosen or contracted into from this position does it satisfy the constraints of justice. In Rawls' theory, a social structure is just if and only if it could have been contracted into by hypothetical agents who have stripped away 'particular allegiances and interests, but retain basic human needs and dependencies'. The idea dramatises the impartiality that is implicit in the idea of justice, since in the original position nobody can indulge in special pleading or bias. Rawls calls the idea 'justice as fairness'.

3 *The difference principle* – This is the principle chosen by rational people from behind the veil of ignorance. The principle requires that social benefits and burdens are allocated in such a way as to make the position of the least well off as good as it can possibly be under the circumstances.

4 *The fairness principle* – Rawls argues first of all that there are in existence such things as natural rights. He then goes on to identify one of these natural rights as being the right to protect resources for future generations. The liberty of an individual may be legitimately constrained if their actions violate the future justice of institutions.

5 *Resourcism* – Rawls' account of justice has been labelled 'resourcist' in that it cites an individual's contribution to and benefit from resources as a criterion for justice. Examples of unjust acts might consist in an able-bodied person not fulfilling their natural capacity at work, or conversely if resources were not equally available to disabled citizens. Each individual's contribution may be calculated by multiplying the length of time worked by the person's natural endowment and by how hard that person works at the job (contribution = time × endowment × achievement). How hard a person works may be calculated by dividing their possible achievement by their actual achievement. A labourer suffering from ill health, perhaps brought about by substandard living conditions, would not be required to contribute as much as someone of good health and aptitude. To expect anything else would be unjust.

Task

What should the laws of a state say about:
- deviant sexual practices between consenting adults?
- the right to suicide?
- the right to take mind-altering drugs?

Research what the current law is on these subjects. Do you think it is adequate? What amendments would you make and why?

Punishment

When the law is broken a state can impose sanctions on the offender through punishment. Punishment is a type of right. It is the right awarded to authority to prohibit certain kinds of conduct and coerce those who contravene this prohibition. The following core features are present in most forms of punishment:

- The imposition of punishment must involve what is normally considered an unwelcome act, e.g. a fine.
- Punishment occurs due to an offence having been committed; even mistakes are infringements of a code, e.g. lack of due care when driving.
- Punishment is imposed on actual or supposed offenders.
- Punishment is intentionally administered by one or another person.
- Punishment is imposed and administered by the authority against which the offence was committed.

Despite their basic nature, the above points are not beyond contention, as one can cite exceptions to one or more. Vicarious punishment, for instance, occurs when someone is punished for another person's crime, and contravenes the third criterion. Accidental punishment proves an exception to the fourth, but by and large all five features hold.

One might, however, employ an anarchist argument and challenge the fact that governments have the right to punish at all. Anarchists hold that social control occurs naturally without the need for a state apparatus, as is the case when a troublesome member of a tribe is ostracised. The anarchist argument is a challenging one, and lays down the gauntlet for its opponents to justify the need for social control as exercised through specialised bodies such as the police or the judiciary.

One defence that has its origins in the political philosophy of John Locke, in his *Second Treatise on Civil Government* (1689), and which has been revivified by Robert Nozick in *Anarchy, State and Utopia* (1974), is the argument that the right to punish is one that every individual possesses in a state of nature. This is a popular theme in Westerns when the characters feel that a serious affront has occurred and believe that they are justified in rounding up a posse to gun down the perpetrator. No new rights emerge with the emergence of a specialised state structure, according to Nozick, and the rights of the individual are only transferred from a state of nature to their place in civilised society. Nevertheless, owing to some people's inability to succeed in achieving justice themselves and to the dangerous character of offenders, a minimal state is formed that has a specialised function (the legal system) and a concentration of force, namely the police and the armed services. For Nozick, as for Locke, institutions are necessary to ensure justice. For him, the fact that a group such as the judiciary have a monopoly over the execution of punishment is a price worth paying.

Underlying Nozick's defence of punishment is the utilitarian argument that punishment ensures social order and that social order is a non-exclusive public good. In other words, it is an advantage that everyone in society benefits from, like clean air. There are other defences of punishment, the most important of which are the argument from deterrence, the argument from retribution and the argument from reform.

The argument from deterrence

The function of deterrence is well illustrated in the case of preventing free-riding – that is, taking advantage of a benefit without paying for it. Deterrence is a coercive method of preventing free-riding. Imagine a train company that introduces conductors on all their trains and imposes a system of heavy fines in order to prevent as many people as possible from getting a free journey. The company's policy illustrates how deterrence works. It presumes that any rational though immoral individual will desist from such misconduct if the cost greatly exceeds the expected benefits. In such an instance, any rational person might consider, in addition to the personal inconvenience of having to pay a substantial fine, the possibility of the train company having to close down because it could not continue to afford the service with so few people paying. Deterrence is not necessary in the case of rational individuals with an internalised sense of justice, and is ineffective when people act irrationally, as in crimes of passion.

Deterrence works as a means to an end due to the relationship between:

- the rate of crime
- the severity of punishment
- the chance of conviction.

The rate of crime will decrease if either or both of the severity of punishment and chance of conviction increase. Likewise, if either or both decrease then the rate of crime will increase. The rate of crime is inversely proportional to the severity of punishment and chance of conviction. I would risk parking my van where I shouldn't if I knew that there were very few traffic wardens on duty and, even if I did get caught, all that would happen was they would be slightly sarcastic. If, however, I knew that town was crawling with traffic wardens and that the penalty for parking in the wrong place was that my van would be confiscated, then I would do the utmost to park in the right place.

Critics of deterrence theory argue that it is impossible to calculate an optimum for the severity of punishment or the chance of conviction, and that this leads to the dangerous state of affairs where punishment has no sense of proportionality. The argument from retribution attempts to offer a theory of punishment that does incorporate a notion of proportionality.

The argument from retribution

Stated formally, the argument from retribution runs as follows:

1 If person X inflicts harm H (H being the measure of harm inflicted)

2 Then person X may have harm H inflicted on him or her.

The above argument might arise out of institutional criteria or a conviction that the criminal deserves to be punished. Retribution differs from revenge in the following respects:

- Revenge may be carried out for a harm which is not a wrong.

- Revenge, unlike retribution, has no necessary limits.

- Revenge is carried out on someone else's behalf, whereas retribution is carried out in the name of an impersonal body such as the state.

- The agent taking revenge cannot be indifferent, whereas retribution has to be dispassionate.

- Revenge can take the form of harming an innocent party, whereas retribution must be directed at the perpetrator.

Thus retributive theorists conclude that retribution and revenge are not synonymous but different.

The argument from rehabilitation and reform

In essence, this is a utilitarian argument that states that the motivating force of punishment should be rehabilitation as opposed to vindication. Rehabilitation helps the perpetrator of a crime to live as a responsible citizen again and restores their rights. Punishment is seen as an instrumental good that has as its end the welfare of every individual in the state. The state

is not a conscious monster as personified in Plato's parable of the beast or as Hobbes' Leviathan, but is made up of particular citizens. Each of these citizens is to be viewed as a priority over the state apparatus. Reformists take the line that an amount of crime is an inevitable part of life, though every adult should take responsibility for their actions. Reform theorists assert that crime is generally committed by insecure people who need help. Punishment, however, has the risk of making such individuals even more insecure. Therefore, reform is the only acceptable justification for punishment.

Review question

Describe and illustrate two criticisms of the view that rehabilitation is the primary aim in punishment.

Authority

A state might think it necessary to limit the freedom of its citizens and implement laws, but with what authority? Much political philosophy is taken up with the notions of legitimate and illegitimate authority. The word 'authority' derives from the Latin *auctoritas*, which has the same root as *auctor* meaning 'author'. An author, like someone in authority, creates and presents ideas that necessitate a response in others. Definitions of the concept of 'authority' are all concerned with the means by which people are persuaded to do as they are told or, to put it more formally, the means by which power, of various sorts and in various contexts, is legitimised. The claim to authority alone is insufficient; there must be some persuasive content in the actions of government. This content usually has to do with either or both of two perceptions:

- Firstly, that those in authority over us have the knowledge, wisdom and experience necessary to ensure that they will govern well (authority on).

- Secondly, that those in authority have the power to coerce us into agreement (authority over).

You will have noticed that there is a difference here between the notion of 'being an authority' and 'being in authority'. This distinction is often made more precise through the terms *de facto* (authority on) and *de jure* (authority over).

In his essay on Bentham's philosophy, J. S. Mill identifies the relevant issues and clarifies them in three central questions: To what authority is it for the good of the people that they should be subject? How are they to be induced to obey that authority? And, by what means are the abuses of that authority to be checked? The third of Mill's questions is an interesting one, for two reasons. On the one hand, it leads him to the view that the people are best placed when the authority that governs them is that of a majority representative government; and, on the other, it leads him to recognise that government, even of this apparently democratic type, may nevertheless lead to injustices committed against individuals and minority groups.

What arises from this exploration of the tyranny of the majority is the question: Can the breaking of a law ever be justified? Can the breaking of a law ever be said to square with the utilitarian end of a thinker such as Mill? Some opponents of utilitarianism take the view that to overthrow an established government is, in itself, an evil act, since even a bad government is preferable to anarchy. You will recognise the Hobbesian view here, although he is by no means the only philosopher to argue it. It is easy to see, also, that even the most corrupt or incompetent government might well seek to use this argument to maintain its own position of privilege and power, regardless of the harm it might be doing to the interests of the people. The issue is that, whilst we are probably content to accept some measure of authority over our lives, there is not necessarily complete agreement as to how much, what type, or which areas of life we feel prepared to submit to the control of others. In other words, whilst we might feel completely happy to submit to authority in principle, we do not feel inclined to submit to a particular authority. Should we feel sufficiently strongly about this issue, it may lead us well beyond civil disobedience and towards revolution. A revolutionary, after all, may be said to be working to achieve the greatest happiness of the greatest number in the long term, even if, in the short term, much misery has to be endured.

Political authority

There are many accounts of the purposes of political authority (government). The following is a summary of the main standpoints:

- *To promote the will of God* – Governments represent the will of God or the gods on earth, and their purpose is to enact laws that reflect divine commandments and help to bring about divinely ordained goals.

- *To serve the interests of the most powerful* – Government is no more than organised domination designed to ensure that the wishes of the most powerful interests in society are carried out, regardless of the wishes of the majority, or of the suffering and injustice that might be caused.

- *To protect people from each other* – This view is the basis of what have become known as 'social contract' theories of government, which argue that people are generally unable to behave in a civilised and law-abiding way unless they are forced to do so by the existence and application of a rigorous system of laws. The purpose of government is to make and enforce laws that require people to treat each other in a relatively decent way, and so help to create a secure and lawful environment in which all of the activities we undertake and from which we achieve wealth and progress may proceed safely and profitably.

- *To promote the general welfare* – According to this theory, the role of government extends further than simply protecting people from harm, and includes also the creation of laws that contribute to the general happiness of the people. These laws may need to include legislation to protect people from exploitation by powerful interest groups in the business, industrial or financial worlds, and may also need to provide services in areas such as education, health and welfare.

- *To conserve a traditional order or culture* – This theory starts from the position that people already live in a lawful environment and already have a culture and a system of government, so that the central purpose of any specific government is seen as the preservation of this culture and social order, as well as of the people's sense of their own nationhood and identity. This is supposed to ensure the survival of the national heritage, but may conflict with individualism and freedom of choice or multiculturalism (the view that a plurality of viewpoints is to be preferred over one).

- *To develop and control the economy* – The role of government, according to Marx's analysis of capitalism, is to assist the development of ever-more sophisticated and effective ways to produce goods. The purpose of government is to promote the expansion of the forces of production.

- *To make people equal* – This theory rests on the notion that it is good and desirable for people to be as equal with one another as possible, on the basis that no one individual is intrinsically better or more valuable than any other. Supporters of this theory would expect their government to seek to remove all inequalities of property, status, wealth, achievement and power.

It is obvious that no political authority could be expected to serve all of these purposes simultaneously since many of them are contradictory and so would conflict with each other. Governments must, therefore, make a choice as to which purposes to follow with absolute conviction.

The source of a government's authority and legitimacy may stem from the notion of a divine right, for example the idea of the divine right of kings has been used for centuries to support and justify monarchies. If a people accepts and does not rebel against a government, then this government's authority is upheld by non-resistance. When a population accepts life under the domination of a dictator, that dictator's authority is legitimised by the passivity and resignation of the people. Legitimate government is also upheld by positive consent, which may be awarded in a variety of ways. One of the best known is enshrined in the American Declaration of Independence, from which the following is an (adapted) extract:

> That to secure these Rights, Governments are instituted among Men, deriving their just Powers from the Consent of the Governed, that whenever any Form of government becomes destructive of these Ends, it is the Right of the People to alter or to abolish it, and to institute new Government … organizing its powers in such Form, as to them shall seem most likely to effect their Safety and Happiness.

One particular aspect of government in this passage concerns the protection of natural rights, including the rights to life, liberty and the pursuit of happiness. These natural rights contribute to the general welfare of society. There are, however, problems with the concept of the 'general welfare'. These arise from differing definitions of exactly what may be said, in any society, to constitute the general welfare, and with the inevitable conflicts between the self-interests of individuals or groups and the paternalistic desire of the government to impose a policy upon all its citizens. This theory depends largely upon acceptance of the view that the individual does not always know what he or she wants and does not always know best. A paternalistic government – that is, one which actively intervenes in day-to-day affairs for the perceived benefits of its citizens – may be perceived to be either enlightened or totalitarian. What is certain is that exercising authority in this way may sometimes, for even the best of governments, mean governing without universal consent and will certainly mean, whether the policy is right or wrong, a degree of unpopularity.

What constitutes the 'best' form of political authority is, of course, quite another question, one that has been argued over by philosophers for centuries. This debate has been less concerned with the making of a final, clear decision than with examining the basis upon which any decision might be made. Conditions vary in different countries and at different historical moments, so that making absolute rules about the nature of 'good government' is clearly not a sensible way forward. The same is true with regard to the argument as to whether or not either its moral or its practical qualities should be given pride of place in evaluating a government's performance, since one of the skills of good government is precisely the recognition that neither can be said to dominate or be dominated by the other. Throughout our discussion we have portrayed the government as an agent of change and protection. The body that is affected by the actions of government is referred to as the state, and, just as there are different theories of government, so also are there varying understandings of what is meant by the 'state'.

Review questions

1 Describe and give illustrations of two examples of authority.

2 Describe and illustrate two instances when it might be considered right to break the law.

The state

Political philosophers work with different definitions and therefore understanding of what is meant by the 'state'. The following have been advanced as possible criteria for inclusion in a definition:

- *A territory of defined border* – One might discount a religious cult from being a state as there are no clearly defined borders despite the presence of leadership and sense of community.

- *A unified populace* – This describes the sense of belonging felt by the members of the state. The citizens of South Africa seem to have more of a shared concept of what it is to be a member of that state and have come to terms with their differences better than the rival and conflicting ethno-nationalisms of Israel and Northern Ireland, where the communities are still divided.

- *The presence of internal sanctions* – By 'internal sanctions' we mean general rules of conduct that enforce obedience and are dictated from within the community. In some tribal cultures, the tribal chief's rule is one of immediate edicts such as 'go to battle' or 'make winter camp'.

- *The presence of external sovereignty* – External sovereignty involves a degree of self-sufficiency. 'Sovereignty' means the possession of power over a piece of land or a body of people. Kenya under British colonial rule cannot be considered a state because the populace were not independent nor were they autonomous; instead they were answerable to a representative of the British government.

- *A centralised apparatus of power* – Feudal England does not count as a state either, as dukes and barons, whilst often in agreement with the monarch, possessed personal armies and could not, therefore, be classified as belonging to a society with a centralised apparatus of power.

Our definition of a state appears to be intimately bound up with the notions of authority and power. The state's borders are defined and its subjects are forced to behave in a certain way by the threat of violence or through non-violent forms of coercion such as a system of fines. In addition, there is a specific apparatus of security to enforce the law and an exclusivity that defines the citizens of the state and excludes others. Does the state so defined have the right to coerce its subjects? Such a question may be termed the problem of political legitimacy.

The problem of political legitimacy

1 A state is defined in terms of force and coercion.

2 Human beings are free.

3 The fundamental status of moral freedom involves being free from coercion.

4 If human beings are naturally free then there cannot be any legitimate form of coercion from any state.

This problem appears to blow out of the water any notion of a legitimate state due to the disparity evident in premise **3**. But a suggested solution surfaces in the form of consenting relations. One might reply that it is permissible for a state to coerce its subjects if these subjects have consented and agreed to such political activity. It is as if I am on a diet and have given you permission to snatch any cakes out of my hand if you observe me eating them in secret. Ordinarily this would be socially unacceptable conduct, but it is justified in this case as I have granted permission.

Such a proposed solution is not without flaws, however, as in practice it appears that many states would coerce their subjects anyway; thus any permission granted from the citizens is gratuitous. One philosopher who developed a detailed theory of the state was the Swiss thinker Jean-Jacques Rousseau.

Review question

Describe and illustrate two defining features of a state.

Rousseau's *Social Contract*

Rousseau is an acute but not a systematic thinker, and one can find loopholes as well as insights in his arguments. He begins *The Social Contract* (1762) with the famous declaration: 'Man is born free but is everywhere in chains'. However, he accepts that humans surrender their natural liberty to ensure stability. This security can be accomplished, argues Rousseau, by the surrender of all rights by every member of the community to the state. The state is thus a sovereign power and its will is the general will, not any particular will. As a sovereign, its control over an individual's property, person and family is absolute. Should an individual's will be in conflict with the sovereign authority, the individual must be 'forced to be free'. In the social contract, individuals gain their civil liberty, limited only by the general will, together with genuine property rights, equality and ennoblement, but lose their natural liberty. Natural liberty is the freedom to gain what one can and keep it, and is limited only by physical capacity and the resources available.

The general will

According to Rousseau, we all have our particular wills, but we do not surrender our power to implement our will in order to be subservient to someone else's will or the will of some class of people. To join in founding a state where such things go on is not a rational choice. We would make our position worse, because in a 'state of nature' we would be vulnerable to powerful individuals and groups without them having the assistance of the machinery of the state.

Jean-Jacques Rousseau (1712–1778)

Political philosophy cannot be divorced from its context, and it would be a mistake to transpose Rousseau's ideas of a society based on the general will onto a twenty-first-century democracy such as Britain. This Swiss philosopher was a Genevan by birth and probably had a similarly small city-state in mind when he wrote the *Social Contract*. During his lifetime Rousseau wrote, in addition to philosophy, the music entries in an encyclopaedia, a short opera that was performed for Louis XV in 1752, a novel and his autobiography. This account of his life, entitled *The Confessions*, records how he variously worked as a servant, engraver, music teacher, and secretary to the French ambassador. He is best known as a political philosopher, and his *Social Contract* and *On Education* led to calls for his arrest, after which he went on the run, staying for a while in Britain as a guest of David Hume. Rousseau's influence can be detected in much contemporary philosophy and, although ambiguous and vague in places, it nevertheless constitutes a heartfelt attempt at reconciling the emotional, passionate aspects of humanity with the rigid structures of society and civility.

Significant works
Discourse on the Origin and Foundation of Inequality among Mankind (1755)
The Social Contract (1762)

The only rational bargain we could make would be one (a) in which everyone surrenders all their power (natural rights) to the state or (b) in which the state carries out the general will, not the particular will of an individual or group of individuals (class).

The reason for condition (a) is as follows: if X and Y are in a state of nature and X is more powerful than Y, then if in a state they only forgo some of their rights and powers and retain others, then X still remains more powerful than Y and Y is at a disadvantage within the state, having, in proportional terms, lost more. In Marxist terms, the working class loses its power and is disadvantaged by the capitalists. The solution to this is that the state takes all power from everyone. Condition (b) attempts to define what an all-powerful state must do. It must do the general will, but in the name of the general will individuals within the state have rights that the state cannot interfere with. So long as the state simply carries out the general will, its liberty will be unfettered.

An act of the general will is one that does not serve the interest of a party or an individual. It is not equivalent to the majority will of the individuals that make up the state (termed 'the will of all'), nor is it equivalent to the will of any clique or elite. It may, however, be expressed by an elite: the guardians of Plato (see chapter 7), an enlightened despot, a democratic body or some sort of plebiscite are all potential means of voicing the general will. Rousseau's view is that rule by direct democracy is probably the best way of articulating the general will, but he recognises that the larger the state, the more likely it is that such a way of ruling will become impractical. As society moves away from direct to representative democracy, the more likely it will be that the government will be hijacked by political parties (groupings of particular wills).

Criticisms of Rousseau

There are some who allege that Rousseau's concept of the general will is an empty formula. A second charge is that even if the concept of a general will can be adequately explained, no one can be sure whether real state action concurs with it or not. Thus, for all practical purposes, a citizen cannot know whether the laws of a state reflect the general will or not. There is nothing that rules out the possibility of the general will coinciding with the desires of an elite, though of course it would not be the general will, for that reason.

Rousseau himself describes the general will as the sum of differences, implying that the general will is somehow a result of the compilation of particular wills. He appears not to mean that it is simply any old resolution that emerges from the clash, conflict and possible concurrence of individual wills. What he means may best be illustrated by criminal behaviour or tyrannical behaviour. The criminal or tyrant wills to act in a way that destabilises the system, and from which he profits. The criminal both steals and upholds property rights (for his property at least); the foolish tyrant both exploits his people and undermines his own authority and status in the process. Both are like people sawing off the branch they are sitting on or engaged in a game they cannot ultimately win. They must, in Rousseau's words, be 'compelled to be free', i.e. be prevented from diminishing their long-term opportunities. This means adhering to the general will, i.e. willing a state of affairs in which the exercise of their will is compatible with the exercise of the will of others. The general will is the reconciliation of the wills of each particular individual in a community.

Rousseau responds to his critics by formulating a series of tests for a legitimate act of the general will. They are as follows:

1 Is the act done simply to advantage one individual at the cost of another?
2 Does the act violate the principle that all citizens are worthy of equal consideration?
3 Is it what each citizen should wish for their long-term welfare?
4 Is it an act that every citizen can be persuaded to accept on the grounds of rational self-interest?

It seems to be the case that much debate over political policy is in fact concerned with whether these criteria are met – or whether the general will is being exercised.

Glossary

Autonomy: the freedom to exercise authority over oneself.

Coercion: the exercise of power by the issue of credible and substantial threats.

Common good: the overall, collective good of the members of a given community.

Consent: the agreement or compliance of individuals to political decisions made by the state.

Ideology: the abstract theories or ideals that lie behind and motivate the practical business of politics.

Justice: the procedure and administration of judgements in accordance with ethical guidelines, which often involve reward or punishment.

Left wing/right wing: 'left wing' describes a political standpoint that is closest to the progressive, liberal side of a party; 'right wing' describes a standpoint that is closer to the conservative, traditional side of a party.

Natural rights: the fundamental rights, for example to life, liberty and the pursuit of happiness, that we possess by virtue of being born.

Obligation: the social, legal or moral duty which entails following or avoiding a course of action.

Power: the ability possessed by an individual or institution to achieve something whether by right, by control or by influence.

State: any politically organised body of individuals in a defined territory who are involved in the exercise of authority.

Suggested reading

- Honderich, T. ed. (1989) *Punishment: The Supposed Justifications*, Oxford, Polity
  Classical collection of philosophical essays on punishment
- Kymlicka, W. (1995) *Contemporary Political Philosophy: An Introduction*, Oxford, Clarendon
  A philosophically astute introduction from various perspectives

- Raphael, D. D. (1990) *Problems of Political Philosophy*, London, Macmillan
  Thorough but slightly donnish analysis of the major themes
- Smith, A. (2001) *Political Philosophy*, Oxford, Polity
  Engaging guide to the subject and a useful set text
- Wolff, J. (1996) *An Introduction to Political Philosophy*, Oxford, OUP
  First port of call that offers a close textual analysis

Note

1 Mill argues this point on the opening page of the fourth chapter of *On Liberty*.

6 Philosophy of science

Experiment escorts us last –
His pungent company
Will not allow an Axiom
An Opportunity. (Emily Dickinson)

Aims

On completion of this chapter you should be able to:

- give an account of the role of observation, experiment and measurement in scientific method
- explain the problem of induction and attempted solutions
- outline the hypothetico-deductive method
- evaluate the reductionist account of scientific development
- evaluate the falsificationist account of scientific development
- evaluate Kuhn's notions of paradigm shifts and incommensurability
- understand the tensions between the realist and instrumentalist accounts of scientific knowledge
- appreciate the different theories concerning scientific laws
- appreciate the aims of science
- understand the difficulties surrounding the claim that science is objective
- outline the philosophical concerns over what should be researched
- give a critical account of the differences between natural and social science.

Philosophers are interested in science for the good reason that it appears to be an epistemic success story. Scientific explanations, theories and models predict what will happen with impressive regularity and can as a result be used for social benefit. This chapter is concerned with epistemological issues in the philosophy of science, and will only use technical examples to illustrate a philosophical point. Popular examples in the philosophy of science include the shift in astronomical perspective from the Ptolemaic model of the universe, which had the earth at its centre, to the Copernican view, which correctly positioned the sun at the centre of the solar system. Darwin's theory of evolution as set out in *The Origin of Species* (1859) is also focused on. Darwin held that animals evolve from simple to complex organisms through a process of natural selection. Thirdly, the advance from Newtonian

to Einsteinian physics in the twentieth century will be mentioned in passing, as it is a classic case of a shift in understanding. The mechanistic, nuts-and-bolts calculations of Newton were enhanced by Einstein's research into particles through the theories of relativity and quantum mechanics, which opened up a new continent of discovery. An acquaintance with the above subject areas is useful but not essential for what follows.

The scientific method

People trust the scientific method to supply factual rather than opinionated judgements, but what is it about the method of observation, experiment and theory that makes it reliable? This section will attempt to illustrate the relationship between these concepts, before focusing on the twin problems of **under-determination** and **over-determination**. As a rule, scientists divide themselves into experimentalists and theoreticians. The former group are assigned the task of finding specific items, while the latter interpret and analyse these findings in an attempt to provide an explanation. The interdependence of experiment and theory can be illustrated in the simple formula:

Theory $\longleftrightarrow$ Experiment

A set of experiments might yield an equation that implies the existence of a specific short-lived particle. It would then be the task of experimentalists to locate such a particle.

Despite the interplay of theory and practice, science is often misrepresented as being solely concerned with either one or the other. On the one hand there is the naïve assumption that scientists develop theories by directly reading results from the external world. This position ignores the all-important conceptual framework in which observations and measurements are set, and is as inaccurate a picture as 'straw-man rationalism', which asserts that knowledge can be obtained through reason alone with no recourse whatsoever to the phenomenal world. The recognition that such straw-man depictions are unwarranted yields the conclusion that when the process used by scientists to formulate **hypotheses** and observation are combined, a cognitive loop develops that includes both experience and reason. Figures 6.1a, 6.1b and 6.1c are offered as summations of what has been said so far.

This holistic picture buttresses the scientific method against sceptical assault. Sceptical

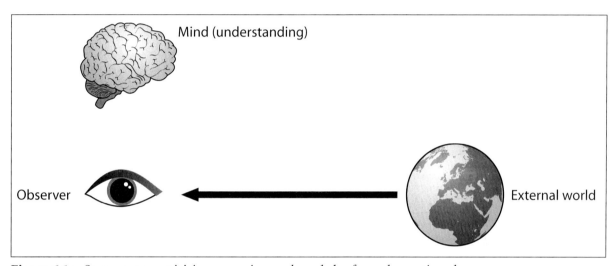

Figure 6.1a *Straw-man empiricism: we gain new knowledge from observation alone*

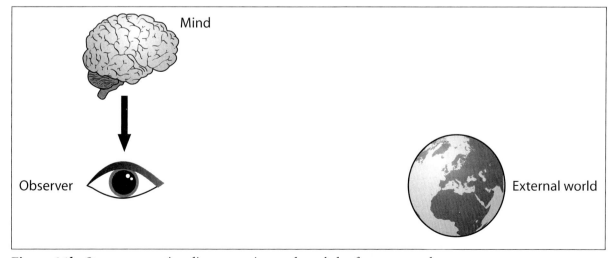

Figure 6.1b *Straw-man rationalism: we gain new knowledge from reason alone*

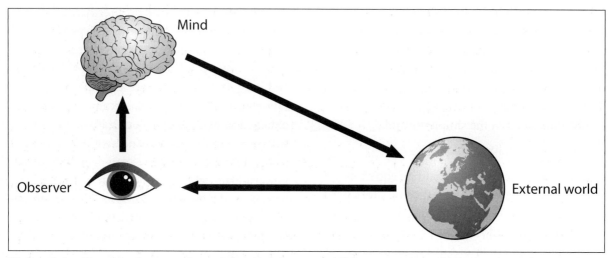

Figure 6.1c *Cognitive loop: we draw deductions from sense-data we receive, which constitutes knowledge of the external world*

arguments from illusion would easily burn straw-man empiricism but are quelled in the cognitive loop model, which gives recognition to the role of reason in judging between conflicting sense-data. Hence we realise that magic is trickery and mirage an illusion by working out that what our senses tell us is in fact impossible.

We now have a fairly robust picture of the scientific method. Over time, the phenomenal data will mature like a fine wine into vintage theories and distinct vineyards of scientific expertise. Observation sentences and measurements (such as volume, frequency and temperature) are first-order operations that, with sufficient accuracy, develop into inductive generalisations and theorems.

> **Task**
>
> Briefly describe a simple experiment from any of the mainstream sciences and explain the role of: hypothesis, observation and theory. Could the theory have been discovered without performing one or more experiments?

Problems with observation

Certain problems arise with the scientist's reliance on observation:

- Observations can never be devoid of theoretical assumptions, and assumptions may be fallacious.

- Wittgenstein draws our attention to the fact that, while public declarations of observation

are accessible, one can never gain knowledge of the personal perception itself. Hence two scientists might be stimulated by the same sense-data and report the same conclusion but be experiencing something very different.

- Observation is experience-laden as well as being theory-laden; thus an experienced entomologist will be able to differentiate and distinguish between various species of wasp, while the average person would not.

- More complex science relies more and more on aided observation in which instruments are used to mediate between the observer and what is observed. As the distance increases between perceiver and that which is perceived, so does the chance of error.

- Observation can only yield a 'for the most part' prediction, and any generalisation, by definition, is fallible and subject to change

A. F. Chalmers argues[1] that the above concerns are indeed valid, yet the scientific method can still claim to be the best we have. He describes it as 'objective yet fallible'. The process by which observations yield theories, which are tested and reappraised through experimentation, is a living, organic process. But if we are too relaxed about the above concerns, then the problem of under-determination presents a damaging prospect. Let us clarify the concepts of under-determination and over-determination.

Under-determination and over-determination

The term 'under-determination' is usually favoured in an analysis of the relationship between data and theory. The same set of data may be compatible with more than one theory. In this case the theory is said to be under-determined by data. One instance of this is found in the case of active transport between cells, where osmosis can be observed, but there are a number of conflicting biological theories as to why it is happening in this way.

A similar problem arises in the study of causality when one event may be in possession of more than one cause. In this case the term 'over-determination' is preferred. One might cite the example of an incestuous royal family in which one member is the monarch's cousin through more than one branch of the family tree. Another example might be if I were to poison my worst enemy and then shoot him. In both cases the event has multiple causes and is over-determined.

The problem of induction

Most scientific research involves some form of extrapolation – that is, the prediction of future patterns from the evidence that has already been accumulated. Yet, according to Hume, just because something has occurred in a certain way does not necessarily mean that it will always happen like that. The problem of **induction** was first noted by this eighteenth-century thinker, who admitted that we could establish facts through observation but challenged the view that because we have observed uniformity in nature in the past it necessarily means that such a pattern will prevail in the future. Such a sceptical argument asserts that any conclusion that is the product of inductive reasoning is not a genuine claim to knowledge, and is nothing more than guesswork. Let us begin by refining the problem of induction into three distinct strands before reviewing attempted solutions.

First, conservative inductivism is the title given to the view that we can predict future occurrences from reading sequences of reactions and events in the past. It is a process that most of us use to acquire knowledge and may be abbreviated as follows:

1 X has always been the case.
2 X will always be the case.

Hume noted that the above argument does not follow as a matter of logic, as there is no necessary entailment involved. Indeed, experience shows us, if nothing else, that we are often misguided in our assumptions. Having always supposed that swans were white, due to the colour of each bird that I have encountered, imagine my surprise on meeting the native black swans of Australia.

Second, revolutionary inductivism predicts change from past results, and may be summarised as follows:

1 X has always been the case.
2 But X will change in time.

The very existence of the revolutionary inductivist argument sheds sceptical doubt on the previous argument from conservative inductivism. There is clearly no good reason for us to accept one view rather than the other.

Third, 'the new problem of induction' as formulated by the American philosopher Nelson Goodman (1906–1998) rests on the contention that uniformity is language-dependent. To assert that the laws of nature are uniform is to make an interesting assertion and nothing more. In order to illustrate this point, Goodman invites us to consider the hypothesis:

Hypothesis 1: 'If all emeralds previously observed were green, then the next emerald will be green.'

This hypothesis encounters certain problems, as mentioned previously, but Goodman goes on to compare it with a second hypothesis:

Hypothesis 2: 'If all emeralds previously observed were grue, then the next emerald will be grue.'

In this statement the term 'grue' means 'green before 2005 and blue thereafter'. Given that Goodman is writing before 2005, inductivism would not be able to separate hypotheses 1 and 2, yet the predicates 'green' and 'grue' are clearly very different, and any successful claim to knowledge would have to specify the difference between them. According to Goodman, we only prefer hypothesis 1 because we rely so much on the inductive way of thinking, but, as Hume has shown, this way of thinking is misguided. How then can we get out of this frustrating malaise? Many attempted solutions have been offered; the most significant of these are discussed below.

Attempted solutions to the problems of induction

- *Induction justifies induction* – This argument draws our attention to the fact that induction has seemed to help us in the past and is, therefore, trustworthy for the present. A vicious circle is drawn by anyone who argues this line, as they use inductive reasoning to justify induction. The point that induction seems to have some value is, however, creditable.

- **Probabilism** – Some philosophers retreat to probability, admitting that induction is indeed a problem and that no scientific assertion is ever foolproof. But, despite our not being able to extrapolate from our past experience, we can nevertheless couch our observations in terms of likelihood. Thus one can assert that, given the fact that litmus paper has always turned red on contact with an acidic solution in the past, it has a greater likelihood to do so in the future, although we cannot be sure that it always will. This flies in the face of Hume's argument, which holds that patterns of past events do not make future ones more probable.

- *Habit versus addiction* – What then would Hume's response be? He believed that induction is a natural instinct or habit inherent in human beings, and that we cannot escape the urge to observe patterns and project them. Hume seeks to explain our instinct for induction but does not excuse it. Indeed, he believed that there was no such justification. A hardening of the Humean position, which comes close to a solution, is the argument that such an instinct is really an addiction and that we can't help ourselves from making inductive inferences. In this case we never have a choice between believing X, where belief X is the product of induction, over believing Y, where belief Y is the product of another method. If we do not have a choice then we cannot be justified in our decision-making, and hence the problem of induction is reduced to a

pseudo-problem as one cannot accuse us of making an ill-informed or illogical decision based on an absence of choice.

- *Pragmatic solution* – Advocates of the pragmatic solution to the problem of induction seek a weak form of justification. Induction, so the argument runs, can do as well as any other method of establishing scientific truth. If pragmatists find a successful method of truth-telling then they can start projecting future events through induction, using induction as a co-opting feature of truth. This theory moves into difficulties, however, when rival theories are equally successful in their predictions, as it does not make clear why induction is successful.

- *The hypothetico-deductive model* – Philosophers of science may draw on the hypothetico-deductive model of science to argue that science does not only use inductive methods. Indeed, induction is only used when one argues from predictions to hypotheses. For example, metals X, Y and Z have expanded when heated, therefore all metals will expand when heated. When the movement occurs in reverse and scientists make predictions from hypotheses, then the process is one of deduction, for example all metals expand when heated, therefore metal X will expand when heated. Popper's philosophy of science, discussed later in this chapter, may be cited as an example of how science can proceed with hypothesis and refutation alone, thus leaving no role for induction. Let us examine the hypothetico-deductive method in more detail.

The hypothetico-deductive method

Various formulations of the hypothetico-deductive method have been made by different philosophers of science, for example Popper, Carnap, Hempel and Quine. After considering a brief outline of the theory we shall examine Hempel's version, which is referred to as the 'covering law' or deductive-nomological method.

Science proceeds by a series of risks, tests and surprises. When scientists are required to offer an explanation, they need to use imaginative guesswork in order to suggest a bold hypothesis, i.e. a suggestion that awaits confirmation. Every hypothesis is tested for the accuracy of its predictions and for potentially devastating results. If the predictions when tested are not refuted then the explanation is awarded the status of a theory and can be said to have been accurately deduced. The scientist has deduced a conclusion from given premises. Consider the following example:

> Hypothesis: All metals expand when heated.
> Fact: Copper is a metal.
> Deduction: Therefore, copper expands when heated.

However, the philosopher of science Peter Lipton notes three problems with this apparently smooth process:

> The hypothetico-deductive method has three weaknesses. It neglects the context of discovery; it is too strict, discounting relevant evidence that is either not entailed by the hypothesis under investigation or not incompatible with it; and it is over-permissive, counting some irrelevant data as relevant.[2]

Thus, when applied to the above example referring to heating copper, there is first of all no account of how the hypothesis is discovered (presumably from experiment). Secondly, it discounts other evidence such as the fact that all material expands when heated. Thirdly, the hypothesis could be viewed as over-permissive as one might only be interested in investigating copper-based metals.

The deductive-nomological model

The covering-law or deductive-nomological model of explanation has been developed by Carl Hempel (1905–1997) in his work *The Philosophy of Natural Science*,[3] and may be summarised as follows:

> A good explanation is a deduction of the fact to be explained (the *explanandum*) from one or more premises (the *explanans*), which include at least one statement of law.

Thus any good explanation should take the following form:

1 Statement of fact ⎫
2 Statement of law ⎬ *explanans*
3 Explanation   *explanandum*

Let us flesh out this skeleton with an example:

1 The plunger of a container is depressed.
2 The pressure and volume of a gas are inversely proportional.
3 There is an increased pressure on the gas in the given container.

Implicit in this theory is the notion that there is a symmetrical relationship between explanation and prediction. Thus explanation is seen as prediction after the event, and prediction as an explanation before the event. But doesn't this thesis present an over-idealised model of explanations? Let us survey the criticisms.

Criticisms of the hypothetico-deductive method

*   *The 'why' regress* – Even when a good explanation is supplied, one can always play the childish game of asking 'Why?' A particularly malevolent critic might try to use this against the covering-law model of Hempel. The philosopher's reply would be that there is no reason to suppose the 'why' regress to be vicious. Like childish curiosity, it expresses an innocent search for more information.

*   *The common cause* – According to Hempel's theory, it appears that from the observation 'Whenever it rains, the barometer reading is low' we can deduce that 'When the barometer reading is low, there will be rainfall'. The barometer's behaviour, however, does not serve as an explanation for rain, and it is in fact the case that both events have a common cause, i.e. a drop in air pressure. This feature does not seem to be incorporated in the hypothetico-deductive method.

*   *The over-determination argument* – This criticism points to an inadequate analysis of cause and effect. Imagine a scenario in which a secret agent on a mission in a distant land has his water bottle poisoned by his worst enemy. However, on straying into the desert he gets eaten by a camel. The following prediction holds:

1 The spy has his water supply poisoned.
2 Anyone who has his water supply poisoned will die.

3 The spy will die in the desert.

The pre-emptive eating of the spy by the oddly carnivorous camel ruins the symmetry of Hempel's *explanans* and *explanandum*. We may hence criticise the covering-law model of explanation for not being able to cope with over-determined evidence.

We find in Hempel's theorising, however, someone who takes the role of science extremely seriously and who stresses the importance of:

- deductive truth
- simple observation
- the coherence of laws
- the role of prediction.

All of these features constitute a good explanation.

Review questions

1 Describe and illustrate two possible solutions to the problem of induction.

2 Describe and illustrate the hypothetico-deductive method in science.

Scientific development
Reductionism

The reductionist account of scientific development holds that the enterprise is essentially engaged in the business of reducing large-scale observations to a more fundamental, underlying level of information. An example of this process was mentioned at the beginning of this chapter, when the Newtonian conception of physics (macro-level) was compared to the Einsteinian one (micro-level).

The first reductionist argument may be termed the 'argument from logical atomism'. The ancient Greeks, following the theory of Leucippus and Democritus, were the first people to coin the term 'atom', meaning that which could not be divided into anything smaller, and although we now know that there are smaller particles in existence the word still carries a resonance of irreducibility. In the twentieth century, under the inspiration of Wittgenstein, scientifically trained philosophers from the Vienna Circle used the word 'atomism' to describe a linguistic theory that judged a proclamation meaningful if and only if it could either be reduced to easily tested observation

Carl Hempel
(1905–1997)

Carl Gustav Hempel was born in Orianenburg in Germany and began a distinguished career at the universities of Göttingen and Heidelberg as a student of mathematics, physics and logic. Hempel developed an interest in philosophy at this time and in particular in the philosophy of science and mathematical logic. Hempel took part in the first conference organised by the logical positivists in 1929 and was so impressed by the philosopher Rudolf Carnap (1891–1970) that he moved to Vienna, where he studied under the tutelage of Carnap and Schlick. During this period of his life, Hempel trained to become a secondary school teacher before his academic success on completion of his doctorate led to appointments in Belgium and subsequently in the American universities of Chicago, Princeton and Berkeley. Hempel eventually grew away from the logical positivist movement, although its influence can still be detected in his 'deductive-nomological model' of scientific explanation. Logical positivists argued that statements are to be classed as meaningful if and only if they are self-evidently true by definition or empirically verifiable. Hempel argued that a good explanation needs to be self-evident, i.e. deductive, and include an established scientific law founded on experience.

Significant work
The Philosophy of Natural Science (1966)

sentences or was a necessary truth. The job of philosophers of science, according to this position, was to test whether scientific statements could be reduced to observations or **protocol sentences** without loss of explanatory meaning. Since its genesis in the 1930s, this school of thought has suffered fatal wounds and gasped its last meaningful utterance. One central figure in its downfall was the Viennese philosopher Karl Popper (1902–1994), who proposed **falsificationism** as an alternative theory and pointed out that reductionism cannot itself be meaningfully reduced to bite-sized propositions that are easy to swallow. Another critic was W. V. O. Quine (1908–2000), who criticised reductionism in his paper 'Two Dogmas of Empiricism' (1951) for over-emphasising the linguistic nature of the reductive operation. For Quine, science was about experience and not a parlour game where observations are rewritten as 'observation sentences'. Quine believed that language is inseparable from experience and that one cannot judge observations such as 'Planet X orbits planet Y' in a neutral, purely semantic context.

The linguistic dimension to reductionism runs into severe difficulties, but exponents have sought solace in ontology, i.e. the philosophical study of existence. It is the job of science, so their argument runs, to reduce entities to what they really consist of and in so doing provide a convincing explanation. Hence one cannot talk with authority about temperature without knowing that what one is really describing is the measurement of the kinetic energy of molecules. Equally, one cannot convincingly analyse human behaviour without a knowledge of human psychology, which may be further reduced to neurophysiology, which in turn may be further reduced. Immediate problems begin to circle overhead.

Problems for reductionism
- How far ought reduction to proceed in its proper explanation? Are all scientists to become particle physicists?
- Some reduction is impractical and as far as we know impossible – for example, in the case of subatomic particles, which have a very mysterious nature indeed.

- What is being reduced exactly? Is it substance, property, meaning or description? When reduction has taken place, what sort of thing are we left with? The process seems to raise more questions than it answers.
- It is apparent that macro-level descriptions supply necessary information that is not present after reduction has taken place. If one wishes to account for the wood as a whole, one loses something in moving to an individual analysis of each tree.
- In **social sciences** such as psychology, many thinkers hold that, although thought is essentially physical, a great deal is lost in reductionist accounts.

Reductionists believe that it is the business of science to dispel popular myths and misconceptions based on a naive or commonsensical analysis of the intricacies of the universe. This seems a fair point, until one unearths the many examples of explanatory poverty after reduction has taken place. Reductionism contains the assumption that there is a scientific reality that can be revealed and discovered, while, as we will see from our exposition of scientific instrumentalism later in this chapter, many thinkers hold that access to such truths is impossible and that we can only use science as a predictive tool.

> **Task**
> Choose one example from any field of scientific enquiry and explain how one main theory can be reduced to more fundamental observations. What benefits do you think that this process may have?

Falsificationism
Falsificationism is a rival theory to reductionism in explaining the nature of scientific development. Falsificationism holds that hypotheses are meaningful if and only if they can be proved false. The most prominent falsificationist, Karl Popper, took Hume's problem of induction very seriously indeed, and concluded that we could not make universal generalisations from an acquaintance with a finite amount of data. For Popper, the goal of

science was not to find out which generalisations are true, but which were false. Hence his contribution to the philosophy of science is termed 'falsificationism'. Falsificationism differs from **verificationism** (the position adopted by Ayer, which states that statements are meaningful if they are able to be proved true or false) in a number of important respects, the most important of which is that falsification concerns the difference between science and non-science, the latter being called 'pseudo-science' or 'metaphysics' by Popper. The demarcation criterion used in Ayer's verificationism, in contrast, is between sense and nonsense. Popper is willing to accept that there are groups of claims concerning religion, metaphysics and psychology that, despite being unfalsifiable, have content and are to be considered meaningful. This contrasts with the views of Ayer, who believed that any statement that is neither tautological nor testable should be considered meaningless, Popper awarded the title of 'mystic status' to certain pronouncements, believing that they may be useful in the future to create theories that are falsifiable.

A further difference lies in Popper's rejection of observation as a reliable method to validate a scientific theory. In contrast to verificationists like Ayer, who believe that sense-data verifies scientific fact, Popper holds that observation is:

- fallible, i.e. subject to future correction; and
- theory-laden, i.e. shaped by our assumptions.

If sensory verification is flawed, then what demarcation criteria do falsificationists advance for us to judge between science and pseudo-science? The answer lies in what Popper, somewhat informally, calls a 'proper scientific attitude'. In practice, this involves scientists stating in advance what test outcomes would falsify the theory. Such honesty is lacking in pseudo-scientific theories that seem able to explain any eventuality. Popper cites the Marxist theory of history, Freudian psychoanalysis and Adlerian psychology as examples of bad science. Sigmund Freud (1856–1939) was the first thinker to introduce the term 'psychoanalysis'. It would be impossible to summarise his work in a few lines but suffice to say that he suggested an

'unconscious' level to human thought that had a destructive, sexual content and often conflicted with the regulating, 'conscious' level. Freud employed many methods to prove his theory, one being the interpretation of dreams. But how might one prove such an interpretation as 'In the symbolism of dreams, a house represents the female genitalia'? Propositions of this ilk did not pass Popper's test and rendered much psychoanalysis meaningless. Another example of 'bad science' in Popper's view were the theories of Karl Marx (see chapter 12). Marx was a philosopher of history and an economist who interpreted history as the struggle between classes. An example of this interpretation might include the statement: 'The literature of any age reflects how men and women have fought to free themselves from exploitation and oppression'. But would such a proposition pass Popper's falsificationist test? It could not, and as a consequence most Marxian philosophy, despite its claim to be a reputable scientific theory, was rejected as non-refutable pseudo-science. Adlerian psychology, which sought to explain human behaviour in terms of inferiority and superiority complexes, is singled out for the following special treatment:

> Once, in 1919, I reported to him a case which to me did not seem particularly Adlerian, but which he found no difficulty in analysing in terms of his theory of inferiority feelings, although he had not even seen the child. Slightly shocked, I asked him how he could be so sure. 'Because of my thousandfold experience', he replied; whereupon I could not help saying: 'And with this new case, I suppose, your experience has become thousand-and-one-fold'.[4]

Good science, in contrast, proceeds by a process of falsification rather than confirmation, where genuine scientists make predictions, the failure of which would falsify the theory. Let us compare astrophysics and astrology to illustrate this point. The seismic shift that occurred in the 1920s and 1930s from Newtonian to Einsteinian physics impressed Popper. He cited the example of Einstein as a paragon of good science. Einstein was bold and conjectural. Popper believed that real scientific progress stemmed from risk-taking and subsequent refinement. Einstein disagreed with Newton in believing that light was best conceived of as a wave that could be bent by gravity. As a test of this theory, he made certain conjectural pronouncements as to the position of the planets with respect to the sun. When Eddington carried out these experiments, Einstein's theory was proved correct, yet everyone was left with the clear idea that if the results had been different then the theory would have been proved false. In contrast, consider the following extract from a tabloid horoscope:

> Things are not going according to plan but then your plan had room for improvement. You are now presented with a better option. If you can accept this, you can enjoy a rewarding weekend. But can you accept it? Are you so attached to a particular fixed area that you see every variation as a threat? You are going where you need to be going. You are getting what you require and deserve.

For the falsificationist, the above mixture of vacuous hypotheses and indeterminable ramblings cannot be falsified and as such constitutes the very antithesis of Einsteinian physics.

Popper refers to good scientific theories as those which are 'highly corroborated', i.e. those which have survived many attempts at falsification. Indeed, Popper's account of scientific theories runs along Darwinian lines, with the fittest theory outpacing its rivals. It is important to note, however, that corroboration is an extremely thin notion for Popper, who believes that all scientific laws have zero probability. The canon of science is made up of theories awaiting falsification, not theories that have surpassed the process.

Karl Popper (1902–1994)

Karl Popper's prodigious intellectual talent and prolific philosophical writings put him in the forefront of important Jewish thinkers. This incredibly rich tradition covers many centuries, and includes eminent figures like Maimonides, Spinoza, Marx, Rosenzweig, Wittgenstein, Ayer, Berlin, Einstein and Derrida. Popper himself was born into an assimilated, Christianised family in the Austrian capital, where he worked for a while as a secondary school teacher and peripatetic philosopher. He became the Vienna Circle's most damning critic, drawing attention to the fact that the principle of verification did not support logical positivism, and replacing the tenet with his own principle of falsification. Popper fled Austria in the face of growing anti-Semitism and took up posts in New Zealand and the United Kingdom. He is greatly respected as 'the scientists' philosopher of science' with one Nobel prizewinner (Peter Medawar) describing him as 'incomparably the greatest philosopher of science that has ever been'. Popper showed incredible academic dedication and stamina throughout his life, reading voraciously and rarely taking time off. His classic work of political philosophy *The Open Society and Its Enemies* (1945) consisted of nearly eight hundred pages, and was redrafted twenty-two times before its final completion thousands of miles from a war-torn Europe, to which Popper returned to build up international recognition and a reputation as a tenacious debater. Indeed, he appeared to suffer from 'small man syndrome' in being overly assertive in discussions, and in addition had an inferiority complex about his looks, especially his prominent ears. He consoled himself with Swiss chocolate, which he adored.

Significant works
The Logic of Scientific Discovery (1935)
The Open Society and Its Enemies (1945)
Conjectures and Refutations (1962)

Task

Choose one example from the historical or economic theories of Marx and one example from the psychological theories of Freud and explain in your own words why Popper would disapprove of them.

'Popper don't preach': problems for falsificationism

One *prima facie* problem for the Popperian account is that most of the science we respect is judged as pseudo-science when his criteria are applied. Popper's rejection of foundationalism and empiricism also causes concern, and leaves many doubtful as to the credentials of the science advocated in his version of falsification. A Popperian philosopher may reply to these two lines of concern by first refining what is meant by a scientific theory. All scientific theories, it might be argued, are made up of a core content together with certain auxiliary hypotheses. We can protect the core content of scientific theories, to which we have awarded honour and credence, while at the same time refuting auxiliary theories that swim alongside. Indeed, it is difficult at this moment to see how the existence of DNA could ever be proved false while acknowledging that some refinements in our understanding could take place. The falsificationist responds to the above criticism by arguing that it is legitimate to blame auxiliary hypotheses when things aren't as they should be. This is technically known as the Duhem–Quine thesis.

The Duhem–Quine thesis

In condensed form, this argument holds that it is logical, when faced with recalcitrant data, to question auxiliary theories. Confusingly, Pierre Duhem (1861–1916) and Quine assert subtly different versions of the argument, with the former holding that any mature theory can be protected by adjusting auxiliaries, and the latter taking a stronger line in stating that any beliefs can be legitimately retained if we are prepared to adjust them. For this reason, some philosophers of science refer to the argument singularly as the 'Duhem thesis'. Whatever one ends up calling it, isn't this cheating? When does holding on to core content or one's favourite auxiliary hypothesis

become unreasonable? Popper replied by stating that any *ad hoc* retention is unwarranted. But a more substantial answer was supplied by Popper's colleague and former student Imre Lakatos.

Lakatos' suggestion

The Hungarian philosopher of science Imre Lakatos (1922–1974) responds to the problem of how to deal with anomalous results in otherwise trustworthy theories by drawing some important distinctions. He borrows the same descriptive apparatus as Popper, calling some beliefs 'hard-core theories' and others 'auxiliary assumptions'. But he further distinguishes between progressive and degenerative research programmes. A progressive research programme has problems yet seems to boast a scoreline of sufficient successes as well. A degenerative research programme, however, stores up more and more problems as the project progresses in time. This distinction between problem-generating and solution-generating properties helps Lakatos distinguish between theories such as Newton's predictions as to the behaviour of the planet Mercury in the face of contrary predictions from flat-earthism. As its name suggests, flat-earthism dissents from the view that the world we inhabit is a spherical body spinning in space. Instead, flat-earthers advance the theory that the earth is a disc of unknown size, with the North Pole at its centre, floating in a primordial ice floe. This view creates many difficulties: What lies beyond the ice? How are such phenomena as sunrise, sunset, satellite pictures, moon landings and lunar eclipses to be explained? Flat-earthism's recourse to talk of tricks, illusions and fakes is surely explanatorily impotent. Newtonian astronomy also had its problems, but there is a sufficiently sound body of material to allow the theory to persist. Lakatos' attempted retrieval of falsificationism is not, however, without its own criticisms:

- *The problem of more than one progressive theory* – Your theory might be classed as progressive, but what if a rival scientist's theory is progressing to a greater extent? One might say that your research project has been trumped.

- *The problem of inertia* – How is Lakatos to

classify a theory that appears to be neither progressing nor degenerating but standing still and with a degree of respectability? The philosopher does not seem to have a reply.

- *Hobson's choice* – Your theory might be consigned to the degenerative class, but, if it is the only answer, is it not rational to refer to it?

Despite the obvious problems with falsificationism as outlined above, it has since its first formulation captured the imagination of scientists, who see in it a realistic description of how science works.

Scientific revolutions

The terms 'scientific revolution' and 'paradigm shift' were coined by one of the most important figures in twentieth-century philosophy of science, Thomas Kuhn (1922–1996). A **paradigm** shift occurs when one starts to think about something in a completely different way. The classic example is the shift from a geocentric world view to a heliocentric one during the Copernican revolution in astronomy. Unlike the realism of Popper, Kuhn denied that science was an accumulative endeavour that gradually homed in on the truth. Yet Kuhn vehemently denied being an anti-rationalist or a relativist during his lifetime. Let us begin by exploring Kuhn's notion of the paradigm shift and his cyclical account of scientific progress.

Paradigm shifts

This term has become absurdly widespread, and has even infiltrated management speak. It has many different senses for Kuhn; indeed the philosopher uses the stock phrase in no less than twenty-two different senses throughout his works. The two main usages of 'paradigm shift' are when considering scientific endeavour as a matrix and when considering it as a model.

By 'disciplinary matrix' is meant a conceptual framework (such as Copernican astronomy or Darwinian evolutionary biology) in which a theory develops and is nurtured. Kuhn recognises that science is a social event and seeks to demonstrate the importance of scientists getting together to share definitions, hypotheses, values and commitments. Examples of shared

practice might be edifying adages such as 'Quantitative theories are better than qualitative' or 'Don't posit action at a distance, always posit intermediaries'. Scientists look to each other to help explain science and, through this sociological event, paradigm shifts are born.

There is also a secondary sense of a paradigm shift consisting in a model, i.e. an ideal answer, exemplar or pattern. A paradigm shift in this second sense is the perfect blueprint of how to solve a scientific problem. Exemplars unify the research community, help direct projects and are educational in instructing scientists as to how science should be carried out. An example might be Newton's solution to the problem of planetary motion as mentioned at the beginning of this chapter.

One comparison that Kuhn makes is between science and problem-solving, and is significant in a number of ways. First, it is significant because Kuhn believes there are answers to scientific problems in the same way crosswords have solutions. Second, there are implicit models to show scientists how to solve scientific problems in the same way that someone can explain the different techniques needed to be mastered in order to solve the clues of a cryptic crossword. Third, and worryingly for scientists, any failure to find a solution is a failure of technique on the part of the puzzle-solver, and invites a colleague to step in and do a better job.

The cycle of science

Kuhn believes that science has characteristic phases, which he terms 'normal science' and 'revolutionary science'. As normal science progresses in time, serious anomalies begin to accumulate, until its validity is cast in doubt and a revolution occurs. In the communities of scientists, people previously classed as renegades will become increasingly mainstream and the old guard become marginalised. The physicists Maxwell and Planck declared that scientific truth does not triumph by convincing its opponents and making them see the light, but rather because its opponents eventually die and a new generation grows up that is familiar with the new thinking. The process is shown in Figure 6.2.

Everything is vague and nebulous in the pre-

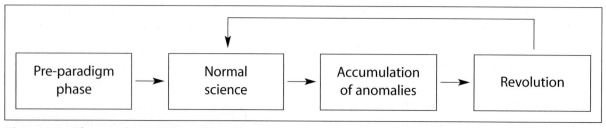

Figure 6.2 *The paradigm shift*

paradigmatic phase, as no agreed exemplars have been set. Take for instance the world of pre-Ptolemaic astronomy. Although the positions of some stars might have been recorded, no cumulative, academic endeavour had occurred. Ptolemy advanced a unified theory that the planets revolve around the earth, but this inevitably created problems. A crisis ensued, and Copernican astronomy took centre stage, yet present refinements show the Copernican view to be already incomplete in some respects. One might compare a scientific revolution to a political one, in that both involve an upheaval, a speedy change, disputes and wrangling between people in power, followed finally by a whole new standard of judgements.

> **Task**
>
> We have used the example of Ptolemaic astronomy giving way to the views of Copernicus. Can you think of another example of a paradigm shift in science?

Incommensurability

Kuhn did not believe that pre- and post-revolutionary science could never be compared, as is often thought. Instead, he believed that the two phases are **incommensurable**, i.e. they do not share a common measure. This milder notion requires unpacking, and may be summarised as follows:

- Pre- and post-revolutionary science have different standards for comparison. Different models contain different standards, which specify what counts as a good solution to a problem and what is worth investigating. If exemplars change, then standards change, which makes any comparison very difficult. A parallel may be drawn between different scientific paradigms and musical genres: how can one say that jazz is better than rock music?

- Pre- and post-revolutionary science provide different fields of data. Kuhn believes that data is theory-laden; in other words, scientific observations are affected by scientific beliefs. What you see depends on what you believe. Hence there is no neutral body of data to adjudicate as to the respective strengths of pre- and post-revolutionary science. In asserting that different data will be meaningful to different scientists, Kuhn comes close to relativism, a description that he tries to shake off.

- In Chapter 10 of Kuhn's *The Structure of Scientific Revolutions* (1970), the author makes the bold claim that pre- and post-revolutionary science occupy different worlds. A weak reading of the statement would interpret it as meaning that different theoretical commitments colour how the world appears to an observer. Yet in later works Kuhn describes himself as a Kantian in the sense that he is sceptical of an external world that isn't influenced by our perceptual capacities. Kant believed that our mind imposes categories such as space and time on the perceptual world. A strong reading, therefore, might interpret the above assertion as meaning that the world itself changes when our theories change!

- Pre- and post-revolutionary science harbour different meanings. In other words, there is no mental language into which the two theories can be translated. For Kuhn, the meanings of terms derive from their role in a scientific theory. The same term, therefore, might have a different meaning for different scientists. When Newton and Einstein write about 'mass' they may be referring to the same type of thing, but are viewing it from different perspectives, and no one can facilitate through a connecting language that is capable of comparing the two meanings. Newton is concerned with the readily observable aspects such as gravity, while Einstein considers mass on a micro-level through the quantum theory of space and time. Kuhn over-stresses this point, given that there is never a perfect translation without loss of meaning, yet we can still appreciate translated works of literature. To extend the above example, one might cite the correspondence principle as a means to bridge Newton's macro-conception of mass and Einstein's micro-conception: correspondence theory defines truth as that which corresponds to whatever is the case. In this example, both Newtonian and Einsteinian physics correspond to reality but on different levels. Further to this, the fact that Einstein's use of the term 'mass' has its origins in Newtonian physics, albeit as a rejection, surely means that there is some correspondence. One might describe Einstein's usage of 'mass' as

being a distant relative, shadowy counterpart or simulacrum of the Newtonian version.

The theme of incommensurability is one that gathers incremental power through the writings of Kuhn, and is an important concept to grasp in order to appreciate his significant contribution to this branch of philosophy.

Review questions

1 Describe and illustrate one argument in favour and one argument against the principle of falsification.

2 Describe and illustrate the view that science progresses through paradigm shifts.

The aims of science
Scientific realism

The philosophy of science is in essence a study in epistemology, and no greater question arises than whether scientific knowledge is a genuine claim to truth. In the next section two rival responses

Thomas Kuhn
(1922–1996)

Professor Thomas S. Kuhn was born in Cincinnati, Ohio, in the United States of America. He went on to become one of the best-known and most influential philosophers of science on the strength of his seminal work *The Structure of Scientific Revolutions* (1962), with over one million copies sold and multiple translations made. Thomas Kuhn read physics at Harvard University before completing his doctorate in 1949. He stayed on at Harvard to teach various courses in science before moving to other teaching posts at California, Berkeley, Princeton and the New York Institute for Humanities. It was while teaching an undergraduate course on science for humanities students at Harvard that inspiration struck for Kuhn's famous notion of paradigm shifts. On preparing a lecture one day, Kuhn referred to Aristotelian physics in order to present some background to modern theories and was struck by how incorrect Aristotle's conception of things like matter and motion was in comparison to Newton's. He realised that Aristotle's physics, rather than being a poor version of Newton's, was a very different yet complete way of thinking that was now obsolete. He famously termed these conceptual frameworks 'paradigms'. Kuhn argued that new paradigms cannot build on old ones but supplant previous theories through a process of scientific revolution. Kuhn's background may have been in physics but he also had research interests in the social and semantic side of science. He enjoyed many accolades throughout his life before succumbing to throat cancer in 1996.

Significant works
The Structure of Scientific Revolutions (1962)
The Road since Structure (1982)

will be compared: scientific realism and instrumentalism. Scientific realism is the view that tried and tested scientific theories inform us as to how the world really is. One might compare the relationship between science and truth to a map and the corresponding terrain. In the same way that a good map is detailed and accurate, so too a scientific theory specifies and pinpoints the right information. For realists, science is in the truth-telling business.

One argument used in favour of scientific realism has been called the argument from miracles. It attempts to reduce the rival standpoint to a position of absurdity by first pointing out that anti-realists never shirk the benefits of science but instead act as if they believe that science informs us about truths. Anyone who claims not to believe that science informs us about how things really are, yet proceeds to fly in an aeroplane, is clearly being hypocritical. If they really believed that science did not correspond to reality then they could not believe the predictions made by scientists. In such circumstances, they would have to excuse their actions with recourse to talk about a miracle occurring on every successful flight. The so-called argument from miracles, however, is founded on the fallacy that false theories cannot make true predictions. One can, with a clear philosophical conscience, adopt an anti-realist position and yet trust the benefits and successes yielded by modern science by arguing that, although the vast majority of false predictions are indeed the product of false theories, it is nevertheless possible that false theories yield true predictions by coincidence (while it cannot be the case that true theories yield false predictions). This may be summarised in tabular form as follows:

	True predictions	False predictions
True theories	All true theories give true predictions	No true theory gives false predictions
False theories	Some false theories give true predictions	Most false theories give false predictions

The pessimistic inductive argument

One argument used to challenge scientific realism is known as the pessimistic inductive argument and it may be set out as follows:

1 Most scientific theories to date have been falsified.
2 If past theories have turned out to be wrong, by simple induction we should predict that our current theories are also incorrect.

If this argument stands, then it is a fairly depressing thought that we are not standing on the firm foundations of scientific truth. This argument challenges the authority of science and scientific realism, questioning the accuracy of past, present and future maps. Pessimistic induction is right to the extent that the history of science is indeed a scrap-yard of failed notions. One may cite the archaic beliefs in the 'aether', bodily humours or phlogiston as choice examples. But is it not a strength of science to have exposed these failures for the fakes they are? The above anti-realist contention seems to use this strength against science, which is suspicious. Scientific realists point out that, given that the mechanism of science consists in eliminating falsehood, our history of obsolete theories is exactly the sort of history we should expect.

Approximate truth

In practice, few philosophers of science support a blasé 'mad-dog realism' that equates science with absolute truth. Rather, they believe that the discipline gives us approximate truth and talk in terms of the 'truth-likeness' or **verisimilitude** of a theory. A plausible scientific realism has to claim that our best-tested, empirically successful theories are approximately true and that later theories get closer to the truth than earlier ones. As we learnt in the earlier section on falsificationism, realists like Popper are even more understated in preferring the term 'highly corroborated'. Yet, is the notion of approximate truth a coherent one? Isn't truth like a light switch that can only be set in an 'on' or 'off' position rather than acting like a dimmer switch?

To accept the 'on–off' binary model of truth does not prohibit a realist from signing up to a notion of approximate truth if one were to argue that the truth of a theory depends on how many sentences included in the theory are true. This appears to solve the problem, but in reality leads to an infinite regress of credited truths and falsehoods, as any one truth may lead to an infinite number of related truths and related falsehoods. This particular conception of approximate truth seems too crude. One way to retrieve the lost thread of argumentation would be to couch the theory in general, comparative terms. Thus one is able to talk about theory X containing more truths and fewer falsehoods than theory Y.

Such a refinement, however, would not have worked in comparing bogus Ptolemaic astronomy with a fairly early version of Copernican astronomy as, despite the latter being true, it was still suffering the birth pangs of a new theory and contained many falsehoods. For example, Copernicus believed that planetary motion consisted in circles within circles rather than ellipses. As falsificationists have noted, all theories are born falsifiable! The neo-Popperian philosophers of science Graham Oddie and Ilkka Niiniluoto (born 1946) have attempted to save 'approximate truth theory' from technical disaster by focusing on the questions asked of rival theories rather than examining the verisimilitude of the theories themselves. In asking the right questions to both and comparing answers, it becomes clearer as to which theory fits reality.

The Lewisian theory of approximate truth

A refreshingly different theory of approximate truth has been formulated by David Lewis (1941–2001), the philosopher most associated with the notion of possible worlds. Lewis's scientific realism may be formulated as follows:

> A theory is approximately true if the actual world is somehow close to the set of possible worlds where the theory is literally (or strictly) true.

Each scientific theory is cast in the frame of a possible world, with the theory that approximates to truth being the one that describes the actual world (that is, the world we are enjoying at the moment) with the greatest accuracy, i.e. which is closest to it. The Lewisian idea of 'the closeness between worlds' as counting as a criterion for truth enables us to explain the gulf between scientific theory and practice. Consider the idealised theories of classical fluid mechanics in relation to how the world really is. The rarefied approach adopted by theoretical physicists has led to the joke that when three scientists – a mathematician, a computer scientist and a physicist – were asked to pick the winner of the Derby, the mathematician studied the form, the computer scientist wrote a program to work out possible winners, while the theoretical physicist began 'Let us begin by imagining a spherical horse in a vacuum'. Yet engineers and architects see in the abstract world of fluid mechanics some important facts that correspond or approximate to their subject matter. According to Lewis's version of approximate truth, one could graph the behaviour of the real world alongside that of rival scientific theories and through comparing their trajectories, in a number of cases, conclude that one theory is superior to others in its truth-tracking ability.

Instrumentalism

The anti-realist account of science, favoured by the school of philosophy known as logical positivism, is termed 'instrumentalism'. Instrumentalists deny that scientific theories aim at truth-telling and instead recommend that they should be viewed as useful instruments of prediction that make precise calculations about what we can observe. Like computers, science acts as a tool that processes observable inputs and produces observable outputs but does not in any respect seek to present a picture of reality. Indeed, the inner workings are so mysterious as to be best left alone. Where the analogy between scientific knowledge and information technology breaks down, however, is that in the case of computers there are experts who can provide an account of how computers work. Positivistic instrumentalism, as the theory is sometimes called, is championed by thinkers such as A. J. Ayer (see chapter 15) because:

- The account is based on verifiable observations.

- The account fits with the anti-realist theory of perception known as 'phenomenalism'. Phenomenalists believe that we can talk meaningfully only about the sense-data presented to us and hence avoid speculation about a metaphysical realm.

Science makes intelligent comments and predictions concerning the phenomenal world of sensory data, but renders the question 'Does the theory tell us how it really is?' as meaningless. Let us examine three instances from the history of the philosophy of science where instrumentalism seems to succeed over scientific realism.

Example 1: *Elan vital*

One strength of instrumentalism is that it seeks to separate bogus science from the genuine article by asking the question, 'Can the theory be directly verified?' Consider the notion of a mysterious life force or *élan vital*, prominent in nineteenth-century biology. Instrumentalists supply the apparatus to judge such a theory as meaningless owing to the fact that one cannot make any direct sensory contact with it, and it is unclear how such an abstruse notion helps us to understand biological phenomena more clearly. Yet can't the same criteria be applied in judging atoms and molecules as nonsensical? Instrumentalists would point out that, unlike accounts of vital forces, atomic theory has specifiable repercussions in things we can discern through observation. Realists suffer a certain embarrassment at having to acknowledge that there is a scientific reality despite our having an incomplete account of it.

Example 2: Newton versus Einstein

According to some accounts, Einstein's theories, which replaced conceptions in classical physics, were highly influenced by the positivistic instrumentalism of Ernst Mach (1838–1916), who rejected metaphysical notions of absolute space. An instrumentalist would view the famous supplanting of Newtonian physics by Einsteinian physics as the play-off between two rival instruments, the conclusion of which is that one has more utility than the other. They do not advocate a trashing of the former, less useful, box of predictive tricks, but warn that one needs to

be careful when using it in the future. Realists, contrariwise, tend towards a less sophisticated portrayal of one theory demolishing another by presenting a more accurate picture of reality.

Example 3: Heisenberg's uncertainty principle

We learn that quantum mechanics cannot be measured or surveyed with reference points outside itself. A quantum system has no determinate position or momentum until the observer interacts with it – for example, with reference to the position of an electron. This gives us Heisenberg's principle: the more accurately one measures a particle's momentum, the less one can know about its position. One attraction of the instrumentalist interpretation of science is that it can incorporate cases such as this, which realism would find it difficult to incorporate into its account. Yet there are issues that demonstrate weaknesses in the instrumentalist approach.

Problems for instrumentalism

In the practical sphere, the instrumentalist account of science relies on a sharp distinction between the theoretical and the observational. One might question whether it is as clear as instrumentalists suppose. Observational terms refer to that which is known to be true 'just by looking', whereas theoretical terms apply to that which requires more than observation. The questions crowd in: Where do we set this theoretical versus non-theoretical boundary? How small does something need to be before it is classified as non-observational? If I can observe something that you can't, are we to classify the item as observational or non-observational? If I am allowed to assist my observation with spectacles, can I rearrange the lenses as two over one eye, and class that which is viewed under a massively powerful optical microscope as non-theoretical? In this sense, instrumentalism is question-begging, but if sufficient answers are made to the above then these criticisms will be abated. One could, for example, draw the distinction between educated and non-educated observations. A lot of training is required to interpret scans, X-rays or what is 'seen' through an optical microscope. In this sense the results are more theory-laden than those perceived by the naked eye.

Secondly, as its name suggests, instrumentalism views science as an instrument, and it follows as a corollary that scientific knowledge is limited by the operational boundaries of such instruments. If I am, therefore, to define temperature as that which can be registered by a mercury thermometer, I am forced to acknowledge that there are no meaningful temperature readings lower than –38 degrees Fahrenheit, at which temperature mercury freezes, or higher than 674 degrees, at which it vaporises. This seems an extremely unsatisfactory state of affairs.

The third criticism that is noteworthy is the accusation that instrumentalism does not constitute a satisfactory explanation. Theory is confined to observation, and we are left with the trite registering of phenomena, accompanied by thin notions of explanation and causation. Instrumentalists, as a whole, adopt a Humean account of causation, and talk in terms of the constant conjunction of cause and effect rather than a logical or 'necessary' connection between these two events. Despite answering the 'how' questions that scientists pose, we are still left wondering why something is the case rather than an alternative.

Scientific knowledge

There are two main accounts of scientific knowledge that may be distinguished here: the causal account and the necessitarian account. Let us examine each in turn.

The causal account

The most famous causal account is advanced by Hume in his *Enquiries Concerning Human Understanding* (see chapter 10). For Hume, scientific knowledge amounts to nothing beyond a familiarity with the constant conjunctions between cause and effect as they arrange themselves in successive patterns of regularity and uniformity. Alternative causal accounts have been suggested in more recent years by philosophers of science such as David Lewis and

Peter Lipton. All causal accounts of scientific knowledge agree that a good explanation in any discipline cites the causal history of the event requiring explanation. By implication, a bad explanation is usually non-causal and falls into the traps of irrelevance, over-determination or a confusion between cause and effect. Lipton's version differs from the Lewisian account of causality in citing a more explicit contrast between appropriate causes. Take for instance a conundrum in biological science in which an evolutionary biologist seeks to answer the question 'Why did subspecies A develop striped markings on its wings whilst subspecies B did not?' Lipton's causal account would seek to explicitly cite a causal explanation in the actual history of subspecies B. Contrariwise, the Lewisian implicit-contrast model of causal explanation would invite us to imagine a possible world in which subspecies B did possess striped markings on its wings and, in comparing this possible world with the situation in the actual world where A is stripy, hope to delineate a fact that is different between these worlds and hence may be offered as a causal explanation. Whichever causal account is preferred, the philosopher has to deal with several criticisms.

Criticisms of the causal account

- Causation is not well understood, and this makes any causal account question-begging. If our explanation requires further expansion then we have cause for concern.

- Not all explanations are causal. Consider examples from mathematics and geometry that seem self-sufficient and, therefore, an exception to the causal account of scientific knowledge.

- Some causes are not explanatory. One might cite the cosmological theory of the big bang as an instance in which one causal explanation leaves many questions unanswered.

- Causality is an interest-relative affair. Causality, like any mode of explanation, is theory-laden, with scientists citing causes that suit their particular interests.

Can the necessitarian account fare any better?

The necessitarian account

The necessitarian account of scientific knowledge holds that a scientific explanation is one that has uncovered a scientific law. The notion of scientific law is intimately bound to philosophical conceptions of necessity, dealt with in the discussion of Hume's fork in chapter 1. The relation may be expressed formally as follows:

> It is a law of science that Fs are B if and only if it is necessarily the case that all Fs are B.

For the variables F and B, one might substitute 'fruit bat' and 'brown'; thus, the observation that all fruit bats are brown holds as a scientific law if and only if it can be proved that there is a necessary connection between being a fruit bat and being brown. The necessitarian account has been recapitulated by the philosopher David Armstrong (born 1926), who points out that the necessary connection in question concerns properties rather than the objects themselves. His refinement may be formulated as:

> It is a law of science that Fs are B if and only if there is a necessary connection between the properties F and B.

Scientific properties might include mass or force that go to give us scientific laws like Boyle's Law or Hooke's Law. In our fruit bat example, one would assert that there is something necessary that binds the properties of 'being a fruit bat' and 'brownness' together. This higher-order property is what is meant by 'necessity', and constitutes the grail quest for scientific research. There are a number of philosophical concepts floating about in the necessitarian account that require further critical attention:

- *The property of necessitation itself* – David Lewis criticises Armstrong's account by asserting that he misuses the term 'necessary' in an *ad hoc* way. Lewis declares wittily that 'something can't be classed as necessary just by being given the name "necessary" just as one can't have large biceps just by being called Armstrong'. Armstrong fails to explain why the mysterious property of necessitation is needed at all.

- *The notion of* a posteriori *necessity* – This is a problem for both Armstrong's and Lewis's

necessitarian accounts of scientific knowledge. Lewis reformulates the theory in his magnum opus *On the Plurality of Worlds* (1986), in which he distinguishes possible worlds from our actual world. For Lewis, possible worlds are no less real than the world we inhabit but, as each world is causally isolated from others, they occupy a very different existence. Anything is possible in possible worlds apart from that which is necessarily false. Thus we can imagine a talking fruit bat, but not a fruit bat that both 'is' and 'is not' with respect to itself. Such a notion of possible worlds has been met with an incredulous stare by critics of Lewis. Talking fruit bats, what will they think of next! But we shall grant Lewis this luxury in order to pursue the notion of *a posteriori* necessity. Any necessitarian account of scientific laws would have to explain why such laws could not have been different. Why, for instance, could force and mass not be related in a different way so as not to produce acceleration? One might even go so far as to conclude that the phrase 'necessary scientific law' is a straightforward logical contradiction, owing to the fact that a scientific law is one that has been drawn from careful consideration of this world and may indeed be different in any number of possible worlds. Necessitarians disagree, and hold that experiments are required in order to investigate the structure of the actual world and that such *a posteriori* investigations yield necessary truths. Along with Kripke, they cite as an example of an *a posteriori* necessary truth the statement 'Water is H_2O'. Clearly all laws of nature do not fall into the same category as the example 'Water is H_2O', which depends on naming a specific substance. Many scientific laws, such as Newton's laws of motion, supply exciting, new information. In such an instance no properties are present, and the scientific law seems removed from the categories of necessity and analyticity.

Science as explanations

Once we understand how and why something works, then we can turn it to practical benefits. Such knowledge requires explanation, however, and it is the business of scientists to explain why something works the way it does rather than another way. For this reason scientists are not crude empiricists, as the opening quotation from Emily Dickinson's poem might lead you to believe, but creative individuals who use their reason and intellect to solve problems. If the aim of science is to offer a good explanation, it is the purpose of the philosophy of science to consider what constitutes a good explanation. Various models of explanation have privileged different candidates such as truth, simplicity, coherence and prediction.

As we have discovered in our previous discussion concerning necessity, labelling a scientific theory or law as 'true' serves up a tangle of philosophical spaghetti. In practice, many scientists rely on metaphors to describe the whys and wherefores of their theories. The movement of gas, for example, might be likened to the motion of billiard balls. In this respect, scientific language comes close to religious language in a similar struggle with the limitations of everyday speech in attempting to describe the technical and complicated. It is important to note, with regard to truth, that although a good explanation should cite truths, not all truths count as explanations. There needs to be a relationship between the phenomena for which an explanation is sought and the actual explanation itself. Thus I cannot explain Fermat's last theorem by declaring that $7 \times 7 = 49$, despite the latter being true, as there is no obvious connection between the two explanations.

Any suggestion of simplicity seems incongruous, due to the complexities of scientific subject matter. The English scholastic philosopher William of Occam (c. 1300–1349) commended us not to needlessly complicate explanations in a caution which became known as Occam's Razor. His razor nevertheless allows complicated solutions to complicated dilemmas. We occasionally hear scientists and mathematicians talk about the beauty and elegance of a theory or proof. One feature of a good explanation that helps us to understand the aesthetic appeal of certain theories may be the fact that each element coheres to give a sense of symmetry or unification. But such a feature surely cannot be classed as an essential aim of scientific research.

One aspect that seems irreplaceable is prediction. Indeed, explanation and prediction have been viewed as different sides of the same coin, yet the facts that make up an explanation are often insufficient to make a scientific prediction. The relationship between the two is illustrated in Hempel's hypothetico-deductive model as outlined above.

Review questions

1 Describe and illustrate the realist view of scientific theory.
2 Describe and illustrate the instrumentalist view of scientific theory.

The objectivity of science

Scientific observations and reports lose their objective status when they presume aspects of the theory under examination. Yet this raises more fundamental questions as to whether scientific observation can ever escape being theory-laden and, if it can't, how we can ever establish which theory is correct. For many philosophers, scientific analysis is always theory-laden, but this in no way hinders the epistemic status of the enterprise. To explain this claim in more detail let us borrow an illustration from the influential work of the Yale philosopher Norwood Russell Hanson (1924–1967):

> Let us consider Johannes Kepler: imagine him on a hill watching the dawn. With him is Tycho Brahe. Kepler regarded the sun as fixed: it was the earth that moved. But Tycho followed Ptolemy and Aristotle in this much at least: the earth was fixed and all other celestial bodies moved around it. *Do Kepler and Tycho see the same thing in the east at dawn?*[5]

The scene is set where one geocentric theorist is admiring the sunrise next to a heliocentric theorist. The question posed is 'Do they see the same thing?' In time-honoured philosophical tradition, it is necessary to draw a distinction at this point, in this case between 'seeing as' and 'seeing that'. The former phrase refers to the theory-neutral, inter-subjective sense-data presented to the observers as the sun rises. It would consist of a round disc of orange light moving slowly upwards, a slight breeze and the gentle lilt of birdsong. Anyone awake at that hour and present on the hillside would experience the same phenomena. Yet if one were to ask Kepler and Tycho to record their experiences ('seeing that') in what philosophers of science call protocol or observation sentences, a different result ensues. This is due to the role played by the interpretative faculty, encountered in an earlier discussion in chapter 1 on representative realism. Thus the sun occurs as a representation in the minds of the observers, but it is then analysed, construed and interpreted by them. This is an inevitable and natural process, the result of which is a theory-laden observation, in which sense-data are placed in a specific conceptual framework. One might note that, even more than being inevitable, such a process is necessary, owing to the fact that many low-level observations are misguided. Consider the case of fire, which in reality consists of waves of tiny particles but which appears to the naked eye as light.

Jerry Fodor draws our attention to the problem-solving properties of perception and from this insight argues that perception cannot be theory-neutral. His argument runs as follows:

1 Phenomena can appear in an ambiguous form, for example, the Necker cube, the Müller-Lyer illusion or Schroder's (Escher's) staircase.

2 We do not perceive such phenomena ambiguously.

3 Our perceptual psychology solves the problem.

4 The problem is solved through an analysis of prior knowledge.

5 An interpretation of phenomena involving prior knowledge is theory-laden.

6 Therefore, perception is theory-laden.

In addition, there are very few scientific observations made today with the naked eye and without the use of specially designed instruments. We use telescopes to scan the planets, and microscopes to search out the intricacies of cellular activity. These complex instruments have clearly been constructed with a

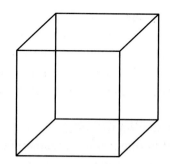

Figure 6.3a *The Necker cube*

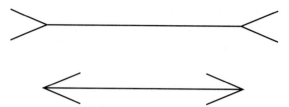

Figure 6.3b *The Müller-Lyer illusion*

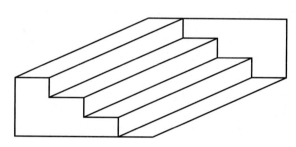

Figure 6.3c *Schroder's staircase*

function in mind, and represent certain assumptions about the nature of the world and how we receive sense-data. One might cite the existence of such specialised perceptual equipment as evidence that observation is theory-relative. Yet this conclusion does not weaken the standing of science if we acknowledge that every theory-laden observation statement is open to reappraisal and testing. Otto Neurath (1882–1945) of the Vienna Circle famously likened the scientific enterprise to a sailing vessel made of many parts, each cohesively attached to the other but subject to repair at any time. He described how scientists are like sailors who are forced to rebuild their ship on the high seas as there is no dry-dock in which to rest and select the best materials. If scientific observations were not theory-laden then this would create a dry-dock in which to repair the vessel but, as we have seen in our examination of the above arguments, observations are theory-laden. The fact that much of science is value-laden raises some important ethical concerns, and it is on these concerns that our attention will next be focused.

Scientific methodology

The main philosophical issue arising out of scientific methodology is whether there ought to be any constraint over what is researched. The Hammer House of Horror extreme of a mad scientist, with maniacal laugh and flask of smoking liquid, is thankfully a part of science fiction, not fact. Most scientists are at any rate thorough-going utilitarians in their motivation to create beneficial cures or labour-saving devices for the good of humanity. Yet how is the balance struck between knowledge, method and value in an arena of rapidly changing norms? Let us first examine the changing social setting for science:

- Whereas scientific knowledge was once owned by the whole scientific community, with increased privatisation spearheaded by the government since the Second World War, today the atmosphere is thick with intellectual property, patenting and copyright issues.

- Whereas scientific knowledge was readily available to the international community of scientists, scientific businesses may be reluctant to part with any information that would put their competitors at an economic advantage.

- Whereas most scientists were first and foremost academics, today many are also shareholders. This economic reality may impinge on their professional research interests.

- Whereas the process of sharing information led to scientific knowledge passing through a rigorous testing process, scientific judgements may be adversely affected by the interests of funding bodies.

- Whereas a balance was sought between funding for expensive and esoteric sciences such as particle physics or astronomy and technologically useful disciplines such as engineering, the latter subjects now attract more interest and investment as more universities enter partnership agreements with industry.

The changing social situation of science impinges directly on the creative work of the scientist and carries wider ethical implications. No clear distinction can be drawn between pure scientific knowledge and its social, technological application. Science is no less science when it is misused. Consider the example of the company who have patented the gene that is implicated in breast cancer and have subsequently refused to allow the availability of cheaper tests for potential risk. In today's climate, scientific discovery means profit for big businesses. Four philosophical positions are adopted by philosophers of science on the issue of research and business, and they are summarised below:

- *The radical left* – This position is militantly anti-industrialist and uses Marxian arguments in its renunciation of private ownership and the power of the investor. Science, according to the radical left, should primarily be a tool to help the poor.

- *The moderate left* – This standpoint champions the rights of minorities affected by the privatisation of science. There is an important sense of scientific duty to society that should be respected, though resulting profit from scientific development is also applauded.

- *The moderate right* – Philosophers of science adopting this standpoint draw our attention to the fact that industry has greatly benefited science and should be encouraged to sponsor university departments. The balance tips towards business and away from pure research and social concern, though they are acknowledged.

- *The radical right* – Authors such as Richard North in *Life on a Modern Planet* (1995) argue that industry and science working together increase the prosperity for everyone and assert that science that isn't in the profit-making game will not survive.

The economic interest in science has an important impact on the enterprise's direction, progress and results. Privatised science that is product-focused and technology-focused appears to be prioritised over academic or evolutionary science. Increased privatisation makes professional scrutiny more value-laden and public scrutiny more important.

In contrast to the scientific methodologies driven by public and private interest are the anarchistic views of the Austrian philosopher of science Paul Feyerabend (1924–1994), as set out in his major work *Against Method: Outline of an Anarchistic Theory of Knowledge* (1975). Feyerabend is the affable *bête noire* of the more conventional philosophies of science advanced in the writings of Popper, Kuhn and Hempel. Feyerabend taught in California where he cut an eccentric dash, often leaving lectures through the window to speed away in his red sports car. He believed that a detailed analysis of the history of science yielded the conclusion that there is no monolithic structure called 'scientific method' that produces results. Success, instead, depends a great deal on luck as well as inspiration. He advocates Millian arguments for the freedom of thought and discussion in research, believing that his philosophy of 'anything goes' will spread the net wider into uncharted seas and hence increase the probability that an important discovery will be made. Feyerabend's advocation extends to his belief that there is nothing special about science and that in an ideal, ideologically neutral society one should be at liberty to choose between scientific and non-scientific world views.

Note the tension between these accounts of scientific method. On the one hand science needs investment, which comes from conservative businesses that expect a return; on the other hand there is an argument that says that scientists should be allowed to play, and will as a consequence of this freedom generate discoveries that are in the long-term public interest.

Scientific research

Any reader familiar with Swift's classic work *Gulliver's Travels* may remember the eponymous hero's visit to the grand academy of Lagado (Part III, Chapter 5). In this chapter, the author takes a satirical swipe at scientists who are wasting valuable resources through apparently valueless research. On his tour of the five hundred laboratories, Gulliver witnesses one professor attempting to extract sunbeams from cucumbers,

another who is trying to reconstitute human excrement into its original foodstuff and a third who is attempting to cure a flatulent dog with a pair of bellows, killing the canine patient on the spot. As is the case with all satire, a serious point lies beneath the surrealism. Three questions are raised:

- How should funding for scientific research be allocated?
- How is the utility of scientific research to be determined?
- Where should the ethical parameters be drawn for scientific research?

There are both external and internal pressures at work in scientific research. External influences are exerted independently of the researcher and may include resource allocation, funding and the scope of the study itself. Internal influences range from the professional interests of the scientists to personal desires for prestige and success. In reality, there is a complex interplay between external and internal influences. An evolutionary biologist such as Richard Dawkins may hold the opinion that his discipline is more worthy and interesting than other, 'softer' sciences. Nevertheless, research into the adaptation of eyes and wings is unlikely to secure more funding than psychology, owing to the latter's utility in the market place. Psychological research can help companies sell more mobile phones!

The most seemingly esoteric branches of theoretical physics will thus find it more difficult to secure research grants. Yet does such an allocation of research funds maximise knowledge and utility? Consider Mill's argument in favour of the freedom of thought and discussion that the future uses or benefits of a given theory cannot be predicted, and thus all avenues of research should be pursued (see chapter 13). Theoretically, this philosophy has mileage, but, in practice, given finite time and resources, more mundane, practical benefits need to be envisaged. The utility of projects such as CERN in Switzerland, where research involves firing particles at high speeds over long distances to observe the reaction when they crash, has been questioned due to the considerable funding needed to keep the operation solvent (this runs into hundreds of millions of pounds). The project intends to locate the last, elusive Higgs particle, which if present at a particular energy would be the final piece of the jigsaw for the standard model of what matter consists of, but for which there is no decisive proof of its existence.

Scientific research is never value-free, but coloured by the interests of the academic community and dependent on the availability of funding. Personal interest can encroach so much as to lead to scientists deliberately falsifying results in order to gain the glory of sponsorship deals. Yet the falsification of results has had a long history, and it is important to remember that good science as well as bad science has fallen victim to such manipulation. Consider the antics of Mendel, who, in his genetic experiments on peas, deliberately falsified his results, which nevertheless turned out to be correct. The fact that some scientists are economical with the truth in how they report their research in the popular press has eroded trust in the impartiality of science by the general public. In Europe's recent BSE scandal, agricultural scientists were looked to as harbingers of truth before it was realised that many of their pronouncements were indecisive and manipulated by those relaying what was said. Peer reviewing in the scientific community, together with an increasingly educated and scientifically literate public, goes some way to restoring confidence in the research enterprise.

The hand-washing argument
Epistemological and ethical concerns meet in the problem of scientific research, when both issues are brought to a head in what may be conveniently termed the hand-washing argument. Some scientists assert that they should be given *carte blanche* to pursue their research irrespective of which direction it takes them in. Researchers, so the argument would run, can wash their hands of any future misuse, as if their research is misused then it is a matter for someone else's moral responsibility and not their own. The sociologist Robert Merton (born 1944) has criticised such an argument as being self-indulgently insular and coined the following epigram to sum up his views: 'Pure science is irresponsible'.

Merton cites the example of a scientist who, as part of the Nazi regime in Germany, designed an index system in the knowledge that it would be used to record the millions of people who were to be murdered. If an index card system is considered as too trivial a kind of knowledge not to make any difference if it was suppressed, Einstein's revelation that $E = mc^2$ constitutes so important a discovery as to necessitate that it be brought to our attention. Yet in his letter to Roosevelt of August 1939, the great physicist suggests a profound feeling of unease verging on culpability. Einstein realised the implications of his discovery in all their fullness: on the one hand the discovery meant cheap fuel, while on the other the possibility of weapons of mass destruction. Science cannot be separated from the world, which means that science cannot be separated from politics.

Task

Discuss the ethical issues raised in the above section. If the possibility exists that research may be used for ill, should it be undertaken? Draw up a pro and con sheet in response to this question. What bearing do these arguments have on the issues of:
- human cloning?
- GM food?
- the ethical issues surrounding using human beings in experiments?

What do you think the philosopher Jean-Jacques Rousseau had in mind when he advocated a return to ignorance?

Natural and social science

In this final section we will explore the main arguments for and against awarding the social sciences of psychology, sociology and economics the same status as physics, chemistry and biology. Many new disciplines have arrived on the curriculum claiming scientific credibility in their titles: sports science, computer science, domestic science. Indeed, one witticism runs that if the subject refers to itself as a science then it probably isn't. In our attempt to determine what is distinctly scientific in terms of methodology, theory formation and objectivity we may draw on some of the previous points outlined in our expositions of Hempel, Popper and Kuhn.

Is psychology a science? One description of the subject runs as follows:

> The scientific study of personality seeks to understand personality as one would the mechanism of a watch, the chemistry of life processes in a mammal or the spectrum of a remote star. That is to say, it aims at objective insights; at the capacity to predict and control what will happen next; and at the establishment of scientific laws of a perfectly general nature.[6]

A problem lies at the heart of this description, and it runs as follows:

1 Scientific method is concerned with objective insight, prediction and the establishment of laws.
2 Social sciences are concerned with the study of human nature.
3 The study of human nature is value-laden, involves many exceptions and cannot be determined.

It appears, therefore, that any attempt to view the study of human beings, their personalities and their social and economic relations in the same light as mechanics, biochemistry or astronomy is flawed. Such an assertion reflects a distinction drawn by two German philosophers of the nineteenth century, Wilhelm Dilthey (1833–1911) and Wilhelm Windelbrand (1848–1915), who separated what they termed the 'nomothetic' from the 'idiographic'. Whereas the former term refers to the establishment of principles and laws in the natural sciences, the latter description reflects the more intuitive and empathetic approach of the social sciences. Yet according to certain formal definitions of science the phrase 'social science' is seen as an oxymoron – that is, an apparent contradiction in terms, for example 'bitter-sweet' (or perhaps 'military intelligence' and 'sports personality'). Social scientists would not agree, however, and their complaint runs along the lines that economics, sociology and psychology are as grounded in experimentation and as successful in making predictions as the traditional disciplines. What are the best principles social sciences can come up with? Let us consider an example from each of the disciplines of economics, sociology and psychology.

Economics

When the economist Paul Samuelson was asked which economic theory would stand the test of time, he cited the principle of comparative advantage developed at the beginning of the nineteenth century by the English economist David Ricardo (1772–1823), who sought to modify Adam Smith's (1723–1790) theory of absolute advantage. Smith held that a country would always trade with goods that were produced more efficiently and as a surplus in comparison to other states. Ricardo held that a country always trades with commodities that are more efficiently produced in comparison with its general productivity. The law also holds in reverse, in that a country will always import goods that are produced less efficiently than the norm. Economic laws concerned with money and trade such as this principle appear scientifically credible; in contrast, any theory concerned with inflation or employment is likely to be tainted by political spin.

Sociology

The positivist sociologist Emile Durkheim (1858–1917) advanced what appears to be a scientific law in his thesis on suicide: someone who lacks social norms and social binding is more at risk than someone who feels integrated into a community. Thus the law would run as follows:

> A high level of social integration produces a low risk of suicide and a low level of social integration produces a high risk of suicide.

In the spirit of scientific enquiry, Durkheim sought to operationalise this thesis through a careful examination of the data and found that the theory fits. A level of subjective evaluation is inherent in the theory, however, as the verdict of suicide is pronounced on the advice of a coroner, who is required to interpret the case as he or she sees fit.

Psychology

Psychology prides itself on being able to test hypotheses regarding human behaviour, to derive predictions that can be tested and in many cases supply surprising results. One such hypothesis may be:

If you process information at a deeper level then you will remember it better.

This hypothesis can be tested by comparing how people remember different lists of words. Take two lists of words describing objects, invite people to remember the type case of the first list (upper or lower case), and ask them meaningful questions about the second list. In most cases the subjects will remember the items on the second list more effectively than the items on the first list, as they have semantically processed the second list of data rather than structurally processing the previous information, which is a more superficial activity. Many theories in psychology, however, fall prey to Popper's falsification principle as they seek to embrace too much evidence.

Task

Discuss the above principles taken from the disciplines of economics, sociology and psychology. Do they count as scientific laws? Write down as many arguments for and against their inclusion as time permits. Can you find any other examples from the social sciences of theories that carry scientific credibility?

One argument against the inclusion of the social sciences in the scientific canon is the claim that there are too many rival approaches to establish any degree of objectivity. Consider the range of approaches one can take when addressing an issue in psychology: behaviourist, psychodynamic, cognitive, biogenic, social-constructivist, feminist, evolutionary. Those defending psychology as a science argue that such disagreement creates a space for objective debate, but critics hold that it indicates a far more serious problem which affects all the social sciences, namely that no paradigm has been established. Social sciences seem in a pre-paradigmatic phase where no common, global consensus has been reached, and hence no social science can truly be classed as scientific. This is a little unfair, as although no dramatic conceptual shifts have occurred in psychology as they have

in physics there is nevertheless a detectable movement from the introspective to the cognitive-psychological approach.

Social scientists point to the fact that, like natural scientists, their research is empirical, systematic and concerned with how observations relate to abstract theory. Many point to Hempel's hypothetico-deductive model as providing a template for their work. In answer to the accusation that social science is value-laden, such apologists may point to the fact that natural science is not value-free either. Yet social science does appear more prone to subjective interpretation than its heavyweight cousins. Natural science itself can be manipulated by value-laden theorising, as in the case of Darwin's theory of evolution being used to legitimate free-market capitalism or harsh social policies.

Review question

Describe and illustrate two challenges to the objectivity of the social sciences.

Revision questions

1 Assess the claim that all scientific theories must be falsifiable.

2 Outline and illustrate the importance of any two of the following terms for the philosophy of science: observation, theory, experiment, proof, scientific law.

3 Evaluate the claim that science progresses in a series of paradigm shifts.

4 Outline and illustrate one argument in defence of scientific realism and one argument in defence of scientific instrumentalism.

5 Assess reductionism.

Discussion questions

- 'Scientific knowledge is not really knowledge as it is based upon induction.' Discuss.
- Is there a distinct scientific method or does anything go?
- Can science ever be value-free?
- What criteria should be used to decide which research should be resourced?
- What disciplines count as science and which as pseudo-science? How does philosophy relate to science?

Glossary

Falsificationism: the process by which a theory is accepted by the scientific community because it counts as a good explanation and has not as yet been proved incorrect.

Hypothesis: a suggested explanation for a given state of affairs that awaits justification.

Incommensurability: when two theories have no common measure or benchmark to make a comparison.

Induction: the intuition that a sequence or pattern will continue in the same form at any point in the future.

Over-determination: the problem that occurs when the exact cause for an event cannot be determined.

Paradigm: a conceptual framework in which observations and interpretations are arranged.

Probabilism: the method of justification that holds that a belief is justified if and only if it is more likely to be the case than not.

Protocol sentences: simple assertions that can easily be checked by observation.

Social science: any subject on the curriculum that looks at human beings through a supposedly scientific method.

Under-determination: the problem that occurs when the scientific evidence leads to more than one explanation.

Verificationism: the process by which a scientific theory is proved true through observational experiment.

Verisimilitude: the quality or attribute of carrying truth.

Suggested reading

- Bird, A. (1998) *Philosophy of Science*, London, UCL Press
  Useful introduction to all the main themes in the philosophy of science
- Chalmers, A. F. (1999) *What Is this Thing Called Science?* Buckingham, Open University Press
  The best introduction to the subject with useful chapters on observation, theory and experiment
- Kuhn, T. S. (1970) *The Structure of Scientific Revolutions*, Chicago, University of Chicago Press
  Primary source for those students wanting to know exactly what Kuhn said about paradigm shifts
- Papineau, D. (1995) 'Methodology' in Grayling, A. C. ed. *Philosophy: A Guide through the Subject*, Oxford, OUP
  A succinct and readable essay that introduces the central themes in a reliable way
- Popper, K. R. (2002) *The Logic of Scientific Discovery*, London, Routledge
  A classical but nonetheless accessible text on falsificationism and scientific procedure

Notes

[1] Chalmers A. F. (1999) *What Is this Thing Called Science?*, Buckingham, Open University Press, chs. 1–3.

[2] Lipton, P. (1991) *Inference to the Best Explanation*, London, Routledge, p. 99.

[3] Hempel, C. (1966) *The Philosophy of Natural Science*, New Jersey, Englewood Cliffs, chs. 5 and 6.

[4] Popper, K. (1963) *Conjectures and Refutations*, London, Routledge and Kegan Paul, p. 35.

[5] Hanson, N. (1958) *Patterns of Discovery*, Cambridge, CUP, ch. 1.

[6] Cattell, R. B. (1981) *Personality and Learning Theory*, vols. I and II, Springer.

PART 2 Thinkers

7 A commentary on Plato's *Republic*

Philosophy is the highest music. (Plato)

Aims

On completion of this chapter you should be able to:

- describe and evaluate Plato's views on morality
- describe and evaluate Plato's views on education and the status of philosophy
- describe and evaluate Plato's views on politics and what constitutes the ideal state
- describe and evaluate Plato's views on knowledge and its relationship to opinion
- understand and evaluate Plato's theory of forms and his notion of the form of the Good
- describe the many different ways in which Plato criticises Athenian democracy, such as the parables of the ship and the beast
- outline and explain the significance of the similes of the sun, the divided line and the cave.

Plato's *Republic* was written in around 375 BC and is a rich, accessible text worthy of its reputation. Like the layers of an onion, the **aesthetic**, pedagogic, ethical, political and epistemological aspects can be peeled away to reveal the work's metaphysical core in Part VII (Books V and VI). The breadth of such a pioneering approach prompted the Cambridge philosopher A. N. Whitehead (1861–1947) to remark that 'the history of Philosophy is a series of footnotes to Plato'.

The title of the dialogue is derived from the poor Latin translation 'republica' of the Greek *politeia*, which means 'ideal state'. Plato sketches out his philosophical fantasy-land, which is held to be a perfect pattern for societies to copy (472c; this and subsequent references correspond to the Stephanus numbers which appear in the margins of most translations of *The Republic*). Plato himself admits that such a thought experiment might cause amusement; nevertheless it has inspired subsequent thinkers, such as Aristotle, Augustine, Thomas More, George Orwell and Aldous Huxley, to follow in a similar vein by outlining utopias or dystopias of their own. (A utopia is an imaginary ideal world, while a dystopia is a satirical portrait of a world which one would not wish to inhabit.)

Plato's *Republic* is an example of an elenctic dialogue – that is, one in which a definition is raised, then exploded and supplanted by a more accurate version. Such supplanting is most obvious in Book I of the text, though one might say that the whole book has as its thrust the task of defining justice in opposition to the initial, cynical attempts advanced by the main characters: Polemarchus, Thrasymachus, Adeimantus and Glaucon. **Elenchus** is an element in the wider genre termed the **Socratic method**, which is a series of questions and answers between dialogue partners in order to establish certain truths. Such a method is still used in law and in counselling today. Plato learnt this technique from his mentor Socrates, who would engage in this mode of discourse with members of the public, sounding out and challenging their views about the important issues in life. Plato believed this to be the most authentic medium for philosophy to take place in and still invites us, after a period of over two thousand years, to join in the argument started in Cephalus' house following a religious festival.

The preliminary arguments

At the start of *The Republic* Socrates and a group of friends are spied from a distance returning from the festival of Bendis, the Thracian equivalent of Artemis (the Thracians were a tribe from northern Greece; Artemis was the Greek goddess of hunting, virginity and the moon). It is suggested[1] that this festival involved a horse race in which the competitors held torches in honour of the goddess. This is an appropriate image for the rest of the book, as Socrates and his dialogue partners embark on their hunt for enlightenment (432).

After some initial jousting (331c–e), in which three definitions of justice are raised and shot down, Thrasymachus attempts to pre-empt further discussions by forwarding his own definition that 'justice or right is simply what is in the interest of the stronger party'. Not to recognise this, he argues, is to engage in high-minded nonsense. He supports his contention by pointing out quite correctly that what counts as legitimate and legally acceptable behaviour in a society is often what those with the real power would wish to encourage; and similarly, what is deplored is often the kind of behaviour that in no way benefits them. Thrasymachus' conception of justice is entirely relativistic, and represents the views of the opposite school of thought to Platonism, known as **sophistry**. Sophists like Thrasymachus earned their keep as professional disputants, and were employed at parties to argue with the guests. Plato contrasts their peddling of opinion with the true knowledge sought by his ideal **philosopher-rulers**.

Plato disagrees with Thrasymachus' account of justice, since he believes that there is only one rationally defensible definition and attempts to sketch this out as a crude outline in the rest of *The Republic*. He does not think, as Thrasymachus does, that talking about justice is really a shorthand way of talking about power. However, in the context of *The Republic* he wishes to begin by setting out the counter-arguments to his position and refuting them. Some of the points he makes against Thrasymachus are poor, but he does have good arguments as well.

Socrates traps Thrasymachus into saying:

- That which counts as just must be simply what is in line with the laws of a given society. This is a position that any consistent relativist would normally take.

- Due to their own stupidity or due to mistakes, what is prescribed by law need not be in every case what the powerful in society would benefit from. Thrasymachus seems trapped into condoning two discrepant notions of justice.

Thrasymachus does not have a clear concept of what justice is, but he is firmly of the opinion that it does not pay and that the just man is misguided: 'it's merely supreme simplicity'. To this Socrates has three counter-arguments, which might carry some weight. First, that justice is an excellence or skill like flute-playing. Second, that even vagabonds develop some conception of respect or 'honour amongst themselves'. Third, that the just individual is always happier than the unjust. *Pro tem* (that is, for the present moment) this puts paid to Thrasymachus' assertions until his arguments are re-cast by Glaucon and Adeimantus. These characters point out that in many arguments for just behaviour (for example, in the first above) justice is recommended not for its own sake but for its consequence (358d). People are just, says Glaucon, 'out of fear of punishment' or 'in order to acquire a reputation'.

People are urged to be just for these sorts of pragmatic, prudential reasons, so that if you gave them the chance to get away with injustice with no loss of reputation, as in the legend of Gyges, they would see little reason for being just. In fact that is what the skilled operator tries to do, to be successfully unjust while not losing reputation or receiving punishment.

> ## Task
> Read the myth of Gyges (359d) and decide what you would do if you found the magic ring. Do you agree with Glaucon that no one would have such iron strength of will to resist getting up to mischief?

The debate so far is summed up by Adeimantus, who briefly argues the following:

- Most defences of moral or just behaviour are plainly inadequate.

- Justice is defended as a means to an end, not as something good in itself (like wisdom).
- If justice is to be defended, it must be in terms of some intrinsic benefit to an individual that unjust behaviour necessarily could not produce.

What has spoilt the argument is the fact that, while much has been said about justice, no genuine effort has been made to forge a real definition of it; a new tack is therefore taken. Surely, argues Plato, we can call both an individual and a society just. If we look closely at what justice amounts to in the case of a society and if we try to map out what a just society is, then we are in a good position to understand what a just individual is; that is to say, we would understand the generic features of justice.

The nature of an ideal society (Books III–IV)

Society, as defined in *The Republic*, is a collection of individuals, who combine out of self-interest and pool their skills in an efficient way with a clear division of labour. It is a self-subsistent unit with many types of craftspeople meeting their basic needs.

Plato argues that if a society's expectations rise beyond the satisfaction of its basic needs then three things happen:

1 A new form of the division of labour appears with an increase in service industries and middlemen of various sorts.
2 Wars will occur as societies compete to gratify their desires at the expense of their neighbours.
3 A society organised enough for war is going to require a strong state machinery and an army.

Plato
(c. 427–347 BC)

Like any hero of the ancient world, Plato's biography is a mixture of mythology and fact. There is little evidence for the belief that he was called Aristocles, acquiring the name Plato, meaning 'broad', on account of his wrestling ability and stature. Plato was a popular Athenian name, and it is likely that he was born in the city-state to aristocratic parents in 427 or 428 BC. Owing to a general disillusionment with the political intrigues of his relatives and associates, he decided on a career in philosophy instead of government, although his philosophy remained politically oriented, focusing on the question of what constitutes ideal leadership in a state.

It is impossible to comment accurately on Plato's personality or character, although one senses an austere, dutiful and loyal individual. Certainly, the fifty-five dialogues and twelve letters are shot through with a sense of injustice at the death of Socrates, his charismatic teacher and friend. Much of Plato's early life was lived under the shadow of the Peloponnesian War and Sparta's victory over Athens. Socrates' circle of friends provided counsel and conversation at a time of unrest. Socrates, having been charged with corrupting the youth of Athens by encouraging subversive thought and belief in one God rather than the Greek pantheon, was forced to drink hemlock in 399. This momentous event echoed and re-echoed through Plato's life and work. Plato's later years were devoted to teaching in the Academy outside Athens, which he founded in around 388 for the provision of literature, science, mathematics and metaphysics. Plato died at eighty years of age, never having married.

Significant works

Crito, Euthyphro, Gorgias, Hippias Major, Hippias Minor, The Laws, Meno, Phaedo, Protagoras, The Republic, Symposium, Theaetetus, Timaeus

A just state needs a properly regulated 'government'. However, it is not at all easy to see how this can be achieved. The tendency today would be to say that we must ensure that the government should reflect the will of the citizens and, customarily though not universally, this is thought to mean active participation on the part of the people, usually through elections. We tend to favour the process of democratic control, yet Plato rejects this solution: first, because any government can shape rather than reflect the popular will; second, because even if the popular will were attended to, the ordinary man is not an expert in government, and to give him real power flies in the face of the principle of specialisation on which civilised society is founded; third, because in any case no government can do what all the people want, only what a sizeable faction would appreciate.

Democracy, for Plato, is therefore:

- illusory
- impractical
- undesirable.

The alternative to democracy is to accept that all societies should have a ruling elite. A just society must have the right sort of elite. Plato's solution to the problem of developing a trained, efficient and just government is to suggest government by a ruling elite who are:

- constitutionally suited by birth to rule;
- educated in the appropriate attitudes we would hope rulers to have;
- debarred by law from exploiting their power unjustly.

Task

Read *The Republic* (368d–374e), making a list of all the occupations that are mentioned in this section. Discuss whether you would like to be a citizen in Plato's ideal state. What advantages and disadvantages lie in living as a philosopher-ruler, an auxiliary or a craftsperson?

Selection by birth

Plato holds that many of the features we would hope a good ruler should possess, such as a courageous temperament, may be more in

evidence in certain groups. Clearly, there is an inherited element in most groups. Thus he makes his **guardians** a caste, and suggests a prohibition on inter-class breeding. However, such a system of class purity is not an end in itself, for it is conceivable that guardians may produce offspring physically or psychologically unsuited for the task of ruling and defending the state. Plato also advocates recruitment into the ruling class from the lower orders when talent is obvious. He proposes a creation myth (415a) to legitimate this process of meritocratic selection – that is, selection by merit – within an **oligarchic** framework (an oligarchy is a society that is structured according to wealth and status). The myth of metals helps people to accept the elite status of the guardian class who 'were fashioned and reared … in the depths of the earth, the earth herself, their mother, brought them up … so now they must think of the land in which they live as their mother and protect her' (414d–e). It is held that this guardian class is made of gold, the auxiliaries of silver and the productive class of bronze. Clearly Plato does not believe that this is literally true, but he probably saw some truth in the myth as illustrating the variety in people's aptitudes. As Plato's suggested eugenics (selective breeding) programme involves infanticide it has led, not surprisingly, to criticism.

Education

Plato often compares the guardians (this term can sometimes refer to the auxiliaries or the philosopher-rulers, depending on context) to watchdogs, yet even the best-bred dog can misbehave without adequate training, so education holds the key to the problem of how to create a just elite. Plato favours both studies that train the mind, such as mathematics, and activities that produce a physically robust group, with a balance being achieved between mental and physical training. In addition he lays the greatest stress on ideological training, without which the abilities developed through education can be misused. Socially corrupting, moral and theological ideas are not to be disseminated, and a purity of outlook must be cultivated. According to him, this will involve wholesale censorship of the arts, but it is crucial if the minds of the rulers are to be 'formed' in the right way. While Plato, in an apparent spirit of equality, allows both male and female philosopher-rulers, recent scholarship[2] has argued that in practice the guardians would almost certainly be male owing to the requisite education and the emphasis on masculine virtues such as 'spirit' throughout the book.

Once the education is complete within this closed society then the ruling class, equipped with the right values, will perform their role justly. In turn, the ordinary citizens will not need to be constantly restrained from undesirable behaviour by legislation, but may form their own rules, being made by education into decent members of the community. With a proper educational system in place the state may withdraw, only interfering in those areas of life where it is competent to do so (for example, not interfering in economic affairs, family matters or religion).

Despite the alleged effectiveness of the education system, Plato proposes that the guardians should be prohibited by law from the acquisition and inheritance of wealth. They are to live the bulk of their life in barracks with neither the comforts of family life nor personal property. This limitation, as Plato recognises, will have little effect if guardians themselves are not educated into accepting it, for a powerful elite can always change a constitution.

Platonic epistemology (Books V–VII)

Art-lovers and philosophers (472–477)

This section of the text is concerned with the nature of philosophical knowledge. It arises when Plato arrives at the conclusion that philosophers should rule. This immediately raises the question of the exact character of the philosopher's expertise. As a preliminary, the philosopher is defined as 'the man who is ready to taste every branch of learning, is glad to learn and never satisfied'. This is, however, imprecise, since the philosopher is not mindlessly interested in the minutiae of learning, motivated by empty-headed curiosity, but wishes to grasp the essential nature of what is understood. Those individuals who run around the countryside in order to attend every lecture or art display are likened to gluttons

and contrasted to the more discerning philosophers who have the tastes of a gourmet.

Thus a philosopher is primarily motivated to find out:

- *not* what things are beautiful *but* what beauty essentially is;
- *not* what acts happen to be good acts *but* what goodness essentially is;
- *not* what physical features the material world has *but* what the entire system of nature is;
- *not* what mathematical equations are correct *but* what any number system is.

Plato says that the philosopher is interested in the **forms** that all particular things embody, not in particular and ephemeral details. A better way to express this notion today would be to say that Plato is interested in the general character of claims to knowledge – that is, what type of claim is being made whenever an aesthetic, moral, scientific or mathematical judgement is passed.

A corollary of Plato's approach is that practising literary critics, moral agents, scientists or mathematicians, in so far as they are not philosophers, have an inadequate grasp of what they are saying. To give just one example: the art critic declaring an El Greco to be beautiful cannot properly understand what he is saying unless he can give an account of what beauty is. For Plato, this means he is a 'man of opinion'. This is a slightly misleading description, since by 'opinion' we normally mean a statement that we cannot adequately justify, whereas what Plato appears to be saying is that the chief defect of everyday knowledge is that we cannot adequately clarify or explain it. It follows that what you cannot clarify you cannot perfectly justify.

Knowledge and opinion (477–480)

Plato identifies three epistemological categories:

- ignorance
- opinion
- knowledge.

He bases this categorisation on:

- the degree of understanding and rational justification present
- the content of this understanding.

The man of opinion concerns himself with this transitory world of flux and change. The philosopher as possessor of knowledge is concerned with the essences or forms of things. Plato often talks as though this is a matter of being in touch with different realms: one ideal and permanent, the other transitory and imperfect. They are called respectively the world of forms and the world of particulars. Philosophers are initially portrayed, not as stargazers looking over the heads of ordinary men, but rather 'those whose hearts are fixed on the true being of each thing'. According to Plato, the philosopher is not someone deprived of ordinary everyday knowledge or opinion, but someone who possesses deeper insight into it. Plato argues that if we know something, then whatever we know can be said to truly exist if indeed what we know is true. If we have got it wrong and what we think we know is not true, then our belief is to be classed as opinion and not knowledge. Knowledge is infallible, attuned to what is real and unchanging. This section of Book VII might seem heavy-going, but read it carefully, substituting 'exists' for 'is' to gain an insight into what the author takes knowledge to be.

The logical structure of Plato's epistemological argument in defence of philosopher-rulers is as follows:

1 Philosophers are concerned with universals; non-philosophers are concerned with particulars (475a–476d).

2 Philosophers have knowledge; non-philosophers only have belief (476d).

3 Knowledge is of what is;[3] ignorance (non-knowledge) is of what is not (476e–477a).

4 Whatever is between what is and what is not must be the object of a faculty between knowledge and ignorance (477a–478d).

5 Belief has a different object from knowledge and ignorance and is between them (477b–478d).

6 Particulars are between what is and what is not (478e–479d).

7 Therefore, philosophers (concerned with universals) have knowledge, non-philosophers (concerned with particulars) have belief (479d–480a).

8 Rulers should possess knowledge rather than belief. Therefore, philosophers should rule (484b–484d).

Plato's epistemology works on a single contour, defining belief as a familiarity with contingent, spatio-temporal objects and citing belief as being half-way between necessity and nonsense. It is not clear, however, whether this sort of knowledge is accessible or how useful it would be in the day-to-day business of government.

Review question

Describe two features of knowledge which, for Plato, distinguish it from opinion.

Qualities required in a philosopher-ruler (484–487)

Plato argues in Book VII (484–487) that because the philosopher pursues eternal realities he or she will be wise, truthful, self-controlled, not grasping about money, brave, generous, just and possessed of an excellent memory. In addition to possessing specialist knowledge of the forms, philosopher-rulers are well balanced, civilised, and not afraid of death, as this merely marks a return to the heavenly realm of pure essences. Later in the text (503c–d), Plato reminds us that a philosopher-ruler should be able to combine intelligence and flair with reliability. Such a ruler is contrasted with three other types of individual: the first is described as bad but clever (519a), the second is uneducated (519b) and the third is an overly academic type who lives purely for intellectual pursuits (519c). We may deduce that the ideal philosopher-ruler is morally upstanding and knowledgeable but with a practical bearing towards the art of government. This, however, is a rather ambitious portrayal of a human being.

The twentieth-century Austrian philosopher Karl Popper criticises Plato's conception of the ideal ruler in *The Open Society and Its Enemies* (1945). According to Popper, Plato poses the wrong question in asking 'Who should rule?'; the question that should be addressed is 'How can we control our rulers?' In other words, what institutional checks and balances can we put in the way of their sovereignty? In addition, Popper criticises Plato's view of education as being elitist and non-egalitarian. Popper asserts that rulers emerging from the Republic would not be good rulers, as they were not trained in originality or initiative and are overly authoritarian.

The ship and the beast (487–495)

In 487b Adeimantus reminds Socrates that philosophers are regarded as 'very odd birds', vicious and completely useless members of society.

Plato responds in two ways. First, he tells the parable of the navigator who is never given licence to chart the course because the crew are too ignorant to appreciate his value (481b–d); philosophers are not appreciated when society is already in a bad way. Second, he explains how in the real world philosophers rarely correspond to their ideal form but are seduced into bad ways. He argues that the exceptional talents of a philosopher if not properly cultivated in the right environment can easily be used to improper effect, for example in the advocacy of popular causes.

Plato argues that gifted natures are not immune from the lure of wealth, power and fame. For a philosophic temperament to turn out right it is necessary to have a society that can support and sustain such a nature in the pursuit of truth.

Let us examine the parables of the ship and the large and powerful animal (sometimes called the parable of the beast).

The parable of the ship

Plato created the parable of the ship to answer the allegation that philosophers tend to be prone to dilettantism and have little relevance in society. This parable explains how it is society's fault that philosophers seem strange and irrelevant. Plato describes a ship (or ships) with a captain who is limited in seamanship but who is nevertheless bigger and stronger than anyone else on board, and therefore has control. The ship represents the state or society that is controlled by the mass of public opinion, which is often misguided. The crew of the ship are depicted as quarrelling with each other as to how the ship should be navigated, each crew member thinking that they are right and therefore should be in control. Plato says that the members of this crew have learnt little about the art of

navigation and believe the art cannot be taught. When one faction of the crew is more successful in taking power than the others, the others will kill them and take control of the ship themselves. Plato says they will also hold in high regard the man who can control the captain of the ship by using force or fraud. The ship's crew represent Plato's old adversaries, the sophists, though one might see in them the character traits of politicians in general. Plato viewed the sophists as corrupt, uninitiated politicians, vying for power through whatever means they could, sinister or otherwise. Perhaps the drugs and drink that they use to try and put the captain out of action symbolise their use of rhetoric. Plato concludes that, with this crew on board, the true navigator will inevitably be regarded as an eccentric and obsolete stargazer: he or she will not be appreciated. The true navigator in Plato's parable is the philosopher-ruler who possesses knowledge of the forms of things necessary to rule over the ship successfully. Plato seeks to explain why philosophers are regarded as slightly strange and detached in society. The sophists, who influence public opinion, believe everything the philosopher might say to be rubbish, and so no one in the society recognises that knowledge of the essential nature of things is in fact necessary to govern successfully, in the same way that knowledge of the stars is essential in navigating effectively or a knowledge of medicine is required for a doctor to successfully treat a patient. Note that the three faculties of ignorance, opinion and knowledge are represented in the parable of the ship by the captain, the crew and the true navigator respectively.

> **Task**
>
> Read Plato's parable of the ship (487e–489c) and draw a picture of the ship that includes each element present in this parable. In a different coloured pen label what each element symbolises.

The parable of the beast

Plato uses the parable of the large and powerful animal to illustrate the corruption of philosophy. He describes a beast that is in the care of a tamer. The tamer aims only at pleasing the beast rather than taming it. The tamer applauds any action the beast does, and in fact studies the beast's attitudes and responses and inappropriately calls this study a science (in the sense of true knowledge). The beast-tamer in this simile is symbolic of Athenian politicians, and the large and powerful animal represents the public. Politicians, like sophists, have no idea as to which of the beast's actions are right or wrong but seem to believe that whatever the beast does is right. Plato is criticising the sophists, the rival school of philosophy from his Academy, by claiming that they only want power and that this is an illegitimate desire for a politician. For Plato, as a moral realist, a politician should be elected as one who has clear knowledge about useful things like justice, holiness, courage and wisdom and who makes sure that the people who are being governed act morally. The philosopher-ruler or 'true beast-tamer' would be of such a temperament that he or she would not seek power as the sophist does, but would rather rule justly and wisely.

In the parable of the large and powerful animal, philosophy is corrupted by sophistry because it gives the name of science to the study of how best to please the animal. One might read this parable today in light of the twentieth-century meta-ethical theory known as emotivism (see chapter 2). Plato criticises any account of ethics that is founded on opinion and emotion. For Plato, morality is not a matter of moods, wants, tastes, desires, reactions, passions, pleasures (all words used in the parable of the beast). Thus Plato's parable outlines the characteristics required in a philosopher-ruler, endorses **moral realism** and criticises sophistry as an unsuitable pastime. Note that the faculties of ignorance, opinion and knowledge are represented in the parable of the beast by the large and powerful animal, the charlatan beast-tamer and, by implication, the properly qualified beast-tamer respectively.

The forgotten metaphors (495–501)

For an author who criticises literature as misleading (377), there is a surprising reliance on the metaphorical in Plato's writing. A defence might rest on the character-building nature of The Republic's illustrations, which never exhibit the needless elaboration that he criticises. Plato allows skilfully articulated knowledge, and only objects to the empty rhetoric and sound-bites of corrupt politicians. The esteem with which the author regards philosophy is evident in a series of metaphors occurring between 495 and 501 that are often overlooked.

After recommending humility to philosopher-rulers by exhorting them to follow the quest for understanding like a slave (494d), philosophy is personified by Plato as an abandoned lover (495b). Wisdom's true lover, namely the philosopher-ruler, has been distracted, perhaps for the reasons suggested in 491c, and leaves her 'deserted and unwed'. This is a state of affairs that does not suit those who should be true philosophers in the literal sense of lovers of wisdom (*sophia*), and they are conceived as victims of circumstance.

In a further simile concerning abandonment, philosophy is likened to an orphan who falls into the hands of 'second-rate interlopers', i.e. the sophists (495c). This second metaphor contrasts with the first in portraying Sophia not as a passive, spurned lover but as a vulnerable, abused child. Some of those who look after philosophy in the absence of philosopher-rulers are just rogues out to get what they can, while others are described as downright wicked. The connecting theme is one of ownership and is further explored in a third metaphor (495d); this is an unswerving attack on sophistry:

> For when they see so good a piece of territory, with all its titles and dignities, unoccupied, a whole crowd of squatters gladly sally out from the meaner trades, at which they have acquired a considerable degree of skill.

The territory represents the study of philosophy, which has been hijacked by those intent on prestige and status rather than the honest business of establishing truths.

Continuing the divine motif running through The Republic, which casts the world of forms as a heavenly realm, philosophy is likened to a temple in a simile occurring towards the end of 495d. The crowd of criminals profaning Wisdom's temple are the sophists and, by implication, the true philosophers are its elite priest caste. Philosophy offers sanctuary for everyone, criminals included, but should not be taken over by those who lack the expertise and vision to be true philosophers.

Section 495 ends with a final simile that might count as evidence that Plato trained as a comic writer early in his career. The simile of the bald-headed little tinker borrows themes from previous illustrations, and likens sophistry[4] to an unsuitable and sinister bridegroom setting out to marry Sophia. Prioritising image over substance in his new suit, he thinks he has a chance owing to the bride's family having fallen on hard times, a comment on the state of philosophy in the fourth century BC. This comic character is of course an unsuitable match for Wisdom.

The notion is consolidated in the botanical simile of 497b, in which philosophy is compared to a foreign seed sown in alien soil, which degenerates into the local growth. The author goes on to outline what philosophy's role in politics should be by talking about philosophical training in terms of nurture and cultivation (498b).

Despite Plato's suspicion of art, the philosopher-ruler is likened to an artist in a significant passage occurring at the end of this section (500e–501c). Using the world of forms as his blueprint or divine pattern, the artist copies Justice, Beauty and Self-Discipline onto a clean canvas upon which an outline of human society has been sketched. In this outline of the social system, human character traits are blended and applied like paint, although sometimes the philosopher-ruler as artist has to delete and start again. The final result is a beautiful picture, entitled *Politeia*, which is of course a masterpiece.

Plato seems to be claiming:

- A perfect society (*Politeia*) should be ruled and designed by philosophers.
- You will not get proper philosophers unless you have a perfect society to nurture them in the right environment.

He appears trapped in a 'chicken or egg' predicament but escapes by bringing in the notion of fortune. It may happen that either the ruler of a country is converted to philosophic ways or a group of genuine philosophers enter upon the political scene.

Plato feels he has done sufficient to show that rule by philosophers is possible, albeit very difficult to achieve. However, precisely because so much depends on the conditioning effect of the social environment, Plato believes that the philosopher must sever all connections with the past. Plato believes in beginning with a blank sheet. The philosopher must be decisively influenced by what Plato calls 'the highest knowledge'; this gives the philosopher the right to draw up a blueprint for society. What is this highest form of knowledge? Plato's reply is that it is knowledge of the form of the Good. The Good is what all things valued as true, beautiful or morally praiseworthy have in common. It enables one to structure 'lesser goods' and to see how far these must be present in the ideal society.

Review question

Outline the qualities of character that Plato thinks are possessed by a philosopher-ruler.

Knowledge of the form of the Good (503–507)

Plato uses 'good' and 'valuable' in the same breath, but the latter term is far less likely to confuse. One might argue that we value moral behaviour, the pursuit of truth, and the creation of beauty. All these things are valued and thought of as goods: the Good, the True and the Beautiful. Just as the philosopher seeks out the common factor in beautiful things – that is, beauty-in-itself – so the philosopher seeks out what all things that are valued have in common – that is, the form of goodness. Only a person who knows how to give each valued pursuit its proper weighting can be relied upon to order a society. Such an individual will possess the 'highest knowledge', which is the supreme wisdom and called in *The Republic* 'knowledge of the form of the Good'. From a Platonic perspective, literature and life are littered with characters who have not known how to order values properly and who are betrayed by their lack of wisdom. Consider the following:

- The Puritan who denies the claims of beauty.
- The dissolute aesthete who sacrifices all for beauty.
- The Inquisitor who subordinates truth for morality.
- The 'mad scientist' who would destroy the world for truth.

All these unwise people know something good but not the form of the Good. As Plato says, there are many who know only the appearance of the Good without grasping its fundamental nature. What then is its fundamental nature? Plato does not spell this out clearly but gives us the following clues:

> The good then is the end of all endeavour, the object on which every heart is set … though it finds it difficult to grasp just what it is; and because it can't handle it with the same assurance as other things it misses any value those other things have. (505e)

This quotation reveals the Good as the goal of philosophy, the centre of a philosopher-ruler's being and that which is essentially indescribable. It is understandable that Christian Platonists went on to equate the Good with God.

Plato makes the point that the Good is what everyone wants, and that everyone desires it because it is useful rather than just being superficially attractive (505). Plato employs two arguments here, the first being an argument from preferences – that is, people prefer genuinely good things to counterfeits. There is also an argument from regression – that is, when people are asked why they want what they are striving for, they are driven to say in the final analysis 'because it is good'. Even if we accept this account, it is still only a formal, empty goal that we are agreeing to accept, and we are still left wanting knowledge of what is good. How, for instance, do we judge between two conflicting accounts of goodness?

The Good is portrayed as the highest form of knowledge sought by philosopher-rulers. The word 'good' in this sense has an application in the field of morals and in the field of non-ethical judgements ('a good day at the races' or 'a good mathematical proof'). A problem arises here, as if the form of the Good presides over both kinds of judgement, it seems to suggest that there is a moral dimension to everything. Plato may be arguing that the perfect act of kindness and the perfect calculation are equal instantiations of the form of the Good. However, does the perfect crime also participate in the form of goodness? If it does, surely this is to some extent contradictory?

In two further arguments, Plato tells us that the Good is not pleasure[5] (the ordinary person's answer) nor is it knowledge (the sophisticated person's answer). In addition, Plato admits that the Good is very difficult to get to know. Plato

needs to emphasise the difficulties of being a ruler in order to justify having his special caste of philosopher-rulers. If any Tom, Dick or Harry can know the form of the Good then we might as well scrap the whole idea of philosopher-rulers. It is nevertheless disappointing that Socrates remains evasive and admits to having no real knowledge of the Good.

Criticisms of the form of the Good

1 Is it legitimate to talk of the Good? Plato appears to assume that 'good' refers to some single thing, or has some unique meaning, which many philosophers would deny. One may criticise Plato's notion of the form of the Good by asserting that 'good' has no absolute, unqualified use but is always defined by some criteria.

2 The form of the Good is not in the world of our experience and seems to be an object of detached rather than practical knowledge. As Glaucon sarcastically puts it, 'the Good seems to be miraculously transcendent'. Aristotle criticises Plato with this in mind in *Nicomachean Ethics* I.6.

3 Plato's concept of the Good is very obscure, and it is not clear how such knowledge would help in solving real-life moral dilemmas. Throughout Book VII of *The Republic* it is granted visionary status with quasi-religious imagery, but it is never clear how knowledge of the form of the Good follows from rational principles.

4 It fails to admit that there is an is–ought gap. For Plato there is no gap between our knowledge of facts and our knowledge of values. Goodness and other values are just as real as other things. One may assert that one is unjustified in saying that 'oughtness' is identical with Goodness, as Plato appears to be doing.

The philosophic knowledge that stands as the preserve of philosopher-rulers is expressed in three similes: the sun, the divided line, and the cave. Let us examine each in turn, and in so doing end our analysis of Book VII.

Review question

Briefly describe Plato's account of the Good.

The simile of the sun (507–509)

In the sun simile the author asserts:

- The sun makes things visible by its light, in the same way that the form of the Good makes things intelligible by giving truth to them.

- The sun gives these things their life, as the form of the Good gives intelligible things their existence.

- Just as the sun is not the same as visibility, so the form of the Good is not the same as knowledge.

- The Good is the source of reality, yet it is not itself that reality, but is beyond it and superior to it in dignity and power.

- The sun might be termed 'the child of the Good'. Just as in the case of children who resemble their parents, the sun has something in common with the Good.

The sun illuminates our understanding of reality just as its absence dooms us to error; apprehension uninformed is apprehension confounded. We do not know how to assess something if we do not have the Good to enlighten us. Plato adds that, just as the sun generates growth, so the Good is in some sense causally responsible for the intelligible world. This is a difficult claim to justify, but there is no doubt that Plato is entirely serious in making it.

Criticisms of the sun simile

- It is not clear whether the Good is the cause of reality or the cause of its being intelligible; likewise it is not clear whether there is some aspect of the world for which the Good is not causally responsible.

- It is not clear in what sense the Good is a cause. 'Cause' can be understood in many different senses (Aristotle uses four quite distinct definitions of 'cause'). The Good might cause reality by being its prior or efficient cause, or it could cause reality by being the end to which everything moves.

- One might further criticise Plato's notion of the Good as advanced in the simile of the sun on emotivist or relativist lines (see chapter 2).

The divided line (510–514)

This construes levels of understanding as though they were segments of a line.

There are four sectors of the line:

A – Philosophy and the form of the Good, the examination of the whole of reality. Plato uses the term 'intelligence' to describe this level of comprehension, and also **'dialectical** thinking'.

B – The world of forms and mathematics, known as 'the sciences', from the Latin *scientia* meaning 'knowledge'.

C – Beliefs based on sense experience, the world of objects.

D – Acquaintance with representations (art, pictures, illusions).

The important point is that all special sciences make certain assumptions (presuppositions), and philosophy subjects all assumptions to rigorous intellectual examination. This is exemplified in later philosophers' works; thus Descartes questions the validity of sense experience, Berkeley the intelligibility of the concept of 'matter' and Hume challenges accepted truisms concerning causality. Plato helpfully draws the line for us and his illustration is copied below.

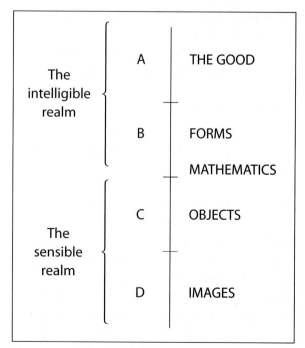

Figure 7.1 *The divided line*

The divided line is a diagram intended to illustrate Plato's theory of knowledge as advanced in the rest of *The Republic*. This figure seeks to emphasise the superior value of philosophical knowledge; hence there is a vertical, epistemological ascent, with the possibility of the seeker of enlightenment achieving knowledge of the forms occupying sections A and B. The line illustration stresses the fact that those in the realm of belief can be ruled by philosophers, since this latter group of individuals have acquired a level of understanding that ranks above illusion. Mathematics is categorised in section B owing to the fact that this discipline involves abstract thought and as such is useful in preparing rulers for the study of philosophy. Abstract notions such as *pi* or square roots will help in the contemplation of the forms. The superior ontological status of the forms is emphasised in the divided line, as is the inferior status of the world of illusion, although their relationship is not entirely clarified.

Criticisms of the divided-line simile

- If we are in a state of true belief rather than of knowledge, it might be argued that we can get along quite well without the forms.

- Secondly, is mathematics really much of a preparation for ethical or political decision-making? The best way to prepare for government is surely to share in the lives of ordinary people.

- One can criticise Plato's rationalist theory of knowledge from an empirical standpoint (see chapter 1).

The simile of the cave (514–521)

Socrates introduces this last, great simile in the style of a Delphic pronouncement. Nevertheless, the cave simile is an accessible illustration and easy to picture. It is a poetic expression of Platonic epistemology as set out in the divided line. The divided line can be mapped onto the simile of the cave, and the previous simile of the sun also plays a significant role. Indeed, the relationship between the three figures has been likened to that between the three paintings of a triptych.

The prisoners in the cave represent the untutored intellects of this world. There are three groupings in the cave:

- chained prisoners – that is, the untutored intellects of this world;

- the unchained;

- the seeker of daylight.

Each of these groups possesses different degrees of understanding. The more perceptive prisoners are those who are able to link admittedly unreal phenomena with one another and predict their sequence. The unchained prisoners grasp somewhat dimly the real nature of the phenomena. Some philosophers have argued that the business of science is simply to order and predict appearances, and there might be a tendency to identify the keen-eyed, chained prisoner with an empiricist or practising scientist. However, it would be more plausible to compare him to a technologist. A theoretical scientist would in all probability be likened by Plato to the unchained prisoner, who sees something of the reality behind the world as it is for laymen but whose grasp goes beyond mere common sense. However, he is operating in a very dim and inadequate light (i.e. he lacks knowledge of the Good); in consequence his sight (understanding) is limited.

The seeker of daylight

In many world religions there is a concept of enlightenment that is usually seen as the possession of a saint, guru, mystic or some other charismatic individual. Plato holds that it is the philosopher who stands in the daylight, though one suspects that his image of the philosopher is not a narrowly academic one. The philosopher sees into the heart of things, informed by reason and knowledge of the form of the Good.

There are two differences between the seeker of daylight and the unchained prisoner. The seeker of daylight sees real things, not models, and sees in better light. This second point implies that the philosopher looks at reality from a different and higher perspective. Many philosophers have been keen to stress that philosophy has a unique vantage point even if they have not wanted to describe it as Plato does.

For Plato it is, as the previous similes make clear, the philosopher's knowledge of the Good (the form of the Good) that makes him especially privileged – all of which seems plausible if not entirely defensible.

Socrates links the unwillingness of the prisoner to return to the cave (516e) with the unwillingness of those who know the form of the Good to get involved in human affairs (quietism). Just as the returned prisoner is treated as a fool when he returns (517a) and is threatened with death, so Plato explains why anyone who descends from contemplation of the divine to human life and its ills will blunder and make a fool of himself when forcibly put on trial and told to discuss shadows and illusions. This is clearly a reference to the trial of Socrates, when 'the wisest man in Athens' unsuccessfully defended himself against charges of impiety and corruption.

Later on in *The Republic* (532a–b), the simile of the cave is used to show the power of dialectic, the final stage in the philosopher's education. Plato's epistemology is best understood if the cave is seen as a realm of ethical misunderstanding; the metaphysical reality of true justice and goodness are contrasted with the deceit and illusion created by the manipulators of opinion. Education is not seen as acquaintance with facts about the world but as knowing what constitutes the good life.

Task

Read Plato's simile of the cave (514a–517d) and draw a picture of this poetic illustration, labelling in a different coloured pen what each element symbolises. How does your cave illustration compare with your earlier ship illustration? Does Plato have the same aim in mind when recounting the cave simile and the parable of the ship?

The notion of forms

In its crudest version, Plato's theory of forms involves the speculation that the 'real world' is wildly different from anything we are acquainted with, we being the chained prisoners. Such a 'real world' is composed of pure forms or essences, which only our minds grasp. Such pure forms have variously been described as ideas, universals, abstractions, species, patterns, the immutable, the immaterial, the unchanging and independent.[6] A form is the element that all particular items with the same name have in common. All men, for example, have manhood or masculinity in common; additionally, all wise men have wisdom in common. Plato describes this as partaking in the form of 'man' or partaking in the form of 'wisdom'. There is nothing particularly wrong with this slightly cumbersome mode of speaking.

For Plato the idea that 'the form of wisdom is wise' is an analytic truth because to assert the opposite, that wisdom is unwise, would not make sense. Every form is the unadulterated, perfect example of what it is meant to be, and it is only in the world of particulars that things become mixed; thus a person might make a wise decision followed by a foolish one. One can nevertheless refine an understanding of the world of forms by recognising the forms as they manifest themselves in particular instances. And one can also recognise a form by noticing its opposite in the sensible realm; thus I come to understand beauty by contrasting it with what is ugly. This point is known as the argument from opposites and holds that we can discover the forms from recognising what is and what is not a certain abstraction in the world of particulars (475e–476a). It is then the job of philosopher-rulers to explain the distinction that they have worked out to the rest of us, for example the difference between being just and unjust.

A second argument employed by Plato to explain the existence of forms is the one-over-the-many argument and follows the above passage in 476b–d, but is explained in greater detail in 596a–597e. Essentially a mathematical argument, this assertion holds that all things in common possess a common denominator, which is their perfect blueprint or form. Some assert that Plato makes a category error in supposing that terms like 'manhood' and 'wisdom' have something in common with everyday objects. Since these 'things' cannot be encountered in this world as Socrates and sausages can, Plato, one might think, is hooked on a theory of meaning according to which words mean the objects they denote or refer to, and thus abstract and general words must have abstract and general objects that they can denote.

The seeker of daylight 'sees' these real essences (the forms), while the unchained prisoner blundering around in the darkened world of the senses simply sees copies or models. This is Plato's way of saying that the prisoner has only an indirect knowledge of the forms. We can see wisdom in the character of Socrates but we do not confront wisdom itself, unless of course we are Platonic philosophers.

The world of forms

One crude mistake is to take Plato's metaphors too literally and suppose that a world of forms is a physical world full of forms just as this world is cluttered with objects. You could picture yourself, for example, strolling past the form of triangularity, despairing with the form of stupidity or sleeping on the form of a bed. You could think of any general term you like – 'car', 'cork' or 'crow' – and populate a Platonic world with appropriate forms, suggesting that all particular cars, corks and crows are mere embodiments of their abstract type. One would even be forced to admit that somewhere in the realm of forms there exists a form of realms. Thus a lot of fun has been had at Plato's expense by the depiction of a realm of ideal quasi-individuals, although it is forgotten that logically Plato cannot be asserting the existence of either a spatially determined world, or anything thronging with individuals. Plato does, however, appear to believe in the ontological independence of the forms. Forms could exist in the absence of a material world. This view may strike us as peculiar, but one must bear in mind that Plato was a mathematician, and even today many mathematicians believe that numbers exist as real entities just like gross physical objects. Even the most reductionist, materialist philosophers have conceded that 'classes' exist as non-material objects and are required to make sense of mathematics and logic.

Criticisms of the forms

- First, there are problems with the world of forms itself. Plato is careful not to allow undesirables into the world of forms, thus preventing it from becoming an ontological slum. He even draws the line at dirt, hair and mud. But it is not clear why there can't be negative forms, such as the form of evil.

- Some forms seem to incorporate others: triangles are made up of straight lines, centipedes of legs and lots of other interesting things; but do these things exist independently as separate forms? Does the form of a straight line exist in addition to the form of a triangle? Does everything participate in the form of a particle?

- When we invent something new, has its form always existed or is it made up of new forms?

- There is also the problem of how forms are embodied in this world. To say that the phenomenal objects of our everyday world partake of them only provokes questions as to how such a relationship works.

- The three fingers argument: Plato's theory of forms seems to hold that large objects participate in the form of largeness, while small objects participate in the form of smallness. The three fingers argument exposes the theory's weakness by illustrating the exception of relative values such as size, weight and shade. Take an average person's middle finger, ring finger and little finger. The middle finger, as largest of the three, must participate in the form of largeness, whereas the little finger participates in the form of smallness. An uncertainty arises, however, in the case of the ring finger: does this digit participate in both largeness and smallness or in mediumness? The three fingers argument seeks to expose an absurdity in Plato's theory of forms.

- The third man argument: A criticism predicted by Plato himself in the *Parmenides*, it follows from 'the one-over-the-many argument'. If we call that which all of a certain species of particulars have in common the form of those particulars, then the form itself must have something in common with the relevant particulars. This would create a third entity, a third man if the particulars were men, and lead to an infinite regress of commonality. A Platonist would respond by emphasising the uniqueness and finality of the forms.

Task

An understanding of the forms is central to an appreciation of the *Republic*. Read a few commentaries on the text and add to this list of criticisms. Can you think of any other problems with Plato's notion of forms?

Review question

Briefly describe Plato's conception of a world of forms.

Platonic education (Book VIII)

To be truly educated in the Platonic sense is to possess knowledge of the forms. This is described in terms of an upward ascent from the twilight world of particulars to a state of enlightenment: 'What is at issue is the conversion of the mind from a kind of twilight to the true day, that climb up into reality which we shall say is true philosophy' (521c).

This section completes Book III's earlier discussion on education in an ideal state that considered the joint education of guardians and auxiliaries. In Book VIII the author concentrates on the education of the philosopher-ruler, and some important points are raised that help us to understand Platonic epistemology. The question is raised (521d): 'What should men study if their minds are to be drawn from the world of change to reality?'

The earlier forms of education such as literature, music and physical training correspond to the world of change and decay, whereas the study of mathematics hones the prospective ruler's rational skills. Mathematics does not rely on sensory data, which Plato seems suspicious of (523–524). The author's primitive rationalism holds that the senses are of no use without reasoned thought. For instance, the sense of sight cannot distinguish between large and small without reason.

Mathematics is seen as essential to a philosopher's education, and is divided into arithmetic, plane geometry and solid geometry, and is approved of due to the fact that such knowledge is eternal and not liable to change and decay (527c). Plato does not admire astronomy or harmonics as much, as they are empirical studies dependent on the senses (529c).

Finally, the 'guardians in the fullest sense' learn dialectic, that is, philosophy or the science of rational argument. Plato retells the similes of the cave (532) and the divided line (533–534) to show how the analysis of argument and the contemplation of goodness itself is the culmination of education. The philosopher-rulers are singled out as being able 'to give account of' whatever is under discussion (534b), and this quality is deemed to be of importance. Six stages of development are identified in Book VIII:

Stage 1	Geometry, arithmetic, physical exercise	Age: childhood
Stage 2	Intense physical training for 2–3 years	Age: 18
Stage 3	Streaming: some remain soldiers (auxiliaries); others are promoted to potential philosopher-rulers and study the art of war	Age: 20
Stage 4	Potential philosopher-rulers study philosophy intensively for 5 years	Age: 30
Stage 5	Practical experience, e.g. military service, for 15 years	Age: 35
Stage 6	The fully formed philosopher-ruler	Age: 50

Platonic psychology (Book IX)

For Plato our behaviour is influenced by three factors within our nature:

- our desires – instinctive or acquired;
- our spirit or character, which is largely a product of training;
- the reason or intellect.

This model of the human psyche resembles the tripartite model offered by Freud: id, ego and superego. Such models are only successful if they illuminate human action and give us a language that more adequately describes how we behave.

The well-balanced individual

Implicit within Plato's analysis is a concept of mental health. An ideal human agent is guided by reason to a course of action that enables him to blend his competing desires into a lifestyle that allows him to express them in an integrated and balanced way. Reason does not repress desires; rather it seeks to harmonise them and give them proper order. Basic human drives for love, power, sex, esteem and stability are not automatically compatible. How many in pursuit of power forfeit the love they crave? How many have lost stability in their life, lured by their sexual appetite? It is surely true to say that if these clamorous emotions are not to wreak havoc in an individual's life (a civil war of the emotions) then reason alone must map out a lifestyle that enables the various drives to co-exist in harmony.

The well-balanced person has such a map. However, the possession and exercise of reason is not sufficient to make him or her well balanced. Having a map and using it are different things. I may think it inappropriate to drink an extra pint of beer, knowing I may miss the train I want to catch, but I still may do so in full knowledge of the fix I'll be putting myself in. In these circumstances what is lacking to get me off the barstool is character or spirit, that mysterious force that also gets you out of bed in the morning when you desire to continue sleeping.

The well-balanced person is thus a unit in which reason commands and organises, aided by character. Character is, according to Plato, the result largely of a sound upbringing.

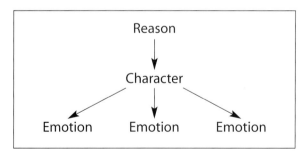

Figure 7.2 *The well-balanced character*

There are problems with this model but, to be fair to Plato, it is probably appropriate to show how this approach not only gives a model of mental health but also enables us to construct a

pathology of personality defects, displaying the diseases of the human soul. The first imperfect society under analysis is a **timarchy** – that is, a society governed by a military elite such as Sparta or Crete at the time of Plato's writing. Timarchic individuals control their emotions, having been brought up to do so, but fail to

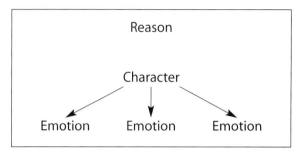

Figure 7.3 *The timarchic character*

explain or understand the course their life takes. The student who allows her desire to excel to overcome more exciting distractions believes that getting on at college is essential for future success and assumes that this is paramount. A very different example is that of a character controlled not by reason but by some strong, inbred force or socially acquired tendency.

The second imperfect society is an **oligarchy** – that is, a society governed by a wealthy elite.

Democratic individuals have no real character, just a string of unstructured emotions all of which have their day and their way. Essentially, the democratic person is a creature of fad, fashion and trend, with no real core, like the passive TV watcher or consumer who responds to green issues one day and buys a flash car the next, who feels for the victims of famine but books a holiday to Disneyland. The democratic type is not necessarily a bad person or an especially indulgent sort. Indulgence will only sometimes have an appeal. There is simply no

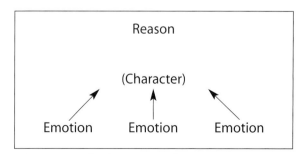

Figure 7.4 *The democratic character*

real hierarchy amongst their feelings. Such stability as they will enjoy in life depends upon the constancy of their emotions. Their best behaviour and their worst is emotive in origin; they are simply devoid of rational resources to restrain or fine-tune their behaviour.

The tyrannical character is possessed of powerful, subterranean drives and fierce emotions, which dominate all other aspects of his or her life. Without reason or character to order impulses, most aspects of life become subordinated to tyrannical drives. Even intellect is forced to accommodate and serve these overriding desires. Plato suggests that such desires would be suppressed in a democratic type by residual elements of character, inbred feelings of decency etc.

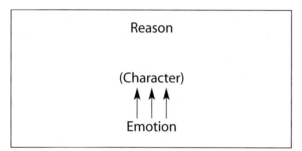

Figure 7.5 *The tyrannical character*

As with most psychological models, there are few people who exactly correspond to any type, though we may find that our behaviour at times can approximate to one type or another. We are all potential tyrants or oligarchs. Plato would argue that certain types of society can expect to produce a higher ratio of one or other type. Democratic society, for example, will produce more democratic types. Plato believes that human nature is very powerfully shaped by the society it grows up in. A healthy psychology, therefore, is far more likely to exist in a society that is not itself sick.

It might be argued that reason, as an element in our nature, is not master but servant of our emotions. Reason cannot tell us what to want, only how to achieve what we want. The concept of reason as conductor and guide to the emotions misses the point that reason has no agenda or goal of its own. A Platonist would respond by arguing that unless reason orchestrates the wails of desire then these wails will inevitably conflict. At the very least, reason can take a long-term

view, draw lessons from experience and try to ensure that the satisfaction of one desire does not frustrate other primary objectives. Reason is active when my urge to speak my mind is balanced against my desire to keep my friends, and so I speak with tactful reserve, knowing that it is better to keep one's friends. Reason fulfils a technical role of identifying emotional conflict and reconciling desires.

Platonic aesthetics (Books X and XI)

Three arguments that attack art and art lovers follow as an appendix to *The Republic* (476b). After a recapitulation of his theory of forms in which he reminds us of the definition of particulars (for example, beds are poor imitations of their perfect essence, the form of a bed), Plato criticises artists for creating imitations of imitations (for example, the picture of a particular bed). Representation (*mimesis*) is viewed by the author as being further removed 'from the throne of truth' (597e). One might criticise *The Republic* itself, a sketch of the ideal state, as being so far removed from the form of justice and therefore obscure. Secondly, Plato argues that such representation appeals to the worst side of people, who like to be misled by illusion. This view is linked to the author's psychological theory as laid out in Book IX. Rationality is prioritised here: 'The dramatic poet produces a similarly bad state of affairs in the mind of the individual, by encouraging the unreasoning part of it' (605b). Plato's third argument against art in Book X is based on the assertion that the arts are morally corrupting, as they allow us to be swept away (605c–e).

In Book XI Plato links his quest for justice with his belief in an afterlife as influenced by the Pythagoreans. His description of an afterlife is cast in the form of the myth of Er, in which a soldier recounts his post-mortem experiences. Plato points to the necessity of an afterlife to reward previously unrewarded acts and to punish previously unpunished acts in this life. The myth of Er shows us that we are responsible for the life we choose and, if we choose correctly, 'all will be well with us' (621d).

1 Explain Plato's distinction between the intelligible and the sensible worlds.

2 Assess Plato's theory of forms.

3 Describe Plato's simile of the cave. How does he use it to support his view of the place accorded to philosopher-rulers in the ideal society?

4 Outline and discuss Plato's distinction between pleasure and the Good.

5 How convincing are the distinctions Plato makes in the divided line? Can this illustration be easily reconciled with the similes of the sun and the cave?

■ Why does Plato believe that philosophers should be entrusted with the government of the state?

■ Are the parables of the ship and the large and powerful animal apt metaphors for democracy?

■ Can knowledge and opinion be distinguished in the way that Plato maintains?

■ What reasons does Plato offer in support of the view that philosopher-rulers must acquire knowledge of the form of the Good?

■ How does Plato develop the simile of the sun, and why is this simile of special significance in his account of the nature of the Good?

Glossary of key terms

Aesthetics: the branch of philosophy dealing with art and beauty. In Plato's time, art consisted of copying images and is viewed in *The Republic* as a corrupting influence.

Dialectic: an alternative name for the science of argument or philosophy.

Elenchus: a form of dialogue in which a definition is requested, for example 'What is justice?' The first attempts at a definition are then rejected and supplanted by a better answer.

Form: the immutable, eternal blueprint and perfect example of anything to which a particular name refers.

Guardians: a general term used in *The Republic* that includes both philosopher-rulers and auxiliaries, and separates them from the class of craftspeople.

Moral realism: the belief that one can assert moral facts, which are accessible through a philosophical education; the opposite of the sophistical relativism advocated by Thrasymachus.

Oligarchy: a state ruled by a small, educated, military elite.

Philosopher-rulers: those gold-standard men and women who have passed the fifty-year training period and are fit to govern Plato's ideal state.

Socratic method: a discussion technique involving questions and answers that encourages you to refine your argument.

Sophistry: a school of commercial philosophers including Thrasymachus, Protagoras, Gorgias and Hippias, which rivalled Plato's Academy. They advertised their ability to teach life skills and are criticised by Plato for manipulating people with rhetoric (the art of persuasion) and lacking knowledge of the forms.

Timarchy: a state ruled by the military.

Suggested reading

- Annas, J. (1981) *An Introduction to Plato's* Republic, Oxford, OUP
  An excellent introduction, Chapters 8, 9 and 10 being useful on the forms
- Hare, R. M. (1982) *Plato*, Oxford, OUP
  A more straightforward book that paints in some background detail
- Pappas, N. (1995) *Plato and the* Republic, London, Routledge
  Enlightening commentary, exactly mapped onto the text
- Strathern, P. (1996) *Plato in 90 Minutes*, Chicago, Ivan R. Dee
  Part of a useful series that provides background, analysis and a selection of quotations for each thinker.
- White, N. P. (1979) *A Companion to Plato's* Republic, Indianapolis, Hackett
  A synopsis of the text preceded by some introductory essays

Notes

1 Kraut, R. ed. (1992) *The Cambridge Companion to Plato*, Cambridge, CUP, p. 228.

2 Hobbs, A. (2001) *Plato and the Hero: Courage, Manliness and the Impersonal Good*, Cambridge, CUP.

3 Annas, in Annas, J. (1981) *An Introduction to Plato's Republic*, Oxford, OUP, pp. 196–197, draws our attention to the two senses of the verb 'to be' in Greek, namely to exist (existential) and to be true (veridical).

4 Also ref. *Gorgias* 459.

5 Also ref. *Protagoras* 354c.

6 Also ref. *Theaetetus* 245e–246c and *Meno* 73d–74e.

8 A commentary on Aristotle's *Nicomachean Ethics*

What is done virtuously is noble and it is done for the sake of the noble. (Aristotle)

Aims

On completion of this chapter you should be able to:

- present a critical account of the concept of *eudaimonia*
- describe Aristotle's conception of the Good and how it differs from that provided by Plato
- outline the argument from functions
- describe and evaluate Aristotle's doctrine of the mean
- explain voluntary, involuntary and non-voluntary action
- explain practical and theoretical wisdom
- evaluate Aristotle's account of pleasure
- evaluate Aristotle's account of contemplation and the good life.

Aristotle's influence over the study of ethics had been greater than that of any other single figure in the history of western philosophy. The *Nicomachean Ethics* constitutes his greatest achievement in the field of moral philosophy and as a textbook for virtue theory tells us how to live a good life. It was Aristotle who added flesh to Plato's skeletal notion of the form of the Good. It was Aristotle who inspired the natural law tradition in the Middle Ages and it is Aristotle's ideas that underpin modern virtue ethics. Let us examine the principal arguments as outlined in this philosopher's major work.

Eudaimonia: the object of life (Book I)

The study of ethics (I.1–3)

The opening sentences of Aristotle's *Nicomachean Ethics* sets out the author's concept of goodness, and in so doing describes the goal or **telos** of humanity:

> Every art and every investigation, and similarly every action and pursuit, is considered to aim at some good. Hence the Good has been rightly defined as 'that at which all things aim'.

Our author appears to fall at the first fence with this opening comment, which commits a formal error in reasoning known as 'the roads to Rome fallacy'. The mistake may be illustrated by a parallel argument:

1 Every road leads to some town.
2 Therefore, there is a particular town to which all roads lead.

The second statement does not follow logically from the first. In the case of Aristotle's version the argument runs:

1 Everything has an aim.
2 Therefore, there is one goal, the Good, to which every aim is directed.

A non-fallacious version occurs at the start of Book I, Chapter 4 (I.4), which asserts that it is a widely held intuition that happiness (***eudaimonia*** in Greek) is the good at which all actions are aimed:

> To resume. Since all knowledge and every pursuit aims at some good, what do we take to be the end of political science – what is the highest of all practical goods? Well, so far as the name goes there is pretty general agreement. 'It is happiness.'

Thus every activity is pursued for the sake of what the agent believes will make them happy. The Greek word *eudaimonia* is popularly translated as 'happiness', but contains the sense of flourishing, self-fulfilment or 'living well'. The translation 'happiness' should not be confused with any sense of psychological hedonism or crude pleasure-seeking. It is the purpose of the first part of the *Nicomachean Ethics* to elucidate the meaning of *eudaimonia* as happiness in the fullest sense of the word.

From the first chapter of Book I, a distinction is drawn between subsidiary goals (the means) and an ultimate goal (the end). Thus the activities of looking after someone, fighting or trading are undertaken in order to secure health, victory or political standing respectively, yet each is part of an intricate causal pattern. Many actions contribute to these subsidiary goals that together aim at personal fulfilment or *eudaimonia*. Indeed, the concept of *eudaimonia* is necessary if a vicious regress of goals is to be avoided. Take, for instance, the saddler's aim to make the best-fitting tack, the aim of which is to

control a horse more effectively, the aim of which is to fight more efficiently in battle, the aim of which is to secure victory, etc. Such a sequence of aims and purposes would continue *ad infinitum* unless one postulates something that is undertaken for its own sake. This end-in-itself is termed 'the Good', a further synonym for *eudaimonia*. But *eudaimonia* is not just convenient to escape a philosophical regress. It is an essential guiding force in showing us how to live our lives (I.1).

The study of the Good is classed as a science (I.2) due to the fact that one is able to gain knowledge of what it is. Indeed, one can teach and learn it, and thus the study falls under the remit of political science, which is concerned with the welfare of the community as a whole. Aristotle wrote a companion volume to the *Nicomachean Ethics* called the *Politics*, in which he defined a just state as one that nurtures and cultivates *eudaimonia*. Aristotle, as a moral realist (see chapter 2), believed that we could talk factually about moral issues, but held that moral and political sciences are not as precise as the

Aristotle
(384–322 BC)

Aristotle was the original polymath (that is, he knew a lot about many different things), and this is reflected in the varied subject matter of his books, which range from literature and logic to philosophy and physics, from metaphysics and marine biology to politics and poetics. He is thought to have written some 550 texts, two-thirds of which have been handed down to us. This learned and sagacious man was born in 384 BC and moved from northern Greece at the tender age of 17 to study under Plato at the Academy in Athens. He left Plato's Academy aged 37, and went on to tutor Alexander the Great before returning to Athens in 335 to found his own academy, called the Lyceum. Political agitations led to the philosopher fleeing the Greek city-state to escape the same fate as Socrates. Indeed, the course of action taken by the two thinkers mirrored their respective moral philosophies, with Aristotle making a phronetic (if not frenetic) decision to run while Socrates a little time before had opted to face the music on a matter of principle. Aristotle wrote three major tracts in moral philosophy, of which the *Nicomachean Ethics* is the most widely read. The title 'Nicomachean' is a family name shared by the author's father and son and has no philosophical significance. Important points are also developed in the *Eudemian Ethics* and the *Magna Moralia*. Aristotle's slightly forced style has been put down to the texts being unfinished lecture notes but this is scholarly speculation.

Significant works
Metaphysics, Physics, Poetics, Politics, Rhetoric (dates of authorship are uncertain)

likes of mathematics, and are satisfied with 'a broad outline of the truth' (I.3). No less skill is involved, but a more flexible approach to the subject matter is required. Take, as a comparison, the difference between horsemanship and the fashioning of weapons: whereas the former is an imprecise art in which one adapts to new situations, the latter is a matter of precision and measurement. In this sense moral education is more akin to horsemanship. Aristotle concludes the third chapter by stating that a 'general education' is required in any moral philosopher, who needs to have experienced many aims, thus putting himself in the best position to judge what authentically counts as good.

Goals and the Good (I.4–5)

Both uneducated and cultured people say that the Good consists in *eudaimonia* (I.4), yet their opinions differ as to what leads to happiness. Subsidiary goals are pursued, such as pleasure, money and fame, but only to achieve the ultimate goal of happiness. These subsidiary aims are often context-dependent, as when one seeks health when ill and money when poor. The distinction between subsidiary or secondary goals and *eudaimonia* as the 'final end' is illustrated in figure 8.1.

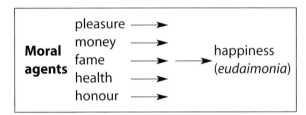

Figure 8.1 *Secondary goals and the ultimate goal*

Having commented on the Good, Aristotle moves on to delineate the sort of knowledge that is required. Note that despite disagreeing with his former teacher, Aristotle borrows many of his descriptive terms from Plato.

As moral philosophy is not an exact science, knowledge in the sense of deduction is not possible. The right course of action is worked out empirically and consists in that which is 'known to us'. Aristotle may be classed as a moral realist due to his conviction that the right course of action can be known factually, but he is not an

ethical absolutist in that he does not believe that a precise course of action applies irrespective of person or predicament. He quotes a verse from Hesiod, who advocates a reflective and individualistic approach to morality.

Three lifestyles are distinguished (I.5): the hedonistic, political and contemplative. The author is disparaging towards the first two, calling the hedonistic lifestyle vulgar and animalistic while condemning a life dedicated to politics as superficial. His approval of the contemplative life is left until Book X, but the fact that he has pinned his colours to this mast raises the question: Is *eudaimonia* theoretical or practical? Tensions certainly exist in the *Nicomachean Ethics*, and there are four alternatives:

- *Eudaimonia* is solely contemplative.
- *Eudaimonia* is solely practical.
- *Eudaimonia* is both contemplative and practical.
- *Eudaimonia* is either contemplative or practical, and one can flourish on taking either route.

There is textual evidence for each option. Certain passages point to a theoretical interpretation of *eudaimonia* (X.7, 1177a12ff.) and (I.7, 1098a16–18), while others argue that *eudaimonia* is practical (I.8, 1098b30ff.) and (I.7, 1097b34). In an attempt to reconcile these differences one might argue that they are mutually supportive. Theory helps practical decision-making. For example, practical life skills such as being organised make it easier not to become embroiled in being too contemplative. This position has scholarly support.[1]

Aristotle's criticisms of Plato (I.6)

Aristotle remained friends with Plato, having spent many years at his Academy, but, as this section shows, disagreed wholeheartedly with the latter's theory of forms. Aristotle's criticisms of the forms are listed below:

- The forms, if they exist, are not ranked by Plato, and it is hence impossible to find an ultimate form to aim at. This criticism seems unfair, as there is an implicit hierarchy of forms in Plato's account, which cites in ascending order: the forms of particulars, abstract forms and the form of forms, namely the Good.

- To talk about the form of the Good is confusing as there are many senses of 'good': of substance, in quality, in quantity, in relation, in time and in space. These may even be further subdivided. The diversity in usage of the word excludes the possibility of a clear science of the Good.

- The Platonic term 'form' does not add anything to normal definite descriptions. Thus there is no clear difference between talking of 'man' and 'man-himself' or the 'form of a man'.

- There are no grounds for supposing that the forms are eternal.

- Plato cites so-called goods, for example intelligence, pleasure, honour, but does not explain why these are good, only that they are contained in the idea of goodness.

- The Platonic concept of the Good does not bear any practical application in everyday affairs.

The argument from functions (I.7–8)

Aristotle reminds us in Chapter 7 of the ethical quest that we have embarked upon – that is, to find the Good to which all our actions are directed. Aristotle believed that the theory of forms was vacuous, but did he suggest anything in its place? Underpinning Aristotelian moral philosophy is the argument from functions, and it is to this that we now turn our attention.

Aristotle distinguishes between three types of Goods:

- those pursued only for the sake of something else;

- those pursued for their own sake and for the sake of something else;

- those pursued for their own sake and not the sake of something else.

Eudaimonia falls into the last of these categories and is hence situated beyond subsidiary goals such as honour, pleasure and reason, which may be classed in the second category. In addition, *eudaimonia* is viewed as self-sufficient, perfect (that is, unable to be improved on) and

necessary in order to fulfil our function as human beings. This last point is an important linchpin in Aristotle's moral system and requires further substantiation. The argument from functions runs thus:

1 Everything in the universe has a function (**ergon**).

2 For human beings not to have a function would make them an implausible exception.

3 All human beings possess a shared function.

4 The characteristic of a function is determined by what is peculiar to the subject.

5 Rationality is the peculiar characteristic of all humans, as nutrition and perception are shared with non-human organisms.

6 Therefore, the activity of reasoning constitutes the function of human beings.

This function is shared universally by 'good and bad' humans alike, just as both good and bad harpists share the common goal of trying to play the harp well. Aristotle adds two further caveats: that reason should be applied to the particular ethical situation and that ideally such a human enterprise should be accompanied by a long life. Chapter 7 is an important section in the *Nicomachean Ethics* and contains many of the work's central features, including Aristotle's teleology, virtue theory, a developed conception of the soul and a distinction between practical and theoretical wisdom. Many of these theories will be referred to later in this commentary.

Having used the argument from functions as a normative instruction on how to live well, the author seeks to paint in the detail. He cites popular support as evidence of the truth of his position (I.8). The argument from popular support lists the following tenets, which are accepted by other philosophers and laity alike. Let us rehearse the tenets nevertheless:

- Happiness is an activity of the soul.
- Happiness enables the individual to prosper.
- Happiness is bound up with virtue, prudence and wisdom.
- Happiness is accompanied by pleasure.
- Happiness is manifest in action.
- Happiness requires external goals.

These external goals, which are also termed 'resources' in the Thomson translation, have been the cause of much attention by commentators despite the casual way in which they are mentioned. The sorts of thing that can inhibit the realisation of happiness, according to Aristotle, include lack of friends, lack of wealth, lack of influence, lack of ancestry, lack of children, an ugly appearance and remaining single. It is as if every individual possesses a personal chart with these headings, the goal of which is to tick each category in order to achieve *eudaimonia*. No one will ever succeed in completing their chart (to which may be added good health and a long life from the previous discussion), but the chart exists as a golden ideal in order to direct our attention. Yet how does all this fit in with the author's claim that happiness consists in virtue? Aristotle has the answer.

Eudaimonia depends on exercising virtues, and not just an ontological state of being in possession of such desirable qualities. External goods or resources, therefore, act as instruments and opportunities for virtuous actions. However generous a spirit an impoverished vagrant might have, he lacks the means to exercise it. Socrates, who was famously poor and ugly, might be generous with his time but would always fall short of the Aristotelian ideal.

> **Task**
>
> Imagine that an Aristotelian philosopher was designing a quiz to test whether someone was happy or not. Draw up a list of the sort of questions you would expect them to ask.

Eudaimonia and fortune (I.9–12)

Self-fulfilment is confirmed as the final aim in life and thus the motivating force behind moral action. One naturally wants to know how it is acquired, whether it is by scholarship, conditioning, divine grace or fortune. Aristotle replies that its achievement lies in the correct combination of moral and intellectual virtue, and hence is largely in our own power to cultivate and is beyond the capacities of children and animals (I.9). Yet *eudaimonia* is not inviolate to fortune. Consider the story of King Priam. Priam, who is favourably depicted in Homer's

Iliad, had his otherwise happy life turned upside down when his son Paris eloped with Helen of Troy. This provoked an alliance of other Greek states against Troy, and one of his other sons, Hector, was killed in the ensuing battle. Priam lost kingly honours through begging for Hector's mortal remains. The Greeks invaded, concealed in their famous wooden horse, and the downtrodden king was finally battered to death with the body of his dead grandson. This digression raises the important question of the relationship between fortune and flourishing. While *eudaimonia* is not dependent on fortune, circumstances do exert some influence. This position is opposed to the stoical point of view, referred to later (VII.13, 1153b19–21), and, to some extent, Platonism.

The question of fortune brings us to the notion of the *eudaimonia* of the dead in Chapter 10. A reference is made to Solon's conversation with Croesus (I.10, 1100a10–18) as it is reported in Herodotus' *Histories*. The latter asked, 'Who is the happiest man in the world?' to which Solon's reply was to cite a dead Athenian who had thrived in business and died an honourable death. Croesus objected and demanded the name of someone who was still alive, yet Solon maintained that in order to accurately ascribe happiness one must consider a complete life, hence he is quoted as saying: 'Wait to see the end'. Aristotle does not seem as strict a judge of *eudaimonia* as Solon, and would be satisfied with a percentage score. Thus, if someone were to act virtuously for the majority of their life but lose *eudaimonia* through misfortune towards the end, on balance an Aristotelian would judge in favour of calling their life happy. Solon's position, in contrast, is that happiness can only ever be judged retrospectively. This certainly raises an interesting issue as to whether posthumous events are to be included in our survey of *eudaimonia*, for example if someone's last will and testament is ignored.

The irrational element of the soul (I.13)

It has already been implied (I.7) that the soul is divided into two elements: the rational and the irrational. The constitution of the first is developed later in Book VI, while the irrational element is sketched out in Book I. 13. The argument proceeds as follows:

1 The soul is part rational and part irrational.
2 The irrational part of the soul shares a common element with all other living things in that it causes nutrition and growth.
3 A second irrational element exists in human beings, which is the source of appetites, desires and emotions, yet is receptive to the rational element.
4 Virtue corresponds to the above classification in that intellectual virtues (wisdom, intelligence, prudence) are part of the rational element, whereas moral virtues (generosity, liberality, self-control) are part of the irrational element.
5 Intellectual virtues develop from learning, while moral virtues develop from habituation (social conditioning).

One might summarise this conception of the human constitution as in figure 8.2. The dotted line shows that the appetitive element of the soul may be made to act in accordance with reason.

Aristotle assumes that there is a fixed number of physical and psychological drives in human beings, including intellectual needs. A fulfilled life is a state of equilibrium in which the incidence of one drive does not conflict with the expression of another. This involves as a minimum requirement the rational control of desire – that is, the prudential management of life. If the desires are jigsaw pieces, then the role of prudence or practical reason is to fit them all together into a

meaningful pattern. However, there will always be conflict at the level of desire, because the desire to find a rational unity in one's preferences co-exists with a more anarchical impulse not to be rational. For Aristotle, this conflict with the rational impulse disappears when one makes following the rational path second nature. It becomes effortless and pleasurable.

One achieves this state of equilibrium by repeatedly following the path of reason and virtue, to the extent that it becomes a habit. A corollary of this is the perception that the imprudent or bad man is heading for an irreconcilable conflict of desires; this is what is meant by unhappiness and as such is incompatible with the enjoyment of pleasure. Thus the unfaithful lover suffers because he also desires the repute, trust and integrity that comes with fidelity. This comes close to saying that vice can be exposed as irrational bungling, and perilously close to suggesting that, since vice can be subjected to dialectical exposure, no one could will vice if they knew it for what it was. The view that evil is a product of ignorance was a Socratic principle.

Criticisms of *eudaimonia*

- There seems to be a slide halfway through Book 1 from claiming that *eudaimonia* consists in successful rational activity to the view that it involves virtue (**arete**). This transition might have been shored up in a more philosophical way.
- It is not clear whether the tension between *eudaimonia* as theoretical wisdom and

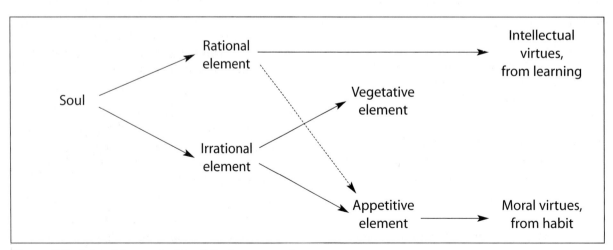

Figure 8.2 *Aristotle's conception of the human soul*

eudaimonia as practical wisdom can be as easily resolved as is suggested by some Aristotelian scholars.

- Two accounts of *eudaimonia* present themselves in the text concerning how the ultimate goal relates to subsidiary goals. The 'dominant' model construes all the subsidiary goals as leading to an exclusive state of happiness, while the 'inclusivist' model sees *eudaimonia* as being composed of individually specifiable goods. In the latter, happiness is a set, the elements of which consist in that which contributes to flourishing and fulfilment. On the whole, Book I seems to favour the inclusivist model, whereas passages occur in Book X to reassert the dominant conception (X.7).

Review questions

1 Outline two reasons why Aristotle rejects Plato's concept of the form of the Good.

2 Explain Aristotle's views that the Good is personal fulfilment and flourishing.

The mean and moral goodness (Book II)

Situationism (II.1–2)

While Plato may be described as the first rationalist, Aristotle was the first empiricist. This is never more evident than in their approaches to moral knowledge, the former believing that the form of the Good can be gained through a philosophical journey in the understanding, while the latter argued that a moral disposition is shaped through action:

> It is the way that we behave in our dealings with other people that makes us just or unjust, and the way that we behave in the face of danger, accustoming ourselves to be timid or confident, that makes us brave or cowardly. (II.1)

For Aristotle, we are born with *a priori* moral capacities or propensities, but these need to be exercised *a posteriori* in order to be made real. Comparisons abound between using parts of our bodies and working at different crafts to illustrate that we cannot be said to be X unless we do X. Those already in a position of being

virtuous can teach intellectual virtue, but this needs to be put into practice through habituation, exercising moral virtue in order that an individual may fulfil their potential.

Ethics as a practical science is situation-dependent, and it may be compared to health or navigation in so far as any cure depends on the illness requiring treatment and any act of navigation begins from one's immediate whereabouts. It is likely that in his lectures Aristotle would have expanded on a great deal of these themes, but in the version edited by his students that we inherit he launches abruptly into a description of the doctrine of the mean. Put simply, this doctrine states: 'While moral qualities are destroyed by excess or deficiency, action in accordance with the mean produces and maintains virtue.' Everyday examples are cited, involving exercise, diet, courage and pleasure. The doctrine of the mean holds that in any sphere, the midpoint between too much and too little is always the correct course of action. (By definition, 'excessive' means 'too much', and the more precise commentator might favour the description of 'maximal' to avoid sounding tautological.) Aristotle's doctrine is deliberately opposed to the hedonists of the time, who advocated a maximisation of pleasure, but also against stoics such as Zeno and Diogenes, who argued in favour of a deficiency of emotion. Many sophists could be categorised as hedonists and many Platonists were stoics.[2] It is important to note that Aristotle is not advocating 'moderation in all things' in the sense of recommending a notionally average amount of each passion. Imagine the absurdity of expecting a moral agent whose family has been tortured to display the same level of righteous indignation as one whose family has not been tortured. The relativity of the mean is emphasised in a later passage (II.6, 1106a35ff.), but before this is further elucidated Aristotle makes some important comments on the human disposition.

Dispositions (II.3–5)

Aristotle argues that if dispositions are shaped by action then they provide a useful 'index' as to whether the moral agent has performed a virtuous act or not (II.3). He goes on to state that, since pleasure and pain are clearly important in the moral sphere, they provide a useful litmus test as to a virtuous character. In Book II, Chapter 4, Aristotle seeks to counter the criticism that we become virtuous solely by actions and that character is irrelevant. He states that such an account of morality would be forced to classify as virtuous those acts that had been committed by accident or coincidence. He believes that, while through a repetition of virtuous acts we may become virtuous, genuine moral virtue requires three criteria: full cognition, that an act is chosen for its own sake, and that an act is chosen by someone of a stable disposition.

If further argumentation is needed as to the role of dispositions in moral decision-making, it is supplied in the following *reductio ad absurdum* (II.5). (A *reductio ad absurdum* is the formal description of an argument that suggests a range of possible options before reducing all of these options except one to absurdity.)

1 Virtue belongs in the sphere of the emotions, the intentions or the dispositions of the moral agent.
2 It cannot belong in the sphere of emotions or feelings, as it is absurd to blame someone for having feelings.
3 It cannot belong in the sphere of the intentions or faculties, as it is absurd to blame someone for having the capability or capacity to do something or not to do something.
4 'So, if the virtues are neither feelings nor faculties, it remains that they are dispositions.'

The author completes this chapter with a formal definition and location of virtue in accordance with the elements of one's personality, as belonging to one's disposition. The Greek word for character **ethos** and its adjective *ethikos* give us the title 'ethics', which is the branch of philosophy that deals with moral action.

The doctrine of the mean (II.6–9)

We have already learnt from a preliminary description (II.2) that Aristotle's normative ethical theory, known as the doctrine of the mean, is characterised by an appropriateness to the ethical situation and an intermediacy between the maximal and the deficient. Taken together, this does not mean that the correct ethical course of action will fall midway between excess and deficiency, as is illustrated in the example of Milo the wrestler (II.6) and in later discussions concerning courage and temperance (II.8). To this outline, the following details are added:

1 The mean is derived from a moral agent's disposition.
2 The mean is an excellence.
3 The mean is intellectually calculated.
4 The mean is relative to each person.
5 The mean is relative to each situation.
6 The mean is that point at which one's function is at its optimum.
7 The mean is that point of perfection when anything is added in gratuity and taken away at cost.
8 The mean provides a blueprint for action.
9 The mean provides the definition of moral virtue.

The fourth and fifth conditions are stipulated against the accusation that the mean is an over-intellectualised, quasi-mathematical notion whose application would be impossible in everyday affairs. Certainly the triumphant declaration in Chapter 6, 'to have these feelings at the right times on the right grounds towards the right people for the right motive and in the right way is to feel them to an intermediate, that is to the best, degree', seems something of a tall order. Yet Aristotle seems to be inviting us to experience this moral sense for ourselves to prove its standing and moral worth. Nevertheless, the rationality of the mean's calculation is brought out in the summary towards the end of the sixth chapter: 'So virtue is a purposive disposition, lying in a mean that is relative to us and determined by a rational principle, and by that which a prudent man would use to determine it.'

The author combines the rationalist and empiricist conceptions of moral knowledge in his account of the mean, in a move that the twentieth-century logician Quine (see chapter 1) would have been proud of had he turned his attention to ethics. Perhaps there are no new ideas in philosophy, just old ones reborn.

Aristotle curiously states towards the end of Book II, Chapter 6, that the mean between too much and too little is, in nature, an extreme of moral goodness, while there also exist certain feelings and actions which, in nature, constitute an absolute deficiency. Having established the notion of an ethical triad, with its three fixed points of excess, deficiency and elevated midpoint, Aristotle appears to be reneging on this theory. He does so in order to avoid an infinite regress created by the polar opposites of the two vices. Given that the mean will always remain at the centre, a regress would be created through asserting that the extreme has a further extreme and deficiency; likewise with deficiency. It may be illustrated as in figure 8.3.

We will survey the main criticisms waged against the doctrine of the mean at the end of this section. For the time being, let us finish recording Aristotle's exposition. Chapter 7 of the *Nicomachean Ethics* is the one that is most familiar to readers as it is in this passage that Aristotle explains the doctrine of the mean with specific examples. A helpful extrapolation from the text appears in the Thomson translation in the form of a table of virtues and vices. This is not part of the text as handed down to us, but one may conjecture that the author used such a medium at this stage in his lecture; a smaller version is featured in the *Eudemian Ethics*. In addition, the glaring error towards the very end of Chapter 7, where in the discussion concerning righteous indignation the spiteful man is

described as rejoicing at his enemies' good fortune rather than bad fortune, as it should read, is only the result of an error in copy-editing.

What is of greater philosophical concern is how justice, in the paragraph following, is treated as a special case. This is developed further in Book V. Justice is singled out for special treatment by Aristotle due to an ambiguity surrounding the Greek word for justice, *dikaiosune*, its many subdivisions and the fact that the notion doesn't seem to accord with any mean state of action. He declares: 'Justice is a kind of mean, but not in the same way as the other excellences' (V.5, 1133b32). Yet his earlier claim (V.2, 1130a24ff.) that injustice is typically motivated by the desire for gain or competitive advantage (*pleonexia*) might supply the following Aristotelian triad:

Greed	**Justice**	**Reticence**
Too much *pleonexia*	Correct amount of *pleonexia*	Deficiency of *pleonexia*

There is a problem with this model, as the author denies (V.11) that it is possible to treat oneself unjustly; thus one cannot steal from oneself. Yet in the case of reticence, where one is reluctant to receive honours or gain, this is what seems to be happening.

Chapter 8 is concerned with the notion of contrariety with each abstraction – excess, mean and deficiency standing contrary to each other. Aristotle argues that the greatest degree of contrast exists between the excess and deficient wings but that the mean is contrary to both

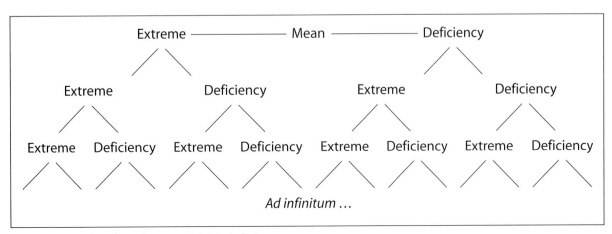

Figure 8.3 *Aristotle seeks to avoid this infinite regress*

while sometimes resembling one more than the other. This added feature of resemblance in a context of contrariety helps to explain the popular misconception that vice takes one opposing position to virtue and not two. Aristotle discusses the cases of courage and temperance, and develops more of a slide-rule conception of virtues. Such a table would appear as:

Excess	Mean	Deficiency
Rashness —— Courage ——————— Cowardice
Licentiousness ——— Temperance —— Abstemiousness

In Chapter 9, the author makes the point that one extreme is always more erroneous than the other, and suggests that this is due to human psychology and how we are tempted. To help us avoid such temptations, Aristotle supplies three practical guidelines: (1) avoid extremes, whether excessive or deficient, as both are contrary to the mean; (2) guard against the errors we feel most prone to fall into – this requires a degree of self-awareness; (3) be wary of pleasure, as this cannot be judged impartially due to its personal nature. Having said this, he makes the point that it is often useful to aim at an excessive or deficient position in order to hit the mean, in the same way as a sailor might aim at a fixed point away from the harbour in the knowledge that the current will take the boat to its destination. Our destination, however, should always be the mean.

Criticisms of the mean

- The strongest criticism is that one can have appropriate, intermediate feelings that are in tune with the mean but directed at the wrong object. An adulterer, for instance, might possess the right measure of lust but direct it towards his mistress rather than his wife.

- Aristotle presumes that there is a correct amount of each emotion; this is a controversial claim. Plato was one philosopher who argued against the supremacy of emotions but even less extreme critics find it hard to believe that there is a correct measure of feelings.

- Aristotle's doctrine of the mean amounts to little more than asserting that we should act in an appropriate way, which does not offer us any meaningful guidelines in the 'real world'.

Aristotelian philosophers may reply that this feature is in fact an advantage as, unlike rule-based theories such as Kant's deontology, which are always subject to exceptions, Aristotle's agent-centred approach, which seeks to analyse the disposition of the person, is more helpful and flexible.

- Aristotle does appear to be issuing moral injunctions against depravity, malice, shamelessness, envy, adultery, theft and murder (II.6). Isn't his assertion that these activities are absolutely wrong a contradiction of the mean?

- The mean as set out in, for example, Book II, Chapter 8, seems an overly abstract mathematical formula based on an aesthetic appreciation of symmetry rather than an understanding of ethics. The author then supplies artificial definitions of vice and virtue to fit his formulae. He never successfully proves that virtue has two opposing vices rather than just one.

- As has already been stated earlier in this commentary on Book II, justice appears to be a problematic exception to the doctrine of the mean, a theme dealt with unsatisfactorily in Book V.

> **Task**
>
> Are there any character traits that we praise as virtuous but which do not lie between the extremes of too much and too little?

> **Review question**
>
> Explain Aristotle's distinction between moral and intellectual virtue.

Action and *akrasia* (Book III)

Voluntary, involuntary and non-voluntary action (III.1)

Book III begins in typically Aristotelian style with a set of distinctions and sub-divisions relating to different kinds of action. Four types of action are distinguished:

- *voluntary action* – any action in which the agent is the originating cause and in which the agent knows the circumstances;

- *involuntary action* – any action performed under constraint or through ignorance;
- *a mixture between voluntary and involuntary action* – one in which the agent is the originating source and in which the agent knows the circumstances but acts through external pressure;
- *non-voluntary action* – a type of involuntary action committed through ignorance.

There is a nautical feel to Aristotle's examples, which I will also adopt. Imagine a scenario in which someone voluntarily purchases a luxury yacht to enjoy his retirement. Unbeknown to him, his arch-rival, having kidnapped his family, may force (that is, an involuntary action) him to give the yacht away in return for freeing the kidnapped family members. The arch-rival might get his just deserts, however, if he is caught in a storm while sailing back and forced to jettison his cargo. In this instance, his action is a mixture of voluntary and involuntary action, as he is in full knowledge of the implications of throwing his belongings overboard, yet needs to do this in order to survive. If, however, he went on to weather the storm and coincidentally find a copy of the *Nicomachean Ethics* on the yacht but burnt it as fuel out of ignorance of the work's edifying contents, then this, according to the above distinction, is to be classed as non-voluntary action as it is committed without knowledge. But if his mistake was drawn to his attention and the villain felt retrospective remorse, then it would revert back to being a type of involuntary action.

Task

Create your own scenario that helps to illustrate the difference between voluntary, involuntary and non-voluntary action.

In summation, Aristotle holds that there are different categories of human action: the compulsory and the voluntary. However, voluntary action is a complex category, since some voluntary actions we claim to be forced to do. Aristotle holds that an act done in ignorance cannot be genuinely voluntary. More problematic is Aristotle's claim that an act is not genuinely voluntary if, from a limited choice of

actions, I choose one that ideally I would sooner not do. Aristotle argues that, if the situation that demands this action isn't both desired by the agent and brought about by the agent, then the action is from one point of view involuntary. If an action is simply brought about by the agent but not desired, then Aristotle calls the action 'non-voluntary'.

Task

Consider the following examples. Can any of them be truly classed as voluntary?
- A police authority is forced to dismiss a senior police officer for misbehaviour at a private party.
- The authorities are forced to put down a dog after it has savaged a child.
- The government is forced to put up with a high level of unemployment as the only way it can see of counteracting inflation.
- A teacher is forced to accept his pupil's excuse about his failure to hand in an essay because he has no means of checking its veracity.
- I am forced to abandon my car because it has broken down and I need to get help.
- I am forced to swerve out of the way of a pensioner as he crosses the road recklessly.
- I was forced to shoot the prisoner because my commanding officer told me to do so.

Ignorance or compulsion are clearly less preferable to an intelligent choice in accordance with virtue. Aristotle is dismissive of the suggestion that every action is really involuntary because there are always external pressures, but he does not go as far as later existentialists, who seem to argue that all actions are voluntary.

Voluntary action for Aristotle needs to be carried out with the full knowledge of:

- the moral agent;
- what he or she is doing;
- who or what is affected;
- the means used;
- the intended result;
- the manner in which the agent acts.

Choice, deliberation and desire (III.2–5)

Chapters 2 to 5 of the third book are concerned with the three elements that combine to make a moral purpose in pursuit of a virtuous act. They are choice, deliberation and desire; the last element, **boulesis**, is translated by Ross as 'rational wish'. Let us examine each concept as it arises and see how this discussion relates to Aristotle's taxonomy of character. The second chapter defines choice as voluntary but draws our attention to the fact that not all voluntary action involves choice, for example spontaneity. Choice, like deliberation and rational desire, is an exclusively human trait and is not shared with non-cognitive animals. Indeed, irrational or incontinent people, according to the Aristotle's survey of characters, are more like animals, as their lives are governed by instinct and appetitive drives.

Aristotle does not believe that children are capable of living a life totally in accordance with virtue, in which the impulses of desire are reduced to a rational coherence which is the product of reflection and embodied in habituation. This is because the harmony that exists in a child's life is at best fortuitous and certainly unlikely to be the product of reflection. Well-disciplined children, it is true, are preferable to ill-disciplined ones, but their lives, however happy they seem, fall short of proper fulfilment, since their existence is only superficially rational, being instead determined by coercive and emotive forces. Children are vulnerable to changes in emotional climate such as falling into bad company or the death of a parent. To avoid this they must develop their rational nature. However, this development of a rational nature will in itself unsettle whatever patterns of behaviour they may have been schooled in when all is brought into question during the years of adolescent rebellion. Virtue, to be virtue, must be ingrained and self-conscious, habitual and rational. In the moral life one has to learn one's craft. Indeed, one can learn a lot through behaving badly. The pain that bad behaviour brings, however, is little spur to behave better if one is insufficiently thoughtful about it. As it says in the Old Testament Book of Proverbs, 'Like a dog returning to its vomit is a fool to his folly'.

Aristotle's taxonomy of character

The word 'taxonomy' is used of any system of classification. Aristotle, like many thinkers in the ancient world, is intent on imposing order on chaos and seems to have had a particular genius at categorisation. He suggests six types of character: the superhuman (god-like), the virtuous, the continent, the incontinent, the vicious and the sub-human. Very little is written about the first and last. Hector from Homer's *Iliad* is cited as an example of the superhuman, but people in this category are so rare as not to warrant attention. Likewise the subhuman or criminally insane character, who occupies a state below normal human immorality, engaging in paedophilia, cannibalism, sadism, gluttony or incest, is glossed over, though Aristotle draws an implicit link between this kind of person and Plato's description of the tyrant as outlined in Book IX of *The Republic*. We are hence left with four orders of merit, of which the virtuous and vicious are fairly self-explanatory although their traits become mixed in the enkratic (continent) and akratic (incontinent) individuals mentioned in Book III, Chapter 2.

Aristotle declares:

> Choice is not shared with man by irrational creatures as desire and temper are. Moreover, the incontinent man acts from desire but not from choice, while contra-wise the continent man acts from choice but not from desire. (1111b5, 31)

This quotation is successful in separating the continent from the incontinent individual, but requires a clearer extrapolation from the text. The Aristotelian ideal is of a person whose choices and desires work together. This is the result of a harmonious relationship between the rational and irrational elements of the soul, first outlined in Book I, Chapter 13. In the case of both continent and incontinent individuals, their non-rational elements (their appetitive and emotional desires) seek to tempt them away from the right course of action, yet it is only the continent, enkratic character who steers the right course despite having the wrong feelings. In the case of the vicious character, their rational element has selected the wrong end, which is misguidedly pursued with conviction. The four alternatives may be represented in tabular form:

Description	Rational element	Irrational element	Resulting action
Virtuous (*arete*)	Correct	Correct	Correct
Continent (***enkrateia***)	Correct	Incorrect	Correct
Incontinent (***akrasia***)	Correct	Incorrect	Incorrect
Vicious (*kakia*)	Incorrect	Incorrect	Incorrect

Let us imagine a scenario where these four individuals meet at a drinks party – the super-human and sub-human have not been invited. After a pleasant evening talking about the finer points of moral philosophy, all become aware that they need to drive home, but the host is so generous that he offers them another glass of wine. The virtuous character, whose reason and appetite speak with the same voice, makes the correct moral choice and declines. Both the enkratic and akratic guests are sorely tempted by the offer; their faculty of rational desire is faulty. Yet it is only in the continent, enkratic individual that reason wins the battle over emotion and appetite. The incontinent partygoer gives way to temptation through lack of will-power (Davidson translates *akrasia* as 'weakness of will') and cannot overcome his desire to have one for the road. The vicious person, who also accepts another drink, does it with the courage of his convictions, unaware that he has selected the wrong end. It is the failure of the irrational element, which 'mishears' the rational element, that causes the wrong choice in the incontinent

person. Luckily, for the continent individual, one's rational wish corrects this state of affairs in the course of action, though Aristotle does not enlarge on how this is achieved.

One problematic assertion that is made, however, is that the continent person cannot be fully said to possess virtue despite the resulting action being the same. A tension exists in the text, attested in the above quotation (III.2) and elsewhere (VII.6), as to how the rational element governs emotions and desires. There seems to be a specific contrast drawn between how rationality enforces appetites such as lust or greed to obey, whereas it seeks to harmonise emotions such as anger or fear. The latter category of emotions responds more to rationality, according to Aristotle, than the former. Thus, one ceases to be angry when one understands the reason for someone's behaviour. In contrast, the correction of appetites needs more severe, long-term planning, for example giving up smoking. In addition to defining incontinence as 'weakness of will', Aristotle characterises it as impetuosity or the failure to deliberate. To an extent, this is in reaction to Plato's denial of the existence of *akrasia*[3] when he asserts that the notion that one can act contrary to what one thinks is at best incoherent. It is nevertheless to the role of deliberation that our author turns in Chapter 3.

Having listed the sort of things that seem interesting to deliberate on, Aristotle condemns them as irrelevant and restricts his discussion to the involvement of deliberation in moral decision-making. The author describes in detail the process of decision-making, shown in an abbreviated form in the flow chart in figure 8.4.

Aristotle seems to be working backwards from this methodology: having first defined right action as the mean, he then considers the notion

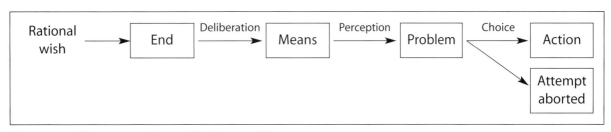

Figure 8.4 *The process of moral decision-making*

of voluntary choice, deliberation and desire (*boulesis*) in Book III, Chapter 4. He begins the fourth chapter by contrasting two accounts of rational wish, the Socratic and sophistical. For Platonists, a moral agent will choose incorrectly if he or she does not desire the Good, which is truly good. In the next chapter, Aristotle takes a Platonic line in arguing that no one is willingly bad. The fact that our author owes much to the Platonic tradition rises to the surface in Book III. Sophists are caricatured as desiring apparent goodness, which, like a cream bun, seems worthwhile but is not conducive to good health. Both Plato and Aristotle, as moral realists, find this position anathema to the good, but the latter argues from a situationist standpoint, i.e. one where a virtuous person judges each act on its own merits.

Chapter 5 begins with the author's assertion that, for good or ill, individuals choose the means they apply and should be held morally responsible for them. Moral action is likened to having children, in that we are held responsible for creating them in spite of what they may end up doing. Such a concept of personal moral responsibility is supported by the actions of judges and legislators. The weight of ethical decision-making ought to be felt in career choices also, as it is pointed out that, in choosing which path to take, one is at the same time deciding what disposition to nurture and what sort of person to become. For Aristotle, human beings are the source of their own actions. In answer to the sophistical query as to whether one can really be blamed for choosing what only appears to be beneficial, the author replies that each agent is held accountable for their judgement as to what counts as good. Even people who cannot control themselves, perhaps from alcohol or drug addiction, at some stage in their lives chose voluntarily to take such a course. Many of the themes raised in Book III concerning choice and culpability are also the concern of the twentieth-century ethicist Jean-Paul Sartre (see chapter 16). While he rejects Aristotelian essentialism, as expressed in the argument from functions, he nevertheless is attracted by absolute moral responsibility.

The importance of prudence (Book VI)

Purposive thought (VI.1–2)

After the detailed discussion on virtue theory that takes place from Books II to V, Book VI is concerned with happiness and the Aristotelian conception of the soul. The archer illustration in Chapter 1 sets virtue theory in its wider teleological context. The author likens each moral agent to an archer who uses their bow, representing virtue theory, to fire the arrows of virtuous action at an intelligently determined target, which is supreme happiness. It is the rational element of the soul, therefore, which directs operations, and Aristotle further classifies this faculty in order to complete the picture sketched out in the last chapter of Book I. He draws a distinction between rationality as concerned with precise subject matter that is not subject to variation (scientific faculty) and the study of things that are capable of variation (calculative faculty). Prudence or practical wisdom (*phronesis*), which is the main theme of Book VI, is another name given to the calculative faculty at work in the moral realm. The completed Aristotelian conception of the soul may be represented as in figure 8.5. Prudence is defined as the excellence of the calculative faculty of the soul, which enables the moral agent to choose the right means to achieve the right ends.

Aristotelean epistemology (VI.3–7)

Five modes of intellectual expression are discussed in Chapters 3–7. These are, in order of examination, pure science, applied science, practical wisdom, intuitive wisdom and theoretical wisdom. They may be allocated to the scientific and calculative faculties of rationality as shown in figure 8.6.

In his analysis of pure science, Aristotle takes a necessitarian view of scientific laws (see Chapter 6). He holds that the laws of science are as they are out of necessity and as such are capable of being learnt from induction, taught by experts and practically demonstrable (VI.3). Applied science is classed as a member of the calculative faculty of the soul because it is the art of producing or creating something which is

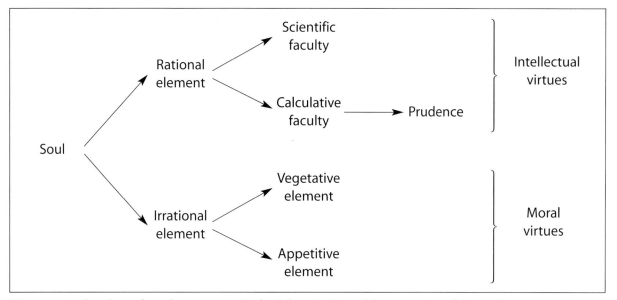

Figure 8.5 *The place of prudence or practical wisdom in Aristotle's conception of the soul*

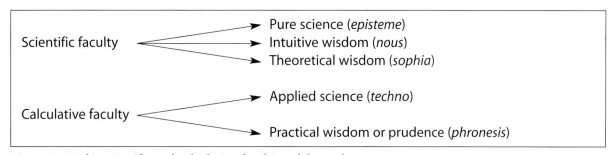

Figure 8.6 *The scientific and calculative faculties of the soul*

contingent, for example a building (VI.4).
Practical wisdom or prudence also forms part of
the calculative faculty, as its subject matter is
personal well-being. Unlike geometry, ethical
concerns regarding well-being are variable due to
their relationship with pleasure and pain, and
also due to the contingency of the situation
(VI.5). Practical wisdom requires separate
treatment in the following section. Intuitive
wisdom involves the formulation of judgements
from the study of particular instances
(induction), and is hence concerned with what
Aristotle calls 'first principles' (VI.6). Theoretical
wisdom, unlike prudence, is of an exclusively
abstract and intellectual nature. It is,
nevertheless, a vital ingredient of supreme
happiness or *eudaimonia*. How are practical and
theoretical wisdom reconciled within
eudaimonia?

Theoretical and practical wisdom (VI.8–11)

The subject of this discussion is at the heart of
Book VI and seems at times unconnected and
discursive. In order to clarify this issue, let us
start with a brief survey of theoretical and
practical wisdom:

• *Theoretical wisdom (***sophia***)* – Unlike
prudence, which is an ongoing process,
theoretical wisdom is described as the most
finished form of knowledge (VI.7). Prudence
is possessed by all animals that need certain
practical abilities in order to survive, but
sophia is viewed as the highest form of
knowledge and is exclusive to human beings.
Whereas prudence is practical and concerned
with particulars (as well as universals when
they apply to ethical arguments), theoretical

wisdom is concerned with universals. Theoretical wisdom, therefore, only uses deduction, while both deduction and induction are used in practical wisdom.

- *Practical wisdom* (phronesis) – Prudence is specifically concerned with the self whereas theoretical wisdom is focused on abstractions (VI.8). Prudence is related to practical issues, which range from political science (legislative and administrative, juridical and deliberative), economics and household management to physical fitness. Prudence involves many auxiliary concepts, which are analysed in (VI.8–11) as resourcefulness (correct deliberation), understanding, judgement, cleverness, and being scrupulous. Understanding is defined in an anti-Platonic way (VI.9) as being concerned with particulars. Together these multifarious aspects contribute to what is generally termed 'maturity'. In contrast, theoretical wisdom involves the capacity for abstract thought.

A useful definition of prudence is given in Book VI:

> Again, prudence is not concerned with universals only; it must also take cognizance of particulars, because it is concerned with conduct, and conduct has its sphere in particular circumstances. That is why some people who do not possess 'theoretical' knowledge are more effective in action (especially if they are experienced) than others who do possess it. For example, suppose that someone knows that light flesh foods are digestible and wholesome, but does not know what kinds are light; he will be less likely to produce health than one who knows that chicken is wholesome. (VI.7, 1141b15)

Thus, someone who is acquainted with the health-inducing properties of eating chicken would be able to benefit while remaining ignorant of the general principle (or major premise). Practical wisdom, nevertheless, as a faculty concerned with both universals and particulars, is required to possess both knowledge of the general rules and particular guidelines. Indeed, this is its great advantage over those who possess only theoretical knowledge or those who possess only acquaintance with particulars. Consider three characters, A, B and C:

A 'Professor Peabody' has only a knowledge of generalised theories; he is stuck in an ivory tower of abstraction and is unable to apply these theories to everyday life. He possesses theoretical wisdom alone.

B 'General Dogsbody' is a military leader who has learnt all the practical maxims ever issued in the history of western philosophy off by heart like a child's times tables and lives according to these. But he is fundamentally stupid and does not possess knowledge of what he has learnt.

C 'Prudence Peabody' (Professor Peabody's daughter) has read Book VI of Aristotle's *Nicomachean Ethics* carefully and possesses both theoretical knowledge of the Good and practical wisdom in understanding how to achieve it.

In Chapter 8, Aristotle illustrates the distinction by contrasting a young student of geometry with an older philosopher. The mathematician is as clever as his elder but does not possess 'practical wisdom of the wise Athenian' (cf. VI.11, 1143b11). Ironically, Plato is cast in the role of the former rather than the latter. There are frequent references to experience as a prerequisite for practical moral decision-making.

Review question

Explain Aristotle's concept of prudence or practical wisdom.

The problem of causal and constitutive means

Aristotle's analysis of prudence (*phronesis*) in Book VI does not pass by trouble-free, however, and there is an apparent conflict in the text between practical wisdom as the 'true apprehension' of the ends of conduct (VI.9, 1142b35) and practical wisdom as knowledge of the means (VI.12, 1144a7–9). The former passage suggests *phronesis* involves choosing both means and end, whereas the latter suggests means alone. One commentator, J. M. Cooper in *Reason and Human Good in Aristotle*,[4] has sought to reconcile this difference by focusing on the phrase 'things leading to an end', which occurs in

Chapter 12. Cooper argues that the textual tension arises from an ambiguity in the notion of 'means'. Two connotations may be distinguished.

- The causal sense – X is a means to Y in that X causes Y, for example spinach builds up my strength.
- The constitutive sense – X is a means to Y in so far as X promotes and is constitutive of Y, for example strength is a component of good health.

Cooper's conclusion is that prudence is both causally contributive to *eudaimonia* in that it involves the capacity to bring it about, but also constitutive of *eudaimonia* in that one cannot be *eudaimon* without possessing practical wisdom.

The interdependence thesis (VI.12–13)

In the closing chapters of Book VI, Aristotle addresses the problem of how practical wisdom relates to virtue. He declares: 'Moral virtue is necessary for prudence' (VI.12, 1144a35). And later he states: 'Prudence is necessary for moral virtue' (VI.13, 1144b26).

They are interdependent: the existence of one is impossible without the existence of the other. To emphasise this point, Aristotle spends a little time detailing two states, which are as close as you can get to prudence and moral virtue but without interdependence. Cleverness is described (VI.12, 1144a24ff.) as practical wisdom without moral virtue, and natural virtue (VI.13, 1144b1ff.) is defined as moral virtue without practical wisdom. Thus in the former one is able to work out the means to achieve something but not the correct means to achieve *eudaimonia*, and in the latter case an individual may be born with the desirable character traits of generosity and courage but lack the reflectiveness or deliberation required for moral virtue. Natural virtue, unlike moral virtue, exists in children and animals (III.8, 1117a8–9) and does not require cognitive awareness of one's moral goals.

Two criticisms are presented against the interdependence thesis. The first stems from the fact that there are differing interpretations over how the interdependence thesis is to be played out.

Criticism 1: the chicken and the egg predicament (Which came first?)

The interdependence thesis does not give a clear indication as to which of the entities came first: prudence or moral virtue. It might be possible that cleverness and natural virtues are the precursors to their more favoured counterparts. An alternative suggestion is made by one commentator[5] who talks about a third type of pseudo-virtue consisting in a predisposition towards habituation. Evidence for this may be found in Book III, Chapter 1.

Criticism 2: the inseparability of the virtues

It seems that Aristotle is led into an absurdity with his assertion: 'For with the presence of the one quality, practical wisdom, will be given all the excellences' (VI.13, 14459–62). This implies that you can't have any virtues at all unless you are prudent, and that the virtues cannot exist independently of each other. Thus one may formulate this criticism:

1 Virtue cannot exist without practical wisdom.
2 If one possesses practical wisdom then one possesses all of the virtues.
3 This implies that one cannot have one virtue without having all of the others.
4 To assert such is an absurdity.

An Aristotelian defence might take the form of arguing that, since actions can be only either right or wrong and we are defining a virtuous action as one that is right, it is inferred that a virtuous action cannot at the same time be wrong. It is, therefore, the presence of moral righteousness that unifies all the virtues.

Pleasure, happiness and contemplation (Book X)

Pleasure (X.1–6)

The opening chapter of Book X acknowledges pleasure as an important motivating force and consequently a useful educational tool. Aristotle has promised us an ethical analysis that is firmly grounded in everyday empirical experience. To ignore this feature of everyday life would therefore be a philosophical *faux pas*. In keeping with the mean, the author strives for the middle ground between the unbridled pleasure-seeking of hedonism and the denunciatory denial found in stoicism.

Eudoxus (Chapter 2) is cited as an example of a hedonist, but one from whom we can learn some important lessons about pleasure such as: all creatures whether rational or irrational are attracted by it; it should not be allowed to control your character; it is sought, just as its opposite (pain) is shunned; it is pursued for the sake of itself and acts as a condiment in enhancing the 'flavour' of other things. Aristotle is wary, however, and concludes that all Eudoxus' arguments prove is that pleasure is good but not in the same league as *eudaimonia*. Even Plato's separation between good and pleasure is wheeled in for support (see *The Republic* (505)).

If the hedonistic views expressed by Eudoxus misfire, then so do those of the stoics and Platonists, who adopt the overly austere view that pleasure is not a good. Aristotle refutes this by stating that anything desired by someone of a rational cast of mind cannot be bad. He assumes that the pleasure-seeking trait in irrational creatures is some sort of subliminal superior instinct manifesting itself. One might equally argue, however, that pleasure-seeking in rational creatures such as ourselves is a subliminal inferior instinct more in keeping with the irrational faculty. The third chapter moves on to assess the argument that pleasure is as much a vice as pain. This point may be set out thus:

	Virtue	Vice
Plato	Stoicism	Pleasure/Pain
Aristotle	Pleasure	Licentiousness/Insensibility

Pleasure, for Aristotle, is the mean between too much and too little; this contrasts with the stoical view that regards any form of pleasure as being an emotive distraction from what is good. Platonic arguments from Book VII of *The Republic* and the *Philebus* are 'footnoted' in passing. He criticises Plato's argument that the Good can be known whereas pleasure is indeterminate. The author likens pleasure and pain to health and illness. Both dichotomies are mixed in practice and we are rarely in perfect health all the time, but that does not stop us recommending health over illness and therefore should not stop us objectively endorsing pleasure.

Clearly the gratification of desire is pleasurable, but the pursuit of pleasure does not lead to happiness, as desires can appear in an undisciplined and irregular fashion. Just as the expression of a desire can drive out another desire, so the enjoyment of one pleasure can dispel another. The pursuit of happiness can turn out to be like chasing a will o' the wisp, which is all the more unsatisfactory because the very rotation of pleasures creates an underlying sense of unfulfilment and all the displeasure that goes with that. One who leads a good life does not need to forsake pleasure, since pleasure is not incompatible with a life in which one's desires are in harmony and one's *telos* attained. However, pleasure is a poor guide to the rational life.

Aristotle extends the definition of pleasure towards the end of the third chapter and points out that it is not a process of replenishment, as when our thirst is slaked or hunger abated. Pleasure has more of a value-added dimension and hence a closer analogy might be that of learning for learning's sake. Immoral pleasures should not be counted as pleasures at all, as they are only attractive to someone with the wrong sort of disposition. To draw a parallel, a cigarette would be pleasurable to a smoker but would make a non-smoker feel ill. The buzz and satisfaction smoking brings is a good thing but not at a detrimental cost to one's health. Aristotle concludes that pleasures can only be recognised as pleasures by someone of a virtuous disposition. He illustrates this with two thought experiments. The first asks whether you would rejuvenate in order to enjoy childish pleasures again in place of adult ones. The second is a response to Plato's story of Gyges (see page 149) and concludes that those of a virtuous character would not indulge in unhealthy 'pleasures' even if they were guaranteed of escaping any social repercussions.

Aristotle likens pleasure to sense perception, in so far as both are perfect, indivisible and self-contained activities (Chapter 4). Pleasure is not a process (the author ignores the perceptions needed for some pleasures), but a complete experience like seeing. I can look at something any number of times or just for an instant and it would not affect my perception of it, just as I can experience prolonged or instantaneous pleasure and feel that both are complete experiences in themselves. Aristotle contrasts pleasure to processes such as building or making a journey and concludes: 'that which is instantaneous is a whole'. Pleasure is instantaneous, whereas processes are made of parts. He extends the metaphor of perception to state that just as my eyesight or hearing cannot be impeded when seeing something clearly, so my pleasure 'sense-faculty' needs to be in good condition. He does not specify what such a faculty is, but one may conclude from the previous discussion in Chapter 3 that it is related to a virtuous disposition. The senses need to be fully functional to gain maximal pleasure from the activity engaged in, while the object of pleasure needs to be in the right condition. Thus the experience of sipping a fine vintage wine would be spoilt if the wine were corked or your taste buds impaired.

Aristotle explores the relationship between pleasure and *eudaimonia* in Chapter 5, and concludes that pleasure is a component of the highest good. A problem is noted in that pleasure appears subjective: some people like flute playing, others chewing sweets or writing. Indeed, often pleasures compete with each other. Which pleasures are we to classify as proper, and which as alien? The author enrols the help of the argument from functions to differentiate between good, bad and neutral pleasures. Good pleasures are those that contribute to a fulfilled human nature, bad pleasures are those that inhibit human flourishing (and consequently should not be classed as pleasures at all), whereas neutral pleasures provide pleasant distractions but are contingent in relation to *eudaimonia*. Whereas functions are divergent amongst species, they are convergent within species: thus 'all donkeys prefer sweepings to gold' and the same things count as good pleasures for all human beings.

Aristotle is no killjoy, but draws a clear distinction between happiness (*eudaimonia*) and pleasure. The former is an end-in-itself and self-sufficient whereas the latter is merely a relaxing diversion yet complementary to prosperity and felicity. One clear way to classify these activities is to observe the actions of a virtuous person. The author puts much sway on virtuous people setting a good example. He asserts that many cul-de-sacs are followed in the field of pleasure by people mistakenly following the pursuits of rich tyrants and copying them on a smaller scale. This behaviour is misguided, as it assumes that such people in power have a clear idea as to what is good for them, when clearly they do not and instead follow the distractions of slaves.

Happiness and contemplation (X.7–8)

Aristotle acknowledges that contemplation is the highest form of human happiness and the purest of pleasures through the following argument:

1 Happiness is an activity in accordance with virtue.
2 Happiness as defined in **1** is the highest good for humanity.
3 The faculty that exercises this highest good is the best faculty.
4 The intellect exercises the highest good through the act of contemplation.
5 Therefore, the intellect is the best human faculty and contemplation the highest human faculty.

Further proof that this is the case is provided in the rest of Chapter 7, where the author asserts that one can engage in contemplation alone as it is closest to our human nature; it has its 'peculiar pleasure', which is often termed 'leisure'; and it exists in a different realm from the practical arts of politics and warfare. The author concludes the section by asserting that, together with a long life, a life of contemplation most truly satisfies human beings: 'Therefore for man, too, the best and most pleasant life is the life of the intellect, since the intellect is in the fullest sense the man. So this life will also be the happiest.'

When one has achieved *eudaimonia* one might be said to be living the contemplative life. In so doing, Aristotle believes human beings come most near being god-like (Chapter 8). Yet this contemplative happiness is at the same time grounded in human experience. The author's virtue theory is practical, situationist and anthropocentric (it stresses human interaction and the importance of feelings as well as the role awarded to the intellect).

Review question

Briefly explain Aristotle's reasons for recommending a life of contemplation.

Ethics and politics (X.9)

The final chapter, though subject to clumsy editing at times, makes a convenient link to the companion volume of this text, entitled the *Politics*. In this work, Aristotle defines an ideal state as that which nurtures and cultivates *eudaimonia*. Our author has always been a pragmatist throughout the text and is concerned with real situations. He is struck by the gulf between the life of contemplative happiness as proposed and the social reality. Education and legislation are seen as corrective processes. Although a receptive audience is required to begin with, Aristotle believes that the state should be in charge of both education and law enforcement, unless a group of individuals can fare better in creating an ordered society themselves. Practical wisdom carries its own authority, which may be used to sound social effect by those skilled in the art of legislation. Aristotle advocates a specialisation of function to prevent the sophists from acting as panjandrums.

There is a tradition of political thought that begins with the notion that there is a definable good life for all human beings. For Aristotle, such a life is rationally defensible in that its goals underlie most of our behaviour whether we recognise it or not. We all seek happiness, and the good life is that life that gets nearest to its attainment. To recommend the good life to anyone is thus to recommend that they apply reason to their behaviour in pursuit of the happiness they want. Within the Aristotelian tradition there is the resultant belief that the state should be some sort of social ringmaster that ensures that people as individuals within a state can lead a good life. This view maintains that any state that allows individuals to lead a good life is a good state, and any state that inhibits the good life is a bad state. Such a state, in not conforming to a pattern that encourages the good life, is said to be not conforming to natural law or violating natural or human rights. A good state creates an environment in which the good life may occur. Like plants bathing in the sun, individuals thrive under the supervision of a benign state.

Revision questions

1 Assess Aristotle's notion of practical wisdom.

2 Outline and illustrate Aristotle's conception of the soul.

3 Evaluate the doctrine of the mean.

4 Explain the difference between voluntary, involuntary and non-voluntary euthanasia.

5 Assess the claim that 'virtue is its own reward'.

Discussion questions

■ Is happiness the goal of every action?

■ What would Aristotle's ideal person be like?

■ Is the capacity to reason a distinctively human activity?

■ How does the doctrine of the mean differ from advocating 'moderation in all things'?

■ How useful is Aristotle's ethical theory for the moral dilemmas faced today?

Glossary of key terms

Akrasia: the word used by Aristotle to describe someone who does wrong whilst realising that they are doing wrong.

Arete: the Greek word for 'virtue', calculated by the doctrine of the mean.

Boulesis: translated as 'rational wish' – that is, the desire to do what is right.

Enkrateia: the word used by Aristotle to describe someone who does the right action despite being drawn to its opposite.

Ergon: the Greek word for 'function'. For Aristotle everything is meant to operate and act in accordance with its nature, including human beings.

Ethos: the Greek word for 'character', which gives us the term 'ethics'. For the ancients, ethics meant the study of what it is to be a noble person.

Eudaimonia: variously translated as 'happiness', 'personal flourishing', 'development' or 'fulfilment'.

Phronesis: prudence or practical wisdom; the intellectual process of working out what the right thing to do is and how one should go about doing it.

Reductio ad absurdum (Latin): a form of argument that offers alternatives before reducing all but one to absurdity thus leaving a clear conclusion.

Sophia: a feminine noun in Greek which means 'wisdom'.

Telos: the goal, purpose, aim or target of an action or series of actions.

Suggested reading

- Barnes, J. (2000) *Aristotle*, Oxford, OUP
  An introduction to the life and works of Aristotle from the Past Masters Series
- Milch, R. (1997) *Cliffs Notes on Aristotle's Ethics*, Lincoln, Nebraska, Cliffs Notes
  Few crib notes exist for philosophical texts; this series also provides notes on some Platonic dialogues
- Rorty, A. O. ed. (1980) *Essays on Aristotle's Ethics*, Berkeley, University of California Press
  An in-depth collection of essays, Nagel's essay on *eudaimonia* being especially useful
- Sherman, N. ed. (1999) *Aristotle's Ethics: Critical Essays*, Lanham, Rowman & Littlefield
  An academic collection that covers all the main themes
- Urmson, J. O. (1988) *Aristotle's Ethics*, Oxford, Blackwell
  The opening gambit for any student of Aristotle's *Nicomachean Ethics*

Notes

1. Cooper, J. M. (1987) 'Contemplation and Happiness: A Reconsideration' in *Synthèse* 72: pp. 187–216.

2. *Apology* 29d–4e, *Republic* Book I, *Gorgias* 492d5ff.

3. *Protagoras* 352–358 and *Meno* 77–78.

4. Cooper, J. M. *Reason and Human Good in Aristotle*, Cambridge, Mass., 1975.

5. Sorabji, R. (1973/4) 'Aristotle on the Role of Intellect in Virtue', *Proceedings of the Aristotelean Society* 74: pp. 107–129.

9 A commentary on Descartes' *Meditations*

One cannot conceive anything so strange and so implausible that it has not already been said by one philosopher or another. (René Descartes)

Aims

On completion of this chapter you should be able to:

- provide a critical account of Cartesian scepticism
- explain Cartesian foundationalism and its quest for certainty
- explain the notion of total deception
- understand and evaluate Descartes' famous assertion *cogito ergo sum*
- evaluate Cartesian dualism with reference to the wax example
- explain and discuss the role of God in the *Meditations* with reference to the ontological argument
- outline and assess Cartesian rationalism with reference to clear and distinct ideas and the trademark argument
- explain Descartes' proof for the existence of material things
- explain the distinction between imagination and understanding
- outline Descartes presentation of the mind–body problem and his intermingling thesis.

The original title of Descartes' classic work is 'Meditations on the first philosophy in which the existence of God and the real distinction between the soul and the body are demonstrated'. This treasure-trove embraces the philosophy of religion, the philosophy of mind and the theory of knowledge. Through elegant and engaging prose, the author outlines his version of the **ontological** argument for the existence of God, refines a more subtle form of substance **dualism** than he is often given credit for, and initiates a debate between fellow rationalists and opposing empiricists that would continue for centuries. Descartes' *Meditations* has justifiably earned its reputation as one of the greatest works of philosophy of all time.

The First Meditation

Some people hold the view that philosophers go around questioning the taken-for-granted views of everyday life in order to indulge in a kind of obtuse eccentricity. This is not correct, and is certainly far from Descartes' intentions. In the First Meditation, he outlines his method of systematic doubt as laid out in his previous work the *Discourse on Method*. He briefs the reader on the task in hand, which consists of an **epistemological** demolition job in order to reconstruct knowledge on firmer foundations. The opening remarks of the First Meditation are reminiscent of an illustration given in the second part of the *Discourse on Method*. Let us quote from this companion text to gain an understanding of the argument:

> It is true that we have no example of people demolishing all the houses in a town for the sole purpose of rebuilding them in a different way to make the streets more beautiful; but one does see many people knock down their own in order to rebuild them, and that even in some cases they have to do this because the houses are in danger of falling down and the foundations are insecure.[1]

Descartes is worried that the foundations of human knowledge as they existed in the seventeenth century were structurally unsafe. He will go on, in the rest of the text, to use *a priori* beliefs, termed 'clear and distinct ideas', as the concrete building blocks for his theory of knowledge.

The author is both a rationalist and a **foundationalist**. He seeks to found human knowledge on the secure foundations of those truths that we can work out through reason alone. Descartes embarks on a search for infallible first principles, rejecting as candidates anything that 'is not completely certain and indubitable'. An element of philosophical paranoia seems to creep in when Descartes promises to reject all beliefs if there is reason for doubting the truth of one of them. The senses are **anthropomorphised** as micro-deceivers that cannot be trusted, as they have lied in the past. Through his musings on thoughts, dreams and sleeping habits, he makes his quest for indubitable truth a personal one, which starts with self-doubt and ends in self-awareness. He meditates, 'I feel this hand, carefully and knowingly', and in the course of the text stretches out this hand tentatively towards God, existence and knowledge.

Descartes lived at a time of great intellectual change, when many previously held convictions in science, theology, politics and art were being challenged. Some people saw the period as a new beginning. For Descartes, a practising mathematician and scientist, it was important that the whole enterprise of knowledge rested upon secure foundations. A sceptic observing humanity trading in one set of opinions for another could doubt whether any set of beliefs was true.

Descartes knew that, from a practical point of view, few of us could act like convinced sceptics, doubting the independent existence of the world, the truths of mathematics etc. But he was also aware that a persistent sceptic could question pretty well anything we claim as truth, and that if we tried to support that claim by invoking some principle or favourite idea the sceptic could doubt that too. He felt, therefore, that the theoretical convictions that make up our view of the world needed to be made immune from the attacks of the sceptic. His strategy was threefold:

- He wanted to find out how far **scepticism** could go (what could not be doubted).
- In doing this he hoped to find some truths that were really self-evident.
- He hoped on the basis of these truths to 'reconstruct' human knowledge on secure foundations, like Archimedes, who declared that if he found the right point he could balance the whole world on it.

He hoped to move from this Archimedean point to establishing a set of first principles; from there he hoped to link up with scientific laws that in turn would imply the particular truths and facts of everyday experience. Descartes' model in this respect was similar to Euclidean geometry, in which apparently self-evident **axioms** are forwarded, postulates and definitions added, and on this basis other truths are seen to follow out of necessity. Theorems are demonstrated by working from first principles. Descartes is aiming for a totally systematic organisation of all human knowledge – that is, a deductive ideal of knowledge, which we could represent as follows:

Self-evident (eternal) truths → First principles → Theories → Everyday facts

Descartes did not sufficiently work out what was involved in this ideal, but this picture of knowledge as a tight logical structure characterises Cartesian rationalism. A slightly later philosopher, Baruch Spinoza (1632–1677), succeeded in organising his own work like a treatise in geometry.

Cartesian scepticism

One cause of doubt with respect to human knowledge arises from the fact that what we take as true is in part based on the evidence of the senses. Evidence from the senses is notoriously unreliable in two ways. First, we may misinterpret what the senses lay before us, for example when we think a stick is a gun from a distance. Second, we may find it difficult at times to distinguish what we imagine from what we hear, for example when we think we hear a bell when there isn't such a sound. There are also, of course, cases where the senses appear to present us with data that is itself deceiving (as in the case of conjuring tricks or puzzle pictures). The senses are the source of error in these cases because had we not eyes, ears etc. we would not be led to make false judgements about what our eyes and ears furnish us with. The cases above show that judgements arising from sense experience can be false.

In most cases, however, sense-data seem to be corrigible. In other words, we do seem able to identify and modify false judgements and to extend and develop our sense experience. We look a little closer and feel the object that we are uncertain about and accordingly frame a judgement that seems based on sounder foundations. That is to say, we do not act as if sense experience is generally an unreliable source. Indeed, it seems difficult to see how we could discover that we were deceived if we held that sense experience as a whole could not at any time be properly assessed.

Part of the reason why we allege that we have been deceived by our senses is that the judgement which we have resultantly framed conflicts with other judgements made about sense-data that we believe to be true. So when I think that a stick looks bent in water but realise it isn't, it is chiefly because my original belief conflicts with other convictions about the stick's rigidity that I am prepared to hold to with more tenacity because these convictions are based on the behaviour of matter in general. If I was prepared to drop these convictions then I might be prepared to say that the stick really is bent, but it would be very costly to do so. This case highlights two important features of judgements of the senses. First, that they are revisable, and it would be difficult to think of an example where they are not. Second, that interpreting sense-data is inevitably part of the general enterprise of understanding our 'world as a whole'. We have no assurance, however, that our overall world view is correct. Judgements from the senses form a provisional body of knowledge and it is precisely this feature that has been regretted by philosophers since Plato as simply not good enough.

Descartes believes that the senses cannot be a source of indubitable knowledge, and a case is made out that constitutes reasonable grounds for saying that he has a good reason to think so. Isolated judgements of the senses do not produce certain knowledge, though one might be forgiven for thinking that they are not a bad starting point. Descartes, however, is ruthless in his condemnation. He first points out that sensory judgement can often be mistaken – let us call this the argument from illusion. He then follows this up with three equally powerful arguments:

- the argument from dreaming;
- the argument based on the possibility of a systematic defect of understanding;
- the arch-demon argument.

The argument from dreaming

It is true that sometimes we trust our senses whereas sometimes we do not. Descartes asks 'How do we know that the whole field of sensory data laid before us is not a dream?' After all, when we dream we take the events that happen within dreams as real, and only retrospectively, when we are awake, do we discover that we are not justified in doing so. While dreaming, we have no means of discovering our mistake, and therefore can entertain the fact that we could be dreaming when framing our ideas of the 'real world'. At any rate, we would not know that we weren't. One is tempted to say that we can distinguish reality from dreams by the more lively feel that reality has, but this is clearly a poor argument, since when one dreams one is completely taken in by the dreams, hence their often disturbing character. Bear in mind that among primitive tribes dreams are often considered as real happenings within some other 'spirit' world.

The fact is that dreams are not identified as dreams by their supposedly unreal feel but because of their inability to connect with circumstances of that experiential world we call reality. The narrative of the dream does not merge into the narrative of everyday life; it does not cohere with waking experience, as when I dream that I have lost all my savings but my bank manager refuses to corroborate this fact. Note, however, that the dream's unreality is something that we discover retrospectively; it is not something that we discover immediately at the moment of dreaming. Given this, one might rush to the conclusion that Descartes has indeed given us good reason to doubt. Could not reality be a dream and dreams sub-dreams within a greater dream?

The trouble with this suggestion is that it proceeds as follows:

1 We suggest that there are two things: dreams and reality.
2 We suggest that these two things can be confused – that is, we can mistake dreams for reality.
3 Finally, we put forward the suggestion that what we take to be reality as a whole could be a dream.

If we claim to know that **2** does occur, we must know the difference between dreams and reality, for you cannot intelligibly suggest that one thing is confused with another if you do not know what the difference between the two things is. It would not be sensible to claim that 'jams' were often confused with 'preserves' if I did not know what the difference between the two was. For Descartes to suggest that we know cases where dreams are wrongly identified with reality would imply that we know the difference between dreams and reality but had erroneously confused the two. This does not imply that we can specify the difference or spell out the criterion, just that we apprehend the difference. To then suggest that all we take to be reality could be taken as a dream is to invite us to ignore our own capacity to differentiate dreams and reality – and why should we do this?

The systematic defect argument

Could it not be the case, argues Descartes, that in thinking out the equations of mathematics or the proofs of geometry we habitually and incorrigibly assess things incorrectly through a systematic defect in our intelligence? Then we would be in a position akin to that of the old man who repeats the same story again and again because he cannot retain the memory of his first telling it. Now the problem with this is that the systematic defect in our understanding is precisely the sort of thing that we wouldn't

expect to know whether we had it or not. Think of what an affirmative answer would look like to the question, 'Is there a systematic defect in our understanding?' Might some alien intelligence make humankind aware of it? There seem few likely ways in which the systematic defect claim could be made good, but it is still a better argument than the previous ones, because the possibility of a systematic defect cannot be precluded even if it could not easily be proved. Human intelligence stands in need of ratification and confirmation; in the absence of that we have a good sceptical argument.

The following considerations may be urged against the systematic defect argument:

- Descartes' examples of the kind of things that could be systematically wrong are not well chosen. He cites examples of simple arithmetic, for example 2 + 2 = 4. Unfortunately, to say we could make an error over a matter like this would seem to involve misunderstanding what the terms '2' and '+' and '=' mean, and they don't seem to mean much other than what we define them to mean. Given how we define them, it is difficult to see how '2 + 2 = 4' could be false without our abandoning the original definitions. A systematic error on our part would need to be a consistent misreading of the formula, and so based on a kind of redefinition and not a proper error. Taking this as read, there are better examples Descartes could have given that do not create the same problem.

- It may be objected that, had we some systematic defect in our understanding, it would be an evolutionary hazard to us that would rapidly endanger the species. However, some species we know have systematic defects in perception and understanding while remaining viable, and not every type of misunderstanding need have a practical consequence. (Cows, for example, are colour blind with no apparent detriment to their well-being.)

- Thirdly, it may be objected that systematic defects can be corrected through the development of our knowledge. For example, we are not naturally aware of gamma rays, but through study of their effects we have got to know about their existence. Again, though we may concede that we can overcome some constitutional deficiencies, it by no means follows that we can overcome them all, and Descartes can dismiss this counter-argument as vain hope.

The arch-demon argument

For some commentators this is Descartes' most powerful argument against our intellectual certainty. The question is raised as to how we know that all our experiences are not being fed to us artificially by some evil intelligence or arch-deceiver. Clearly, if this is true, we would be in no position to either falsify or verify it. Equally, we have no reason to believe that it is true. The thrust of the argument is to suggest that we are totally immersed in a world of complete illusion like characters in a book. However, like characters in a book, we may reach correct conclusions about our imaginary world, and thus the argument constitutes an attack, not on our knowledge as such, but on its worth and status. In doubting the authenticity of our thought processes as a whole, a pathway is laid towards the assertion *cogito ergo sum*, which is implicit in the Second Meditation.

In the few paragraphs that make up the First Meditation, the author tells us a great deal about thoughts. They are to be used as a foundation in his epistemology. They occur in the mind, which is distinct from physical, sensory experiences, as is the faculty of interpreting sense-data. We cannot create new thoughts independently of features we see painted on the external world that surrounds us. The important features of the mental, as the foundation of truth, are identified in a few lines:

> but that arithmetic, geometry, and other such disciplines that discuss only very simple and general things, are not concerned with whether or not they exist in nature, contain something that is certain and beyond doubt. For whether I am awake or asleep, two and three added together make five and a quadrilateral figure has no more than four sides. It seems impossible that one would ever suspect that such clear truths are false.[2]

For Descartes, even God cannot alter these truths before my mind's eye, as God cannot create something that is logically contradictory. The indubitable, for Descartes, enjoys a divine seal of approval.

Review question

Describe any one of Descartes' sceptical arguments.

Task

Prepare a role-play in which two characters, Sceptic and Non-sceptic, are having an argument. Non-sceptic should write down five statements that they believe are impossible or at least very difficult to doubt and then show them to Sceptic, who should challenge them. Swap roles after a while.

The Second Meditation

The opening sentiment of the Second Meditation is a popular one in philosophy, namely the desire to impose order out of chaos. Descartes goes on to liken his epistemological labour to Archimedes levering a heavy object into a position of greater stability. This object is the weight of knowledge, the lever is methodological doubt, and the fulcrum about which the load turns is the notion of clear and distinct ideas. Descartes proceeds by questioning whether we can be certain of anything at all. His argument proceeds in the following way:

1 I consist of both a mind and a body (substance dualism).

2 I can doubt whether I possess a body, including the senses.

3 I can doubt the authorship of thoughts in so far as thoughts may be self-generated or injected into my mind by some supreme being.

4 I cannot doubt, however, that I have a mind that functions as a receptacle for any thoughts.

5 It is, therefore, a necessary truth that I know that such a receptacle as my mind exists. This is the case whether I am being deceived through my thoughts or not.

6 As the only indubitable candidate for personal identity, I know that my mind is 'me' in the truest sense.

Descartes' conclusion, 'I am, I exist', sounds like a precursor to existentialism, although Cartesianism is unlike this later movement in that it holds that humans have a preordained nature or essence. For the author of the *Meditations*, one's essence involves existence. He is careful in the subsequent paragraph, though, not to be too bold about pronouncements to do with personal identity, stating: 'I do not yet understand sufficiently who this "I" is who now necessarily exists'. Despite this admission, even greater uncertainty surrounds the physical. Descartes repeats the arch-demon argument here, with the result that a **physicalist** account of personal identity is reduced to absurdity, as it remains open to doubt, whereas an account of personal identity that depicts the individual as 'a thinking thing, that is, a mind, soul, intellect or reason' is accepted on the grounds that it is genuine, true and indubitable. If evidence is needed that this section of the work is concerned with personal identity, note that the word 'I' is used fifty-eight times in the space of three paragraphs. Embedded in the centre of this sequence resides the suspicion that the author is guilty of the homunculus fallacy. The homunculus fallacy occurs when a philosopher does not offer an explanation for something but asserts that there is another layer of the human mind that is able to solve the problem. This begs the question as to whether there is an end to this layering. Descartes asserts that 'I know that I exist and am asking who is this "I" who I know'. An infinite regress is created by talking about one's personal identity in third-person terms, as one might pose such a question *ad infinitum*: who is the I who knows the I who I know? Descartes does not seem unaware of this, and is quick to define the 'I' who I seek to know as consciousness in general. This consciousness or thinking is used as a catch-all term for many activities: understanding, affirming, denying, willing, not willing, imagining, sensing and of course doubting. The activity of thinking is elevated above the content of the thoughts themselves and offered as the criteria for what makes us fully human. In the case of doubting, the irony of understanding something clearly by considering one's doubts is duly noted by the writer.

The wax example

In this poetic illustration, Descartes takes a piece of wax and records its accidental features: the slight taste of honey, as it has just been extracted from the honeycomb, the scent of flowers, its cool, golden firmness. The same piece of wax is then moved near to a fire and loses each feature in front of our very eyes! The wax is now tasteless, without scent, colourless, hot, liquid and malleable, yet any observer would testify that it is the same wax. Through using this example, Descartes seeks to demonstrate the function of the mind as an interpreter. The senses record that which is particular, extended, flexible and changeable, whereas it is the mind that is able to register and understand what is going on. To use a modern-day example courtesy of John Searle, both computers and humans can process information, but only the human mind can attach meaning and use reason through interpreting the information processed. Descartes argues that animals, while capable of sensory perception, are not conscious or aware of what is being perceived (29).

Following in the footnotes of Plato, Descartes describes the mind as that which is concerned with the immutable essences of things, such as wax itself. If this were not the case, we would justifiably mistake other people as empty shells or mindless automata. Yet because of the mind's faculty of judgement we are able to 'see', in the sense of 'understand', that which lies beyond the surface of things and avoid scepticism concerning other minds. One knows the wax more clearly and perfectly through understanding what wax is, just as one knows oneself more clearly by reflecting on what it is to be a human being. At this stage in the Second Meditation, Descartes becomes aware of his own relationship to that which he is observing and understanding. Like Sartre centuries later, who defines his own existence in relation to the surrounding phenomena, Descartes seeks to define his identity in terms of perceiving and interpreting the external world: 'Likewise, if from the fact that I touch it, I judge that the wax exists, it follows that I exist'.

Cogito ergo sum

Descartes' famous pronouncement *cogito ergo sum*, 'I think therefore I am', is not to be found in the *Meditations*.[3] The above, however, constitutes an argument in the same vein that may be summarised as 'I judge therefore I am'. As the linchpin of Descartes' theory, *cogito ergo sum*, as a philosophical statement, deserves attention. The phrase is not original; a thousand years before, St Augustine had stated *dubito ergo sum*, 'I doubt therefore I am'. It is widely accepted that the *cogito* is an indubitable premise and a legitimate, if somewhat uninformative, starting point of Descartes' philosophy. It is in a unique category of judgements, which have only to be voiced to be seen as true or certain, rather like the axioms in Euclid, which are not argued for but are taken as certain in order that theorems might be proved. The philosopher Franz Brentano (1838–1917) argued that if we feel truth claims need backing up by other supporting judgements there must be some judgements that do not need backing up; he called these 'the evident'. Descartes clearly views Euclid's axioms as a prototype of what the first principles of philosophy might be, and though he and later philosophers accepted that there are indeed 'truths of reason', 'eternal truths' etc. he does succeed in demonstrating in the *Meditations* that these can be doubted. They can be doubted by assuming there is an arch-demon.

The *cogito*, on the other hand, cannot be doubted. I might speak of some principle about which I feel there is no question, for example 'nothing comes from nothing', but then raise the question about whether my confidence in its truth might not be misplaced. My feelings of complete confidence in its truth might be pathological, the product of some psychological illness or demonic deception. Clearly the fact that I cannot see how it could be false or conceive of any kind of objection to it might be just what you might expect from such a malaise or piece of witchcraft. Thinking that I exist, however, seems in a different league, since I cannot sketch a theoretical situation in which I could be wrong. Any attempt to do so, whether by talk of demons or brain quirks or whatever, seems to involve reference to my existence. I can,

it seems, sketch a rather peculiar situation in which I could erroneously believe 'nothing comes from nothing', whereas I cannot sketch a situation in which I erroneously believe that I exist. There does not seem to be any situation conceivable in which it would be incorrect for me to believe I exist. It is of course perfectly possible to visualise a situation in which someone would be wrong to believe they didn't exist, due to insanity. But the fact remains that no one can dream up a predicament in which they erroneously believe they exist.

The *cogito* as a tautology

Some philosophers have suggested that *cogito ergo sum* is really a **tautology**, and this weakens its claim as a firm foundation for knowledge. By 'tautology' is meant any statement that is true by definition. The reason why one cannot envisage a situation in which someone could erroneously believe *cogito ergo sum* is because *cogito ergo sum* is not the type of proposition that can meaningfully be negated. To put it another way, *cogito ergo non sum* makes no sense or is clearly an instance of self-contradiction. Following the terminology of chapter 1, we might call it 'analytic'. If we look at examples of tautologies, such as 'All bachelors are unmarried' or 'Eggs are eggs', they do not seem to be telling us anything new, and it is this point that critics use against the *cogito*. The criticism states that the fact that the *cogito* is tautological weakens its standing. However, the following replies may be given:

- Even if it were tautological it would be no more so than the truths of mathematics, which Descartes has shown one may doubt. If it were tautological, that would not account for it being indubitable in the way Descartes says it is. I can sketch a situation in which I erroneously believe '2 + 2 = 4' but not one in which I erroneously think I exist. To refer to both beliefs as tautologies seems unhelpful in explaining why one is indubitable in a much stronger way than the other.

- It is by no means clear that the *cogito* is a tautology. It would be if 'I think' meant something like 'I (existing thing) think therefore I exist'. Equally, it is perfectly true to say that that which sings exists. Thinking is one clear manifestation of existence, and so is singing, but no one supposes that 'existence' is part of the definition of singing or for that matter thinking.

- A different tack would be to suggest that what Descartes means by 'I think' is 'I am aware', and by 'exist' he means 'to be conscious', so we could paraphrase *cogito ergo sum* as 'I am aware therefore I am conscious'. Read like this, the statement looks truly tautological. In fact it is just saying, 'I am conscious'. He views this as the primary perception and this does not have to be expressed in a particular form of words. If the *cogito* is a tautology, it voices a primary fact which can be put in a non-tautological fashion as 'I am conscious'. We return to the fact that there are no conceivable circumstances in which one could erroneously believe this.

In reply, to call the *cogito* a tautology:

- fails to clarify its special character;
- is difficult to support on the ordinary meanings of the terms;
- misses the point that it is just a cute way of expressing the fundamental factual insight that one cannot doubt one's own existence.

The *cogito* as a referential tautology

This leads to the suggestion that the statement 'I exist' is a referential tautology. This claim means that 'I' is the sort of term that can only be used if that to which the term refers exists. To give an example, if I were to say, 'This is my dog but he's not here', it would seem odd. We normally use 'This' to point to something that is within our field of vision, and not to speak like this seems to undercut the conventions governing the use of the term and so produce a kind of gobbledegook. Thus we could look at 'This is my dog, he's here' as a funny kind of tautology, a referential tautology. In a similar way, we could say that 'I exist' cannot be doubted for the simple reason that a claim like 'I do not exist' completely ignores the conventions governing the use of the term 'I'. 'I' is a term reserved in our language for conscious beings to attribute to themselves. 'I

exist' is only indubitable for the trivial reason that 'I do not exist' is unspeakable or, to be more exact, if said, would not convey any meaning. Quite apart from such remarks as 'Don't mind me, I don't exist', I could foresee someone making a video of themselves for posterity and saying on the soundtrack, 'Although you are watching me, I no longer exist'. This would not look to me like a violation of English or any other language. The whole concept of 'referential tautology' seems unsatisfactory. Imagine holding up a picture of Spot and saying, 'This is my dog but he's not here'. While one might agree that the statement *cogito ergo sum* is a funny sort of statement, to discount it does not seem appropriate either.

Review questions

1 Briefly explain what is meant by the assertion 'I think therefore I am'.

2 Explain the purpose of the wax example.

Task

Resume your roles as Sceptic and Non-sceptic. How would a sceptic challenge the statement, 'I think therefore I am'? Is it a successful criticism to condemn the statement as tautological?

The Third Meditation

As its title suggests, Descartes' *Meditations* is a spiritual work and the product of a sincerely held religious faith. Its main concern is to prove God's existence, and the author starts by clearing his mind to prepare for the task in hand:

> I will erase from my thought all images of physical things or, since this is almost impossible, I will regard them as nothing, as false and empty, addressing only myself and looking more deeply into myself. (30)

Descartes' methodological doubt is one strand of an all-pervading **apophaticism**, or negative theology, that reflects the distinction between being and nothingness, existence and non-existence, certainty and uncertainty. His writings portray a contemplative, trying to understand the nature of thought itself. Descartes has already attempted to categorise thought in the Second Meditation, and this trend is continued in the opening paragraphs of the Third Meditation and elsewhere.[4] He talks about modes of thinking as categorisable, although, as is stated later in the Sixth Meditation, consciousness is indivisible. There are, nevertheless, instances when one does not have any control over what one is thinking about – that is, the content of one's thoughts. Perceptions are presented to the mind, and one is left presuming a type of representative realism in supposing that an external world exists to generate such images and that the images themselves resemble the world from which they originated.

This account is inadequate philosophically, as it remains prone to sceptical attack through arguments from deception, defects and dreaming. What is required to satisfy the author is a clear and distinct conviction such as accompanies arithmetical certainties like 2 + 2 = 4. In this case, to accept any other answer would be to endorse a logical contradiction. If, however, it is possible to be deceived about everyday occurrences, perhaps *a priori* deception is also a possibility and some god is actively pulling the non-material wool over our mind's eye. Yet, according to Descartes, God is the rock of ages upon which all certainties and truths are founded. How could God deceive us? An examination of God and God's relation to ideas is required.

Before a family of ontological arguments are recorded, the ground is prepared by the writer, who distinguishes between three kinds of ideas: the innate, the acquired and the fabricated. It is in the sphere of ideas that proof for God's existence must be sought, as ideas stemming from the external world that are presented to me against my will are often the source of error. For example, when I observe the sun, it is presented to me as a small disc, whereas astronomical reasoning assures me that it is several times larger than the earth. Similarly, fabricated thoughts about such mythical beasts as sirens and satyrs are invented by me and are known to be fictitious. Instead of relying on sensory evidence, I must put my trust in the natural light of reason in order to establish God's existence. The results are as follows:

Ontological argument 1: the trademark argument

In this argument, Descartes seems to be asserting that the idea of God is so impressive that it cannot have originated from our imagination or elsewhere, but can only have originated from God. At the same time, the fact that I can recognise this perfection means that there is something about me that is special. It is as if the perfect creator has left His trademark on His creation. The writer uses an analysis of causality as summarised below:

1 I am aware of my own imperfection.
2 I cannot be aware of my own imperfection without having an idea of perfection.
3 This conception must have an origin, as something cannot come from nothing.
4 The cause of the idea of perfection must have at least as much perfection as the notion itself.
5 The idea of perfection cannot originate in me, as I am imperfect.
6 Therefore, there must be a perfect cause for the idea of perfection, which we call God.

The analogy that Descartes goes on to draw exposes this argument's weakness. He argues that something that is hot must have been made hot by another entity possessing at least the same amount of heat. However, it does not follow from this that the idea of God must have been created by something divine.

Descartes shows his debt to Plato's theory of forms when he declares:

> Thus it is evident to me by the natural light of reason that my ideas are like images of some kind that can easily fall short of the perfection of the things from which they are derived, but they cannot contain something that is greater or more perfect than themselves. (36)

The idea of God is thus a particular manifestation of the divine form. The above argument presumes that people do have a conception of what God is like, which places this ontological argument in the realm of religious experience.

Ontological argument 2: *a priori* perfection

1 The finite exists in relation to the infinite.

2 I am aware of my own finite existence.

3 I must, therefore, be aware prior to **2** of the existence of an infinite existence.

4 This infinite existence that I am aware of may be termed 'God'.

In this argument, based on the existence of both the finite and infinite, the ontological argument meets the argument from religious experience in so far as it is about how one's feeling of being finite instils a sense of wonder and dependency. In keeping with the negative or apophatic tradition in theology, one is able to understand the infinite through the finite. Yet God remains incomprehensible: 'It is the nature of the infinite not to be comprehended by me, who am finite'.

Ontological argument 3: God as a clear and distinct idea

Descartes declares:

> This idea of a supremely perfect and infinite being is also clear and distinct to the highest degree because whatever I perceive clearly and distinctly as real and true, and as containing some perfection, is completely included in it. (39)

Thus I come to know that God exists by considering the idea of God. The realisation dawns that God's essence involves existence, and it is as necessary a truth to talk about God existing as it is to talk about a triangle having three sides and interior angles that add up to 180 degrees or that a mountain necessarily involves an adjoining, flat plain.

Ontological argument 4: from epistemology

This version takes the form of a thought experiment in which the reader is invited to imagine that they possess the potential to become omniscient – that is, all-knowing. Through this meditation, one gradually is made aware of the fact that I am judging my potential omniscience against the real omniscience of God. Using similar reasoning to Aquinas in the fourth of his Five Ways, Descartes argues that, in thinking of my potential epistemological perfection, I come to understand that God's

actual epistemological perfection necessarily exists. Descartes concludes with an ideational law, asserting that 'the content of a thought can only be produced by an actual, rather than potential being'. If this were not the case, the foundation stone *cogito ergo sum* would no longer make sense.

Ontological argument 5: from existence

This is another argument from causation, but concerns itself with the cause of my existence. Descartes is struck by the fact that it was difficult for thinking things such as ourselves to emerge from nothing. What then was the cause of my existence, and who or what sustains and conserves my existence during the individual moments of my life? Through introspection I realise that I do not possess such power of self-generation; therefore, my existence depends on something apart and distinct from me. The author concludes that, as the idea of God's perfections is a part of my waking existence, it can only be God who is the author of my existence. That is not to deny the biological facts of life but to trace, through reason, the train of causality involving secondary perfections back to the ultimate cause of all perfections, which we may call God. Just as we know that our parents are responsible for our accidental character traits and appearance, we come to realise that the capacity to think and reason is God's 'trademark imprinted on his work' (43). Descartes ends this section with an appropriate doxology in praise of God, but returns to the subject again on the last pages of the Fifth Meditation.

Review question

Describe Descartes' ontological argument for the existence of God.

Task

The ontological argument is vital to Descartes' quest for knowledge. But does the ontological argument, in any of its variations, work? Draw up a list of criticisms, referring to chapter 3 on the philosophy of religion as well as to external sources.

The Fourth Meditation

Struck by a sense of frailty and dependency, the author of the Fourth Meditation finds solace in his contemplation of the divine. Descartes believed that there are two existent substances, mind and matter, and held that, whatever my discoveries may be, thoughts and ideas are always in the realm of the non-physical. The dualist account of personal identity views humankind as occupying an intermediate position between an omniscient, infinite, immaterial deity and a fallible, finite, physical universe – that is, between life and lifelessness, between being and nothingness:

> I am like some kind of intermediate between God and nothingness or I am so constituted between the supreme being and non-being that, in so far as I was created by the supreme being, there is nothing in me by which I can be mistaken or led into error. (45)

Considering that God is incapable of deception, owing to no moral imperfection existing in the divine nature, it is unclear why God has permitted his creation to be prone to making mistakes. This is an aspect of the problem of metaphysical evil: why, if there is an omnipotent God, isn't the world perfect? Error is defined by Descartes in a way that links the notion of choosing to that of knowing. He believes that, in comparison with God, the human memory and intellect is a poor imitation. However, in the case of the will or volition – that is, deciding to do something rather than not – we are remarkably like God; in fact we are made in God's image, *imago dei*. Our freedom is of a slightly less perfect kind, as we do not make a divinely informed choice, yet we are nevertheless in a position to choose between alternatives. It is when my choosing extends beyond my understanding that errors occur and I make mistaken judgements or bad choices (48). The opposite category to error is termed 'clear and distinct', and Descartes supplies examples including knowledge of one's own existence (*cogito ergo sum*), knowledge of God's existence through the family of ontological arguments, and knowledge of analytic truths such as those found in mathematics.

Clear and distinct ideas

Descartes puts great stress on the concept of clear and distinct ideas, and we need to look at the classification in more detail. He argues that the concept is the hallmark of certain truth and, provided we identify a judgement as possessing this feature, we cannot go wrong. It is, however, not a concept he explains very well, describing this category of ideas somewhat tautologically as: manifest, considered as one ought, free from doubt. Such characterisations seem to say that clear and distinct ideas are ideas that are in some way 'unmistakable', 'indubitable', 'correctly conceived'. This seems to leave Descartes saying that we will never go wrong if we accept only ideas that we find it impossible to find fault with. This should be no news to anyone and seems trivially true, rather as if someone were to tell us that the way to find a reliable car is to find one that doesn't break down.

Descartes, however, does seem to have in mind separate meanings for the two terms 'clear' and 'distinct'. 'Clear' means 'present to the mind', whereas 'distinct' means 'separate' and 'not confused'. For Descartes the judgement 'I've got a pain in my leg' is clear but not distinct. I know about the pain, but I am wrong in so far as I attribute the pain to my leg. The pain isn't in my leg in the same way that my veins are; it's in the mind. It's not just that the judgement is ill phrased. The point is that it is confused. As it stands, it cannot be defended, although we are sure that in a confused way it expresses a truth. It is this concept of defensible truth that is the core of what Descartes means by clear and distinct ideas.

Clear and distinct ideas, for Descartes, are judgements that are either properly grounded or need no independent justification. The latter type may be termed self-evident axioms, and include:

'I think therefore I am.'

'Nothing can come from nothing.'

'What is done cannot be undone.'

'A straight line is the shortest distance between two points.'

These statements require no separate proof, since it could be suggested that any doubt expressed about them simply cannot be understood. If sceptics were to question them, it would not be clear what they would be suggesting. Equally, anything deducible from such axioms by a clear process of reasoning would be similarly immune from sceptical challenge.

Descartes divides the clear and distinct into the self-evident and the theoretically unquestionable. His ideal of knowledge is of a system analogous to Euclidean geometry, where all proper claims (clear and distinct ideas) have either axiomatic or theorem status, axioms being the class of self-evident truths and theorems being the class of truths deducible from axioms. Descartes does not believe that knowledge progresses exactly along the same lines as geometry. We do not begin with the axioms and spin everything else out of them. After all, even in mathematics we get theorems which are seemingly unhooked from their axiom set. Take Fermat's Last Theorem:

There are no positive integers, x, y, z or n satisfying $x^n + y^n = z^n$ for $n > 2$.

Fermat claimed to have found a proof for this theorem, which was subsequently lost. Such was his reputation that this theorem was held to be correct even though it was not proved until the 1990s. The problem was that, although the statement is consistent with the basic principles of arithmetic, no one was able to show that it follows from them. In Descartes' view, this would not have been clear and distinct, and we ought to suspend belief in it. It is only at this later stage that isolated theorems become clear and distinct. 'Clear and distinct' describes how they stand to the enquiring mind, not the confused senses.

Descartes evidently felt that what is true of mathematics is true of knowledge in general. We assemble science piecemeal. A good example from Descartes' time is Boyle's Law, which generalises the relationship between the volume, pressure and temperature of gases. It was not known why gases should behave as Boyle alleged, until the kinetic theory of gases was devised at a later date. Once that theory was in place, Boyle's Law could be deduced, and so become even more clear and distinct. However, to be completely clear and distinct, the kinetic theory would in turn have to be portrayed as the logical corollary of some more fundamental, unquestionable, axiomatic truth. Here, we see that to be clear and distinct is to be part of a systematic ordering of knowledge, to belong to a system the foundations of which are beyond dispute. I do not pretend that Descartes makes this apparent, but it does seem implicit in what he says.

The Fifth Meditation

Having established in the Second Meditation that he exists as a thinking thing, the author turns his attention to proving the existence of material things in the Fifth Meditation. This meditation begins in Platonic vein with an argument from recollection about 'true and immutable natures', an attestation to the fact that knowledge is something rather than nothing, which is reminiscent of *The Republic* 477b in its juxtaposition of opinion and knowledge. Descartes seeks to prove the existence of the external world by first noting that our observation of it seems to accord with human nature. My perceptions, however, are not produced by me but are presented to me against my will. That which is perceived, in addition, seems to possess a nature of its own. For example, a triangle possesses a definition or properties that exist independent of my existence. It is concluded that these perceptions, registered in the mind, are of something rather than nothing. Descartes compares the revelation that an external world exists to the previously unveiled truth that God exists. Just as I can come to know that God exists through contemplating the idea of God, I can also come to the realisation that there is a world external to me through meditating on my perceptions.

Descartes succeeds in proving beyond question that he exists, no matter what else he can doubt. But it does not follow from the fact that I have perceptions that there is anything other than conscious states, or that perceptions are caused by or mirror a world different and separate from conscious states. Descartes feels obliged to prove the existence of such an external world. He could argue that a good God would not allow us to arrive at such preposterous beliefs if they happened to be wrong, but Descartes' position is that a good God would not allow us to get the wrong idea if the idea itself was clear and distinct. But it is not apparent that his belief in the external world is in this category.

He accepts that our perceptions are:

- outside our control (we do not choose them);
- often 'livelier' and more impressive than the products of our imagination.

Obviously, these facts could be used to support a belief in the external world, but they do not make such a belief inescapable, simply probable.

Descartes' approach is to first of all identify the mind as essentially identical with its thoughts. He goes on to draw a contrast between conception and imagination. This is consolidated in the Sixth Meditation, where he argues that we can think of the concept of a thousand-sided figure (a chiliagon) but we cannot imagine it. Our imaginations seem restricted to the sort of things we have seen. We can distinguish our faculty of conception from our faculty of imagination in a way that makes the former more intimately connected with our essential nature than the latter. Presumably, he holds that imagination is a more dependent faculty and not dependent on thought alone, as otherwise we should be able to imagine everything we can think of, and clearly we cannot. This brings us to Descartes' next move. He clearly appreciates that perceptions do not depend on conception. What I will see next has little to do with what I am thinking of. Conscious thought, therefore, cannot be the cause of perceptions. Descartes supports this view with another consideration: the features of our perceptions in terms of their variety and originality are such that the mind as described by Descartes is an unlikely candidate to be the cause of them.

There are therefore two alternatives: either perceptions are caused by an external world or they are caused by God. Descartes rejects the second alternative on the grounds that God is no deceiver and we are deceived from time to time through our perceptions.

The Cartesian circle

One of the most famous criticisms of Descartes is the accusation that the Fifth Meditation contains circular reasoning, making the argument fallacious. The problem arises because the philosopher accepts two premises simultaneously:

1 I know that I perceive the truth clearly and distinctly because God exists and is not a deceiver.
2 I know that God exists and is not a deceiver because I perceive this truth clearly and distinctly.

Attempts to circumvent the Cartesian circle involve seeking assurance that God's existence is a special, self-evident certainty prior to other clear and distinct ideas, such as $2 + 3 = 5$. The ontological argument, therefore, does not rely on God for its validity but stands alone as proof and guarantee of God's existence and by extension obvious truth.

Proof of an external world

The following argument summarises Descartes' defence of an external world:

1 Belief in an external world is natural.
2 The mind is primarily its conceptions.
3 Imagination and perception do not depend just on conception.
4 Belief in an external world is required to explain the phenomena of imagination and perception.
5 The existence of an all-perfect God is the surest guarantee of the existence of an external world.

Put negatively, Descartes is trying to tell us that there is no intelligible way of accounting for the existence and character of perception without conceding an external world. Berkeleyan idealism and phenomenalism (see chapter 1) would not make sense for him. Despite many apparent leaps in the argument, he believes that belief in the external world, like the *cogito* and belief in God, is clear, distinct and certain. There follows a discussion on necessary truth. For Descartes, any discussion on necessary truth revolves around the concepts of essence and existence. The essence of a certain thing involves the existence of a clear and distinct idea about that thing:

- The essence of a triangle is to have three sides; to negate this clear and distinct idea would be self-contradictory.

- The essence of a mountain is to have lower environs; to negate this clear and distinct idea would be self-contradictory.

- The essence of God involves existence; to negate this clear and distinct idea would be self-contradictory.

Whereas the first two examples may work in theory, without any such triangle existing or without any mountain actually existing, the third example must work in practice – God has always and will always be an existent being: 'I am not free to think of God without existence' (54).

What then are we to make of this world of particulars, which besiege our thoughts from every direction? According to the above arguments and the fact that God would not deceive us, we are to think of the existence of the external world as a clear and distinct idea, although I may well remain misguided as to what the external world is like, as if a clear view were sporadically obscured by a mist of ignorance. The necessity for the divine in Descartes' epistemology is recapitulated at the end of the Fifth Meditation when he declares, 'all knowledge depends only on the knowledge of the true God' (57). This view has led some critics to accuse Descartes of using

Réne Descartes (1596–1650)

René Descartes was born in La Haye in France, later renamed 'La Haye-Descartes' in his honour. He embodied the intimate relationship that the two disciplines of mathematics and philosophy had enjoyed since early Greece. Descartes studied mathematics and logic under the Jesuits at La Flèche College from January 1604, only a few months after it had opened, and continued a love affair with the subject throughout his education at the military school at Breda, where he studied mathematics with mechanics under the Dutch scientist Isaac Beeckman. After spending some time travelling around Europe, he decided to adopt Holland as his home country for the next twenty years. Descartes established a school of mathematical physics decades before Newton and he is most remembered for inventing the x, y and z axes in graphs, called 'Cartesian coordinates' in his memory. There were three main bones of contention between the Cartesians and the Newtonians: absolute space, atoms and the laws of attraction. For Newton, space was a neutral medium in which objects moved. Cartesians denied the existence of true vacuums, assuming them to be full of rarefied inert matter. Newtonians viewed atoms as uniform, infinitely dense and indivisible, whereas Cartesians disputed all three claims. Newton suggested that all bodies attract one another proportional to their mass and inversely proportional to the square of their distance (gravity). Cartesians thought this sounded very occult, and explained such movements as due to the direct action of forces of impulsion known as vortices. Descartes believed that it was possible to lay out science as a hierarchy of truths in which each level of truth was seen as an elaboration or an expansion of a higher-level truth. This was to be achieved not through the discovery of new facts but through the exercise of one's rationality. In his refusal to work before midday, his strange diet and intermittent contributions in lectures, Descartes remains a role model for philosophy students today. His views on religion and the mind, however, have fallen out of fashion.

Significant works
Discourse on Method (1637)
Meditations (1641)
Principles of Philosophy (1644)

God to fill certain gaps in his philosophy just in order to escape an infinite regress.

The Sixth Meditation

Many of the themes and motifs running throughout the text come to fruition in the sixth and final Meditation. The author seeks to provide a more exact analysis of personal identity at the beginning of the section, by comparing the faculties of imagination and understanding. By 'imagination' Descartes does not mean a sense of creativity, as when we say that so-and-so has a fertile imagination, but means the sense of perception or imaging. On the other hand, 'understanding' is construed as that sense whereby the mind 'turns back on itself in some way and reflects on one of the ideas that are inside itself' (58), in contrast to 'imaging', where the mind focuses on an article apart from itself. This distinction is illustrated by juxtaposing our perceptions of a triangle and a chiliagon (thousand-sided figure). We can both imagine a triangle and understand what a triangle is whereas, despite understanding the concept of a chiliagon, we cannot conjure up an image of it in our mind. This shows a limitation of the human mind, but also has a bearing on how we conceive of ourselves. This theme is revisited later on in the Sixth Meditation when Descartes concludes that he is essentially a thinking thing in so far as he possesses an understanding of clear and distinct ideas (52).

There follows a clearly laid out discussion on sensations, which raises the mind–body problem. Descartes recognises the explanatory poverty as to how these two substances interact (60), but such uncertainty does not dissuade him from dualism, which he defends by a number of arguments in the final section of the work. The first is an argument from dependency:

1 I have a distinct idea of my mind and I have a distinct idea of my body.
2 I can imagine existing without my body.
3 I cannot imagine existing without my mind.
4 Therefore, my mind and body are separate entities and I am more truly my mind – that is, my non-extended thinking.

Descartes' two-substance theory, which sees the body as a member of a closed physical system bound by deterministic laws and the mind as a non-extended entity whose sole attribute is thought in all its forms, was not noticeably an improvement on the medieval perspective. The next argument in this section takes the form of a *reductio ad absurdum* to prove that the physical exists in addition to the mental.

1 Ideas are presented to me against my wish.
2 Such ideas must emanate from somewhere as real as the ideas themselves.
3 This somewhere is either the external world, God or an agent of God.
4 I have a strong sense that these ideas are from the external world.
5 It would be contrary to God's benevolent nature to deceive me, and God controls His agents.
6 Such ideas can only originate from the physical realm. Therefore the physical realm exists.

One can also take faith in the fact that, although I am often deceived about the world of particulars, my senses are not willingly deceiving me, as this would be to construe them anthropomorphically. Rather, God has imbued me with the natural light of reason to calculate, for example, the respective size of the planets for myself. This creates a major puzzle about how the body interacts with the mind and vice versa. Strictly speaking, for Descartes the mind, having no extension, is not anywhere. It cannot be inside the body or in the brain. Descartes hazarded that the mind was similar in one respect to the pilot of a ship controlling the body via the delicately balanced 'animal spirits' in the pineal gland, diffused throughout the body and therefore influenced by events in any part of the body. This does not seem to flow from the tenets of epistemological dualism, however, and seems an *ad hoc* manoeuvre on the author's part. Equally, Descartes has no need to tell a story of how the mind influences the body or vice versa and no need to describe a pseudo-physical pattern of interaction. Mind–body interaction must be unlike the interaction of two bodies. Yet there are many instances in his works where Descartes appears to go beyond crude substance dualism.[5] This usually takes the form of asserting the existence of an extended realm, a realm of thought and an uncertainty as to how the two realms interact in the pineal gland. This has led some commentators to go as far as to re-label Descartes' philosophy of mind as 'trialism' rather than dualism, as there seem to be three kinds of things: mind, matter and their interaction.

There is also the difficulty that the movements of any physical object, including our bodies, ought on Cartesian principles to be explicable through the specification of physical causes. If that is indeed so, and if it is the case that the bulk of our behaviour is the movement of our bodies, is it not the case that the mind will seem somewhat redundant, or simply a non-explanatory concomitant of physically determined behaviour? The first view that the mind is redundant led to materialism. The second view led to a doctrine called epiphenomenalism. In this century Cartesian dualism has been under attack from two sources:

- Materialists, or physicalists, who identify the mind with the brain (the mind–brain identity theory) or with the structural properties that the brain exhibits.

- Behaviourists, who, seeking to exorcise the doctrine of the ghost in the machine, find the postulate of 'mental substance', 'inner life', 'subjectivity' etc. either unnecessary or mistaken. All we want to say about people, they argue, can be said about their observable behaviour; there is no need to refer to some inner mental state to make sense of our discourse about human thought and action.

The intermingling thesis

The pilot–ship **disanalogy** is often cited as one of importance in Descartes' description of how the mind and body interact. Whereas an analogy compares two things that are alike, a disanalogy compares two things that are dissimilar. It runs as follows:

> Nature also teaches by means of the sensations of pain, hunger, thirst etc., that I am not present to my body only in the way that a pilot is present to a

ship, but that I am very closely joined to it and almost merged with it to such an extent that, together with it, I compose a single entity. (64)

We learn here that the mind–body interaction is not just one of giving direction, as a pilot of a ship steers the right course. Instead, Descartes presents a holistic account emphasising the fact that I am a single entity and illustrating the fact by encouraging us to reflect on what happens when we feel the sensations of pain, hunger or thirst: such sensations are present inseparably in mind and body. '[I am thus] the thorough mixing together of mind and body, that is to say composed of a body and a mind' (64), and 'a completely unified and integral thing' (67). Might Descartes, with a bit of twentieth-century neuroscientific persuasion, have become a biological naturalist?[6]

This relationship is divinely orchestrated, and consists in my registering sensations in terms of pleasure and pain in order to signify what is beneficial or harmful to my well-being. A problem is created here as, if we assert that God has created us and that God cannot perform any act that would frustrate His benevolent and compassionate purpose, why do poisons hold an agreeable taste for us or why, in the case of dropsy, do we feel thirsty when taking a drink worsens the condition? Descartes' answer to this last dilemma is laid out in four parts. First, the argument from indivisibility is stated (67), where the author contrasts consciousness to body parts. Second, Descartes outlines a seventeenth-century mechanistic view of how the body's nervous system works, comparing it with clockwork. Third, Descartes admits to a necessary correspondence between mind and body. Fourth, he entertains a mind–brain interaction where the mental sensation does not correspond to the brain state. He argues that this is neither the case nor would it be beneficial, so our design is clearly the work of a beneficent artisan. In addition, the sensations brought about by dropsy are unavoidable exceptions, as in the vast majority of cases the desire for water is beneficial. On the last page of the *Meditations*, Descartes admits that the physical is at best an inductive, *a posteriori* medium, and only *a priori* knowledge can be classed as certain and can only be found in the sphere of the mental.

If all subsequent philosophy is described as footnotes to Plato, then all subsequent philosophy of mind is footnotes to Descartes. The three main problems surrounding consciousness are present even if only implicitly in the *Meditations*: the whole work is concerned with personal identity and how we stand before our creator, the problem of other minds is hinted at in the Second Meditation when the author observes passers-by in the street, and, having proved the existence of both mind and body, Descartes bequeaths us the mind–body problem. A Seventh Meditation in which this last dilemma was solved would have been nice. The author himself is categorised as a substance dualist, but has spawned many refinements such as occasionalism, parallelism, epiphenomenalism and property dualism. This is not to suppose, however, that Descartes has not exerted an influence on physicalist or idealist doctrines. Descartes was a proficient scientist in his own right and held an interest in anatomy, identifying the pineal gland as a possible source of consciousness owing to the fact that it did not seem to have a symmetrical equivalent like other parts of the brain. In addition, a rudimentary knowledge of the nervous system is displayed in the Sixth Meditation. As far as idealism is concerned, Berkeley had certainly read Descartes, and appears influenced by his scepticism and prioritisation of the mental. In trawling through any work on the philosophy of mind it is difficult not to encounter echoes of Cartesianism.

Review question

Explain how Descartes distinguishes between imagination and the intellect.

Task

Having proved to his own satisfaction that our thoughts are real and that an external world exists, Descartes raises the problem of how these two worlds interact. This problem is only raised in the Sixth Meditation and not answered. How do you think the author would have answered the problem if he had written a Seventh Meditation?

Revision questions

1 Evaluate the distinction drawn by Descartes between mind and body.

2 Explain the role of one of the following in Descartes' philosophy: God, doubt, mathematics, thought.

3 Assess the concept of clear and distinct ideas.

4 Describe the wax example and its purpose.

5 Briefly explain the distinction between the imagination and the intellect.

Discussion questions

- Is Descartes correct in asserting that we are thinking things and nothing more?
- How does the author prove the existence of the external world? Is this line of argument immune from further sceptical attack?
- Which formulation of the ontological argument is the most coherent?
- What role does science play in Descartes' philosophy?
- How might the proposition *cogito ergo sum* be criticised?

Glossary of key terms

Anthropomorphise: to describe the non-human (for example, angels, aliens, animals) in human terms.

Apophatic theology: descriptions of God that are of a negative nature, for example that God is not comprehensible or not finite.

Axiom: a statement that we can be sure about and use as a basis for our reasoning.

Disanalogy: a figure of speech in which two things are compared in order to illustrate their difference.

Dualism: the belief that there are two kinds of things in existence: the physical and the mental.

Epistemology: the study of how knowledge is acquired and tested.

Foundationalism: the theory of justification that seeks to build an edifice of knowledge on indubitable truths.

Ontology: the study of existence or 'what there is'.

Physicalism: the theory of mind which holds that thoughts are essentially physical events.

Reductio ad absurdum: the structure of a logical argument in which options are outlined before any number are disproved (or reduced to absurdity), leaving only the conclusion.

Scepticism: a philosophical movement that uses doubt to establish what is certain.

Tautology: any statement the opposite of which does not make logical sense.

Suggested reading

- Cottingham, J. (2000) *Descartes*, Oxford, Blackwell
  An accessible introduction to Cartesian thought

- Cottingham, J. ed. (1998) *Descartes*, Oxford, OUP
  A lengthier volume edited by the same author, which contains useful chapters

- Dicker, G. (1993) *Descartes: An Analytical and Historical Introduction*, Oxford, OUP
  This is a detailed commentary, which will suit a more advanced reader

- Rorty, A. O. ed. (1986) *Essays on Descartes' Meditations*, California, California Press
  A compendium of scholarly contributions on the main issues arising in the text

- Williams, B. (1990) *Descartes: The Project of Pure Enquiry*, London, Penguin
  A comprehensive survey of Descartes' contribution to philosophy

Notes

1 Descartes, R. (1968) *Discourse on Method*, London, Penguin, p. 37 and Replies 7, AT 7:537.

2 Descartes, R. (2000) *Meditations and Other Metaphysical Writings*, London, Penguin, p.20; hereafter page references to the *Meditations* are given in brackets and refer to this edition.

3 The *cogito* appears at the start of the Fourth Discourse on Method.

4 Modes of thinking: 'but then the I … senses' (26). In addition the author classifies: images, choices, emotions and judgements (32); innate, acquired and fabricated ideas (33); thoughts about God, things and the features of things (35); knowing and choosing (46); clear versus confused ideas (51); imagining and understanding (57). Ryle focuses on many of the above as sub-headings in *The Concept of Mind* in order to provide an alternative behaviourist account.

5 Descartes, Letter to Elisabeth of 21 May 1643.

6 Consider the following: 'Secondly, I perceive that the mind is not affected immediately by all the parts of the body but only by the brain or, perhaps, only by one small part of the brain, namely the part in which the common sense is said to be/ Finally I perceive that any of the motions that occur in the part of the brain that affects the mind immediately trigger only one particular sensation in it' (68).

10 A commentary on Hume's *Enquiry Concerning Human Understanding*

Truth springs from argument amongst friends. (David Hume)

Aims

On completion of this chapter you should be able to:

- provide a detailed account of what Hume means by 'ideas' and 'impressions' and explain how the two notions are related

- explain the principles of association

- describe and assess Hume's fork

- explain the problem of induction

- describe what Hume means by the principle of custom

- describe the notions of imagination and belief

- evaluate the Humean account of causality, including an analysis of constant conjunction and necessary connection

- explain what is meant by liberty and necessity.

The *Enquiry Concerning Human Understanding* begins with Hume seeking clarification as to the nature of the enterprise he will shortly embark on. He points out that philosophy can exist at both a popular level and an abstruse, speculative level that seeks to offer guidance on the conduct of life and seeks to understand the principles that govern our thought and action. The latter brand of philosophy seems to have little practical application and can lead to a lack of proportion, even a lack of humanity, and can easily be dismissed by those of a more practical turn of mind. Hume defends philosophy by arguing that the mental skills the philosopher acquires are useful in any culture, and that an understanding of how people think, reason and act may have benefits for people's understanding of concrete situations, just as a gruesome grasp of anatomy may help the painter draw a particular picture. He does, however, concede that philosophy is a risky business, and an error at the first stage in one's theorising may have knock-on consequences for all subsequent stages of a philosopher's thought. Furthermore, much philosophy of the metaphysical kind is not 'properly a science' but comes about from 'the fruitless efforts of human vanity which would penetrate into subjects utterly inaccessible to the human understanding'. Hume blames this 'craft of popular superstition' on the efforts of priests and theologians who befog the human intellect with weird and wonderful notions. Hume wants no truck with this sort of philosophy, and proposes as an alternative 'to enquire seriously into the nature of human understanding, and to show, from an exact analysis of its powers and capacity, that it is by no means fitted to such remote and abstruse subjects'. What he proposes is a species of mental cartography, in which the same kind of progress can be made as has been made in the mapping of the heavens by astronomers.

Of the origin of ideas (Section II)

Hume chooses the method of introspection in order to achieve a proper grasp of human understanding, and he begins by examining the contents of our consciousness, the furniture of the mind. He introduces a twofold categorisation of these contents, which can be classified as either ideas or impressions. It is important to note that Hume views the introspective survey of the mind's contents as a relatively unproblematic study. He views it as the application of the 'experimental' methods of Newton, so successful in the study of natural objects, to new material. Hume views himself as systematising our knowledge of the mental, just as Newton systematised our knowledge of the natural world. One could argue, however, that the methods used by Hume differ very radically from those used by the natural scientists of his age or indeed of any age. Hume's understanding of the procedures of natural scientists seems at best defective, and the procedures of Hume and those of natural scientists are ill-suited to answer the questions he sets himself, as philosophy is by nature metaphysical.

Hume is in the business of modelling philosophy on the natural sciences, just as Descartes was in the business of modelling philosophy on mathematics. Both try to buy in new machinery, in the hope of cutting a swathe through ancient philosophical dilemmas. However, it does not seem clear how the author is going to avoid:

- creating a contradictory anti-metaphysical metaphysical system of his own;
- discovering the limits of human understanding and the nature of human knowledge without at the same time floundering on those very limits.

There is the constant danger that we shall not discover the true limits of our understanding but simply display them. This leads to the important question 'How should we proceed in philosophy?' to which Hume answers, 'like a kind of natural scientist'. This is the thought that might have crossed the mind of many an eighteenth-century gentleman viewing the success of Newton's efforts. The German philosopher G. W. F. Hegel (1770–1831) said that Hume treats philosophical subjects 'as an educated, thoughtful man', which might sound like a compliment but is in fact Hegel's way of saying that Hume's methods are not rigorously philosophical.

Our mental furniture
Impressions

Just as a room may be full of tables and chairs, so, argues Hume, our mind is full of **impressions**. 'Impressions' is a term he introduces, almost apologetically, as a neologism, or a new employment of the term. Hume's analysis of impressions is discussed in detail below.

Impressions are perceptions (ideas are another sort of perception)
Impressions are feelings or sentiments

To identify impressions with perceptions creates no problems, as we can treat the words as synonyms. To include the category of feelings as part of the definition of impressions, however, seems to add to that picture, since 'perception' implies a degree of recognition while 'feeling' does not. Perception involves an element of judgement and for that reason can be wrong, whereas feelings are a condition of one's mind or body, which can neither be right nor wrong; they are just there. To perceive a jellyfish and to have the feeling of being in contact with one are not the same sort of affair.

Impressions are sensations, passions and emotions

One might question the wisdom of listing these elements of thought together, and especially of including passions such as sadness with non-emotive conditions such as the experience of diving into cold water. The former is not a specific local reaction. To call both 'impressions' might not in fact serve to make the term clearer.

Impressions are a force to be reckoned with

Hume does not describe impressions as either objects or powers but describes them in the text as things that:

- 'make us perceive';
- 'strike the eyes';

- 'are admitted through the organs, the organs of perception';
- 'are conveyed by our senses';
- 'enter the mind'.

Hume talks about impressions as though they were objects travelling along a strange path from the external world to the inner recesses of our mind. It is as if the world could be populated by impressions even if there were no one present to be affected by them. He has a tendency to **reify** impressions and to describe them almost as things rolling separately through chambers labelled 'senses', 'organs', 'mind' etc. Impressions are not defined as the self-generated product of the perceiver or as the **effects** of an external **cause**, but are credited with a quasi-autonomous existence. It is not surprising therefore that when Hume surveys his impressions – that is, the contents of his understanding – he can find no support for **belief** in an external world or the self.

Impressions vary in their 'liveliness'
A defining feature of impressions is that they are all more 'lively' than **ideas** and therefore cannot be confused with them. Hume talks about impressions as varying in their liveliness and at times as being 'faint' or 'obscure'. This feature of impressions has nothing to do with content, as I could have a lively impression of something faint, like an old etching or a pastel shade. The liveliness of an impression is according to Hume a function of the force with which it strikes us. Again he falls into the trap of treating impressions like things, in this case rather like incoming missiles. Incoming missiles of course have an existence even before they hit us, but one could not say the same of impressions.

Clearly, if the force of an impression is not a product of its content, awareness of its liveliness can only come about if I have some sort of impression of that, an impression of the impression's effect. I could then in turn have an impression based on that impression, and so on *ad infinitum*. In fact, to distinguish any idea from an impression I must know it to be more lively than an idea, which means I must form an impression of each impression. The same would apply for each second-order impression, which

must appear distinct from mere ideas by virtue of a third-order impression, and so on *ad infinitum*. On the other hand we could give up talk of the liveliness of impressions.

Impressions are complex or simple
An impression of a red patch would be simple; an impression of the Eiffel Tower would be complex. Hume divides impressions into the simple and the complex and views complex impressions as in fact batteries of simple impressions. Complex and simple impressions differ in their content; they do not differ as feelings. Simple impressions are those which we form simple ideas of; Hume is thinking of things like colours, sounds, the feeling of anger. As experiences, these vary quite a lot. We never just perceive red but a red something. A sound, like any impression, has duration, and is a particular pattern of waves or oscillations. Equally, anger is felt as a varying collection of emotional and bodily stimuli. Hume's view is that our field of consciousness is made up of complex impressions and these are, in turn, 'made up' of simple impressions. The fact that an impression forms part of a more complex impression does not make it simple. Complex impressions can form part of still more complex impressions. The simplicity of an impression must be a matter independent of its ability to be part of something else – that is, it must be intrinsically simple. We are left in the position of having to say that the simple impression is what the simple idea represents. Reaching a clear view of what a simple idea is seems the necessary pre-condition to arriving at a definition of the 'simple impression'. Without a clear notion of 'simple impressions' it would be futile to define 'complex impression', though we can see even at this stage that a 'complex impression' has got to be something more than a collection of simple impressions. (The Eiffel Tower is not just the feeling of steeliness added to the feeling of height and the feeling of being in Paris etc.)

Impressions are internal or external, depending on whether they are 'outward sentiment or inward sentiment'
Although Hume wishes to draw some sort of distinction between internal and external

sentiments, he holds that our body is something that we find out about via our impressions: 'Properly speaking, it is not our body we perceive when we regard our limbs and members but certain impressions which enter by our senses'. For Hume, impressions do not come labelled 'inner' and 'outer'. Only through thinking about our impressions do we reach a position where we can allocate some of them (passions, pain, bodily feelings) to one category and others (perceptions) to a different group. We could not reach such a position, argues Hume, 'without a certain reasoning and experience'. Inner and outer impressions do not differ in liveliness, and Hume has a problem here in explaining how we come to mark the distinction, how we get to know the difference. At first sight this looks like a discovery that cannot come about through just surveying our impressions. A Humean answer might consist in the argument that the different kind of impressions happen to fall for us naturally into two teams: outer impressions that happen to bunch together over time and inner impressions that form another discrete association. They also seem to be triggered by 'impressions of sensation', and are reactive rather than truly original. For Hume, the answer must ultimately lie in how the ideas 'associate' or link together, but it is difficult to see how he can construct an account in which the mind and its thought processes do not play a creative and constructive role.

Task

The following questions may be raised for discussion:

Is it clear what an impression is? Is Hume's description satisfactory?

Is it indeed the case that our experience is made up, at least in part, of Humean impressions?

The relationship of impressions to ideas is something we can look at after we have completed an examination of Hume's account of ideas.

Ideas

Hume's analysis of ideas is discussed below.

Ideas are perceptions
Ideas are thoughts

To have an idea of something is to have some kind of awareness of it, and it is therefore appropriate to refer to ideas as perceptions. The problem is that many ideas are of things that cannot possibly be perceived in any normal sense of that word, for example the number 9 or logical validity, so little is gained by viewing thought as a sub-species of perception. To think up a prediction or think of doing something is not really to perceive. There are currently no percipients (those who are perceiving) of the assassination of the Queen of England, though I can imagine it and hold an idea of it in my mind. It is difficult to see what Hume gains from calling thought a sub-species, just as in the section on impressions there seemed not much to be gained by viewing all feelings as perceptions.

Ideas are less lively than impressions, but nevertheless vary in liveliness, as is the case with impressions

Ideas, according to Hume, can vary in liveliness, and we can sense differences between them. Ideas in the memory, for instance, are livelier than ideas in the **imagination**.[1] It is difficult to see how Hume can maintain this without believing that we have 'impressions of ideas'. Clearly this allows us in turn to form ideas of this special group of impressions – that is, the impressions ideas make. These new ideas could then, in theory, make a particular impression on the mind which could be the object of a further idea, and so on *ad infinitum*. Talking of the liveliness of ideas, like talking of the liveliness of impressions, seems to trap us into an infinite regress. The trouble is that for Hume 'liveliness' is the ultimate criterion for dividing 'impressions' from 'ideas'. In theory, an idea has simply to get more lively for it to be an impression. The insane, as Hume admits, through the liveliness of their ideas have no internal means of distinguishing their ideas from reality. Nor of course would we, if as a matter of fact our perceptions did not organise themselves into the lively and not so lively. According to Humean psychology, if my thought of stupidity grows lively enough I will either believe I perceive it or actually feel stupid.

Ideas are images and copies of impressions or possible impressions

Ideas are defined as 'copies' or 'faint images' of impressions (13). They resemble them in every way but liveliness. The confusion between an idea and an image, copy or mental picture is notorious. Hume declares that images may be associated with ideas, but unlike them are not the possessors of meanings. When I form an idea of a desk I do not simply make a ghostly copy of it in my mind, for clearly I would need to have an idea of what the desk was in the first place to make the copy at all. Even if the copy were simply deposited in my mind by unknown causes it doesn't become the idea of the desk without my recognition. I can't even take it as the idea of the desk, since it would be deficient in a whole range of features which the desk had, for example it would only be one-dimensional. The problem of construing ideas as 'mental pictures' is made immeasurably more complicated by our difficulties in specifying appropriate mental pictures for the likes of, for example, the smell of bromide, the square root of –2, Beethoven's 5th Symphony, monetarism. This fundamental error is at the root of much of Hume's later difficulties. When he asks 'Can we form in our minds an idea of 1?' he is all too often demanding that we paint a mental picture in order to depict things in concrete terms.

Ideas are either simple or complex

Ideas for Hume are either simple or complex. A simple idea is not susceptible to division or separation, whereas a complex idea is susceptible to division and is compounded out of simple ideas. An example of the first type of simple idea would be the notion 'greyness', and an example of the second type would be the notion 'horse'. Hume's analogies are drawn from 'mechanics' or 'chemistry'; the latter yields a comparable distinction between elements and compounds. A compound such as water consists of the elements of hydrogen and oxygen, and in the same way our idea of a concept such as God is made up of

the elements of intelligence, wisdom and benevolence (14). As a consequence, if the percipient is unaware of simple ideas, then the requisite complex ideas cannot be formed in the mind (15–17).

There are two ways in which Hume could explain what a simple idea is. He could:

- Define it as that which a simple impression represents; but this depends on us knowing what a simple impression is! After all, in an earlier part of this commentary, we had to define a simple impression as the object of a simple idea, so this looks like circular reasoning.
- Show that simple ideas are the sort that cannot be analysed.

For Hume a simple idea is one about which one can say very little. A complex idea can be the subject of more expansive comment. You can say a lot more about 'horses' than about 'grey'. A simple idea, for that reason, is far more likely to be a predicate than a subject. On the surface, one might think that a tolerably clear distinction has been drawn and that the idea of a simple idea is pretty acceptable. This is not the case. To start with we must get away from the idea of physical simplicity. In Hume's day advanced enthusiasts for atomic theory might have held that the atom was the simplest thing you could get in the physical world (though the atom is not in Hume's terms a simple idea – on the contrary, there is quite a lot to be said about it). Of course a physicist would say that an individual 'photon' was simpler than the shade of grey, since any shade of grey is made up of photons.

Hume's simple ideas are not the ideas of something possessed of an ideal physical simplicity. A simple idea is logically simple. By this he does not mean ideas that cannot be subject to a particular kind of logical analysis; Hume is suspicious of ideas like 'soul' and 'substance' precisely because they defy the kind of logical analysis he supports. Ideas are logically simple for Hume because they are, as it were, termini for his preferred technique of analysis. You break down a complex idea like 'horse' into other ideas like 'four-legged' or 'fleshy'. Words like 'fleshy' can then be broken down into 'pink' and 'soft' etc. and here you reach a kind of linguistic bedrock. What can you say about 'pink'?

One might criticise Hume by asserting that we are not thereby offering a proper analysis of the term, but are just explaining it or discussing it in a narrower or more detailed way. Through adopting such a method, we end up with a vocabulary of terms that we cannot analyse further. It is as if we have boiled the sauce on our cooking stove to such an extent that it has reduced and reduced until we have nothing to serve with dinner. Thus we find that simple ideas are simple only in the sense that they defeat further analysis on Humean lines. 'Simple' means 'unanalysable', while 'complex' means 'analysable'. This will not do because 'simple' and 'unanalysable' are not synonyms in Hume's work. Some terms that are judged unanalysable by Hume are thought of not as simple but as meaningless. It all seems to depend on the process of Humean analysis being clear and it is not evident that it is; nor does Hume offer an adequate description of the process, trading to some extent on misleading mechanical analogies.

Ideas are particular

Although we might want to say that simple ideas are concepts that can only function as end-points of Humean analysis, it is by no means obvious for vast ranges of concepts whether they will fall into this category. You might look back over the terms used in this paragraph and ask yourself how many of them express simple concepts. There is something wrong in making a claim about the logical simplicity of an idea depend solely on its vulnerability to a particular technique of analysis. After all, there is a sense in which terms like 'pink', which is, so far as Hume is concerned, a paradigm case of what a simple idea should be like, are more complex than they look. For 'pink' is a general term or 'universal' that covers a whole range of shades, all of which are pink.

Of the association of ideas (Section III)

Hume proposes three ways in which ideas are connected (18–19) – that is, in which they can evoke one another:

- *Resemblance* – This refers not only to the resemblance between the categories of ideas and impressions but within the two sets themselves. Despite ideas being fainter than impressions, Hume argues that there is a family resemblance, with ideas resembling impressions. There is a problem as to how we could get to know that this relationship existed. Presumably it would have to be based on an impression of resemblance. This would seem a very different sort of impression, and it is not clear whether it would be simple or complex.

- *Contiguity* – By this Hume means the proximity between ideas in space and time. Some ideas may depict objects that are spatially or temporally contiguous, which makes us naturally think of them occurring together, like Christmas Day and Boxing Day.

- *Causation* – The relationship between impressions and ideas is discussed as though it were a cause-and-effect relationship. Considering Hume's views on causation, there does not seem to be a very stable connection between impressions and ideas, and it may more accurately be described as a conjunction. This leads on to the theme of causation, which will be dealt with in more detail later in this commentary.

For Hume, a causal relationship is simply one of constant association. A always follows B in space and time. Thus we grow to expect B after A despite the fact that B can, in theory, occur without A and vice versa. Therefore:

1 There is no *a priori* reason why a simple idea should not occur in the absence of a simple impression.
2 The resemblance between simple ideas (and ideas in general) and impressions is strictly fortuitous; they are in essence discrete phenomena. Like causes and effects seen from the Humean standpoint, there is no hidden connection to link them or ensure that things must be as they are.

Perhaps Hume falls prisoner to his own philosophy on this point. There is little option for him but to say that the relationships he discerns between impressions and ideas are the relationships he happens to detect by the experimental method. Things could turn out otherwise. What he is offering is an empirical generalisation of how things are. However, it is also an empirical fact according to Hume that some ideas, for example the idea of necessary connection, are not based on impressions. This fact cannot be used to invalidate such ideas unless you can show that sound ideas have to be based on impressions. There is no way a genuinely 'experimental method' can do this. Hume is in fact posing as an empirical scientist in order to establish normative conclusions. He could get away with it if he just restricted himself to pointing out that ideas not derived from impressions just happen not to be meaningful, but this, in its broadest sense, would mean that they would not be able to be discussed.

If it is to be claimed that ideas and impressions are causally related, Hume's theory is plunged into confusion. First, a causal relationship is defined as a relationship holding between our ideas of things, and impressions are neither ideas nor things. Second, we form an idea of a causal relationship as a result of the spatial connection between things; according to Hume a cause and its effect are always spatially contiguous, whereas impressions and ideas are not so situated. Third, if there is a causal relationship it must be no different from other causal relationships as described by Hume, a fortuitous connection. Hume believes that there are only the three types of connection mentioned above that make one idea prompt another. In order to prove that this is indeed the case he invites the reader to perform an internal thought experiment to see if any more can be classified.

Review questions

1 Briefly explain Hume's distinction between ideas and impressions.

2 Describe the implications of the distinction between ideas and impressions for epistemology.

David Hume (1711–1776)

Hume was a well-educated, down-to-earth Scotsman, the second son of a minor landowner from Ninewells, a small town between Perth and Edinburgh. He was educated at Edinburgh University as a lawyer, a career pursued by many thinkers with philosophical aspirations, and became a friend of the famous economist Adam Smith. He spent three years in France from 1734, to write and study, and after some time in London returned to Scotland to become tutor to the Marquess of Annandale in 1748. *An Enquiry Concerning Human Understanding* was published in the same year, and initiated what was to become the most productive period of Hume's academic career. In the following decade, he was best known as a historian and political commentator. He returned to France for the period 1763–1766 to work in the diplomatic service. Hume was a pivotal figure in the Enlightenment period, championing reason over **custom**, logic over tradition and encouraging a healthy dose of scepticism to unsettle our unfounded certainties. He famously declared, however, that all his sceptical doubts were forgotten when he was playing backgammon with his friends.

Significant works

A Treatise of Human Nature (1739–1740)
An Enquiry Concerning Human Understanding (1748)
An Enquiry Concerning the Principles of Morals (1751)
Dialogues Concerning Natural Religion (1778)

Sceptical doubts concerning the operations of the understanding (Section IV)

Part I: Hume's fork

At the very start of this part, the author draws his famous distinction between *a priori* and *a posteriori* knowledge, in what has become known as **Hume's fork** (see chapter 1). Hume's distinction lies between propositions that assert relations between ideas and those that assert matters of fact.

Mathematics is cited as an example of the sort of truths that fall into the first category, and Pythagoras' theorem (20) is rehearsed in full to give the reader the idea. These types of truth are discoverable by the mere operation of thought, and are impossible to deny without self-contradiction; thus many other kinds of propositions are included in this set.

The second strand of *a posteriori* truths includes scientific and historical facts, and these are only discoverable through experience (21). In addition, these statements are always open, in principle, to doubt – that is, their denial describes a possible though not usually an actual state of affairs. Hume focuses on this feature for the rest of this section, and examines the causal link between facts and the events leading up to their establishment together with the 'arbitrary' nature of their epistemic standing.

Having established that there are two kinds of truth, Hume asks in which category a statement like 'A causes B' would fall? He suggests that it is part of the second, *a posteriori*, category, termed 'matters of fact', for the reason that if one knew only the event or object labelled as a cause one would not, by dwelling on such an idea, be able to anticipate any of its effects. The cause-and-effect connection is thus not discoverable by thought alone (22). Hume invites us to consider some examples:

- I believe as a matter of fact that my friend is in France because I heard him shouting 'Goodbye, I'm going to France'.

- I believe as a matter of fact, on finding a watch on a desert island, that someone left it there, because of my past sensory experiences of watchmakers and the fact that human artefacts are not made by other creatures.

- I believe as a matter of fact that there is another person present in a dark room because of the clear auditory sensations that I receive.

Hume employs further thought experiments and illustrations in the next paragraph (23), first by inviting us to imagine that we were the first person on earth, like Adam in the Genesis account. Would we be able, by contemplating the idea of the various earthly elements such as water, to work out their properties? Hume argues that we would not, and that the relation between the 'secret powers' of things – that is, their nature – and their sensible qualities – that is, their observable properties – is worked out through experience. Natural scientists are the finest examples of individuals who are able to discover lots of interesting facts, ranging from the chemical composition required to make an explosive to the dietary habits of tigers, all through a simple procedure of observation and experience. Throughout this paragraph the author prefers to talk about causes as 'objects' even though we usually talk about causes as 'events': bread does not cause us to grow; only the eating and digesting of it does that. This preference for 'object' not 'event' language is an important feature of Hume's approach and a necessary requirement for the philosopher's next move.

Hume has gone to great efforts to emphasise the process of empirical evidence leading to what we can safely describe as true facts. He then analyses this process in such a detailed way as to start unravelling the certainty that bound this category of truths together. Admittedly, if I were to appear by magic in this world without prior knowledge as to how it worked I would not be able to, for instance, predict the outcome of one billiard ball hitting another. I would have to become acquainted with the laws of physics as they hold in this world. I learn through observation and possess an instinct for induction, which detects and is able to predict sequences of events. But what grounds do I have for believing that these orders and sequences will hold in the future, other than a desirous expectation, which Hume calls custom? Custom is motivated by a human desire for a complete explanation and the pragmatic need for a sufficient explanation in order to manage one's practical concerns. It would indeed be an unsettling world if cause and effect worked interchangeably and at random. It is nevertheless conceivable for there to be any number of options; returning to the billiard balls, the potted ball might as plausibly with regard to the laws of logic stay at rest, return to its original position or even leap in the air (25). Certainly, this revelation, called in paragraph 28 'a kind of merit of our very ignorance', breeds modesty in any empiricist who recognises it and who settles for generalisations that are open to refinement over ultimate pronouncements concerning cause and effect (26). Even applied mathematics that contains an empirical dimension is affected by this possibility of change and the need therefore for humility (27).

Task

Draw up two lists of statements that should be classed as:

- relations between ideas
- matters of fact.

Is this, as Hume intends it to be, an exhaustive account of human knowledge?

Part II: the problem of induction

Hume draws our attention to the fact that, as a rule, certain effects follow from certain causes. From experience we infer (29) that these causes will produce these effects, and these effects alone. The following is not, however, a logically valid inference:

1 All As have caused effect B.

2 Therefore, any future A will cause effect B.

The argument is not a good deduction unless we add:

1(b) All causes will always have their usual effects.

The additional premise raises the question: What reason do I have for believing this? If I cannot find a logical reason, then it seems to be just an irrational and unjustifiable assumption. This uncertainty is illustrated in paragraph 29 with the author's bread example: How do I know that because eating bread has always provided sustenance that it always will? We often reason in our everyday lives as though premise **1(b)** is correct, and Hume seeks to explain why we do this. The additional premise, which states that matters will continue to go on as they have before, is sometimes dignified with the title 'the principle of the uniformity of nature' or 'the principle of induction'. It proves to be a reasonably practical assumption. The same causes do by and large have the same effects, and we do seem to cope quite well if we assume that identical situations will have identical outcomes. According to the author, we think like this due to the irrational force of habit and custom – that is, the conditioning effect of our environment. We do not think like this because we are compelled by force of logic. We do not know how such a way of thinking could be rationally defended.

We could of course say that making the assumption that the world will run in a regular way, namely that causes will have their customary effects, is a reasonable thing to do, because, so far, matters have turned out just like this. However, this could only be considered a good argument in defence of the principle if we assume that matters must continue to go on as they have hitherto. We would of course have to appeal to the principle of uniformity to defend this last assumption, and this is where we came in. For Hume, inductive arguments are neither deductively valid nor rationally defensible, and yet they form the bulk of our reasoning in everyday life. As Bertrand Russell said, 'Hume's philosophy represents the bankruptcy of eighteenth century reasonableness'.

Some possible answers

1 One could adopt the view that there is really no need for a good argument to be a valid, deductive argument, and claim that a valid, deductive argument is only one species of good, rational argument. One could even go further and state that good, rational arguments have certain features that deductive arguments share with inductive

arguments. Hume, it could be said, is setting up the deductive argument as the sole ideal of rational argument, and in that respect is being unduly restrictive.

2 One could argue that Hume, in demanding a different type of justification for the principle of uniformity, is being himself unreasonable. What kind of justification is he after? Isn't the type of defence we offered what we normally mean by 'justification'? This is the response favoured by linguistic philosophers, who tend to allege that there is something unintelligible about Hume's request for justification.

3 One could allege that the principle of uniformity is an *a priori* principle that either is known to be true *a priori* or is essential to the construction of intelligible experience. These points are not incompatible positions. Variants of this approach all owe their origin to Kant. The general thrust is that we are bound to take the principle for granted.

4 One could argue that since the principle has proved a useful, practical assumption, it must be true. Pragmatists argue that what we call true is any useful assertion. Accepting that general thesis, a useful principle is a true one. There are, however, general difficulties with pragmatism and its equating of 'the true' with 'the useful'.

5 One could suggest that inductive arguments could be doctored to make them resemble deductive arguments, for example:
   - Water habitually weakens acid.
   - This is water.
   - Therefore, it will probably weaken acid.

You could allege that in this case the conclusion is strictly entailed by the premises, as in a deductive argument. This, however, does not seem to help much, because you can deny the conclusion and assert the premises. The only thing stopping you would be an appeal to the principle of uniformity itself, which functions as a background or hidden premise of the argument. If we can deny the conclusion and assert the premises we do not have a good deductive-style argument here.

Review question

Outline what is meant by the problem of induction and describe Hume's attempt at a solution.

Task

Is there a solution to the problem of induction? Discuss the merits and demerits of the above solutions and decide which one you think is the best solution.

Sceptical solution of these doubts (Section V)

Part I: the principle of custom

It is helpful to devise causal laws of the form 'X causes Y', because they serve as rules of thumb when it comes to co-ordinating our activity within this world. Such rules are not rules about specific events, but are about types of event. X stands for a range of individual phenomena, as does Y. The natural tendency towards and affinity with this operation is part of what Hume terms 'habit' or 'custom'. He begins Section V by informing us that we stand in need of being rescued from the more extreme strands of scepticism as promulgated by such thinkers as Epictetus (c. 55–135). Custom is then outlined as the way human beings cope in their everyday affairs. It fits in with the natural constitution of the human mind, which finds it a waste of energy to keep questioning all the time; Hume judges this as a form of indolence, but elsewhere declares that his sceptical doubts are forgotten when he is playing backgammon with his friends. He is quick to point out and emphasise in a later paragraph (36) that 'in all reasonings from experience, there is a step taken by the mind which is not supported by any argument or process of the understanding'. Instead, the presumption of cause and effect being connected in a way that lends itself to prediction is seen to supply the required or 'customary' explanation created by the contiguity of ideas. We are otherwise left wondering what the 'secret power' is in A that makes it cause B (35). The philosopher continues (36):

> Without the influence of custom, we should be entirely ignorant of every matter of fact beyond

what is immediately present to the memory and senses. We should never know how to adjust means to ends, or to employ our natural powers in the production of any effect. There would be an end at once of all action, as well as of the chief part of speculation.

This quotation eulogises the indispensable nature of custom in the purely mental spheres of memory and perception as well as in the applied field of everyday life. The author illustrates this with the simple example (38) of the weather being associated with a particular temperature.

> **Task**
>
> John Stuart Mill takes up the theme of custom in his work of political philosophy, *On Liberty*. What does Mill say about custom, and how is this influenced by Hume's position?

Part II: imagination and belief

The preceding discussion on the subject of custom leads to a distinction in Hume's philosophy of mind between imagination as the act of conceiving a possibility and the act of believing that involves endorsing such a conception as likely or more probable.

The imagination mixes, separates, imagines and depicts the succession of impressions or sense-data received from the external world (39) and has the power to arrange such items in novel ways; the author uses the example of a centaur. The faculty of belief, however, though inextricably linked to the faculty of the imagination, has a further 'annex', which is the power to award assent, credence or plausibility to the images. Thus one might not believe in the existence of centaurs despite having the power to imagine what they would look like. In the following paragraphs, the author strives towards a tighter definition of the faculty of belief. He observes that believable ideas are more realistic in their vivacity and livelier form (40), and goes on to declare that belief 'makes [ideas] appear of greater importance; enforces them in the mind; and renders them the governing principle of our actions'. In answer to the question 'On what grounds do we consider an idea more believable than others?' Hume relies on the three features identified in paragraph 19: resemblance (41),

contiguity (42) and causation (43). Thus we might believe that someone is our friend when we experience a set of emotions on presentation of their picture, which engenders in us certain feelings that attest to the fact that this is our friend. In another example, the author points to how the music, incense, ornate vestments and decorations inspire feelings of devotion in many churchgoers, thus making the faith more palatable. Further sources of credibility involve ideas being contiguous, as when familiar scenery makes us believe that we are homeward bound, and causation, as when we presume when presented with a picture of a person that he or she existed.

In all this we should remember that, though Hume succeeds, in his own eyes, in demonstrating the frailty of human reason, he does claim that in a way nature knows best. Nature conditions us to think in a way that aids our survival. Even if we cannot justify the way in which we think, nature has arranged a fruitful outcome. Hume does not explain to us why nature bestows on us the seemingly inaccurate idea of necessary connection (discussed below). Hume thinks that ideas that we believe to be true are imprinted upon us with great force by factors like custom, and also by current impressions. We believe something, as opposed to imagining something, when the idea of that something is present to our mind with greater force. The force of the idea is a product of a variety of external factors: custom, association, the actual presence of the object of the idea. Beliefs are powerful ideas. According to Hume, we cannot choose what we believe, and if ultimately we cannot justify all the beliefs we hold there is little we can do about it:

> belief is something felt by the mind, which distinguishes the ideas of judgement from the fictions of the imagination. It gives them more weight and influence; makes them appear of greater importance; enforces them in the mind; and renders them the governing principle of our action.

Of probability (Section VI)

Although we are able to conceive of many options, we believe in the more probable ones. Hence if there is a die with many of the sides marked in the same way, we are justified in believing that this marking is more likely than not to appear on rolling. Hume reminds us of the billiard-ball illustration, but whereas in paragraph 25 he talked of hundreds of options he now refines this comment by pointing out that these are hundreds of imaginable options; while owing to past experience the most believable result involves the potted ball moving instead of remaining motionless, 'belief is nothing but a firmer and stronger conception of an object than what attends the mere fictions of the imagination'. There are many occasions, however, when the results are not as well known as billiards. The medicinal effects of rhubarb on different people is cited as an example.

Review question

Briefly explain one of Hume's sceptical arguments.

Of the idea of necessary connection (Section VII)

Causality

Hume defines an event as an artificially isolated phenomenon, picked out from a continuum of happenings. Romeo's serenading of Juliet can be called an event, but during it he is consuming oxygen, creating sound waves etc. – all of which influences and is influenced by the surrounding ecosystem, which in turn is shaped and in turn shapes the entire history of the universe. This is a version of holism. To throw a spotlight on one aspect of the history of the whole universe is to impose an intellectual boundary upon that which is not actually separate. To break the entire world process into discrete events can be looked upon as an act of abstraction. To ask what causes an event thus is to draw attention to an item within a process and its genesis. For Hume the task is to explain the origin of views about causal connections, and in particular the view that there is something natural or necessary about effects following on from causes.

To do this he compares:

- the received concept of the cause–effect relationship; and

- the description of a causal situation as Hume sees it (that is, in terms of ideas and impressions).

For Hume, this is like testing a hypothesis against 'experience', but it should be seen as testing a hypothesis against the Humean construction of experience. For the author, the cause-and-effect link is a relationship of ideas. The idea of relations is itself a complex idea, but it is not clearly spelt out how this idea is composed of simple ideas. In addition, it is not obvious that all the elements in this complex idea can be copies of simple impressions. However, we will shunt aside the vexed question of whether even the existence of the idea of causal connections is explicable within Hume's theory of knowledge, and turn to how Hume tests such hypotheses against experience through his method of introspection.

Testing the causal hypothesis

The first thing to note about Hume's methods is that in describing the raw causal situation he prefers to talk of causes and effects as 'objects'. Can you tell, he argues, by looking at an object what effects it is likely to have? This is very misleading, because by and large it is events that give rise to effects. Effects are also classed as events. Causes do not cause objects but *events* to happen; this is not a trivial point. Hume's preference for this rather strange way of talking, in object-language rather than event-language, increases the plausibility of his views. It is easy to provide two independent descriptions of objects involved in a causal situation. Descriptions of events within the causal situation do not seem to have the same degree of logical independence. To take Hume's favourite example, there is nothing in the description of billiard ball X that implies that it will move billiard ball Y. However, a description of the movement and momentum of X, which ends in collision with Y, is difficult to give without a reference to its collision with and impact on Y. Whether a cause is an object or an event for Hume, a cause is at the least:

- spatially contiguous with its effect;
- temporally contiguous with its effect.

Spatial contiguity

Spatial contiguity means for Hume something like 'touching', being 'next to' or 'adjacent'. A cause and its effect are alongside one another in space. There is an initial problem here. Consider the following illustration:

1 A   B
2   AB

The problem lies in the fact that both the examples above can be viewed as spatially contiguous if we suppose that on the second line there is empty space between the A and the B. Hume was unhappy about the Newtonian concept of empty space, but did accept 'action at a distance' as forwarded in Newtonian but not Cartesian physics. He did not wish to deny gravity, but suggested that the influence of an object upon another over a distance occurred if they were in some way materially linked. This still comes close to saying that a cause does not need to be spatially contiguous to its effect. Even if we get round this definitional problem, there is the worrying fact that not all causes and effects appear to be spatially contiguous (often for the good reason that not all of them appear to be in space).

> ### Task
>
> When we get away from Hume's very restricted diet of examples involving billiard balls and the like, his thesis of spatial contiguity seems less plausible. Discuss the following examples and how they might prove problematic for Hume:
>
> - The smell of gas caused wholesale panic.
> - The push of the button caused the death of millions.
> - Impressions cause us to have ideas.
> - My desire for vengeance caused me to lie in wait for my enemy.
> - The execution of the king caused a popular uprising.

In the last example, cause and effect cannot lie side by side, for it is essential that the cause be complete (the event must have happened) before the result occurs. In what way can events that are not temporally simultaneous be spatially contiguous? Few causes are both temporally simultaneous and spatially contiguous, for the very good reason that if an event is temporally simultaneous with another event we are likely to look for some third factor that would explain their occurrence rather than explain one by the other.

Temporal contiguity

Temporal contiguity is no happier a notion for Hume: ask yourself what time interval should exist between two events before we could not call them 'temporally contiguous'. Clearly there is no definite answer that can be offered here, unless we say there must exist no time interval between the two events; but this would imply that the two events were simultaneous and would in effect deny that causes are temporally prior to effects.

Necessary connection

For Hume there is a third element involved in our identification of causal relationships. We feel causes to be bound necessarily to their effects. This is an element that Hume cannot find in the world of impressions. Causes and effects can be genuinely spatially and temporally contiguous, but this necessary connection is to Hume illusory. Hume does not believe that causes and effects are necessarily connected precisely because he cannot account for it as a fact of perception. He cannot point to some locus within the causal relation and say, 'Here it is – here is the necessary connection!' The surprising thing is that Hume thinks you ought to spot something among our sense-data and identify it as 'the necessary connection'. Clearly, were we able to say, 'Look over there, that's the necessary connection', such a perceptual fact would be like any other fact of perception – that is, a matter of contingency and not of necessity. A cause would just happen to be necessarily connected with its effect in the same way as it just happened to be blue or round etc. This would be an odd state of affairs.

Hume is right in believing that the propositions that describe causes and the propositions that describe effects are not related in any straightforward deductive way and are obviously not logically equivalent.

1 If 'A' describes cause X,
2 And if 'B' describes effect Y,

3 Then the conditional 'if A then B' is not a valid, deductive inference.

When people say: 'X necessarily causes Y', they are not thought to be asserting that 'A implies B', but that Y would not have occurred without X. My potting a billiard ball necessarily means that the potted ball moved; in other words, if I hadn't hit the cue ball accurately in a specific direction then it wouldn't have moved in the particular way it did, but that is not to say that there is any logical connection between my shot and the subsequent movement. If, however, logical necessity is not the intended sense and if there is no impression to label 'necessary connection' (50–51), Hume's view is that the idea of necessary connection must have arisen through some species of conditioning. We grow to expect Y whenever X occurs, because X and Y are continually found together in relationships of spatial and temporary contiguity. It is important to note that Hume is explaining away rather than clarifying the idea of necessary connection. He is giving a causal account of how we get stuck with this distinctly dicey idea. He is not suggesting that the idea of necessary connection simply means the impressions built up in us by the likes of conditioning. The correct idea of that sequence of impressions would be a copy of it, not an idea of necessary connection. Nor is he providing an analysis in terms of simple ideas and impressions of the idea of necessary connection. If Hume is right in his general theory of ideas and impressions, he must show how even this mistaken idea can be derived from impressions. After all, all ideas are supposed to be ultimately copies of impressions. Hume has only explained how the idea of necessary connection could crop up, not how we come to have the idea in the first place. Hume has got his work cut out to explain how the idea occurs in our mind in the first place. It might have been wiser to dub the idea a meaningless verbal formula, as occurred in later philosophies of mind.

Hume's account of the origin of the idea of necessary connection

It is important to note that Hume is offering a causal account of the origin of 'necessary connection'. The constant conjunction of causes and effects engenders in the human mind a subjective feeling of necessity, that A causes B. As a consequence, therefore:

- There is no intrinsic connection between cause and effect. They are fortuitously connected (58).
- They must have been constantly conjoined (temporally and spatially contiguous).

Note too that part of Hume's thesis is that we acknowledge that one thing causes another:

- if they are spatially contiguous;
- if they are temporally contiguous;
- if they are constantly found to be so.

One might suggest that this is not a sufficient condition to justify a causal proposition. Crows often build their nests in the lower branches of trees before a bad winter, but it would be unfair to blame them for the inclement weather or even presume the weather will be bad just because of our ornithological conclusions, as there might not have been a suitable place elsewhere in the tree. Hume's conditions are met in many circumstances where we do not go on to make a causal claim. One can also suggest that the points cited above are not necessary connections for a causal claim to be met. We have already explained why a cause does not have to be temporally and spatially contiguous to its effect; nor need it be found constantly conjoined with its effect. To declare with impunity that Oliver Cromwell caused the dissolution of the Long Parliament does not require us to acquaint ourselves with lots of Oliver Cromwells. Equally, we may assert that eating a cake caused a flood of memories to overwhelm Proust without alleging that this is always the consequence of eating cake.

If constant conjunction were required before we concluded 'A caused B', any occurrence of A in isolation from B would weaken our tendency to make that link. This does not happen. The fact that I often see fire but no damage does not weaken my belief that fire causes great damage. In the cases where we postulate causes that are unobservable, for example sub-atomic particles, anti-matter etc., we cannot be said to find impressions constantly conjoined. We may give certain predictable and constant effects a particular cause, but that cause is not observed to be constantly spatially and temporally contiguous to the effects; it is not observed at all. Of course we may think of certain unobservable causes as constantly conjoined in the Humean way, but that is not the same type of affair as the regular succession of impressions that Hume believes gives rise to the idea of causal connections.

The absence of spatial and temporal contiguity and the lack of constant conjunction seem no bar to asserting a causal connection, and the presence of all three elements is no guarantee of it. It is possible to refer to something as a cause which is not spatially contiguous, not temporally contiguous and not constantly conjoined. Consider, for instance, the statement: 'The big bang caused the present state of our galaxy'. The big bang might have created the spatial dimension of the universe, but much has happened since and we have not observed this event or found it to be 'constantly conjoined'.

Liberty and necessity (Section VIII)

Section VIII continues many of the themes outlined in Section V concerning the role of habit in the philosophy of mind. It also raises the philosophical problem of whether our actions are performed freely or whether they are **determined**. The author wishes to move the debate on from definitions to real argument, which he does, but in a tentative and rather inconclusive way. Having briefly surveyed the territory and reminded us of his previous findings (64), Hume points out that the processes of human thought, as far as the relations of ideas and impressions are concerned, is generally the same regardless of nationality and profession; yet people do exhibit different dispositions. Only philosophers are expert and keen-sighted enough to determine where and how this moulding of minds takes place. The tension discovered in 68–69 is that, while human characters are inconstant, everyone is similarly influenced by the same 'conjunction between motives and voluntary actions'. The same relation exists between motives and action as has

been identified in the previous sections between cause and effect.

The position adopted by the author is known as compatibilism due to the fact that he holds that free will is compatible with determinism. Determinism is the view that human beings are subject to the same physically determined laws as other objects in the universe, and as such cannot be said to be free to act. There are two opposing notions: first, the view that we have free will and our lives are not determined; second, that our lives are determined and that we do not have free will. Both opposing standpoints are referred to as incompatibilism. The compatibilist argument seems to be subtle to the point of advancing an emasculated version of determinism but, in order to be fair, let us outline Hume's position in more detail.

Hume has established what he calls a 'uniformity in nature' – that is to say, we experience 'the constant and regular conjunction of similar events'. As perceptive beings we spot patterns and sequences of events and in so doing learn how the world is. Hume does not elaborate on the uniformity of nature as this would be to steal the thunder from investigative scientists. Instead, he draws our attention to the fact that we exist as part of a universe that obeys physical laws and consequently are subject to the same physical laws as other physical things. Yet we are also conscious beings with attitudes, emotions and aspirations that affect our actions. All things being equal, we are not constrained like a prisoner in a cell but are free to exercise choice while free from constraint. Hume defines voluntary action as the freedom to choose while free from constraint. He is happy to observe us exercising freedom of choice through voluntary action in a physically determined universe. Indeed, he believes that it is a necessary condition for moral responsibility because if the world did not exhibit uniformity and determination we would have been cast into an arbitrary world of randomness where moral judgement would not make sense. Hume is interested in the legal implications of compatibilism and concludes that, far from exempting criminals from blame, his analysis binds the offender to the offence in a firmer way.

In the final paragraphs Hume indulges in some theological speculation, and argues that as his doctrine of deterministic holism admits to the presence of evil (that is, that there are flaws in the system) this either reflects badly on the first mover (that is, God), or else human beings are totally free and their actions are contingent. Having dismissed the notion of personal liberty, these last thoughts are perhaps intended as a criticism of the cosmological argument (see chapter 3) to accompany those set out so eloquently in the *Dialogues Concerning Natural Religion*.

Task

Do we really have free will or are our lives determined by our material natures in a material world? Organise a discussion and record the arguments for and against the idea that we have free will.

Revision questions

1 Explain how, according to Hume, the idea of necessary connection arises.

2 Critically evaluate the Humean account of causation.

3 Outline and explain the difference between ideas and impressions.

4 Outline Hume's three principles of the association of ideas.

5 Critically assess Hume's claim that knowledge is either concerned with relations between ideas or matters of fact.

Discussion questions

■ How has Hume's theory of perception influenced phenomenalism?

■ Does Hume's empiricism contribute anything to epistemology apart from a sense of modesty?

■ How do we become conditioned into believing in induction?

■ Is truth really only a matter of probability beyond which we cannot reach?

■ Given Hume's views on causality, why do you think that he criticised the cosmological and teleological arguments for the existence of God?

Glossary of key terms

Belief: described as an addition to the imagination in so far as it is the act of endorsing or signing up to a particular idea.

Causation: causation or causality is the philosophical study of the relationship between entities in time and space.

Cause: that which is seen to produce an event.

Contiguity: the word Hume uses to describe things being in close proximity – that is, next to each other in space or time.

Custom: the process of conditioning, whereby we come habitually to expect a given effect after a given cause.

Determinism: the view that everything in the universe is the product of a prior cause.

Effect: that which follows another event and which becomes causally linked to it through the process of inductive reasoning.

Hume's fork: the notion that truth comes in two forms: the experiential, called 'matters of fact', and the logical, termed 'relations of ideas'.

Ideas: an idea is the mental picture we have of something gained originally from an impression; twentieth-century philosophers call this a phenomenon or 'sense-datum'.

Imagination: the faculty of imagination enables us to form images and hold concepts in our minds.

Impressions: the immediate and lively sense experience that we receive in our conscious lives.

Reify: to treat something that has no independent existence as a solid and separate thing. For example, the state of Britain could not exist if all Britons were abducted by aliens, but you could imagine someone talking as if it could.

Suggested reading

- Ayer, A. J. (1980) *Hume*, Oxford, OUP
  Classic introduction to Hume from one of his most ardent fans

- Baillie, J. (2000) *Hume on Morality*, London, Routledge
  The second chapter offers an analysis of ideas and impressions

- Fate Norton, D. ed. (1997) *The Cambridge Companion to Hume*, Cambridge, CUP
  The earlier articles in this compendium are of particular relevance

- Noonan, H. (1999) *Hume on Knowledge*, London, Routledge
  The third chapter offers a useful take on causality

- Stroud, B. (1990) *Hume*, London, Routledge
  A sound introduction to the issues raised in the *Enquiry*

Note

1 Hume, D. (1975) *An Enquiry Concerning Human Understanding*, Oxford, Clarendon Press, paras 11–12; hereafter references in brackets are to paragraphs within sections of the *Enquiry* and refer to this edition.

11 A commentary on Nietzsche's *Beyond Good and Evil*

It is better to out-monster the monster than to be quietly devoured.
(Friedrich Nietzsche)

Aims

On completion of this chapter you should be able to:

- give an account of Nietzsche's critique of past philosophers
- evaluate Nietzsche's account of truth and interpretation
- evaluate Nietzsche's theory of the will to power
- understand the distinction drawn between the pre-moral, moral and extra-moral periods
- give an account of Nietzsche's critique of religion
- give an account of Nietzsche's history of morality
- evaluate Nietzsche's depiction of the new philosopher and his superiority and nobility
- give an account of Nietzsche's critique of modern ideas.

To his followers Nietzsche's insights into the human condition constitute the most perceptive of all time; to his critics the Nietzschean canon seems overly rhetorical and adolescent in its fetishisation of vitality and virility. The title of the tract *Beyond Good and Evil* is borrowed from Hindu scriptures, possibly *The Upanishads*, in which the doctrine of *advaita* teaches that human enlightenment involves the transcendence of every form of duality, including the division between good and evil. The success of Nietzsche's enterprise then is to be judged on how far he achieves such a move.

On the prejudices of philosophers (Part I)

Beyond Good and Evil begins with the memorable line, 'Supposing truth is a woman, what then?' Nietzsche's epistemological argument is that there is no such thing as absolute truth set apart from the world we inhabit and that any metaphysical quest for meaning is misguided. Womankind in the above quotation epitomises the illusory nature of truth and the predetermined physical world in which we live. Throughout Part I Nietzsche lampoons various thinkers who have sought to give an account of truth: Plato, the Stoics, Christ, Descartes, Kant, Berkeley, Hegel, Spinoza, Schopenhauer. He believes that past philosophers commit the fallacy of prejudice, apportioning praise or blame to an argument as a result of certain presuppositions they have taken for granted. The groundless presuppositions or prejudgements that Nietzsche accuses past philosophers of include the notions that:

- truth exists to be discovered;
- logic is absolute;
- we possess an immortal soul;
- there is a separate, metaphysical 'I' in existence.

To contemplate any of the above is equivalent to taking seriously the riddle of the Sphinx. The Sphinx was a mythical creature of ancient Greece who stopped travellers to ask them pointless questions. The question 'What is truth?' falls into this meaningless category.

Nietzsche is intrigued by our motivation in approaching philosophy. Why are you reading this page, for example? In asking the question 'Why do we want to know the truth?' he poses a more fundamental question than his predecessors, who sought to answer 'What is truth?' Nietzsche's new species of philosopher will hold a light up to human nature as it really is.

For Nietzsche, philosophy and the philosopher cannot be separated, as they are mutually inclusive. Even logic, provocatively called 'fictitious' and 'superstitious' in the text, bears a human presence behind the apparent autonomy of ps and qs:

> In the philosopher, on the contrary, there is nothing whatever impersonal; and above all, his morality bears decided and decisive testimony to *who he is.* (I.6)

Philosophy is a subjective discipline and moral philosophy is personal. There is a tension between a belief and its opposite (the Hegelian dialectic), and this tension is a personal force felt by each individual thinker who encounters truth and deception. Such a force is one manifestation of the **will to power** and is described as 'life-advancing, life-preserving, species-preserving, perhaps even species breeding' (I.4). Yet we are not just talking about the human sex drive or, as Schopenhauer called it, 'the will to life', but something altogether more aesthetic that locates us beyond our animal identity, moving us closer to the ideal of *Übermensch* (the superman or human ideal).

It is this quasi-sexual, aspirational drive that underpins all our actions. Nietzsche uses the example of academics. He admits that there are in existence some real men of science who treat study as an end in itself but most use knowledge as a tool to cultivate a reputation for learning and assume gravitas in order to assert their will

Friedrich Nietzsche (1844–1900)

The life of Friedrich Nietzsche reads like a chronology of illness, which may go some way towards explaining the importance attached to health, strength and vitality in his work. His father died of a congenital brain disease when Nietzsche was five years old; as a schoolboy the young Friedrich missed many lessons owing to severe headaches; on joining the army he received a chest injury when mounting a horse. Ironically he worked as a medical orderly in the Franco-Prussian war before being discharged on sick leave. To an extent, Nietzsche blamed his sickness on the spiritual crisis he experienced after moving academic disciplines from philology to philosophy. He felt confronted by the raw reality of life as he saw it from a perspective of strong nihilism and, like Darwin on formulating his theory of the survival of the fittest, such a philosophy made him feel nauseous. Migraines and worsening eyesight hastened the philosopher's decline. He experienced bouts of depression, suffering a complete breakdown in 1889, eleven years before his death on 25 August 1900. The bulk of Nietzsche's work was produced in the period before his eventual mental collapse while he was living in rural isolation in lodgings and hotel rooms. His demise was advanced by progressive syphilis, possibly contracted from a prostitute in his youth. He remained a philosopher in the truest sense: a gifted thinker who gives us insights into the human condition.

Significant works

The Birth of Tragedy (1872)
Human, All Too Human (1878)
The Gay Science (1882)
Thus Spoke Zarathustra (1885)
Beyond Good and Evil (1886)

On the Genealogy of Morals (1887)
The Anti-Christ (1888)
Ecce Homo (autobiographical, 1888)
Twilight of the Idols (1889)

to power over their less-educated students. Imagine the case of a professor who name-drops, uses complicated jargon and refers to books you haven't read. This person, Nietzsche maintains, is asserting his or her will to power over you; their 'real interest' lies in a different direction to the assumed role of educator. In addition, the example of Epicurus is cited with reference to his rejection of the Platonic model of well-being, which emphasises the role of reason over the emotions. Nietzsche argues that it was the drive to be better than Plato that motivated Epicurus to write his plethora of tracts and not a detached desire for the truth. This view of ourselves and other animals emerges with some feelings of embarrassment and foolishness on our behalf yet with a conviction that carries a certain beauty and strength of argument (I.8). Not to behave in this way would be to contradict our nature in the same way as the misguided stoical school. Stoics were that group of ancient Greek philosophers who advocated detachment from worldly success and its trappings. Despite Nietzsche's inability to succeed in forming relationships or in accruing material wealth, he always admitted that these were what he wanted, like every other human being.

Task

Nietzsche was greatly influenced by another German philosopher called Arthur Schopenhauer. Find out what Schopenhauer's main ideas were and in particular what he meant by 'the will to life'.

Nietzsche advocates a methodology borrowed from his previous area of expertise, that of philology, the study of the origin of words. Philosophers are to adopt the same strategies as someone who is tracing their family tree, hoping that patient research into their ancestry will yield important truths about who they are. Nietzsche holds that he is asking a different sort of philosophical question. Unlike his predecessors, who prided themselves on discoveries (for example, the existence of the synthetic *a priori* in the case of Kant), Nietzsche's enquiry asks: 'What is the motivating force in asking such a question? Why is this belief necessary?'

Nietzsche and the will to power

The answer to all the questions posed in Part I lies in the will to power. The suggestion is made that our whole way of acting is controlled by our will to power – that is, the desire to assert ourselves. We do not fundamentally seek an elusive condition called happiness but ever-increasing opportunities to assert our will. This is not necessarily what we would claim to be doing or even what we think we are doing but it is nonetheless what we are always directly or indirectly up to. Being hypocritical, we will not always admit it; lacking insight, we may not always appreciate it.

The will to power is our motive both in setting our general course for life and in entering into or conducting social relationships. The child, the parent, the lover, the moralist, quite as much as the tycoon or the army officer, seeks power. People have children in order to exert power over them. Lovers seek to emotionally chain one another. Moralists seek to enforce ways of behaving that they find attractive and helpful to them. Power, according to Nietzsche, is the expression of the will towards one goal: establishing a situation in which one's will may be further expressed to greater effect. This is the goal we are programmed to pursue. For Nietzsche, this is just how we are made and his view stands or falls on whether such a theory adequately describes how people act.

An individual's will to power lies beyond the desire for truth. Nietzsche reminds us of the age-old conundrum as to whether we have knowledge of reality or only the appearance of things. For Nietzsche, reality is the will to power. A choice lies for philosophers between a theory of knowledge that seeks to avoid error and the more extravagant strong nihilism that seeks a 'cartful of beautiful possibilities over a handful of certainty' (I.10). In choosing the latter one creates something that is far more inspirational and progressive.

For Nietzsche, the will to power is a more important faculty than Kant's synthetic *a priori*, which had caused so much rejoicing in the German philosophical community. By contrast, *Beyond Good and Evil* was largely ignored. For Nietzsche, Kant's idea appeals only to those who seek a hiding place or antidote to the sensual and life-enhancing. Nietzsche's Copernican revolution in philosophy involves the rejection of outmoded beliefs, just as the Ptolemaic conception that the planets revolved around the earth was rejected. The notion that our faculties are governed by each of our 'selves' is supplanted by the admission that our self is ruled by the will to power. Each of our relationships is characterised by this drive. It is the will to power that deserves the status occupied by the atom in modern science or the soul in the Judeao-Christian world view. Nietzsche criticises rival explanations such as science, in particular physics and physiology (I.17, 22), religion (I.12) and idealism (I.15).

Nietzsche describes the will to power as 'the drive to self-preservation' and 'the desire to vent one's strength' (I.13). He explains that the will is not just a will to reproduce but a complicated process involving separate stages. A commanding thought starts the process, accompanied by a sensation of leaving something and moving towards something else. This makes the agent act and develop a sense of superiority and assertiveness. Each element constitutes a self-sufficient system of commanding and obedience: 'a primordial, total household of the soul' (I.20), shared by every member of the human race. Human nature, like any other nature, does not obey a set of laws but draws certain conclusions about nature. Nietzsche's psychological insight holds that 'the emotions of hatred, envy, covetousness and lust for domination as life-conditioning emotions [are] something which must fundamentally and essentially be present in the total economy of life' (I.23). This thought is an exhilarating one, like the excitement of someone embarking on an adventurous voyage who nevertheless feels nauseous, as they are struck by the reality of its brutality and potential danger. Nietzsche sails over the straits of established moral guidelines to the uncharted waters of meta-ethics. He sets out to steer a course beyond good and evil.

On the Genealogy of Morals (1887)

Much of what Nietzsche says about truth and interpretation can be found in a companion

volume called *On the Genealogy of Morals* that we will mention in passing at this point in the discussion. There is no independent category of objective truth for Nietzsche; instead a word or idea gains its meaning when it is coined and used as common currency. A study of the origins of moral ideas is undertaken in the three essays collectively known as *On the Genealogy of Morals*, viewed by the author as a sequel to *Beyond Good and Evil*. Nietzsche holds that the word 'good' originally stood opposed to 'bad' as synonymous with what is low, vulgar or plebeian. Only through the advent and ascendancy of a weak but cunning priestly caste at odds with a life-affirming warrior caste did the meaning of bad change and blend with the notion of evil and impurity – thus first establishing the distinction 'good' and 'evil'.

Nietzsche's support for the values of the warrior caste and his disdain for the weak has led scholars to speculate that his philosophy foreshadowed and influenced the atrocities of Nazi Germany. Two points may be made in the philosopher's defence. First, despite depicting the Jewish people as an example of the priestly caste par excellence, responsible for the slave revolt in morals and giving the world a conscience, there is little ground for accusing Nietzsche of actual anti-Semitism. Second, Nietzsche's sister Elizabeth edited and manipulated Friedrich's work in a ploy to impress Adolf Hitler. This started a trend of misreading such passages as the blond beast (*Genealogy of Morals* I.2, II.17), which is more a rhetorical flourish than racist propaganda. Having conceded these points, on reading such passages as quoted below, one is made aware of the social implications of key strands in Nietzsche's nihilistic non-cognitivism and how they contributed to the tragic events in Nazi Germany. Consider the following passage in which the author describes the pleasures of violation and the right to cruelty:

> This enjoyment will be prized all the more highly, the lower the creditor stands in the social order, and can easily appear to him as the choicest morsel, even as a foretaste of a higher rank. By means of the 'punishment' inflicted on the debtor, the creditor partakes of a *privilege of the masters*: at last, he too has the opportunity to experience the uplifting

feeling of being entitled to despise and mistreat someone as 'beneath him' – or at least, in cases where the actual power and execution of punishment has already passed to the 'authorities', to see this person despised and mistreated. So this compensation consists in an entitlement and right to cruelty. (*Genealogy of Morals* II.5)[1]

This extract sees Nietzsche exposing the raw side of human nature. We need to be clear what his aim is. Is it to assert an empirical fact about humanity or is it to endorse a certain type of behaviour? To phrase this point in technical terms: Is Nietzsche asserting an 'is' or an 'ought' (see chapter 2)? Nietzsche's influence on National Socialism was most fairly summed up at the Nuremberg trials:

> Without doubt, the late philosophy of Nietzsche cannot be identified with the brutal simplicity of National Socialism. Nevertheless, National Socialism was wont to glorify Nietzsche as one of its ancestors. And justly so, for he was the first to formulate in a coherent manner criticism of the traditional values of humanism; and also, because his conception of the government of the masses by masters knowing no restraint is a preview of the Nazi regime. (17 January 1946)

The Nuremberg transcripts go on to record other philosophical influences on Nazism from Machiavelli to Hegel.

Review question

Briefly describe what Nietzsche means by 'the will to power'.

The free spirit (Part II)

T. S. Eliot famously remarked that 'human kind cannot bear very much reality'. The same sentiment underpins Part II of *Beyond Good and Evil*, where Nietzsche rails against the human need for a security blanket or comfort zone that shields us from the harsh truth that life is the will to power. He reworks the Eden myth from the first book of Genesis, portraying the will to power as the natural, pre-lapsarian (before the fall of Adam and Eve) state of innocence and the categories of good and evil as the poisoned fruit of the tree of knowledge. Such concepts as good and evil are a deceptive masquerade that

inevitably makes those who partake more stupid: 'the stupidity of moral indignation', which no philosopher can take seriously. Adam and Eve, the archetypal man and woman, are urged to hide, not out of guilt, but so as to avoid such a flawed quest for moral enlightenment. The good that lies beyond goodness is that solitude of a free spirit, the urge to wage war openly and not be repressed, to shun the golden trelliswork of a false Eden.

Nietzsche's new philosophers learn that everything revolves around the will to power. Their journey is similar to the course taken by Plato's philosopher-rulers, yet Nietzschean *Übermenschen* seek freedom rather than truth. Their natural abode is the secret citadel of individualism and individuality. Yet they descend to the common masses in order to define their superiority. Nietzsche preaches a doctrine of predestination for these lovers of wisdom. Yet the title 'lovers of wisdom' is ironic because the knowledge they achieve is the realisation that we are animals wallowing in excrement as well as in learning and that we have the same basic appetites as goats or monkeys: 'a scientific head set on a monkey's body … with the passion to tear at things with our teeth'. This is the only truth that can be borne on the current of the Ganges, that ancient river of truth, despite people's reluctance to admit it. Friends who refuse to accept its validity should be either shunned or at worst tolerated as ignoramuses. Yet such a reality yields a certain light-headed *allegrissimo* (a sense of fun or happiness). Such excitement is not in keeping with the solemn, staid and stiff German culture but more in keeping with the 'delicious cruelty' of Machiavelli, whose writings make us heady and let 'us breathe the subtle, dry air of Florence'. Even Plato, that most noted of anti-aesthetes among philosophers, surely needs a draught of the life-affirming from time to time.

The transition from man to superman occurs beyond the witness of others. 'Superman' refers to those individuals who are seen by Nietzsche as the new philosophers who can transcend the faults and failings of their humanity. The Nietzschean superman is compared to Theseus, the hero in Greek legend who killed the minotaur in order to marry his beloved. As Theseus fought his adversary in a labyrinth, so the new breed of philosophers pass through a moral maze, their goal being the freedom that lies beyond the bounds of good and evil. Some potential *Übermenschen* will die in their noble yet perilous quest. The diet of *Übermenschen,* or men of free spirit, is very different from that of the average human being. Nietzsche notes this was recognised in India through the Hindu caste system, in Greece in Plato's myth of metals, and celebrated in the militaristic imagery of Islam.

The term 'esoteric' means lofty, aesthetic, highbrow and is used to describe the assent by certain individuals to *Übermensch* status. The difference between Nietzsche's 'aristocracy' and Plato's 'seekers of daylight' lies in the opposing roles awarded to the emotions and reason. Nietzsche prioritises the former whereas Plato emphasises the latter. It is only when the new philosophers reach their mountain top that the pure air can be breathed. It is contrasted to incense, used in Christian worship as a symbol of purity, a symbolism reversed by the author. Nietzsche goes on to point out that by 'will to power' is not meant the hot and savage virility, anger and ambition of youth but something more magnificent and profound.

Three stages of history
Nietzsche identifies three stages of history in relation to ethical judgements:

- the *pre-moral* period of mankind, in which right and wrong are derived from the consequences of an action (consequentialism);
- the *moral* period of mankind, in which right and wrong are determined by the intention of the moral agent (deontology);
- the *extra-moral* period of mankind, when the reasons for the above derivations and determinants are exposed.

Nietzsche admires certain aspects of the morality found in the pre-moral period; he eulogises aspects of classical Greek culture in *The Birth of Tragedy*. The Confucian past of China is alluded to (II.32) and one can understand how the author would have seen in this male-dominated, hierarchical ethical system based on duty and obedience[2] the same features that are prevalent in all ancient cultures and which reflect the essential nature of the human craving for power and a natural affinity for rank. Both the pre-moral and the moral phases are to be burnt off as dross, to leave the *Übermensch* as the alchemical gold of the extra-moral domain. Such a process of overcoming may be paralleled with the temporary phase termed by Marx 'the dictatorship of the proletariat' (see chapter 12). When the Nietzschean supermen succeed in their defeat of consequentialism and deontology a new existence emerges, a new form of humanity awaiting expression ripples beneath its transparent skin. The human desire for untruth stems from a fear of what the extra-moral reveals: a class conflict between the weak and the strong. A similar classification of moral history is developed in Nietzsche's *Twilight of the Idols*.

Twilight of the Idols (1889)
In this rhetorical and provocative work, published late in Nietzsche's career, five stages of history are identified in order to explain previous philosophers' obsession with finding out the truth or what happens in the real world:

Stage 1: the Socratic
The works of Plato advance the view that the real world is not the one perceived by us; instead we are dislocated from the pure world of forms, which we can only reach through reason.

Stage 2: the Christian
The two-kingdoms ethic of Christianity holds that the real world cannot be known in our earthly existence; it is only attainable in the future through good works performed in the present.

Stage 3: the Kantian
This moral philosophy of the Enlightenment advanced the view that the real world is not something we can ever understand in this life, but we need a sense of what it is to give our lives meaning.

Stage 4: the positivistic
The rise of science in the nineteenth century condemned metaphysics as factually nonsensical and something that can be dispensed with and replaced by scientific facts.

Stage 5: the extra-moral (Nietzschean)

Nietzsche acts as a cultural critic here, declaring that the four previous stages of moral history are **decadent** and hypocritical. Instead, we need to engage critically and destructively with the real world in order to revaluate values. The author draws our attention to the fact that during stages 1–3 the soul and the other-worldly characteristics are privileged as ascendant values by the weak in order to gain advantage over the strong. Such an analysis (cf. parts II–V of *Beyond Good and Evil*) leads to a criticism of Nietzsche that accuses the philosopher of presenting pseudo-history. One might dismiss the Nietzschean enterprise of analysing previous, primitive societies and drawing conclusions from them about the way we live as unconvincing owing to the fact that although causal links are made they are not accounted for. Nietzsche draws our attention to certain facts in the past and marries them to subsequent events without proving the connection to be true or false.

Nietzsche and morality

In Part II, Sections 33–34, of *Beyond Good and Evil*, Nietzsche puts Christian morality on trial, accusing it of hypocritically preaching self-sacrifice and renunciation, yet being the most powerful seductress of all. The author believes in an aesthetic antidote to the ethical. Our aesthetic goal blurs the distinction between appearance and truth, and exists in contrast to the 'civil world' in which dwell straightforward categories of right and wrong, or 'yes' and 'no'. It is a philosopher's role or duty to look beyond. For the philosopher, a bad character is as illusory as a good one. What really exists are our drives. In Part II, Section 36, the author tells us of the elemental substance of which everything in the universe consists. It lies behind the drives and emotions as well as physical things and is governed by the will to power; such is the will to power that it is as divine as it is demonic (II.37). For Nietzsche, the moral period began its death throes at the time of the French Revolution, in 1789, which produced the essentially corrupt ideology of socialism but has now progressed into the extra-moral phase.

Nietzsche criticises the twin pursuits of happiness and evil as equally misguided, declaring that 'happiness and virtue are no arguments'. The author himself, however, appears to be advocating certain virtues throughout the work, for example those of independence and strength. The next section (II.40) describes the will to power as so valuable a force that it needs protective clothing in the form of a mask. Even comparing it to something else (in the form of an image or parable) should expose a valuable truth that the listener would find hard to bear. Ironically, this will to power, of which the sole truth consists, is best disguised as a paradox, fit for the contemplation of mystics. Language is a suitable cover, but the proverbial vessel is not empty but brimming with the most delicate and profound reality.

The new species of philosophers who are able to deal with such a reality must pass a stringent test of self-mastery made up of six stages. These consist in a litany of baptismal promises:

- Do you renounce your loved ones?
- Do you renounce nationalism?
- Do you renounce feelings of pity?
- Do you renounce the quest for knowledge?
- Do you renounce faith in detachment?
- Do you renounce the need to pursue virtue?

If any individual can coldly answer 'yes' to all then they are 'christened' as new philosophers or followers of the prophet **Zarathustra**, and are ready to attempt their flight beyond good and evil. Nietzsche preaches an elite individualism and describes as contradictory the phrase 'common good'.

In the final section of Part II, the author criticises modern ideas that help propagate the slave morality of the **herd**. A problem arises, however, in so far as he seems to be advocating a normative ethical system, rather than progressing to the territory beyond.

The religious nature (Part III)

Part III of *Beyond Good and Evil* starts with the striking image of Nietzsche hunting down the 'big game' of the human soul, God and belief in heaven. Academics have been useless in tracking down such quarry to date as they lack the courage to enter dangerous terrain and address the bigger picture, just as they lack subtlety and keen-sightedness to follow the trail left by those of a religious persuasion (III.45). Nietzsche's analysis extends to all four points of the compass. He disapproves of, but does not count as dangerous, the gruff, northern Protestantism of England and Germany. He believes that the most decadent and misguided form of religion is the Catholicism of southern Europe (III.46). He seems less critical of the figure referred to as the oriental slave, perhaps a reference to Christ, and believes that the muscular Christianity of the Celtic fringe is, to an extent, an exception to the rule as it is borne out of hardship and characterised by asceticism (III.48).

Beyond Good and Evil nevertheless gives us an idea as to why its author disapproves of the Christian ideal. His hostility to Christianity is intense. He describes it as the most extreme thinkable form of corruption, together with alcohol (VIII. 252). Christianity, to Nietzsche, is a decadent product of feminine rather than masculine instincts. It is a religion of the weak, the herd, the lower orders and a sign of their triumph over the healthier instincts of superior types. Nietzsche can smell out Christian leanings at some distance, finding them in most philosophers, including Plato and Socrates, whom he regards as decadent pre-Christian seducers of the Ancient World. He finds the roots of Christian morality in Judaism and the theology of St Paul. Insidiously it gives rise to socialism or anarchism, and has equally infectious counterparts in the East, such as in the Buddhist doctrine of compassion (*karuna*).

Nietzsche is hostile towards religion because:

- He classes it as a form of self-mutilation, although he admits to being unclear as to whether 'solitude, fasting and sexual abstinence' follow from or contribute to this. Religion is described as a type of neurosis (III.47).

- He believes that it is impossible to deny one's drives and 'become a saint', and comments that the only reason why saints hold sway is that people enjoy entertaining the idea that they

too can transcend their weakness and possess special, otherworldly powers.

- It is the most cunning and successful form in which the values of the *Chandala* (Hindu term meaning 'outcaste' or 'lower orders') are broadcast.

- The instincts of religious people are decadent. They are not Nietzsche's instincts nor are they those of the **Dionysian**, pre-Christian world – Christianity embodies the **Apollonian** desire for an absolute truth where one can shelter from reality. Nietzsche is led to what he believes is a this-worldly, life-affirming stance, which accepts the fact that people differ enormously in quality.

Nietzsche uses the word 'decadent' in a specific way in this section. 'Decadent' can mean degenerate, declining in power or rotting. However, Nietzsche uses 'decadent' to mean morally repulsive. Nietzsche writes about decadent tendencies triumphing over millennia and over the healthy vigour of the ancient world and the Renaissance. This seems to imply that what is decadent can nonetheless be very powerful. The only advantageous mindset that religiosity can bring is an appreciation of the world as was found in pre-moral spirituality and subsequently lost with the advent of Christianity, which preaches a creed of fear. Nietzsche draws some unflattering portraits: the noble savage with unrefined popular piety; the oriental who is seduced by the promise of something ecstatic and elevating; the adolescent girl who substitutes religious devotion for sexuality; and the old woman who becomes more religious as she nears death.

Religion, like every facet of human life, is characterised and governed by the will to power but manifests itself in a more feminine and manipulative form. Lacking physical strength, the saint can only exercise his will to power through psychological warfare and spiritual belittling, which caused the heroes of old from the warrior caste to submit and pay homage. The values of the warrior caste are reflected in some pre-moral literature such as the Old Testament, which Nietzsche admires, but he thinks it a travesty that it should be joined to the subversive and life-denying New Testament to form the Bible.

Nietzsche once declared that the only person out of the whole New Testament who was worthy of praise was Pontius Pilate. It was Pilate who rose above the mob rule of the crowd and the pacifism of Christ, remaining pragmatically 'beyond good and evil', in a state of empowered indifference, and it was Pilate who expressed the central tenet of epistemic perspectivism when he asked 'What is truth?'

Nietzsche may have been anti-Christian but he was not necessarily opposed to all aspects of every religion. He admired the liberating nature of Buddhism[3] and the life-affirming, heroic values of the Jewish Torah, together with its grand narrative style.[4] Nietzsche came from a religious background; his father and grandfathers were Lutheran pastors, and he initially studied theology at university, switching to an academic career in philology only when he had lost his religious faith. In a social comment (III.53), the author points out that while theism is in decline, a life-denying, quasi-Christian morality still spreads like an epidemic.

Nietzsche argues in a more philosophical passage (III.54) that philosophy by nature is anti-Christian in many respects but especially in its success at disproving the soul. Since its first formulation, philosophers have attacked (*Attentat* means 'attack') Descartes' famous epigram 'I think therefore I am' as an analytic truth – that is, a statement in which the predicates are contained in the subject and which according to Descartes proves that we have souls. Nietzsche believes that a religious doctrine of the soul contradicts the notion of **eternal return**, which teaches that atoms are physical (I.12); in addition he believes that the ascetic notion of sacrifice contradicts the superior aesthetic values of pleasure, strength and health.

Nietzsche's three rungs argument (III.55) exemplifies his anti-Christianity and method of pseudo-history. He describes three stages in religious history, all involving sacrifice and corresponding to the descriptions laid out earlier in Part II, Section 32:

- pre-moral: the practice of human sacrifice to appease the gods;
- moral: the practice of sacrificing our strongest and best instincts for God;
- extra-moral: the sacrifice of God in favour of atheism.

Renouncing God in this way carries as its corollary a rejection of conventional normative morality: one cannot, like followers of Schopenhauer and Buddhists, reject one but not the other. This point is well expressed in another work:

> When one gives up Christian belief one thereby deprives oneself of the right to Christian morality. For the latter is absolutely not self-evident: one must make this point clear again and again in spite of English shallowpates. Christianity is a system, a consistently thought out and complete view of things. If one breaks out of a fundamental idea, the belief in God, one thereby breaks the whole thing to pieces: one has nothing of any consequence left in one's hands.[5]

In his assumed role as prophet, Nietzsche forecasts that the notion of religion will be dismissed as nothing more than a childish superstition and of no more than historical interest. There was already a shift occurring in the German middle classes, who wondered at the existence of religion with 'dumb amazement', having been acculturated by hard work, family and national concerns (III.58). In the following section, Nietzsche echoes the sentiment of Oscar Wilde that 'deep down we are all superficial people'. There are some 'philosophers and artists', he argues, who try and reverse this through postulating something that lies beneath the surfaces of things; examples may include Plato's theory of forms. Nietzsche cites religion as the epitome of this wrong-headed view, borne as it is out of weakness and an inability to counter the pessimism that nihilism brings. To escape the harsh reality of the will to power with recourse to love of one's neighbour for the sake of God is the most misguided conception that has ever been entertained (III.60). In true Machiavellian fashion, Nietzsche advocates that religion should nevertheless be 'made use of' by the *Übermensch* for political ends and to emphasise the pecking order. This line hardens in the last section of Part III, in which the author claims that religion is contrary to the rhythm of nature in so far as it allows things to exist that rightly ought to perish. The 'ought' in this phrase, rather than being an imperative, appears to be given more factual status. For Nietzsche, the fact that this current has been quelled shows what is wrong with the inhabitants of Europe at the time of his writing.

In an adaptation of Protagoras' phrase, the author construes humankind as 'the animal man, the measuring animal'; by extension, that which exists contrary to our animal nature, for example Christianity, can never fulfil us. One is presented with a Nietzschean version of virtue theory where noble traits such as courage are accepted but qualities such as kindness are rejected. Which extrapolation of Aristotle's virtue theory are we to choose from: the Nietzschean or the theological? Both positions are very critical of each other, for example in Nietzsche's understanding of what he terms 'the three dangerous dietary prescriptions' of Christianity: solitude, fasting and sexual abstinence (III.47). He offers a characteristically historical account of how such practices came to be accepted in *On the Genealogy of Morals*. Mesmerised under 'the spell of society and peace', mankind's animal instincts were forced to turn inwards in what Nietzsche classes as a process of devolution and internalisation:

> These half-animals who were happily adapted to a life of wilderness, war, nomadism, and adventure were affected in a similar way to the creatures of the sea when they were forced either to adapt to life on land or to perish – in a single stroke, all their instincts were devalued and 'suspended'.[6]

Behind the author's accusations lurks the suggestion that Christianity's dominance is like the dominance of a parasite – that is, ultimately degenerative. It is decadent because it puts the survival of the human race at risk. Christianity, with its notions of equality and its suppression of excellence, is ultimately a source of biological degeneracy or at any rate a bar on future development.

Review question

Briefly describe Nietzsche's account of the religious nature.

Task

Part IV of *Beyond Good and Evil* consists of a selection of maxims. Read and discuss the following sections: 65a, 69, 75, 76, 78, 115, 116, 117, 132, 139, 146, 153.

On the natural history of morals (Part V)

In Part V, Nietzsche draws on the historical framework as previously described. The moral period, though later than the pre-moral period, is still young and inept in contrast to the extra-moral. It is seen as ironic that morality, which is subject to 'live, grow, beget and perish' in a cyclical, organic process, should be viewed inorganically as a science of morals. Nietzsche goes on to point out that morality can't be a science owing to the problem of relative values. This is a point that moral realists such as Aristotle, who talked about a science of morals in the opening sections of the *Nicomachean Ethics*, fail to recognise. Such ethicists confuse the realm of faith with the realm of fact, as is evinced through their trite, unscientific language, which the author likens to the naivety of children or the platitudes of old women. Thus the non-cognitive position is affirmed and the cognitive standpoint denied in light of the truth that 'the essence of the world is the will to power'. The appropriate response is not pessimism but celebration. Nietzsche reminds us that even Schopenhauer, the most pessimistic of all philosophers, played the flute, just as earlier the author conjectured that Plato kept a copy of Aristophanes' plays under the pillow of his death bed (II.28).

A full and fruitful exposition of Nietzsche's emotivism follows (V.187). The author declares that 'all moralities are only a sign language of the emotions' in so far as they variously intend endorsement, assurance, contentment, catharsis, nemesis or transcendence. In contrast, Kant's categorical imperative is a moral system driven by the desire to forget oneself as a being defined by the will to power. Instead, deontology preaches duty, obedience and suppression. Kant's moral system, like all others, contradicts nature and reality. The unnaturalness of this view of the world is illustrated through a series of oxymorons (apparent contradictions) such as arbitrary laws, spiritual discipline and limited horizons. Previous theories, from stoicism in the pre-Christian era to Comte's sociology (he refers to Comte's home town of 'Port-Royal') and from the seventeenth-century Protestant work ethic to utilitarianism, are constrained by the same grammar of foolishness and error. Such an error is expressed through arbitrary laws that are mistaken for moral certainties and which constitute the antithesis of freedom and inspiration. Indeed the desire to let go (*laisser aller*) is forsaken for other ends found in religion, reason or art. Any of these attempts at spiritual education amount to nothing short of slavery and a protraction of the individual's will.

According to Nietzschean emotivism, guidelines are nothing more or less than a communication of personal likes and dislikes. Strictly speaking, the emotivist theory of ethics, as presented by Stevenson and Ayer in the 1930s, was not a theory about how people should operate but a linguistic analysis of ethical judgements. According to this theory, a moral statement is ultimately an expression of preference. When I say 'X is good' it can be analysed, not in the same terms as a factual utterance but as a statement of individual taste, as though I were saying 'Hurray for X' or 'X!!!' Nietzsche, however, is not writing primarily about the meaning of ethical judgements but about the aims people have in forwarding them. Nietzsche surveys the moral game and, regardless of what individuals are actually saying or meaning to say, alleges that when we assert 'X is good' this is equivalent to stating 'X heightens my sense of power', and when we assert 'X is bad and irrational' this is equivalent to saying 'X hinders my will to power'. Nietzsche's strong emotivism[7] goes further when he identifies certain emotions present in the ethical field and advocates their advantage in spite of their abuse by the herd:

> There are certain strong and dangerous drives, such as enterprisingness, foolhardiness, revengefulness, craft, rapacity, ambition, which hitherto had not only to be honoured from the point of view of their social utility – under different names, naturally,

from those chosen here – but also mightily developed and cultivated. (V.201)

The opposite values of consideration, pity, fairness, mildness and mutual aid are ineffective in one's assertion of the will to power and inappropriately endorsed by the herd. Thus Nietzsche calls for a reappropriation of the pre-Socratic values and the deposition of base, dishonourable herd instincts.

Nietzsche moves on to comment on the sociological manifestations of this as observed in countries with a strong Protestant work ethic like England and Germany. Yet even the leisure enjoyed in southern Europe is interrupted by 'intercalated' fast days to constrain and subdue the spirit. Further evidence exists in the Christian church's 'sublimation of sexual desire into love'. Platonic ethics, as espoused in dialogues such as the *Gorgias*, are cited as another contributing factor. Plato argues that once the elite develop knowledge of 'the Good' then they are qualified to judge what particular things are good or bad. The moral truth found beyond the mouth of the cave is that 'goodness is good'. For Nietzsche there are no absolute categories of righteousness and wrongdoing.

Task

Nietzsche lectured on Plato when he was a professional philosopher and was influenced by some of Socrates' adversaries. Read *Gorgias* 483 and the speeches of Thrasymachus and Glaucon in Books I and II of *The Republic*, recording any similarities and differences you notice between the line advanced in these passages and Nietzsche's philosophy.

Nietzsche alludes to the faith-versus-reason debate in theology, implying that the same tension exists in the field of ethics, the only difference being that the topic of contention is the good rather than God. Three responses are identified (V.191) across the instinct–reason spectrum: the Platonic emphasises the reign of reason over instinct; the more subtle Socratic sees a place for both reason and instinct; while the Nietzschean prioritises the instinctive. Socrates is described as an ironic deceiver who plays with reason while separately knowing its weakness. The Socratic method itself corresponds well to a Nietzschean analysis in being a public way to assert one's will to power while never acknowledging that there is a fixed point of truth and that most positions are mistaken. Various illustrations of the will to deception follow: our inaccurate appreciation of foreign music or language, our haphazard skim reading of a novel, the approximation involved in any instance of perception. The psychological insight of constructing what is not present is likened to the interpretation of a particular work of art by a creative faculty separate from the senses. Nietzsche proceeds to talk of such a faculty as existing in interplay between light and darkness in the same way that dreams and waking experiences interweave. One can detect a Nietzschean influence on Freud (V.192–194). The darker realm of instinct acts as a theatre for aspirations, dreams and happiness. The author uses the familiar image of flight and ascension to illustrate the natural tendency of the free spirit or superman, as opposed to the fixed and earthly preoccupations of the herd.

The next section (V.194) starts on a relativistic note, talking about a table of virtues. The table is concerned with the theme of possession and consists first in a description of three moral agents: the man who wants to possess a woman's body for sexual gratification, the man who wants to possess a woman's mind for the sake of manipulation, and the man who wants to possess a woman's 'soul' for the pleasure of unravelling her inner secrets. The second moral agent seeks to create a need in her for a man and, in fulfilling the identity of 'a man', the lover is satisfied though he can remain behind a mask as a phantom identity. The third character, the most power-crazed of all, desires the possession of his partner to the greatest extent and in such a way as may be identified with the Christian ideals of love and marriage. The desire for the possession of power is also prevalent on a societal scale, expressed in Nietzsche's Machiavellian epigram: 'it is a mask of him which rules the hearts of the people'. The human craving for power is evident too in familial relationships as in the case of parents wanting to possess their offspring. The example of fathers having the power of life and death over their children is used from ancient Rome to illustrate this *a fortiori*.

Three shorter sections follow (V.195–197). The first is an analysis of the Jewish faith, though it seems Christianised in certain respects. The author accuses Judaism of inverting the values of life-denial and life-affirmation, of demoting that which is rich, atheistic, violent, immoral or sensual to the pejorative category of evil, so even the description 'worldly' holds a resonance of disapproval. In addition, the holy poor or *anawim* – that is, the herd or mob – are unjustifiably exalted. Nietzsche advocates anything committed out of an aesthetic desire for power, whether this is termed in the moral period 'good' or 'bad'. The author's emotivism leads him to judge that moral psychologists are better qualified to comment on the night sky of human subliminal desires than the moral philosopher.

The image of man as beast of prey (V.197) is reminiscent of a metaphor used in *On the Genealogy of Morals* and continues a motif of 'man as animal' that runs through the work. Nietzsche is keen to stress health and vitality as expressed through nature and condemns any attempt at reading in to such natural processes the themes of suffering or moral degeneration. The rhythm of nature is the law of the jungle and pulsates with an intense, tropical heat that contrasts with the tepid temperature of the moral period. Yet the author seems to contradict himself in asserting:

1 Nature is free of all values.

2 Therefore, we cannot condemn nature for being morally degenerate.

3 But what is natural is health-inducing and life-affirming and ought to be pursued.

Nietzsche believes that all normative ethical theories possess a common ground, which resides in the desire to suppress natural passions and inclinations. They deceptively smell enticing but are flavoured with little more than a grain of salt, and are hence as valueless as they are flavourless. This has been the case from the time of the stoics to the ethics of Spinoza in the seventeenth century, but a new age of the extra-moral is being inaugurated through Nietzsche's work. The author criticises Aristotelian virtue theory as advocating a 'harmless mean'.

The antithesis of life-affirming values is the slavish, timid morality of the herd and it is to this form of psychological pathology that the rest of Part V is dedicated. Given our nature, its most fruitful expression is to command rather than be subservient. The herd mentality is dangerously undiscerning about what authority to obey and is contrary to evolution. It even infests those in power, who amount to nothing more than 'bell-wethers' (castrated male sheep with a bell around their necks that are used by the shepherd to lead his flock). True leaders are empowered, solitary individuals (V.203). Yet isn't Nietzsche's value judgement that the individual instinct is better than the herd instinct an equally arbitrary one?

One way that the values of the herd may be promulgated is in a mixing of the races. This causes a *psychomachia*, an internal battle of the emotions, 'contrary drives and values which struggle with one another and rarely leave one another in peace' (V.200). The author of *Beyond Good and Evil* appears to commit two fallacies. In criticising people of mixed race, such as St Augustine, who was brought up in North Africa of European descent, he commits the *ad hominem* fallacy (this occurs when one criticises the arguer rather than the argument). In his conviction that things are their origins, he commits the genetic fallacy. Yet the author is concerned only with supplying acute insights and not with the labour of logic and one is left wondering whether what he says bears a ring of psychological truth. A seeming contradiction exists in the author's works as, on the one hand, he argues against jingoistic and nationalistic fervour yet he speaks out against mixing racial identity (V.200). The tension can be reconciled in the belief that both may contain an expression of insecurity and as such constitute manifestations of herd mentality.

The opening sentence of Part V, Section 201, is laced with irony as Nietzsche criticises Christian morality for being in effect 'immoral' in its promulgation of herd values that ultimately put the human race on a devolutionary course. He declares that this is far

from the claim of neighbourly love cited in the Christian code of conduct. Nietzsche argues that even if genuine pity were exercised those of us who live in the extra-moral period realise that it is only the product of our emotions. The author draws a link between the pre-moral period and the extra-moral period, admiring many features of the former and hoping that they will be manifest in the latter. Any act of pity, he argues, was viewed neutrally in ancient Rome and if advised was done so scornfully and pragmatically. One may imagine an emperor sparing the life of a gladiator in order to reward bravery, appease the crowd or ensure further combat another day. Those values, termed 'strong and dangerous drives', that exist in antithesis to pity, are perceived as contrary to social utility by the herd and hence have nowhere to go other than to be subverted. This extract ends with a comment on the nature of punishment in a herd-led state in which everything is a reaction from fear. The author comments that those living under this misapprehension are even afraid to punish criminals and instead live under the contradiction that is a 'timid imperative'.

The new ethical enlightenment termed the extra-moral period supplies a meta-ethical answer to the question 'What is good and evil?' through informing us that each consists in emotions and the will to power. Thus Socrates' dilemmas are answered and we are able to taste for ourselves the forbidden fruit of Eden. This truth leads the free spirit to a higher realm of consciousness but is defiled by the herd instinct and its misguided, monolithic claim to be the sole source of morality through its various incarnations: Christianity, Buddhism, anarchism, democracy, Marxism or socialism – indeed, any collective ideology that entails some notion of equality. In contrast, the master morality advocates a return to the natural state of inequality, suffering and survival of the fittest. The task of the new philosophy, that has Nietzsche as its prophet and herald, is to reverse this trend of 'antithetical evaluations and to revalue and reverse 'eternal values' (V.203). The new leader will challenge the herd instinct, dominant in Europe through utilitarianism and

Christianity, so as to dwarf this trend. The new leaders will have hearts of brass, will keep to the new path, shattering the false idolatry of the herd and in so doing bring humanity to fruition.

Nietzsche on his fellow philosophers

Nietzsche lampoons those philosophers who give a rational basis to morality, accusing them of failing to look at the real phenomena of morality – that is, how morality actually works. To attempt to represent one's morality as rational is simply to be in the business of pushing its claims in a bogus way. To the author of *Beyond Good and Evil* all moral systems are arbitrary limitations of free choice. Nietzsche criticises previous philosophers who have failed to realise this and instead have ended up defending a conventional morality and have helped to perpetuate decadence as agents of the herd. Let us look at each school chronologically.

The Greeks: immorality and intellectual error

According to Nietzsche, Socrates has the instincts of a herd animal but also a high degree of cunning. He is perceived as someone who ironically is capable of spinning a yarn, knowing it to be false. Without very much evidence, Nietzsche considers Socrates to be 'disingenuous' enough not to believe in what he says when he argues that immoral behaviour stems from ignorance of the good (V.190–191). Plato, according to Nietzsche, was more innocent and 'without the craftiness of the plebeian', and wanted to prove that reason and instinct move towards one goal, towards the good.

The Germans: the rationality of moral choice

Kant is subjected to special vilification. Nietzsche's perception of Kant is of someone who is professorial but typically Teutonic and stupid, not realising that his views on the moral law are simply a subconscious desire to bind his fellow men to his beliefs. Most moralists, according to Nietzsche, have these hidden agendas in mind – even if they are actually hidden from themselves (V.187).

Schopenhauer, who finds the principle of morals to be 'harm no one and do right when you can', is similarly faulted. Nietzsche is disappointed with him. Such a principle is one that a weakling would adopt. In a world dominated by the will to power there is no reason why that principle should recommend itself to the *Übermensch*. It seems another ploy by the herd, disguised as a universally acceptable moral principle.

The British utilitarians: uncouth pleasure-seekers

Nietzsche is especially scornful of Mill and his cohorts owing to their outdated adherence to class structure and a quasi-religious moral code. They recognise that the basis of morality is not divine law and divorce morality from religion but then completely sell out to herd morality by suggesting that the basis of morality is the greatest happiness of the greatest number. This is what the herd would recommend: 'always look after the majority'. The very success of the utilitarians in getting this message across infuriates Nietzsche. They seem to be trying to get Christian ethics in through the back door. They are dullards who haven't worked out the consequences of abandoning the religious underpinning of morality. Whereas Mill was an agnostic, Nietzsche was an out-and-out atheist. Nietzsche's disapproval of utilitarianism stems from a belief that they act as a kind of secular restraint on the development of the revaluation of values.

The rest of Part V develops the history of morality as outlined in Part II with particular reference to the moral period and how it must lead to the extra-moral period. It has already been established (II.55) that the moral epoch is concerned with natures but has misdiagnosed the true nature of mankind. In Part V, Nietzsche hopes that the Socratic trend to prioritise reason over instinct will be reversed and in place advocates a strong emotivism.

Review question

Outline and explain Nietzsche's criticisms of any two other philosophers.

We scholars (Part VI)

This part, the title of which perhaps reads more accurately as 'We learned ones', is Nietzsche's equivalent of Part VII of Plato's *Republic*. For Nietzsche, true philosophers are independent individuals who despise pettiness, possess the ability to command and make decisions that are not governed by over-specialised knowledge or an over-developed sense of conscience. They understand the nature of virtue, and are war-like and masculine. The term 'men of knowledge' is used ironically as the knowledge possessed is that knowledge is a smokescreen for power.

The stronger species of scepticism referred to in Part VI is not the epistemological doubt of Descartes but a brave, new and bold form of moral doubt, 'the scepticism of audacious manliness'. It is embodied by the eighteenth-century German monarch Frederick the Great. In a similar way to epistemic scepticism, this ethical brand is self-possessing and liberating. It undermines past presumptions in order to reconstruct and reap the reward:

> Whether as intrepidity of eye, as bravery and sternness of dissecting hand, or as tenacious will for perilous voyages of discovery, for North Pole expeditions of the spirit beneath desolate and dangerous skies. (VI.209)

The new philosophers are sceptics in so far as they doubt moral certainty and, more positively, critics in so far as they possess certain traits that critics bear:

> I mean certainty in standards of value, conscious employment of a unity of method, instructed courage, independence and ability to justify oneself; indeed they confess to taking a pleasure in negating and dissecting and to a certain self-possessed cruelty which knows how to wield the knife with certainty and deftness even when the heart bleeds. (VI.210)

The new philosophers value what is life-affirming, employ the methodology of the will to power and are justified by the natural order of things. Nietzsche develops a unique form of poetic empiricism in reading conclusions from the rhythm of nature and human psychology. He also advocates that we are to experiment in our moral lives. Philosophers are the real men of science (VI.211). The fact that no limitations are set, indeed cannot be set in a world located beyond good and evil, has spurred attacks against Nietzsche as a corrupting influence, yet this is often due to misreading. The above paragraph, for instance, refers not to the gratuitous knife-wielding of a psychopath but the surgical precision and detachment of a professional physician who executes his work for the good of humanity.

If Nietzsche is misinterpreted with reference to knife-wielding, he is also misconstrued in his advocating that we should philosophise with a hammer (VI.211). Undoubtedly he wishes to knock down certain moral prejudices, but the hammer referred to is a musical hammer that acts more like a tuning fork and carries an aesthetic connotation. Philosophy, as Nietzsche defines it, is a creative process of re-evaluation and hence is necessarily concerned with the future, as is reflected in the book's subtitle: *Prelude to a Philosophy of the Future.* Philosophers are concerned with new horizons and how the human ideal of enlargement, greatness and spaciousness can be achieved. Note that the untrodden path of the future leads not to enlightenment of the human condition but to its enlargement: 'He shall be the greatest who can be the most solitary, the most concealed, the most divergent, the man beyond good and evil' (VI.212). The opposite individual is one who possesses the sensibilities of the herd, who inevitably is 'timely' in the sense of being tied to mundane concerns of the present and who lacks vision and drive. Socrates is cited as a paragon of one who possesses the herd instincts of pleasure-seeking and a sense of equality. He is called a 'plebeian' for this reason and likened to a physician who injures himself.

The last section of Part VI argues that Nietzschean 'philosopher-rulers' are born and not made. Unlike instructed scholars, the new breed of philosopher possesses a natural unselfconsciousness in thought and aptitude. Nietzsche contrasts this with his contemporaneous philosophers who trudge through their work in a pedestrian manner and whose coarse feet should never be allowed on such hallowed carpet.

Task

The term 'postmodernism' is used to describe a twentieth-century philosophical movement. Find out what the main beliefs of postmodernists are and how Nietzsche might be counted as an influence.

What is noble? (Part IX)

All of Nietzsche's main philosophical themes are referred to in Part IX of *Beyond Good and Evil*, yet the piece is shot through with a heartfelt melancholia and pathos as if the author in his perfectionism wished the natural order of things to be somehow different, though he is resolute in facing his convictions about reality unflinchingly. He points to human successes such as the story of the elevation of aristocracies at the expense of the herd:

> Let us admit to ourselves unflinchingly how every higher culture on earth has hitherto begun. Men of a still natural nature, barbarians in every fearful sense of the word, men of prey still in possession of an unbroken strength of will and lust for power, threw themselves upon weaker, more civilised, more peaceful, perhaps cattle-raising races, or upon old mellow cultures, the last vital forces in which were even then flickering out in a glittering firework display of spirit and corruption. (IX.257)

One is free to criticise the author's historical analysis but underpinning and colouring such judgement is a moral philosophy that seems far from meta-ethical. Nietzsche appears to read off values from nature and advocate the psychological superiority of dominance and masculinity over 'humanitarian illusions'. The oppressor is thus more of a complete human being in his capacity as 'a more complete beast' than the oppressed. And any ordering of people into rank, caste or class is inevitable. In the same way that emotivists believe that moral propositions can be translated into statements concerned with emotions, so Nietzsche holds that expressions of emotions can be translated into statements of power or 'life'. When such instincts of power or life are denied, it is said that they have been corrupted. The author uses the example of advocating liberty, equality and fraternity in the French Revolution. Instead

society should rightly be construed as a means or 'scaffolding' upon which the *Übermensch* can be raised (IX.258).

Given that 'life is will to power' is the only fundamental principle or primordial fact, then any contrary philosophy is not only misguided but dangerous to humanity. Nietzsche gives an indication (IX.259) as to why his kind of ideal society would degenerate into a constant battle of *Übermenschen* by stating that an equilibrium is maintained between those of similar strengths, and it is only the herd tendency to elevate this notion of equilibrium to the status of a fundamental principle that is corrupting. It is natural for injury to take place between those of different and, therefore, competing statuses, and any denial of this fact results in a neurotic obsession with cleanliness (IX.271) and the desire to establish a sanitised state with 'no organic functions'.

In the closing section of *Beyond Good and Evil*, a contrast is drawn between the advantageous master morality and the inferior, futile slave morality. The superman's suppression of the herd can only lead to progress:

> Exploration does not pertain to a corrupt or imperfect or primitive society: it pertains to the *essence* of the living thing as a fundamental organic function, it is a consequence of the intrinsic will to power which is precisely the will of life. (IX.259)

The above quotation is typically Nietzschean in that it draws on essentialism and naturalism in order to justify the exploitation of the weak-willed by the psychologically strong and brass-hearted *Übermenschen*. In many places, perhaps as a result of his countryside ramblings, Nietzsche points to the rhythm of nature as warrant for his philosophy of will to power. The bird-of-prey analogy in *On the Genealogy of Morals* (I.13) is an example of this motif and raises questions as to the social implications of such a theory. Where does Nietzsche's philosophy lead? In painting a portrait of the superman, Nietzsche appears to be giving us an unfair choice: either we are to choose the path of the knightly aristocrat who acts and grows spontaneously, is powerful and domineering, a man of good taste and in the mould of a

Homeric hero or Greek god; or we are to choose leaders who are compassionate. This is a false choice if we can envisage leaders who embody both sets of characteristics. The philosopher has not proved how the two sets of traits are necessarily in conflict and mutually exclusive. It would, however, be a daring philosopher who would argue that Christian values and Nietzschean values could be combined.

The next section (IX.260) is concerned with the distinction between slave and master moralities, with the latter being praised as noble. Nietzsche's ethic of power and plenitude is exemplified by the hard-hearted Viking spirit and juxtaposed against the herd-hearted morality of pity. Nietzsche goes on to outline the central tenets of each:

The morality of the rulers includes:

- resemblance and respect for ones ancestors (atavism);
- healthy scepticism of modernity;
- equality amongst the *Übermenschen*;
- the lowly status of non-*Übermenschen*;
- the natural requirement for opponent and adversary.

The morality of the slaves includes:

- mistrust of the human condition;
- an advocation of 'useful qualities' to endure the human condition (for example, kindness, patience, humility).

In a linguistic argument developed in *On the Genealogy of Morals*, the author goes on to explain the origins of the terms 'good' and 'evil' in respect of the herd's fear of master amorality. Indeed readers might at this stage be harbouring a secret admiration for the herd, who seem exceedingly adept at holding dominion over the so-called 'supermen'. Perhaps Nietzsche's depiction of their feminine and dishonest manipulation is just sour grapes. The virtue of honesty, favoured normatively by Nietzsche together with the characteristics of freedom, strength and masculinity, is contrasted with vanity (IX.261) as an irrational belief that occurs when someone has an inaccurately over-inflated conception of themselves. It is caused by the mixing of master and slave blood.

Nietzsche's tripartite definition of moral history into pre-moral, moral and extra-moral periods is implicit in IX.262. The author praises the pre-moral for providing favourable conditions for a society to struggle and thus gain strength from enduring such severe conditions. Once this tension has relaxed in the moral period, corruption ensues and it is during this period that the contrast between the Aristotelian virtues of mediocrity and the Nietzschean virtues of 'growth and up-stirring' is at its clearest. In turn, the extra-moral period sees the individual come of age as artist, law-giver and ultimate survivor. This elite has a reverence for power, an instinct for rank and a disregard for what the herd deems worthy of respect (IX.263). Their caste of mind is viewed as an ancestral memory and psychological remnant, which exists in spite of attempts at education or refinement. The *Übermenschen* are so in tune with this primal law or natural justice that it is a form of injustice for the herd not to surrender to these elite souls who move about each other like celestial bodies (IX.265). As members of a tribe or lovers have a specialised and intimate way of communicating, so *Übermenschen* and *Menschen* communicate their experiences through languages defined respectively as noble and common (IX.268). Nietzsche believes, however, that language bewitches us into thinking that there are discoverable moral truths whereas in fact the reality is only will to power.

Review question

Briefly describe Nietzsche's description of the new philosopher.

Revision questions

1 Describe Nietzsche's distinction between the pre-moral, moral and extra-moral periods.

2 Evaluate the claim that Nietzsche's account of religious belief is unphilosophical.

3 Evaluate Nietzsche's grounds for believing in the *Übermensch*.

4 Can it be said that Nietzsche develops a new ethic? If so, to what extent is it liberating?

5 Outline and explain the significance of *one* of the following terms in relation to Nietzsche's thought: nihilism, atheism, militarism, existentialism, emotivism.

Discussion questions

- Can you think of a situation in which the participants are not asserting their will to power?
- Would it be right for Nietzsche to criticise people for expressing their will to power in a particular way?
- Nietzsche says that prostitution is more honest than marriage. What does he mean by this remark? Is he right?
- Why does Nietzsche say one should be ashamed of one's morality? How does he view morality and why, in his view, should there be anything to be ashamed of?
- What is the distinction between a simple act and an act that aims at the will to power? If we had an act before us, how would we know which category to put it in?

Glossary of key terms

Apollonian: an adjective used by Nietzsche to describe the fundamental impulse and desire to create order out of chaos. Named after the Greek god of illumination and truth. Nietzsche saw pre-Socratic Greece as a culture caught between two poles, the Dionysian and the Apollonian. He advises a return to Dionysianism as a remedy for the malaise of modernity.

Decadence: any corrupting force, prevalent in the moral age, that suppresses 'the superior' in their quest for power.

Dionysian: an adjective used by Nietzsche to describe the desire to achieve a heightened feeling of power; named after the Greek god of chaos, fruitfulness, ecstasy and inebriation.

Eternal return: the view that, given an infinite amount of time and a finite amount of matter in the universe, this matter repeats itself eternally in a sort of cosmological recycling scheme.

Herd: the majority of people, who are weak-willed individuals incapable of greatness yet who stifle the strong.

Übermensch: sometimes translated as 'superman' or 'overman'. The superior individuals of any race, who are able to create their own values and fashion their own lives.

Will to power: the process, as observed in the natural world, of asserting oneself over someone or something.

Zarathustra: an alternative name for the Persian prophet Zoroaster, seen by Nietzsche as the first person to cast life in terms of a struggle between good and evil, light and dark, and therefore the appropriate person to transcend such a misleading ethical dualism. Zarathustra is used as a rhetorical mouthpiece to advance prophecies and aphorisms in Nietzsche's magnum opus *Thus Spoke Zarathustra*, published in full in 1892.

Suggested reading

- Ansell-Pearson, K. (1994) *An Introduction to Nietzsche as Political Thinker*, Cambridge, CUP
  An eloquent exposition of Nietzsche's thought in relation to political philosophy
- Danto, A. (1965) *Nietzsche as Philosopher*, London, Macmillan
  Chapter 3 explores Nietzsche's views on language and truth
- Hayman, R. (1995) *Nietzsche: A Critical Life*, London, Weidenfeld & Nicolson
  Biography interspersed with philosophical arguments
- Nietzsche, F. (1977) trans. & ed. Hollingdale, R. J. *A Nietzsche Reader*, Oxford, OUP
  Extracts from Nietzsche's complete works from *The Birth of Tragedy* to *Ecce Homo*
- Tanner, M. (1996) *Nietzsche*, Oxford, OUP
  Introduction to Nietzsche's philosophy from a devotee

Notes

[1] Consider also *Genealogy of Morals* II.6: 'To witness suffering'.

[2] Kant is referred to as a Chinaman for this reason in VI.210.

[3] *Genealogy of Morals* III.7, despite Christianity also seeming to advocate detachment (Matthew 10, Verses 37–39).

[4] *Genealogy of Morals* III.22 and *Beyond Good and Evil* 52.

[5] *Twilight of the Idols*, 'Expeditions of an Untimely Man', Section 5, p. 69.

[6] *Genealogy of Morals* II.16. Cf. Glaucon's arguments in Book II of Plato's *Republic*.

[7] *Genealogy of Morals* III.19.

12 A commentary on Marx and Engels' *The German Ideology*

Philosophers have only interpreted the world in different ways; the point, however, is to change it. (Karl Marx)

Aims

On completion of this chapter you should be able to:

- give an account of Marx's criticism of the Young Hegelians
- explain the key notions of historical materialism
- explain the concept of praxis
- evaluate Marx and Engels' account of the division of labour and its historical development
- explain and evaluate the concept of alienation
- explain the concept of ideology and the Marxian alternative
- evaluate the notion of class conflict
- evaluate the notions of revolution and the establishment of a communist society
- explain Marx and Engels' anti-essentialism
- evaluate the implicit communist ethic of emancipation
- evaluate the claim of Marxism to have scientific status.

The German Ideology should really have been entitled 'Against German Ideology' as, in the course of its pages, its co-authors Karl Marx and Friedrich Engels embark on a systematic reappraisal of the 'ideological philosophy' advanced by Georg Friedrich Hegel (1770–1831), which was widespread in various forms in universities at the time. It was their purpose to debunk the fashionable followers of Hegel and to correct and complete Hegel's work by giving it a 'turn' towards materialism. An ideological philosophy is one which bases its values on any theological, cultural or moral set of beliefs. The authors' materialist criticism of **ideology** continues from the Preface into the first section of Part I. Marx and Engels are keen to redirect philosophy away from the metaphysics of Hegel and his followers towards the study of empirical reality on a social level. The work was not published in the authors'

lifetimes but nevertheless contains the most significant of Marx's themes. These abridged extracts provide a lucid introduction to Marxian thought as it was being developed.

As a point of reference, the adjective 'Marxian' is preferred by scholars to describe the actual works of Karl Marx over the word 'Marxist', which is reserved to describe the followers of Marx, who have sometimes used the author's philosophy for their own ends. This led Marx to famously declare, on hearing about another minor Parisian party describing itself as Marxist: 'one thing is for sure and that is that I am not a Marxist'. Let us examine what Marx and Engels really did argue.

Preface

Despite its introductory brevity, the Preface to *The German Ideology* contains a useful defence of materialism. Materialism or physicalism is the view that we are material beings in a material world and bound by material laws. The opposite philosophical position may be termed 'metaphysicalism': this is the contention that there is something beyond the physical, for example important ideas. These important ideas are arranged into a coherent system with identifiable goals and termed 'an ideology'. Marx and Engels (from here on 'Marx' for convenience) seek to liberate humanity from the false conceptions of idealism, essentialism and other metaphysicalist dogmas, instead drawing attention to the empirical and economic reality of daily life. The opening lines of *The German Ideology* refer to the Feuerbachian contention that God is not an independently existent being but nothing more than a self-generated projection, who we in turn come to worship. Marx goes on to argue that all ideology falls into this category, and he seeks to eradicate it. Such a rescue procedure from the imaginary, mythical world of German ideology, and in particular Hegelianism, is akin to a religious absolution, medical cure or pardon from imprisonment. It is a process of complete emancipation (liberation) and not just a political reaction against the middle class. The Young Hegelians (discussed below) face a barrage of mockery in the opening sections of *The German Ideology*, where they are described as 'sheep in wolves' clothing' for the good reason that despite their promise of revolutionary ideas they 'merely imitate in philosophic form the conceptions of the German middle class'. Marx's much-quoted adage that invites philosophers to change the world rather than to interpret it is worth recalling at this point. The authors criticise the Young Hegelians from the outset for putting an analysis of ideas before an analysis of the material conditions of existence, and parody this mistake by likening it to the idealist belief that one dies from the idea of drowning rather than from the reality of water-filled lungs.

Feuerbach: opposition of the materialist and idealist outlook (Part I)

The illusions of German ideology (I.A.I)

The authors' materialist criticism of idealism continues from the Preface into the first section of Part I. The style is similar to that of logical positivism in the twentieth century, with Marx seeking to free political philosophy from Hegelian metaphysics in order to replace such meaningless jargon, not with more of the same as the Young Hegelians were apt to do, but with an empirical study of reality that would make philosophy look a very different discipline. So who was Hegel and who were the Young Hegelians?

The Young Hegelians[1] were a group of philosophers whose influence on Marx is evident from a close reading of *The German Ideology*. They included Ludwig Feuerbach, Max Stirner and Bruno Bauer. Feuerbach's notion of **alienation** in particular made an impression on Marx, though 'The Thesis on Feuerbach' criticises the philosopher's materialism for not allowing sufficient importance to the individual.

Hegel believed that the sum of individual human minds exerted a power over history, which he termed 'the world spirit'. This world spirit could be traced through the course of history and was always advancing towards a state of self-understanding and greater liberty. History could be divided into Greek, Roman and German phases, with each contributing towards the development of humankind. The abstract concept of 'man' is rejected by Marx, who nevertheless appears to retain the notion of human development, and claims that it may be categorised in distinct stages. This is described in the next section of *The German Ideology* (I.A.II).

Hegel's philosophy of history included the following features:

- Human thought, variously called 'consciousness' or 'reason', cannot be separated from its historical context.
- Ideas are always changing.
- Ideas develop through a process of dialectic where any thought (the thesis) has an opposite

(the antithesis), while there exists between the thesis and antithesis a refined compromise (the synthesis). We have already witnessed an example of this procedure in action in the field of epistemology when Kant synthesised the rationalism of Descartes (thesis) with the empiricism of Hume (antithesis).

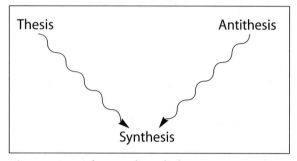

Figure 12.1 *The Hegelian dialectic*

- The world spirit is always advancing and progressing.
- There are no fixed, eternal truths.

Marx sought to subvert Hegel's idealism by arguing that the pattern of history can only be scientifically predicted through an analysis of the material conditions of human beings and not their ideas. Marx flirted with Young Hegelianism during his time at university, but rejected its tenets after this short flirtation. The Young Hegelians refused to attach any importance to the state and believed that one could cure the ills of humanity by inaugurating a change in consciousness. The Old Hegelians, in contrast, believed in the bonds of society and the importance of the state. For Marx, both suffer from the same metaphysical or 'religious' delusions, falling victim to **false consciousness** and failing to ground their beliefs in the empirical reality of human experience. Two graphic metaphors are used to illustrate this point in the opening section of Part I. The first likens Hegelianism to a putrefying or decomposing substance that is replaced with a fresh alternative. The second metaphor likens Hegel to a capitalist businessman who is out to sell his notion of 'absolute spirit', and having failed in this venture is replaced by the Young and Old Hegelians, who attempt to trade with shoddy, cut-price versions that are even worse.

Marx sought to explain why both Young and Old Hegelian concepts of the state were internally self-destructive and proffered an alternative, stable model of his own. Marx's alternative is one in which 'powers alienated by the state are reabsorbed into civil society'. Marx does not think that the state should be abolished.

First premises of materialist method (I.A.II)

Marx believed that history was shaped by an individual's desire for physical welfare. History is seen as a set of economic arrangements through which human beings seek to maximise their physical comfort in providing food, shelter and other material necessities. Such a view is:

- materialist, in that human beings are conceived as physical entities, without a spirit or soul (for Marx, even our consciousness is shaped by material conditions);
- determinist, in that it holds that everything, including human action, is the result of physical causes.

Yet the authors of *The German Ideology* should not be viewed as mechanistically materialistic or deterministic, as they acknowledge the existence of consciousness, but hold it to be materially determined. Marx declares later in this section that 'life is not determined by consciousness, but consciousness by life'. Marx enlarges upon this sentiment when he asserts that 'circumstances make men just as much as men make circumstances' (I.B.I). The title of this section, 'First Premises of Materialist Method', has a rationalist ring to it, and one might be forgiven for expecting deductive argument to proceed from agreed premises. Marx is staunchly empirical, however, emphasising the fact that his analysis is 'empirically verifiable', able to be proved true from observation. The authors favour words like 'active', 'direct', 'definite', 'positive' and 'practical', thus contrasting their down-to-earth realism with the airy-fairy idealism of Hegelian philosophy.

The first premise of Marx's argument is the observation that human beings exist and history is made through their existence. He quickly embarks on a detailed analysis of the physical existence of human beings, concluding that, while it has previously been suggested that human existence is distinct from that of other life-forms due to metaphysical criteria such as the presence of a mind or soul, the real difference lies in the **means of production**. Human beings are unique in that they produce their own means of subsistence, and it is this process that shapes human identity or 'consciousness'. Two key Marxian terms need to be discussed at this stage in the proceedings:

- the means of production – that is, how things are made;
- the **relations of production** (forms of intercourse) – that is, the association between those individuals who are involved in the manufacture of products. These relations are necessary in order to develop the means of production at each historical stage.

> ### Task
> Consider the example of a factory that makes a particular kind of equipment. The means of production would be employed in a dozen or so stages in which the various parts are assembled, fitted and tested. In this example the relations of production would be, on the one hand, the factory owner, whose power may be exercised through managers and supervisors, and, on the other hand, the workforce who work on the production line. Think of your own example to illustrate the means and relations of production from any period of history.

For Marx, the relations of production are determined by the means of production which underly them: as the population grows, new means of production develop all the time. The relations between nations and within nations depend on the level of productive development in each. The division of labour develops as production does. The term 'division of labour' is a technical term in economics and refers to the specialisation of function in a workforce. Consider the example of the famous English furniture maker Thomas Chippendale, who employed a variety of journeymen to cut, chisel, assemble and upholster his famous chairs. The labour is divided into specialist areas rather than

the workers being equally skilled at every task, as the former arrangement is considered more efficient. Three major phases are detected by the authors in early history that illustrate the growth in the division of labour:

1 *Primitive communism:* early tribal culture in which the first communities live off the land. The social structure is familial, yet this patriarchalism eventually turns into a relationship of master and slave.
2 *The slave state:* prevalent in ancient Greece and Rome, a transition is made from a rural to an urban setting and there is a clear demarcation between master and slave.
3 *The feudal state:* the feudal state is exemplified in medieval Europe, where the sole means of production were land and labour and the relations of production were between serf and feudal lord.

As one historical phase followed another, the means and relations of production changed. Thus urban societies may be distinguished from rural ones and industrial from commercial. Each phase of history is determined by the ownership of resources – that is, the materials, instruments and products of labour. One might cite an example from the third phase of the feudal lord who buys the seed for his farm, owns the agricultural implements and sells the harvest, while the serf toils in the fields for free to ensure a productive crop, but is allowed an acre for his own provision. It is through the above phases of history that one class's ownership of private property emerges as dominant. This class, the precursors of which were the masters or feudal lords of history, is termed 'capitalist'. Marx believed that the phase in which he was writing could accurately be called 'the capitalist age'. The tension between the means and relations of production, called a 'dialectical movement' in Hegel's terminology, inevitably leads to **revolution** (a theme taken up later in I.D.IV). Note that Marx is not against private property but against private ownership of the means of production in a capitalist society. Thus he would not object to the serf or labourer owning his own spade, but he would object to anyone owning a vast acreage and not farming it himself, instead hiring other people to do so. I become a capitalist by owning many more spades than I can use.

According to Marx, ideology as expressed through the legal, moral and metaphysical beliefs of a given population develop in relation to the productive forces of that group. He describes its development as being like an echo or a reflex. To think otherwise is to view the world through a *camera obscura* – that is, an instrument that projects images of the material world onto a screen. Marx, by contrast, wishes to view the material objects first-hand and without the metaphysical mediation of Hegel. It is this method that is advised rather than the collection of dry facts or imaginary explanations. Implicit in this Marxian account of history is the view that, if properly undertaken, philosophy itself will dissolve into redundancy.

History: fundamental conditions (I.A.III)

The next section details the four moments in human development. In each case it is production that lies at the heart of things. It is from production that distribution, exchange and consumption follow. The four moments of primary historical relations are as follows:

1 *Subsistence:* human existence pre-determines human needs; we cannot escape these nor can we escape the necessity of fulfilling these material requirements. History is made through their satisfaction.
2 *New needs:* the second moment involves the realisation of how these primary needs (food, drink, shelter, clothing etc.) can be satisfied. Thus one needs the expertise, essential materials and equipment in order to build a shelter.
3 *Families:* the third moment is reproduction. Communists view the family unit, as glorified in Hegel's philosophy, as a stage in history with no inherent value. Patriarchalism for Marx sows the seed of class conflict as a precursor to **capitalism**.
4 *Society:* the fourth moment is the creation of social relations. Any mode of production entails relations of production, which are themselves social forces. Humans become

'conscious' only when these four moments of historical development have been accomplished.

Human consciousness is expressed through language, which is described as 'practical consciousness' in the text, and which is as old as human thought and equally determined by the means and relations of production. Marx reasons that if consciousness is shaped by social background then language must be too. There is no point in using language unless we can effectively express ourselves to other people; this entails an audience to which we address our thoughts and which shapes our mode of expression. Consciousness, it is pointed out, develops in stages like history and progresses from an awareness of one's environment (animal consciousness) to a social awareness or tribal consciousness. Then, as the population grows and the division of labour proceeds, consciousness becomes separated from its material roots, and the first ideologies are born in the form of theology, philosophy and ethics. The division of labour builds an ideological superstructure on the foundations of social relations.

Private property and communism (I.A.IV)

Marx lived during a phase which he called 'the capitalist age' or 'capitalist mode of production'. In this age the means of production were chiefly capital (including money and plant) and the labour of the workforce. The relations of production centred round the bargain struck by capitalist and **proletariat** (the working class). The proletariat had nothing to sell but its labour, and it was in the capitalists' interest to buy such labour for the lowest possible price in the form of the workers' wages. Since modern workers had no land to sell, unlike the serfs of feudal times, they must sell their labour or face dire poverty. Marx eloquently describes the predicament of the industrial workers prostituting themselves in the factories of 'fat cat' capitalists. As the workers cannot possess ownership rights over anything they produce, they feel removed from their work and are described as alienated. The workers have no ownership over anything except their labour power, which is a necessary condition for the capitalist to make profits. Marx, however, alleges that the workers are exploited as they do not get the full value of their labour. He argues that there is a fundamental conflict between the wages sought by the worker and the profits sought by the capitalist. The capitalist class is motivated by profit. It is a fundamental part of capitalist psychology to want members of society to be in need of some commodity, a need that can only be satisfied by capitalists. The capitalist goal is to put other members of society in a position where they find it difficult to satisfy their own needs from their own resources. Thus a capitalist who produces gloves will want the greatest possible need for gloves. Marx believes that this capitalist desire is unfraternal, inhumane and dictated by the system in which capitalists and workers operate.

The themes of private property and alienation are further developed in the section under analysis. Marx's example of the husband as family bread-winner may seem outdated to modern minds, but the conviction that lies behind this example is that property and labour are the same thing and unified in the role of the wage earner. Marx's notion of private property is further developed in I.A.IV. He seeks to illustrate the link between private property and labour by seeing them as two sides of the same coin. The working man, as was traditionally the case in Marx's day, has a specified role in the process of manufacture; Marx termed this 'the division of labour'. The result of this labour, i.e. the end product, involves the workers' wages and the manufactured goods. These become private property and contain within themselves the seeds of class conflict. The fact that the division of labour leads to conflict between self-interest and communal interest means that private property is the source of social conflict and from a Marxian perspective should belong to its immediate producers. Such a conflict is enshrined in the state, which only reflects the interests of the dominant class. The state as it is described in this extract is not the autonomous demi-god of Hegel, but an agent of class conflict and alienation brought about through its guarding the right to private property.

Alienation is created through the division of labour. The manufactured product becomes physically alienated from its manufacturer, while the workers themselves are aliens in the workplace. They feel that they do not belong: 'man's own deed becomes an alien power to him, which enslaves him instead of being controlled by him'. Marx contrasts this divisive state of affairs with the idyllic picture of communist life where one can enjoy earthy leisure pursuits, the essential business of food production and intellectual endeavours all in the same day without being constrained to one activity. For Marx, this communist utopia is a global vision to be realised after the revolution. Marx quotes the British economist Adam Smith (1723–1790), echoing an earlier reference in *The German Ideology* to the relations between nations and the internal structure of nations being determined by the level of productive development. In this passage Marx refers to the forces of production or 'the law of supply and demand' controlling the fortune and misfortune of the global community. Marx's objection to Adam Smith's invisible hand argument (see chapter 5 for a discussion of this concept) is twofold:

- Marx does not think that it happens in real life.
- Marx believes that even if it did it would mark a deficient human system. A worthy society does not rely on some invisible power to provide benefits but on collective, reasoned decision-making by its citizens.

The notion of practical materialism (praxis) is reinforced when Marx argues that freedom can only be achieved through social liberation and not through ideology as the Young Hegelians would have us believe. Yet a communist revolution and the abolition of alienation can only be achieved on two conditions:

- immiseration: when the conditions of the proletariat masses become intolerable;
- when the world-historical developments have brought everyone to the same level – otherwise revolution will only occur on a local basis and be quashed by counter-revolutionary neighbour states.

Briefly describe two ways in which Marx and Engels attack the Young Hegelians.

Alienation

To understand Marx one needs to understand the concept of alienation. Marx reworks what is essentially a Hegelian idea, giving it a specific non-metaphysical usage in his writing. At the start of his *Lectures on Aesthetics* Hegel tells the story of a small child throwing a stone into a lake in order to watch the expanding ripple effect on the water's surface. The child does this to imprint a little of herself onto the world. She is surprised and delighted that the world has been transformed in this small way by her activity and that this particular effect somehow reflects, or is an expression of, herself. Hegel distinguishes three different stages in this act. First, the immediate exercise of the agent's power. Second, the feeling of alienation, otherness or separation from the thing affected. Third, the realisation that power can transform something about the world.

When Marx uses the term 'alienation', he is referring to a social fact rather than a purely psychological state. For Marx there are four defining dimensions to the concept:

- The object of alienation is something other than ourselves.
- This something should be under our control.
- This something, however, is not under our control and may in fact be capable of exercising power over us.
- This relationship makes self-affirmation impossible.

Alienation occurs when something which by its very nature belongs to us is encountered as alien. Capitalism breeds alienation. One example of an alienated social institution might be the police force. The authority vested in the police force is encountered as alien and can be used against any member of the community. Marx believes that such a power should be reappropriated – taken away from the elite body of the police (who would be disbanded) and reclaimed by those who make up civil society. For Marx, our essence as human beings lies in being part of a collective body of individuals who work together for the common benefit. One can be distracted from this goal (by religion) or one can be denied this goal (by a capitalist state).

Alienation in the sphere of economics or labour constitutes the most important form of alienation for Marx. It has four expressions:

- *Alienation of the immediate producer from the product.* This could only be rectified in a capitalist economy if I were paid sufficient to buy everything I made, but then the factory would close.
- *Alienation from the process of production.* The conditions in which I am active are not decided by me but by someone else.
- *Alienation from others.* Fellow workers are seen as potential rivals. Capitalists are similarly alienated by the competitive system they create.
- *Alienation from my Species-Being or Species-Essence.* This phrase is borrowed from Feuerbach but without his metaphysical connotations. For Marx, our Species-Being consists in being part of a free, conscious group engaged in the collective act of developing powers to satisfy our human needs. Capitalism alienates us from our Species-Being by breaking the connection between needs and powers. Our powers become overly specialised in the workplace and are directed away from our real needs.

Civil society and the conception of history (I.B.I)

Marx develops his philosophy of history in the second section of Part I, entitled 'The Illusion of the Epoch'. A simile used throughout this section likens the idealist's conception of history to a spectre or an illusion, a metaphysical ghost in a materialist machine. Instead, society is identified as 'the true source and theatre of all history'. This is due to the fact that society is made up of family units and extended familial relationships, which are determined by productive forces (earlier identified as the means and relations of production) and control the course of history. To argue otherwise is not only to misattribute the purpose of historical events but to misread the nature of history, which in effect is the history of nature and humankind's relation to it.

> **Task**
>
> Marx uses examples from the cotton, sugar and coffee industries to illustrate how world trade produces world history, and shows that history is made in a material way and not through abstract ideas. From your own research give other examples of how production shapes history.

According to Marx, world history develops due to material progress rather than the Hegelian world spirit, but this is not to ignore the role of the individual and the effects of his or her response to material conditions. Marx argues that revolution as the driving force of history is made up of the individual actions of humankind in answer to the social and economic conditions which prevail. But is the Marxian analysis of history correct?

Marx has variously been accused of inconsistency and lack of clarity in *The German Ideology*. In part this is unfair as, although the text is hard work at times, it was never meant for publication and was abandoned still in note form 'to the gnawing criticism of mice'. Indeed, on discovery the manuscript was partly chewed by these rodents. Let me outline some gnawing criticisms of my own:

- One might deny that the lives of human beings are so rigidly determined. Alternatively, one might accept that there is a degree of pre-determination, but disagree with Marx over the influences. Human beings, one might assert, are multi-dimensional, and the Marxian analysis has not given sufficient attention to religious, political or emotional motivation. In fact, historical examples abound to show how we are influenced by ideas over material production: the Crusades show the power of religion; the voyages of Columbus attest to the enterprising spirit and urge to discover; nationalism and racism cause such atrocities as the Holocaust. Indeed, Marxism itself might be cited as the ideological cause of revolutions. This criticism may just be arguing the opposite but it uses the same historical methodology to

reach a very different conclusion, so why should we take Marx's word for it? Marx would reply that ideas are themselves material forces, just one of many that drive human action. An analysis of the accuracy of this view falls in the remit of the philosophy of mind.

- One might protest that the communist ideal is not as attractive an affair as portrayed in the text. There must be something wrong with a theory that promises utopia but gives us radically flawed regimes every time it is tried. The fault might lie in Marx's analysis of human beings or in his assumptions about social organisations.

- Marx and Engels denounce ideology and metaphysics yet seem to offer an ideology of their own. It would be difficult to convince a sceptic that their selection and interpretation of empirical data was not driven by a set of preconceived ideas. Secondly their analysis seems to be imbued with a strong moral conviction. Marx holds that nothing exists beyond the material world. Yet value, by definition, is extra-material. The Marxian canon contains many value judgements and this is an explicit contradiction of the criticisms they make of other thinkers.

- One of the most famous attacks on Marxian thought came from Karl Popper, who termed the communist analysis of history 'historicism' and accused it of not following proper scientific procedure (see p. 128). Marx does not state a clear set of criteria by which his theory of history can be proved true or false. Instead, the accuracy of what he has said is assumed.

Feuerbach: philosophic, and real, liberation (I.B.II)

The next section of the text contains a number of criticisms of the Young Hegelian philosopher Ludwig Feuerbach (1804–1872) and concludes that by Marx's standard he is neither a communist nor a materialist. Marx first claims that Feuerbach is not a revolutionary and, as all communists are by definition members of a revolutionary party, he cannot be classed as a communist. Feuerbach believed that human beings' essence was their existence and that their mode of existence satisfied their essence. The importance of the working class or proletariat for Marxian thought is brought to the fore early on in *The German Ideology*, and this is re-emphasised when Marx criticises this analysis on the grounds that if it is true then it leaves no hope for those who are exploited in the workplace and left impoverished; their essence seems preordained and their lives condemned to material misery. In contrast to Marx, Feuerbach sees liberation as an intellectual freeing from false ideas, whereas for Marx emancipation involves 'real means' such as technological or agricultural improvement. Feuerbach's philosophy is one of ideas rather than action, and may be accused of quietism.

Communists are practical materialists who aim to help people achieve equal access to resources and are contrasted with 'materialists' such as Feuerbach who, when confronted with 'the scrofulous, overworked and consumptive starvelings' of nineteenth-century Europe, retreat into their ideas and are hence no better than idealists. Marx cites the philosophical problem of perception as further evidence that his historical materialism is right. Whereas theories of perception rehearsed in an academic theatre only create technical problems, a materialist outlook enables one to perceive the reality. Examples are provided from the agricultural landscape around Germany where one can see in the typical cherry trees a means of production imported many centuries ago but one that is still determining the lives of the community in which it is planted (similar examples are given from England and Italy).

Ruling class and ruling ideas (I.B.III)

The argument that 'the ideas of the ruling class are in every epoch the ruling ideas' is not original to Marx. Thrasymachus entertains the same notion at the start of Plato's *Republic*. What is of interest here is how the study of ideology and history meet, and the communist conviction that material and intellectual production are dominated by the same class. Marx uses an example from eighteenth-century England: the power struggle between monarchy, aristocracy and democracy, and how this gave birth to the notion that power could be shared in a balanced constitution, an idea that took on the mantle of an 'eternal law' by the time the century came to an end. Marx held that the division of labour leads to the emergence of a class of ideologists who come into conflict with the productive classes (the proletariat); the mode of intercourse between these classes acts as an impediment to progress, and revolution ensues. In the French Revolution of 1789, the **bourgeoisie** revolted against the aristocracy, who were standing in the way of the development of French commerce and industry. Each revolution appeals to a broader class of people, and the cycle of revolution can only be broken when class rule ends under **communism**. The revolution of the proletariat will appeal to the whole of society and overturn social division.

Marx ends this section with another attack on Hegelian idealism, accusing Hegelians of committing three fallacies:

- *the* ad hominem *fallacy*, when they confuse those with empirical power with philosophers who have powerful ideas;
- *the intentional fallacy*, when specific purposes are awarded to historical events with no warrant in order to prove that some great principle is at work;
- *the fallacy of rhetoric*, when some abstraction such as 'self-consciousness' is invented to fill an explanatory gap between material reality and idealist conjecture.

Marx declares bitingly that any shopkeeper worth their salt has a better idea as to his customers' identities than these idealist philosophers with their nonsensical talk of essences.

Review question

Describe the distinction drawn by Marx and Engels between the proletariat and the bourgeoisie.

Division of labour: town and country (I.C.I)

For Marx, the most extreme form of the division of labour is found in the separation between town and country. He embarks on a contrastive analysis of rural and urban economies, and in so doing identifies the origins of the present two-class society, the birth of the superstructure and the domination by one class (the capitalists) of the superstructure. To understand the superstructure fully, we must analyse the origins and reality of the economic substructure. Rural and urban societies are equally divisive and restrictive as far as the relations of production are concerned, but Marx is in no way advocating a rural idyll, believing that class conflict is altogether more noticeable and raw in the urban jungle. The rural proletariat work in an environment that is dominated by nature, while their urban counterparts work in an environment that is artificial and dominated by artefacts. While rural workers are unified by familial and tribal bonds, urban workers are unified by the process of economic exchange. Rural work exists as an exchange between humankind and nature, with the work equally requiring mental and physical skill, and the landowner's dominant relationship is set in a context of the wider community. In contrast, the urban workers' exchange is between fellow humans; there is a sharp distinction drawn between mental and physical work, and the capitalist class dominates by being in possession of money. The antagonism between town and country is itself a form of subjection, which can only be broken down by communism.

The division of town and country leads to the division of commerce and production and the emergence of two classes: merchants and manufacturers. The capitalist society that Marx criticises is a two-class society and, since these two classes are at war, or as the authors prefer 'in conflict', this is in turn reflected in all the other institutions of the superstructure whether the members of society realise it or not. In a capitalist society, the capitalist class will hold the dominant position over the state apparatus (government, judiciary and police), culture (religion, art, the mass media) and the economic and educational systems. In a capitalist society, every organ of the state serves to perpetuate the power and interests of the dominant, capitalist class.

Task

Discuss how the interests of the capitalist class might be served by the police, religion, art, the mass media and the education system. What case would a Marxist make for each?

The inherent weakness in the capitalist system as Marx sees it lies in the numerical strength of the proletariat when united. (Note that Nietzsche employs a similar argument in explanation of the herd's apparent strength.) Another weakness is the power of the capitalists, who in their ruthless pursuit of profit will drive the workers to revolution and in the process force the workers to realise that only in their unity can economic salvation be achieved. This realisation will rid the proletariat of their previous false consciousness imposed by capitalist culture. Without feeling sorry for the 'haves', Marx believes that those with the capital are as much victims of the system as the 'have-nots'.

The workers, having achieved emancipation, will work together for communal goals, producing a highly advanced and technologically developed society, which would enable all to perfect their skills in a community of artists without the need for protective guilds. Equality in the form of collective ownership may, however, require a state powerful enough to enforce it. This intermediate state between revolution and the establishment of a communist society is termed 'the dictatorship of the proletariat' and will eventually wane with the success of the universal or communist class. In a communist society the means of production will be owned by the immediate users. These users will enjoy the protection of the state but there will not be a separate state mechanism that exists apart from the users. The state in a communist society will have its locus of power in the soviet, or collective, of workers.

The rise of manufacturing (I.C.II)

The majority of section C on 'The Real Basis of Ideology' is concerned with how material factors have influenced historical change. Many specific examples are given, which range from the inaccurate account of Henry VIII ordering the death of 72,000 peasants to arbitrary judgements about such things as maritime law developed in the Italian trading port of Amalfi.

The opening story of how the medieval guild system collapsed due to an increase in mechanisation seems further evidence as to how the mode of production changes social relations. As the guild system disappears, workers feel less supported, lose pride in their craftsmanship and become more focused on the wage they are earning from the emerging capitalist clan. Marx also comments on how the world at large develops in this phase of history: the boom in manufacture leads to an increase in importing and exporting, expanding colonisation, protectionist tariffs, trade wars and real wars culminating in England's domination of the high seas and as a consequence trade. We have now entered the capitalist age of banks and stock markets, of big industry and technological development. Profit and scientific advancement destroy ideology, religion and ethics, but this is of no surprise to Marx, who viewed religion as akin to a belief in ghouls and ghosts that was destined to evaporate eventually. Commercial towns and cities dominate the countryside, cash transactions take precedence over crafts, and national identity is subsumed by the roles of workers and factory owners. All relations depend on capital. Welcome to the capitalist age.

The relation of state and law and property (I.C.III)

This section begins with an analysis of the historical development of property. Marx states that the first form of property had to be movable (thus discounting land) and developed through

Karl Marx
(1818–1883)

Karl Marx was the original champagne socialist, in the literal sense of loving life's luxuries while maintaining an unswerving devotion to rescuing the proletariat from their predicament. *The German Ideology* was penned late at night, usually after a game of chess, through a thick fog of cigar smoke and perhaps over a glass of brandy. Marx was born in the town of Trier in Germany's Rhineland, a stone's throw from the Moselle river, near where his middle-class parents owned a small vineyard. From his days as a student, Marx earned the reputation as someone who enjoyed a drink, and he regularly embarked on raucous pub-crawls. He changed his studies from law to philosophy at university before pursuing a career as a journalist and editor of the *Rheinische Zeitung*. It is one of life's ironies that this philosopher, who spent most of his life writing about money, should have spent most of it in dire poverty. His years spent as a political exile in London's Soho were particularly impoverished, and Marx had to be regularly helped out by his close friend and co-author Friedrich Engels. The contrast between the swarthy, rabbinic Marx and the angular, teutonic Engels could not have been more striking. Engels supplied enthusiasm, organisation, cash and important practical knowledge, having impressed Marx with his work *The Condition of the Working Class in England* (1845), which consisted of a social history of the living and working conditions of cotton mill workers in Lancashire. Engels' father jointly owned one such mill in Manchester, and his son eventually ended up working for the family business, socialising with the bourgeoisie while at weekends co-authoring subversive communist tracts with Marx. Both thinkers flirted with *la dolce vita* – indeed Marx was proud to have married into the aristocracy – but both remained committed to the communist cause. One might even argue that such an acquaintance with capitalism was necessary to formulate an accurate criticism.

Significant works
The German Ideology (1846; with Engels)
The Communist Manifesto (1848; with Engels)
Capital (1867)

the middle and feudal ages to the present capitalist climate in which the 'purest' form of property is in the form of capital, which is owned neither by the collective populus nor by the state. Indeed, the state is owned by the capitalist class, who lend it money and resources, Marx describes it as 'nothing more than the form of organisation which the bourgeoisie necessarily adopt, both for internal and external purposes, for the mutual guarantee of their property and interests'. The state is thus a means for the rich to safeguard their ill-gotten gains and to assert their common interests through the laws of the state. The authors of *The German Ideology* do not dwell on the subject of law for very long but their message is clear: the law is not built on any principle of justice in a capitalist society but is an expression of the will of the ruling class.

Review question

Briefly describe Marx and Engels' account of human nature.

Individuals, class and community (I.D.I)

The authors begin this section with a historical account of how the capitalist class or bourgeoisie developed from the urban burgher class of the Middle Ages, who were successful in overthrowing the feudal aristocracy. The feudal system could not support large-scale manufacture, which led to revolutionary change, led by the bourgeoisie, whereby the old social structure was swept aside. The increased material advantage of the bourgeoisie in turn spawned the propertyless proletariat. Marx notes that it is competition, created by the capitalist system, which turns individual against individual and breeds class hatred. In this he is unlike his fellow nineteenth-century thinker Friedrich Nietzsche, who argued in works such as *Thus Spake Zarathustra* that conflict is noble and character-building. Marxism contains an implicit moral judgement that this state of affairs is unjust and that human beings could do better for themselves. There might be points of agreement, however, as Marx advocates revolution and the establishment of a universal class in order to create a genuine community in which individuals are free from class-based indoctrination (the word 'estate' is occasionally

substituted for 'class' in the text). Many passages in Marx's writings advance ideas that rest easily in the company of existentialism (see chapter 16). Freedom is a unifying theme in the extract under discussion, and Marx argues that:

- The abolition of the state and the division of labour followed by the establishment of a communist society will lead to personal liberty.
- Freedom means neither autonomy nor non-interference. Freedom is the ability to exercise power. We exercise power in order to satisfy human needs. Marx distinguishes between an individual's personal life and their role as determined by their class, believing that an end to class will set the individual free and enable them to be themselves. This is a theme later taken up by the French existentialist and Marxist Jean-Paul Sartre (1905–1980).
- Freedom in a capitalist society is illusory, propagated by the myth that one is free to make of life whatever one wants to. In reality, those living in such a situation are more susceptible to the violence of social conditions. The proletarians may be free of feudal ties but they cannot maintain themselves in existence without selling their labour. They enter the labour market naked.

Although it is unfair to class all Marxist regimes as odious, it is true to say that the restrictions on personal liberty appear greater than in western democracies. It is important to note the form of freedom that is being advocated in this part of *The German Ideology*: for Marx the amount of freedom in a society is to be gauged by the range of opportunities available to each of its citizens. Thus, in conditions of freedom, one may be able to develop any talent, become an influential politician, enjoy a cultured life and receive an excellent education. The bourgeois freedom of the West, in contrast, offers freedom from restriction; thus, one can speak freely, go anywhere, vote for anyone and read what one wants. Marxists argue that this is illusory freedom as, unless the individual is very rich, their range of actual opportunities is in fact negligible. Marx criticises the social contract theory of Rousseau (defended in the twentieth century by thinkers such as Rawls) by stating that the idea of sacrificing some freedom for protection in fact amounts to nothing more than banding together to share in the unpredictable storms of fortune.

> **Task**
>
> Research one society in the course of history that has described itself as Marxist. What, in your opinion, were the strengths and weaknesses of this regime? How long did it last, and was it true to the original views of Marx?

Forms of intercourse (I.D.II)

Communism achieves unity among individuals while at the same time preserving each person's individuality and giving them control over their environment. Pre-communist societies encourage people to develop split personalities made up of who they are and what class they belong to. The category 'class' may incorporate a number of factors such as occupation, marital status and social position. Marx and Engels rework the Aristotelian terminology of 'essence', designating the inner nature of the entity, and 'accident', which refers to arbitrary features of a thing. Marx argues that, whereas one's individual persona is essential, one's class persona is as accidental as having, for instance, blue or brown eyes. One's essential persona may be materially determined through the forces of production, but it should not be stultified either by ideology or by an unfair distribution of the means of production.

Marx goes on to discuss the dependence of the relations of production (termed 'forms of intercourse') on the forces of production. Marx asserts that the relations of production evolve as the means of production develop. Sometimes, however, the means of production outstrip the relations of production and a glitch occurs in the process, termed a 'contradiction'. A social system may remain in place while technological advancement moves on. If this is the case, it does not take long for the slowly developing mode of intercourse to impede or become a fetter on the productive forces. Revolution ensues. It may be the case that the means develop faster than the relations of production; the same revolutionary fate awaits this situation, however, as it is only by violent change that the forms of intercourse can be made to meet the new forces of production. Marx calls such revolutions 'collisions' and categorises them as all-embracing collisions, collisions between various classes, 'contradictions of consciousness' or battles of ideas and political conflicts. All revolutions or collisions have as their common denominator the fact that they involve the contradiction of productive forces with the relations of production. This is the true dialectic, first outlined as an idea by Hegel, and applied by Marx to social circumstances.

Conquest (I.D.III)

In this short section the authors examine the argument that 'violence, war, pillage, murder, robbery etc. [have] been the driving force of history'. They explain this by simply stating that violence and war are modes of intercourse or relations of production and that conquest was caused by material factors in the conquerors' home. Marx uses the instance of the fall of the Roman Empire as an example of an event that is explicable purely in terms of the mode of intercourse and its relation to the means of production. An increase in the barbarian population, whose social system was dependent on war, led to its expansion into the Roman Empire, whose social and economic development was weakened by its dependence on slavery. Further to this example of how historical materialism offers the only accurate diagnosis of revolution, the authors supply evidence from the practice of plunder and conquest, arguing that the conquerors tend to adopt the material conditions of the conquered state.

War involves the capture of resources from the enemy. The authors argue that the act of capturing resources, in addition to having an effect on those who lose their property, has important consequences for the plunderers themselves. Thus the marauding hordes, on looting their goods, buy into the social and economic conditions of the state from which they have plundered them. In so doing they submit to the means and relations of production of that captured society. During the ensuing peace the conquerors must continue production and adopt the same means as the conquered. An example of this might be the Norman conquest of Ireland, when the conquerors gradually became 'more Irish than the Irish themselves', adopting their dress, customs and language. The analysis here dramatically ignores any psychological explanations for conquest such as the lust for power from a feeling of inferiority, or greed. If one could defend such a psychological profile then it would present real problems for Marx and Engels.

Contradictions of big industry: revolution (I.D.IV)

The final section of Part I is written with characteristic Marxian passion, and prophesies the path towards revolution. The starting point is the observation that 'big industry', or big business as we might say, swallows up small businesses. This results in a contradiction between the means of production and what is deemed private property. Consider the example of a successful farmer buying the neighbouring, smaller, family farms around his land and developing a factory farm. Whereas in the past he had both owned and worked on his farm, now he owns a vast acreage and employs tenant farmers to milk the cows, grow crops and rear livestock. Marx sees the growth of big business as the first step towards revolution. Revolution will entail first the destabilising and then the reappropriation of private property and the establishment of a communist society. In the period leading up to this revolution, successful businesses will naturally compete with each other and such competition will increase the pressure on these enterprises to gain as much property while paying as little as possible in wages. Alienation of the workers will follow as the means of production become completely divorced from those immediately engaged in the process of manufacture.

Marx writes like an Old Testament prophet foretelling the destruction of the present capitalist age and promising salvation to humankind and a promised land for the workers: 'never, in any earlier period, have the productive forces taken on a form so indifferent to the intercourse of the individuals as individuals'.

Such individuals have little interest in their work or in accumulating wealth. They might as well spend the little they earn from poorly paid factory work on a holiday in the sun and cheap ale. Such social and economic conditions can only, for Marx, hasten revolution and therein lies the rub: he wrote in the nineteenth century and yet we are reading the text now; one would have expected a revolution of some sort to have occurred. Present-day followers of Marx argue that revolution has been avoided because of:

- revisionism, with people misreading Marxian literature;
- nationalism, which distracts followers from their true vocation;
- charismatic leaders, who win the people over to their erroneous ways of thinking;
- interference from capitalist countries, for example the geographical location of Cuba right next to the largest capitalist country in the world has not helped the communist cause.

Following from a point in our earlier discussion on freedom, many Marxists would add that the endemic vices of communist states such as restrictions, militarism and censorship stem from difficulties in implementing Marxism and do not emanate directly from Marx's ideas.

Marx draws our attention to the fact that all previous attempts at revolution failed, as they were partial, due to underdeveloped means of production. The capitalists had not developed enough, and the proletariat, the only class through which revolution can be achieved, had not been sufficiently alienated. The time is at hand, however, when the universal class of workers will believe that they should commit themselves to the revolutionary cause; in this way their 'self-activity' and material life will combine, shots will be fired and, after a brief period of proletarian domination, the universal, communist ideal will be accomplished. The whole of history, for Marx and Engels, points to this fact: that humans through a process of estrangement will develop a mind for revolution and restoration. The authors round off the last section of Part I with a numbered conclusion as follows:

1 'Destructive forces' evolve through the means and relations of production, and a class is created which bears the burden of society (the proletariat). The proletariat develops a communist consciousness by contemplating their situation and ridding themselves of their false consciousness.

2 Revolution ensues directed at the capitalist class and at the state.

3 For this revolution to be successful it needs to remove the division of labour altogether and in so doing destroy all classes.

4 For the establishment of the communist ideal of a universal class to be successful, a wholesale change of consciousness on a mass scale is required.

Revolution can only occur when the working class understand the nature of their material existence and are able to distinguish between their 'actual will' and their 'real will'. One's actual will is what one thinks one wants, and this is manipulated in capitalist societies (consider all the adverts selling expensive luxuries on the television). In contrast, one's real will is what one needs and rationally should desire. In Marx's view, this is revolution. Any proletarian who is unaware of this fact might be described in Marxian terminology as being a victim of false consciousness, in other words distracted by a deceptive day-dream. One can only be awoken from these delusions of grandeur by revolutionary struggle in which one's actual will and real will coincide.

Review questions

1 Briefly describe Marx and Engels' account of human history.

2 Outline and explain the Marxian account of revolution.

Task

Imagine that you are a political leader whipping up support for the Marxist cause. Write an impassioned speech convincing your listeners of the truth of Marx's analysis. Include as many key themes advanced in *The German Ideology* as you can.

Selections from Parts II and III
Kant and liberalism (206)

Let us now look at selections from the rest of the original text that have a bearing on what has been previously discussed. The extract concerned with Kant and liberalism gives examples from the history of Germany as to how economic conditions can lead to the development of harmful ideologies, which can in turn affect economic conditions. Eighteenth-century Germany is portrayed as a divided, stagnant country that was behind the times with regard to industry, trade and agriculture. Marx argues angrily that this nurtured the petty and parochial moral philosophy of Kant, whose emphasis on 'the good will' infected the three hundred or so German states which were formed along the lines of the Holy Roman Empire. An ideology such as Kant's exists in contrast to the ideologies of big businesses, as discussed in the preceding sections, and in contradiction to the interests of this capitalist class. Until the 1840s, Germany remained blinded by ideological illusion, supporting Britain, who wanted to exploit it, and ignoring France, who wanted to develop it.

The language of property (245)

Marx and Engels launch an attack on the Young Hegelian philosopher Max Stirner (1806–1856) and the little-known French poet Destutt de Tracy, who considered the notions of 'property' and 'personality' to be identical because the words share the same root – *eigen* and *Eigentum* in German, *propre* and *propriété* in French. Stirner and de Tracy then assert that private property cannot be abolished as it is identical with one's self. To argue otherwise would be as absurd as to assert that one can stop having something as personal as a stomach ache in a communist society. The authors of *The German Ideology* think that this etymological argument is nonsense and refute it by making clear that something that is unsaleable cannot be classed as property, thus stomach pain or even a shabby coat do not enter the economic sphere as they do not command anyone's labour.

Philosophy and reality (254)

Marx complains that his account of materialism as laid out in works such as the *Critique of Hegel's Philosophy of Right* and *The Jewish Question* has been misunderstood because he was obliged to write in philosophical jargon. This frustrates Marx, as his materialism precisely contrasts philosophy, the study of ideas, with praxis as the analysis of reality and implementation of practical activity. He compares philosophy to masturbation, as both are futile and fantastical unlike praxis or sexual fulfilment, which is productive.

Personal versus general interests (265)

The next extract begins by discussing Stirner's technical question as to whether the contradiction between self-interest and general interest is real or apparent. In the course of the discussion, however, some interesting points are raised over the themes of alienation and communist amorality. Stirner himself is referred to at various intervals throughout *The German Ideology* as 'Saint Max' in a sarcastic jibe at his interest in high-flown ideological concerns, which Marx puts on a par with religious faith. Marx's reply to the original question considers the process of how personal interests become general interests. He describes a process of objectification or reification whereby the individual becomes so preoccupied by their interests that their interests take on a life of their own and are awarded the same status as religious objects of worship. According to Marx and Engels (who despite being an atheist was a little more tolerant of faith than his co-author), such ideological idolatry can be dissolved, as can religious idolatry, by historical materialism. For Marx, self-sacrifice and egoism do not exist in a Hegelian dialectic, but they are both materially determined like everything else. Indeed, self-interest is a necessary form of self-assertion, the motivating force for revolution, which in turn destroys any need for self-sacrifice, as everyone in a communist society is satisfied by receiving what they require. This is provided according to their need and produced according to their ability.

One-sided development (284)

Twenty pages later Marx seems to strike a moral rather than amoral tone, condemning the 'one-sided, crippled' natures produced by living in a capitalist society. Instead he praises the multi-faceted individual who takes part in a variety of activities. This, he adds, is only produced when empirical circumstances allow individuals to develop a world outlook or 'intercourse'.

Will as the basis of right (357)

The authors raise the old philosophical problem as to whether the law is based on the consent of individuals (the will) or the power of the state. They agree with Hobbes that it is the latter, and add that any state and its set of laws are based on the material lives of individuals. Whereas in earlier passages the relations of production have been depicted as stemming from the means of production, in the context of law the connection is portrayed as one of mutual entailment: 'their mode of production and form of intercourse, which mutually determine one another … is the real basis of the state'. The authors restate their earlier conviction that the ruling classes determine the ruling ideas and that at present this is the capitalist class. Only when the productive classes take over after the revolution shall their wills be recognised. This extract ends with the historical observation that inherited laws, as in the case of Roman law and the English judicial system, often appear to originate from a source that is above the material and productive forces of society. Marx assures us that this view is illusory and that any society's acceptance of such laws may be explained in terms of materialism.

Artistic talent (430)

Marx's vision of a communist utopia is one in which art and culture flourish. It is necessary, in order to cultivate this scenario, to understand the economic forces at work in the art world. Artistic talent cannot be divorced from the socio-economic context, whether this is Raphael's Rome, Leonardo's Florence or Titian's Venice. The skills of the artist are determined by:

- the technical advances made in art in that society;

- the organisation of that society;
- the local division of labour;
- the international division of labour and in particular that of countries which are in a relation of production with that of the artist.

No artists can survive on their own talents, immune from the reality of supply and demand. The great works produced by Raphael, Leonardo and Titian are produced *with* inventive talent not *because* of it. Their economic antecedent is the wealth of the Roman Catholic merchants from their respective cities who commissioned the work in the first place. Communist society, of all the alternatives, with its emphasis on equal access to resources, is the one in which art will most successfully thrive. This is because everyone will be encouraged to have a go without the social labels of artists and non-artists.

Utilitarianism (448)

Utilitarianism, or 'the theory of usefulness' as Marx ironically terms it, is a typically bourgeois philosophy. The notion that the greatest happiness of the greatest number is the prime aim of life fits naturally into a capitalist system, which extols the greatest wealth for the greatest number. Utilitarianism is nothing more than a metaphysical expression of bourgeois ideology. The authors continue with their history of ideas, tracing the origins of utilitarianism from the political philosophies of Hobbes and Locke in the seventeenth century, who justified the exploitation of the poor through the omnipotent actions of the state, to the views of the physiocrats Claude Adrien Helvetius (1715–1771) and Paul-Henri Holbach (1723–1789), who wrote on economics in eighteenth-century France. The predominant view in this period was that as long as the wealthy elite was large enough then the principle of utility had been satisfied and it was immaterial to the point of being expected that some citizens would be poor. Such injustice was given a scientific gloss by the nineteenth-century utilitarians William Godwin (1756–1836), Jeremy Bentham (1748–1832) and James Mill (1773–1836) (J. S. Mill's father). Marx says that all utilitarianism does at his present time of

writing is defend the status quo. One might allege that Marx and Engels in the final analysis are utilitarians, despite not admitting it, as they seek in their vision of the universal communist state a happy life for all.

The philosophy of enjoyment (458)

This is a philosophy that has its roots in ancient Greece and which is popular amongst the French, according to the authors, because of their natural *joie de vivre*. This philosophy holds that the purpose of life is to enjoy oneself. Marx condemns such a standpoint as 'never anything but the ingenious language of certain social circles who had the privilege of enjoyment'. According to Marx, the capitalist class, having developed after the decline of feudalism, wanted to justify its own actions and used the doctrine of hedonism for this purpose. Yet when addressing the proletariat, the bourgeoisie preach a form of asceticism and self-denial, and are guilty of hypocrisy. Communism shatters the basis of all metaphysical moral theories, whether puritanical or hedonistic. Marx seems to be invoking an implicit theory of morality without realising it.

Needs and conditions (474)

This extract is a satirical attack on the Young Hegelian Max Stirner. Like all members of this philosophical school, Stirner believed that humans could only achieve liberation through a journey towards self-realisation. Marx, of course, disagreed and believed that any freedom could only be realised if the material forces of production permitted it. In the past the forces of production have restricted satisfaction to only a few; indeed, history might be said to have developed through a framework of contradiction between the satisfied and the frustrated: freemen and slaves, nobles and serfs, the bourgeoisie and the proletariat. The authors mock the distanced, patronising outlook of nineteenth-century philosophers by suggesting that this division is between the human and inhuman. In a reference to the preceding section describing the conditions necessary for revolution, Marx informs us that these productive forces have not quite reached the right level yet, but watch this space. We are still watching.

The free development of individuals (482)

In this section the authors continue to attack Stirner, who is given the nickname Sancho (a reference to the credulous sidekick of the romantic hero Don Quixote in Cervantes' novel of the same name). This is an ironic name, as it is the very romanticism of idealism that is in fact the cause of the fetters that keep the proletariat in their chains. The passage is written in the style of a conclusion, and many materialist themes such as liberation, revolution and communism are recapped. Each individual is charged with the responsibility of breaking these chains of oppression, as this is the goal of communism. As we have seen, it is achieved through the abolition of private property and the division of labour.

Language and thought (491)

This short piece launches a further attack on philosophy, which from the days of Plato has divided the world into the realm of thought, which is occupied by ideologists, and the sensuous world, which is the preserve of everyone else. The two realms do not share the same language, and Marx criticises the jargonistic, incomprehensible language of philosophy (faults that he could be said to share himself at times). The division of labour has led to the creation of professional ideologists in the form of philosophers and has led to the creation of an ailing German philosophy. For Marx, there is no such division between worlds or between ways of describing them. Thought and language are manifestations of actual life.

'True' socialism (501)

This is an attack on a group of young writers who call themselves 'socialist' but who believe that a purer form of socialism exists in the realm of 'pure thought'. Marx condemns this literary movement for mixing German philosophical notions with French socialism and as being fundamentally an erroneous ideology.

Theses on Feuerbach

Feuerbach's philosophy calls itself materialistic but is, in effect, only a set of ungrounded theories about the material. In order for philosophy to provide answers it needs to be founded in the empirical and provable world of the senses, the sensuous realm and not in some Platonic world of forms (see chapter 7). From this practical vantage point one can observe the social and economic forces at work in the changing course of history. Feuerbach's condemnation of religion becomes a secular ideology and makes all the same mistakes that religion does. Marx enjoys describing the Young Hegelians in religious terms such as 'Saint Max' or in this passage as 'the Holy Family'. Having denied any religious essence, Feuerbach remains in the mire of metaphysics by espousing a human essence in which the human reality is 'the ensemble of social relations'. Marx concludes by saying that Feuerbach's 'contemplative materialism' is a contradiction in terms and, like everything else, is a product of social relations. If one wants to make life better the only way forward is to change these social relations through praxis not philosophy.

Revision questions

1 Outline and explain Marx's notion that the abolition of private ownership is central to the communist revolution.

2 Assess Marx and Engels' view that ideology is illusory.

3 Explain and illustrate what is meant by 'alienation'.

4 Evaluate Marx and Engels' materialist theory of history.

5 Outline and explain what is meant by 'the bourgeoisie'.

Discussion questions

- 'Marxism is a scientific system free from any ethical judgement' (Lenin). How scientific is it? And is it free from moral judgement?
- Is Marx right to advocate the abolition of private ownership?
- Is a classless society ever possible?
- What would life be like in a communist utopia? What do you think might be criticised after dinner?
- 'Circumstances make men, just as men make circumstances.' What does Marx mean by this statement?

Glossary of key terms

Alienation: the process in a capitalist state whereby workers become distanced from the fruits of their labour, from themselves and from each other.

Bourgeoisie: the bourgeoisie own the means of production. They may be referred to as the capitalist class. They are distinct from the proletariat, who have only their labour to sell. The petty bourgeoisie exist between these two opposed classes and comprise small business people as well as intellectual labourers such as teachers, priests, lawyers and clerks.

Capitalism: the system by which production is controlled by capital, or any political philosophy advocating such a system.

Communism: the political standpoint that advocates an equitable distribution of resources, 'from each according to their ability, to each according to their needs'.

False consciousness: any mistaken belief among the proletariat that prevents them from understanding the dynamics of class struggle and its injustice. For example, an instance of false consciousness might occur if members of the proletariat see immigrant workers as their competitors rather than as their co-workers in the struggle against capitalism and the bourgeoisie.

Ideology: a term borrowed from French writers of the eighteenth century which refers to any body of ideas or system of beliefs.

Means of production: the physical manufacture of goods, including what is used, what is produced and the means by which it is delivered.

Proletariat: those individuals who are involved in the manufacture of goods but who do not own what they make.

Relations of production: in order to produce, human beings enter into relations of production. Marx provides examples which include the family, the tribe, and the relations of slave and master, serf and feudal lord, businessman and proletarian. The phrase is interchangeable with 'forms of intercourse' in the text.

Revolution: the overthrowing (possibly violent) of the prevailing system.

Suggested reading

- Cohen, G. (2000) *Karl Marx's Theory of History*, Oxford, OUP
  A detailed analysis of Marx's philosophy of history
- McLellan, D. (1999) *Thought of Karl Marx: An Introduction*, Basingstoke, Macmillan
  Almost anything from this Marxian scholar is suitable; this volume combines commentary and selected extracts
- Miller, R. (1984) *Analyzing Marx*, Princeton, Princeton University Press
  A readable survey of Marx in relation to morality, power and history
- Rius (1998) *Marx for Beginners*, Duxford, Icon Books
  This series provides a useful resource for those beginning philosophy
- Singer, P. (1980) *Marx*, Oxford, OUP
  Readable introduction that covers themes such as class conflict and alienation

Note

[1] For more on the Young Hegelians refer to pp. 25–26 of C. J. Arthur's introduction in D. McLellan (1993) *The Young Hegelians and Karl Marx*, Aldershot, Gregg Revivals.

13 A commentary on Mill's *On Liberty*

Ask yourself whether you are happy and you cease to be so.
(John Stuart Mill)

Aims

On completion of this chapter you should be able to:

- provide a critical account of Mill's view of liberty
- describe Mill's defence of democracy
- explain what is meant by the tyranny of the majority
- give a critical account of the harm principle
- survey the arguments cited in favour of freedom of thought, expression and action
- describe the arguments in support of variety and individualism
- explain how freedom is reconciled with the power of the state
- evaluate the intrinsic and instrumental value of freedom
- evaluate the wider application of Mill's principles.

Mill wrote a copious amount of philosophy although he is known primarily for his defence of **utilitarianism** in the field of moral philosophy and his exploration of **negative freedom** in his seminal work on political philosophy, entitled *On Liberty*. This might best be described as a work of practical ethics or applied utilitarianism. Both the notions of utilitarianism and liberty can be expressed as neat philosophical principles which constitute the foundations of Millian thought. They run as follows:

- *The principle of utility* – 'An act is to be classed as morally right if, and only if, it leads to the greatest happiness of the greatest number';
- *The principle of liberty* – 'Human beings, individually or collectively, should never interfere with another person's freedom unless it is for self-protection or to prevent harm to others'.

Let us examine the principle of liberty in context, beginning with its first formulation in the opening chapter.

Introductory (Chapter 1)
'Utility in the largest sense'

Mill lays his cards on the table in the opening paragraph and informs his readership that he is embarking on an exploration of political freedom and not an examination of the free will debate more suited to the philosophy of mind. After a whirlwind tour of many of the concepts dealt with in the work (including **democracy**, power, the **tyranny of the majority**, custom and religion), Mill seems to start again halfway through the first chapter when he introduces the principle of liberty.[1] This principle has the status of an axiom or acceptable starting-point for an argument. According to Mill, it is derived from the right to self-protection, which is often taken as an agreed moral principle. Mill's project in *On Liberty* seems rather like the attempt by Jeremy Bentham (1748–1832) to develop a morality from one single principle, although in Mill's case the principle of liberty is also to be linked to the principle of utility. The relationship between liberty and happiness may, at first glance, seem asymmetrical but Mill praises freedom for enabling social progress which contributes to an increase in happiness (59). Mill is a moral realist (see chapter 2) and believes that one can attain moral truths such as 'happiness is the universal goal' or 'torture is wrong as it involves suffering'. From this realist standpoint Mill seeks to address important questions in the political sphere such as 'How much freedom should the citizens in an ideal state be allowed?'

The tyranny of the majority

The author goes on to criticise the tyranny of the majority stating:

> The will of the people, moreover, practically means the will of the most numerous or the most active *part* of the people – the majority, or those who succeed in making themselves accepted as the majority; the people, consequently, *may* desire to oppress a part of their number, and precautions are as much needed against this as against any other abuse of power. (62)

Mill condemns any such 'vulgar and enslaving' bullying by the majority as a misrepresentation of the utilitarian formula, which sets to achieve the greatest happiness of the *greatest* number of citizens and not the greater happiness of the *greater* number. One can imagine a primitive community of ten individuals in which two are oppressed by the dominant eight. A thoroughgoing utilitarian would argue that this oppression is immoral as it prevents the society achieving the maximum amount of happiness, which would be ten out of ten.

The introductory chapter provides a key to why Mill introduces the principle of liberty in the first place. A sketch is provided of the historical development of **liberalism**, democracy and religious toleration after the overthrow of tyranny. Like his fellow nineteenth-century philosophers Marx and Nietzsche, the author of *On Liberty* strives to strike an empirical note through his analysis of the relations of power through the course of history. Mill maps out the 'vulture-like' antagonism of ancient dictatorships, the emergence and establishment of democracy and a period when the technological fruits of democracy can be

enjoyed. Democracy is justified on utilitarian grounds as it encourages progress, which leads to prosperity, but a danger lurks in the undergrowth. This danger is described as a new form of democratic tyranny, the tyranny of the majority, the despotism of public opinion or the 'yoke of opinion'. The tyranny of the majority is also evident in the social field. Examples of social tyranny, in which people feel controlled by the views of the majority, might include diet, dress or the pressure to conform to behavioural norms.

Mill fashions his principle of liberty as a counterblast to this democratic tyranny, on the understanding that a positive, liberal framework can be established as an alternative. Mill puts forward an almost Marxian view: 'Where there is an ascendant class, a large portion of the morality of the country emanates from its class interests and its feeling of class superiority'. He believed that liberty was under threat and needed to be defended: in the 1850s, Mill claimed that the ideas of Auguste Comte were undermining it; this is referred to later in the first chapter. Mill felt the need to write *On Liberty* in defence of freedom from constraint by an overly paternalistic state.

The principle of liberty

After his initial exploration of the above themes, the author formulates his notion of freedom. Let us examine this principle of liberty as it is set out in the text:

> That principle is that the sole end for which mankind are warranted, individually or collectively, in interfering with the liberty of action of any of their number is self-protection. That the only purpose for which power can be rightfully exercised over any member of a civilised community, against his will, is to prevent harm to others. His own good, either physical or moral, is not a sufficient warrant. (68)

This detailed version of the principle of liberty needs to be broken down into its constituent parts:

- The fact that Mill describes this notion as a 'principle' means that he believes it to be a watertight statement. The rest of the work adds clauses here and there to make the principle serviceable but the first chapter contains its most complete formulation.

- Mill refers to 'the sole end for which mankind are warranted'. This is a teleological statement and one that refers to a clear goal. Like the ancient Greek philosopher Aristotle, who wrote about teleology, Mill has a clear view of what human nature consists of and, therefore, of what ought to be pursued to fulfil it. Human nature, for Mill, consists in being able to reason and in having a desire for happiness. Human nature by definition is shared by everyone and justifies the moral worth of actions.

- Mill emphasises that the state is justified in 'interfering' with individuals or groups of individuals in order to prevent harm to others. This interference may involve the use of force, but note that it is specifically aimed at actions and not beliefs.

- The phrase 'civilised community' suggests that uncivilised nations can be dominated and Mill adds children and those who are mentally incapable to this category. This view has a long history, dating back to Aristotle, but runs into the criticism from cultural relativism that any assertion that one state is more civilised than another is itself a product of cultural conditioning or 'custom'.

- The phrase 'against his will' suggests that the individual's willing agreement to enter society will lead to demands that cannot be refused, for example taxation or military service. Mill does not give us a clear account of how this will is determined.

- The clause that mentions preventing harm to others has been termed the **harm principle** and exists as a utilitarian sub-clause within the wider principle. The emphasis on security is obviously a very important limitation on liberty. Security is as significant a goal for Mill as liberty. We cannot enjoy our liberty if we are being harmed; so the lover of liberty must accept the need to prevent harm.

- 'Harm' requires further clarification: the principle seems to work with regard to physical harm but mental harm seems more difficult to determine. In addition, we might view something as potentially harmful but also potentially beneficial. The principle does not give us clear instructions on how to act in this situation.

- 'His own good, either physical or moral, is not a sufficient warrant' is an important expansion of the scope of the principle. It is in contradistinction to the harm principle, since it means we can harm ourselves. A paternalistic state cannot, under Mill's principle, interfere with the individual's freedom on the grounds that the state knows what is best for the individual.

> **Task**
>
> We have mentioned that the notion of harm is a problematic one. What definition can you give of the term 'harm'? Draw up a list of what might be included in this category. Are there any circumstances in which the harms that you have identified should be allowed? What does Mill say about constructive or **contingent harm** in Chapter 4?

Criticisms of the principle of liberty

The principle of liberty may be a useful guide, or an ideal to aim for, but it is not likely to serve as a complete solution. To try to achieve a complete solution undervalues the complexity of the question. This is shown by the fact that the rest of *On Liberty* seems in places to contradict itself (as do other aspects of Mill's thought expressed in other books). It could be said that it is better to base the relationship of the individual to society on a series of 'rules of thumb' that will allow scope for the complexity of the matter to be appreciated. In general, the principle of liberty is insufficient as a guide to the totality of relations between individuals and society.

A second criticism might involve the fact that the distinction between **self-regarding action** and action which affects others cannot in the end be sustained. This notion is at the centre of the principle and is expressed in the conviction that society can interfere only if an action harms another; otherwise there should be freedom. Actions that do not harm others but which are harmful to the agent cannot be punished or stopped. As a consequentialist, Mill must accept that all actions, or indeed inaction, affect other people in some ways. Consider the example of alcohol abuse and how it affects many more people than just the drinker.

Mill accepts that there is such a thing as contingent, constructive or secondary harm, but says that in the interests of liberty the less severe forms of this should be ignored. Society should seek to prevent them by education. Thus society should not take preventative steps to stop the harm that may result from individuals abusing their liberty 'for the sake of the greater good of human freedom'. Mill adopts a long-term solution to short-term harm. For example, he will put up with some immediate problems from drunkenness, but hope that such a policy of education will persuade people not to drink so much alcohol in the long term.

A third problem arises for the author over what he means by 'harm'. Harm can mean material or mental harm, yet Mill is unwilling to admit the latter. What if the majority of the population is distressed mentally by some act of individuality which Mill allows? Such mental harm may be as severe as material harm.

In our society the law generally recognises the negative consequences of mental harm, as for example in the notion of mental cruelty in divorce cases and laws against slander. Even Mill seems to admit this when he says that some things should be permitted in private which are not permitted in public. In addition are we to interfere with someone's liberty if their actions are considered potentially harmful, and how is this to be measured?

The case of self-harming seems to be an exception. Society has power over children and those mentally incapable of looking after themselves, so why not over other people who are generally weak-willed? Where do we draw the line? Is a vicious person, a drunk or a drug addict capable of looking after him- or herself?

Kinds of liberty

Liberty, according to Mill, is not a matter of an inalienable, abstract right as defended in the French Revolution. He does not accept that there are natural human rights and agrees with Hume's and Bentham's dismissal of this idea. Only occasionally does Mill use the word 'right', preferring instead to speak of 'interests'. Three types of liberty are mentioned at the end of the introductory chapter as a foretaste of what is to come:

- *liberty of conscience* – freedom concerning thoughts, feelings and opinions;
- *liberty of tastes* – **positive freedom** that enables us to choose how we want to live;
- *liberty among individuals* – freedom to join with others in a common cause that does not involve harm.

All three categories involve the 'freedom to pursue our own good in our own way, so long as we do not attempt to deprive others of theirs, or impede their efforts to obtain it' (72). This is a slightly different formulation of the principle of liberty. The freedom of the individual, Mill says, leads to a free society. No free society is possible if individuals are not free. A free society must surely simply mean an independent self-governing one. So, the principle of liberty is a patriotic requirement for national sovereignty. This is a very old argument for freedom, dating back to Roman authors. The arguments for liberty in the rest of the book explain why Mill supports liberty. The 'one very simple principle' of liberty that Mill talks about, however, appears on closer examination to be neither singular nor simple.

Review question

State Mill's harm principle and outline any two objections to it.

Of the liberty of thought and discussion (Chapter 2)

A market place of ideas

The second chapter of *On Liberty* tackles the question of free speech and whether there should be any limitations. Arguments that defend free speech by asserting that we should be free to criticise the government are taken as a given, although Mill admits that the nineteenth century still has to deal with questions concerning the freedom of the press. In the course of the second

John Stuart Mill
(1806–1873)

The most famous autobiographical fact that most people recall about Mill is to do with his precocious education: he solved mathematical problems and developed an acquaintance with standard Greek at the age of three and learnt Latin at eight years of age. One fact that is often overlooked, however, and one that is well attested in his autobiography, was that he found his early education enjoyable and he was proud to be allowed to work at the same desk as his father. His father was a Scottish academic and contemporary of Jeremy Bentham; they lived next door to each other in London. James Mill adopted Bentham's utilitarianism and his son gave much attention to it in order to retrieve this normative ethical theory from the hole that had been dug by its critics. The eldest of nine children, Mill appears from the pages of his life story as a bookish and brittle child. But one can see emerging from the pages in which he describes the stream of academic acquaintances invited to dinner at their London home and the long walks he had with his father the roots of his philosophical ideas concerning the freedom of discussion and the importance of individuality. He embarked upon a thirty-five year career with the British East India Company, starting as a clerk and soon enjoying a promotion to 'chief conductor of the correspondence with India'. He found time to write a prodigious amount of philosophical work covering ethics, epistemology, logic and political writing; his best-known political essay is *On Liberty*. Mill's wife Harriet Hardy Taylor collaborated on his writing of this text. They had enjoyed an intimate friendship for twenty years before her first husband died and they eventually married in 1852.

Significant works:

System of Logic (1843)
On Liberty (1859)

Utilitarianism (1861)
The Subjection of Women (1869)

---

chapter, Mill offers epistemological, utilitarian, naturalistic and logical defences of free speech. His epistemological justification rests on the fact that free speech derives from truth and clarifies falsehood. Mill argues that one should be allowed to voice one's opinion as, if it is true, then it will be useful, if it is false it will act as a contrast to the truth, and if it is partially true then it will be useful in part.

It is from such a market place of ideas in which theories are displayed and exchanged that truth, like profit, emanates (76–78). To silence an opinion would be to incorrectly assume that you are right and that is to assume infallibility. Mill believes that no human being can make this claim and reminds us of the dangers that assuming infallibility brings.

He argues:

- It is perfectly conceivable for the majority of humanity to be misguided (76).

- To silence any opinion is to unjustifiably assume that you have access to absolute truth, which is a claim none of us can make (77).

- We assume that we are always right because of cultural conditioning or, to borrow Hume's term, because of 'custom'.

- Any number of past beliefs have had to be refined due to error (78).

- Even the Roman Catholic Church, which is held up by the author as the epitome of absolutism, uses a method of discourse in which both sides of the argument are explored and tested when deciding on whether to canonise a candidate. This method is called 'playing devil's advocate' (81).

- Our certainty about belief X is an attitude belonging to us and not to the truth (81).

For Mill truth and usefulness are two sides of the same coin and, as a consequence, if we are to suppress truth by not allowing freedom of thought and discussion then we are putting ourselves at a disadvantage. Even if we are not sure what the benefits of a truth are, we cannot afford to say that such information will never be useful to us in the future.

A series of examples follow that illustrate the dangers of assuming infallibility. The first example is that of Socrates, who, through inviting his fellow Athenians to question received opinion in order to attain something close to the truth, was unjustly executed. The second example is that of Jesus Christ, who despite preaching an ethic of love and forgiveness was cruelly executed. Although Mill is not religious he believes that Christian ethics are a force for the good and to some extent compatible with the greatest happiness of the greatest number. He criticises those in first-century Palestine at the crucifixion who assumed a position of infallible judgement over another, which led to the unhappy consequences. The author draws our attention to the irony that the Stoic philosopher Marcus Aurelius persecuted Christians while at the same time he espoused a similar moral code.

On pages 87–90, Mill outlines and rejects Dr Johnson's 'fires of persecution' argument, which holds that fires of persecution are a good thing and necessary to burn off falsity, leaving us with the alchemical gold of truth. Mill replies with three arguments, the first being that such a position as that adopted by Dr Johnson presumes that a finite number of truths exist and that these have already been discovered. If this is the case then the persecution of new candidates cannot harm us as we have already collected enough truths but, Mill argues, we haven't. Second, Mill points out that Johnson's position holds that historically no truth has ever been harmed by persecution, which is blatantly untrue. The author uses a series of religious examples but one might as accurately draw on instances from science such as the trial of Galileo. Third, Mill condemns the view that 'truth will always prevail over persecution' as sentimental nonsense.

Mill's purpose in outlining these arguments in favour of freedom of thought and discussion become clearer when he admits to certain worries about the increase in religious intolerance at the time he wrote *On Liberty* (1859). He mentions two specific examples in passing: that of Thomas Pooley, a Cornishman sentenced to death for atheist grafiti but later pardoned, and that of two witnesses at the Old Bailey whose testimonies were viewed as less trustworthy owing to their lack of religious beliefs. Mill draws the reader's attention to the remnants of bigotry that live on and warns of the dangers of such inflexibility of thought.

> **Task**
>
> Discuss the meaning of the following sayings and proverbs:
> - The devil rides on the backs of those who are certain.
> - Orthodoxy is the heresy that won.
> - The truth shouldn't be subject to consequences.
>
> What relevance do they have for Mill's epistemology as set out at the start of Chapter 2?

The search for truth

In keeping with the nineteenth-century preoccupation with 'great thinkers', Mill advances the view that without freedom of expression the creative genius of innovative minds would be silenced along with the resultant insights. For Mill, truth flourishes more abundantly in heterodoxy than in **orthodoxy**. Truths are refined and extended through debate in a public forum and it is members of such a society which benefit in the long run from the resulting discoveries: 'the well-being of mankind may almost be measured by the number and gravity of the truths which have reached the point of being uncontested'. Mill's argument here prefigures Popper's falsification principle (see chapter 6) and the subsequent versions devised by Lakatos and Feyerabend in the philosophy of science.

> **Task**
>
> Find out as much as you can about the philosopher Paul Feyerabend. What does he say about the way science develops? Are there any similarities between Feyerabend's account of scientific method and the arguments advanced by Mill in Chapters 2, 3 and 4 of *On Liberty*?

Received opinion

Mill focuses on our attitude to received opinions in the next section of Chapter 2 (96–108). He starts by praising three examples of the 'yoke of authority' being broken: the Reformation, the Enlightenment and the period of German Romanticism. In each instance, the freedom of thought and discussion was exercised. In the case of the Reformation, the German monk Martin Luther suggested a return to a simpler, Bible-based faith and condemned the way in which Christianity was practised at the time. Then the Enlightenment witnessed fresh and original ideas in science that changed how people saw the world. Third, Goethe and Fichte reacted to the Enlightenment preoccupation with reason by stressing the importance of the human imagination. In each of these cases, new life was breathed into received opinion. To assume received opinion without investigation and challenge is to dwell in superstition.

Mill's analysis of our treatment of received opinions raises the following points:

- An academic dialectic between 'two sets of conflicting reasons' is best suited to establish truths. Here the author seems to be defending a type of Hegelian dialectic (see chapter 12).

- Such a dialectic is particularly suited to the fields of religion, ethics and politics (98). This may be because in these fields there does not seem to be a precise answer and a more subtle approach is required that adapts extreme positions on both sides.

- Mill quotes Cicero, who argued that you should know your opponent's case better than your own (99). This is how the solution to a problem is sought, through a detailed knowledge of the opposing standpoints so that an accurate compromise can be reached.

Experts and everyman

Mill moves on to explore the objection that we don't need to investigate the vast majority of issues but can leave this to a band of experts in that sphere. The author replies by asserting that freedom of thought and discussion is needed among experts as not even an authority is infallible. Second, he points out a similar

distinction in religious life where, in Roman Catholicism, a separation is drawn between the laity, who accept church teaching on trust, and educated individuals or clergy, who accept theological doctrine on conviction. Mill says that any self-respecting Protestant should be wary of this practice and instead decide on issues through their own conscience and understanding. Mill believes that if beliefs are accepted without question then the original meaning of the said belief will be lost, thus leaving the believer with only 'the shell and husk'. Religion is cited as the prime example of this torpor (102–105). The example of Christian ethics is used to illustrate how a belief can stagnate if it is not being questioned and tested for weaknesses.

Many people, Mill alleges, sign up to the Christian conviction that one is to love one's neighbour and not seek comfort in material possessions. He argues that in reality most appear to be reciting this without any critical appreciation. The fact that the belief is blandly accepted and not discussed means that it exercises less power in the moral agent's mind: 'Both teachers and learners go to sleep at their post as soon as there is no enemy in the field' (105).

Yet is it inevitable that when any belief becomes accepted it is destined to perish? Mill believes that this tendency is real but needs to be avoided. The success of humanity is to be judged on how many useful doctrines resist this decline. There are certain ways in which one can keep beliefs alive: such as the Socratic method of question and answer, the medieval practice of disputation or the use of criticism (termed 'negative logic') popular in the nineteenth century.

Partial truth

Mill feels it necessary to underscore the importance of investigating partial truths, hinted at earlier in the chapter. One allows freedom of speech because if what is said is right then it will be useful; if it is profoundly misguided then it will act as a useful contrast; and if it contains a partial truth then this truth can be eventually distilled. The author appears to expound a kind of coherentism here in which previous beliefs are replaced by more accurate ones. He goes on to provide two examples of partial truths in the field of political philosophy. The first is the insight of Rousseau that we should seek what satisfies us most and reject those things that appear artificial. The second is the truth contained in the rival dialectic between order (conservatism) and reform (radicalism). In reality both positions have some truth despite being frequently pitted against each other in the political sphere.

A further objection is examined: 'One cannot refine or improve upon the Christian moral code as it is complete and absolute'. This would have been a popular view held by Mill's readers in nineteenth-century Britain. Mill argues that even this view deserves to be challenged. He points out that there is no singular insight that counts as 'Christian morality' due to the fact that Christian moral teaching is made up of many different strands: the Old Testament, the Gospels, Pauline literature, early church teaching and the influence of early Greek philosophy. In addition, Mill says that there is room for debate given that Christian ethics is often accused of being too negative and life-denying in ignoring 'magnanimity, high-mindedness, personal dignity, even the sense of honour'. The author is not necessarily criticising Christianity in this passage, though he may well agree with the arguments being raised, but asserting that Christianity can be challenged. Indeed for anyone to call themselves Christian with any justification means that they have an obligation to critically engage with this system of beliefs.

Mill concludes with some final points:

- Those entrenched in their prejudices will never be convinced but the 'calmer and more disinterested bystander' may benefit (115).
- The argument from free speech is fourfold: first, we cannot silence an opinion that is true and may benefit us; second, we cannot silence an opinion that may contain a partial truth; third, knowledge only counts as knowledge if it is critically examined; fourth, beliefs lose their power if they are not regularly challenged.
- Mill adds as an appendix that such challenges should not take the form of sarcastic, invective fallacious diatribes, but even if they do this is

not a legal issue but a matter of good sense and civility.

Task

Mill stands out as the great champion of free speech, but are there no limits at all? Discuss the following as possible exceptions: pornography, holocaust denial, incitement to religious or racial hatred.

Mill's arguments have been seen as the great classic defence of free speech and free expression in the tradition started by John Milton's *Areopagitica* in the seventeenth century. Chapter 2 stands apart from the rest of the text in so far as its defence of freedom of thought and discussion does not refer to the 'no harm' clause of the principle of liberty. Mill appears to allow complete freedom of thought and discussion, without reference to the harm that this might cause others, whereas liberty of action is limited by the harm principle: 'no one pretends actions should be as free as opinions' (119).

Mill believes that thoughts are of such a different constitution that they cannot be treated in the same way as actions. There is a problem here, which Mill in the end fails to solve. What is the link between freedom of thought and freedom of action? Let us briefly rehearse the main criticisms against Mill's argument in favour of free thought and expression.

Criticisms of Chapter 2

- It is more or less an axiom of philosophy (indeed of all forms of study worth the name) that humanity is fallible. It is of course difficult to demonstrate without falling into paradox or even fallacy. How do we know that human beings are fallible? Because Mill tells us so, yet Mill, by his own account, must be fallible because he is human.
- Is it really true that complete freedom of expression is useful for society? Mill says utility must be the starting point for any ethical discussion, including a discussion of liberty, but, if liberty leads to the collapse of a tolerant, liberal society and the imposition of a bloody tyranny, it would seem not to have been very useful. Hence, in the end, liberal societies tend to ban the most extreme false

opinions because they will destroy society if allowed to become too prevalent.

- Mill allows absolute freedom of discussion, but in other respects restricts freedom so that actions do not harm others. He ignores the fact that free speech may cause harm, for example it may be intellectually harmful to be exposed as an individual to false ideas. Other classes of opinion may also cause harm and are also candidates for censorship: racial prejudice, libel and slander, false business information, bad advertising, the spreading of rumours, pornography, violent films, official secrets, contempt of court, invasion of privacy. There is a case for limiting the expression of all of these but Mill does not, on the whole, accept it.

- Mill's principle of liberty applies to actions but not to expression. It is difficult to say that expression is not a form of action. If a book is published and sold, actions are performed; debate and speech involve actions. In the opening pages of the third chapter of *On Liberty*, there is condemnation of the mob orator who incites the mob to attack corn-dealers in time of famine and demagogues who whip up a crowd of starving people against the rich. This drives a coach and horses through his claim that freedom of expression is absolute, and would seem to me at least to justify the imposition of censorship in various sorts of cases. Mill appears to be offering contradictory advice.

- Mill's analysis seems to be based on too idealised a view of human nature. He believes in the perfectibility of humanity and the power of education. The antidote to evil tastes and pursuits is not law but education. Mill talks of Rousseau's ideas regarding human perfectibility as coming like a 'bombshell' in the eighteenth century.

- Finally, Mill seems unclear whether he believes in truth or not. He is certainly not an absolutist but does not seem like a relativist either. The best term to describe his epistemological position is 'realist' as he believes that human knowledge and human morality correspond to something real, but this is not further elaborated in the text.

Review question

Briefly describe the epistemological benefits of allowing freedom of thought and discussion.

Of individuality, as one of the elements of well-being (Chapter 3)

A market place of lifestyles

The third chapter of *On Liberty* examines the relationship between freedom, individuality and happiness. Mill describes the type of individuality under discussion in what appears to be another principle:

> It is that there should be different experiments of living; that free scope should be given to varieties of character, short of injury to others; and that the worth of different modes of life should be proved practically. (120)

This principle of individuality seems in keeping with the principle of liberty as laid out in the first chapter. Mill emphasises the fact that we should be allowed to be free to develop our characters and styles of living as long as this does not cause harm. He warns us of the fact that opinions and acts are often inseparable in their moral culpability, illustrating this with the story about an excited mob outside a corn-dealer's house and how in this instance even freedom of expression needs to be curbed. Nevertheless, Mill keenly advocates a market place of lifestyles or 'experiments of living' in order to increase diversity. He believes that such individual spontaneity has intrinsic worth and awards originality the status of a secondary maxim to that of the greatest happiness of the greatest number. Mill goes on to expand on the concept of individuality by arguing the following points:

- Individuality is encouraged as long as it does not interfere with the freedom of others.

- Individuality is cited as the 'chief ingredient' in social progress.

- Individuality is a necessary part of civilisation, education and culture.

- Individuality is said to have intrinsic worth.

- The importance of individuality is only recognised by a few scholars, for example the German scholar Baron Wilhelm von Humboldt (1767–1835), who argued that a good is only a good if we decide to do it ourselves. Thus an unintended good is not a proper good. Von Humboldt influenced Mill's argument in praise of individuality and Marx's criticism of the 'invisible hand' argument.

Mill describes a Hegelian dialectic between everyone on the one hand striving to be totally different and on the other copying one another completely. The synthesis exists through achieving a balance of accepting those insights gained through previous human experience, while at the same time critically engaging with every aspect of this body of knowledge. Certain dangers lie in accepting custom straight off:

- One may not be interpreting it correctly.

- The particular custom may not be suitable to one's character or situation.

- Accepting custom for its own sake seems not so much an inauthentic choice as not a choice at all.

Mill points out that human nature is defined by the freedom to choose a plan of life; this is what we mean by 'positive freedom'. If this were not the case then there wouldn't be anything to separate us from animals or machines.

Mill considers some objections in the course of the third chapter. The first qualm is that individuality may lead to those with strong and dangerous impulses taking over and suppressing the weak. Mill reasons that strong impulses are a type of energy that may be put to good use as well as bad. He argues that historically there might have been times of excessive passion but, at the time of writing, in the nineteenth century, people are in danger of a deficiency. The author blames the influence of Calvinism, with its emphasis on God's will rather than self-will and the suppression of human nature, for this shortfall. He likens the 'cramped and dwarfed' followers of such doctrines to absurdly trimmed topiary! Mill's ideal character is the mean between the excessive self-control of a churchman like John Knox and an emotionally incontinent character such as Alcibiades. For the author, the Athenian general Pericles has the right mixture of control and spirit. In a sense one might describe Pericles as filling the mould of an ideal human being in respect of getting the balance right.

The theme of there being an ideal human nature runs throughout *On Liberty* and is expressed in the third chapter through a series of images in which the author contrasts humans to animals and machines. Mill argues that the most desirable characteristics are those found in certain great thinkers, those people of genius who make important discoveries that we all benefit from. The nineteenth century saw a great many technological advances and Mill witnessed the beneficial effects of these discoveries, made by great minds. His argument is essentially a utilitarian one. Mill argues that society should nurture freedom so that genius can flourish as, when genius flourishes, new discoveries are made that contribute to the health and welfare of the greatest possible number of people. Implicit in Mill's discussion are a number of other features of genius. Mill draws a series of comparisons in the space of a few pages. They are summarised in the following table:

Comparison	Image of genius
Salt of the earth	Genius preserves truth and adds flavour to life.
Stagnant pool	Genius injects new life, like oxygen, into dead ideas.
Cattle	Genius does not follow the lead of others.
Machines	Genius tries something different.
Electricity through dead matter	Genius critically engages with the subject.
Growth	Genius needs to be nurtured by society.
Breaking the mould	Genius is not confined by a narrow view of human nature.
Breaking the chains	Genius is not constrained by social norms or custom.
The Niagara Falls	Genius can be erratic but spectacular.

Task

Who do we class as a genius? Write a short speech defending a genius of your choice. Perhaps you have chosen Einstein, Shakespeare or Gandhi? Write a list of characteristics that all geniuses have in common.

Mill argues that through encouraging individuality, even to the point of eccentricity, genius will be nurtured and this will contribute to the greatest happiness of the greatest number and raise society above the level of mediocrity. It should be an essential feature of society, therefore, that people do not feel constrained by social norms or the pressure to conform. In a famous passage (133), Mill declares that humans are not like sheep in so far as they have individual needs. Just as they appear in different shapes and sizes, which are superficial differences, so they have different characters and need an array of lifestyle choices from which to choose. In the remaining pages of the third chapter, the author contrasts the ideal of a society that encourages individuality to one such as China that, according to Mill, advances the ideal of making everyone alike. Mill warns that the same fate awaits Europe if it does not take heed of his argument.

Three defences of originality are offered in the course of this chapter, which we shall call the argument from choice, the naturalist argument and the argument from likenesses.

The argument from choice

Mill's moral argument is based on the caveat that people are only moral through exercising choice and if people myopically adhere to social norms for the sake of social norms then no true moral decision is being made. Following someone's good example certainly has its place but it must be done critically and autonomously. Mill praises individuality for encouraging choice in contrast to the compressed and structured moral development of conformists in society. For Mill, choice is good and we should not imitate, or act according to custom, but choose how we shall live. This is good for the individual and an essential part of being human. But unless we have freedom, we cannot choose. Choice is a form of mental exercise, which stretches the brain in the same way that physical exercise improves the body. Mill's idea of the 'higher pleasures' is also involved here. As is well known, Mill modified Benthamite utilitarianism by saying that some forms of pleasure were better than others: poetry was better than push-pin. So, in order to develop a taste for these higher pleasures, people had to exercise choice, had to have the freedom to experiment. Mill talks of 'experiments of living', and these are a way in which the individual finds out what gives him pleasure. So, even without the notion of higher pleasures, utilitarianism presupposes the ability to choose what actions give us most pleasure and least pain. We are all different and it is through choice that we find out what tastes and pursuits give us most pleasure. Not everyone will be able to take advantage of this freedom to choose and not everyone will wish to do so. Some will be too timid or stupid not to follow convention. But it is important that society gives freedom to everyone, so that those who can benefit will take advantage of this freedom.

The naturalist argument

There is a distinctly Aristotelian feel to the third chapter (for example, 124–127). Mill held that Aristotle's teachings were utilitarian in essence, so it is not outlandish for us to brand Mill as a closet virtue theorist in return. He mentions the importance of well-being in the chapter title, talks of his 'love of virtue', criticises societies that exhibit excesses and deficiencies of spontaneity, advocates a certain type of disposition, stresses the importance of realising personal preferences, cites pleasure as a necessary element in fulfilment and describes individuality as an integral part of human nature (criticising Calvinism for ignoring this). Mill even admits that if he were religious then he would view God as a designer delighting in the diversity of his creation. In summation, Mill's argument is that freedom and individuality are the only way to lead a fulfilled life and achieve the *summum bonum* (the greatest good). Such a fulfilled life, Mill contends, needs to be tailored to suit each individual.

The argument from likenesses

1 Liberty is proven to be good.
2 Despotism is the opposite of liberty.
3 Despotism is the opposite of individuality.
4 Individuality, like liberty, leads to the good.

In its strict logical form this argument does not work but contains some worth if one is willing to admit that individuality, like liberty, leads to progress and improvement. The argument is teleological in the sense of justifying anything that leads to utility, and may be criticised on the grounds that the same end may be achievable by some benign dictatorship.

Mill's defence of individuality or originality is essentially utilitarian: 'each person becomes more valuable to himself, and is, therefore, capable of being more valuable to others'.

Criticisms of individualism

- Mill is unclear as to what experiments in living he has in mind: communal living, polygamy, monasticism? Whereas Mill gives plenty of examples in Chapter 2 of new ideas, he does not give us many examples of new styles of living.

- There are problems in reconciling Mill's argument as laid out in Chapter 2 with certain points arising in Chapter 3. The major difference is that the harm principle applies to freedom of action but not to freedom of thought and expression (except in the case of incitement).

- There are contradictions in Chapter 3 itself. Is it for the sake of the individual or of society in the future that Mill encourages freedom of action? The answer is that it is for both since individual development will foster society's development. But it is possible to envisage a conflict between the two purposes. Society may think that my experiment in living is actually rather harmful while I may insist that I enjoy it and that in the long run it will benefit mankind if only everyone else could learn to adapt to it.

- There seems to be some tension between Mill's conception of humans as progressive beings and the idea that public opinion is conformist and repressive. If man is so progressive, why does he produce such a regressive public opinion?

- Is Mill's elitism consistent with his liberalism, individualism and belief in liberty? One commentator, Maurice Cowling, suspected that Mill was in the end an elitist and an opponent of liberty, who wanted liberty for the time being until his elite group of utilitarians had conquered the universe, when we would all be told that the truth had been found, and now there was really no need to quarrel with it. This is to take what Mill says farther than the evidence allows, but it nevertheless suggests that there may be a real tension in Mill's arguments. What, to take another tack, would Mill say if we were to suggest that individualism would lead to a sort of hedonistic stagnation, everyone completely absorbed in their happiness-pursuing experiments of living in a universal California? Would he still want liberty if it were not a progressive force?

Review question

State Mill's principle of individuality and outline any two of Mill's applications of that principle.

Of the limits to the authority of society over the individual (Chapter 4)

The fourth chapter tells us what is under discussion in the first sentence: 'What, then, is the rightful limit to the sovereignty of the individual over himself?' In other words, when should individuality be limited? Mill's answer is twofold:

- in order to prevent harm;
- if the individual is not sharing the labour involved in protecting society.

The author rejects Rousseau's model of a social contract, but believes in the thinner notion that each member of a state has a *quid pro quo* duty or agreement towards that state that needs to be enforced through law or public disapproval if not observed. Apart from that, any self-regarding action should not be interfered with. Mill points out that many such activities, for example educating oneself, are beneficial. The freedom of choice enjoyed in a liberal society far outweighs any potential evils though we are reminded of the importance of behaving responsibly. If a citizen chooses badly from the moral market place of ideas, we are justified in voicing our disapproval, but should only have recourse to punitive actions in the case of real moral vice.

Mill goes on to consider whether the distinction between self- and other-regarding action holds, and concludes that 'no person is an entirely isolated being' (146). He points out that some harmful self-regarding actions can affect others, and hence be re-categorised as harmful other-regarding actions that are subject to state intervention. One example is given: someone is spending so much on themselves as to not be able to pay their debts. Mill argues that apparent self-regarding actions can easily turn into harmful other-regarding actions and as such should be stopped by the government. Mill's main line of defence is consequentialism. He uses the example of drunkenness, stating that, whereas one cannot condemn the act itself, one is justified in condemning it if its result leads to general unhappiness. Imagine the consternation citizens would feel if a member of their police force was drunk on duty. The author goes on to separate such significant harm from what he terms 'contingent harm'.

Contingent harm

Experiments in living are to be allowed even if they lead to contingent or constructive harm, but disallowed if they lead to serious harm. We limit contingent harm at the cost of liberty and education; any state that does not allow this learning curve lets 'its members grow up mere children'. Mill makes the case against a coercive moral police by arguing that such a force prevents genuine decisions and runs the risk of interfering in the wrong place. This argument is substantiated by a series of examples of illegitimate interference:

- a majority imposing a dietary restriction on a minority, for example not eating pork in a Muslim state (153);

- a majority enforcing religious belief and practice on a minority, for example for Roman Catholics to ban Protestant worship and a married clergy in a Catholic country (154);
- the state interfering with the leisure activities of its citizens, for example the Puritans banning music and dancing (154);
- the state interfering with the expenditure of individuals, for example the sumptuary laws in America – Mill, following the French commentator on American affairs Alexis de Toqueville, cites America as an example of a state that introduces sumptuary laws (that is, laws that impose a ceiling on individual spending) (155);
- the state interfering with trade unions, for example in objecting to their campaigning against piecework (156);
- the state prohibiting the sale of alcohol, as was the case in the American state of Maine at the time of writing (156);
- the state interfering with the times when people are allowed to work, for example the campaign to keep Sunday as a day of rest (158);
- a majority persecuting a minority over their views on marriage, for example the persecution of Mormons because of their views on polygamy (160).

Chapter 4 champions freedom, but is it for its own sake or because it is instrumental in achieving the greatest happiness of the greatest number? Let us briefly rehearse some of the relevant arguments.

Intrinsic and instrumental freedom

Mill could open a whole canning factory of worms with his deceptively trouble-free claim that freedom is a good thing. One such problem is whether liberty is valued for its own sake, i.e. is intrinsically valuable, or whether it is a means to achieve other ends, i.e. an instrument.

There are three possibilities:

1 Mill may value liberty as an end (the intrinsicalist view).
2 Mill may value liberty as a means to an end (the instrumentalist view).

3 Mill may value liberty both as an end and as a means (partly for its own sake).

There is more textual evidence for the second position but the fact that in a number of key places in *On Liberty* Mill appears to assign freedom intrinsic worth means that the third possibility is an accurate compromise.

Let us briefly detail the instrumentalist arguments. The first fact to bear in mind is that the text is written against a background of utilitarianism and as such holds liberty as important if and only if it leads to an increase in happiness or the prevention of harm. For Mill, utility is the ultimate appeal on all ethical questions. The second fact to bear in mind when surveying the instrumentalist case is that Mill discounts the freedom of children, the mentally infirm and so-called barbarians. This suggests that he does not believe in a universal, human right to freedom but only grants this privilege to those at a certain stage of development. These two points are synthesised in the second chapter, where Mill's argument appears to be that liberty is valued because it leads to intellectual progress and such development enhances the greatest happiness of the greatest number and minimises pain.

Any reader cannot ignore the passages in *On Liberty* where Mill seems to argue that freedom is good in itself. The second chapter offers a virtually unqualified defence of free speech that is only refined at the beginning of the third chapter in the corn-dealer illustration. The argument from contingent harm in Chapter 4 advocates allowing drinking, even if it results in harm, for the sake of freedom, although this is defended by consequentialism in the wider sense. Finally, Mill expresses his dislike for too many 'antecedent precautions' in the fifth chapter, as they may limit freedom. He declares that 'all restraint *qua* restraint, is an evil', and later in the chapter refuses to allow us to sell ourselves into slavery – that is, he disallows us to be free not to be free. Why is this the case if he does not see intrinsic worth in the virtue? The tension between the instrumentalist and intrinsicalist positions may seem to make Mill's theory of liberty confused, yet, for the author, the practical outcome is the same: act in such a way as to

exercise freedom as long as it is not to the detriment of other people.

Applications (Chapter 5)

Mill occupies the middle ground between **libertarianism** and **paternalism** in so far as he justifies weak intervention by the state in cases where harm would otherwise be caused to its citizens. The examples cited in the fifth chapter are pictured against the scenery of weak paternalism as developed in Chapter 4.

The Millian form of weak legal paternalism seeks to cultivate higher pleasures, and interference is only warranted if less desirable attributes need to be discouraged. The government's laws are, therefore, allowed to warn or express distaste as part of the learning process necessary for a society of maximum utility.

The applications recorded in the fifth and final chapter of *On Liberty* are carefully chosen to support Mill's theory. He reminds us of what this is in the form of two principles (163):

- 'That the individual is not accountable to society for his actions in so far as these concern the interests of no person but himself.'

- 'Secondly, that for actions as are prejudicial to the interests of others, the individual is accountable and may be subjected either to social or to legal punishment if society is of the opinion that one or other is requisite for its protection.'

The harm referred to in the second principle is of a very serious kind and not just the loss felt when one fails in an exam or comes off badly in a business transaction. For this reason Mill quickly endorses competition and free trade. There follows a selection of case scenarios that intend to strike a balance between freedom and harm prevention.

1 The sale of poisons (165)

Mill argues that the sale of poisons should not be restricted, for the sake of the consumer's freedom. Owing to their lethal contents, such products should be clearly labelled. On utilitarian grounds, however, as they can be used to good effect, it is not deemed appropriate for the state to interfere with their sale.

2 The bridge example (166)

On the whole the text is concerned with the practical business of negative liberty – that is, the specifics of being free to do or not to do act X. In the bridge example, Mill declares his hand with regard to positive freedom, asserting that 'liberty consists in doing what one desires'. From this it is inferred that it is justifiable to warn a person of a potentially dangerous bridge and to prevent someone from crossing a really dangerous bridge on the presumption that they do not want to fall in the river. This seems so close to common sense as to appear vacuous. But Mill uses it as an example of real harm prevention.

3 Drunkenness (167)

The potential carnage from drunken behaviour may be as serious as a dangerous bridge but the difference lies in the fact that drunken misdemeanours are potential, and as we cannot presume a crime will take place then the state is not justified in intervening in this instance. A similar example is noted with regard to idleness and how this might result in serious negligence.

4 Sex and gambling (169)

Mill points out that the instigation of harm is in a different logical category to committing harm, and admits that it is not easy to know how to restrict such instigators, for example pimps and bookmakers. He attempts a Hegelian dialectic that synthesises the facts that on the one hand we are to be tolerant, while on the other we believe the resultant activity to be immoral (it exploits the weak-willed in society, thus subverting their autonomy). Mill's compromising synthesis takes the form of allowing sexual freedom and gambling to take place in private but not to occur openly in case the moral welfare of society is affected.

5 The sale of stimulants (171)

In his discussion of the restrictions any state can justifiably impose, Mill examines whether it is right to tax alcohol in order to restrict its sale. He admits that drink carries the real potential to be injurious, but also concedes that this is not a foregone conclusion. He sidesteps the predicament with characteristic shrewdness by claiming that stimulants are not necessities and may be heavily taxed to generate revenue for the Treasury.

6 Freedom of association (172)

One might read the term 'association' in the sense of 'acquaintances', but Mill probably means something more general and provocative such as the membership of trade unions.

7 Slavery (173)

He appears equally adamant that we should not be free to become slaves and renounce freedom. He dwells on the logical contradiction involved in asserting that freedom is good while wanting not to be free. Interestingly, the author links slavery with marriage and goes on to defend the right of a partner to seek a divorce (174). Mill brings up the notion of third parties who are involved in a divorce, such as children, but takes the line that leads to the least possible harm for those interested parties.

8 Education (176)

Mill is keen to look after the welfare needs of children but believes that it is not the role of the state to provide their education. He concedes that in the case of very poor children then this is warranted and that annual state-run exams are needed, but in keeping with his notion of a minimalist state he believes that private schools should be the norm and that parents need to take responsibility.

9 Government (180)

The final section of *On Liberty* contains a condemnation of an overly active government. Mill believes that this is dangerous for three reasons. First, it may lead to jobs being done inefficiently by public servants. Second, it robs people of an educational opportunity. Third, it unnecessarily adds to the power of the state with regard to councils, industries and charities. Mill envisages local enterprises and voluntary organisations taking over many of these responsibilities. Mill admits to the need for a centralised body to inform these decentralised groups, but he lobbies for the minimum possible state.

Review question

State Mill's principle of liberty and outline any two of Mill's applications of that principle.

Glossary of key terms

Contingent harm: Mill allows a certain amount of harm for the benefit of learning from one's mistakes. This is termed 'contingent' or 'constructive' harm.

Democracy: a Greek word literally meaning 'power of the people'.

Harm principle: the clause built into Mill's principle of liberty that argues one is justified in limiting freedom if the action would have resulted in harm.

Liberalism/libertarianism: the political ideology that holds that a state is necessary but it should not intervene excessively at the cost of individuality and freedom.

Negative freedom: freedom from constraint, whereby individuals can decide what actions to do or not to do.

Orthodoxy: any set of beliefs that are accepted as true without question by a faith community. Heretical beliefs conflict with those established as orthodox.

Paternalism: the pejorative description of a state that acts like a parent in telling its citizens what they are allowed to do.

Positive freedom: the capacity enjoyed by human beings of being able to set goals in life rather than having them set by authority.

Self-regarding action: any action committed with a direct consequence to oneself, as opposed to actions that affect others (termed 'other-regarding action').

Tyranny of the majority: the situation where a larger group of individuals impose their decision-making on the minority under the guise of a democratic process.

Utilitarianism: the normative ethical theory that holds that an action is right if it leads to the greatest happiness of the greatest number.

Suggested reading

- Donner, W. (1991) *The Liberal Self*, Ithaca, Cornell University Press
  Scholarly survey of liberalism, the later chapters being especially useful
- Dworkin, G. ed. (1997) *Mill's* On Liberty, Maryland, Rowman & Littlefield
  Series of critical essays on the main themes of *On Liberty*
- Gray, J. (1983) *Mill on Liberty: A Defence*, London, RKP
  A scholarly defence of Mill that tries to reconcile *On Liberty* and *Utilitarianism*
- Gray, J. and Smith, G. W. (1991) *J. S. Mill* On Liberty *in Focus*, London, Routledge
  A complete version of the text followed by famous articles on Mill by noted philosophers
- Riley, J. (1998) *Mill on Liberty*, London, Routledge
  This work offers a close commentary on the text and supplementary chapters

Note

¹ J. S. Mill (1985) *On Liberty*, London, Penguin, p. 68; hereafter the page numbers given in brackets in the text refer to this edition.

14

A commentary on Russell's *The Problems of Philosophy*

Many people would sooner die than think. In fact they do.
(Bertrand Russell)

Aims

On completion of this chapter you should be able to:

- offer an account of Russell's sense-data theory and his distinction between appearance and reality
- understand the terms 'knowledge by acquaintance' and 'knowledge by description'
- evaluate Russell's theory of induction
- evaluate Russell's laws of thought
- evaluate Russell's account of *a priori* knowledge
- evaluate Russell's theory of universals
- provide an account of Russell's critique of Berkeley, Kant and Hegel
- understand Russell's views on the philosophical enterprise.

There are a great number of problems in philosophy and in a sense the title of Russell's work is a misnomer as only one philosophical problem is focused upon, that of categorising knowledge. Matters of interest in ethics and the philosophy of science are touched upon only briefly. The book is, nevertheless, of interest as a systematic exploration of epistemology by one of the most influential thinkers in the British analytic tradition. In a companion volume, Russell describes his approach:

> For my part, I have found that, when I wish to write a book on some subject, I must first soak myself in detail, until all the separate parts of the subject-matter are familiar; then, some day, if I am fortunate, I perceive the whole, with all its parts duly interrelated. After that, I only have to write down what I have seen. The nearest analogy is first walking all over a mountain in a mist, until every path and ridge and valley is separately familiar, and then, from a distance, seeing the mountain whole and clear in bright sunshine.[1]

The above quotation goes some way towards illustrating the distinction between what may be termed 'epistemic' and 'epistemological'. Both words share the same Greek origin from *episteme* meaning 'knowledge', but whereas the first concerns the specifics of what we know, the second term refers more philosophically to how we know what we know. Epistemology is depicted by Russell, in the above illustration, as a clear, sunlit view of a mountain as seen from afar.

Any reader of *The Problems of Philosophy* will become aware of the author's methodical and painstaking exploration into the difference between appearance and reality, his categorisation of how we come to know phenomena presented to our senses *a posteriori* and how *a priori* knowledge is in fact a description of the relations between phenomena. Russell agrees with Plato in asserting that there is a mysterious reality behind or beyond what is apparent, but believes that we are not in any position to comment authoritatively on such a realm. Let us begin our examination of Russell's epistemological journey.

Appearance and reality (Chapter 1)

We find in the opening chapter of *The Problems of Philosophy* Bertrand Russell seated in his study at Trinity College, Cambridge. One can imagine the scene, sometime between 1910 and 1912, as the philosopher looks up from his desk at the view over Great Court with its manicured lawns, trickling fountain and sixteenth-century buildings in mellow, golden stone. Russell, in the style of Descartes, is contemplating the epistemological question 'Is there any knowledge in the world which is so certain that no reasonable man could doubt it?' His gaze passes around his study over the familiar items he sees every day: the chairs, desk and papers strewn on top of the desk. Russell's gaze settles on an oblong coffee table in the centre of the room and he engages in what has subsequently become a famous meditation on the distinction between appearance and reality.

From the start a dichotomy is established between the straightforward interpretations of everyday objects favoured by those of a practical bent as opposed to a critical interpretation that is the preserve of the philosopher. Russell is preparing the ground for his version of scepticism, his theory of **universals** and his views on the status of philosophy and science. The first important philosophical distinction that is made is that between **sensations** and **sense-data**. They are not the same thing. When the author views the coffee table carefully he becomes aware of the varying hues of what he had previously described as 'brown'. He gets up from his desk and walks around the piece of furniture, noting its different shades in the light, registering on close analysis the varying textures of rough and smooth in the figure and flame of the wood. He taps it and the sound resonates with a different hollowness with respect to its different parts. In conclusion, the table is made up of many different descriptive aspects that are insufficiently grouped together under general terms such as 'brown', 'smooth' and 'hollow sounding'. Such discrete observations are termed 'sensations' and present themselves to the observer as experiences. They are 'signs of some property which perhaps causes all the sensations' and which are termed 'sense-data'. Sense-data are the things known to us through sensations yet belong with sensations in the realm of appearance. Whether the table exists in reality is a further sceptical question raised later. It might be helpful to look on sensations as the flash cards of experience, while viewing sense-data as the pattern depicted on these flash cards and '**matter**', or the external world, as the actual objects being depicted.

Suffice to say at this stage that Russell, through an appeal to intuition, is confident that sensations relate to sense-data and that together sensations and sense-data count as the 'appearance' of an object. He is sceptical about whether there are corresponding objects to the sense-data in 'the real world'. Russell defends his distinction between sensations and general descriptions by reminding us of the accuracy with which the trained, acute, observant eye of an artist or scientist (for instance, when studying microscopic detail) can notice features that a blundering layperson would miss. Indeed, anyone who has tried to draw a still life or landscape will admit to noticing details that had been previously ignored. This goes to show, says Russell, that there has been, under our very noses, a category of perception that has been literally and philosophically overlooked.

The distinction between appearance and reality is a threadbare one, having been discussed since the time of Plato. We have on the one hand the apparent – that is, the careless, ordinary, everyday, experiential, evident, unreflective, immediately known, direct aspect of objects. This exists in contrast to the real 'form of something that is wholly true', that which can be inferred from appearance but which counts as the reality of objects. The gap that exists between appearance and reality leads Russell to employ the following sceptical argument, which we can call the argument from perceptual relativism:

1 There is disagreement concerning an object's colour, texture, shape.
2 Therefore, we cannot talk meaningfully about the real table in terms of appearance.

Russell seeks clarification as to what is meant by the term 'real object' and concludes that it is something material that we can be sure actually exists in the external world. In the second half of the chapter, a discussion develops about immaterialism or **idealism**, the view usually associated with the Anglo-Irish philosopher George Berkeley (1685–1753), who held that the only entities that could be classed as real were ideas and the minds in which ideas occur. Berkeley rejects the notion of material things – that is, space-occupying objects that are made of a distinct, unified and unconscious matter – but does not reject belief in 'physical things', by which he means anything that is independent of other things and which are ordered in a different way to how they appear in the form of sense-data. For Berkeley, these physical things continue to exist in the mind of God when they are not being observed. Russell sees in such a conception something that is identifiable with his own sceptical epistemology. Like Berkeley, he does not draw any distinction between the material and the physical, holding that in total there are three entities involved in perception: the sensation, sense-data and the mysterious real or material thing which stands in a causal relationship to the sense-data. Thus when we look carefully at an object such as a table a multitude of sensations are presented to us which lead us to believe that there are sense-data to which they belong and it is likely that there is an independent reality generating such sense-data but in a way that we can never know whether such a realm of physical objects actually corresponds to what is seen.

To embark on some preliminary criticisms:

- Russell seems to be addressing two different matters here: how something appears and what something is. He asserts that we can only talk meaningfully about one type of knowledge, labelled in Chapter 5 as acquaintance and description, but not both. This is plainly untrue as we have many ways of talking, ranging from the mundane or metaphorical to the technical and scientific. To prioritise one species of discourse over another is purely the product of an unfounded value judgement. The author offers us an unfair choice based on the obvious difference between appearance and reality.
- The argument from perceptual relativism seems simplistic and flawed. The assertion of a vulgar

perceptual relativism that an object appears different from different angles does not seem in the same category as ethical or aesthetic relativism. In practice one can differentiate between the literal standpoint of an observer (whether viewing an object under artificial light, through blue spectacles or when colour blind) and the verdict as to what colour or shape or texture an object actually is. Similarly, we understand that general descriptions such as 'brown' cover different shades. The author appears prejudiced in judging the appearance of an object by a passer-by as any less accurate than its appearance to a scientist peering down a microscope.

- The American philosopher Hilary Putnam (born 1926) has argued that Russell ignores the possibility that the object viewed might be of uniform texture, colour and shape and that there is another mysterious feature of it that we haven't discovered yet which makes it appear varied from different angles. This is certainly an imaginative criticism, but let us continue on Russell's journey and explore the nature of matter as laid out in the second and third chapters.

The existence of matter (Chapter 2)

The second chapter of *The Problems of Philosophy* takes up the opening dispute concerning the existence of matter. This section follows a sceptical line of enquiry and follows in the footsteps of Descartes by referring to arguments from dreaming, deception and delusion. Russell's sceptical attack runs as follows:

1 Appearance is different from reality.
2 We can only be certain of appearances.
3 We are, therefore, uncertain about reality.
4 We can reasonably doubt the reality of X.

Two arguments are raised in the course of the text in an attempt to infer the existence of real things from the existence of the sense-data we know for sure through sensations. The first argument we may term the 'argument from public experience' and is illustrated when the author invites us to imagine him at a dinner party in his study. The table with which we have become acquainted has a tablecloth draped over it. Russell spends the morning in town buying all sorts of party food which he methodically sets out in anticipation of his friends' arrival. Now imagine all his guests seated around the table at various intervals, each enjoying their own sensory experiences as well as the sumptuous fare. We do not know what each of the boffins is thinking about but, when Russell asks for the olives and someone passes the requisite dish, it ceases to be an aspect of an individual guest's sense-data and becomes an object in the public sphere, what the author terms 'a public neutral object'. The first defence of a material world relies on the fact that other people know what we are talking about and, as this is indisputably the case, it seems more probable that there are objects that transcend private experience.

This appears a typically Russellian common-sense argument but, as the author admits, it runs headlong into the problem of other minds. The difficulty occurs in supposing that it is indisputably the case that there are people sitting around the table, as the only evidence we have is the sense-data presented to us and it is precisely the reality behind this layer of perception that we are trying to establish. This argument is not as successful as might be hoped but there is a counterpart that attempts to sway any doubters. Let us call this the 'argument from simplicity'. It begins with Russell's admission that:

> No logical absurdity results from the hypothesis that the world consists of myself and my thoughts and feelings and sensations, and that everything is mere fancy.[2]

The external world, including its inhabitants, may be mere fancy but Russell says that there is no real evidence for this and, as a consequence, it seems an eccentric position to hold. Implicit in the author's dismissal of solipsism is the principle made famous by the thirteenth-century Franciscan monk William of Occam, who held that a simple solution to a simple problem should always be preferred over a needlessly complicated one. This principle is generally accepted in the sphere of scientific research but does not appear to hold elsewhere. Russell's

second defence of a material world is that such a hypothesis, although not proved, is simpler and more plausible than solipsism.

The second defence is illustrated by Russell's cat example. Here he invites the reader to imagine a feline visitor to the philosopher's study. As the author is working he looks up from time to time to see the college cat asleep on a chair, perhaps rubbing herself against a table leg before slipping out of the open door. The three episodes are presented to the observer in the form of sense-data and when one asks the question 'Is there a material cat in Russell's study to which the sense-data correspond?' two alternatives are possible. The first is to suppose that Russell is subject to disconnected feline flash cards of experience that occur whilst he is writing; the second supposes that the sense-data do correspond to a real cat which moves around the study independently when not being observed. Russell believes that, although he has not proved it with certainty, the second alternative is to be favoured as it is beyond all reasonable doubt and that is as much as a philosophical argument can hope for. The first choice, that the cat somehow disappears between sightings, seems to exclude the possibility of the cat possessing thoughts, such as hunger. Thus, if one saw Russell in the quad stroking his feline friend, one could not say that the cat was enjoying it nor, if solipsism is to be granted any ground, could one say that Russell was either, as fellow human beings hold the same status as the rest of the furniture of perception. Such arguments appear to Russell as counter-intuitive and he relies, throughout the text, on a natural and intrinsic common sense that may be appealed to in awkward philosophical situations. *The Problems of Philosophy* was written as 'a shilling shocker' to interest the general public in philosophy but appears at times to use the sort of common-sense arguments that the general public would advance anyway and, as a result, seems a bit of a con.

In a similar vein to Cartesian methodological doubt, Russellian scepticism starts with the uncertainties surrounding perception but, unlike Descartes' representative realism, the author of *The Problems of Philosophy* advances a version of **phenomenalism** inherited from his godfather, John Stuart Mill.

The first steps in Russell's phenomenalism raised in the second chapter are:

- The separation of sense-data from the intrinsic nature or independent existence of objects. Russell asserts that we can only have knowledge of the former category.

- His philosophical method in dealing with perception turns into a linguistic analysis: 'when I look at my table and see a certain brown colour, what is quite certain at once is not "I am seeing a brown colour", but rather, "a brown colour is being seen"' (8).

Russell shares Descartes' ambition to establish a degree of certainty concerning the external world or 'public, neutral objects'. The stakes are raised when the uncertainty over the nature of matter is linked to the problem of other minds. The latter is only mentioned in passing in *The Meditations* but carries the threat of creating an ethical and epistemological desert if the existence of other minds is denied.

Review question

Outline and explain one of Russell's sceptical arguments.

The nature of matter (Chapter 3)

Two further facets are added to Russellian phenomenalism in the third chapter. First is the rejection of the view that the perceived object ceases to exist when it is not being perceived. The author argues that, despite sense-data literally disappearing from view, such items continue to exist through the continuation of material reality that lies behind the appearance:

> The colour ceases to exist if I shut my eyes, the sensation of hardness ceases to exist if I remove my arm from contact with the table, the sound ceases to exist if I cease to rap the table with my knuckles. But I do not believe that when all these things cease the table ceases. On the contrary, I believe that it is because the table exists continuously that all these sense-data will reappear when I open my eyes, replace my arm, and begin again to rap with my knuckles. (13)

Russell believes that objects exist behind the veil of appearances in spite of our only having access to phenomenal data. This raises the next set of questions, which concern the nature of the external world and the nature of our understanding of it.

Russell offers a scientific analysis of the veil of perception and concludes that the laws of physics and the immediacy of sense-data can be reconciled if we talk in terms of real and apparent worlds. The 'apparent world' is how sensations appear to us, while the term 'real world' describes a realm beyond our senses from which sense-data emanate. Thus we may sense a light (part of the apparent world) which is, in fact, being produced by wave motion (part of the real world).

It becomes evident on reading the third chapter that Russell believes any reliance on direct sensory information is unphilosophical.

Russell's argument against direct realism may be summarised as follows:

1 An acquaintance with sense-data leads out of curiosity to scientific inquiry.

2 Scientific inquiry has yielded certain conclusions (e.g. that light, heat and sound are all due to wave motions).

3 These conclusions tell us that the ordinary, direct realist view of the material world is false.

4 Therefore, direct realism is misleading and false.

Russell draws a distinction between appearance and reality and equates everyday experience with the former and scientific enquiry with the latter. He extends this distinction to one between real and apparent space before going on to explore how the two categories are connected. Let us examine the examples he uses to help explain this notion. The first involves a coin lying on a table in his study. The author walks around the table observing the coin from many different angles. He concludes that it appears circular from an aerial perspective and elliptical from the various sideways sensations. From such an analysis he infers that the coin is indeed circular and notes that it is a feature of circular coins that they appear elliptical when viewed from the side. Such observations, Russell insists, are of apparent space whereas the conceptualisation of all coins as circular occurs in real space. The distinction is neo-Platonic with the ancient Greek philosopher illustrating the distinction between sensory perception and understanding by using the metaphor of two different spaces: inside and outside the cave. Real space is inhabited by physical objects while apparent space is populated by sensations. Our sensory organs provide a pathway between the two worlds. Our senses do not supply direct knowledge of the real world as is asserted by direct realists but a mediated commentary concerning the correspondence or relations of things. We do not see what is, but what is is what is seen.

Russell attempts to illustrate the difference between real and apparent space through an illustration about time. Let us continue with our poetic licence and imagine the guests at Russell's party. Some are entertained by his philosophical ramblings while others are bored senseless. For the interested guests, the time flies by, while for the uninterested audience, the hours pass at a snail's pace. In any case, the clock in the philosopher's study registers accurately how much time has elapsed. The guests' impressions of how long the party lasted represent the private, apparent world of sense-data whereas the clock corresponds to the public reality. There is an important correspondence between the clock and the personal conceptions of the guests as each looks up to check how much time has elapsed. They check to see how their sense-data correspond to the physical reality through public experience. Russell clearly believes that there is such a reality but he did not always hold such a view, having previously subscribed to the idealism of Bishop Berkeley. In the next chapter he lays these idealist ghosts to rest.

Idealism (Chapter 4)

The author's critique of the idealist theory of perception at this stage in the proceedings serves to bolster his own phenomenalist account of perception through exposing the inadequacies of a rival theory. Some readers have detected passages in the Berkeleyan canon that come close to phenomenalism, which makes this philosophy too close for comfort. Berkeley held that 'whatever can be known to exist, must be in some sense mental'. This sounds like Russell's own opening premise that our sensations and sense-data rely on us. For this reason Russell grants that Berkeley's reasoning thus far is 'valid'. He proceeds to expose the fallacious nature of the rest of the idealist argument, which irresponsibly moves to the conclusion that there is nothing beyond the sensory domain. In fact, throughout the four chapters we have so far commented on, a consistent motif has been the notion of causality and the notion that sense-data cannot have appeared from nowhere. (Philosophers of religion might be surprised to note this, given Russell's insistence that the cosmological argument is wrong in supporting a necessary cause for the universe.) Russell's intention in criticising Berkeley is to marry his own thesis to the scientific enterprise, while rejecting Berkeley's offering as eccentric, theistic and philosophically flawed. The author of *The Problems of Philosophy* formulates the following criticisms:

- Berkeley uses the word 'idea' in an ambiguous way. The method of close linguistic analysis adopted by the British analytic tradition has its origins in moves like this. Russell exposes two senses of the word 'idea' in Berkeley's writing. The first is as a unit of understanding, for example X has just thought about skunks, while the second is an object of thought, for example the smell of a skunk. Through confusing the object of thought with the act of understanding, Berkeley concludes erroneously that there is nothing apart from thoughts. For example, early on in the first dialogue[3] between Hylas and Philonous, the latter asks: 'Can you frame to yourself an idea of sensible pain or pleasure in general, abstracted from every particular idea of heat, cold, tastes, smells etc?' Hylas replies that he cannot, to which Philonous declares, 'doth it not therefore follow, that sensible pain is nothing distinct from those sensations or ideas?' The answer follows that this is undeniable and that such 'particular ideas' are thus purely mental.

- Berkeley asserts that there are two things in existence, the mind and its perceptions, yet physical accounts can be offered of both in terms of the brain as a bodily organ and perceptions being registered wave motion. Russell appeals to a more scientifically sophisticated readership.

- Implicit in Berkeleyan idealism is the confusion between judgement (knowledge that) and acquaintance (knowledge of). This distinction is the most important in the whole text and is expanded upon in Chapter 5.

> **Task**
>
> What were Berkeley's views on epistemology? Produce a poster presentation on Berkeley's philosophy with an image of the philosopher, a brief biography and an outline of his idealist theory of perception. What similarities and differences are there between Berkeley's account and that of Russell?

Knowledge by acquaintance and knowledge by description (Chapter 5)

The author, having distinguished between 'knowledge of things' and 'knowledge of truths' in the last pages of the fourth chapter, further divides these categories into subdivisions termed 'acquaintance' and 'description'. He then proceeds to distinguish between 'ambiguous' and 'definite' description later in this chapter as if he were mapping the forks in the road of his mountainous ascent. Let us summarise these epistemological distinctions diagrammatically for ease of reference (see figure 14.1).

Knowledge of truths is logically independent from the knowledge we gain from sense-data, which is termed variously in the text 'acquaintance' or 'knowledge of things'. I might happen upon a rare species of orchid on a mountain expedition and, in spite of my acquaintance gained from detailed study of the detail of its leaf shape, the colour of its petals and its delicate perfume, remain unsure as to what it is (knowledge of truth). For Russell, however, knowledge of things is a superior category to knowledge of truths as the former produces the latter and is of greater certainty. This gives Russell his fundamental epistemological principle which influenced the school of logical positivism: 'Every proposition which we can understand must be composed wholly of constituents with which we are acquainted' (32).

The world of abstract universals, explored in the ninth chapter, is essentially different from acquaintance and consists in inferential pieces of reasoning. Knowledge of things is *a posteriori* whereas knowledge of truths is *a priori*. Let us leave the *a priori* category of universals until they are explored thoroughly in Chapters 8, 9 and 10 and first explore knowledge of things.

Certain features of acquaintance are recorded: it is essentially a simpler type of knowledge than the others and is logically independent from knowledge of truths. Acquaintance is the product of direct awareness but does not involve inference and does not provide any clues as to the essence of the 'acquaintee'. Nevertheless, acquaintance is awarded pride of place as the foundation of truth.

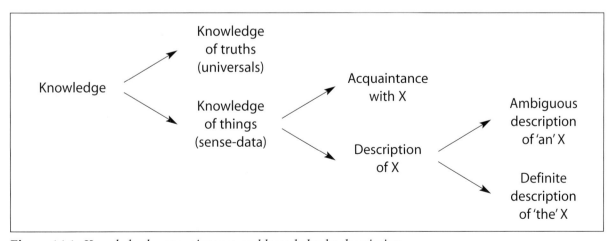

Figure 14.1 *Knowledge by acquaintance and knowledge by description*

Five types of acquaintance are identified in Chapter 5:

- acquaintance with sense-data, the foundation of our knowledge;
- acquaintance with past experience – that is, memory;
- acquaintance through introspection, e.g. the sensation of desires such as lust;
- acquaintance with 'self', very cautiously defined as that which is acquainted with sense-data;
- acquaintance with universals – that is, abstract ideas (enlarged upon in Chapter 9).

To return to the orchid example again, when I first catch sight of this beautiful alpine flower, I am confronted with a set of sensations containing sense-data. This pleasant memory might occur to me at some time in the future when once again I experience the same sense-data, presented to what Wordsworth called 'the inner eye'. I am aware of both the delight that this memory brings and am self-consciously aware that I am aware. In turn, I understand that all orchids are flowers. When, on completing my mountain trek, I return to my cabin and look up the plant in an encyclopaedia of flowers, then I am in search of a description. I do not expect to find a definite description of the exact flower I saw that very morning on a particular slope, but my curiosity is slaked by an indefinite description of the type of plant species (Russell terms this category 'ambiguous description'). In reverse, I might have been browsing through this book in a moment of leisure and developed knowledge that there is in existence some such plant that fits the general description. Despite not having ever seen one, I know through description that such a species exists.

Knowledge from acquaintance is a far more reliable category than knowledge by description as it is based on the phenomena of experience. Indeed, Russell believes that his version of phenomenalism provides the most successful antidote to scepticism out of all the theories of perception. From knowledge by acquaintance and knowledge by description, there exists a sliding epistemic scale that Russell indicates with an example of his own involving the first

German Chancellor Otto von Bismarck (1815–1898). If one were to meet this esteemed Prussian, then one may be described as having knowledge by acquaintance; because of his illustrious career you may be called 'well acquainted'. If however, you learn facts about him from news reports or via a friend's account, then, given the fact that what you hear is true, you may be said to have knowledge by description. We will never get to meet Bismarck but can only learn about him from history books. This is also an example of knowledge by description but exists further down the scale and, as it is further removed from acquaintance, is less reliable. There is always the chance of a psychotic historian making up information. A more technical problem is created for our author, however, in the shape of sentences that seem to be authentic knowledge by acquaintance, such as 'Bismarck was born in 1815', but which contain imaginary descriptions. Russell's common-sense philosophy of language asserts:

1 Any sentence that is not nonsense has significance.
2 Any significant sentence has semantic value.
3 If a sentence as a whole has semantic value then each of its constituent expressions must have semantic value.
4 The semantic value of a sentence is related to what the sentence refers to.
5 If any sentence containing a singular term is to have semantic value then the singular term must refer to something.

Thus in our example above one can equate the definite descriptions 'Bismarck' and '1815' to something that can be traced back to sense-data. But what if one is confronted with the following example: 'The king of the world is a lizard'? The Austrian psychologist and philosopher Alexius Meinong (1853–1920) suggests a realm of non-existent things that are nevertheless capable of being the objects of thought and in which the above 'king of the world' would live. Russell rejects this theory and instead asserts that such sentences as the example cited above, in spite of appearing to be a normal subject–predicate type of sentence, do not share the same logical form.

In order to expose this, the proposition needs to be broken down into three separable components:

1 There is at least one thing that is 'the king of the world'.
2 There is at most one thing that is 'the king of the world'.
3 Whatever thing 'the king of the world' is is a lizard.

Russell's theory is empiricist and we are invited at this stage to sport binoculars and go and test the claims contained above. We will, of course, conclude that there is no such person as the king of the world and thus reject the validity of the premises. In such a way Russell founds all knowledge by description on knowledge by acquaintance.

Review question

Outline Russell's phenomenalist theory of perception.

On induction (Chapter 6)

Knowledge by acquaintance, as outlined by Russell in Chapter 5, consists of our experience of sense-data as mediated through experience. The problem of **induction**, an age-old philosophical conundrum first described by Hume in the eighteenth century, holds that we have no assurance that the same flash cards of experience will occur in a similar situation in the future, nor can we be guaranteed the same sequences of experience as have pertained in the past. Russell illustrates this point through two meteorological examples. The first involves the co-existence of thunder and lightning, where we expect one to follow the other. In a strictly logical sense, however, there is no necessary relationship between the sudden bolt of lightning and the rumble of thunder. It is only owing to the fact that we are familiar with one event following the other that we come to expect the same pattern. This is likened by the author to conditioning in animals when, through an unwavering adherence to routine, the animal comes to expect the same sequence. Thus, if you stop your pony and trap every time you pass a pub on the way home, the animal in the end stops for you whether you desire a drink or not.

Russell has to be careful here, as he has relied on the role of subjective instinct, which he terms 'natural' and 'intrinsic' in earlier chapters. If he then condemns an instinct for induction, it would seem inconsistent. But such a problem would shoot his theory of knowledge out of the water, because if we admit to not being able to make any necessary connections then we cannot talk meaningfully about the relation of different sense-data nor can we suppose that the same physical objects are causing the sense-data from behind the screen of phenomena. The author avoids these apparent pitfalls by arguing that induction is a matter of probability and that probability is not concerned with proof. He offers the following epistemological principles, quoted in full, to explain how induction is concerned with offering the most likely occurrence in a given situation:

1 The greater number of cases in which a thing of the sort A has been found associated with a thing of the sort B, the more probable it is that A is always associated with B (if no cases of failure of association are known).
2 Under the same circumstances, a sufficient number of cases of the association of A and B will make it nearly certain that A is always associated with B, and will make this general law approach certainty without limit (37).

Russell goes on to explain what is meant by a general law in the next chapter but is satisfied at this stage in the work to accept induction as a useful means to divine association that brings us closer to certainty. Russell is adamant that this application of probability does not constitute in any way an explanation for what is occurring. Thus the man who has only seen white swans is justified in expecting the next swan he sees to be white, as he cannot be expected to calculate that some swans are black on the evidence presented to him. We are condemned to wander the mountainside as tourists, observing its flora and fauna of sense-data without ever understanding anything beyond. This is something we have to accept.

On our knowledge of general principles (Chapter 7)

Russell is now in search of general principles that may be extracted from an analysis of phenomena through acquaintance. These general principles hold in the vale of sense-data but never pertain to the mysterious reality beyond. They nevertheless provide a category of truths that we can be as certain about as our experiences. Three examples of general principles are cited:

- mathematical truths
- self-evident logical principles
- knowledge of ethical value.

If we have sat through enough episodes of *Sesame Street* as children then we will realise that the simple laws of arithmetic hold in any given number of situations involving cookies, children or muppets. And if we award epistemological credence to the principle of induction then why should we exclude mathematics? And if mathematics, why not the laws of logic? Russell gives the example of the following simple inference:

1 If yesterday was the 15th then today is the 16th.

2 Yesterday was the 15th.

3 Therefore, today must be the 16th.

The most important word in this deduction is the word 'if' as it admits the limits of our knowledge. There may be all sorts of evil demons at work to create a matrix of consciousness that differs from reality. This does not affect Russellian epistemology, however, as we are only awarding status to experiences and corresponding general principles. We are not commenting on their eternal and actual validity. The author continues to provide other examples from formal logic, which he terms 'the laws of thought', though he clarifies this description in Chapter 8. They include:

- The law of identity: that whatever exists exists.
- The law of contradiction: nothing can both exist and not exist.
- The law of the excluded middle: everything must either exist or not exist.

Task

Discuss the above laws. Are they absolutely beyond sceptical challenge? Can you think of any exceptions to any one of them, for instance when something exists and does not exist at the same time?

This discussion takes place within the traditional debate among philosophers between empiricism and rationalism (see chapter 1). Russell is suitably diplomatic in his adjudication:

> Thus, while admitting that all knowledge is elicited and caused by experience, we shall nevertheless hold that some knowledge is *a priori*, in the sense that the experience which makes us think of it does not suffice to prove it, but merely so directs our attention that we see its truth without requiring any proof from experience. (41)

Russell recognises the role of reason in organising the knowledge gained from acquaintance and description while at the same time he draws our attention to the fact that *a posteriori* foundations lie at the base of such knowledge (the role of *a priori* knowledge is dealt with by the author in his analysis of Kant in Chapter 8).

There remains for us only to mention the third strain of general principle held by Russell to be authoritative and bear the hallmark of certainty and that is knowledge of moral value. Russell's moral philosophy is close to that of the Cambridge philosopher G. E. Moore (1873–1958) and is generally described as **ethical subjectivism**. It is the view that all moral statements are self-generated expressions of our personal convictions. Russell's meta-ethical theory is the precursor to emotivism and prescriptivism. But, despite categorising moral judgements as factually meaningless like these offshoots, Russell stresses the importance of ethical intuition, which he believes acquaints us with how we should or should not behave. Such

For the extensive seventy-year period when Bertrand Russell was academically active, he was well known in the media and the popular imagination as Britain's foremost philosopher. Having achieved widespread recognition in intellectual circles with the publication of *Principia Mathematica* between 1910 and 1913, Russell gained notoriety for his liberal views on politics, religion and education in writings such as *Marriage and Morals* (1929) and *Why I Am Not a Christian* (1957). He campaigned fervently against nuclear weapons and was often pictured on news broadcasts and, slightly incongruously, at sit-ins and demonstrations. On one occasion, when Russell had been arrested, the officer in charge of recording his personal details asked him his occupation. On replying 'philosopher', he was asked by the curious policeman, 'What does a philosopher do then?' Russell replied with sonorous gravitas, 'I think'. On another occasion when the wife of the American poet T. S. Eliot was in a London taxi, the cab driver began the conversation by saying, 'I had that Bertrand Russell in my cab the other day. I asked him the meaning of life, and do you know the bugger couldn't tell me'. Such was the style of Russell's philosophy with its anti-metaphysical bias. He influenced the logical positivist school and the Anglo-Saxon analytic tradition, of which he is often described as the founding father. Russell appeared as a gaunt, silver-haired Cambridge don who enjoyed taking afternoon tea in the Orchard Tearoom in Grantchester and dining at high table in Trinity College.

Significant works
Principia Mathematica (1910–1913)
The Problems of Philosophy (1912)
A History of Western Philosophy (1945)

a conviction was translated into the philosopher's life and he became an active campaigner for nuclear disarmament in the 1960s. Although he admits morality to the factually nonsensical camp, he grants that we possess a 'non-logical *a priori* knowledge' that tells us what is ethically valuable.

How *a priori* knowledge is possible (Chapter 8)

Russell has shown so far that we acquire knowledge from direct acquaintance with sense-data and indirect knowledge from descriptions of sense-data. He points out at this stage that we can possess knowledge of the relationship between sense-data or phenomena through reason, and asks to what sort of knowledge this second category belongs. Might it be viewed as unadulterated *a priori* knowledge? He draws on Kant's metaphysical system for inspiration, reminding the reader that pre-Kantian

epistemology viewed all knowledge as belonging to one of two groups:

- knowledge gained through reason, e.g. tautologies such as 'All bald men are bald';
- knowledge gained through experience, e.g. 'We are born to die'.

Kant's reworking of the first category recognised that in the case of mathematical expressions such as $7 + 5 = 12$, the truth is not contained within the statement as it is in logically necessary propositions and is consequently not a purely analytic sentence. One needs first of all to become acquainted with what '5', '+', '7', '=' and '12' actually designate. Kant was strongly influenced by Hume's work on causality and believed that the proposition 'Every event has a cause' fell into a similar classification. Thus for Kant there are three types of knowledge, with a third category added to the previous two, namely synthetic *a priori* knowledge.

Russell adopts Kant's metaphysical categories of noumena (things in themselves) and phenomena (things as they appear) but disagrees with Kant over the nature of our perception of sense-data. Whereas Kant, following the rationalist tradition, believed that the human mind organises sense-data into categories such as time and space, Russell held the view that our minds only register the phenomena as they appear to us. Russell's contribution is to deny the existence of pure *a priori* truth altogether. He reminds us that the thing-in-itself or, to borrow the Kantian nomenclature, the noumena, cannot be known, as only the phenomena, that veil of experience between us and the existing world, can be analysed meaningfully. This analysis does not involve any metaphysical tricks of the mind but a straightforward reading off of the sense-data.

Russell disagrees with Kant over the nature of *a priori* statements, arguing that our minds are as much part of the material world as any of the noumena and hence may be subject to change; we might wake up tomorrow and conceive that $2 + 2 = 5$. *A priori* truths assert something unchanging, however, and should rightly be attached to the phenomenal world whose relations they describe. Assertions such as 'All bald men are bald' and '$2 + 2 = 4$' are only truths because of the phenomena represented and not through any independent reasoning. The same applies to the so-called laws of thought already listed, which are, of course, not about thought but about phenomena:

> Thus the law of contradiction is about things, and not merely about thoughts; and although belief in the law of contradiction is a thought, the law of contradiction itself is not a thought, but a fact concerning the things in the world. (50)

For the author, all *a priori* statements refer to the world of sensation and sense-data, perhaps less obviously in the case of logical formulae than the explicit Cartesian example 'Every mountain has a valley', yet without exception. If you want to know about pure thought, then you have to enter a different realm altogether: the world of universals.

Task

What did Kant say about our perception and interpretation of the external world? Produce a poster presentation about Kant's epistemology. Include an image of the philosopher, a brief biography and an outline of Kant's theory of perception. What similarities and differences are there between Kant's account and that of Russell?

The world of universals (Chapter 9)

Following his analysis in Chapter 8, Russell reiterates the question, 'What kind of a thing is *a priori* knowledge?' The answer is that *a priori* knowledge 'deals exclusively with the relations of universals' (59). The meaning of the Russellian term 'universal' is much the same as Plato's notion of forms. Russell gives credit to Plato and resurrects the ancient Greek philosopher's 'one over the many' argument, which describes many of the same things sharing one essence. Russell is fascinated with what sort of a thing this essence is and whether it is indeed, as Plato believes, more real than the particulars or phenomena of day-to-day experience. Some of Plato's epistemology is given a twentieth-century make-over and a linguistic sheen. Let us call Russell's neo-Platonic defence of the forms the 'argument from relations', and see how it explains the realm of pure thought.

Russell has already established that particular phenomena exist and that relations exist between such sense-data. He cites as evidence the existence of prepositions in the language we use to describe one set of sense-data coming after another or certain phenomena existing alongside others. Many verbs and adjectives have the same function. For Russell, the study of philosophy has been too long obsessed with the existence of nouns and their properties, asking questions such as 'Does God exist?' or 'What action is right?' Metaphysically this has led to two belief systems known as **monism** and **monadism**. The first holds that there is only one substance of which the universe consists, and the second, while admitting that there might be more than one substance, is determined that no relations exist between such substances. The author of *The*

Problems of Philosophy believes that this is blatantly untrue as we are confronted with a multitude of sense-data every day, which suggests at least one material cause behind them.

Russell wants to explore the relations between phenomena and to focus on the nature of such relations. One such interconnection between particulars is resemblance, for example the resemblance between all things that happen to be white.[4] Resemblance is an example of a relation between phenomena; another might be triangularity. Both are examples of what Russell terms 'universals'. Universals are understood through the medium of thought. Thus we establish in our minds a link between one phenomenon that is white and the set of sense-data that we have previously categorised as white. Terms which describe relations between sense-data, such as 'is white' or 'is north of', are firmly rooted in the phenomenal world, yet the relationship they outline would still exist if there were no one there to perceive it. Towards the end of Chapter 8 the author distinguishes between the world of existence and the world of being. The world of existence is the phenomenal world of sense-data, whereas the world of being is a realm that is inhabited by universals: the relations between sense-data.

On our knowledge of universals (Chapter 10)

Russell's epistemology as outlined in the tenth chapter of *The Problems of Philosophy* synthesises the distinction detailed in the fifth and ninth chapters. We learnt in Chapter 5 that knowledge of sense-data can be gained through first-hand acquaintance and also through description. In addition, Russell explained in Chapter 9 that there are abstract relations between sense-data that he terms 'universals'. He begins the tenth chapter by announcing that the same distinction applies to universals as applies to sense-data. Russell's terminology varies slightly throughout the text and he loosely calls sense-data 'phenomena', 'objects', 'substantives' and 'particulars'. As we cannot ever access the noumenal world beyond sense-data, we can only talk meaningfully about sense-data (particulars)

and their relations (universals). How then does the acquaintance–description distinction apply to universals?

Russell bombards the reader with a plethora of *a priori* examples to illustrate his answer to this question. He begins by reminding us of what sort of universal relations there are:

- *Sensible qualities:* this is the most immediate universal according to Russell, who uses the example of all white particulars sharing the property of whiteness and hence having this connection.

- *Universal relations in space:* Russell reminds us that he is still at work in his study by illustrating universal relations in space by the position of text on a page. Thus some words might be to the right or left of others.

- *Universal relations in time:* perhaps the chime of a college clock resounding over the tranquillity of Trinity College inspired the author's third example of the relation of particulars (the chimes) to time.

- *The relation of relations:* thus having established relations between two sets of two particulars, one is at liberty to compare the relations themselves. For example, one might say that the contrast between the shades of these two beech trees is greater than that between these two birch trees.

Having reminded us of his theory of universals, the author returns to the problem of defining *a priori* knowledge and bravely issues the following hypothesis: 'All *a priori* knowledge deals exclusively with the relations of universals'.

In truly scientific fashion, the best way of testing a hypothesis is to disprove it and the only way that the philosopher can think of disproving the above is to show that, in fact, through the medium of pure thought, one can work out that 'all of one class of particulars belong to some other class'. If Russell succeeds then the rationalists were right all along and there is a category of pure *a priori* knowledge. If he cannot, then Russell is vindicated and he has shown that:

1 *A priori* knowledge is concerned exclusively with the relations of universals.

2 One establishes the relations of universals through an empirical study of sense-data.

3 Sense-data are the foundations of our knowledge.

There is almost an audible drum roll as Russell appears on stage to pull his epistemological rabbit out of a hat, but notice that to prove his theory correct he must fail in this task. He does this admirably. Thus in the classic example of 2 + 2 = 4, we do not learn anything apart from the fact that any couple of items added to any other couple makes a foursome and no further details. In addition we have established a general rule that makes it unnecessary to keep checking empirically, although the relation is grounded in empirical observation. Similarly we can cite as *a priori* the proposition 'All men are mortal' in light of evidence in its support and lack of evidence to the contrary. It is, at this stage, unnecessary to keep testing the statement through acquaintance when we have so much inductive data and can now cite the proposition as an instance of knowledge by description. From such detailed descriptions we can even work out *a priori* propositions that do not have any instances. Russell gives the examples of multiplication tables and infinity. There is an air that loose ends are being tied up and the discussion is coming to an end. In fact, there are five more chapters to go, but we shall conclude this commentary with an overall look at Russell's thoughts on the nature of the philosophical enterprise.

Review question

Outline Russell's account of *a priori* knowledge and explain what is meant by the term 'universal'.

Task

What similarities and differences are there between Russell's theory of universals and Plato's theory of forms?

The limitations of philosophical knowledge (Chapter 14)

There follows some propaganda on behalf of the British analytic tradition. It singles out the metaphysics of Hegel and Kant for special treatment as examples of how not to proceed. Russell's argument is that any philosophy grounded in our experience of phenomena, as is presented in this text, which was written as an introduction to the discipline, is incompatible with metaphysics. He has already proved that all knowledge is rooted in the sense-data we perceive and that even universal relations, which he terms 'pure *a priori*' in Chapter 14, are in fact not instances of pure reasoning but extrapolations from the phenomenal world. It can only be a flagrant breach of truth then to adopt any system of belief that professes 'metaphysical reasoning, such things as the fundamental dogmas of religion, the essential rationality of the universe, the illusoriness of matter, the unreality of all evil, and so on'.

The eighteenth-century German metaphysician Friedrich Hegel appears to have committed most of these crimes. His philosophy had already been slated by Marx in the previous century (see chapter 12) and Russell adds his own criticisms in this volume. Russell eloquently outlines the gist of Hegel's argument that we can construct an absolute picture of reality through the course of history by adopting the method of dialectic. Thus thoughts are incomplete and need to be synthesised with their opposite (the antithesis) in order for us to advance closer to the ultimate, harmonious truth, which is non-spatial, timeless, devoid of evil and amounts to a god's-eye view of everything. As one can see, this is a far cry from Russell's philosophy of what you see is what you get! The author explains such a grandiose system as fulfilling a very human need for security in the form of *ad personam* answers to the big questions. This is not the function of philosophy for Russell, who declares that science and philosophy are engaged in the same sort of enterprise.

Russell criticises Hegel for arguing from the natures of things and not from an acquaintance with observable phenomena. Thus for the German metaphysician there is something within the nature of an incomplete abstraction that links with its opposite, that in turn links with its synthesis, that in turn links with absolute reality. Russell likens this procedure to someone scaling a rock-face with grappling irons. It has been proved, however, that the only links or 'relations' that can be established are between reliable descriptions and that which is described through universals. One cannot move from acquaintance to metaphysical speculation to the nature of that which is known: 'thus we are left to the piecemeal investigation of the world, and are unable to know the characters of those parts of the universe that are remote from our experience'.

Kant also receives a reprimand from Russell, who contradicts his notion that space and time are illusory properties, imposed on phenomena by our minds. The author points out that mathematics has proved the possibility of infinity in space and time and hence reduced any objections to unfounded mental prejudices typical of metaphysicians. He is also at pains to point out that this way of philosophising is not dull in being limited to the realm of sense-data and their relations. In fact, this view is exactly wrong, as logic engages with hypothetical worlds in which sense-data might be arranged in different ways. The American David Lewis (1941–2001) is one philosopher in the analytic tradition who explored this avenue in greater depth.

The closing chapter of *The Problems of Philosophy* contains some reflections on the value of the philosophical enterprise. This is a challenging question that philosophers need to answer in order to justify their continued role. Admittedly, philosophers' adversaries will look for some material benefits from this cerebral and abstract discipline, but the question remains: 'What does philosophy add?' Russell suggests that:

- Philosophy acts as a meta-science ordering and unifying scientific knowledge like a benign, though at times convoluted, filing system.

- Philosophy trains the mind to avoid fallacies, poor reasoning and 'the prejudices derived from common sense, from the habitual beliefs of [one's] age or [one's nation]' (91).

- Philosophy, through its inevitable uncertainty and contemplation of the unsolvable, generates a sense of wonder and awe and encourages intellectual creativity.

Task

One of the skills gained through studying philosophy is the ability to argue convincingly. Organise a formal debate in which there are both advocates and adversaries of philosophy. To hone your debating technique, you could choose the side that least represents your personal opinion, e.g. if you are a fan of philosophy try attacking it as a pretentious and worthless waste of time. Did you arrive at any further apologetic arguments in favour of the subject that were overlooked by Russell?

Revision questions

1 Outline and explain the difference between sensation, sense-data and physical objects.

2 Assess Russell's phenomenalist theory of perception.

3 Evaluate Russell's treatment of inductive principles.

4 Outline and explain two examples of universals used by Russell in *The Problems of Philosophy*.

5 Outline and explain the difference between knowledge by acquaintance and knowledge by description.

Discussion questions

■ How would the views of Russell and Berkeley differ as to the nature of the oval table in the former's study?

■ Assess the view that Russell's philosophy is closer to empiricism than rationalism?

■ How successful are Russell's arguments for the existence of matter?

■ How much does Russell's theory of universals have in common with Plato's theory of forms?

■ Does Russell make a convincing case for the value of philosophy?

Glossary of key terms

Ethical subjectivism: the meta-ethical theory expounded by Russell. It holds that moral statements are value judgements but nevertheless meaningful.

Idealism: the view, popularised by George Berkeley, that all existent substances are mental – that is, only our ideas and our minds exist.

Induction: the process of reasoning by which sense-data are collected from particular instances and used to predict forthcoming patterns of events.

Matter: the name given to the physical objects or the external world in contrast to the realm of sense-data. This is not a neutral term for Russell as in his preliminary chapter he criticises idealists who assert that there is no such thing as matter.

Monadism: the belief, advanced by Leibniz in his *Monadology* (1714), that the universe is conceivably made up of more than one substance but that such substances cannot relate to each other.

Monism: the belief that the universe is made up of a single substance whether mental or physical. Contrary theories such as dualism depend on there being more than one.

Phenomenalism: the theory of perception that holds that we can only talk meaningfully about our direct sensory experiences.

Sensations: the medium through which sense-data are presented to the human mind in the act of perception.

Sense-data (singular: sense-datum): the individual colours, shapes, textures, aromas or sounds that we experience. This is the world of phenomena or appearances from which the most fundamental kind of knowledge is gained.

Universals: expressions of the abstract relations between sense-data.

Suggested reading

- Baggini, J. (2002) *Philosophy Key Texts*, Basingstoke, Palgrave
  This compendium has a chapter on *The Problems* and a useful bibliography
- Bell, B. R. (1972) *Bertrand Russell*, London, Lutterworth Press
  An introduction to Russell's philosophy in the Modern Masters series
- Berkeley, G. (1988) *Principles of Knowledge and Three Dialogues*, London, Penguin
  A familiarity with this work aids an understanding of Chapter 4 of *The Problems of Philosophy*
- Grayling, A. C. (1996) *Russell*, Oxford, OUP
  Standard introduction to Russell's philosophy in the Past Masters series
- Pears, D. F. (1972) *Bertrand Russell and the British Tradition in Philosophy*, London, Fontana
  This work cites Russell in the context of analytic philosophy

Notes

1 Russell, B. (1993) *A History of Western Philosophy*, London, Routledge, p. 138.

2 Russell, B. (1998) *The Problems of Philosophy*, Oxford, OUP, p. 10; hereafter page references to *The Problems of Philosophy* are given in brackets and refer to this edition.

3 Students of Russell will find an acquaintance with Berkeley a useful asset. Start with *Three Dialogues between Hylas and Philonous* edited by Roger Woolhouse.

4 Plato, *Meno* 74.

15 A commentary on Ayer's *Language, Truth and Logic*

The traditional disputes of philosophers are, for the most part, as unwarranted as they are unfruitful. (A. J. Ayer)

Aims

On completion of this chapter you should be able to:

- evaluate Ayer's views on the nature of philosophy as analysis
- evaluate the verification principle, its formulation and uses
- describe what is meant by 'linguistic phenomenalism'
- understand the distinction between explicit and in-use definitions
- describe Ayer's treatment of induction
- evaluate Ayer's account of *a priori* knowledge
- evaluate Ayer's view of the status of science and mathematics
- evaluate the emotivist theory of ethics and aesthetics
- evaluate Ayer's criticisms of metaphysics and theology
- outline Ayer's criticisms of other philosophers.

The author of *Language, Truth and Logic* sets about his task with the evangelical fervency of a new convert. One biographer describes his intention as follows:

> A lot of anger and revolutionary zeal went into the writing of *Language, Truth and Logic*, and its arguments had very radical practical implications: if they were accepted, religion would wither away, ideology would perish, science would flourish, social hierarchies would collapse, and, Ayer hoped, people would become more sceptical in their moral convictions, more tolerant of others' points of view.[1]

Ayer's enthusiasm, however, led to a number of errors and consequently *Language, Truth and Logic* has been an undergraduate punch-bag for philosophical generations since its first publication in 1936. Few thinkers would sign up to the view that this work was a faultless textbook of logical positivism, yet to condemn Ayer, as Sartre did, as a conman would be to ignore the wider importance and impact of the school of philosophical thought known as the analytic tradition.

The elimination of metaphysics (Chapter 1)

Ayer's aim in writing *Language, Truth and Logic* was to rid **philosophy** of its anti-scientific prejudice and ensure it had a more secure status. His aim was to sort all philosophical thought into two groups labelled 'sense' and 'nonsense', and, in true Humean fashion, to burn the latter. He declares in the first chapter: 'For our object is merely to show that philosophy, as a genuine branch of knowledge, must be distinguished from metaphysics'.[2]

Ayer does not only wish to draw our attention to the fact that one cannot argue from empirical premises to a metaphysical conclusion, but that any metaphysical statement, of any shape or form, is factually nonsensical. In the field of ethics, for instance, Ayer's argument is not just that we cannot move from a fact to a value (see section on the is–ought controversy in chapter 2), but that values are of a suspect nature by virtue of being values.

Alfred Jules Ayer
(1910–1989)

A. J. Ayer's father was a Swiss Calvinist and his mother came from a Dutch Jewish family. He always felt like an outsider in the upper echelons of English society. Having enjoyed a privileged education at Eton and Oxford, he courageously joined the Welsh Guards in 1939 and later worked for the Secret Service in Africa, the USA and France. The Second World War marked a life-changing experience for the young philosopher, who continued to travel extensively throughout the rest of his life. Accounts report him to be self-absorbed, precocious and dispassionate, as well as being a charismatic companion and inspirational teacher. These traits prompted Wittgenstein's disparaging remark that 'Freddie Ayer is clever all the time'. Ayer enjoyed a hedonistic lifestyle of drinking, dancing and womanising and is reported to have had around 150 love affairs in the course of his life. As a point of trivia, Ayer's third wife was the mother of TV chef Nigella Lawson.

There are many stories about Ayer: at one notorious party he is supposed to have single-handedly intervened to stop Mike Tyson assaulting Naomi Campbell. Descriptions at the time, however, were more mundane:

> [Ayer] was told at a party that Mike Tyson was upstairs raping a model. 'We can't have that', he said, and forged upstairs only to find that Tyson was talking quietly to the model and that she was clearly delighted. Not having any grounds to intervene, but feeling that it would be ignominious to retreat, he said, 'Mr Tyson, you're the physical champion of the world and I am one of the intellectual champions. I think it's high time that we met.' (*The Tatler* December 1988 – January 1989)

To many he will be remembered as the scientifically minded thinker who sought to rid philosophy of unfounded **metaphysics**. To others, closer to him, he will be remembered as a loyal Spurs supporter who exuded *joie de vivre*, loved puzzles and danced a mean samba.

Significant works
Language, Truth and Logic (1936)
The Problem of Knowledge (1956)
The Central Questions of Philosophy (1972)

Ayer uses a linguistic test, known as the principle of verification, to distinguish between fruitful subjects for philosophers to study and unfruitful cul-de-sacs. Ayer is by no means a nihilist – that is, someone who believes that there is no meaning to life – but a linguistic philosopher who concludes that the question 'What is the meaning of life?' is nonsensical. His approach was shaped by Wittgenstein's famous remark at the end of his *Tractatus Logico Philosophicus*: 'whereof one cannot speak, thereof one must remain silent'. Ayer was also influenced by the anti-metaphysical bias of the Vienna Circle, especially Moritz Schlick. The Vienna Circle consisted of a number of Viennese scientists and mathematicians who were interested in philosophy but who sought to rid the subject of unprovable make-believe.

Ayer's method rests on the following *reductio ad absurdum*:

1 Knowledge claims are either experiential or deductive.
2 If claim X is neither experiential nor deductive then it is not a claim to knowledge and may be termed 'factually nonsensical'.

By 'experiential', Ayer means that the claim may be proved true by sensory experience, perhaps by means of experiment. By 'deductive', Ayer means that which can be proved true through the laws of logic. In the tradition of philosophical discourse, the author tries to predict his opponents' replies so as to advance counter-arguments in order to strengthen his position. Two criticisms from potential opponents are examined. The first is the notion of intellectual **empiricism**, an epistemic sixth sense that enables you to judge the truth of a statement without recourse to experience or logic. The second argument holds that even if the philosopher is right and methods other than the empirical are misguided then it still doesn't prove the non-existence of metaphysical realities such as God, objective moral truth or the soul. Ayer responds by detailing his intention in this work to analyse the conclusions of arguments, whether produced by intuition or not. He then issues a modal defence of his position (see chapter 1), stating that it is a law of logic that we cannot move from a general discussion about what is possible to conclusions about what is necessarily true. To assert that God, objective moral truths and a soul may exist does not entail that they do exist.

The author's promise to analyse the conclusions of arguments epitomises the linguistic methodology adopted throughout the text and one which he contrasts with the method adopted by Immanuel Kant. Kant distinguished between a realm of experience (the phenomenal world) and a realm of essences (the noumenal world) and, like Ayer, held that you could not infer something about one from a feature of the other. Kant, however, stated this as a matter of fact rather than as a matter of logic and is criticised by Ayer for straying beyond the bounds of meaning into metaphysics. Ayer borrows Hume's fork to dig over past philosophy. And in so doing unearths Kant's exception to Hume's fork, the synthetic *a priori*, which is examined later in the fourth chapter of *Language, Truth and Logic*. In pursuing the line he does, Ayer hopes to avoid Wittgenstein's criticism that any distinction between empirical facts and **tautologies** entails an experience of both realms, which one clearly hasn't got. He also hopes to spurn the gauntlet thrown down by the moral philosopher F. C. Bradley (1846–1924) that one cannot disprove metaphysics without at the same time advancing a metaphysical theory. It is by no

means clear that the author ever succeeds in avoiding this second refutation. Indeed, to engage in any epistemological enterprise is to engage with general truth claims that lie beyond the phenomenal and the physical. If truth is acquired through language, logic and experience, in order to avoid the accusation that meaning is metaphysical, then Ayer would have to assert that truth is contained in these things in the same way that eliminativists argue that thoughts are contained in brain waves. Ayer appears to give scant regard to such a project.

Ayer continues with a brief synopsis of the verification principle, which sets out the criteria of a statement's truthfulness. Take any putative (that is, conjectured or hypothetical) proposition, and ask whether it is empirically verifiable (provable through experiment) or tautological (true by definition). If the answer is affirmative in either one case or the other, then the statement may be said to possess literal significance. An example of an empirically verifiable statement might be: 'Calcium burns with a brick red flame'. This proposition can be proved true or false by burning the appropriate substance and noting the result. The statement 'Calcium burns with a brick red flame' is, therefore, factually meaningful. An example of a tautology or logically necessary statement might be 'Bachelors are unmarried men'. This proposition, in English or any other language, is known to be true, from definition, by anyone acquainted with the meaning of the words. If a proposition does not fall into these two categories then it is judged by the verification theory to be a pseudo-proposition and, though it may possess emotional significance, does not possess literal significance.

Ayer honeymooned in Vienna in 1932 and was invited to meetings of the Vienna Circle, a group of philosophers with scientific backgrounds who sought to eliminate metaphysics from philosophy. His relationship with logical positivism lasted a lifetime, unlike his marriage to Renée Lees. Ayer possessed only rudimentary German and a basic scientific knowledge, but was seduced by the apparent certainty of their approach. One member of the Vienna Circle, a rotund polymath named Otto Neurath, would regularly interrupt the discussions with cries of 'Metaphysics!' if he thought that the speaker was straying into unscientific waters. Another member, the physicist Moritz Schlick, impressed Ayer greatly. Ayer sought to graft the methods of the Vienna Circle onto the diseased branches of British philosophy. He uses one of Schlick's examples of a meaningful statement in the first chapter: 'There are mountains on the farther side of the moon.' This statement awaits justification but may be classed as meaningful in the knowledge that one day it may be empirically tested (as it could be in 1969 when men landed on the moon). Schlick's example draws a distinction between what is verifiable in principle and what is verifiable in practice. Ayer distances himself from the strong **verificationism** of Schlick in allowing the inclusion of the laws of science in the factually meaningful realm. Schlick, contrariwise, believes that such laws cannot conclusively be established through raw experience or discrete observation and thus terms them 'an important kind of nonsense'. Ayer is more convincing in respect of his inclusion of general propositions which can be empirically verifiable somewhere down the line, such as scientific laws and historical facts. He is aware that the verification principle will judge many propositions meaningless if applied in the strong sense of that which we conclusively prove to be true. Instead, Ayer's weaker form of verificationism is more in keeping with his philosophical hero David Hume's views on **induction**, namely that 'that which is proved to be true beyond reasonable doubt is meaningful'. It is sufficient to judge a statement true according to probability.

The fact that Ayer's verificationism stretches to general laws is illustrated in three examples: 'Arsenic is poisonous', 'All men are mortal' and 'A body tends to expand when it is heated'. General propositions of law cannot be granted the status of an analytic proposition due to being, at best, inductive. There is always the slightest chance that an exception to the law exists. To take the above examples, it does not require a particularly imaginative cast of mind to envisage a state of affairs where our blood has evolved an immunity

to arsenic, a scientific researcher genetically reverses the ageing process, or creates a strange substance in which the lattices of atoms contract rather than expand when heated. It is conceivable that exceptions to every rule exist and it is an impossible task to test for every contingency. Similarly propositions about the remote past contain so many testimonies and revisions that we cannot award them the same ranking as tautologies. Nevertheless, the above propositions seem to possess significance through being probable. A third category exists in the form of statements that are confutable (proved false) by experience, for example 'Calcium burns with a green flame'. Such statements are judged possible though not definitive, in so far as circumstances may occur when a previously confuted hypothesis becomes true. To assert that there are future circumstances when calcium might burn with a green flame, and not a red flame as it does at present, is not to assert a logical contradiction. Yet one would have to term such assertions 'possible' rather than 'probable'.

The following proposition is cited as an example of a statement that is meaningless: 'The Absolute enters into, but is itself incapable of, evolution and progress'. The proposition is consigned to the flames of nonsensicality owing to it being neither provable by experiment nor true by definition. This seems unfair as it seems to consist in a rephrasal of the tautology: 'that which is already perfect cannot become more perfect'.

The author moves from the certain truth of logical propositions, through meaningful statements concerning possible and probable truth to examples of factual nonsense. Three examples of nonsense are cited:

- The first victim in front of the firing squad is the mild Cartesian contention that because our senses are unreliable we cannot be certain that what we perceive is real. Ayer condemns this as nonsense due to an internal contradiction. We only know that our senses have been unreliable by subsequent sensory verification, for example when we realise our mistake by taking a closer look. One feels that solipsism would have been a more heavyweight opponent for someone who felt able to take on Mike Tyson.

- The second example of nonsensical metaphysics is the monist versus pluralist debate as to whether reality is made of one substance or many. Ayer destroys this by stating that there will never be a circumstance when such claims can be proved true or false.

- The third candidate for eviction is the metaphysical debate between realists and idealists over whether objects are real or illusory. Ayer cites work by his favourite painter Goya as an example of that which may be real or illusory and condemns the dispute for being unverifiable:

> We may accordingly define a metaphysical sentence as a sentence which purports to express a genuine proposition, but does, in fact, express neither a tautology nor an empirical hypothesis. And as tautologies and empirical hypotheses form the entire class of significant propositions, we are justified in concluding that all metaphysical assertions are nonsensical. (24)

The author offers an explanation from the evolution of language for the proliferation of metaphysics. He says that out of convenience we use a single word to describe a thing made up of many complex properties. Metaphysicians commit a category error if they suppose that this shorthand infers the existence of such simple entities (things-in-themselves) behind the complex appearance, as the object cannot be defined apart from its appearance. This notion is complicated by his insistence that statements that assert the non-existence of something are nevertheless meaningful. For example, I am able to assert with impunity that 'Unicorns are fictitious' and even assert statements about these non-existent unicorns, such as 'All unicorns are white'.

The main criticism at the time came from the Oxford philosopher of language J. L. Austin (1911–1960), who maintained that language use was descriptive and could only be evaluated according to the effectiveness of how ideas are communicated to other language users rather than in sitting in judgement over its subject matter:

> We have a pretty rough idea of what pigs look like, what they smell like, and how they normally behave; and no doubt, if something didn't look at all right for a pig, behave as pigs do, or make pig-like noises and smells, we'd say that it wasn't a pig. But are there – do there *have* to be – statements of the form, 'It looks…', 'It sounds…', 'It smells…', of which we could say straight off that 'That is a pig' entails them? Plainly not. We learn the word 'pig', as we learn the vast majority of words for ordinary things, ostensively – by being told, in the presence of the animal, '*That* is a pig'.[3]

Austin argues that perception precedes and exists alongside language and it is a misleading emphasis to state, as Ayer's linguistic **phenomenalism** seems to, that language entails perception. One might criticise Ayer, in a similarly agricultural vein, for putting the cart before the horse. We have already considered some notable exceptions to the author's verification principle in a previous section on **emotivism** (see chapter 2). This battery of criticisms can be used here to damaging effect. Most notable are the scientific statements which must be judged meaningless by Ayer but which are valued as indispensable by the scientific establishment. Consider the case of the space–time continuum. This is a theoretical construct that adds the fourth dimension of time to the traditional Cartesian co-ordinates known as the x, y and z axes. The notion of four dimensions is neither tautological nor observable, yet few would categorise this notion as meaningless.

The second explanation that Ayer offers for the evolution of metaphysics surrounds the confusion between existential and attributive propositions. An existential proposition is any sentence that asserts that something exists; the author uses the example 'martyrs exist'. An attributive proposition is any sentence that contains a description that tells us something about the subject of the sentence, for example 'martyrs suffer'. Ayer insists that existence should not be classed as an attribute and that metaphyicians, through making this linguistic error, end up convincing themselves that they have proved the existence of all sorts of wild and woolly things. The prime example of a metaphysical argument that would be judged meaningless by Ayer is Anselm's ontological argument in which the saint distinguishes between existence in our understanding (the idea of God) and existence in reality (the existence of God). Ayer judges the first category to be meaningless as there is no way of testing it. Ayer adds that just as it is fallacious to assume that statements of the form 'X exists' are attributive propositions so it is erroneous to believe that statements of the form 'X does not exist' are attributive propositions as well. The author uses the example of 'Unicorns are fictitious'. It is a consequence of this, and one that Ayer does not spell out very well, that attributive propositions do not necessarily refer to an existent thing. One might assert, for instance, the statement 'All unicorns have one horn'. In this linguistic analysis, 'existence' means 'that which we can observe' and that exists in reality and not in the realm of thought. There is no room for the fanciful in Ayer's concentration camp of the mind.

Task

Place a tick or cross next to the following statements according to whether you think that they are verifiable by Ayer's criteria. Discuss any statements that you are not sure about. Why do they present a problem for Ayer's verification principle?

Statement	Verifiable or not
1 Each human has a soul.	
2 I am going into town tonight.	
3 There will be a nuclear holocaust.	
4 Sodium burns with a yellow flame.	
5 Sodium burns with a white flame.	
6 I am sitting here talking to you.	
7 The battle of Hastings was fought in 1066.	
8 Having extra-marital affairs is wrong.	
9 Emotivism is right.	
10 God does not exist.	

The closing pages of the first chapter reject the rejoinder that metaphysics is 'misplaced poetry'. One might imagine a writer gaining aesthetic effect from references to the absolute,

transcendent or essential. But Ayer holds that poetry, in spite of often being false, is in fact in possession of some meaning, whereas metaphysics is not. Consider the poetic proposition 'A butterfly is a flower in flight'. This metaphor is literally false; both poet and philosopher are aware of this. Yet the poet seeks to convey a truth by making the comparison. Such a comparison can be reduced to experiential propositions that may be tested. So, for instance, one might compare the similarities of both the shape and colour of blooms and butterflies. Such an over-zealous analysis might spoil one's aesthetic appreciation but is nevertheless possible, whereas metaphysics cannot escape the classification of factual nonsense. Oscar Wilde once quipped that 'so much bad poetry is the product of genuine emotion'. Ayer might have added that so much bad philosophy is as well.

Review question

Briefly explain two ways in which Ayer attacks metaphysics.

The function of philosophy (Chapter 2)

The question 'What is philosophy?' is itself a philosophical question and Ayer is keen to set out what philosophy does and does not consist in:

> If the philosopher is to uphold his claim to make a special contribution to the stock of our knowledge, he must not attempt to formulate speculative truths, or to look for first principles, or to make *a priori* judgements about the validity of our empirical beliefs. (36–37)

The job of a philosopher is instead to provide a critical analysis of science and to separate metaphysics from linguistic and factual truths. Ayer's opening rejection of philosophy as the presentation of some grand 'deductive system' contains both notable similarities and differences to Plato's analogy of the divided line as laid out in *The Republic* (511). Let us remind ourselves of the diagram used by Plato to distinguish between knowledge and opinion (figure 15.1).

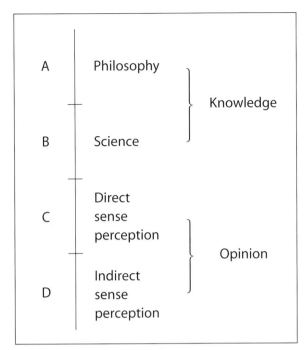

Figure 15.1 *Plato's model*

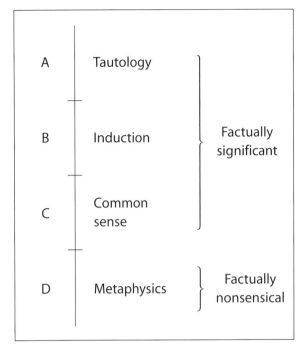

Figure 15.2 *Ayer's model*

The analogy of the divided line in Plato's *Republic* illustrates an epistemological ascent from shadows, through acquaintance with objects, to conclusions about these objects (science) and finally to an understanding of essences and the nature of goodness itself. Ayer reverses this trend, demoting metaphysics to the bottom of the line (figure 15.2). Ayer's section C is very much like Plato's in its subject matter but Ayer is careful to talk in terms of sense-content or sense experience in keeping with the brand of phenomenalism ascribed to at the date of authorship. Section C is important for Ayer, as it is the medium for empirical research. There are points of contact between the Ayerian and Platonic notions of sections A and B. Plato describes the workings of section B as follows:

> the mind uses the originals of the visible order in their turn as images, and has to base its inquiries on assumptions [hypotheses] and proceed from them not to a first principle but to a conclusion. (*Republic* 510b)

This is a description of induction, summarised by Ayer later in the second chapter as 'certain empirical generalisations which are derived from past experience [and] will hold good also in the future' (34). As Ayer points out, a reliance on induction is problematic as one can neither make the logical leap from empirical science to logic, nor justify principles with the same empirical data used to formulate them, as this is circular and fallacious. Ayer falls into the trap of circular reasoning later in the chapter when he argues:

> On the contrary, we know that it must be possible to define material things in terms of sense-contents, because it is only by the occurrence of certain sense-contents that the existence of any material thing can ever be in the least degree verified. (39)

The pinnacle of knowledge for Plato resides in the realm of essences or forms and culminates in the necessary acclamation that goodness is good. The category of logical necessity is, for Ayer, the high point of our knowledge. Both philosophers agree that *a priori* truth is important but radically disagree over the inclusion of ethics. As Plato set out to define philosophy in contrast to sophistry so Ayer defines philosophy in contrast to metaphysics.

The central argument of the second chapter is that it is a total misunderstanding of what philosophy is to suppose that philosophers are able to proffer a complete and holistic explanation of reality. Chapter 2 begins with a refutation of coherentism to this end. The author goes on to recommend a theory of justification based on a study of the reliability of observable phenomena. Cartesian foundationalism is then savaged on the grounds that its cornerstone, *cogito ergo sum*, is not logically necessary. Any proposition, according to Ayer, that is logically certain must be a necessary truth: one whose negation is self-contradictory. In other words, if I were to say the opposite, then what I have said would not make sense.

Ayer argues that the statement 'I think therefore I am a thinking thing' can be reduced to 'I think', and that this in turn can be further expressed by the sentence 'There is a thought now'. This refinement cannot be a logically necessary proposition because its opposite, 'There is not a thought now', is not self-contradictory.

Underpinning the above anti-rationalism is the conviction that such a task is impossible as any deductive system is dependent on induction to supply the premises and can thus be challenged with standard Humean scepticism. Ayer draws on Hume's bundle theory to argue that a thought at a given moment is insufficient to constitute a 'single self'. Ayer's linguistic phenomenalism led him to construe thoughts as nothing more than discrete experiences.

Ayer admits that any study of reality 'as a whole' is logically flawed, for we can never achieve a bird's-eye view of it from some metaphysical perspective, as we are inevitably a part of it. Ayer goes on to criticise the Gestalt psychologists at the end of the chapter for the same reason (44). This was a movement that arose towards the beginning of the twentieth century as a reaction to behaviourism. Behaviourism attempted to reduce all psychology to descriptions of human conduct. The Gestalt school, which takes its name from the German, meaning 'form' or 'overall shape', used as their *modus operandi* the slogan 'the whole is worth more than the sum of its parts' and sought to analyse human psychology in general and perception in particular in a holistic way. So, for example, they might comment on the prior causes that affected how one perceives an ambiguous shape or on one's personality traits and their significance. Gestalt psychologists did not see the point in breaking down the whole to its constituent parts. As a scientific movement, it represented the antithesis of Ayer's reductionism.

Having rejected the notion that philosophy can occupy a metaphysical vantage point, the author goes on to reject the view that philosophy can exist alongside the other sciences. Ayer does not believe that it is possible to have a legitimate form of speculation that is not grounded in empirical study. Philosophy, in its critical justification of science, has to be an empirical study. In practice, this entails the active categorising of meaningful and meaningless statements, spotting inconsistencies and presiding over empirical verification. Empirical verification ranges from the examination of common-sense beliefs to intricate scientific measurements. Ayer cites electrons as an example. Electrons cannot themselves be observed but a physicist can fire light of a certain energy at a metal surface to dislodge an electron and trace the path of light. Ayer stresses that the primary warrant for scientific theories is their success in practice. For instance, through an understanding of the flow of electricity, one is able to produce many practical electronic benefits, such as a computer, as a practical verification of one's understanding. Philosophy is a critical rather than speculative process that demonstrates the self-consistency of beliefs and provides criteria for their justification. In such a capacity, philosophers work within science.

This is where Ayer wants to be, despite knowing little about the sciences due to his predominately classical education at Eton and Oxford. He nevertheless wanted to deal in indubitable truths. Yet a problem emerges in elevating science whilst downgrading metaphysical theories in that you are left in confusion over how to deal with 'scientific theories', which take on the guise of oxymorons, concerned as they are with both science and theory. This is a further manifestation of the dilemma referred to by philosophers of science as the problem of induction (see chapter 6). Having observed a pattern in your experiments, you may want to grant your findings the status of 'a theory'. Even though Hume was an empiricist he lived under no false apprehensions that such empiricism was watertight. A pattern or uniformity of experiences that has held in the past and about which we have formulated a scientific theory is under no necessary obligation to hold in the future. Ayer takes a stronger line on the problem of induction and argues awkwardly that it is not a proper problem because no solution can be found for it. Ayer behaves like those annoying people who respond by saying 'You are asking the wrong question' before suggesting the question that you should have asked and to which they have a rehearsed answer. Having argued in Chapter 1 that all meaningful statements are either tautological or empirically verifiable, Ayer goes a step further here and asserts that all meaningful questions are those to which you can respond with answers that are either tautological or empirically verifiable. This unearths a problem with Ayerian, analytic philosophy in that it moves from arguing that there are no real metaphysical answers to asserting that there are no meaningful metaphysical questions. Opponents reply that if there are no such questions then philosophy as we know it does not exist. Ayer's insistence that the problem of induction is a pseudo-problem rests on the technicality that a possible answer would have to take one of two forms. First, one would have to move from matters of fact (your experiences) to a tautology, which is impossible. Second, one would have to justify the matters of fact with other related experiences, which seems sharp practice. The author retreats to his pragmatism.

Ayer has already described the many routes that lead an unsuspecting traveller into metaphysics: one can make a category error, confuse existential and attributive propositions or strive for poetic effect. A further error arises through not accepting his phenomenalist theory of perception. Ayer develops the bundle theories of Hume and Russell to argue that perception of material things consists in bundles of sensory experiences. All phenomena are made up of such bundles and we can translate any sentence that describes the phenomena into a sentence that describes the appropriate bundle of sensations. Hence the theory is given the grand title 'linguistic phenomenalism'. The theory is further developed in the third chapter of the book. Ayer does not criticise the history of philosophy for

being a long streak of metaphysics. Instead he highlights a number of examples of philosophers who have tried and in the main succeeded in philosophising analytically.

Review question

Outline Ayer's view on what philosophy can and cannot achieve.

Task

Read pages 38–42 of *Language, Truth and Logic* and make a list of the names of all the philosophers referred to. Then draw up a table as below and write a sentence summary indicating why Ayer has chosen this thinker as an example of an analytic philosopher.

Locke	
Berkeley	
Hume	

The nature of philosophical analysis (Chapter 3)

Ayer viewed philosophical analysis as analysis of language and in turn saw language as the preserve of logic. That is to say, language obeyed logical rules:

> Language is a purely logical activity; and it is in this logical activity, and not in any empirical study of the linguistic habits of any group of people, that philosophical analysis consists. (62)

This is by no means an uncontroversial claim, but while we are sharpening the knives of criticism let us examine Ayer's linguistic analysis in more detail. The author starts by asserting that the field of study for the philosopher concerns the definitions of things. He then goes on to draw a distinction between explicit definitions that supply replacement words or synonyms and 'definitions in use'. The first type is unphilosophical in nature and can be confined to crosswords and parlour games. In defining the word 'oculist', for instance, one may put forward the alternative symbol 'eye doctor'. The second type focuses philosophical attention and is intended to dispel misunderstanding and assert the existential implications of definite descriptions. 'Definitions in use' are analytical and critical in that they unpack concepts, make them more precise, formalised and unambiguous. Ayer cites two examples:

1 'The round square cannot exist.' This proposition may be translated more accurately as: 'No one thing can be both square and round.'
2 'The author of *Waverley* was Scotch [*sic*].' This proposition may be translated more accurately as: 'One person, and one person only, wrote *Waverley*, and that person was Scottish.'

The first example demonstrates how a definite description, i.e. any expression preceded by the word 'the', is unpacked and made explicit. In the second example, one is left in no doubt that, despite there being lots of authors in existence, the proposition under analysis refers to only one, who happened to be Sir Walter Scott. Philosophy as linguistic analysis attempts to increase our understanding of the building blocks of discourse, a thing which metaphysics could never do. Empirical verificationism accompanies this enterprise, testing the '**atomic propositions**', which are deduced from the sentences under analysis.

Ayer points to Russell's treatment of definite descriptions as a paradigm of how philosophy should work. Russell sought to explain how a sentence such as 'The king of France is bald' was misleading to the uninitiated as, through its use, it appears that there is such a person as the present king of France, which we know empirically not to be the case.

Ayer believes that we can move from an analysis of the meaning of a statement to assert something about existence. For example, the concept of a square circle does not make sense; one might argue that it is logically contradictory. From this fact I can conclude that the concept has no referent. In other words there is no such thing in existence as a square circle. However, there is nothing logically contradictory in the statement 'The king of France is bald' despite the king of France not existing. In order to find out whether this statement is true one needs to bypass *a priori* truth and use good old-fashioned observation. Having gone to France and investigated the state of affairs, one can assert that the assertion does not apply as there is no such person.

Ayer describes the function of philosophy to be the enumeration of types of sentences in any language before examining their relations of equivalence. The turgid and uninspiring way this is put across belies Ayer's popularity and charismatic power as a teacher in University College London, Oxford and the USA. Nevertheless, any student enrolling in the hope of gaining pearls of wisdom about the human condition or how one ought to live would be sorely disappointed if this was how philosophy was taught. In contrast to his friend Isaiah Berlin, Ayer conceives philosophy as pure linguistic analysis and excludes philosophy in its literal sense of love of wisdom from the agenda.

In the second half of the chapter, Ayer's description of language links to his phenomenalist theory of perception. A word, according to Ayer, is a symbol that represents a sensory experience. Each word is a logical construction that describes a specific experience that is open to empirical verification. Underpinning Ayer's linguistic phenomenalism is the conviction that language and perceptual experience work in the same way. When we perceive phenomena P from a certain angle, there are other angles that are not directly perceived but exist as potentialities. For example, a coin viewed from above appears circular whereas when viewed from a sideways angle it seems elliptical. Its elliptical shape exists as a potentiality and feature of the object even when the coin is being perceived from above. In this respect Ayer may be termed a naive or reductive phenomenalist rather than an eliminative phenomenalist. The latter position holds that the sum of reality consists in a collection of sensory experiences without connections. As a whole range of synonyms exist as potential adjectives for the object being described (though only one is actualised at a given moment in conversation), so sense-contents and descriptive definitions are made real by use but do not exist as metaphysical entities elsewhere. Perceptions are defined by the relationship that exists between themselves and, likewise, the same is true of words. Such perceptual relationships are awarded a special nomenclature in Ayer's text. This may, by extrapolation, be used with respect to language:

- *Direct resemblance:* no difference or an infinitesimal difference between them, for example the same object seen from the same angle or the same word used in the same token instance.
- *Indirect resemblance:* the same type of object seen in the same context or a similar word used in the same way.
- *Direct continuity:* this occurs when a succession of objects appear in the same context or when the same word appears in the same context in a sentence again and again.
- *Indirect continuity:* this occurs when an object repeatedly appears in related contexts or when a similar word appears in related contexts.
- *Possible sense-content:* when an object or a word might have been perceived or used but wasn't, i.e. when the specific conditions weren't fulfilled.

The relationship between language and phenomena is formally linguistic and contingent. Language and perception are related by their shared psychological effect.

Ambiguous symbols, the same word referring to different things, are explained with reference to logic. Consider the following sentence: 'Ayer is the most wicked man in Oxford'. Such a sentence holds different meanings that centre around an ambiguity in the word 'wicked'. Person A might state the above in order to rebuke Ayer for being a morally corrupt character. Person B, on the other hand, who happens to be well versed in the phraseology of 1990s youth culture, might declare the above because they liked Ayer's trainers. A problem is created for Ayer where the same sensible form (the word) has alternative meanings or significance. Ayer responds by noting that ambiguous words such as 'wicked' may embrace many meanings, some of which exist as a potential when the symbol is used in a particular sense.

Ayer was tutored by Gilbert Ryle at Oxford and there are evident similarities in their mutual impatience with metaphysics. Ayer uses similar examples to Ryle, for example his analysis of the terms 'constitution' and 'team'. Such words as 'constitution' are umbrella terms that cover many elements in the same set. Ryle uses the example of a 'team' to make the same point. For Ayer, all symbols are words that function as sets describing a number of elements or features. These may be actually present or potentially present in any one usage. In a further Rylean move, Ayer conjures the thought experiment that any sentence can, in principle, be translated into a statement about sense-data or phenomena.

A philosophical problem termed the 'problem of perception' arises from this linguistic phenomenalism. It is unclear how the phenomena or sense-content relate to material things. Later in his philosophical career Ayer argued that a material world does exist behind sense experiences owing to the fact that other people enjoy the same experiences, but he is yet to commit to this view in *Language, Truth and Logic.* Instead the visual and tactual 'depth' – that is, the distance between perceiver and phenomena perceived – is discussed. Two examples are provided, one of shape and the other of colour. Both experiences are described in the most clinical, scientific terms but one is left wondering whether this theory of perception is successful in avoiding the classification of 'metaphysical'.

Review question

Outline Ayer's phenomenalist theory of perception.

The *a priori* (Chapter 4)

Ayer's epistemic patron saint was the famous eighteenth-century empiricist David Hume. Hume was renowned for his 'fork model of knowledge' (see chapter 1), which advanced the view that knowledge is either one of two sorts: tautological or empirically verifiable. Hume held that despite its commonsensical importance, observation data is not immune from sceptical attack. Ayer gives greater weighting to empiricism but spends the fourth chapter of this text deciding how an empiricist ought to view *a priori* truth, traditionally the preserve of rationalism. Ayer raises the question as to the relationship between *a posteriori* and *a priori* knowledge at the start of Chapter 4. It is fashioned as follows:

> But if empiricism is correct no proposition which has a factual content can be necessary or certain. Accordingly the empiricist must deal with the truths of logic and mathematics in one of the two following ways: he must say either that they are not necessary truths, in which case he must account for the universal conviction that they are, and then he must explain how a proposition which is empty of all factual content can be true and useful and surprising. (65)

Two replies are presented. The first, exemplified by Mill, is that tautologies aren't really tautologies. The second is that *a priori* knowledge belongs in another realm from the factual. Ayer travels down this second route and concludes that 'there can be no *a priori* knowledge of reality'. Mill's line of thought is brought to the dissecting table first. Mill argues that necessary truths are only inductive generalisations that are granted infallible status owing to their span over 'an extremely large number of instances'. Necessary truths differ only in a matter of degree rather than kind to hypotheses verified in the natural sciences. Ayer rejects this argument but admits our knowledge needs experience. Necessary truths, as exemplified in the laws of mathematics and logic, proceed through a process of trial and error. Nevertheless, he is sure that *a priori* knowledge has the status of being (1) universal – true in every case in this world – and (2) necessary – true in every case in all possible worlds.

The author goes about proving this contention by examining a selection of analytic propositions. The first is '2 × 5 = 10'. He makes the passing remark that, even if I intend to mislead someone into believing that '2 × 5 = 9', I am only deceiving them about the truth. He argues that even if I were to perform an experiment and end up calculating that '2 × 5 = 9', I would conclude that my experiment failed. The fact is that '2 × 5 = 9' is never going to be the best explanation because it grates with the truth. Next, Ayer draws us a Cartesian illustration to make a similar point as above. He states that, if I were to work out that the interior angles of a Euclidean triangle did not add up to 180°, I would not conclude that not all Euclidean triangles exhibit the same properties but that either our calculation is wrong or else the triangle is not Euclidean.

A further instance is borrowed from logic: 'A proposition must be either true or false'. Ayer followed Russell in his belief that behind mathematics are certain laws of logic that are necessarily true and certain. Ayer concludes, contrary to Mill's argument, that 'the truths of logic and mathematics are analytic propositions or tautologies'. The dilemma remains for Ayer as to how such analytic truths can involve facts. The problem is never more evident than in Kant's notion of the synthetic *a priori*, a notion that Ayer never seems to tackle head on but which has the potential to weaken Ayerian epistemology as it challenges the categories laid out in the principle of verification. According to the author of *Language, Truth and Logic*, Kant defines analyticity as the citing of any proposition in which the predicate is contained in the concept of the thing, e.g. a bald man is bald or all bodies are extended. Synthetic statements cite new information in addition to the thing. Ayer gives the awkward example of 'All bodies are heavy', which one might rephrase as: 'Any body in a gravitational field has weight'. Thus whereas one understands that 'All bodies have an innate mass', or as Ayer puts it 'are extended', just by thinking about the idea of bodies, one needs to have studied bodies *a posteriori* to work out that weight = mass × gravitational pull. Thus in a setting such as space, where there is no gravitational pull, the body is weightless yet possesses an innate mass as a body, in all conditions and in all possible worlds.

Ayer's criticism of the synthetic *a priori*

According to Ayer, Kant's mistake arises out of the confusion of two separate criteria: the principle of contradiction in the case of analytic propositions and subjectivity in the case of synthetic statements. Ayer seeks to build a brick wall between analytic and synthetic propositions to emphasise their separateness:

> We say that a proposition is analytic when its validity depends solely on the definitions of the symbols it contains, and synthetic when its validity is determined by the facts of experience. (73)

Ayer does not seem to critically engage with the notion of the synthetic *a priori* but restates the position of Hume and supplies lots of examples of analytic statements to emphasise the difference between them and subjective judgements. He reads like the Englishman abroad who thinks that shouting louder will make him better understood. The examples cited are as follows:

- Either *p* is true or *p* is not true!
- Nothing can be coloured in different ways at the same time with respect to the same part of itself.
- If all Bretons are Frenchmen, and all Frenchmen Europeans, then all Bretons are Europeans.

In contrast to synthetic statements that contain observations about the world that can be tested empirically, analytic statements are true because they follow certain necessary laws of logic. They nevertheless can tell us new things by drawing previously unnoticed connections and through revealing 'unsuspected implications'.

After a few gripes about Kant's vague use of the term 'concept' and his assumption that every sentence takes a subject and predicate form, the author moves on to the meatier contention that Kant does not supply clear criteria for judging statements to be analytic or synthetic. Kant's mistake in positing a category of synthetic *a priori* truth was similar to that of Socrates when

illustrating the existence of *a priori* knowledge to Meno's slave.[4] Both thinkers' analysis of analytic statements only tells us something about the truths themselves, namely that they are necessary and do not convey facts about the world or inform us about our minds. In this respect, Platonic psychology and Kantian metaphysics lead the reader further into the woods. Geometry is used as a model to demonstrate the relationship between *a priori* truths and worldly facts and Ayer goes on to say that tautologies are linguistic truths.

Task

The American logician W. V. O. Quine, like Ayer, visited the Vienna Circle and is credited with bringing logical positivism to the United States of America. In many ways his analysis of analytic statements is more subtle than that of Ayer and provides a useful contrast. Research what Quine says about analytic statements and summarise it in a paragraph.

Critique of ethics and theology (Chapter 6)

Having examined synthetic statements and analytic statements in the preceding chapters, Ayer moves on to evaluate judgements concerning the ethical, aesthetic and theological. It is clear to any onlooker that statements in these subject areas are not analytic but Ayer sets out to prove that, despite their grammatical appearance, they are not synthetic either. For the author of *Language, Truth and Logic*, metaphysical utterances are neither true by definition nor provable by experiment. He focuses on moral statements first and classifies four kinds of moral proposition:

1 Definitions of moral terms: e.g. 'Abortion is the wilful termination of a foetus'.
2 Statements recording moral experience: e.g. 'I believe that abortion is wrong'.
3 Moral exhortations: e.g. 'You should not have an abortion'.
4 Ethical judgements: e.g. 'Abortion is wrong'.

Ayer argues that whereas the first two categories contain some degree of meaning the second two lack any factual significance. The first classification consists of definitions and as such is a necessary feature of language. The second group of statements is concerned with experience and as a result can be tested – that is, one can actively find out whether P is happier than Q, X approves of Y, or whether all Zs believe that suicide is wrong. The literal sense of these examples is not part of an ethical study, however, but more an aspect of the social sciences. These two categories apart, moral statements are exclusively value judgements. Ayer makes clear (105) that his examination is of a meta-ethical nature and is not concerned with a sociological observation of how people operate; nor is it a normative theory that offers advice.

The first port of call on his meta-ethical journey is the relationship between ethical and non-ethical terms. He argues that, *prima facie*, utilitarianism (the view that right and wrong are a matter of generating happiness) and subjectivism (the view that right and wrong are a matter of personal approval) seem to involve a metric that may be tested. Yet if one applies a simple law of contradiction one sees that both theories fail to account for the following scenarios:

1 A utilitarian asserts: 'I ought to do X because X is pleasurable'; but one can equally assert without contradiction: 'I ought to do X and X is not pleasurable'.
2 A subjectivist asserts: 'I ought to do X because I approve of X being done'; but one can equally assert without contradiction: 'I ought to do X even though I do not approve of X being done'.

A useful criticism of any theory is one that shows up a weakness in that theory. If one were to assert the opposite view then one has not successfully criticised anything but provided an arbitrary choice for onlookers to make. In the above example it is still uncertain whether I ought to pursue pleasure as my goal or not. For Ayer all metaphysics consists of is the provision of arbitrary choice.

In due course, the author turns his critical eye to intuitionism and absolutism. The fact that Ayer groups these theories together is significant as he holds that both are hard-line cognitive positions that award ethical propositions fact status, in contrast to the theories analysed above that claim ethical judgements are synthetic truths. The roots of both intuitionism and absolutism, like so much in philosophy, can be found in the works of Plato. Plato's notion of the form of the good held that the statement 'Goodness is good' counts as a necessary truth that when contemplated by philosophers will yield moral assurance as well as epistemic certainty. Ayer's argument is that, while such propositions as 'Eggs are eggs' or 'All bachelors are unmarried' count as logically necessary propositions because we are familiar with the subject matter, in the case of goodness we are not. Later in Chapter 6, the same argument is used against theological statements. Such a criticism is powerful but needs to have been spelt out in clearer terms as the author seems to set up absolutism as a straw man in order to torch it with the conclusion that, owing to the notorious problem of ethical relativism, absolutist propositions are to be rendered unverifiable.

Ayer goes on to sketch out his emotivist theory of meta-ethics. He argues:

1 Ethical statements are neither tautologies nor empirically verifiable.
2 Ethical statements are unanalysable 'pseudo-concepts'.
3 Ethical statements simply evince – that is, indicate approval or disapproval.
4 In addition to expressing feelings, ethical statements are calculated to arouse feelings in others.

Ayer's terminology is a bit clumsy at this stage and one is left pondering the notion of what a 'pseudo-concept' might be. Surely something is either a concept or not? Followers of Ayer might prefer the term 'pseudo-proposition' to draw attention to the linguistic nature of the author's analysis. Ayer cites the example of the proposition 'You were wrong to steal my money'. This is neither true by definition nor are we able to create a definitive experiment to prove its truth. Instead it is an expression of the victim's outrage and intends to arouse remorse in the perpetrator or potential perpetrators. Ayer's non-cognitive theory of ethics develops Russellian subjectivism but diverges from this standpoint in not classifying moral statements as genuine. Ayer describes each moral utterance as a 'pure expression of feeling' like a cry of joy or disgust. The author proceeds to analyse the expression of such feelings, concluding that despite the possession of an emotion entailing its articulation – for example being sad means you whinge and whine a lot – this articulation does not follow necessarily. Likewise expression does not imply possession. The position is thus refined to the assertion: 'If person P expresses a feeling F at time T, it must logically follow that at time T, P is experiencing a feeling related to F (though not necessarily F itself)'. Thus even in the case of an actor pretending to be sad, their feelings must be related to sadness even if they are being outwardly deceptive.

One of the works that challenged the author the most on going up to Christ Church College, Oxford, was G. E. Moore's *Principia Ethica* and it is to the intuitionist challenge to non-cognitivism that Ayer turns next. The challenge questions the efficacy of ethical discourse and considers whether, if moral language is meaningless, this means that all participants in ethical discussions are talking nonsense. Emotivism appears to rule out all moral discourse as meaningless but, as Moore argues, we clearly engage in genuine ethical dispute all the time. Ayer replies that such disputes often appear genuine if they involve factual content. One might imagine a debate surrounding the banning of smoking which centres around scientific evidence over whether the chances of lung cancer are increased. Nevertheless, non-factual ethical discussion is only a sophistical exercise in persuading the other side that they are misguided and takes place without any proof or validity to substantiate either side's claims. It is condemned as 'mere abuse'. Indeed, Ayer throws down the gauntlet in the form of a thought experiment that invites the reader to construct an ethical argument that is meaningful but irreducible to logical or empirical verification. As proof of his emotivist theory of ethics, he points to the normative theories of utilitarianism, Kantianism and virtue theory being based on the emotions of happiness, fear and contentment respectively (117).

Ethics and aesthetics are both construed as matters of personal preference or taste. Ayer enjoyed art and literature but did not write much on these subjects due to a reluctance to persuade others of his personal opinion. Aesthetics receives a brief acknowledgement in Chapter 6 before an examination of the philosophy of religion is undertaken. Ayer links the passages about morality to those concerned with theology by advancing the psychological notion that a fear of invoking God's displeasure might explain the origins of moral utterance. Ayer goes on to examine the argument from religious experience as a possible candidate for an inductive truth. Despite there being nothing to separate the propositions 'I am experiencing God' from 'I am experiencing yellowness', the latter is empirically verifiable whereas the former is not and hence is rejected; by the same process agnosticism (the standpoint which holds that God is a possibility) and atheism (the belief that God does not exist) are consigned to the flames of meaningless utterances. Ayer explains the need for transcendent propositions in the same way as he earlier explained the desire to create a category of synthetic *a priori* out of an awe inspired in less developed minds. Mysticism is conceived as an eccentric way of raising propositions, in a similar manner to luck, and equally doomed to create statements of insignificance owing to these statements not being verifiable.

Review question

Describe Ayer's account of the nature of morality and outline any two of Ayer's examples.

Ayer's hallucination

The final section of this commentary is given up to clarifying what has come to be termed Ayer's 'near-death experience'. It is a popular misconception of Ayer's critics that his near-death experience during the summer of 1988 changed his views on the meaning of life. There is no evidence in Ayer's own accounts or in secondary sources that this was the case and strictly speaking the event cannot even be classed as a near-death experience. Let us examine the experience first of all as Ayer describes it:

I am particularly fond of smoked salmon, and one evening I carelessly tossed a slice of it into my throat. It went down the wrong way and almost immediately the graph recording my heart beats plummeted.

The ward sister rushed to the rescue, but she was unable to prevent my heart from stopping. She and the doctor subsequently told me that I died in this sense for four minutes, and I have no reason to disbelieve them … The only memory that I have of an experience closely encompassing my death is very vivid. I was confronted by a red light, exceedingly bright, and also very painful even when I turned away from it. I was aware that this light was responsible for the government of the universe. Among its ministers were two creatures who had been put in charge of space. These ministers periodically inspected space and had recently carried out such an inspection. They had, however, failed to do their work properly, with the result that space, like a badly fitting jigsaw puzzle, was slightly out of joint.

Ayer goes on to tell of how he tried to attract the ministers' attention in order to rectify this matter. The account is of interest to us for a number of reasons. It is characteristically bombastic, with Ayer describing the doctor in attendance as being very much in awe of him. The fact that the philosopher's brain did not cease to function but that his heart stopped for four minutes means that the incident should not be classed as a near-death experience but as a hallucination, and a typically Ayerian hallucination at that, with the prosaic professor attempting to fix the universe like a child's jigsaw puzzle. If any image is to be counted as fitting for his philosophy it should be this one.

In a further article entitled 'Postscript to a Postmortem',[5] Ayer underscores his conviction that the most likely explanation of the above was that his brain continued for four minutes without a fresh blood supply from the dysfunctional heart. He discards the Christian belief in the resurrection of the body due to the uncertainty as to what form our resurrected bodies would take but has more time for the doctrine of reincarnation, which he considers a less outlandish suggestion. Ayer remains a thoroughgoing logical positivist to the end, however, and makes the point that any conjectural positing as to the significance of this incident would be literally senseless. He quotes his American counterpart in the analytic school, W. V. O. Quine, that in this enquiry 'there is no fact of the matter that we can seek to discover'.

Revision questions

1 Assess Ayer's attempt to eliminate metaphysics from philosophy.

2 Critically examine linguistic phenomenalism.

3 Explain the place of *a priori* knowledge in Ayer's empiricist philosophy.

4 Outline and explain Ayer's response to the problem of induction.

5 Assess Ayer's claim that all religious utterances are factually meaningless.

Discussion questions

- Does Ayer present a metaphysical theory of his own?
- What would Ayer's ideal philosophy course look like and would anyone enrol?
- Can we ever talk meaningfully about morals?
- Can we ever talk meaningfully about the past and future?
- Is Ayer's description of a near-death experience meaningful?

Glossary of key terms

A priori: the term that covers all claims to knowledge that exist independent of experience or experiment.

Atomic propositions: statements that concern single experiences that can be verified by observation.

Emotivism: the theory of ethics that holds that any moral proposition is an expression of the speaker's feelings or emotions.

Empiricism: the philosophical movement, popular in the Anglo-Saxon world, that emphasises common sense, experience, logic and unambiguous terminology.

Induction: the inference of general rules from known events in order to predict the occurrence of future events with greater accuracy.

Metaphysics: literally meaning 'beyond the scope of physics'; Ayer uses this term to cover any aspect of the subject that is neither analytic nor scientifically verifiable.

Phenomenalism: Ayer adheres to this theory of perception, which holds that we have access to only actual or potential sensory (auditory, tactual) experience and nothing more.

Philosophy: according to Ayer philosophy is the study of 'definitions in use' and justification by the scientific method.

Tautology: any statement the opposite of which would involve a contradiction. Tautologies repeat the same information and are hence necessarily true.

Verificationism: an account of how something might be proved true. In the weak sense, as Ayer outlines, this involves probability, in contrast to strong verificationism, which strives for certainty.

Suggested reading

- Edmonds, D. and Eidinow, J. (2001) *Wittgenstein's Poker*, London, Faber & Faber
  An entertaining read that provides background to philosophy at this time

- Gower, B. ed. (1987) *Logical Positivism in Perspective*, London, Croom Helm
  A series of essays written to commemorate the fiftieth anniversary of *Language, Truth and Logic*

- Hanfling, O. (1981) *Logical Positivism*, Oxford, Blackwell
  A clear analysis of Ayer's concerns; an anthology of logical positivism was produced by the same author in the same year

- Macdonald, G. and Wright, C. eds. (1986) *Fact, Science and Morality*, Oxford, Blackwell
  A series of serious essays that cover all the main issues in detail

- Martin, R. M. (2001) *On Ayer*, Belmont, Wadsworth
  A useful study guide to the chapters commented on above

Notes

1 Rogers, B. (2000) *A. J. Ayer: A Life*, London, Vintage, p. 121.

2 Ayer, A. J. (1990) *Language, Truth and Logic*, Harmondsworth, Penguin, p. 23; hereafter page references to *Language, Truth and Logic* are given in brackets and refer to this edition.

3 Austin, J. L. (1962) *Sense and Sensibilia*, Oxford, Clarendon, Lecture X, pp. 120–121.

4 Plato, *Meno* 84–86.

5 *The Spectator*, 15 October 1988.

16 A commentary on Sartre's *Existentialism and Humanism*

If you are lonely when you are alone, you are in bad company.
(Jean-Paul Sartre)

Aims

On completion of this chapter you should be able to:

- explain the central teachings of the philosophical movement known as existentialism
- understand the existentialist claim that existence precedes essence
- evaluate Sartre's atheism
- evaluate Sartre's refutation of determinism
- explain and criticise the notions of anguish, abandonment and despair
- outline Sartre's existentialist ethic of choice and responsibility
- describe and assess the notions of subjectivism and intersubjectivity
- describe and discuss Sartre's conception of bad faith.

What is existentialism? Existentialism is the name of a philosophical perspective, in the same way that Marxism and feminism are philosophical perspectives. Existentialists believe that in contrasting existence and non-existence, or 'being and nothingness', one can offer an accurate analysis of life, the universe and everything. A useful account of existentialism occurs in Sartre's *Nausea*, a novel written shortly before *Existentialism and Humanism* and a useful starting point for our commentary. In the following passage from Sartre's novel *Nausea*, the narrator is struck by the fact that perceptions, the objects perceived and the perceiver exist independent of each other and for no good reason:

> Everything was full, everything was active, there was no unaccented beat, everything, even the most imperceptible movement, was made of existence. And all those existents which were bustling about the tree came from nowhere and were going nowhere. All of a sudden they existed and then, all of a sudden, they no longer existed: existence has

no memory; it retains nothing of what has disappeared; not even a recollection. Existence is everywhere, to infinity, superfluous, always and everywhere; existence – which is never limited by anything but existence.[1]

Each element in the universe's giant ecosystem is as meaningless as the next. The realisation by any thoughtful atheist that so many things exist without a God to award them significance conspires to make those who contemplate this state of affairs feel nauseous, as if they had eaten and drunk too much.

Nausea (1938)

The mental life of *Nausea*'s central character, the diarist Antoine Roquentin, is certainly a rich one. He is conscious of the external world around him: a pebble, a knife, a tree; of other-minded individuals such as the customers of a café and its staff. Roquentin, in addition, is conscious of specific thoughts such as the emotions of disgust or embarrassment, the awareness of time passing, a dream or day dream, the 'fading memory of a lover's smile'. He is also conscious of consciousness and the relationship between consciousness and contingency. For Sartre, consciousness is the process whereby an object, person or thought allows itself to be encountered by the perceiver. Through this process the perceiver is struck by the fact that such a thing does not exist out of necessity but exists superfluously. In turn, this rejection of the necessity of existence engenders within the subject a stomach-churning feeling of abandonment and meaninglessness, termed 'nausea'.[2] This is a permanent mid-life crisis where each experience is rendered as insignificant as 'little flakes of sunlight on the surface of a cold, dark sea'.[3] Nausea is a property of the contingency found in the surrounding articles and events of everyday life:

> His blue cotton shirt stands out cheerfully against the chocolate-coloured wall. That too brings on the Nausea. Or rather it is the Nausea. The Nausea isn't inside me: I can feel it over there on the wall, on the braces, everywhere around me. It is one with the café, it is I who am inside it.[4]

Through observing life in a café or in a park, Roquentin registers a succession of independent existents devoid of meaning, which contribute to an overall sense of absurdity. These reflections on the meaninglessness and absurdity of existence led some readers to accuse existentialism of being a subversive philosophy. The lecture *Existentialism and Humanism* is the author's rebuttal of criticisms waged against many of the themes laid out in *Nausea*. Sartre argues that, despite our feelings of nausea and despair, we are still responsible for making moral choices and decisions.

Existentialism and Humanism: an introduction

Sartre's lecture *Existentialism and Humanism* may be better translated as 'Existentialism is a Humanism'. It is a transitional work between the author's magnum opus *Being and Nothingness* and his later work *Critique of Dialectical Reason*. The author's purpose in delivering the lecture *Existentialism and Humanism* is established from the start and is a defence of existentialism against

the criticisms waged by, amongst others, communists and Christians. The criticisms made against Sartre's philosophy are fourfold:

- *Quietism:* this asserts that existentialism encourages inaction (a communist criticism).
- *Pessimism:* this asserts that existentialism leads to a depressingly negative view of life (a 'common criticism').
- *Subjectivism:* this asserts that existentialism emphasises the individual over society (a communist criticism).
- *Relativism:* this asserts that existentialism propounds the subversive view that there are no moral truths (a Christian criticism).

Communist criticisms

The first criticism, attributed to members of the communist party, accuses existentialists of dwelling in a 'quietism of despair'. **Quietism** (or pietism) is originally a theological term meaning the distancing of oneself from society in order to reflect on spiritual or philosophical matters. Sartre's critics are reproaching the existentialist movement for being too contemplative and therefore ineffective in helping people. Such 'mountain top experiences' enjoyed by philosophers should be translated into practical assistance in the market place of everyday life. Existentialism is viewed as a selfish luxury, the preserve of the unethical and a privilege of the rich. Sartre's critics assert that it is not even the case that such contemplation leads to hope but that it fosters pessimism and despair.

Existentialism is a failed philosophy, so the argument goes, if it fails to acknowledge the relationship of each individual to the rest of society. The communists blame the Cartesian heritage of self-absorption that invites us to think about our own thoughts and our own existence as opposed to the material needs of others. Ironically, towards the end of his career Sartre felt that existentialism could breathe renewed energy into communism.

Christian criticisms

In shaking off the moral restraints of Christianity, one danger predicted by Christian critics of existentialism is a tendency towards ignominious, shameful or dishonourable behaviour. Existentialism is equated with mean, vulgar, ugly and scandalous acts. As a result, purer pleasures such as an innocent delight in new life (the image is presented of an infant's smile) will be lost, no clear moral guidance accepted and debate or comment on other people's actions will be rendered meaningless. This scenario is construed as, at best, a travesty and at worst a serious danger. Note that this lecture was being presented to an audience in 1945 when the extent of the Nazi atrocities was only gradually being realised and people were faced with the question of how such an event could have occurred in the heart of twentieth-century, Christian Europe. Religious thinkers advanced the view that the crimes of the Second World War happened because the perpetrators ignored the Judaeo-Christian ethic that demands we transcend our capacity for animal violence. These commentators were naturally suspicious of any moral system that seemed to argue differently. Yet Sartre goes on, in this lecture, to outline a secular existentialist ethic of transcendence.

Sartre's defence

Ironically, the communist criticism of existentialism has been used against Christianity and the Christian criticism of existentialism has been used against communism. Sartre attempts to escape such circular wrangling. His defence is to equate existentialism with humanism, a term that means a non-religious system of beliefs that advocates shared values, such as respect for one another and responsibility for future generations. It is this humanistic existentialism that addresses the real problems of suffering and poverty.

Before an existentialist ethic is asserted, however, Sartre tells us what his philosophy is not.

- Existentialism is not naturalism in that it does not provide a ready-made definition of human nature.

- Existentialism is not traditionalism in that it does not sycophantically support the establishment.

- Existentialism is not romanticism in that it does not offer an overly romantic view of humanity.

In fact, this school of thought appears to be optimistic and pessimistic in equal measures.

Review question

Outline the criticisms that Sartre says have been made against existentialism.

The paper knife argument

The paper knife argument defines existentialism as a rejection of both theism and **essentialism**. Indeed, Sartre holds that in rejecting belief in God (theism) one is forced to deny the existence of a pre-figured human essence (essentialism). Sartre believes that the only being that would be powerful enough to create an essence is God but takes it as given that God does not exist and so concludes that human beings cannot be said to possess an essence. It is not clear, however, where the essences of things originate from, nor whether it is more plausible to argue that because we don't have essences then God does not exist or rather assume that because God does not exist then we cannot possess essences. Sartre seems to be making the first claim at the end of the book and the second claim at the start. It is, therefore, a moot point as to whether the 'first principle of existentialism', that human existence precedes essence, depends on the non-existence of God. If it does, the slogan cannot claim to be a first principle and Sartre needs to justify his atheism with philosophical argument.

Four possible standpoints may be adopted on the issue of essentialism and the existence of God. One might accept belief in God and believe that such a divine intelligence has created us in accordance with some blueprint. The thirteenth-century theologian St Thomas Aquinas adopted this line. Alternatively, one might believe that human beings possess a pre-determined essence, shaped not by God but by our nature and function, in the style of Aristotelian philosophy. The Danish theologian and philosopher Søren Kierkegaard (1813–1855) represents a third possibility: he believes in the existence of God yet denies a pre-determined human essence. Sartre rejects both the belief in an all-powerful deity and a universal human essence.

By 'essence', Sartre means the definition of a thing, created in the mind of an artisan before its production. Definitions describe an object's purpose or end: to cut paper in the case of a paper knife, or to be read as in the case of a book. His reasoning proceeds as follows:

1 In order to manufacture X we need to have an idea of what X will be.
2 In order to have an idea of what X will be, we need to know what X will do.
3 Thus, an understanding of the essence of X precedes the existence of X and is based on the purpose of X.

Note that any essence must already be in existence in order to be understood. Sartre says that we can observe the same relationship in the divine act of creation as defended by theists. God acts as the supernal (heavenly) artisan or designer and each individual is created according to a pre-existent prototype. Sartre goes on to say that if God does not exist then mankind lacks a prototype and is free to choose how to live. It is as if human beings in acknowledging their power to create and decide on what is morally acceptable make themselves into gods. Two problems are immediately evident: the formula 'existence precedes essence' does not seem necessarily to require atheism; secondly, having dispensed with God, we could look for alternative sources to establish the essence of humanity, for example biological naturalism, Marxist materialism or utilitarianism.

The human condition

Sartre enlarges upon the doctrine of existence preceding essence, stating:

> What do we mean by saying that existence precedes essence? We mean that man first of all exists, encounters himself, surges up in the world – and defines himself afterwards. If man as the existentialist sees him is not definable, it is because to begin with he is nothing. He will not be anything until later, and then he will be what he makes of himself. Thus, there is no human nature, because there is no God to have a conception of it. Man simply is.[5]

There are many midnight snares hidden in this doctrine to catch the unaware, not least of which is the fact that the phrase 'existence precedes essence' entails an essence that Sartre seems to be denying. Commentators have pointed out the inherent contradiction:

> Although he [Sartre] rejects the idea that human beings have any essence, he takes the essence of human beings to be that they are free when he declares: 'man is free, man is freedom'.[6]

Essence by definition precedes existence and Sartre adamantly denies that humans possess such a thing. Nevertheless, the author believes that every human being shares a freedom to create oneself as one wants to be created and decide how to act responsibly. This universal human attribute is sometimes called 'human nature' or, even more confusingly, 'essence' in the text, but might be unambiguously referred to as 'the human condition'.

In arguing that the only thing we have in common is the freedom to act, the author of *Existentialism and Humanism* grounds his thought in the field of moral philosophy. The argument proceeds as follows: having stated that existence precedes essence in the case of human beings and having granted that the only feature all humans have in common is their freedom, Sartre spells out the implications of this freedom. The process involves an initial movement of the mind that begins a causal sequence of decision-making and acts of will. This freedom carries with it a very great responsibility. So great in fact that it can weigh down the moral agent with its gravity, a sensation the author terms 'anguish'. In deciding what to do we are also advertising our preferences to the rest of humanity and inevitably affecting how we view other people. So, for instance, in deciding to get married, I am at one and the same time advocating marriage to fellow humans in my position. In deciding to adopt a racist attitude, I inevitably enter into a judgemental relationship towards other people. In the case of Christianity, this decision involves separating mankind into the saved and the damned, and, in the case of communism, into the proletariat and the bourgeoisie. It is this notion that the author had in mind when he penned the non-sequitur 'In fashioning myself I fashion man' (30). Sartre adopts a neo-Kantian position through describing human society as a kingdom. The term echoes Kant's description of the ideal society as a kingdom of ends. Each individual who is part of this society is viewed as a legislator 'deciding for the whole of mankind'. In fact, the categorical imperative appears in a more or less complete version at this stage in Sartre's lecture, translated into the colloquial plea, 'What would happen if everyone did so?'

Review question

Briefly explain the relevance of Sartre's paper knife illustration to his view of the human condition.

Task

Select four quotations from page 28 of *Existentialism and Humanism* on the theme of the human condition. Discuss whether the author's notion that existence precedes essence leads to moral responsibility or to insecurity and pessimism.

A brief history of existentialism

Existentialism has a long pedigree and can trace its ancestry through Pascal and St Augustine to Socrates. Traces are even found in the Bible. However, as a distinctive aspect of European culture it can be said to begin in the middle of the nineteenth century with the writings of the Danish theologian Søren Kierkegaard and the German philologist Friedrich Nietzsche. In addition to Nietzsche and Kierkegaard, a number of other prominent existentialist thinkers are discussed in the introduction to Philip Mairet's translation of *Existentialism and Humanism*. Let us examine first the influence on Sartre of the theistic existentialists Kierkegaard, Jaspers and Marcel and then the atheistic existentialist Heidegger.

Kierkegaard

Kierkegaard maintained that the outlook of nineteenth-century Europe by and large is not Christian but a surrogate: Christianity is represented as a comfortable creed, perfectly consistent with current bourgeois lifestyles, requiring a nominal assent in order that the mass ranks of Christians can be parcelled up and zip-coded for heaven. If people have doubts then there are on hand professors and pastors who, with demonstrable arguments from the Bible, science or philosophy (e.g. the proofs of the existence of God), can allay such scepticism if they are paid the requisite attention. To Kierkegaard this is all a travesty. Christianity is not a set of socially approved doctrines but an 'existential communication' speaking to each individual in turn. In order to make clear what he means by this, we must make a brief digression.

Through education, one comes across a good many bodies of knowledge: history, geography, physics, biology etc. This is 'objective knowledge' since it is possessed by a great number of people who accept the same rules, principles and facts. No matter what you accumulate in the way of objective knowledge, there is always something that falls outside it. We meet these solid and respectable bodies of knowledge like history, philosophy and physics within our existence, and outside our existence they have no reality at all. There are, therefore, two things: objective knowledge and existential understanding. The existence that we seek to understand is not just the process by which we come to endorse, support and understand systems of knowledge but also the process of making moral decisions, the process of loving, hating and organising our life's plan. In sum the whole of an individual's life is encompassed by the term 'existence'. To understand existence is not something that can be done by the scientific since one's involvement with the social enterprise that is science is itself part of the subject. The same can be said of philosophy if by philosophy we mean the analysis of ideas and arguments rather than a sense of personal discovery on the way to self-understanding.

For Kierkegaard, to attempt to comprehend existence is to pursue wisdom. This ultimately leads to the insight into the human condition afforded by Christianity. Progress is made by trying in all seriousness to understand existence and one's place in it and then trying to live out that understanding to be what one takes oneself to be. For example, if one believes that man is just an animal then one must try to live as an animal; if one cannot do this without guilt or self-deception, one must give up that particular understanding of existence and try again, hoping to learn from one's error. Kierkegaard's works are littered with 'existential sketches' of people enmeshed in contradictory and unsustainable perceptions, unable to live by what they believe or believe in how they live. This begins the notable association of existentialism with literature, a mantle that Sartre adopts with admirable success.

Jaspers

Karl Jaspers (1883–1969) was a scientist by training but like many existentialists felt that the scientific method failed to provide a conclusive and final picture of reality as we actually experience it. Science, argues Jaspers, imposes limits on that which it studies, just as Kierkegaard had suggested. It is a specific way of approaching reality, a particular way of existing. To understand existence as a whole is the task set for reason. To exist is to go on a journey of exploration; reason is an attempt to map out the track taken. Jaspers has many things to say about reason in this sense. It aims at clarity, openness, unity and so on, and interestingly, though it may use the terms of ordinary objective language, it is chiefly in the business of using concepts as signs and statements as pointers to what cannot be stated. What Jaspers appears to be saying is that analogical and symbolic talk of the kind so often found in religion is most properly suited to the expression of rational existential understanding. Jaspers rejects religious orthodoxy, however, because it is not personally acquired. He favours knowledge which is attested by the conscience and won in the encounter with life's hazards. Jaspers believes that true religion and philosophy spring most properly from limit-situations. During the dark days of Nazi power, Jaspers was deeply moved by the writings of the Hebrew prophets. He did not personally find the Christian faith alone adequate for his life situation.

Marcel

Gabriel Marcel (1889–1973) was brought up as an atheist but converted to Roman Catholicism in 1929. Like many existentialists he had considerable literary gifts and wrote plays as well as philosophy. His thought, though, is distressingly cryptic, despite being deeply rooted in his own experience. When he served in the First World War, Marcel's job involved both keeping records of casualties and visiting the families of soldiers killed in action and explaining to them what had happened. This impressed upon him that there are two ways of accounting for things. In the first instance, an experience such as bereavement is just a matter-of-fact way of registering that someone has died. In the second instance, however, it is a matter of personal adjustment on all levels to one of life's mysteries. By mystery, he did not mean that it was a problem that had to be solved, rather that it was a fact that one had to enter into. Other mysteries nominated by Marcel include the existence of others, the world, evil, God and birth. Through entering into these events in the same way as one's spirit enters into and possesses one's body, one comes to terms with 'being' and this is the foundation of faith. Marcel, in a typically existentialist way, argues that one can avoid doing this through the ceaseless, empty activity and chatter that characterises inauthentic existence.

Heidegger

It is often quite erroneously supposed that all existentialists are atheists. This is not true, but there have been some very notable existentialists who were, pre-eminently Nietzsche (see chapter 11), Heidegger, Camus and, of course, Sartre.

Heidegger was educated by the Jesuits and studied under the great German Jewish philosopher Husserl before deposing him in a conspiracy with the Nazi authorities and taking over his university teaching. He remained compliant during the restrictions imposed on academic freedom by the Nazis, a fact which has tarnished his reputation. For Heidegger, European culture had pretty well gone wrong from the days of Plato onwards. He remained unimpressed by its considerable scientific advances, which he saw as simply increasing man's technical grasp on the environment, extending our practical understanding of how things work (seen from the limiting perspective of our intelligence). Heidegger wanted to remind us of the 'mystery of being'. By this he means that it is necessary to look at reality in a broader and in a more open way – that is, outside the framework of our customary concepts and pre-conceptions, which must be set aside. In his first works Heidegger spoke as though this was a reductive, precise, analytical exercise; in his later works he spoke as though this was an opportunity for the intuitive grasp of the poet who, like Wordsworth, 'saw into the heart of things'. Heidegger sought to emphasise the sheer contingency of our world. It is, but it need not be. Every second that it exists is fortuitous. In *Nausea* Sartre repeatedly makes the same point that everything that exists exists instead of nothing, but nothing too is a possibility. Every individual lives on the same terms and everyone is a conscious item in reality. In him, 'being finds expression'. He too lives with the possibility of his own 'non-being'. He is thrown into a world and must orientate himself to it. Man rapidly learns to adjust to physical reality, turning things into tools, but he has special problems with his fellow creatures.

Within the pages of Heidegger, we find a withering condemnation of social existence. Man is radically dependent upon his fellows. His self-concept stems from the definition of others. He lives for their approval. His life is a constant effort to be what others want him to be or require him to be. Nor are the others any better; we are all in the same bondage. None of us is a genuine self, everyone is determined by what 'they' will think, say or do. Our moral judgements are second-hand; we all work with a common-sense view of the world for which no one is responsible. The only escape from this ensnarement of life is to come to terms with the terms of our existence, to recognise that society cannot die on our behalf, that each man through his death is isolated and that life is 'being unto death'. To lead life with the constant recollection of death is to liberate oneself from the social pressures, to lead an 'authentic existence', to make of one's life a project and to gain a self worth talking about.

So long as man is equipped with a sense of his own 'non-being', referred to in the Middle Ages as the 'recollection of death', man perceives himself as free and indeed is free. Man generally does not realise this possibility, according to Heidegger. He diverts himself and evades the truth. He consumes his life with chatter, curiosity in both public and private forms of self-deception. He lives for the future, in terms of plans that are somehow thought to provide a sense and rationale to his life that cannot be found in the present. Heidegger claims that we are 'given to ourselves' but that 'human life' rapidly descends to the 'inauthentic and commonplace'. This is a secular version of the biblical myth of the Fall. We are 'saved' through the call to authentic existence expressed in us as the voice of conscience, and stimulated by the presentiment of death.

Sartre

The themes of freedom and authentic existence are taken up forcefully by Sartre. For the author of *Existentialism and Humanism* the world can be divided into the in-itself (things) and the for-itself (human consciousness). Sartre gives this distinction between **being-in-itself** and **being-for-itself** an interesting twist. Think of what you are, form a picture or general idea of yourself, your nature. Now straight away there are two selves present: the self being thought of and the self thinking. The self being thought of is your notion of what you have been up to this point, but thinking about yourself is a further development of your consciousness, a change in yourself, so your general picture of what you are has left this out and is, to a certain extent, untrue. Consciousness is not, therefore, a solid, complete, full and given thing. It is a process of self-creation, continual improvisation based on a rejection of what it has been up to this moment.

Sartre does not believe in human nature; we are what we become. You cannot rationally think of yourself as something fixed and limited, for even to do that is an exercise of your freedom; it's your decision. For Sartre, inauthentic existence consists precisely in thinking of oneself as fixed, as unfree or as a thing. We are all familiar with people saying things like 'I can't possibly do that' or 'I'm afraid I'm not the sort of person who ...'. Such people, in one way or another, set limits to their range of action and deny their radical freedom. All this, argues Sartre, is part of the willed deception of everyday life (**bad faith**). Sartre wants no truck with theories that help human beings to see themselves as unavoidably constrained in their actions. Hence he opposes Freudian psychoanalysis, behaviourism and all other deterministic philosophies. These simply give individuals excuses for their own refusal to recognise personal freedom. Equally, he has little time for Christianity with its concept of a divinely created human nature and God-given values to which all must subscribe. As Sartre sees it, we are all free to create our own values. Man is not made for any purpose; he must find his own purpose.

Of course, Sartre recognises that we have physical limits – our size, our shape, our disabilities. He argues that none of this has to be put up with – after all, we can commit suicide and are free to do so. Thus, if we prefer to live and be blind rather than to be dead, we choose to be blind. We choose to live with and relate to our blindness.

Anguish

'Anguish' is the term used by Sartre to describe the realisation that there is no *a priori* justification for moral decision-making, while at the same time being aware that it is incumbent on us to make a moral decision; it is a 'moment of complete and profound responsibility'. Sartre illustrates the weight of anguish felt by moral

Jean-Paul Sartre (1905–1980)

Sartre was the epitome of French intellectual chic, inspiring his followers to dress in the existentialist uniform of black beret and turtle neck sweater and to socialise in the cafés of Paris where they would discuss their atheist and communist views. Sartre was a Parisian, of German extraction on his mother's side. She was a relation of the musician and Christian missionary Albert Schweitzer (1875–1965). In his autobiographical work *Words* Sartre recalls the restrictive, Protestant atmosphere of his upbringing and how he developed a fascination with literature from an early age, recoiling from the rough and tumble of the playground. Later in his life, Sartre was deeply and personally engaged in many political disputes, including the French resistance against Nazism, the struggle to free Algeria from French occupation and various staunch defences of French communism. Sartre personified the adage that the pen is mightier than the sword with various satirical plays and articles in the newspaper *Le Monde*. When he died on 15 April 1980, one commentator mourned the loss of a moral compass that would register an august opinion on most contemporary issues. Sartre wrote with a serious commitment to freedom, social equality and shared responsibility, but favoured freedom as a central theme. His hatred of constraint and determinism was mirrored in his personal life as much as in his philosophical writings: he did not covet material possessions and once gave away all his books. He rejected commitment to any single lover, even his long-term partner Simone de Beauvoir, whom he affectionately referred to as 'the beaver'.

Significant works
Nausea (1938)
In Camera and Other Plays (1943)
Being and Nothingness (1943)
Existentialism and Humanism (1945)
Critique of Dialectical Reason (1959)

agents by telling the Old Testament story of Abraham and Isaac. Kierkegaard had written an important meditation on this episode a number of years before, in his work *Fear and Trembling* (1843). The story tells of how 'the father of Judaism', Abraham, having prayed with his wife Sarah to have a child, was granted such a gift by God, who then put the devoted patriarch to the test by ordering him to sacrifice his son. The old man leads Isaac up mount Horeb on the back of a donkey before binding him (the story is often referred to as the *Haggadah* or binding of Isaac). When he raises his knife in obedience to God's command he is told to stop and sacrifice a ram instead, which he finds caught by its horns in the nearby scrub. This powerful story is intended to show the faithful that the Jewish God does not require human sacrifices of this sort, which were common in many pagan religions at the time. Sartre refers to it as a prime example of moral angst. He casts each human being in the role of Abraham. Each of us has an uneasy conscience, disturbed by the adrenaline of moral decision-making. Yet, as Sartre puts it: 'it is still I myself who must decide / it is only I who choose / I am Abraham' (31–32). Our heartfelt anguish, however, isn't necessarily a bad thing if it heightens the sense of moral responsibility. This degree of accountability would make us view every other human being as dear to us as a child, even if we are only in a professional relationship, as in the case of a commanding officer and his soldiers. The Jewish existentialist Martin Buber (1878–1965) later referred to this outlook as an 'I–thou' relationship, as opposed to an 'I–it' encounter, where one human being treats the other as an object or empty role.

Abandonment

Sartre's version of existentialism has much in common with that of Nietzsche. The latter declared in his *The Gay Science* (1882) that 'God is dead', which is not to say that God was ever alive, but that humanity invented such a conception and is now free to dispense with it. The Sartrean version of 'God is dead' philosophy is summed up in the term 'abandonment'. It is a feeling of **existential angst** at being alone in the universe without any supernatural assistance to help us decide what to do. Sartre has rejected the Aristotelian solution of working out our essence in order to calculate what we ought to do. He also rejects the Nietzschean response, which is to trample the concept of 'ought' into the ground and to live by our drives and whatever asserts the will to power. Instead, Sartre's position rejects the essentialist 'is' but reaffirms a moral 'ought'. The author dispels the Enlightenment myth that attempts to establish a set of *a priori* moral truths through our ability to reason. Such moral realism as espoused by Kant in the shadow of Plato's 'intelligible heaven' of forms denies our freedom. Instead, the absence of God intensifies the freedom we experience as moral decision-makers and reconstructs humanity in the image of God. We are empowered to choose our actions as we think fit, without excuse, without limitation and without the confinement of dogma. In so doing we are free to transcend our own humanity.

Task

Look at the painting entitled *The Scream* (1893) by Munch. What do you think the artist was trying to portray in the piece?

Sartre's student

Sartre exemplifies the human predicament of abandonment with the story of one of his philosophy students who approached him for help. The young man was faced with the dilemma of whether to avenge the death of his brother and fight for France against the Germans or whether to stay at home and care for his vulnerable and doting mother who was separated from her husband, the boy's father. The author points out that no normative ethical theory can assist his decision, as there are no *a priori* moral truths. One cannot, on utilitarian grounds, predict a national collectivity of happiness in contrast to his mother's distress as the military operation may fail. It is unclear which is the greater virtue: devotion to one's family or to one's country. Christianity fails to provide clear advice as to which actions are more in keeping with God's divine plan. Kant's categorical imperative creates a paradox in which one cannot escape treating someone as a means rather than an end. To escape this slough of despond, Sartre advocates the prioritising of feelings over abstract values: 'In the end it is feeling that counts; the direction in which it is really pushing me is the one I ought to choose' (38).

Sartre appears to be advocating a subtle linguistic theory here that smacks of certain elements of behaviourism. Any statement that involves my asserting 'I feel X' may be translated into one in which I am asserting 'I have already chosen X and am already committed to this course of action'. One manifestation of this choice that is already made is my search for an adviser who I already know will confirm my intuition even though I might pretend that I am searching for impartiality.

The Jesuit

Sartre cites a further example to illustrate the theme of abandonment. When Sartre was in prison for his work for the Resistance in the summer of 1940, he met a Jesuit priest, who, like many religious people, claimed that he did not choose the religious life, but that God had chosen him and communicated such a choice through various calamities that befell him: an unhappy and impoverished childhood, an aborted love affair and failure to pass the entrance examination for the military. This anecdote is not of philosophical relevance because of the claims it makes about God but because it illustrates the link between abandonment and anguish, freedom and choice. It is ourselves alone who possess the freedom to interpret the significance of an act in any way we see fit, and is like the Abrahamic story in this respect. This view has important epistemic, ontological and ethical implications. Sartre argues that signs do not possess objective meaning and that significance is a thing thrust upon them by the perceiver. Ontologically, this means that we are free to 'decide our being' (39). Such freedom of choice, described rhetorically as 'abandonment', yields to the human reality of anguish, the pressure of making decisions.

Despair

In the next paragraph, the author examines the notion of despair (39). 'Despair' is the term Sartre uses to describe the realisation that we are free to act but our actions can often be in vain; as a consequence 'we should act without hope'. He harks back to an earlier conclusion that we act according to the strength of our feelings (37). This raises the question as to whether there should be any constraints to the strength of our feeling. Sartre again reinforces his atheism, declaring 'there is no God and no prevenient design' but makes the point that freedom of choice is bound, nevertheless, to take place within the realm of possibilities and is therefore a matter of probability. The realisation that we are limited by possibilities engenders a feeling of despair in the free-spirited individual. This feeling of despair is heightened by the knowledge that it is always possible that my actions are somehow thwarted. So, for instance, a late-running tram might cause me to miss a meeting. Or, owing to unforeseen political circumstances, my comrades in a political party (Sartre uses the communist party as an example) might abandon the struggle they promised to continue after my death. Such grounds for despair draw our attention to other people's freedom: 'there is no human nature which I can take as foundational /

men are free agents and will decide, tomorrow, what man is then to be' (40).

I partake in this freedom and am then bound to commit an action. The notion of despair inevitably leads back to the reality of anguish. I am not able to abandon such anguish or refrain from choice as only God would have the power to do this and there is no such being. Inaction, then, is a type of action in that it entails choice and consequences. Pascal had argued some centuries before that agnosticism is itself a choice – a choice to be unsure about God's existence. Every choice is then an action and it is nonsensical to talk in counterfactual terms: 'If I had lived under circumstance X then I would have been able to achieve result Y', where Y might be a successful love affair, a best seller or the procreation of a loving family:

> There is no love apart from the deeds of love; no potentiality of love other than that which is manifest in loving; there is no genius other than that which is expressed in works of art. (41)

At this stage of the lecture (42–44), Sartre returns to the initial accusations that he intended to refute at the start. The pessimistic criticism that existentialism is morally impotent is dismissed and attention is focused on the optimistic criticism that existentialism idealises free choice. This criticism asserts that human beings are not free agents but rather bound by 'determining factors, psychic or organic'. Sartre cites the examples of cowardice and heroism and concludes that there is no such thing as a pre-determined temperament and that one can only use such descriptions if they have been given actual value in actions. Again Sartre stresses human responsibility, but somewhat incongruously seems to have a pre-conceived notion that heroism is morally more praiseworthy than cowardice. This may indeed be the case but it does not seem to follow from his analysis.

Review question

Briefly explain what Sartre means by the following terms: abandonment, anguish and despair.

Task

Discuss the validity of the following criticisms of Sartre's viewpoint. How would he have responded to them?

- The text is overly rhetorical and only interested in persuading by use of memorable phrases, forcefully asserted but not argued.
- There are too many non-sequiturs such as 'In fashioning myself I fashion man'.
- The lecture seems self-contradictory in places, for example the author says man has no essence but then says that part of the definition of being human is to be free.
- The view that humans do not possess an essence is overly simplistic and unscientific.
- Sartre's account of freedom is absurdly optimistic.
- Sartre assumes rather than proves the non-existence of God.
- *Existentialism and Humanism* fails in all its main aims and does not answer its critics.

Intersubjectivity

Sartre borrows the same descriptive apparatus as the seventeenth-century rationalist René Descartes in the *Meditations*. Descartes uses the terms 'essence' and 'existence' but differs from Sartre in believing that human beings possess an essence founded in their thought.[7] Sartre takes as his starting point the Cartesian **cogito**, not out of any bourgeois egomania but out of the need to explore our existence. Unlike the contingency of tables, chairs, stones and all other objects, human beings remain unique in their possession of a necessary, absolute truth: existence through thought. We can establish our own existence through introspection, 'the immediate sense of oneself'. Yet this subjectivity does not remain inward looking and self-absorbed but is necessarily interactive owing to the existence of other people. The theme of interaction between minds is prevalent through much of Sartre's writings (e.g. in the author's play *Huis Clos*, variously translated as 'No Escape', 'No Exit' or 'In Camera') and is termed **intersubjectivity**. The author declares: 'I cannot obtain any truth whatsoever about myself, except through the mediation of another' (45).

Our interaction with each other and with the world around us, which Sartre phrases in Marxian terms as 'the necessities of being in the world', constitute that which all human beings have in common. It is the human universality of condition and is shared by humankind, irrespective of time (epoch), place or cultural milieu. But this does not constitute human essence as our interaction with each other and the world is in flux and subject to changes brought about by our conscious desires and decision-making.

Sartre condenses his message into a particularly rich passage where he compares the absolute nature of moral commitment, gained through our freedom, to the relative cultural context in which we find ourselves placed (47). The same tension exists within Descartes' famous proposition 'I think therefore I am' (the *cogito*), which stands as a necessary truth about my existence and a personal truth about me at any given time and place. Sartre defines our existence as that which is exercised through personal choice. Any absolute truth about existence is at one and the same time absolute and a moment in our actual existence and is in no sense something separate, rarefied or abstracted. At a deeper level, the universal condition of humanity is characterised by freedom more than thought. The category of 'thought' itself covers a range of activities – breathing, eating, sleeping or behaving in various ways – and is localised in particular brainwaves; thought is thus relative to the various activities that go to make up our personal histories.

Sartre erects another signpost to remind his readers of the journey this lecture promised to take – that is, to respond to the accusations that existentialism is anarchic, immoral and valueless. The theme of freedom is again stressed, this time with reference to the French novelist André Gide's notion of the *acte gratuit*. In Gide's comic novel *The Caves of the Vatican*, a character stabs himself in the thigh as an expression of freedom (*disponibilité*). It is a deliberately gratuitous act in response to his sense of liberation and one which foreshadows an episode in Sartre's *The Age of Reason* when the novel's central character, a philosophy teacher called Mathieu, pins his hand to a table with a knife in order to outdo a student that he is drinking with and wants to impress. He later wonders about the alternative, less painful actions that he might have taken to exercise his freedom and why he chose such a gratuitous and dramatic gesture:

> It was not only to defy Ivich that he had stuck the knife into his hand; it was a challenge to Jacques, and Brunet, and Daniel, and to his whole life. 'I'm a ghastly kind of fool,' he thought. 'Brunet was right in saying that I'm a grown-up child'. But he couldn't help being pleased. Ivich looked at Mathieu's hand, nailed to the table, and the blood gathering around the blade. Then she looked at Mathieu; her expression had entirely changed.
> 'Why did you do that?' she said, gently.
> 'Why did you?' said Mathieu, stiffly.[8]

Task

What does Sartre mean by 'freedom'? Write a paragraph explaining the author's justification for the following assertions, made in *Being and Nothingness*.

1 There are no accidents in life.
2 In war there are no innocent victims.
3 In a certain way I choose being born.

Sartre takes examples from real life to prove the merits of his assertions, and in the next few paragraphs focuses on relationships (49). The line taken is that moral decisions are neither in accordance with *a priori* moral certainties that are set in stone, nor are they *ad hoc*, capricious decisions made on the spur of the moment. The author draws a parallel between aesthetics and ethics, though is quick to declaim that he is not advocating an aesthetic moral theory as Nietzsche did in *Beyond Good and Evil*:

> In life, a man commits himself, draws his own portrait and there is nothing but that portrait. (42)

> Let us say that the moral choice is comparable to the construction of a work of art. (48)

The comparison being drawn between the aesthetic and ethical is concerned with subjectivity rather than objectivity and in this respect is similar to non-cognitivism, though Sartre would depart from the view that ethical statements are to be classed as meaningless. 'Subjective' means creative, inventive, experimental and, in the case of the ethical, it means that it is interactive. Art, for Sartre, in the truest sense does not consist in the ready-made or in painting with numbers but means a work of inspiration sketched upon a blank canvas. Moral agents are both the creator and *tabula rasa* upon which their lives are inscribed. In the style of Wilde's eponymous hero Dorian Gray, each of us paints an invisible picture of ourselves throughout life to which is added a daub of detail or colour through each action we choose. The 'moral problem' is at one and the same time always the same, namely what does one create?

Bad faith

'Bad faith' is a term used by Sartre in this lecture and in the most famous textbook of existentialism, *Being and Nothingness*, to describe the human propensity to self-deceive. The opposite is good faith or **authenticity**. People deceive themselves – that is, act in bad faith – if they fail to acknowledge and act in accordance with the feelings of anguish; in so doing they reify themselves, choosing to live inauthentically as beings-in-themselves. Critics of Sartre have alleged that he makes a number of fundamental mistakes in arguing this line:

- Sartre assumes a set of ethical standards.
- Bad faith might be better for us.
- Mechanisms for bad faith such as wishful thinking, cynicism or incomprehension seem out of our control.
- He overestimates the extent of our freedom.

In response to these points the author argues that those acting in bad faith are making a straightforward factual error and that drawing attention to this does not imply a moral judgement. Yet it seems inadequate just to summon the individual to authenticity without giving any indication as to how to act.

Sartre goes on to argue that other people play a devastating role in forcing one to think of oneself as an image, a particular kind of being instead of as a 'no-thing'. To recognise other people is to be aware of them categorising and classifying you. You can struggle to present yourself as you wish to be seen, but you cannot escape the definition the other thrusts upon you. You cannot avoid the label imposed on you but can only engage in a struggle over it. Sartre claims that other people are a menace or, as he puts it more colourfully at the end of the play *No Exit*, 'Hell is other people'. It is, nevertheless, in the context of our relationships with others that we must exercise our own freedom and achieve authentic existence. Sartre argues that you can only do this if you are prepared to engage in the struggle for their freedom. Throughout his life, Sartre was engaged in politics and everyday affairs.

In summation, Sartre offers a criterion by which to judge acts, described in more detail in his magnum opus *Being and Nothingness*. One is to act out of good faith and to avoid acting out of bad faith, as this is self-deception. In so doing, one becomes a better person. This is the process of amelioration or progress referred to in the text (50). The argument may be expressed as follows:

1. In the case of human beings, our existence precedes our essence.
2. We are a 'project' whose values are self-imposed.
3. Such personal values also have universal value.
4. Those who do not choose through anguish suffer from self-deception.
5. Anguish is a condition of action.
6. Existentialism as a path to authenticity and action is the antithesis of quietism and pessimism.

The above existentialist view of ethics is well articulated by Mary Warnock in the following passage:

> A choice, Sartre says, is the assertion of a value; and a value is necessarily universal. Subjectivity, from which existentialism starts, entails only that each man chooses himself; but this necessarily means that he is choosing everyone else as well … since my choice for myself involves a choice for others, Sartre argues that it is always appropriate to raise the question, 'What would happen if everyone did as you were doing?'[9]

One might criticise aspects of the above argument; certainly the third proposition begs proof and one might argue in opposition that diversity in human taste is more worth while. A more general criticism is that the author dwells on the 'how' aspect of moral action – that is, whether something is committed in good or bad faith – and not 'what' the action consists in. Any heinous crime is justified according to Sartre's criteria of good faith unless the author is prepared to state that 'all morally acceptable actions involve respect for others', which is surely an example of an *a priori* moral truth, which he denies.

Two heroines

Sartre criticises those who cannot face themselves in good faith as cowards and terms those who, like Descartes, believe their existence is necessary as 'scum'. This latter description is closer to the English 'froth' as in the title of Boris Vian's satire of Sartre, *The Froth on the Daydream,* and signifies the contingent and ephemeral nature of human life in contrast to their mistaken over-inflated conception of it.

Two literary cases are cited: the first is the case of Maggie Tulliver in *The Mill on the Floss,* who sacrifices herself for a lost love; the second is La Sanseverina in Stendhal's *Charterhouse of Parma,* who sacrifices conjugal love for the sake of passion. Sartre points out that, while the intentions of these respective characters are far removed from each other, the effect on their lives is nevertheless very close – that is, 'to sacrifice oneself upon the plane of passion' in order to be free. The heroine in George Eliot's *The Mill on the Floss* (1860) exhibits some notably existentialist traits in her anguish in decision-making, her resistance to constraint and her intuition for intersubjectivity and strength of feeling. All are exemplified in a dialogue that takes place between Stephen and Maggie in their rooms at the inn in Book VI, Chapter 14, which reads like an excerpt from *No Exit*:

> 'No, I don't sacrifice you, I couldn't sacrifice you', she said as soon as she could speak again; 'but I can't believe in a good for you, that I feel – that we both feel is wrong towards others. We can't choose happiness either for ourselves or for another; we can't tell where that will lie. We can only choose whether we can indulge ourselves in the present moment or whether we will renounce that for the sake of obeying the divine voice within us, for the

sake of being true to all the motives that sanctify our lives.'[10]

Sartre believes that we cannot make a moral judgement on the content of choices but only on whether they are free choices. The decisions made by Maggie Tulliver and La Sanseverina are opposed to morality but are made in good faith upon the plane of free commitment.

Review question

Briefly describe what Sartre would class as an 'inauthentic' moral life.

Final thoughts

Existentialism and Humanism was a response to the critics of Sartre who accused him of espousing an amoral philosophy. The author disagrees and claims that he is a thoroughgoing humanist, but not one who delights in the fripperies of human achievement. Instead he is struck by the gravity of our present predicament in being faced with fresh moral responsibility: 'man is still to be determined'. The criticisms first outlined at the start of the text are revisited again at the end. Let us rehearse them for the last time, together with Sartre's defence:

- *Quietism (the communist criticism):* Sartre argues that existentialism is a philosophy of action (24 and 44) and that human beings commit themselves through action and in so doing draw their own portraits. Through a sense of anguish one recognises the responsibility of choice and through despair one does not learn to give up but learns to act without self-deception or illusion.

- *Pessimism (the popular criticism):* Sartre replies that it is ironic that this is the popular criticism of existentialism because it is 'the wisdom of the people' that is pessimistic. Existentialism is optimistic in confronting people with the possibility of choice rather than determinism: 'the destiny of man is placed within himself' (44).

- *Subjectivism (the communist criticism):* Sartre is proud that subjectivism is the foundation stone of existentialism as there cannot be a more secure foundation than the *cogito* – that is, one's immediate sense of oneself. Yet this is no narrow subjectivism but a point of departure that leads to intersubjectivity and the insight that other people are a necessary condition of our existence; it is through our interaction with others that we recognise what we have chosen to be.

- *Relativism (the Christian criticism):* Sartre believes that the only absolute moral truth is that we are committed to choice and must take responsibility for our actions. This appears to many as a useful piece of advice in a 'post-religious' society. It is not true that we cannot criticise others, although we cannot as such talk of moral progress as realists would like (50). Existentialists can criticise others in a logical way if their choices are founded upon the error of bad faith. Any individual who hides behind human nature or determinism is a self-deceiver and is not making a free choice.

Sartre's aim is to turn humanism into an existentialist ethical theory rather than an essentialist one. Just as an artist is free to choose what to paint, human beings are free to choose what they are to be and, as a corollary, are not determined but transcendent and 'self-surpassing'. This is the philosophy of existential humanism, slightly disrupted in the final furlong by the author's assertion that his views are founded on a consistent atheism but would still make sense if God existed. This appears to be in contradiction but is perhaps a rhetorical attempt to draw the reader's attention to the fact that religious people have more grounds to be pessimistic whereas existentialists should be optimistic in light of what has been said.

Revision question

1 Outline and illustrate one of the following concepts: abandonment, anguish, despair, authenticity, bad faith (self-deception).

2 Assess the notion that human 'existence precedes essence'.

3 Outline and illustrate one criticism alleged against existentialism that Sartre refutes in *Existentialism and Humanism*.

4 Evaluate the role of choice in Sartre's existentialism.

5 Sartre draws on many literary examples in the text (from Zola to George Eliot). Select one of these examples and explain its significance for existentialism.

Discussion questions

- How successful is Sartre at meeting his critics?
- How is it possible to be both religious and an existentialist?
- Is Sartre's view of human freedom too idealistic?
- Is Sartre right to assert that 'in choosing for myself I choose for all mankind'?
- How can Sartre expect existentialists to remain optimistic in a climate of abandonment, anguish and despair?

Glossary of key terms

Authenticity: our awareness of anguish, abandonment and despair and our ability to make an appropriate response. Being authentic is realising human finitude and our approaching death; to ignore this is to live a lie.

Bad faith: a form of self-deception where we objectify ourselves, e.g. by conceiving of ourselves as a role rather than as a person.

Being-in-itself: the term used by Sartre to describe inanimate objects such as cauliflowers, moss and stones whose essence precedes existence and whose existence is consequently shaped by the laws of nature.

Being-for-itself: the term used by Sartre to describe human beings who are free to decide for themselves how they behave and what they believe.

Cogito: the *cogito* refers to Descartes' famous saying in his *Discourse on Method*, *cogito ergo sum*, meaning 'I think therefore I am'. Sartre uses our thinking as a starting-point for his moral philosophy.

Essentialism: the belief that we are free to describe human beings as having a pre-determined 'essence'.

Existential angst: a general term to describe the feelings of anguish, abandonment and despair.

Facticity: the notion that despite being free as human beings to create ourselves we are inevitably bound by certain material conditions and physical limitations.

Intersubjectivity: the Sartrean view that others are indispensable to my existence. Human beings live within a network of freethinking individuals where one person's choice will affect another's and vice versa.

Quietism: the accusation that philosophy is an impractical, rarified and useless activity.

Suggested reading

- Kamber, R. (1999) *On Sartre*, Belmont, Wadsworth
  This work supplies background information and contains a useful introduction to Sartre's ethics
- McCulloch, G. (1994) *Using Sartre*, London, Routledge
  This volume focuses on Sartre's ontology and suits a more advanced readership
- Macquarrie, J. (1976) *Existentialism*, Harmondsworth, Penguin
  An elderly introduction to existentialism that is still worth consulting

- Matthew, E. (1996) *Twentieth Century French Philosophy*, Oxford, OUP
  Chapter 4 is on Sartre but the rest of the book provides useful background reading
- Warnock, M. (1967) *Existentialist Ethics*, London, Macmillan
  Classic introduction to Sartre's moral philosophy

Notes

[1] Sartre, J.-P. (1981) *Nausea*, Harmondsworth, Penguin, p. 190.

[2] Ibid. p. 188.

[3] Ibid. p. 218.

[4] Ibid. p. 35.

[5] Sartre, J.-P. (1980) *Existentialism and Humanism*, London, Methuen, p. 28; hereafter page references to *Existentialism and Humanism* are given in brackets and refer to this edition.

[6] Warburton, N. 'A Student's Guide to Jean-Paul Sartre's *Existentialism and Humanism*' in *Philosophy Now* 15 Spring/Summer 1996, pp. 27–31.

[7] Descartes, R. (2000) *The Meditations and Other Metaphysical Writings*, London, Penguin, p. 26.

[8] Sartre, J.-P. (1974) *The Age of Reason*, Harmondsworth, Penguin, ch. 11, p. 195.

[9] Warnock, M. (1967) *Existentialist Ethics*, London, Macmillan, p. 40.

[10] Eliot, G. (1994) *The Mill on the Floss*, London, Penguin, p. 489.

PART 3 Appendices

Appendix 1

Introduction to aesthetics

The purest and most thoughtful minds are those which love colour the most. (John Ruskin)

Events like the Turner Prize regularly fuel controversy by rewarding artists with substantial sums of money for work which apparently consists in the mundane: a pile of bricks, an unmade bed, a flashing light bulb. The question 'Why is this art?' is a challenging one and too broad for exposition in a short appendix like this; nevertheless I would like to introduce some of the arguments to whet your appetite and also to illustrate how this branch of philosophy, known as aesthetics, is in many ways a theatre for many of the arguments already examined in the preceding text.

The word 'aesthetics' derives from the Greek *aesthesis* meaning 'perception'. But art is not just of epistemological interest because it depends upon sensory perception but because some thinkers (we shall call them 'cognitivists') hold that there are objective criteria that enable us to know what counts as art and what does not. The cognitive school of thought attempts to provide objective criteria to describe what counts as aesthetically valuable, while non-cognitivism consigns aesthetic judgement to the realm of belief and opinion. These opposing standpoints are represented by the relative positions of Plato and Ayer, which could not be further removed from each other. Whereas the ancient Greek philosopher was suspicious of how artists were swept away on a tide of inspiration (e.g. *The Laws* 719c), A. J. Ayer was a keen patron of the arts and believed them to be a force for the good; whereas Plato believed we could define beauty, the twentieth-century empiricist held that aesthetic pronouncements were literally meaningless.

This short appendix considers one possible criterion for art, before linking the principle to some examples and surveying the main non-cognitive criticisms. There are many other questions in the philosophy of art such as: Is beauty definable? Is art beyond the realm of moral responsibility? What is the relationship between the percipient, the artist and the work of art? For the moment, however, we are concerned with the problem of how art is to be recognised.

There is as much skill involved in the interpretation and criticism of art as there is in its manufacture. Such a skill of interpretation involves, to borrow a Quinean image, spinning a web of intellectual engagement about points of reference chosen and deemed appropriate by the 'aesthetic patient' or onlooker. There is not one exclusive, fossilised account of art that is right while others are wrong. Cognitivism holds that any approach needs to be critical, as the work of art *qua* art needs to reward interest. In upshot, let us call this the principle of attentive engagement and express it as follows:

> An entity may be classed as art if, and only if, our critical attention is engaged and rewarded.

What is attentive engagement? I am attentively engaged if I am able to see more and more things of interest in a work, simultaneously appreciating the representing vehicle while at the same time learning new respect for the thing represented. I am attentively engaged if my mind is stirred to think and feel something about the exhibit. This is largely dependent on the eloquence of technique of the artist, and how he or she uses skill to subtle and delicate effect to illustrate a depth of richness and content. That is not to say that art rests solely upon the technical ability or craft of the aesthetic agent – the artist – but that such technique is a necessary component. Russell is incorrect in citing the proposition 'A bad poet is a poet' as an example of a logically necessary truth, as a writer of verse only earns his or her status as a poet if the verse is classed as poetry rather than doggerel. This is

Bedroom in Arles *by Vincent van Gogh*

My Bed *by Tracey Emin*

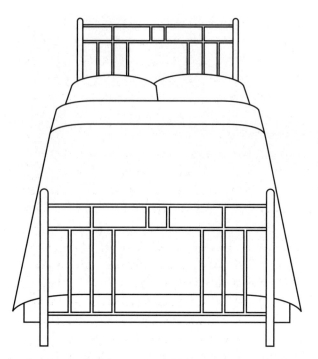

Sketch of a bed by my mum

an old cognitive argument that goes back to the first book of Plato's *Republic*, where he argues that a mathematician is so called because mathematicians get their sums right not wrong. But is there a right and wrong in art?

Task

How does the principle of attentive engagement work? Consider the three examples above. Does a close analysis reward your interest? Which would you classify as a work of art?
- *Bedroom in Arles* (1888) by Vincent van Gogh
- *My Bed* (1998) by Tracey Emin
- Sketch of a bed by my mum

Emin's bed buys into an ideology inspired by Marcel Duchamp's 'readymade pieces'. Readymade art is that branch of conceptual art where the exhibitor takes an everyday object and displays it in a gallery to encourage the viewing public to meditate on its significance. This has led to the argument that it is the position a work holds in a recognised art gallery that defines the piece as art. To borrow the title from one of Nelson Goodman's articles, the question should not be 'What is art' but 'Where is art?' Does this stand up to interrogation? One might assert that the readymade school commits a circular argument

by asserting that art is displayed in a gallery while defining what is displayed in a gallery as art. This does not provide a definition and, while the gallery setting may help aesthetic appreciation through practical measures such as lighting, silence and space, context cannot create art. Non-cognitivists reply that we are misguided in our search for definitions in cases such as this, as the subject matter does not concern the explicable or measurable. Questions that start 'What is…' for the most part do not have answers.

The readymade school of art is of course right in asserting that art does not exist in a vacuum but is always in a conceptual framework. The depiction of beds in the above works carries a resonance of the arguments against art advanced by Plato in Book X of *The Republic*, where he uses the example of beds. Plato was suspicious of art as he saw it as a morally corrupting force. A problem arises for the Platonist in how to clarify a work of art, because art seems to be more than an object as it buys into the abstract world of forms. Works of art provide a third classification of existing things – that is, things that depict particulars, are a particular, yet reflect elements from the metaphysical world of essences. This Platonic terminology might help us to define what art is, i.e. that which transcends the particular and universal. Yet observers might be interested in particulars and not find deep and meaningful essences (the forms) attentively engaging at all. Cognitivists escape this point by arguing that their remit is not to normatively instruct people on what they should or shouldn't like but to define art as that which rewards attention, of whatever nature it might be. This is a much thinner notion compared with the bold promise encountered earlier to define the objective criteria for art.

The principle of attentive engagement runs into other difficulties:

- *Disinterested engagement:* Might it not be the case that a work should be still classed as art if it engenders disinterested engagement, as when I plough through a novel by Agatha Christie to find out 'whodunit'? The difference between disinterested engagement and attentive engagement seems to lie in an individual's motivation. If the only reason why I finish the crime novel is to be entertained I might just as well have played a round of golf or a computer game, neither of which counts as art.

- *Too attentive an engagement:* A critic may allege that there are no limitations placed on my attentive engagement as outlined in the above principle. Do I not, therefore, run the risk of overinterpretation, as when an overly zealous reader analyses each phrase of a poem at the cost of appreciating the piece as a whole? In this case, practical criticism is being misused and it would be unfair to take this as a paradigm case.

- *Attentive engagement in a non-aesthetic object:* Why can't I be said to attentively engage in a non-aesthetic object? One might counter this by asserting that, although I may have my attention engaged when watching an autopsy or admiring an artefact in a museum, it is an engagement that is not deliberately created by an artist for that purpose.

- *The intentional fallacy:* A further criticism might involve trapping any advocate of the argument from attentive engagement in a fallacy known as the intentional fallacy. The intentional fallacy as applied to the study of aesthetics holds that the private intentions of the artist can never be known as they occupy a privileged and inaccessible realm of subjectivity and are, therefore, irrelevant to the piece of work as art. Yet if details about the artist's psychology, intentions and life situation were

known about, perhaps through diaries or an interview, would not this add to the perceiver's attentive engagement? Are not exponents of the argument from attentive engagement duty-bound to enquire into such details? The appeal of *My Bed*, it has been alleged, is that it reflects the feelings of angst and dejection experienced by a jilted lover when Tracey Emin successfully turned a crisis in her own life into art, at the suggestion of a friend. In a way, the argument from attentive engagement is a response to the intentional fallacy and entails that if the artist's intentions add to active interest then they are worth reflecting upon. It is essential, though, to see such predictions as the artist's private state and an addition to an already engaging piece of art rather than the sole source of attentive engagement.

The few thoughts outlined above merely provide an aperitif to aesthetics as well as a digestif at the end of this book. This is an issue that engages many philosophers' attention and is always a good way to start an argument.

> **Task**
>
> Organise a formal debate between two groups of people, one proposing the motion that Emin's *My Bed* is art and the other opposing it. You should start by appointing a chairperson to keep order. Begin with a short speech from each of the camps outlining their opposing views. At the end of the discussion take a vote on the motion: for, against or abstaining.

Suggested reading

- Budd, M. (1996) *Values of Art*, London, Penguin
- Hanfling, O. ed. (1992) *Philosophical Aesthetics: An Introduction*, Oxford, Blackwell
- Lyas, C. (1997) *Aesthetics*, UCL Press
- Sheppard, A. (1987) *Aesthetics: An Introduction to the Philosophy of Art*, Oxford, OUP
- Warburton, N. (2003) *The Art Question*, London, Routledge

Appendix 2 Critical thinking

The fact of twilight does not mean we cannot distinguish between day and night. (Samuel Johnson)

Philosophy is more of a way of thinking than a body of knowledge that needs to be learnt. Many philosophy graduates will admit that, while they cannot always remember which famous thinker said what, they nevertheless feel equipped with the skills of reasoning and critical judgement, which can be readily applied to new and diverse subject matter. While philosophy is concerned with ultimate questions of reality, the methods analytic philosophers use have recently found a place in the curriculum as a discrete discipline called 'critical thinking'. This appendix seeks to introduce the important notions of inference and fallacy that are often emphasised in courses on critical thinking.

Inference

We can draw a distinction between statements (also referred to as propositions, judgements or premises) and inferences. Inferences can have any number of statements in them; the important point is that they must be arranged in support of some conclusion. Consider the following argument:

1 Bob is either mad or bad.
2 He isn't mad.
3 Therefore, he is bad.

In premises **1** and **2** we are mounting an argument designed to establish the conclusion. If both premises **1** and **2** are true, the conclusion has got to be true; philosophers would say 'it follows'. In fact it *cannot not* be true; it follows necessarily. Such an argument in which the conclusion follows necessarily from the premises is called a valid argument or syllogism. Look at the next example:

1 Bob is French, German or English.
2 He certainly isn't French.
3 Therefore, he must be English.

This is an invalid argument even if the premises are both true, because the conclusion doesn't follow from the premises. Consider the third example:

1 Gandhi was either Russian or Chinese.
2 He wasn't Russian.
3 Therefore, Gandhi must have been Chinese.

This argument is an example of a valid inference. If we accept the premises then the conclusion follows necessarily. This may sound strange as the first premise is quite obviously false, which makes it a bad argument to use in the real world if you want to make a point, but the inference as a piece of inference is a perfectly valid one. A valid inference is, therefore, not an argument which establishes a true conclusion or even has true premises but one which, if we suppose hypothetically that the premises are acceptable, we are bound to accept as the conclusion that follows logically from them.

Ultimately, if we believe an inference to be valid we do so because it seems intuitively to be logical. Throughout the history of philosophy, logicians have been interested in cataloguing the main types of valid inference in much the same way as botanists might be interested in recording types of plants. Logicians look beyond the contents of an argument to how it works, i.e. its form. Consider the following:

1 All cows eat grass.
2 Daisy is a cow.
3 Therefore, Daisy eats grass.

One may substitute almost anything for 'Daisy' and anything for 'grass' and as long as you do it for every instance of the word you will end up with a valid argument. A philosopher might formalise the argument using variables instead of real names:

1 All As are Bs.

2 X is an A.

3 Therefore, X is a B.

Another type of inference can be summarised as follows:

1 Either p or q.

2 Not p.

3 Therefore q.

An inference is signalled by an 'argument-indicating' expression such as 'therefore', 'so', 'thus' or 'hence' that show the move from the premises to the conclusion. The expressions 'since', 'follows from' and 'for' refer back from the conclusion to the premises.

Statement logic is concerned with arguments in which complex statements are built up from simple ones by four kinds of operation. These operations are as follows:

- Negation: e.g. it is not the case that X.
- Conjunction: e.g. statement X and statement Y.
- Disjunction: e.g. statement X or statement Y.
- Conditionalisation: e.g. if X then Y.

The complex sentences used in arguments are made up of the above operations. For example, 'If infanticide is wrong then so is abortion'. Philosophers employ formal arguments to express themselves in the clearest possible terms.

> **Task**
>
> Write out an example of a formally valid inference.

Fallacy

A good argument is the product of logical reasoning or one that is backed up with evidence. It is insufficient to say that an argument is good because it comes from a particular source or because it sounds convincing. Bad arguments such as these are called 'fallacies'. There follows a list of the top ten fallacies or mistakes in reasoning. It is noteworthy that many famous philosophers have committed one or more of these errors.

1 *The* ad hominem *fallacy:* one commits the *ad hominem* fallacy by criticising the person rather than their argument. One apportions praise or blame according to who the arguer is rather than the validity of what they say. Such detail is of course immaterial. Nietzsche is a prime example of a philosopher who argued *ad hominem*, for instance calling John Stuart Mill 'a boring old frog'.

2 *The* ad baculum *fallacy:* one commits the *ad baculum* fallacy by accepting an argument from those in authority out of fear of the consequences of not accepting it. We hope that those in authority state the argument because it is correct.

3 *The gambler's fallacy:* this is the misapprehension that the probability of something being true is affected by what has occurred previously. A gambler who has lost on a regular basis keeps betting, on the misguided conviction that their luck will change.

4 *The* ad populum *fallacy:* one commits the *ad populum* fallacy by apportioning praise or blame to an argument according to the majority view. This is an example of fallacious reasoning due to the fact that most people might be wrong, as in the Middle Ages when everyone thought that the world was flat.

5 *The* ad personam *fallacy:* one commits the *ad personam* fallacy by apportioning praise or blame to an argument because it makes one feel better to do so. Hume is one philosopher who warns us against this when he states that if the view that morality might not be based on reason makes us insecure or uncomfortable then this is not sufficient grounds for dismissing the argument.

6 *Circular arguments:* one commits the circular fallacy by appealing to an aspect of the very argument one is seeking to verify. The most famous example of this is the Cartesian circle in which Descartes justifies his notion of 'clear and distinct ideas' because the notion itself is 'a clear and distinct idea'.

7 *Fallacies of rhetoric:* one commits the fallacy of rhetoric by apportioning praise or blame to an argument because it sounds convincing. If an argument sounds convincing then it needs further investigation and may indeed be proved correct but just because the likes of politicians use long words, alliteration or Ciceronian rhetoric (listing things in groups of three) does not add anything to the argument's veracity.

8 *Arguments from analogy:* one commits the fallacy of analogy by apportioning praise or blame to an argument that makes a comparison. Plato is the prime example of a philosopher who uses lots of picture language to make us understand his philosophical arguments. This is what makes his texts so accessible but one must be careful not to think this also makes his arguments more plausible.

9 *Ambiguous arguments:* this is a straightforward dirty trick, though it might not be intentional. It involves using a term or concept in different ways in the course of the same argument to make one's point of view sound more believable. Bertrand Russell accuses George Berkeley of using the word 'idea' in different ways in his dialogues.

10 *Slippery slope arguments:* the misapprehension that something will inevitably lead to something disadvantageous when this has not been proved. Many examples occur in practical ethics where, for instance, someone arguing against euthanasia might assert that it will lead to a general devaluing of life. This might be the case but legalising euthanasia does not necessarily entail a devaluing of life.

> **Task**
>
> To check whether you have understood all of the above fallacies, write out examples of your own invention. Keep adding to the above list of fallacies as there are many more.

Suggested reading

- Baggini, J. and Fosl, P. S. (2003) *The Philosopher's Toolkit*, Oxford, Blackwell

- Fisher, A. (2000) *The Logic of Real Arguments*, Cambridge, CUP

- Fisher, A. (2001) *Critical Thinking: An Introduction*, Cambridge, CUP

- Thomson, A. (2000) *Critical Reasoning*, London, Routledge

- Van den Brink-Budgen, R. (2000) *Critical Thinking for Students*, Oxford, How to Books

- Warburton, N. (2000) *Thinking from A–Z*, London, Routledge

Appendix 3

An alphabet of advice on study skills for philosophy

The excellence of any art lies in its perfection. (John Keats)

Analysing a text

Philosophical writing is often inaccessible and you should always seek to persevere. Any first reading is to gain an acquaintance with the subject while subsequent readings and re-readings are required for the text's subtle flavour to be released. Identify the time of day when your powers of concentration are at their best. Select a peaceful environment, though not too soporific, and settle down ready to make notes. Rather than adopting a Blitzkrieg approach, it is better to wage a war of attrition by gradually working on a text in manageable pieces. Give your brain a chance to rest in between assaults. Reading in this context should always involve writing and any notes should be accompanied by page numbers for ease of reference. It may be useful to have a specific question in mind, perhaps one from a past exam paper. Often auditory learners (see page 338) find reading and discussing in small groups more efficient. In addition to reading in this way, it is important to look at some of the author's other works as suggested in the profiles in this book and to make reference to critical commentaries. Biographies and autobiographies may also count as a useful feeding ground for information, despite including non-philosophical material. Finally, make connections between different areas of study and cross-reference authors with each other or with any relevant arguments gleaned from analysing philosophical themes.

Bibliographies

Bibliographies should consist of a single list of relevant books and articles added at the end of a piece of writing. Make sure that the bibliography contains all the sources you have used in the text and adopt the Harvard system (sometimes referred to as the author–date system). In this system the work is referred to in the body of your text by the author's surname and the date of publication, and in the bibliography the full details are given: the author's surname, initials, date of publication of the edition cited, italicised title, location of publication and publisher. A complete reference for this work, for example, would read:

> Phelan, J. W. (2005) *Philosophy: Themes and Thinkers*, Cambridge, CUP

Books and articles should be listed in alphabetical order of author surnames. In the case of an article appearing in an edited collection it should read:

> Phelan, J. W. (2004) 'A. J. Ayer' in J. Baggini and J. Stangroom (eds.) *Great Thinkers A–Z*, London, Continuum

If reference is made to more than one article by the same author in a single year the date entry might read (2005a) and (2005b). These references should be listed in full in the bibliography. References should appear after quotations in the following style and within parentheses: (Phelan 2005: 72). This reference cites author, date of publication and page number where the quotation is to be found. If reference is made to a journal article don't forget to cite author, date, article title, journal title, volume, edition and page numbers. All of this may seem a nuisance but it is extremely useful for someone following up a reference. It is advisable, therefore, to keep a note of such details as you research.

Command, context and content

When writing essays remember the three Cs. Look at the root command of the question as this gives you a specific idea of what to do or how to do it. Essay questions that begin with the commands Appraise, Assess, Consider, Discuss, Evaluate or, more generally, How far does … ? require an answer that weighs one approach against another. You are required to examine the different views on the topic and advance an opinion of your own. To create a sense of depth, criticise some of the criticisms. Alternatively, root commands that include Define, Describe, Explain, Illustrate, Outline, Relate and State seek a descriptive, factual answer that details the main points without evaluation.

Bring in examples and illustrations to help the reader understand the argument. The use of examples is also a useful indication in assessed work as to how much of the material is understood by the writer! Remember to PEE regularly, i.e. make the Point, illustrate with an Example and Explain how the example is relevant. The opening paragraph of an answer should set certain limits to the range of the enquiry and explain the context in which you are writing (in more advanced work this will involve declaring your perspective, e.g. feminist, Marxist, rational-scientific). Philosophy is a wide-ranging discipline and it helps to know the angle from which the author is approaching the question.

You should also give an idea of the essay's content. This requires planning. An easy strategy to remember is to state briefly what you are going to say in the introduction, say it and then summarise what has been said in the conclusion. As the poet Philip Larkin pointed out, every essay should have 'a beginning, a muddle and an end'.

Discussion

Convivial debate is the natural medium for philosophy, a fact that attracts many to the subject in the first place. Yet the art of philosophical discussion is one that requires practice. Consider the following guidelines:

- Discussions should revolve around a specific issue or set of questions.

- It is desirable that every member of the group should contribute.

- No one should feel compelled to contribute if they enjoy listening.

- To avoid bush fires of debate breaking out at random, only one person should talk at any given time.

- It may be desirable to appoint a chairperson to ensure on-task discussion and that no budding Wittgenstein is hogging the limelight.

- Each contribution should follow from what has previously been said in the form of clarification, questioning or extrapolation. This enables one to record a route through a given problem.

Socrates was one of the most famous interlocutors in the history of philosophy and many points can be gleaned from reading the Platonic dialogues in which he is the central character. Socrates' aim was always to elucidate, scrutinise and challenge rather than crush his opponents into the ground. His method involves systematic questioning in the hope of getting closer to the truth. The sort of questions he asked were: What do you think about that? What do you mean by that? Give an example of the sort of thing you mean. Does that necessarily follow from what you have been saying? Are you not assuming … ? How do you know?

Exam technique

The two main points of advice for exam technique are, first, to follow the root command (e.g. don't outline when you are asked to assess and vice versa). Second, match your time and effort to the mark allocation. It is a wasted opportunity to spend more time than is necessary on low-tariff, confidence-giving questions while the richer fruit remain unpicked. If there is a choice of questions, then read through the options twice before deciding which question to tackle. Underline the key words of any question as this will often expose any subtleties or nuances which invite an original response. Take time to construct a quick plan of campaign based on your revision as this will create structure and focus in an answer and avoid poor sequencing of paragraphs. The first line of any answer should meet the question head on and arrest the attention of the reader.

Refer regularly to your plan as you are writing in order to keep on task and avoid falling into a pre-rehearsed reminiscence of facts. It is important to have practised exam answers under timed conditions beforehand. Any errors in timing, spelling or legibility can be identified at this stage and ironed out. Taking exams is a taxing business, so eat a good breakfast beforehand with slow-releasing energy foods such as bananas and muesli.

Footnotes and endnotes

Make use of footnotes, or endnotes, if you wish your additions to be less intrusive on the main line of argument. Insert the relevant number at the end of the sentence which corresponds to the addition cited at the bottom of the page (if it is a footnote) or at the end of the essay (if it is an endnote).

General abbreviations

Despite being unacceptable in a formal piece of writing, shorthand is an extremely useful time-saving device to use when note-taking during lectures. Invent your own abbreviations as well as using the following more commonly used examples:

Therefore	∴
Because	∵
Eighteenth century	C_{18}
Number	# or no.
Does not equal	≠
Approximately equal to	≈
Change	Δ
Between	|·|
Less than X	< X
Greater than X	> X

With	$\overline{w}$
Nomination (adapt for any 'ion' ending)	nom^n
Increasing	inc ↑
Decreasing	dec ↓
And	&, +
Especially	esp.
Should, would, could	shd, wd, cd
Very	v.
And so on	etc.
That is to say	i.e. (*id est*)
Namely	viz.
Compare/contrast	cf.
Note well	NB (*nota bene*)
For example	e.g. (*exempli gratia*)
Pages	pp.
If and only if	iff

How to plan an essay

Start on a piece of work as soon as possible to give yourself as much time to read around the problem. You might begin with a mind map or spider diagram with the essay title in the middle of a blank piece of paper turned sideways; scatter your ideas around the central question before linking connected ideas with a coloured pen. Once you have connected your points, decide on their logical sequence before beginning writing.

Alternatively you might try the card technique of essay preparation: write the relevant arguments (quotations, strengths, weaknesses, counter-criticisms) on a series of small cards, arranging them in different sequences until you are satisfied you have the most fitting order. Sometimes it is easier to write the introduction and the conclusion after finishing the main text, when your mind is clearly focused on what has been said. Use the cards as cues when you are writing the piece and for later revision. A third alternative to the spider diagram or card technique is the matrix or chart method. After identifying the required information, divide a blank page into two or four sections. Label each section with a relevant heading and organise your notes under the relevant label. Work on the order of the sections together with the sequencing within each subdivision. Remember to attribute arguments that are not your own and remember to give clear signposts or signals throughout the answer (perhaps at the start of alternate paragraphs) to remind the reader of the issue under examination.

Internet

Once you have become acquainted with the central arguments in a given text or theme, subsidiary points may be gleaned from the Internet. Enter the keywords in a search engine such as Google or try an online philosophy encyclopaedia such as Stanford or Routledge. Philosophy magazines also provide links to the web as well as their own useful sites.

Joining paragraphs

The careful use of paragraphs in any philosophy essay will help the reader. A paragraph is a unit of thought of no prescribed length and should work like an essay in miniature, containing a beginning, middle and end. Smooth transitions that join paragraphs are of central importance so as to make the essay flow as a unified whole. Although each different paragraph should move into new territory, there needs to be a connection between the first line of any new thought and the last line of the preceding paragraph. It is important to plan the sequence of your paragraphs before you write, perhaps by using the card technique as outlined above. This will allow you to form an overview of your argument and choose how to present your case to its best advantage. Always choose stronger arguments to explore first as this strengthens your position.

Keeping time

You should have an idea of how long you are willing to spend on a piece of work even when you are not writing under exam conditions. Timing, however, becomes even more important in an exam. Distribute effort accordingly by awarding more time for high-tariff questions. This seems an obvious point, but it is often not put into practice.

Learning

Educational research, originally carried out in New Zealand, divides learners into four categories: visual learners, auditory learners, those who prefer reading and writing, and kinaesthetic learners. In practice, most people are a mixture of the four types but it is worth reflecting for a moment on how you learn most effectively, as this helps in note-taking and revision. Visual learners prefer mind maps, diagrams, charts and anything that stimulates the visual senses. Auditory learners, on the other hand, retain most information when listening and benefit from studying in discussion groups or even using tape recordings to help with revision. Many philosophy students fall into the third category, armed with a wheelbarrow of paperwork and a selection of highlighting pens. Kinaesthetic learners, who are of a more practical caste of mind and learn from hands-on experience, are afforded fewer opportunities in philosophy, although they might enjoy some of the tasks suggested in Hayward, J., Jones, G. and Mason, M. (2000) *Exploring Ethics*, John Murray.

Mind maps®

Many students use mind mapping to help retain the required information. Mind maps stimulate the creative and imaginative right side of the brain as well as the logical, analytic left side. There are some simple rules to follow:

- Use a central image (it has to be a picture).
- Add key themes with thick black lines.
- Aim for about five key themes as human beings find it easier to remember things in fives (unlike tigers, who remember things in threes).
- With thin lines connecting to the respective thick lines, add connecting subtopics.
- Use coloured pens.
- Use capital letters.
- Use lots of images.

Note-taking

Note-taking is a necessary skill to master in lectures and the library. You should not aim to write every detail down like a transcript but listen carefully and select the key points and main ideas. Work out a numbering or lettering system to be used as a framework, e.g. I, II, III; A, B, C; 1, 2, 3; a, b, c; i, ii, iii. In secondary literature, the main ideas are often summarised in the preface, introduction or at the beginning of each chapter. Write on one side of your note pad and leave plenty of space as you may want to add more information later. Use your own shorthand, putting a dash for words you miss if the speaker goes too fast, to fill in later. If the speaker says something is important then don't forget to highlight it. At a more leisurely time you can draw attention to important themes by underlining, using capitals, circles, boxes or colours.

Organisation

Many people find it difficult to meet deadlines and achieve the best product in the time allowed without staying up all night in the company of Mr Marlboro and Mr Nescafé. This is sometimes due to being faced with an unacceptably heavy workload, which needs to be reduced, but is often due to poor organisational skills and lack of time management. Draw up a plan of your average week to see whether you achieve the correct balance between work and leisure. Count how many times you think about a piece of work or pick up the relevant paperwork without doing anything about it. As with cold swimming pools, it is better to dive straight in than splash around in the shallows. The moral of the story is to start work as soon as possible. For longer pieces of work with a distant deadline, it may be more useful to draw up a plan in advance using a time management circle. Draw a circle and divide it into the number of segments that will match the number of weeks or days available. Label the stages in the assignment's life cycle, for example finding books, recording arguments, seeking extra help from your teacher, first draft, second draft. Place the circle in a place where you can see it for ease of reference.

Proof-reading

A. J. Ayer was particularly proud of writing *Language, Truth and Logic* straight off without a second draft; the result is a repetitive and unstylish harangue. All submitted work should be carefully proof-read out of courtesy to the reader. The following guidelines might be of assistance:

- Do not proof-read immediately but approach the piece of work afresh after a period of time as only then will you spot certain errors.
- Proof-read for meaning first – Does it make sense?
- Common errors include a mixture of past and present tenses, omitted speech marks and apostrophes, omission of small connecting words such as 'of', 'that' and 'to'.
- If you are unsure where to apply punctuation, read the essay aloud, adding commas when you feel there is a natural pause.

- Check for spelling errors (if unsure use a dictionary); commonly misspelled words in philosophy essays are 'necessary', 'simile', 'argument' and 'intelligible'.

- Check that words and names are spelled consistently throughout the piece of work and that your handwriting is legible.

Quoting technique

A useful rule of thumb to remember is that if you can articulate the idea as well as the author then you do not need to rely on a direct quotation. Only choose quotations that count as evidence to shore up your argument. Philosophers prefer to use longer quotations that incorporate important facets of an argument rather than short, mid-sentence quotations that demonstrate familiarity with a text. If you need to use shorter quotations in your prose use single quotation marks, except for quotations within quotations, when double marks should be used.

A comma is often required before mid-sentence quotations, but not if the sense flows on smoothly from your sentence into the quotation. The free-standing quotations favoured in philosophical writing should be separated from the text, set off by a colon and a blank line, and indented. Single quotation marks around the entire passage should be used and don't forget to reference quotations accurately by adding in brackets the author, year of publication and page or paragraph number, e.g. (Phelan 2005, p. 340); this work must then be listed in the detailed bibliography at the end of the piece of work.

Revision

It is first necessary to measure the scale of the task: remind yourself of what you need to know (refer to the subject course booklet) and how much time you have got to revise in. Focus on the topics that you know least well and try to make the revision inventive and varied. You need to be familiar with the timing and shape of the exam, so use past questions as the main focus of revision. While other students learn vocabulary, formulae and dates, arguments are the meat and drink of a philosopher. Reduce each topic to ten interesting points to learn by heart; these might include a definition, a quotation, a strength, criticism and counter-criticism. Select a comfortable environment that is conducive to

work and use this location as a regular venue for revision to help you slip into the pattern of study as quickly as possible. Reflect on what time of the day or night you function best and use the rest of the time to relax. A quality 3–4 hours per day is better than an eternity of sitting in your bedroom flicking through a file of notes and not taking anything in. Be proactive: consult a 'successful' student, revise in a group if it helps, use highlighters, summary cards, tape recorders, study guides and visually memorable mind maps. Get your family to test you on the work and to provide a selection of treats as encouragement. Revise up until the final hour and ignore people who tell you, 'If you don't know it now then you'll never know it'.

Synoptic study

Many courses in philosophy (such as the AQA A level) require a lengthier piece of writing that counts as coursework and is called a 'synoptic study'. Many of the snippets of advice already mentioned are relevant, but a few guidelines may be issued in addition. Start as soon as possible with your research and use primary sources as your first port of call. Follow your own line of enquiry rather than flocking sheep-like around

the obvious points. Assignments of between fifteen and twenty sides require a clearer direction to stop them becoming rambling and unfocused. It is useful to read an example of a good assignment in advance, together with the exam board's assessment objectives. Draw up a careful itinerary for the journey ahead and try to avoid a scatter technique of unconnected arguments. Critically engage with the material to avoid slipping into a history-of-ideas approach as this is not required in philosophy. Cultivate a formal, academic style that avoids colloquialisms, slang or abbreviated bullet points. Your first draft should be completed in good time and if possible be looked at by a willing proof-reader.

Teaching and learning

Anthony Kenny once remarked that there is no shallow end to philosophy and this fact makes its teaching and learning cumbersome at times. The situation has been helped in recent years by the publication of basic study guides by Baggini, Morton, Warburton, and Horner and Westacott. These provide sound foundations upon which to build. A common problem encountered by philosophy students is the jargonistic nature of the subject and you should always be armed with a glossary at first. In addition, learning can be enhanced by balloon, formal and devil's advocate debates. Useful revision exercises include drawing up pro and con sheets and making sentence summaries of the arguments.

University interviews

With increased competition for limited places, many universities request a formal interview with the philosopher in residence. There is no shortage of interview advice on offer, ranging from the useful (dress smartly, prepare answers to obvious questions such as 'Why here?' and 'Why philosophy?') to the disturbing (help avoid nerves by imagining the interviewer in the nude). Whether naked or fully clothed, the interviewers will be professional academics and therefore used to dealing with freshly baked ideas that are sometimes a little soft. Avoid ducking the question with paltry responses such as 'We haven't covered that yet' or 'I don't know' and instead try and intuit an answer from what you have studied. Although some arrows might misfire, others will hit their target. Avoid too many metaphors.

Videos

There are useful videos available for teaching philosophy such as *The Examined Life* series and Alain de Botton's *The Consolations of Philosophy*. Often lecturers refer to editions of *Star Trek*, the Royal Institute Christmas lectures or films with a philosophical undercurrent such as *The Matrix*. There are a number of strategies that can be useful when taking notes from television recordings:

- Identify key questions before the programme to help focus the purpose of your notes.
- Be prepared to catch ideas from different parts of the programme as they are often constructed for dramatic effect rather than in a logical sequence.
- Most people need to use the pause facility or watch the video more than once to add supplementary notes.

Writing philosophy

Don't start writing in a haphazard, directionless way but sketch a plan before you begin so that you have a map of the mountain before its ascent. Construct your essay as a reasoned argument so that it has form and so that the reader can follow the line of your thinking. Use the same terms as the question to give shape to your answer and to avoid straying into irrelevancies. The first sentence of an answer and the first sentence of subsequent paragraphs should address the question without fuss. Leave a healthy margin to allow for comments or future thoughts and annotations. Remember that, in most cases, you are addressing an intelligent reader who is well acquainted with the text so avoid story-telling and background information and go for the philosophical jugular. Give some thought to the phraseology you use; it is always useful to have a dictionary and thesaurus to hand. Do the words you use convey the exact meaning you wish them to? Do you have a small group of favoured words that you return to? Build up a bank of adjectives and try to extend your critical vocabulary. Mix long, illustrative sentences with shorter, pithy ones. Good introductions tend to analyse the question under consideration. Explain any particular theory or ambiguous concepts. The main body of the text will provide a more detailed evaluation but don't try to solve the ultimate question of reality that has baffled gifted philosophers for centuries; instead offer a close reading of the relevant literature and focus on a specific weakness. Assume that the reader disagrees with you and that you have to convince him or her with good evidence and examples. Show where the evidence comes from and that it is reliable. Ask yourself: Would this stand up in a court of law? Show that

you have considered any possible arguments that might contradict your case. Conclusions are often poorly written and, in exam style answers, it is advisable to stop writing rather than offer a weak ending. Good conclusions restate the argument and explain how you arrived at your endpoint. Be courageous and state where you think the heart of the argument is to be found. The last sentence should express your final conclusion or stress that there are two or more views that cannot be resolved. Most importantly of all: be clear. The reader should not have to read any sentence twice to be sure of its meaning. For more information consult Martinich, P. (2001) *Philosophical Writing*, Oxford, Blackwell.

X and Y

Consider the appearance of an answer and how it is laid out on the page. Often formal expressions of an argument, using the variables X and Y, express the point in the clearest possible terms. X and Y can represent universals (any X) or particulars (person Y). To express an

argument formally, finish the sentence with a colon, leave a line and indent, for example:

For any X iff X then also Y.

Other formal philosophical expressions, which form the basis of propositional calculus and may be of use, include:

Symbol	Formal name	Meaning	Example	
&	Conjunction	And	$p \& q$	p and q
~	Negation	Not	$\sim p$	Not p
⊃	Conditional	If … then	$p \supset q$	If p then q
v	Disjunction	Or	$p \vee q$	p or q
iff	Biconditional	If and only if	p iff q	p, if and only if q

ZZZ: keeping awake

Philosophy is an in-depth study and requires good powers of concentration. Inevitably you will find it difficult to concentrate at times but you can do certain things to help:

- Start early in the day.
- Aim for shorter bursts rather than tedious slogs.

- Burn lemon oil in an aromatherapy burner.
- Seek a quiet, comfortable environment in which you can spread out your work.
- Use quiet music if it helps.
- Take regular breaks and drinks (non-alcoholic).
- Avoid hunger, interruptions and itches.

Index

duty: in intuitionism 40
in Kant 27–9, 37, 232
Dworkin, Ronald 106, 107

economics 144
Eddington, Sir Arthur Stanley 11, 129
education: in Aristotle 169, 186
in Mill 264, 269, 275
in Plato 151–2, 160, 162
effect 16, 208, 212, 217–20, **221**
Einstein, Albert 11, 128, 136, 143
and Newton 120, 129, 132–3
élan vital 136
elenchus 148, **165**
eliminativism, materialist 80–2, **97**, 295, 303
Emin, Tracey 329, 330, 331
emotivism 20, 31–2, 43–4, 155, 158, 286, 309
and Ayer 43, 46, 233, 306–7
and Nietzsche 32, 232–4, 236, 238
empiricism **21**, 130, **309**
and Aristotle 173–6
and Ayer 295, 300–1, 302, 305
and foundationalism 9–11
and Hume 6, 212, 213–14, 300
and knowledge 4–6, 7
and Nietzsche 237
and scepticism 16
'straw-man' 121–2
see also Locke, John
energy conservation argument 81–2
Engels, Friedrich 102, 242–60, 252
enkrateia 178–9, **187**
Enlightenment ethics 28, 29, 31–2, 228
epiphenomenalism 74, **97**, 204
epistemology 4–21, **21**, **205**; *see also* knowledge
ergon (function) 170, **187**
error-avoidance theories 10
essentialism 238, 243, 312–13, 318, **324**
ethics 23–49
Christian 267–8
and general principles 45, 286–7
and law 107, 110–11
normative 23–32, **49**, 307, 319
practical 32–8, 261, 334
and science 143
utilitarian 23–7, 261, *265*, 271, 306–7
see also deontology; meta-ethics; moral realism; virtue theory
ethos 30, 174, **187**
eudaimonia 36, 167–73, 183, **187**
and contemplation 169, 185–6
and pleasure 184–5
and the soul 171–2
and virtue 30, 32, 34, 167, 171
and wisdom 181–2
euthanasia 27, 35–6, 334
evil: in Aristotle 172
in Hume 221
metaphysical 66, 198
moral/natural 66
in Nietzsche 226, 227, 234
theodicies 66–9
evolution 120, 145
existence and essence 193, 200–1, 249–50, 312–13, 320, 324
existence of God 15, 51, 55–63
cosmological (first cause) argument 55–7, **71**, 221, 282
faith argument 64–5
and idealism 18
and illative sense 65
miracle argument 69
moral argument 57, 69–70
ontological argument 59–61, 71, 195–7, 297–8
pragmatic argument 63
and problem of evil 59, 66–9
religious experience argument 61–3, 197, 307

teleological (design) argument 57–9, 66, **71**
existentialism: criticisms of 311–12
and ethics 313–14, 317–18, 320–3
history of 314–17
and Marx 253
and Nietzsche 48, 314, 318
and psychological continuity 95
and Sartre 310–25
experience: and beliefs 10
and knowledge 4–5, 12, 215, 217, 294, 304
and language 9, 127, 302–3
as subjective 76, 82–3
see also empiricism
experience, religious, argument from 61–3, 197, 307
experiment *see* theory

fact and value *see* is–ought distinction
facticity **324**
faith and reason 56, 63–5, 233
falsificationism 100, 127–31, 145, **146**, 266
and religious belief 53–5
feminism, and abortion 34
Fermat, Pierre *64*, 139, 199
Feuerbach, Ludwig A. 243, 248, 249–50, 259
Feyerabend, Paul 142, 266
fideism 64–5
Flew, Anthony 53–5
Fodor, Jerry 140
folk psychology 80–1, **97**
forms 161, 164, **165**, 196, 288
criticisms of 161, 169–70
of the Good 156–60, 170
and is–ought distinction 41, 157
and knowledge 152–3, 154, 155, 162
and Nietzsche 228, 231
Foster, John 74
foundationalism 9–11, 130, **205**
and Descartes 10, 189, 300
free-rider problem 112
free will 67, 198, 220
freedom 104–8
and authority 104–5, 108, 109, 113
criticisms of 263–4
and individuality 99–100, 263–4, 269–72
intrinsic/instrumental 273–4
and law 107–8
and liberalism 99–100
in Marx 253–4
meaning 104
in Mill 261–76
positive/negative 104–5, 261, 264, 270, 275, **276**
and rights 105–7
in Rousseau 117
in Sartre 253, 313, 316–20, 321, 322
of thought and expression 142, 264–9, 272
Frege, Gottlob 61
Freud, Sigmund 35, 128, 162, 234, 317
functionalism 80–1, **97**
functions, in Aristotle 41, 170–1

gambler's fallacy 333
genetic fallacy 235
Gestalt psychology 300
Gettier, E. L. 13–14
God, attributes 51–2, 55, 59, 66, **71**, 197–8
see also existence of God
Godwin, William 258
good life 1, 23, 36, 47, 186
Goodman, Nelson 123, 330
goodness/the Good: and intuitionism 40–1
in Nietzsche 226, 227
in Plato 41, 156–7, 158–60, 162, 170, 184, 233, 299, 306

and realism 38
see also eudaimonia
government *see* authority, political; state
Graham, George 88–9
guardians 118, 151–2, 162, **165**

Hanson, Norwood Russell 139–40
happiness 26, 27, 34, 35, 307
in Bentham 23–4, 25, 261
in Mill 25, 29, 100, 236, 261–2, 263, 266, 271
in Nietzsche 229
in virtue theory *see* eudaimonia
Hare, R. M. 44–5, 46, 54
harm, contingent 263, 264, 273, 274, **276**
harm principle 263, 268–9, 272, 274, **276**
Hart, H. L. A. 107
hedonism 24–5, 27, 169, 173, 184, 258
Hegel, G. W. F. 207, 254, 267
and Marx 242, 243–4, 246, 248, 250, 290
and Russell 290–1
Heidegger, Martin 1, 315–16
Heisenberg, Werner Karl 136
Helvetius, Claude Adrien 258
Hempel, Carl Gustav 124, 125–6, *126*, 139
herd 229–30, 233–6, 237, 239, **240**, 251
Hick, John 53, 54, 62–3
history: in Hegel 243–4
in Marx 244–6, 248–9, 251–2, 254–7
in Nietzsche 228–9, 231, 232–6, 238–9
Hobbes, Thomas *109*
and law 108–10, 114
Leviathan 108–10
and rights 106, 108, 110
and the state 103, 106, 109–10, 257, 258
Holbach, Paul-Henri 258
holism *see* coherentism
homunculus fallacy 73, 193
human nature 29, 199, 226
in Marx 243, 248–9
in Mill 263, 268–9, 270, 272
in Sartre 312–14, 316–17, 319–20, 321
and social sciences 144
humanism, and existentialism 312, 324
Humboldt, Wilhelm von 270
Hume, Basil 59
Hume, David 1, 52, 69, 207, *212*, 264
Dialogues Concerning Natural Religion 58–9, 221
and emotivism 43
Enquiry Concerning Human Understanding 6, 69, 137, 206–21
and knowledge 6–8, 43, 137, 207–16, 295, 304
and liberty and necessity 220–1
and scepticism 16, 58, 123–4, 158, *212*, 213–16, 300
and teleological argument 58–9, 63
see also bundle theory; causation; impressions; induction
hypothesis 121, 124–5, 130, 144–5, **146**
hypothetico-deductive method 124–6, 139, 145

ideal utilitarianism 26–7
idealism **21**, **292**
and Marx 243–4, 250, 259
and perception 18–19, 21, 200, 204
and Russell 279, 282–3
subjective 18–19
transcendent 19
ideas: association of 211–12
in Berkeley 18, 282–3, 334
in Descartes 10, 189, 196–7, 198–9, 201, 202

in Hume 207–11, 216, 217, 219, **221**
identity, personal: bundle theories 75, 94–5, 96, 300
and continuity 95–6
in Descartes 192–3, 198–9, 202–4
identity theory 77–80, 91, 193
ideology 99, 101, **260**
left/right-wing 99, **119**, 141
and Marx and Engels 102, 242–3, 246–7, 249–50, 256, 258–9
see also anarchism; conservatism; liberalism; socialism
ignorance-avoidance theories 11, 91
illative sense 65
illusion: in Descartes 15, 190–2
and realism 17–18, 20, 158
and science 122
imagination: in Descartes 74, 200, 202
in Hume 209, 216, **221**
imperative 45
categorical 27–30, 232–3, 314, 319
and existence of God 69–70
hypothetical 27
impressions 207–9, 211–12, 216, 217, 219–20, **221**
incommensurability 132–3, **146**
individuality **31**, 311
and liberalism 99–100, 263–4, 269–74
in Nietzsche 227, 229
and socialism 102, 254
induction **146**, **292**, **309**
in Aristotle 180, 181–2
in Ayer 296, 299–301
in Hume 123–4, 127, 213, 214, 285, 296
in Russell 285
inductivism 123
inference 12, 13, 45, 214, 332–3
instrumentalism 135–7, 273–4
intelligence, artificial 83, 88–9, **97**
intentional fallacy 250, 331
intentionality 28, 79, 80, 83, 88, **97**
interactionism 74
interests: personal and general 115, 247, 257
and rights 99–100
intersubjectivity 139, 320–2, 323, 324, **325**
introspection 73, 94, **97**, 207, 217, 284, 320
and behaviourism 85–6
intuitionism 38, 39–41, 286–7, 306, 307
invisible hand argument 101, 247, 270
Irenaeus of Lyon, St 66
is–ought distinction 32, 39, 41–3, **49**, 157, 293

Jackson, Fred 87–8
James, William 62
Jaspers, Karl 315
Johnson, Samuel 18, 266, 332
justice 25, 29, 32, 101, **119**
in Aristotle 175, 176
and law 110–11
in Plato 110, 149–50
retributive 110–11
justification **21**, 55
and coherentism 11–12
externalist theory of 12–13
and foundationalism 9–11, 299–300
internalist theories of 13
of knowledge 9–14, 215
and reliabilism 12–13

Kant, Immanuel *29*, 37, *48*, 295
and categorical imperative 27–30, 232–3
and deontology 27–8, 35, 307
and good will 28–9, 256
and idealism 19
and moral argument 69–70

psychology 128, 144–5, 300
  in Plato 162–4
punishment 100, 111–13, 235
Putnam, Hilary 15–16, 86, 279
Pyrrho of Elis 14

qualia 83, 87–8, **97**
qualities, primary and secondary 5, 17,
  18
quantum mechanics 120, 136
quietism 160, 250, 311, 322, 323, **325**
Quine, Willard Van Orman: and
  falsificationism 130
  and hypothetico-deductive method
    124
  and knowledge 7, 8–9, *8*, 174–5,
    305, 308
  and reductionism 127

Rachels, James 35
rationalism 5, 10, **21**, 74
  and Aristotle 174–5
  and Descartes 189, 202
  and knowledge 4–6, 7, 158–9, 304
  and Plato 5, 158–9, 162, 225
  'straw-man' 121
Rawls, John 110–11, 254
realism: naive/direct 17–18, 281–2
  representative/indirect 18, 20, 21,
    140, 196, 199–200, 280
  scientific 133–5
  see also moral realism
reason: and character 163–4, 172, 225
  and ethics 28–9, 37, 45
  and faith 56, 63–5, 233
  and function 170, 286
  and science 121–2
  sufficient reason principle 47, 57
  and virtue theory 32
  see also rationalism
reductio ad absurdum 60, 174, **187**, 202,
  205, 294
reductionism, scientific 126–7, 300
Regan, Thomas 38
regress, infinite 10, 14, 55, 57, **71**, 73,
  125, 135, 175
Reid, Thomas, and memory 95–6
reify, reification 208, **221**, 257, 322
relations of production 245, 246, 251,
  254, 256, 257, **260**
relativism: moral 46–7, 149, 158, 263,
    306, 311, 324
  perceptual 278–9
  and science 132
relativity theory 120, 143
reliabilism 12–14
religion 51–71
  and divine attributes 51–2
  and language 52–5
  in Marx 252, 259
  in Nietzsche 229–32
  see also belief; Christianity; existence
    of God; faith and reason
return, eternal 231, **240**
revolution: in Marx 245, 247, 249–50,
    251, 253–6, **260**
  scientific 131–2
  and utilitarianism 114
rhetoric, fallacy of 250, 333–4
Ricardo, David 144
rights 105–7, **119**, 264
  animal rights 36–8
  and government 115, 117–18
  and interests 99–100
  and justice 111
  and law 110
  as moral entitlements 106
  as renunciations 106
  as side constraints 107
  as trumps 106–7
roads to Rome fallacy 167
Roman Catholicism 34, *56*

Ross, W. D. 40
Rousseau, Jean-Jacques *117*
  criticisms of 118, 253–4
  and freedom 104–5, 117, 269, 272
  and political philosophy 99, 268
  and social contract 117–18, 253–4,
    272
rule utilitarianism 26, 27
Ruskin, John 328
Russell, Bertrand 1, *8*, *93*, *287*
  and existence of God 57
  and general principles 286–7
  and moral value 286–7, 306
  and other minds 91, 280, 281
  The Problems of Philosophy 277–92
  and scepticism 16, 278–81
  see also knowledge; language;
    phenomenalism
Ryle, Gilbert 75, 84, *84*, 206 n.4, 303

Samuelson, Paul 144
Sartre, Jean-Paul 1, 33, *317*
  and Ayer 293
  and bad faith 317, 322–3, 324
  and existence and essence 193,
    312–13, 320, 322, 324
  Existentialism and Humanism
    310–25
  and intersubjectivity 320–2, 323
  Nausea 310–11, 316
  see also abandonment; anguish;
    choice; freedom
scepticism 13, 14–17, **21**, **205**
  Cartesian 15–16, 158, 189–92, 196,
    204, 279–81
  and foundationalism 10–11
  Humean 16, 58, 123, 212, 213–16,
    300
  Nietzschean 237
  Russellian 16, 278–81
  and scientific method 121–2, 123
  and solipsism 16–17, 20
Schleiermacher, Friedrich 67
Schlick, Moritz 126, 294, 296
Schopenhauer, Arthur *48*, 59, *236*
  and nihilism 47–8, 232
  and will to life *48*, 224, 225
science 120–46
  aims of 133–9
  development of 126–33
  as explanations 138–9
  objectivity of 122, 139–43, 144
  and philosophy 81, 300
  privatisation of 141–2
  and realism 133–5
  and reductionism 126–7
  scientific method 120–6, 141–2, 144,
    266
  scientific research 142–3
  scientific revolutions 131–2
  see also falsificationism;
    hypothetico-deductive method;
    induction; instrumentalism;
    knowledge
Searle, John 42, 82–3, 88, 193
selection, natural 120
self: in Hume 75, 94
  in Parfit 75, 95
  in Sartre 316
  see also mind
self-ascription problem 93–4
sensations 19, 20, 278–9, 281–2, **292**,
  301
sense-data 7, 9, 17–21, **21**, **292**
  fallibility 10–11, 189–92
  and phenomenalism 20, 280–5, 286,
    287–90, 292
  and scepticism 14–16, 278–80
  and science 121–2, 128, 136, 139–40
  see also impressions
simplicity, explanatory 139, 280
Singer, Peter 27, 33, 37–8

situationism 173, 180, 186
slippery slope arguments 334
Smith, Adam 101, 144, *212*, 247
social science 127, 143–5, **146**
socialism 101–2, 229, 230, 259; *see also*
  communism
society: in Kant 314
  in Marx 246, 248–9, 251, 253
  in Mill 263–4, 266, 268–72
  in Plato 110, 150–6, 163–4
sociology 144
Socrates, and ethics 23, 236, 237
Socratic method 148, **165**, 234, 267,
  336
solipsism 16–17, 20, **21**, 91, 280, 296–7
sophia (wisdom) 155–6, 181–2, **187**
sophistry 1, 149, 154–6, **165**, 173, 180,
  186
soul: in Aristotle 171–2, 180
  in Descartes 74
  in Nietzsche 226, 231
Spinoza, Baruch 189, 234
state 99, 116–18, **119**
  and anarchy 102–3
  in Aristotle 186
  and authority 113–16
  and coercion 116–17
  and general will 117–18
  in Hobbes 103, 106, 109–10, 257,
    258
  and justice 112
  and law 107–8, 109–10
  and legitimacy 116–17
  and liberalism 100
  in Marx 244, 245, 247, 251, 253,
    256, 257
  in Mill 262, 263, 272–5
  in Plato 150–2
statements: analytic/synthetic 6–9, *8*,
    194, 225–6, 231, 287–8, 304–5
  atomic 302, **309**
  existential/attributive 297–8, 301
  meaningful 52–3, 295–301
  moral 43–4, 233, 305–6
  religious 52–5
  scientific 126–7
Stevenson, C. L. 44, 233
Stirner, Max 243, 256, 257, 258–9
stoicism 14, 173, 184, 225
study skills 335–42
subjectivism, ethical 25, 224, 286–7,
    292, 306–7, 311, 323–4
substance dualism *see* dualism
suffering, and existence of God 59,
  66–7
suicide 28, 35, 317
supervenience 76–7, 83, **97**
Swift, Jonathan 142
Swinburne, Richard 63, 74

tautology 61, **205**, **309**
  in Ayer 43, 44, 295, 296, 301, 304–6
  cogito as 194–5
  in Hume 6, 43
teleological argument 57–9, 63, 66, **71**
teleology, and ethics 31, *56*, 180, 263,
  272
telos (goal) 57, 167–8, 184, **187**
theism 51, 57, 63, **71**, 312
theodicy 66–9, **71**
theology, natural 69
theory: error-avoiding 10
  and experiment 121, 300–1
  and hypothesis 124–5, 130
  ignorance-avoiding 11, 91
  and observation 122, 128, 132,
    136–7, 141, 145
Thomism *56*, 57
Thomson, Judith Jarvis 33
timarchy 163, **165**
tolerance, and liberalism 100
transcendentalism 91

truth **21**
  analytic/synthetic 8–9
  approximate 134–5
  and coherentism 11, 12, 14, 266–7
  contingent 16
  in Descartes 189, 192, 194, 197,
    200–1
  in Hume 6, 43, 213, 221
  and justification 9, 14
  in Mill 265–9, 304
  moral 38–9, 46–7
  necessary *see* tautology
  in Nietzsche 223–4, 226, 230, 235
  partial 267–8
  in Russell 10–11, 283, 286, 328
  and science 134–5, 139, 143, 300
  self-evident *see* tautology
  theories of 14, 133
  see also a posteriori knowledge; *a
    priori* knowledge; verificationism
Turing, Alan 89
type–token distinction 79, 91
tyranny of the majority 25, 114, 261,
  262, **276**

Übermensch, in Nietzsche 224, 227–8,
    231, 234, 236, 238–9, **240**
uncertainty principle 136, 291
under-determination 122, 123, **146**
universalisability: and categorical
    imperative 28–30, 34, 35
  and prescriptivism 45
universals 153, 182, 211
  in Russell 278, 283–4, 288–90, **292**
utilitarianism 23–7, 114, **276**
  and liberalism 100
  and Marx 258
  and Nietzsche 235, 236
  and practical ethics 34, 35, 36, 37
  strengths of 25
  types of 26–7, 35, 37–8
utility principle 24, 25, 27, 261

Van Gogh, Vincent 329
veil of ignorance 111
verificationism 52–3, *129*, **146**, **309**
  in Ayer 43, 53, 128, 294–6, 300–1,
    302, 304
verisimilitude 134–5, **146**
Vienna Circle 53, *84*, 126, *129*, 140,
  294, 295–6
virtue theory 27, 307
  and abortion 34
  in Aristotle 30, 31–2, 34, 167, 171,
    172–4, 180, 183–6, 271
  and euthanasia 36
  in MacIntyre 30
  in Nietzsche 232, 234–5, 237

Warnock, Mary 322
Whitehead, A. N. 148
Wilde, Oscar 4, 43, 231, 298, 322
will to power 224–6, 227–8, 229,
    230–1, 233–5, 236, 237, 238–9,
    240, 318
William of Occam 139, 280
Wind in the Willows 61–2
Windelbrand, Wilhelm 144
wisdom, in Aristotle 181–2
Wisdom, John 53
Wittgenstein, Ludwig 54, *93*, 126
  and Ayer *84*, 294, *294*, 295
  and other minds 92–3
  private language argument 88, 92–3,
    122
Wong, David, and relativism 47

Young Hegelians 243–4, 247, 249, 256,
  259

Zarathustra 229, **240**